Jewish Law and Legal Theory

The International Library of Essays in Law and Legal Theory
Series Editor: Tom D. Campbell

Schools

Natural Law, Vols I & II *John Finnis*
Justice *Thomas Morawetz*
Law and Economics, Vols I & II *Jules Coleman and Jeffrey Lange*
Critical Legal Studies *James Boyle*
Marxian Legal Theory *Csaba Varga*
Legal Reasoning, Vols I & II *Aulis Aarnio and D. Neil MacCormick*
Legal Positivism *Mario Jori*
American Legal Theory *Robert Samuel Summers*
Postmodernism and Law *Dennis Patterson*
Law and History *David Sugarman*
Law and Language *Fred Schauer*
Sociological Theories of Law *Kahei Rokumoto*
Rights *Carlos Nino*
Law and Psychology *Martin Lyon Levine*
Feminist Legal Theory, Vols I & II *Frances Olsen*
Law and Society *Roger Cotterell*
Contemporary Criminological Theory *Francis T. Cullen and Velmer S. Burton Jr.*

Areas

Criminal Law *Thomas Morawetz*
Tort Law *Ernest J. Weinrib*
Contract Law, Vols I & II *Larry Alexander*
Anti-Discrimination Law *Christopher McCrudden*
Consumer Law *Iain Ramsay*
International Law *Martti Koskenniemi*
Property Law, Vols I & II *Elizabeth Mensch and Alan Freeman*
Constitutional Law *Mark V. Tushnet*
Procedure *D.J. Galligan*
Evidence and Proof *William Twining and Alex Stein*
Company Law *Sally Wheeler*
Privacy, Vols I & II *Raymond Wacks*
Lawyers' Ethics *David J. Luban*
Administrative Law *D.J. Galligan*
Child Law *Harry D. Krause*
Family Law, Vols I & II *Harry D. Krause*
Welfare Law *Peter Robson*
Medicine and the Law *Bernard M. Dickens*
Commercial Law *Ross Cranston*
Environmental Law *Michael C. Blumm*
Conflict of Laws *Richard Fentiman*
Law and Religion *Wojciech Sadurski*
Human Rights Law *Philip Alston*
European Community Law, Vols I & II *Francis Snyder*
Tax Law, Vols I & II *Patricia D. White*
Media Law *Eric Barendt*
Labour Law *David L. Gregory*
Alternative Dispute Resolution *Michael D.A. Freeman*

Legal Cultures

Comparative Legal Cultures *Csaba Varga*
Law and Anthropology *Peter Sack*
Hindu Law and Legal Theory *Ved Nanda*
Islamic Law and Legal Theory *Ian Edge*
Chinese Law and Legal Theory *Michael Palmer*
Socialist Law *W. Butler*
Common Law *Michael Arnheim*
Japanese Law and Legal Theory *Koichiro Fujikura*
Law and Development *Anthony Carty*
Jewish Law and Legal Theory *Martin P. Golding*
Legal Education *Martin Lyon Levine*
Civil Law *Ralf Rogowski*

Future Volumes

African Law and Legal Theory and Cumulative index.

Jewish Law and Legal Theory

Edited by

Martin P. Golding

Professor of Philosophy and Professor of Law
Duke University

NEW YORK UNIVERSITY PRESS
REFERENCE COLLECTION

First published in the U.S.A. in 1993 by
NEW YORK UNIVERSITY PRESS
Washington Square
New York NY 10003

Library of Congress Cataloging-in-Publication Data
Jewish law and legal theory / edited by Martin P. Golding.
p. cm. – (The International library of essays in law and legal theory. Legal cultures ; 4)
Includes bibliographical references.
ISBN 0-8147-3049-3
1. Jewish law. I. Golding, Martin P. (Martin Philip), 1930–
II. Series.
LAW <General Jewi 1993>
296.1'8—dc20

93-27808
CIP

Contents

PART IV ETHICAL CONCEPTS IN SUBSTANTIVE LAW

PART V THE JURISTIC PROCESS IN JEWISH LEGAL THEORY

PART VI SELECTED TOPICS IN JEWISH JURISPRUDENCE

Public Law

Criminal Law

Unjust Enrichment

Acknowledgements

The editors and publishers wish to thank the following for permission to use copyright material.

Norman Lamm and Aaron Kirschenbaum (1979), 'Freedom and Constraint in the Jewish Juridical Process', *Cardozo Law Review*, **1**, pp. 99–133. Copyright © Norman Lamm and Aaron Kirschenbaum. This article originally appeared in 1 Cardozo Law Review 99 (1979).

E J Brill, Leiden for essays: Shmuel Shilo (1978), 'Maimonides on "Dina de-Malkhuta Dina" (The Law of the State is Law)', *The Jewish Law Annual*, **1**, pp. 146–67; Nahum Rakover (1980), 'Unjust Enrichment', *The Jewish Law Annual*, **3**, pp. 9–32; Norman Solomon (1980), 'Concepts of *Zeh Neheneh*... in the Analytic School', *The Jewish Law Annual*, **3**, pp. 49–62.

Diné Israel for essays: Arnold Enker (1973), 'Self-Incrimination in Jewish Law – a Review Essay', *Diné Israel*, **4**, pp. 107–24; Aaron Levine (1977), 'The Just Price Doctrine in Judaic Law – an Economic Analysis', *Diné Israel*, **8**, pp. 7–31.

L'Eylah for essays: Daniel B. Sinclair (1986), 'Maimonides and Natural Law Theory', *L'Eylah*, **22**, pp. 35–40; Daniel B. Sinclair (1990), 'Legal Reasoning in Maimonidean Jurisprudence', *L'Eylah*, **29**, pp. 32–5.

Harvard Law Review Association for the essay: Moshe Silberg (1961), 'Law and Morals in Jewish Jurisprudence', *Harvard Law Review*, **75**, pp. 306, 308–31.

Israel Law Review for the essay: Shmuel Shilo (1978), 'On One Aspect of Law and Morals in Jewish Law: *Lifnim Mishurat Hadin*', *Israel Law Review*, **13**, pp. 359–90.

Jewish Law Association for the essay: Nahum Rakover (1990), 'The "Law" and the Noahides', *Jewish Law Association Studies: The Boston Conference Volume*, **4**, pp. 169–180. Copyright © Scholars Press, U.S.A.

Juridical Review for the essay: Isaac Herzog (1929), 'Moral Rights and Duties in Jewish Law', *Juridical Review*, **41**, pp. 60–70.

Jerusalem Center for Public Affairs for the essay: Menachem Elon (1983), 'Power and Authority: Halachic Stance of the Traditional Community and Its Contemporary Implications', in *Kinship and Consent: The Jewish Political Tradition and Its Contemporary Uses*, Washington DC: University Press of America, pp. 183–213.

New York University Press for the essay: David M. Feldman (1968), 'The Structure of Jewish Law', in *Birth Control in Jewish Law*, New York: New York University Press, pp. 3–18. Reprinted by permission. Reprinted in M.M. Kellner (ed.) (1978), *Contemporary Jewish Ethics*, pp. 21–37, New York: San Hedrin Press.

Ohio State University Press for the essay: Aharon Lichtenstein (1975), 'Does Jewish Tradition Recognize an Ethic Independent of Halakha?', Ohio State University Press, pp. 62–88.

Religious Ethics, Incorporated for the essay: Aaron Kirschenbaum (1980), 'The Bystander's Duty to Rescue in Jewish Law', *Journal of Religious Ethics*, **8**, pp. 204–26.

Jeffrey I. Roth (1988), 'The Justification for Controversy Under Jewish Law', *California Law Review*, **76**, pp. 337–87. Copyright © Jeffrey I. Roth.

Tel Aviv University Studies in Law for the essay: Aaron Kirschenbaum (1980–82), 'Jewish Law and the Abuse of Rights', *Tel Aviv University Studies in Law*, **5**, pp. 98–114.

David Weiss Halivni (1978), 'Can a Religious Law be Immoral?', in *Perspectives on Jews and Judaism: Essays in Honor of Wolfe Kelman*, New York: The Rabbinical Assembly. Reprinted by permission.

Ernest Weinrib (1990), 'Rescue and Restitution', *S'vara*, **1**, pp. 59–65. Copyright © Ernest Weinrib.

Every effort has been made to trace all the copyright holders, but if any have been inadvertently overlooked the publishers will be pleased to make the necessary arrangements at the first opportunity.

Series Preface

The International Library of Law and Legal Theory is designed to provide important research materials in an accessible form. Each volume contains essays of central theoretical importance in its subject area. The series as a whole makes available an extensive range of valuable material which will be of considerable interest to those involved in the research, teaching and study of law.

The series has been divided into three sections. The Schools section is intended to represent the main distinctive approaches and topics of special concern to groups of scholars. The Areas section takes in the main branches of law with an emphasis on essays which present analytical and theoretical insights of broad application. The section on Legal Cultures makes available the distinctive legal theories of different legal traditions and takes up topics of general comparative and developmental concern.

I have been delighted and impressed by the way in which the editors of the individual volumes have set about the difficult task of selecting, ordering and presenting essays from the immense quantity of academic legal writing published in journals throughout the world. Editors were asked to pick out those essays from law, philosophy and social science journals which they consider to be fundamental for the understanding of law, as seen from the perspective of a particular approach or sphere of legal interest. This is not an easy task and many difficult decisions have had to be made in order to ensure that a representative sample of the best journal essays available takes account of the scope of each topic or school.

I should like to express my thanks to all the volume editors for their willing participation and scholarly judgement. The interest and enthusiasm which the project has generated is well illustrated by the fact that an original projection of 12 volumes drawn up in 1989 has now become a list of some 60 volumes. I must also acknowledge the vision, persistence and constant cheerfulness of John Irwin and the marvellous work done by Mrs Margaret O'Reilly and Sonia Hubbard.

TOM D. CAMPBELL
Series Editor
The Faculty of Law
The Australian National University

Introduction

This collection of essays is intended to introduce the English-language reader to a discussion of issues in the theory of Jewish law. Of Jewish law it has been said that it is 'an independent legal system embracing most of the subjects to be found in any system of positive law'.[1] But it also embraces much more. The traditional term for Jewish law, in its widest sense, is 'halakhah'; aside from such standard 'civil' or 'secular' law subjects as contracts and torts, the halakhah includes 'religious' and 'ritual' or 'ceremonial' law. The meaning of the term is often traced to the Hebrew *halokh*, 'to walk'. Thus, halakhah has been understood as 'a way of life', the distinctively Jewish way of life, so that Jewish law is inseparable from the Jewish religion.[2] It is understandable therefore that various essays in this volume should touch on topics of theological concern, but how the relation between the law and Judaism is to be defined in depth is not dealt with; nor do the essays explore the reasons for ritual laws.[3] In making his selections, the editor has chosen to emphasize, in the main, subjects in the philosophy of law and jurisprudential analysis that have arisen for legal systems generally and which would be of interest to readers who approach the field from the perspective of any modern legal system.

Jewish law may well be the world's oldest operative legal system. Aside from the Hebrew Bible, its literary sources go back at least to the middle of the third century of the common era and continue into the present. Until almost the end of the 18th century the halakhah, in both its civil and religious parts, by and large governed relations among Jews in all their communities.[4] These communities were organized bodies with their own institutions: Jewish courts were functioning agencies and rabbis were judges and legal scholars who elaborated and applied the law to changing circumstances (see Chapter 20, 'Power and Authority', by Justice Menachem Elon). By the beginning of the 19th century, however, this situation no longer universally obtained, for reasons too complex to be detailed here. Whereas it was once the case that a Jew could avoid the authority of the community only by conversion to another faith, adherence to Jewish law increasingly became a matter of individual choice for people who otherwise still identified themselves as Jews. (It should be noted that in the State of Israel, however, questions of personal status and family law initially fall under the jurisdiction of religious courts – rabbinic courts in the case of Jews.) Moreover by the beginning of the 20th century, the plenitude of communal legal authority had eroded in most corners of the world. Yet to this very day the halakhah has continued to be investigated, elaborated and applied, even though it has ceased to be effective everywhere.

Brief surveys of the literary sources of Jewish law may be found in footnotes to various essays in this volume, particularly those by Lamm and Kirschenbaum (Chapter 15) and by Roth (Chapter 16); the main classic sources are surveyed in the piece by Feldman (Chapter 1). If the literature *about* Jewish law is large,[5] and it is, the literature *in* Jewish law is massive.[6] A standard English translation (Soncino) of the Babylonian Talmud, for instance, runs to nearly 20 closely-printed thin-paper volumes. It has been estimated that well over 250,000 responsa (answers to legal questions) have been written, most of them dealing with 'civil' law matters. Although the literature in and about Jewish law is largely in Hebrew, a number of significant publications have appeared in English in recent years. A highly recommended English-language account of the substantive law that corresponds to a modern system, known as *mishpat ivri* (see below), as well as the theory of Jewish law, is edited by Menachem Elon (1975), *The Principles of Jewish Law*, Jerusalem: Keter Publishing House.[7]

Since the halakhah is a religious legal system, questions have been raised as to the appropriate methodology for its investigation. Is it possible, without distortion, to study Jewish law from a secular point of view; that is, from a perspective that does not accept the presuppositions of the system's own practitioners? Or does the investigator have to be a committed adherent? These are disputed questions; the reader will recognize, here, an issue analogous to that raised in general legal theory by the late H.L.A. Hart's distinction between the internal and external points of view.[8] Furthermore, if Jewish civil law elements were to be incorporated into a secular law system, would they still be Jewish law?[9] This latter question has generated an ideological debate between those Israeli legal scholars who fear that such incorporation would result in a dilution of the essentially religious constitution of Jewish law, and those who feel that incorporation would bring the secular law system more into line with the Jewish character of the State. In any case, as important as they are, these and other methodological and definitional questions are not taken up in this collection, except incidentally. Instead, the reader is referred to the articles in *Modern Research in Jewish Law* (Leiden, 1980), edited by Professor Bernard S. Jackson. It was not thought appropriate to reprint any one of these articles without reprinting others. An essay in this collection that deals with some methodological issues in Jewish law research is Professor Shmuel Shilo's 'The Contrast between Mishpat Ivri and Halakhah' (Chapter 3).[10]

The Table of Contents indicates the orientation of this collection. Although the titles of the essays are highly descriptive of their subject matter, a few words should be said by way of introduction to the approach and structure of the volume.

After a brief account in Chapter 1 of the classic literary sources of Jewish law (Feldman, 'The Structure of Jewish Law'), we turn to two essays that deal with how the field of Jewish law is to be identified and the jurisprudential assumptions involved in that identification (Elon, 'The Legal System of Jewish Law' and Yuter, 'Legal Positivism and Contemporary *Halakhic* Discourse'). Both of these essays adopt (but only in passing, in the former piece) a 'positivistic' approach as to how the constituents of Jewish law are to be identified. Roughly speaking, they adopt a version, appropriate to the system at hand, of Hans Kelsen's doctrine of the 'Basic Norm'. Whether a positivistic approach to Jewish law can be fully maintained is dependent, however, on how one views the relation between ethics and law, and on the role of moral concepts and 'reason' in the elaboration of the law. These topics are dealt with in a number of the essays in this collection, enabling readers to come to their own conclusions on the issue. The editor has his doubts as to the adequacy of a Kelsenite approach.[11]

Sandwiched between the above mentioned essays is Shilo's 'The Contrast between Mishpat Ivri and Halakhah'. The reason for this placement is that a good deal of Justice Elon's essay is devoted to explaining the concept of mishpat ivri. As Elon indicates, the term 'mishpat ivri' is a coinage of the 20th century. It is used as a name for that part of Jewish law that corresponds to a modern legal system. Is there a basis in the classical sources for separating out mishpat ivri, so conceived, from the rest of the halakhah? Although this question is discussed by Elon, it will be useful to say a bit about it at this point. We can consider only two possibilities.

The classical sources (see Elon, footnote 6) do intimate a distinction between those matters that are between man and God (*bain adam la-makom*) and matters that are between man and his fellow (*bain adam la-havero*). 'For transgressions from man to God the Day of Atonement effects atonement; for transgressions between man and his fellow man the Day of Atonement does not effect atonement until he shall have first appeased his fellow man' (Mishnah, Yoma, 8:9; third century). Yet the separation of the system into 'civil' or 'secular' and religious parts is in many ways artificial. A central concept, perhaps *the* central concept, of the halakhah is that of *mitzvah*, commandment – divine commandment. 'Mitzvah' might be called the keyword of Jewish jurisprudence, just as John Austin said of 'command' in general jurisprudence. The law of the goring ox (Exodus, 21) is as much a divine commandment[12] as any of the Ten Commandments is.

Another distinction recognized in the classical sources is that between *mammona* (monetary matters) and *issura* (forbidden things). 'The essential criterion of ... *mammona*,' says Chief Rabbi Isaac Herzog, 'is that what is comprised in [this term] is subject to waiver or forbearance.' As Herzog explains, the waiver or forbearance of the party that has suffered a wrong or who is entitled to a right coming within this category at once removes it from the concern of the body-politic as represented by its authorized agencies. 'This is not the case with other departments of the law.'[13] This distinction has important legal consequences that may seem paradoxical in light of Herzog's explanation. For in contrast to forbidden things, monetary matters are to a significant extent subject both to rabbinic and communal enactment ('takkanah'), and to community practices and common expectations, in ways that affect a party's legal rights.

By itself, however, the distinction between monetary matters and forbidden things does not succeed in identifying that area of halakhah (i.e., mishpat ivri) which corresponds to a modern legal system. To be sure, most and perhaps all of the halakhah concerned with mammona would also be dealt with in a modern system; but such topics as family law and personal status, which are largely in the issura area, are also subsumed under a modern system. The issura area, however, covers much that falls outside the latter (e.g., forbidden foods as well as forbidden marriages).

While there may be no basis in the classical sources of Jewish law for isolating the area of mishpat ivri from the rest of the halakhah (and no one maintains that the isolation is absolute anyway), this collection of essays nevertheless focuses on that part of the halakhah that roughly corresponds to a modern secular legal system and on the sort of philosophical and jurisprudential issues that have been raised in connection with such systems. Still, the reader will find that quite a number of the essays deal with other aspects of the halakhah which could well be included in a different kind of collection based on the philosophy of Jewish law and religion.

Parts II, III and IV deal with the relation between Jewish law, natural law and ethics. This relation is complex; because the essays examine it in a variety of different contexts, it is difficult to generalize about their treatments. Very roughly speaking, two issues are considered. First, what role do natural law notions and ethical principles play in Jewish legal thought and in the elaboration of the halakhah? And second, is Jewish law subservient to natural law and ethical principles? These may be distinct issues and are as difficult to disentangle for Jewish law and legal theory as for other systems. Plainly, these issues have a bearing on whether a 'positivistic' approach to the identification of the constituents of Jewish law is adequate. Relevant to these issues, also, is Chapter 15 by Lamm and Kirschenbaum ('Freedom and Constraint in the Jewish Judicial Process') in Part V.

Thus, the reader will find that essays from different sections, as well as those from the same section, complement, supplement and sometimes constitute partial criticisms of other pieces. So, for instance, Chapter 5 by Professor Rakover in Part II ('The "Law" and the Noahides') is supplemented in various ways by Professor Shilo in Chapter 19 of Part VI ('Maimonides on "Dina De-Malkhuta Dina" (The Law of the State is Law)'), though the context of each is quite distinct. As will be evident from Chapter 5 by Rakover, Jewish law and legal theory recognize the existence of other legal systems developed and enforced by non-Jewish political entities. Maimonides's views on the scope of these systems and the authority that they exert over the Jewish residents in a non-Jewish state are examined by Shilo (Chapter 19).

Parts V and VI deal with topics that are raised in respect of other legal systems as well as the halakhah. But the flavour of these treatments is unique to Jewish law. Again, various chapters complement, supplement and sometimes constitute partial criticisms of others. (Compare, for example, the discussion of the famous talmudic passage of the 'oven of Achnai' in Chapter 8 by the late Justice Silberg (page 310 of the original) and in Professor Englard's 'Majority Decision and Individual Truth' (Chapter 17).) In Part V, on the juristic process of legal elaboration, the essays discuss a pervasive feature of the legal tradition from its earliest post-biblical literary sources – disputes over questions of law. Here, the reader will find analogues to a much debated subject in Anglo-American jurisprudence, as generated by the work of Professor Ronald Dworkin: is there a uniquely 'right answer' to every question of law?[14] As far as I am aware, the earliest mentions of this subject in connection with any legal system occur in classical Jewish legal materials.

The selection of topics for coverage in Part VI posed difficulties of choice, given limitations of space. Among the many subjects not included are family law and the status of Jewish law in foreign courts which, in the US at least, have raised both constitutional and halakhic questions, particularly in the area of divorce. Neither are there essays on issues in bioethics or medico-legal questions, in which an extensive literature exists in English. Nor on so-called biblical law.[15] (On these and other topics, see the bibliographies cited in footnote 5 below.) It is hoped nevertheless that the topics selected will give the reader a representative sample of what the jurisprudence of Jewish law is like.

Most of the essays in this collection might be described as analytical-historical, written in the mishpat ivri mode. Although many pieces refer to decisions on questions of law, none could be characterized as a legal responsum. It will also be noticed that this collection does not contain selections from any of the classic Jewish philosophers who wrote extensively on the theory of Jewish law. Moreover, with the exception of Maimonides (1135–1204), there are no essays devoted to an exposition of the views of any particular jurist or philosopher. The reason for making an exception in his case is the enormous influence he exerted on Jewish legal thought; many subsequent discussions begin and end with him.

With one exception (Silberg's 'Law and Morals in Jewish Jurisprudence' (Chapter 8), where the editor has deleted the translator's note), only whole articles have been reprinted. Some of the essays are fairly lengthy, while others are quite short. Because of space limitations, a short contribution has on occasion been selected over a much longer piece on the same topic by the same author. This is the case, for example, with Professor Rakover's

'The "Law" and the Noahides' (Chapter 5).[16] Also, with the exception of Chapter 1 (Feldman's 'The Structure of Jewish Law'), no selection has been drawn from single-author books. It should be noted that the abbreviations, transliterations and sometimes even the translations of the same passages are not uniform; note that the editor has not wanted to tinker with the texts in order to introduce uniformity.

Finally, the editor wishes to thank the Research Council of the Faculty of Arts and Sciences of Duke University for a grant that enabled him to complete this work.

Notes

1 B. Lifshitz (1990), 'Israeli Law and Jewish Law – Interaction and Independence', *Israel Law Review*, **24**, 507.

2 'Halakhah' also has a more restricted meaning. 'In practice [halakhah] has the same meaning as [hóros] (literally "boundary") which means *regula*, and especially a statement of the law, a juristic principle, in antithesis to case law [ma'aseh]. ...' S. Lieberman (1962), *Hellenism in Jewish Palestine*, 2nd ed., New York: Jewish Theological Seminary, p. 83, n. 3. Leiberman notes the suggestion that the term derives from a Babylonian word, *ilku* (tax, a fixed land tax).

3 Closest to dealing with the theme of Judaism and the law is Chapter 6, 'Judaism and Natural Law', by Professor J. David Bleich. While Bleich's essay is written from an 'orthodox' perspective, it is especially useful for its extensive references to a variety of Jewish writings bearing on natural law. In general, the editor has sought to avoid denominational debates over the scope and authority of the ('religious') halakhah. For that, see articles in *Judaism*, **29** (Winter 1980).

4 See the still useful three-volume work by Salo W. Baron (1942), *The Jewish Community*, New York: Jewish Publication Society.

5 N. Rakover (ed.) (1990), *The Multi-Language Bibliography of Jewish Law*, Jerusalem: The Library of Jewish Law; P.H. Weisbard and D. Schonberg (eds) (1989), *Jewish Law: Bibliography of Sources and Scholarship in English*, Littleton, Colorado: F.B. Rothman; R. Warburg (1986), 'A Bibliographic Guide to *Mishpat Ivri*: Books and Articles in English', *National Jewish Law Review*, **1**, 61–135. A computer search in the *Legal Resource Index* will show recent articles in English. A work that deserves mention here is Aaron Kirschenbaum (1991), *Equity in Jewish Law*, 2 vols, Hoboken, N.J. and New York: Ktav Publishing House and Yeshira University Press, which deals with many topics covered in this collection.

6 For an account of the halakhic literature of the classical period, see Shmuel Safrai (ed.) (1987), *The Literature of the Sages*, Assen/Maastricht and Philadelphia: Van Gorcum and Fortress Press. For a comprehensive account up to the present, see Manachem Elon (1993), *Jewish Law: History, Sources, Principles*, Philadelphia: Jewish Publication Society, a four-volume English translation of a work in Hebrew.

7 The articles in this volume (over 700 double-column pages), some of them quite lengthy, were originally printed in 1972 in *Encyclopaedia Judaica*.

8 See H.L.A. Hart (1961), *The Concept of Law*, Oxford: Clarendon Press; relatedly, on the interpretative attitude, see Ronald Dworkin (1986), *Law's Empire*, Cambridge, MA.: Harvard University Press.

9 As noted above, this incorporation has occurred in Israeli law with respect to personal status and family law. In addition, reference to the halakhah is found in many decisions of the Israeli secular courts. The Foundations of Law Act (1980) provides that a court has to turn to 'the principles of freedom, justice, equity and peace of Israel's heritage' when it finds no solution to a legal question in statute law, case law or by way of analogy.

10 Shilo draws the contrast in terms of the differing methodological approaches of mishpat ivri and the traditional halakhah, including their respective approaches to manuscript materials. On the latter point now see, however, Moshe Bleich (1993), 'The Role of Manuscripts in Halakhic Decision-Making', *Tradition*, **27**, 22–55.

11 Perhaps a distinction should be drawn between a Kelsenite legal scientist who is engaged in the second-order activity of describing a given legal system (which is how I regard the mishpat ivri researcher) and the practitioner within the system (the poseq, the decisor). It could be argued that the criteria by which the former determines the contents of the system are not necessarily identical to those employed by the latter.

12 According to a talmudic source, there are 613 commandments; in fact, a genre of halakhic literature developed which was devoted to determining the constituents of this set of 613. In his Book of Commandments, Moses Maimonides (1135–1204), the great philosopher and jurist, formulates the mitzvah of the goring ox in abstract terms: 'to judge the laws of the ox'. The law of the goring ox was understood as a duty of the courts to judge cases of property damage and personal injury caused by animals. Many rules are subsumed under this law which, in the Talmud, takes up most of the first six chapters of the tractate Bava Kama.

13 Isaac Herzog (1936), I, *The Main Institutions of Jewish Law*, London: Soncino Press, pp. xix f. Five volumes of this work were projected, but only two appeared. This may be considered as one of the first important productions in mishpat ivri in English. Rabbi Herzog (1888–1959) was chief rabbi of the Irish Free State from 1921, becoming chief rabbi of Palestine in 1936, and later of the State of Israel.

14 R. Dworkin (1978), *Taking Rights Seriously*, Cambridge, MA: Harvard University Press, revised edition.

15 The Bible, particularly the Pentateuch (The Five Books of Moses; the Torah, in one meaning of the term) is of course the central text in all of Jewish law. The present collection of essays, however, is concerned with the law and theory of law presented in the rabbinic juristic tradition, the halakhah and its subdivisions. For an overview of the use of the Bible in the tannaitic period (first to third centuries), see Rimon Kasher, 'The Interpretation of Scripture in Rabbinic Literature' in M.J. Mulder (ed.) (1988), *Mikra*, Assen/Maastricht and Philadelphia: Van Gorcum and Fortress Press, pp. 547–94. See also the article entitled 'Interpretation' in M. Elon (ed.) (1975), *The Principles of Jewish Law*, Jerusalem: Keter Publishing House. It might be added that talmudic rabbis recognized that it was not feasible to enforce various biblical laws, some of which, they contended, were never meant to be enforced but which instead comprised a sort of ideal law. Thus, in the criminal law area, alongside the ideal scriptural law, there existed the exigency jurisdictions of the king and the rabbinic courts in order to preserve social peace. See the essays on Criminal law by Professors Enker and Kirschenbaum in Part VI of this collection (Chapters 21 and 22).

16 For his longer and more detailed treatment, see N. Rakover (1991), 'Jewish Law and the Noahide Obligation to Preserve Social Order', *Cardozo Law Review*, **12**, 1073–1136. For a book-length study in a more theological vein, see David Novak (1983), *The Image of the Non-Jew in Judaism: An Historical and Constructive Study of the Noahide Law*, New York and Toronto: E. Mellen Press.

Part I
General Aspects of Jewish Law and Legal Theory

[1]

1.
The Structure of Jewish Law

DAVID M. FELDMAN

The Talmud

Supreme in authority—the "fundamental law"—is the Torah in its narrower sense, which means the Pentateuch, the Five Books of Moses. In its broader sense, the "Torah" encompasses all of developed Jewish religious law and lore. From the legal standpoint, even the remainder of the Bible serves as an auxiliary basis; when the Rabbis speak of a "biblical law," they are referring to commandments or ordinances that derive from the Pentateuch alone. The word "derive" here is used advisedly, for ordinances not found literally in the Pentateuchal text but which the Rabbis deduced therefrom by agreed-upon rules of interpretation are also called *d'oraita* [from the Torah]. Amplification of biblical law to include safeguards—a "fence around the law"—or ordinances, observances, or even new enactments *(takkanot)* instituted by classic rabbinical authority, are called *d'rabbanan* [from the Rabbis].[1]

The conventional division is between *Torah shebikh'tav*, the Written Torah, and *Torah sheb'al peh*, the Oral Law. "By the side of Scripture there had always gone an unwritten tradition, in part interpreting and applying the written Torah, in part supplementing it," says George Foot Moore in his study of Talmudic Judaism.[2] This oral interpretation is, in turn, divisible into two essential forms: In defining what the Torah requires in the matter of practice ("the way wherein they should walk and the thing which they should do" [Exodus 18:20]), the *halakhah* (from *halokh*, to go, to walk) was devised. The detailed application of Torah law was systematically formulated, and the ordinances and observances were defined and regulated in accordance, again, with agreed-upon rules or canons of legal decision. Hence, *halakhah* is the law or a particular law. Where, on the other hand, the oral law yielded extralegal teaching such as moral maxims, legends, philosophical and historical speculation, theological observations, and the like, these became known as *aggadah* [the narrative]. *Halakhah* and *aggadah* are the two great currents in the oral tradition.[3]

The earliest widely accepted reduction to writing of the legal matter of the oral law was the work of R. Judah the Patriarch (*HaNasi*, known simply as "Rabbi," d. 219) and was called the *Mishnah* [the *disciplina*, or manual of study]. Before his time, R. Akiva (d. 132) and his pupil R. Meir had essayed earlier compositions of the *Mishnah*, but that of "Rabbi" promptly became the canonical one. The word *Mishnah* derives from a root meaning "to study"; hence its definition as a manual or the repository of relayed teaching. It is indeed the cornerstone of all later law, for the Talmud, with all its vast size, is primarily a commentary and exposition of the Mishnaic nucleus. Traditional material formally omitted from the Mishnah, moreover, is given due consideration by the Talmud. Described by the general term *baraita* [outside], this material becomes an aid to explaining the Mishnah and stands alongside it in the Talmud's discussions. The word *baraita* covers other definitive corpora of law as well, though they have individual names, such as the *Tosefta* [Supplement] which is now a separately printed collection of remnants of earlier compilations of halakhah that found no place in Rabbi's official *disciplina*. Also, the *Mekhilta*, *Sifra*, and *Sifrei* are included in this general term, although they are works of *Midrash* rather than Mishnah.

Midrash is an important term for our purposes: The word means "exposition" and refers to large extra-Talmudic collections of biblical interpretation. Like the Oral Law itself and unlike the Mishnah, there are Midrash collections of both halakhah and aggadah. The three mentioned above are halakhic *Midrashim* on books of the Pentateuch and are largely contemporaneous with the Mishnah. On the other hand, the *Rabbah* collection of Midrash comprises aggadic elaboration of, and homilies upon, the Five Books of Moses as well as the Books of Ruth, Song of Songs, Ecclesiastes, and so on, which date anywhere from the sixth century to the eleventh. But these, like the *Tanhuma*, another cycle of *aggadic* Midrash, are based on material of much earlier vintage.

Since the Mishnah is the fundament of the Talmud, its six divisions, called Orders, are the divisions of the Talmud itself. The Six Orders are further divided into sixty-three tractates called *massekhtot*. The word's root is akin to that of the Latin *textus*, both meaning, a weaving together, hence a text or treatise.[4] The third of the Six Orders, for example, is *Nashim*, meaning Women, and contains seven tractates, the first of which is *Y'vamot*, literally "Sisters-in-law" or Levirate Wives. Because this tractate contains the pivotal *baraita* about contraception, as well as references to the duty of procreation, it is referred to frequently in this study. Other tractates in the Order *Nashim*, such as *Kiddushin* [Betrothals] and *K'tubot* and *Gittin* [Writs of Marriage and of Divorce] also contain much material relevant to our subject, as does *Niddah* [The Menstruant] from the sixth Order *Tohorot* which deals with ritual purities. Since the Talmudic discussion of any subject within the tractates, however, follows not a logical but an organic sequence, and since all of Jewish law is interconnected, with analogies adduced from one sphere to the other, references from the whole of the Talmud are brought to bear on the subject at hand in the relevant literature. Source texts from tractate *Shabbat* of the second Order [*Moed*, "Appointed Times"], or from tractate *Sanhedrin* [The High Court] of the fourth Order [*N'zikin*, "Torts"], or from any number of other tractates, necessarily figure in our discussion as well.

Infinitely more voluminous than the Mishnah itself, the large body of analysis, discussion, dissection, and commentary on the Mishnah is called *G'mara*, meaning, in Aramaic, "the study."[5] In Hebrew "the study" is the "Talmud." By usage, Talmud refers to both Mishnah and *G'mara* together and hence, leaving to one side the great collections of Midrash, "the Talmud" is the comprehensive term for the large corpus of official formulations of oral law and lore. The Talmudic period, if it is said to begin with early Mishnaic times, comprises a span of at least six centuries. The ongoing argumentation, commentary, and refinement continued for at least three centuries after the redaction of the Mishnah and was brought to a close about the year 500. This scholastic activity took place primarily in the academies of Babylonia—Sura, Nehardea, and Pumbedita—where the Sages lived under Zoroastrian rule. Back in Palestine, a parallel development was taking place: the comments and interpretive teaching of the Sages there were sifted and set down in writing about a century earlier than was the case in Babylonia. The Talmud of Babylonia is much more exhaustive than the Palestinian Talmud and, for many and various reasons, predominated throughout subsequent Jewish history as the object of intensive study and as the reigning authority in Jewish law.[6] Hence, "the Talmud" means the Babylonian recension thereof, although *TB* as opposed to *TP* is used for accurate footnote reference.

Post-Talmudic Codes

The first important stratum of interpretation after the period of the Talmud is that of the Geonim. With Babylonia still the center of the Jewish world, the heads of its higher academies bore the title of *Gaon* [Excellency] and taught the Torah to students from near and far. In addition to the Responsa which they wrote as answers to queries in matters of law and faith, they were the first to compose systematic codes of halakhah by summing up in logical arrangement the conclusions of Talmudic discussion. The first of these is the *She'iltot* of R. Ahai Gaon (d. 760), a leading scholar of Pumbedita. The book contains 191 discourses, arranged according to the sections of the Torah as read in the synagogue, and seeking to explain the commandments therein in the light of the Talmud and other halakhic works.[7] The *Halakhot G'dolot* by R. Simon Kaira of the ninth century is another early example of an ambitious attempt to arrange topically the material of Jewish law and offer the decisions. After him, the estimable R. Hai Gaon and others produced some important partial codes in the next century and a half.

The scene shifts to North Africa where Talmudic studies flourished at the beginning of the second millennium. Chief among the commentators of this school was R. Hananel of Kairawan, who combined three convergent streams of learning: the Palestinian, the Babylonian, and the European. His annotations are of the greatest importance and appear alongside the text in printed editions of the Talmud.

For our purposes, the important product of the North African school is the work of R. Isaac of Fez, Isaac Al Fasi (1013—1073). Like the *Halakhot G'dolot* on which it was modeled, this "Alfasi" is a codex which closely follows the Talmud but which omits when it can all the discussion leading up to the legal conclusions. By including an opinion of one of the Sages, Al Fasi stamps it as the norm (halakhah); by simply ignoring another opinion he shows it to be rejected. His greatest influence lies in this, his role as decisor [*posek*] of the halakhah, for in the Talmud the debates on doubtful points often leave a matter undetermined. Al Fasi helps us to understand the meaning of the text as well: "We have, therefore, in the Alfasi, a work which is a commentary and a code at the same time. The commentary is implied; the code is manifest. And both are in the form of an abridged Talmud."[8]

Rashi and Tosafot

The commentary par excellence on the Talmud was, however, being composed by Al Fasi's younger contemporary on a different continent. Rashi, the acronym for R. Sh'lomo Yitzhaki (1040–1105) of the French province of Champagne, lived in an era of thriving Talmudic study in Europe after its decline in Babylonia. It was the century when R. Samuel HaNaggid of Granada in Spain had composed his systematic *Introduction to the Talmud* and when the pupils of the illustrious Rabbenu Gershom of Mayence—among whom Rashi's teacher is to be counted—founded many schools. From his teacher Rashi had learned the value of keeping written notes. Out of his classroom explanations to his disciples, there came the great Commentary on the Talmud. Based on earlier notes of R. Gershom's school, his Commentary is largely the result of his own keen insight, comprehensive mastery of all of Talmudic literature, awareness of the pupil's difficulty, and an unrivaled felicity of style. Here, too, however, we deal not with a "dictionary," with commentation which merely explains obscure passages—although that it does magnificently—but with a legally decisive presentation of the essence and applicability of the Talmudic argument.[9]

In the several schools that rose up under the influence of Rashi's popular intellectual activity, his notebook came to serve as a text. Known as the *konteros*, after the Latin *commentarius*, it was and is formally studied along with the Talmud and has opened to great numbers what had been virtually a sealed book.

Among the most eminent teachers of the next generation utilizing this companion text, were members of Rashi's own family. The central debate on the birth control *baraita* in this study has as its principals Rashi on one side and his grandson R. Jacob ben Meir of Rameru on the other. The latter is known as *Rabbenu Yaakov Tam*, "Our Rabbi Jacob the Unblemished," after the biblical description of Jacob as *tam*, meaning whole, simple, unblemished. To Rabbenu Tam pupils flocked in large numbers, some from countries as distant as Bohemia and Russia, and he was consulted by Rabbis from near and far. Rabbenu Tam "possessed a remarkably original, broad yet subtle intellect, and his writings display keen penetration and singular vigor of thought."[10] These words apply as well to the other masters of the new species of Talmudic literature initiated by Rabbenu Tam. Under the general heading of *Tosafot* (literally, "Supplements"); this type of commentation does much more than supplement the *konteros*, which served as its point of departure. The *Tosafot* aim at profounder depths, dissecting a Talmudic passage or Rashi's accepted commentary with the scalpel of subtle and forceful logic, against the background of an all-embracing mastery of the principles and content of the Talmud. Rabbenu Tam in particular "took pleasure," a modern biographer of Rashi puts it, "in raising ingenious objections to Rashi's explanations and in proposing original solutions," as did the other Tosafists. He continues,

> Yet, it would be a mistake to see in the *Tosafot* nothing but the taste for controversy or the love of discussion. . .the Tosafists even more than Rashi sought to deduce the Halakhah. . .and to discover analogies permitting the solution of new cases.[11]

A large part of Rabbenu Tam's contribution is contained in his *Sefer HaYashar*, but his pupils quote him in the *Tosafot* on just about every other page of the Talmud. Another prolific writer of Tosafot, a nephew of Rabbenu Tam, was R. Isaac of Dampierre, known as "Ri". In all standard editions of the Talmud since the first Bomberg (printed) edition of 1523, the text is flanked by Rashi and Tosafot facing one another and lending it their respective modes of illumination. Many Tosafot, other than those appearing in editions of the Talmud, were composed during this time and later published separately. The Tosafot of R. Isaiah da Trani of thirteenth-century Italy—known as *Tos'fot RiD*— is an important example.

Maimonides' Code

While such commentation proceeded apace, the work of proper and systematic codification awaited a successor to Al Fasi. It found one in the son of a disciple of his disciple—R. Moses ben Maimon, "Rambam" (1135–1204) of Cordova in Spain, deservedly the most famous Jew of the Middle Ages. Not the least of many achievements of Maimonides was the greatest single work of halakhah ever produced—a monumental code of Jewish law. He called it the *Mishneh Torah*, the "Second Torah," because thenceforth no other book "would be needed" in determining the law. He states his purpose in the Introduction as that of offering the student the developed law conveniently accessible, making it unnecessary to consult any intervening work. Arranged in architectural orderliness and written with brilliant lucidity, the Code comprises all of Talmudic and Geonic law in fourteen grand divisions, or books, which total one thousand chapters. (In the Hebrew numerical system, 14 is *Yad*, which gave the book its more popular name *Yad HaHazakah*, the "Strong Hand.") This marvel of structure, scope, and clarity commands the awesome respect of scholars to this day and must be reckoned with in any analysis of the halakhah. Yet it suffered from the defects of its virtues: Intending it as a single, complete, practical handbook, Maimonides chose to exclude even the minimum of Talmudic discussion and, of course to omit the citation of authorities for his decisions. Less understandable is his omission of the views of the Franco-German scholars. Dogmatically, in clean but categoric propositions, Maimonides laid down the law. His work thus became the target of the strictures of R. Abraham ben David of Posquieres in Southern France, and subsequent editions of the Code have Ben David's demurrals printed on the margin or as a kind of inset within the text. Other scholars of that and later generations endeavor to supply the missing source references (as in the Commentary, *Maggid Mishneh*) and the Franco-German material (*Hagahot Maimuniyot*), as well as to meet the objections of Ben David (*Migdal Oz*), or elucidate the material generally (*Mishneh LaMelekh*). Several of these commentaries are likewise printed with the Code itself, so that the regal masterpiece, with *nos'ei kelav*, its "armament bearers," now reigns supreme, unique and impregnable.

Ben David himself, despite his opposition to Maimonides' method of code-making, contributes a small work to this genre—a partial code. He collected the laws of *Niddah*, the treatment of which he concluded with a compact discourse on proper marital relations; hence the importance to our subject of this work, which he called *Ba'alei HaNefesh*. An earlier work of Maimonides, his *Commentary to the Mishnah*, is also relevant.

The Thirteenth Century Scholars and Asheri's Code

Some sort of a union between the Spanish and the French-German schools is exemplified by the mid-thirteenth-century Code, called *Sefer Mitzvot Gadol* (*SMaG*). Here the material is grouped around the 613 biblical commands, divided into positive and negative ones, under which are given the Talmudic deductions therefrom and other material less closely connected. The views of the Tosafists of the Rhineland are given a hearing along with those of Maimonides, serving as a bridge of acquaintance between the two. A generation later Rabbi Isaac of Corbeil wrote his compendium called *Sefer Mitzvot Katan* [*SMaK*], which proved highly popular among laymen and scholars alike and which, too, figures in our treatment here. So does an important thirteenth-century Code called the *Mord'khai* by R. Mordecai ben Hillel of Nuremberg (d.1298). Actually less of a code in the usual sense than a digest of opinions, decisions, and Responsa, the *Mord'khai* is held in high esteem by scholars to whom it served as a comprehensive source book.

Another code-like commentary from this period, or commentary that offers a digest of Talmudic debate, is the *Beit HaB'hirah* of R. Menahem HaMeiri (1249-1315) of Perpignan, Southern France. Written in the lucid style of his model Maimonides, this work is a running commentary to most of the tractates of the Talmud, many of which, unfortunately, were not published until the nineteenth century when the work quickly became a popular study companion. His ability to interpret, distill, and set forth the essence of the Talmud and of other authorities had instant appeal among students. His own newly coined phrases in referring to these authorities became well known: Al Fasi was the "Greatest of Decisors"; Rashi, the "Greatest of Teachers," and Maimonides the "Greatest of Systematizers."[12]

The "great reconciler" between the two schools was the foremost Talmudic scholar of his age, R. Moses ben Nahman—Nahmanides, ("Ramban," 1195-1270) who lived in Spain but who had learned his Talmud from French masters. He esteemed their method, the analytic method of subtle dialectic, and blended it with the local Spanish approach, the method of synthesis, of erudite systematization. Much more important than his partial Code, *Torat HaAdam*, on mourning customs, are Nahmanides' analytic commentaries and *novellae* on the tractates of the Talmud, where his genius yields new insights and resolutions of difficulties. Of course, his superb Commentary to the Bible itself, which is ample in both erudition and keenness, must be mentioned. Also, a small tract, important for our study, the *Iggeret HaKodesh* on the subject of sexual relations, has been ascribed to him as well.[13]

Nahmanides' most outstanding pupil was R. Solomon ben Adret ("Rashba," 1215-1310), who compiled codes of particular sections of the halakhah and who, too, is better known for his incisive *novellae* on the Talmud, to say nothing of his Responsa. Three thousand of his Responsa have been published.

As the famous Rabbi of Barcelona, Ben Adret was host one day to R. Asher ben Yehiel (1250–1327), who had fled there from the pillage and persecution visited upon the Jews of medieval Germany. Rabbenu Asher (Asheri or, better, "Rosh") was appointed Rabbi at Toledo and achieved renown as a scholar, teacher, and judge. His fame for our purposes rests upon his Abstract of the Talmud which followed the example of Al Fasi (and like it, was called "*Halakhot*"), but was enriched by the opinions of the later authorities, Maimonides and the Tosafists. His Abstract was marked by scholastic acumen and met with a ready reception in his old and new homes. Some parts of the Talmud itself were the object of a running commentary by Asheri; he has, moreover, authored separate Tosafot of his own to many tractates. All of these, together with one of his Responsa, figure prominently in our study. Rabbenu Y'ruham (d. 1340), author of a significant code not infrequently consulted, is reckoned among the pupils of Asheri.

The Tur Code

The next landmark code was that of Asheri's son, Jacob, who, next to Maimonides, is the most resourceful of all codifiers. He took the *Mishneh Torah* as his model, but his work is the independent creation of an original mind. He gives neither sources nor proof but generally cites the post-Talmudic authorities by name. Rabbinic studies had developed rapidly since the period of Maimonides two centuries earlier and, as R. Jacob says in the Introduction to his work, there was then hardly a point of law on which there were no differences of opinion.

Like that of his father and Nahmanides, the work of R. Jacob combined the French-German dialectics with Spanish systematics, and answered all the requirements of a code for the next two centuries. Even then, the new codices adopted his system and arrangement, about which more must be said: His book is called *Tur*, short for *Arba'ah Turim*, the Four Rows (after Exodus 28:17, the four rows of stones on the High Priest's breastplate). The first of the Four is called *Orah Hayyim* [Way of Life] and comprises the laws of Sabbath, festivals, daily prayers, and so on. The second is *Yoreh Deah* and deals with forbidden and permitted foods, as well as vows and purity regulations. The third is *Even HaEzer*, which treats of marriage, divorce, sexual relations, and the like. The fourth is *Hoshen HaMisphat*, collating civil and criminal law, inheritance, property, etc. The name of the third of the Four Rows, that of *Even HaEzer*, alludes to the phrase *ezer k'negdo* in Genesis, where the woman is called man's "helpmeet." Later codes adopted this highly serviceable arrangement, and even the section numbers within each of the Four Rows became standard. Hence, *E.H.* appears frequently in our footnotes, with *E.H.* 1 and *E.H.* 23 signifying the same relevant section in either the *Tur* or the later codes or commentaries thereon. Responsa books, too, have designated either sections or entire volumes accordingly: Vol. *E.H.*, Vol. *O.H.*, etc. R. Jacob's *Tur* succeeded as the standard Code even in his own lifetime and, on account of its conciliatory yet definitive nature, displaced many similar works of before and after.

The two centuries that elapsed between the *Tur* and the *Shulhan Arukh* saw little that was novel in the field of complete codes. Some partial efforts, such as a work on the liturgy alone, called *Sefer Abudarham*, of R. David Abudarham of Seville (d. 1345) may be mentioned, as well as *Maharil*, the custom compilation on the authority of R. Jacob Halevi Mollin of the Rhineland (d. 1427). A highly popular work, translated into many European languages, was the *Sefer HaHinnukh* of R. Aaron Halevy of thirteenth- and fourteenth-century Barcelona. This is a catalog of the commandments according to the weekly Torah reading, accompanied by much legal definition and moral edification. While significant new codes may not have been produced, the study of Talmud was far from neglected. This was the period of the great *Rishonim*, the Early Authorities, so called because they date from before the *Shulhan Arukh*. In addition to Nahmanides, Ben Adret, and Asheri mentioned above, these include R. Nissim, Ritva, R. Aaron Halevi, R. Isaac bar Sheshet—even R. Yosef Habib, whose *Nimmukei Yosef* Commentary to Al Fasi's Abstract is an important source—and many others. A work called *Shittah M'kubetzet* of the seventeenth century preserves some of the literary fruit of these *Rishonim*, much of it not otherwise available in their volumes of *novellae*.

The Shulhan Arukh

After the expulsion of the Jews from Spain and Portugal towards the end of the fifteenth century, they found themselves scattered throughout many lands—Turkey, Holland, Asia Minor, Palestine, and so on. This upheaval undermined the power of the "custom of the country"; in some places mixed communities arose, made up of Spanish, Italian, German, and other Jews. Only one who had mastered the immense material gathered since the *Tur* and whose prestige was commensurate could meet the challenge of dislocation and reestablish legal and customary order. R. Joseph Karo, scholar and mystic of Safed, qualified; moreover, he possessed the literary capacity necessary to reduce the existing codices to one Code. He began by writing his *Beit Yosef*, ostensibly a commentary to the *Tur*, but actually an independent, self-contained work. This was the result of twenty years of painstaking examination and study of every line and phrase in the *Tur*, supplying analysis and sources. After spending twelve more years in revision, he set out the conclusions of *Beit Yosef* in brief and called them the *Shulhan Arukh* [the "Set Table"], where the student could find what he wanted prepared and accessible. His ranking pillars of authority are Al Fasi, Maimonides, and Asheri; he usually adopts an opinion held by any two of the three. Some determination independent of antecedent authority is also evident in his great Code. Along with an insufficient acquaintance with the Ashkenazi (Polish-German) practice, this feature invited opposition—which might very well have been fatal to his Code were it not that the lack was overcome by R. Moses Isserles of Poland. The latter's *Glosses*, reflecting Ashkenazic differences in accepted practice, became the *Mappah* ["the Table Cloth"] to the *Shulkan Arukh*. Still, acceptance was far from won. It took a while before Karo's Code, even thus augmented, could triumph over another code of that time, or overcome the criticism of R. Solomon Luria.

Luria found much to criticize in the *Shulhan Arukh* and brought forth his own competing Code-Commentary in its place. He maintains that his own is closer to the original Talmud and, therefore, more authoritative. Since, after all, the Talmud is the final "court of appeal," and all subsequent literature must be judged in terms of its faithfulness to the original Talmudic law,[14] his claim could not be ignored. The other competing Code was that of R. Mordecai Jaffe, who had been preparing a comprehensive code before the *Beit Yosef*, then the *Shulhan Arukh*, and then the *Mappah* had appeared. In each case, he welcomed news of these efforts only to find them lacking as far as he was concerned. His own Code, called *L'vush*, paraphrases rather than quotes the earlier authorities, which makes for a highly readable work. It follows the divisions of the *Tur* and *Shulhan Arukh*, except that the first of the Four Rows, *Orah Hayyim*, is divided into two. Also contemporaneous is a small code-like tract, emanating from Karo's circle of mystics in Safed, called the *Sefer Haredim*.

The Later Authorities

The commentators and decisors after the *Shulhan Arukh* are known by the inclusive term *Aharonim*, the Later Authorities. Some of them helped make the *Shulhan Arukh* the accepted standard work it became. R. David ben Samuel HaLevy (author of *Turei Zahav*, the "*Taz*") and R. Shabb'tai ben Meir HaKohen (*Siftei Kohen*, the "*Shakh*") offered their Commentaries to Karo's Code, in the middle of the seventeenth century, questioning or defending its decisions and adding refinements and new "case law."

In keeping, however, with what was stated above, that the Talmud is really the final authority, the *Aharonim* are formally considered inferior to the earlier masters. In the Talmud itself, none of the Amoraim (Sages of the *G'mara*) may contradict the words of the *Tannaim* (Mishnaic Sages). Every exponent of the Law is—in the phrase of a medieval Commentator to the Mishnah—superior "as a matter of assumption" (*min ha-s'tam*) to those of succeeding generations.[15] Where faithful transmission of authentic tradition is involved, such retrospective deference is proper. Less proper but quite understandable is the sentiment expressed by a contemporary of the above two expositors of the *Shulhan Arukh*. R. Aaron Kaidanover (d. 1676) wrote to a colleague:

> You have given attention to the later authorities (*Shakh* and *Taz*). My studies are limited, thank God, to the Talmud and older authorities. Why should we nibble at the bones of later teachers when we can feast on the meat spread

> upon the golden tables of Talmud, Al Fasi, Maimonides, Asheri. . .on which everything depends. The later writers confuse a man's mind and memory. You would, therefore, do better to sell their books and buy an edition of the *Tur* with Joseph Karo's commentary.[16]

But the hierarchy here is one of learning, rather than of authority. According to the canons of rabbinic decision, the latter-day master—assuming his awareness of earlier rulings which he may show to be inadequate or inapplicable—is, by virtue of that cumulative knowledge, to be deferred to. The principle is then *halakhah k'batra'ei*—the law follows the latest ruling.[17]

Competent in logic and learning and cumulative in legal precedent and refinement, the writings of *"Shakh"* and *"Taz"* gained their merited acceptance and were printed alongside the text of the *Shulhan Arukh*. So were many others—such as *Beit Sh'muel* of R. Samuel ben Uri on the *Even HaEzer* section—far too numerous to mention; they will be identified as they enter our discussion. The result was that Karo's Code became the new citadel, after Talmud, Maimonides and Tur, around which there clustered commentaries and glosses. The incomparable Elijah, "Gaon" of Vilna in the eighteenth century, chose the medium of commentation upon the *Shulhan Arukh* for his magnum opus in rabbinical writing.

In 1863, R. Solomon Ganzfried compiled a laymen's handbook of some everyday laws; he called it the *Kitzur* (abridged) *Shulhan Arukh*. It remains in wide use and high usefulness, and has been translated into English—but under the extravagant title, "Code of Jewish Law."[18] Unabridged digests of one or more of the Four Rows of the *Shulhan Arukh* also were composed, distilling again the continuing legal development. The overarching achievement in this realm is the *Arukh HaShulhan*, a grand restatement of the entire Code and of subsequent legislation, not without independent judgments, in most felicitous language. The work of R. Yehiel M. Epstein at the turn of this century, it enjoys widespread popularity and esteem.

Works based on the *Shulhan Arukh*, or even volumes of Responsa, were not at all the only literary media for the *Aharonim*. Some have their say, in the present treatment, through the instrumentality of Commentaries to the Talmud, which continue to be authored up to the present time. Some, such as the colorful R. Jacob Emden (d. 1776), utilize all three of these categories and several more as well.

The Extralegal Tributaries

Our subject draws heavily on the mainstream of Codes and Code Commentaries, of course. But if the authoritativeness of works in the legal complex is a function of their sequence or position in a framework, or of their fidelity to basic Talmud law, such is not the case with the extralegal tributaries. Even the Bible Commentaries, so many of which contribute to the picture presented in this study, would not, by the mere fact of being attached to the Bible, be able to overrule official interpretation of scripture. The latter properly finds its elaboration in Commentaries to the Talmud and to the Codes. Philosophic works of the Middle Ages partake of the same status: they are extralegal and, as elements in the "Jewish mind," help shape the picture, but are only auxiliary to the legal process. They require no sequential sketch at this time; when introduced in this study, they are briefly characterized in the body or the footnotes.

Some are in a special category and do merit mention here. The *Sefer Hasidim*, for one, contains the literary testament of three leading spirits of Hasidism (Pietism) in medieval Germany (five centuries before the Hasidic movement of R. Israel Ba'al Shem Tov, in the eighteenth century), and, in particular, of the writings of R. Judah the Hasid. The book often resembles a mass of casual jottings, with numbered paragraphs, yet is

> . . .undoubtedly one of the most important and remarkable products of Jewish literature. No other work of the period provides us with so deep an insight into the real life of the Jewish community. . .in the most intimate connection with every day life.[19]

The author's "historical position," according to a modern scholar, is akin to that of Francis of Assisi.[20] The book became popular in many circles and is even quoted in legal contexts by some Responsa.

Menorat HaMaor ["The Lamp of Light"] is the name of two separate but similar books, both worthy of special mention here. The first is by R. Israel Ibn Al Nekawa of Toledo, who died in 1391. The book is a fine example of popular ethico-philosophic writing, although not very original. It is primarily a compilation of hundreds of beautiful maxims regarding the practice of virtue and of various virtues, garnered from all corners of Talmudic literature and skillfully woven together. The second is by R. Isaac Aboab of the same city, who died in 1492. It resembles the method and content of its namesake work but surpasses it in intellectual level and narrative competence. Both of these frequently reprinted classics contain a section on proper conjugal relations.

Another literary creation in a special category is the Zohar, which book, or group of books by that name, is the Bible of Kabbalah, of Jewish mysticism. It is the very cornerstone of the entire mystic movement, which became a substantial factor in Jewish life for six centuries after the Zohar's appearance in the thirteenth century. All later mystical works merely use its passages as a basis for further development.

Its mode of appearance was rather quaint and is still a matter of debate: The Zohar is ascribed to the Tanna (of the Mishnah) R. Simon ben Yohai with the assistance of an assembly of Sages initiated into the secrets of mysticism. It made its appearance at the end of the thirteenth century through the Kabbalist, Moses De Leon. This "Book of Splendor" was accepted by his contemporaries, though it did not lack for those who doubted its antiquity. After the Zohar's authority grew, voices of challenge to its antiquity or genuineness became louder, and, by the nineteenth century, a fair-sized literature on the subject had grown up with scholars taking various positions as to how much and which, if any, elements were of ancient origin.[21]

The mystic orientation was a dominant influence in the lives of many. The term mystic in this connection refers to a wide gamut of attitudes or motifs: from a dark, theurgic occultism to an enlightened, romantic suprarationalism, or an inwardness of religious experience. The author of the *Shulhan Arukh* was a mystic, but he intended his Code to be a bare statement of the inherited law, uninfluenced and unadorned.[22] Something of the role that mysticism did play in the development of our subject will become evident [later in this book]. This includes the contribution of the Zohar's spiritual descendants as well, such as *Sefer Haredim*, already mentioned, and the estimable *Sh'nei Luhot HaB'rit* (The *"ShLaH"*) of R. Isaiah Hurwitz (d. 1628).

The Responsa Literature

Because the pivotal baraita on the birth control question was not included by the major Codes the door was opened to its extensive consideration by another body of literature. The Responsa are formal replies to legal queries addressed to the scholars of all generations. We have already referred to some, from as soon after the Talmud as the Geonic period. As Jewish life developed in the various countries of sojourn, historical, political, and economic changes raised many new legal problems. The Tosafists and *Rishonim*, too, had authored Responsa and, after the dislocation caused by the Spanish expulsion, much literature of this type emanated from Turkey, Poland, and Palestine. Most of the great codifiers and commentators mentioned above are also authors of Responsa. The period of the *Aharonim* saw the issuance of a huge number of Responsa, and the process continues to this very moment.

In the main, Responsa are replies to queries submitted by Rabbis to their more learned colleagues concerning questions not specifically dealt with in the *Shulhan Arukh* or other Codes. They are characterized by personal attention to a specific case at hand. The data are given and the Respondent analyzes the legal literature bearing upon the case, cites analogies and the rulings of previous authorities, and comes up with an answer of "forbidden" or "permitted" or with advice on steps to be taken to resolve the issue or problem.[23] Highly individual, the question and the answer appertain primarily to the person involved, although they become part of "case law" and enter the legal mainstream as precedent authority. But further characterization of this unique literature, or even identification of the leading Respondents, is best not undertaken at this time.[24]

Notes

1. In Maimonides' Introduction to his *Commentary on the Mishnah*, he defines biblical laws as (1) laws expressly stated in the Torah; (2) laws derived from the Torah by interpretation; and (3) certain laws not derived from the Torah but regarded as "*halakhot* to Moses from Sinai." This last phrase is understood by Asheri (in *Rosh* to *Hilkhot Mikvaot*, Ch. 1) to include laws as clearly accepted or as anciently established as if they were derived from Moses on Sinai.

2. G. F. Moore, *Judaism* (Cambridge, 1927), I, 251. The tradition is referred to in the New Testament as *paradosis ton presbyteron*, the "tradition of the Elders." Mark 7:2-13. See also Hermann L. Strack, *Introduction to the Talmud and Midrash* (Philadelphia, 1931), Part I, Ch. 2.

3. See, e.g., Strack, *op. cit.*, Part I, Ch. 1.

4. See, e.g., George Horowitz, *The Spirit of Jewish Law* (New York, 1953). Appendix I, for contents of the Six Orders of the Mishnah; also Ben Zion Bokser, *The Wisdom of the Talmud* (New York, 1951) for much informative material.

5. Strack, *op. cit.*, p. 5.

6. See Ch. I, "An Introduction to the Palestinian Talmud," in Louis Ginzberg, *On Jewish Law and Lore* (Philadelphia, 1962).

7. See, e.g., Meyer Waxman, *A History of Jewish Literature* (second ed.), I. 281 ff. S.K. Mirsky, in the Introduction to his edition of *She'iltot d'Rav Ahai Gaon*, maintains that this work incorporates material of Talmudic times.

8. Samuel Daiches, *The Study of the Talmud in Spain* (London, 1921), quoted by Horowitz, *op. cit.*, p. 50. See also Ch. 5, "The Codification of Jewish Law," in Ginzberg, *op. cit.* On medieval rabbinic studies generally, see S.W. Baron, "The Reign of Law" in *A Social and Religious History of the Jews*, second ed. (Philadelphia, 1958), VI, Ch. XXVII.

9. See the fine biography by M. Liber, *Rashi* (Philadelphia, 1926).

10. Liber, *op. cit.*, p. 188.

11. *Ibid.*, pp. 191-192.

12. He refers to them respectively as *g'dolei ha-pos'kim, g'dolei ha-rabbanim, g'dolei ha-m'habb'rim.*

13. On the question of the authorship of *Iggeret HaKodesh*, see David M. Feldman, *Birth Control, etc.*, Ch. 4, Note 89.

14. See, I.H. Weiss, *Dor Dor V'Dor'shav*, III, 215 ff. See also Feldman, *op. cit.* Ch. II, p. 213, on Luria's *Introduction to Bava Kamma*. Cf. Note 17, below.

15. *Tos'fot Yom Tov to Eduyot*, I, 5. Cf. *TB Shabbat* 112b: "If the Early Ones were as angels, we are as humans, etc."

16. *Resp. Nahalat Shivah* (Warsaw, 1884), No. 50. See N. H. Dembitzer, *K'lilat Yofi*, p. 62.

17. The principle is Geonic (*see Iggeret R. Sh'rira Gaon*, ed. Levin, p.38); it is explained by, e.g., Alfasi to *Eiruvin* (end); Asheri to *Sanhedrin* (IV, 6); and by R. Joseph Kolon (d. 1480) in his *Responsa*, Nos. 84 and 94, the latter relayed by Isserles to *Hoshen Mishpat*, 25,2 (end). See also *Pri M'gadim, K'lalim* No. 8, Preface to *Yoreh Deah*.

18. For significant variations in phraseology, with respect to sexual matters, in *Shulhan Arukh*, the *Kitzur*, and their antecedents, see Feldman, *op. cit.* pp. 70 ff.

19. Gershom Scholem, *Major Trends In Jewish Mysticism* (Schocken, 1941), p. 83.

20. F.I. Baer, quoted by Scholem, *loc. cit.* The two men lived at about the same time and had similar pietistic influences upon their communities.

21. See Scholem, *op. cit.* Chs. 5 and 6; Waxman, *op. cit.*, II, 392 ff.

22. See "The Shulhan Arukh: Enduring Code of Jewish Law," by Isadore Twersky, in *Judaism: A Quarterly Journal* (Spring, 1967), pp. 146, 149, 153.

23. Partial collections of references to the Responsa have been appended to the *Tur* or to the *Shulhan Arukh* in the form of Commentaries thereto. The *K'neset HaG'dolah* of 17th-century R. Hayyim Benvenisti is an example of the first; *Sha'arei T'shuvah* to *Sh. Ar. Orah Hayyim* and *Pit'hei T'shuvah* to the other three sections, the latter by 19th-century R. Zvi Hirsch Eisenstadt, are examples of the second. Far more exhaustive is *Otzar HaPoskim*, a monumental project recently undertaken by a collegium of scholars in Jerusalem. The initial volumes, on the opening *simanim* of *Even HaEzer*, have already appeared.

24. See Solomon Freehof, *The Responsa Literature* (Philadelphia, 1955), esp. Chs. 1 and 2.

[2]

THE LEGAL SYSTEM OF JEWISH LAW*

MENACHEM ELON**

I. INTRODUCTION

Jurisprudence is one of the areas of intellectual and social endeavor in which Jews have played a decisive role, both in developing legal theory and in applying it to everyday life. It seems to me that this development and application stem from the special place legal thought has always occupied in Jewish culture.

Until relatively recent times, the study of *halakhah*, Jewish law, was one of the main components of a young Jew's course of study. Plato's theory that the study of laws should be a central factor in determining a young person's education[1] was implemented in the Jewish educational system in ancient times. The Scriptural injunction, "[a]nd you shall teach them [the laws] diligently to your children,"[2] and the Talmudic dictum that "the study of Torah is equal in value to all of them [i.e. the other commandments] combined"[3] served as the basis for early childhood education. From an early age Jewish children were encouraged to apply themselves to the study of such complicated subjects as the laws of acquisition and evidence as well as to the study of the practical and less abstract laws of benedictions and festivals, all contained in various Talmudic tractates. The ancient historian Flavius Josephus summarized this educational approach when he attributed the following command to Moses: "Let the children also learn the laws, as the first thing they are taught, which will be the best thing they can be taught, and will be the cause of their future felicity."[4] In fact, every Jewish child was a potential jurist who was conversant with

---

* This article is based on the first Gruss Lecture given by Justice Menachem Elon, Caroline and Joseph S. Gruss Professor of Talmudic Civil Law, New York University School of Law, November 12, 1984.

** Justice of the Supreme Court of Israel; Professor of Law, Hebrew University, Jerusalem, Israel.

1. PLATO, CRITO 50,d.
2. *Deuteronomy* 6:7.
3. *Mishnah Peah* 1:1.
4. FLAVIUS JOSEPHUS, ANTIQUITIES OF THE JEWS part IV, 8, 12 (W.

the processes of legal thought and who was particularly sensitive to the problems of justice and equity which lie at the foundations of every legal system.

Intense legal analysis permeates all parts of *halakhah* and applies to its ritual[5] sections as well as to its civil[6] sections. Legal concepts are basic to the entire *halakhic* system. Critical analysis, legal terminology, methods of interpretation, and all the other methods of explication and legal creativity are common to all branches of *halakhah*.

II. Development of the Jewish Legal System

A. *Methods of Analysis of Jewish Law*

Anyone who has participated in a Talmudic discussion will realize that there is no difference between a discussion of civil law and a discussion of the law of sacrificial offerings or ritual impurity, as regards the use of legal concepts and terminology or in the way the laws are discussed. Thus, many general principles are common to all areas of *halakhah*. For example, the doctrine that an action by an agent is legally equivalent to an action by the principal is applied in the *Mishnah*, the primary codification of oral *halakhah*, to a purely religious issue. The *Mishnah* in *Berakhot* states: "If he who recites the *Tefillah* [the central prayer in the liturgy] makes a mistake, it is a bad omen for him; and if he is the cantor (*Shaliaḥ Ẓibbur*), it is a bad omen for those who appointed him, because a person's agent is as himself."[7] Thus, even the relationship between the congregation and the cantor is understood within the framework of principal and agent.[8]

Whiston trans. 1st ed. 1737). This command is found in Josephus' rendition of Moses' final oration to the Jewish people.

5. The precepts and commandments which deal exclusively with man's relationship with the Deity (*bein adam la-makom*).

6. Those topics which deal with the ordering of relations between individuals and society (*bein adam la-haveiro*). This article uses "civil law" and "Jewish law" as synonymous with the Hebrew term "*Mishpat Ivri*." For an explanation of *Mishpat Ivri*, *see infra* note 28.

7. *Mishnah Berakhot* 5:5. This is the solitary *Mishnaic* reference to this principle. In other Talmudic sources, the laws of agency apply in the same way to purely *religious* matters, as they do to marriage, divorce, recovery of debt, and similar matters.

8. Religious legal principles are often based on civil principles. This mutual interaction between the religious and civil sections of *halakhah* is

While the civil and ritual areas of Jewish law share a common source, methodology, and conceptualization, there is a fundamental difference between these two areas. This distinction was already pointed out in the *Mishnaic* era when the Sages differentiated between *issura*, religious matters, and *mamona*, mostly matters of civil law.[9] The following examples illustrate this distinction between *issura* and *mamona*.

Freedom of contract exists with respect to monetary matters.[10] The parties to any monetary transaction may establish the relationship between themselves as they please without regard to Jewish law. As Nahmanides[11] explained, in such matters the Torah itself did not establish its norms as *jus cogens*, but only as *jus dispositivum*.[12]

Another example is that of illegal contract. According to Jewish law, the perpetration of a religious offense in the course of a civil transaction will not affect the legal validity of the transaction.[13] This is contrary to the rule of other legal systems that *ex turpi causa non oritur actio* (a cause of action does not arise from a base claim).

The distinction between civil and ritual matters is of great importance with regard to the scope of the application of the doctrine of *dina de-malkhuta dina*, that the law of the land (the government under whose reign Jews lived) is valid law.[14] Jewish law recognizes the validity of various provisions of alien legal systems in civil matters, even if those provisions are contrary to Jewish law. However, the law of the secular authority is not valid if it is inconsistent with a Jewish ritual precept.[15]

While the *halakhic* authorities and communal leaders

---

attributable to their common origin. *See* 1 M. ELON, JEWISH LAW, HISTORY, SOURCES, PRINCIPLES 151-58 (2d ed. 1978) (Hebrew). This book is currently being translated into English.

9. *See, e.g.*, *Mishnah Yevamot* 15:3, *Eduyyot* 1:12.

10. *Tosefta Kiddushin* 3:8.

11. R. Moses ben Nahman, the thirteenth century Spanish scholar who settled in Jerusalem in his later years.

12. RAMBAN (Nahmanides), COMMENTARY on *Bava Batra* 126b.

13. Bava Meẓia 65a, Rashi commenting. (See under "*Gelima Lo Mafkinan Minei*"); PISKEI HA-ROSH ch. 5, No. 19, *Bava Mezia*; MAIMONIDES, YAD, at *Mekhirah* 30:7.

14. *Nedarim* 28a; *Gittin* 10b; *Bava Kama* 113a-b; *Bava Batra* 54b-55a.

15. *See* R. SIMEON DURAN, RESPONSA (TASHBEẒ) 1:158.

were given wide discretion to develop Jewish legal institutions to respond to changing economic and social conditions, they were subject to one major limitation: proposed changes could not infringe on the basic concepts of justice, morality, equity, and freedom. It was for this reason that Rabbi Isaac ben Sheshet Perfet[16] voided a contract in which the debtor agreed that his person be seized in the event of non-payment.[17] Jewish law views imprisonment for debt as an infringement of human liberty. Although freedom of contract is an accepted principle, as indicated above, no person can stipulate to the loss of his freedom. For the same reason, Jewish law would not recognize the validity of an alien law unless it applied equally to all members of the community without discrimination. As Maimonides stated in the twelfth century:

> The principle of the matter is the following: any law that the king will enact which applies generally and not only to a single individual is not thievery; and whenever he will take from a particular individual only, except by law applicable to everyone, this is unlawful and robbery.[18]

Similarly, the levy of a monetary fine by a government against an entire group because of the misdeeds of individuals is termed "total robbery," because it is contrary to the principles of Jewish law which forbid collective punishment or punishment of one person for the misdeeds of another.[19]

The basic distinction between the *religious* part of *halakhah* and its *civil* component was clearly expressed by the *halakhic* authorities. Rabbi Judah Loew of Prague[20] explained this distinction as follows:

> There are three components [to *halakhah*]:

---

16. A fourteenth century *halakhist* active in Spain and North Africa also known by his acronym, Ribash.

17. Ribash, Responsa No. 484. *See also* Elon, *The Sources and Nature of Jewish Law and its Application in the State of Israel*, 3 Israel L.R. 88, 111-14 (1968).

18. Maimonides, Yad, at *Gezelah* 5:14.

19. *See* Ribash, Responsa (ha-Ḥadashot) No. 9. In support, Ribash cites to *Genesis* 18:25, *Numbers* 16:22, and *Pesahim* 113. *See also Deuteronomy* 24:15 and *II Kings* 14:6.

20. Scholar and philosopher active in Prague in the sixteenth century known by his acronym, Maharal.

1. Laws between man and his fellow;

2. Matters of Torah;

3. Performance of precepts . . . . The laws [between man and his fellow] are not identical with matters of Torah [or the performance of precepts], for the laws stand by themselves, the matters of Torah stand by themselves, and the performance of precepts also stands by itself. Regarding the laws, a person must understand their roots so as not to obligate the innocent or acquit the guilty, which [determination] is a matter depending on human logic, [and should not be undertaken] until the depths of the law are penetrated. This is not a matter of Torah but only of human logic and it may not be found in the Torah. Those laws which are written in the Torah only present the main thrust of the law in question but not everything which applies to the relationship between man and his fellow is written in the Torah . . . .[21]

Of special interest on this subject is the explanation offered by Rabbi Israel Lipschutz.[22] In the last *Mishnah* of *Bava Batra*, Rabbi Ishmael said: "If a person desires to become wise, let him occupy himself in the study of civil law for there is no field in the Torah greater than that, for it is like a swelling fountain."[23] Commenting on this *Mishnah*, Rabbi Lipschutz observed:

> Nowhere in ritual law did the Torah allow human intelligence to soar as high as it can, to penetrate, to investigate, and to decide as it sees fit—as it did in civil law. In that branch, the Torah has given man an unlimited field to weigh, to judge, and to draw conclusions according to his discretion to such an extent that most of the laws of litigation, on which there is a great mass of material like a harvest wagon full of sheaves, were encapsulated in the Torah in one sentence: "You shall judge your fellow in justice."[24] Since human intelligence is likely to err in

---

21. MAHARAL, DEREKH HAYYIM on *Mishnah Avot* 1:1 (*see* under "*Heim Hayu Omerim Shelosha Devarim*").

22. Nineteenth century scholar in Germany who composed one of the basic commentaries on the *Mishnah*.

23. *Bava Batra* 10:8.

24. *Leviticus* 19:15.

> this delicate matter, our early Sages of the *Mishnah* and the Talmud, gathered together—and they numbered a multitude of the nation's greatest men—and laid down for us the fundamentals and the roots applying to such matters. But there is still room for the judge to veer to the right or to the left, to compare one thing to another, or to make distinctions which are occasionally as fine as a hair. Therefore, occupation with civil law will sharpen a person's intelligence to scrutinize a matter well in order that he arrive exactly at the truth . . . .[25]

This dichotomy between the *religious* part of the *halakhah* and its *civil* component was forcefully expressed by Rabbi Simeon Shkop:[26]

> The laws which fall in the category of monetary law which govern the relations of a person and his neighbor are different from the other commands of the Torah. All of the other commands constitute the admonitions of the Torah in positive or negative form and the obligation of obeying them rests mainly on the duty to carry out God's command. But monetary matters are different; before it is incumbent on us to carry out the command of God to make a payment or return an object, a legal obligation must exist . . . . There is another fundamental principle involved here. When we deal with a legal right or the acquisition of an object or of a property lien, we do not concern ourselves with the question of the observance of a religious commandment but of the circumstances determining who has a right to the object or who, according to legal principles, may take possession of the object. Therefore, the general principles governing cases on monetary matters which the Sages laid down were determined by logical considerations that according to legal principles a particular result

25. RABBI ISRAEL LIPSCHUTZ, TIFERET ISRAEL on *Bava Batra* 10:8. For a further discussion see the instructive comments on this subject made by Rabbi Jacob Anatoli, a thirteenth century scholar in southern France, in his work MALMAD HA-TALMIDIM 71b-72b (Mekiẓei Nirdamim ed. Lyck 1866) (commenting on the weekly portion *Mishpatim*). For an English translation see Elon, *More about Research into Jewish Law*, in MODERN RESEARCH IN JEWISH LAW 66, 68 n.5 (B. Jackson ed. 1980).

26. The dean of the Talmudic Academy of Grodno, Lithuania at the beginning of this century.

> was proper . . . . The commandment prohibiting theft is that one should not steal from his neighbor an object that according to legal principles belongs to his neighbor.[27]

In other words, theft occurs only when one takes something which the *law* has concluded does not belong to him. Rabbi Shkop's argument, which had been made by earlier scholars in a less articulate form, is extremely important for modern research in Jewish law. These remarks were made not by a professor of law desirous of dressing Jewish law in a scientific-academic veneer which is not indigenous to the system of Jewish law. Rather, they emanate from a practitioner of original, indigenous Jewish legal thought in a form typical of and acceptable to the analytical methodology of the great Lithuanian and Polish Talmudic academies of recent generations.[28]

In summary, *halakhah* is, on the one hand, uniform and interrelated in that its components have a common religious source,[29] a common method of thought and analysis, and an interdependence between its *ritual* commandments and its *civil* precepts. Conversely, *halakhah*, as it has crystallized, has recognized an essential and fundamental distinction between *issura* and *mamona*, the latter generally corresponding to most of what is included in the corpus juris of contemporary legal systems. This basic distinction offered greater flexibility and an extraordinary potential for development to the civil part of *halakhah*, that part which is most affected by and subject to changes in economic and social life.

---

27. 2 R. Simeon Shkop, Shaarei Yosher at gate 5, ch. 1.

28. The term *Mishpat Ivri* is now accepted as referring to those matters of *halakhah* whose equivalent is dealt with in modern legal systems—matters pertaining to relations between man and his fellow and society. The term was first used at the turn of this century to circumscribe the bounds of the legal research and teaching to be undertaken. Today the term *Mishpat Ivri*, as defined above, is accepted by both the legal practitioner and the researcher. This Article uses the term "Jewish law" as synonymous with *Mishpat Ivri*. For a more complete discussion, see 1 M. Elon, *supra* note 8, at 146-51; Elon, *supra* note 25, at 67-71; Englard, *Research in Jewish Law—Its Nature and Function* in Modern Research in Jewish Law 22-27 (B. Jackson, ed. 1980).

29. On the religious-national nature of Jewish law, see 1 M. Elon, *supra* note 8, at 5-6.

B. *Historical Development of Jewish Law*

To analyze the corpus of Jewish law as a legal system with methods of classification and legal principles equivalent to those of modern jurisprudence, we must briefly consider the historical development of Jewish law. The foundation of Jewish law and its basic norm, or as Professor Kelsen put it, its *Grundnorm*,[30] is the written Torah, and the body of oral law which grew continually until it was crystallized in the teachings codified in the *Mishnah* and in both the Jerusalem and the Babylonian Talmuds which followed it. This Talmudic literature is the basic material of Jewish law and constitutes the point of departure of any study or discussion of *halakhah*. However, for all their authority, the Talmudic sources are only the foundation of the Jewish legal system. The system continued to develop as a living body of law for more than 1,300 years beginning with the close of the Talmudic period in the fifth century until the onset of the Emancipation at the end of the eighteenth century. Post-Talmudic *halakhic* literature constitutes most of the corpus of Jewish law. Unfortunately, until the last few decades, those scholars who engaged in the scientific study of Jewish law preoccupied themselves with the legal thought of the Biblical and Talmudic periods.

Scientific research into Jewish law, as distinguished from the traditional study of *halakhah* in the study halls of the Talmudic academies, began in the early modern era. The pioneers of such research include John Selden[31] in the seventeenth century, Johann David Michaelis in the eighteenth century,[32] and Eduard Gans,[33] J.L. Saalschütz,[34] Samuel

30. *See* H. KELSEN, PURE THEORY OF LAW 193-278 (1967).

31. For a catalogue of Selden's works, see S. EISENSTADT, EIN MISHPAT (Legal Bibliography) 102, 126, 151, 207, 337, 359 (1931) (Hebrew).

32. J.D. MICHAELIS, MOSAISCHES RECHT (Reutlingen 1785-93); MOSAISCHES PEINLICHES RECHT NEBST EINER VERGLEICHUNG DES HEUTIGEN PEINLICHEN RECHTS MIT DEMSELBEN (Braunschweig u. Hildesheim 1778); J. D. MICHAELIS, ABHANDLUNGEN VON DEN EHEGESETZEN MOSES, WELCHE DIE HEYRATHEN IN DIE NAHE FREUNDSCHAFT UNTERSAGEN (Göttingen 1768).

33. Gans, *Die Grundzüge des mosaisch-talmudischen Erbrechts*, 1 ZEITSCHRIFT FÜR DIE WISSENSCHAFT DES JUDENTUMS (Zunz ed.) 419-71 (1823).

34. J.L. SAALSCHÜTZ, DAS MOSAISCHE RECHT MIT BERÜCKSICHTIGUNG DES SPÄTERN JÜDISCHEN (Berlin 1846-48).

Mayer,[35] and Joseph Salvdor[36] in the nineteenth century. These scholars analyzed Jewish law in the Biblical and Talmudic periods. They compared Jewish law with other legal systems, delved into the ethical values and philosophical postulates expressed in Jewish legal institutions, and studied the historical and literary aspects of the sources of Jewish law. In their view, the Talmudic period was the *terminus ad quem* of Jewish law.

Another group of prominent scholars of Jewish law includes Hirsch Fassel,[37] Zacharias Frankel,[38] Leopold Auerbach,[39] and Moses Bloch[40] in the previous century and M.W. Rapaport[41] and Asher Gulak[42] in the present century, who focussed on the work of the great medieval codifiers.[43] However, even these scholars neglected the main repository of post-Talmudic Jewish law, the responsa literature.

The indifference to the development of Jewish law in the

---

35. S. Mayer, Die Rechte der Israeliten, Athener und Römer, mit Rücksicht auf die neuen Gesetzgebungen (Leipzig 1865, 1868).

36. J. Salvdor, Historie des institutions de Moïse et du peuple Hébreu (Paris 1828).

37. H. Fassel, Das Mosaisch-Rabbinische Strafgesetz und strafrechtliche Gerichts-Verfahren (1870).

38. Z. Frankel, Entwurf einer Geschichte der Literatur der nachtalmudischen Responsen (Breslau 1865); Z. Frankel, Der gerichtliche Beweis nach mosaisch-talmudischen Rechte—Ein Beitrag zur Kenntniss des mosaisch-talmudischen Criminal und Civilrechts (Berlin 1864); Frankel, *Ueber manches Polizeiliche des Talmudischen Rechts*, 1 Monatsschrift für Geschichte und Wissenschaft des Judentums 243-61 (1851-1852).

39. L. Auerbach, Das jüdische Obligationenrecht nach den Quellen und mit besonderer Berücksichtigung des römischen und deutschen Rechts, systematisch dargestellt (1870).

40. M. Bloch, Die Vormundschaft nach mosaisch-talmudischen Rechte (1904); M. Bloch, Das mosaisch-talmudische Strafgerichtsverfahren (1901); M. Bloch, Das mosaisch-talmudische Besitzrecht (1897); M. Bloch, Das mosaisch-talmudische Polizeirecht (1897); M. Bloch, Der Vertrag nach mosaisch-talmudischen Rechte (1803); M. Bloch, Das mosaisch-talmudische Erbrecht (1890).

41. M.W. Rapaport, Der Talmud und sein Recht (1912).

42. A. Gulak, Yesodei ha-Mishpat ha-Ivri (Foundations of Jewish Law) (1923) (Hebrew).

43. Such as, Rabbi Isaac Alfasi (eleventh century, North Africa); Maimonides; Rabbi Jacob of the Turim (fourteenth century, Germany and Spain); Rabbi Joseph Caro of the Shulhan Arukh (sixteenth century, Turkey and Israel).

post-Talmudic period is primarily attributable to a mistaken and truncated view of legal creativity after the compilation of the Talmud.[44] These scholars viewed the study of Jewish law in the post-Talmudic period as dialectics for its own sake and as sterile scholasticism, confined within the walls of the study hall and devoid of innovation and vital creative force. This distorted image of Jewish history has been corrected by leading Jewish historians of the last and the present generations.[45] An exact and penetrating examination of the Jewish legal system in the post-Talmudic period demonstrates its continuing vitality.

After the compilation of the Babylon Talmud, *halakhic* creativity continued in the major Jewish center in Babylonia until the middle of the eleventh century.[46] From the eighth century on, various forms of *halakhic* literature emerged including considerable responsa literature. Responsa constituted the case law of the Jewish legal system. They were authoritative opinions given by *halakhic* authorities in all areas of Jewish law in response to questions which arose out of actual situations. To some extent, the responsa resemble the *Responsa Prudentium* of Roman law[47] and particularly—as far as their authority and creative substance are concerned—the *Fatwa* of Islamic law.[48]

Until the eleventh century, the world Jewish community looked to one spiritual center. That center was originally in the land of Israel and later moved to Babylon. The situation changed after the eleventh century when each Jewish community in the diaspora became dependent on its own spiritual leaders.[49] Such local centers included, among others, North Africa, Spain (Sepharad), northern France and Germany (Ashkenaz), Southern France, Poland, Turkey, Italy,

44. For an in-depth discussion of this phenomenon, see 1 M. ELON, *supra* note 8, at 136-42.

45. *See* H. BEN-SASSON, *The Middle Ages* in A HISTORY OF THE JEWISH PEOPLE 389-92, 393-723 (H. Ben-Sasson ed. 1976).

46. This era, spanning from the seventh (sixth?) to the eleventh centuries, is known as the *geonic* period.

47. *See* H. JOLOWICZ, HISTORICAL INTRODUCTION TO THE STUDY OF ROMAN LAW 369-72 (1952).

48. *See Fatwa* in 2 THE ENCYCLOPAEDIA OF ISLAM 866 (1960-1971).

49. For an analysis of both the internal and external historical reasons for this change see 1 M. ELON, *supra* note 8, 62-64 & n.215.

and the land of Israel. In all these centers, enormous creativity in Jewish law continued in the writing of commentaries on the Talmud, of legal codes, and of thousands of volumes of responsa. According to the most reliable estimates, the responsa volumes include some three hundred thousand legal opinions covering all areas of Jewish law. Most significantly, this enormous mass of material came into being against the background, and as a result of, the application of Jewish law to practical day-to-day life.

C. *The Role of Judicial Autonomy in the Development of Jewish Law*

The pre-Emancipation Jewish communities throughout the diaspora were given the right to manage their internal affairs. This right was realized in the judicial automomy of the Jewish courts which were authorized by the general government to resolve legal disputes which arose within the Jewish community between individual Jews, between the individual Jew and the community, and between communities.

Jewish courts were empowered to impose sanctions ranging from fines to imprisonment. We know of Jewish prisons administered by the Jewish community and staffed by Jewish jailers. We are given the names of various jailers and prisons and some deliberations regarding *halakhic* problems concerning the administration of prisons.[50]

Jewish judicial autonomy existed for two reasons: first, the intense desire of the Jewish community to maintain its religious-national legal system and second, the prevailing

---

50. Elon, *ha-Maasar ba-Mishpat ha-Ivri* (Imprisonment in Jewish Law) in JUBILEE VOLUME FOR PINHAS ROZEN 171, 183-94 (H. Cohen ed. 1962) (Hebrew); 1 M. ELON, *supra* note 8, at 11, 664-65. The jailers' names were Isaac Shpekel and Aaron Katz. In Cracow we hear of one jail called "*Dudik*" and another named "*The new Dudik*" (*der neier Dudik*), which was apparently designated for women prisoners. A seventeenth century responsum from Poland by Rabbi Ephraim ben Jacob ha-Kohen, RESPONSA SHAAR EFRAYIM No. 83, discusses whether a room which is used as a prison requires a mezuza. (A mezuza is a parchment containing verses from the Bible which is affixed to the doorpost of permanent Jewish homes.) The argument is made that a mezuza is not required because, inter alia, a jail is hopefully a temporary residence only and because a prisoner stays there against his will. The conclusion is that a mezuza is required.

medieval legal and political concept of statehood. The medieval judicial systems were personal and not territorial in their application. They were based on the individual's membership in one of several corporate groups such as the barons, the burghers, or the guilds. The decentralized general government agreed to grant judicial autonomy to the Jews within its borders for theological reasons or, primarily, in exchange for large sums of money. This corporate existence is evidenced by the various Charters of Privilege which medieval governments granted to Jewish communities and which granted the Jews, inter alia, judicial autonomy.[51]

The responsa literature and the various enactments adopted by *halakhic* scholars and medieval Jewish communities are the most accurate gauges of Jewish judicial autonomy. The responsa literature, in particular, serves as a window into daily life in the various communities of the diaspora. A study of responsa literature prior to the sixteenth century reveals that nearly eighty percent of the responsa dealt with matters of civil, criminal, and public administrative law while only about twenty percent of the opinions concerned ritual law.[52] This preponderance of civil issues demonstrates that the areas which occupied the Jewish community and its leadership were those in which significant social and economic changes occurred. The *halakhic* authorities and the lay leadership were required to respond to these changes and supply new solutions.

The change of understanding regarding the vitality of Jewish legal history in the Middle Ages brought with it a change of emphasis in the study of Jewish law in the post-Talmudic period. The new approach is evident in the works of scholars such as Abraham Hayyim Freimann[53] and Simha Asaf.[54] The work of scholars in the field of Jewish law in the

---

51. *See* 1 M. ELON, *supra* note 8, at 32-34.

52. For results of this study, see INSTITUTE FOR RESEARCH IN JEWISH LAW, MAFTEAH HA-SHEELOT VE-HA-TESHUVOT, SHUT HA-ROSH (Digest of Responsa Literature) at Introduction (1965) (Hebrew). These proportions did not change until the advent of the Emancipation.

53. *See, e.g.*, A. FREIMANN, SEDER KIDDUSHIN VE-NISSUIN AHAREI HATIMAT HA-TALMUD (Marriage in the Post-Talmudic Era) (1945) (Hebrew).

54. *See, e.g.*, S. ASAF, BATEI DIN VE-SIDREIHEM AHAREI HATIMAT HA-TALMUD (The Judicial System in the Post-Talmudic Era) (1924) (Hebrew);

last few decades especially illustrates this substantive change in approach.

Law, as a reflection of life itself, constantly evolves. Its function is to find solutions for problems which arise out of life in every generation and in every place. The existence of Jewish judicial autonomy and the fact that *halakhah* functioned as a living body of law guaranteed the continuous development of Jewish law. In Jewish law, as in any other legal system, development occurs by way of its creative sources—the legal sources.[55] Such development occurred not only in civil matters, to which substantive and far-reaching additions were made in the post-Talmudic period, but also in the creation and development of new branches of law.

Yehezkel Kaufmann, a great scholar of Jewish religion and history, argued: "It was judicial autonomy which truly transformed the Jewish people in the diaspora into 'a state within a state'."[56] This assessment is not only true from a socio-political standpoint; it also finds expression in the nature of Jewish law in the post-Talmudic period when new substantive branches of law were created, branches that are typical of a system functioning quasi-independently. From the tenth century, Jewish law developed a comprehensive system of public administrative law, a sophisticated tax system,[57] and impressive mechanisms for dealing with conflict of laws issues both within the Jewish legal system and between Jewish law and alien systems.[58] A sophisticated criminal justice system was developed in some Jewish communities.[59] Such development should not always be equated with progress. Occasionally, practical Jewish law absorbed laws

---

HA-ONESHIN AHAREI HATIMAT HA-TALMUD (Punishment in the Post-Talmudic Era) (1922) (Hebrew).

55. *See* 1 M. ELON, *supra* note 8, at 219-22, 239-828. The legal sources include interpretation, legislation (*takkanot*), custom, case law (*maaseh*), and legal logic (*sevara*).

56. 1 Y. KAUFMANN, GOLAH VE-NEKHAR (Exile and Statelessness) 518 (1954) (Hebrew).

57. *See* M. ELON, *Taxation* in PRINCIPLES OF JEWISH LAW 662-701 (M. Elon ed. 1975).

58. *See* M. ELON, *Conflict of Laws* in PRINCIPLES OF JEWISH LAW at 715-24.

59. For an instructive deliberation in an Israeli Supreme Court judgment, see C.A. 543/79, *Nagar v. State of Israel*, 35 P.D. (1) 113, 163-70 (1984).

which were foreign to its spirit and incompatible with its principles and which were eventually eliminated.[60]

III. Public Administrative Law: An Illustration of the Development of Jewish Law

A. *Majority Rule and the Constitution of the Majority*

The emergence of a body of public administrative law in the medieval period is an example of the resiliency of Jewish legal thought. The decline of the Babylonian center (which was referred to earlier), which had wielded spiritual authority over all Jewish communities, permitted each Jewish community to reach maturity. The leadership of an individual person[61] was replaced with community rule in the form of elected or appointed representatives. This change raised questions regarding the organization of the community. Among the questions dealt with were: how representatives should be elected, what was the legal relationship between the individual and communal institutions and between different communities, and how the tax burden should be apportioned. Talmudic *halakhah* did not provide explicit solutions to many of these problems and they are discussed in thousands of responsa written in the various Jewish centers.

The question of majority rule serves as an example. The principle of majority rule is discussed in the Talmud with regard to the vote of judges in a court decision[62] and to a *praesumptio juris*,[63] but not in connection with political leadership. In a community council, which was often composed, for instance, of seven members,[64] does the opinion of four members bind the other three who voted against a proposed action?

While according to Talmudic law the majority cannot force its opinion on the minority in private civil law, such as

60. For a fuller discussion of the variegated development of Jewish law, see, *e.g.*, 1 M. Elon, *supra* note 8, at 37-39 & n.115, 700-12.

61. In the land of Israel the leader was known as the *Nasi* (Patriarch); in the Babylonian period the leader was the *Resh Galuta* (Exilarch).

62. *Mishnah Sanhedrin* 1:6.

63. *Hullin* 10b-11a.

64. The concept of the "seven elders of the town" appears already in the Talmud. Megilla 26a. In the medieval period, the number of members of the council varied.

in matters of partnership,[65] the question of majority rule in public law is not discussed in the Talmud. In European law of the twelfth century, the prevailing opinion was that a communal decision was invalid unless it was unanimous.[66] After incisive discussion of the question,[67] most *halakhic* authorities concluded that the majority decision does obligate the minority. *Halakhic* scholars justified this conclusion primarily by asserting that communal rule could not be viable otherwise. As Rabbi Asher ben Jehiel[68] wrote: "If you do not say so, the community will never be able to function, for when will a whole community agree to one opinion?"[69]

Halakhic authorities now had to address the question of how a majority is constituted. When a community elects its representatives, do all the members of the community have equal votes, or should a wealthy member's vote be worth more than that of a poor person? Since the wealthy were primarily responsible for financing communal expenditures and bore a heavier tax load, they claimed a greater role in communal decision making. Authorities also had to decide whether unlearned and unschooled members of the community had a vote equal to that of a scholar.

Various legal systems have dealt with such questions. In the Middle Ages the accepted view, in those systems which accepted the validity of majority rule, was that a majority is to be constituted of the rich and the learned. Thus, the Fourth Lateran Council in 1215 held that in choosing archbishops, the person on whom "the greater portion or the more healthy portion" of the voters agree should be chosen.[70]

For a certain period of time, Jewish legal scholars also ruled that the majority must be "of the leaders" among the

65. *See* PISKEI HA-ROSH, ch. 2 No. 11 *Bava Batra* (a single tenant of a common courtyard can prevent the majority from engaging in specified activities in the courtyard).

66. 1 M. ELON, *supra* note 8, at 582 n.114.

67. *See id.* at 580-87.

68. A great *halakhic* scholar active in Germany and, later, Spain in the thirteenth and fourteenth centuries.

69. R. ASHER BEN JEHIEL, RESPONSA 6:7.

70. Baer, *ha-Hathalot ve-ha-Yesodot shel Irgun ha-Kehilah ha-Yehudit bi-Yemei ha-Beinayim* (Origins of Jewish Communal Organization in the Middle Ages) 15 ZION 1, 37-38 (1950) (Hebrew).

community who were the wealthy and the scholarly.[71]

However, the Jewish public did not accept that ruling and hundreds of responsa present detailed discussions on the relative electoral rights of the rich and the poor, the unschooled and the scholarly. Eventually in the fifteenth century, we find alternative solutions in the responsa literature. Some *halakhic* authority gave equal votes to all members of the community, adopting the principle of "one person one vote." As one responsum concluded: "In this matter there is no difference whether the majority is constituted of rich or poor men, scholars or laymen."[72] Other authorities fashioned rules which assured equal influence to the various groups which represented the whole community[73] and still others suggested different solutions.[74]

B. *Orderly Public Administration as a Basis for Legislation*

Several responsa discuss basic questions regarding limitations on the power of the majority. They discuss whether there are basic rights of which the majority cannot deprive the minority and whether the majority may infringe on the principles of equity, justice, and orderly public administration.

In one Spanish Jewish community, the council decided to do away with the post of communal comptroller, whose function was to inspect the management of communal institutions. The council consisted of wealthy men and dignitaries and it seems that they had some special interest in avoiding inspection. There was great opposition to this decision in the community at large and Rabbi Solomon ben Abraham Adret[75] agreed with the opposition and announced that the

---

71. *See* L. FINKELSTEIN, JEWISH SELF-GOVERNMENT IN THE MIDDLE AGES 121 (1924); R. SOLOMON ADRET (Rashba), RESPONSA 3:443; R. YOM TOV ISHBILI (Ritba), COMMENTARY on *Avodah Zarah* 36b. *See also Shaarei Zedek in* TESHUVOT HA-GEONIM, part 4, gate 4, No. 16; R. ISAAC ALFASI (ha-Rif), RESPONSA No. 13.

72. R. ELIJAH MIZRAHI, RESPONSA No. 53 at 145-46 (1946).

73. *See, e.g.*, R. MENAHEM KROCHMAL, RESPONSA ZEMAH ZEDEK No. 2.

74. *See* Elon, *On Power and Authority: Halachic Stance of the Traditional Community and Its Contemporary Implications* in KINSHIP AND CONSENT 183, 196-99 (D. Elazar ed. 1983).

75. The leading *halakhist* in Spain in the late thirteenth and early fourteenth centuries, known by his acronym Rashba.

decision was null and void because it contradicted orderly public administration and would impair the management of the community's affairs.[76]

C. *Protection of the Minority's Rights—Limitations on the Majority's Powers*

The following cases demonstrate the limitations of the majority's power to tax when the proposed tax violates equitable principles. In a thirteenth century community in Germany a minimum tax was imposed on all members without exception. The majority decided that no plea of hardship would excuse payment. One member of the community argued that he was poverty stricken and could not possibly pay the tax. A court, composed of three *halakhic* scholars of Mainz, voided the enactment. The court reasoned that no enactment which obliges a person to pay what he does not possess can be valid. Holding that the majority has no authority to adopt such an enactment the court asked rhetorically: "Because they are many, may they be thieves?"[77] This rule, "because they are many, may they be thieves" (*Atu rabim gazlanim ninhu*) appears in the Talmud in the context of the actual theft of an individual's property by the community.[78] The judges of Mainz adapted this principle to the field of taxation and it thereby became a basic principle in Jewish administrative law.

The principle of protecting the minority was not only intended to protect the poor, as is evident from the following example. A Spanish community, acting through a majority of its members, imposed a tax on the property of one of its affluent members. The person's property was situated in another community which also collected taxes on it. The Rashba ruled that double taxation on that property constitutes an infringement of justice. He characterized the infringement as theft by the majority and the citizen was only obliged to pay taxes on the property to the government of the situs.[79]

These rulings in the field of Jewish public-administrative

---

76. Rashba, Responsa 2:279.
77. Maharah Or Zarua, Responsa No. 222.
78. *Bava Batra* 100a.
79. Rashba, Responsa 5:178.

law and many other responsa offer an accurate depiction of Jewish life in the diaspora. While medieval Jewish history does contain pogroms, plagues, crusades, and massacres, these calamities were not the dominant features of this era. The predominant characteristic of medieval Jewish life was the interaction of the community and the individual within the framework of Jewish internal rule, based on Jewish law, its principles, and its sources. This led to tremendous creativity in all areas of substantive law and in the various branches of the philosophy of law. The history of this era includes not only what happened, or could have happened, to the Barukh of Mainz in the poem by Saul Tchernichovsky,[80] but also, and more importantly, the decision by Rabbi Barukh the son of Samuel, one of the judges of Mainz, who fiercely defended the right of a person not to pay taxes beyond his means and transformed the Talmudic saying "[t]he majority cannot be thieves" into a cornerstone of Jewish democratic theory.[81]

IV. The Abolition of Jewish Legal Autonomy

A fundamental change took place in the practical application of Jewish law at the end of the eighteenth century. Jewish judicial autonomy in Europe was annulled at the onset of the Emancipation. Practical judicial activity in the Jewish communities became limited to the ritual aspects of the *halakhah*.[82] With the end of Jewish judicial autonomy, the subject matter of the responsa changes drastically. The vast majority of the responsa now dealt with ritual matters—such as laws relating to prayer, benedictions, holy days, and dietary matters—and to a limited extent with matters of family law. Conversely, matters from the legal system of Jewish law constitute a negligible proportion of the post-Emancipation responsa. The few responsa which deal with civil law matters seem divorced from a living body of law. It is true that in the great Talmudical academies, the *yeshivot*, students continued to study all areas of Jewish law. Nonetheless, practical life

80. *Baruch of Mayence* in E. Silberschlag, Saul Tchernichovsky Poet of Revolt 114-34 (1968).

81. *See supra* text accompanying note 77.

82. For the reasons of this decisive change in Jewish judicial autonomy, see 1 M. Elon, *supra* note 8, at 65-72.

was henceforth regulated by the legal systems of the countries in which the Jews lived, a situation which a large proportion of Jews viewed favorably as desirable integration into general public life.

The inevitable result was that the development of Jewish civil, criminal, and public law ceased except through academic and theoretical study.[83] However, no legal system can be sustained by academic study alone. This new state of affairs had serious consequences for the Jewish legal system particularly since it was the nineteenth century that brought with it great economic, industrial, and social changes. Jewish law was not required to meet the new challenges. The ensuing vacuum can be filled by two means: interpretation grounded on a socio-historical approach with the object of solving new problems through existing Jewish case law, and enactments (*Takkanot*) that would pertain to areas that are not solved by interpretation.

Law in the modern state is territorial. The same courts judge all people without regard to religion or national origin. A modern state is not prepared to grant judicial autonomy to an ethnic minority living within its boundaries. The only possibility for again applying Jewish law to practical life, therefore, lay in its being incorporated into the legal system of a modern state. That possibility arose with the advent of the Zionist movement which ultimately led to the establishment of the Jewish state.

V. Jewish Law in the State of Israel

The possibility of the integration of Jewish law into the legal system of the future Jewish state was first discussed by Jewish scholars at the onset of the Zionist movement at the beginning of this century. As the feasibility of establishing a state became apparent the discussion intensified. The matter has remained on the national agenda, particularly among jurists.

The subject is both wide in scope and complex in content and is far beyond the scope of this Article.[84] One basic

83. In Eastern countries, which were not affected by the Emancipation, Jewish judicial autonomy continued and therefore Jewish law continued to develop in all areas. *Id.* at 72-73.

84. *Id.* at 74-94.

issue, however, should be emphasized. The subject of Jewish law should not be confused with the problem of the relationship of religion and the state, an extremely sensitive issue which is greatly disputed by various groups in Israeli society. What is proposed is the incorporation of that part of *halakhah* which is included in the various legal systems of modern states, that is, the legal sections of *halakhah*, not its ritual portions. As was demonstrated, even in previous times *halakhic* scholars drew a distinction between the civil and ritual components of *halakhah*. While the line they drew is not identical to that between law and religion, the existence of such a division in the world of *halakhah* is itself sufficient to serve as a guideline for discussion of the place of Jewish law in the State of Israel.

A law which was enacted by the Knesset (Israeli Parliament) four years ago offers a compromise between the different viewpoints on the incorporation of Talmudic civil law into the Israeli legal system. The law is entitled "The Fundamentals of Law" and contains two clauses. One clause repeals article 46 of the King's Order in Council which was enacted during the period of the British Mandate over Palestine in 1922. Article 46 provided that whenever there is a lacuna in the law of Palestine, reference should be made to English common law and equity.[85] The other clause contains the following provision replacing article 46: "Where a court is required to decide a legal question for which there is no answer in statutory law, judicial predecent, or by analogy, the question shall be determined in the light of the principles of freedom, justice, equity, and peace of the Jewish heritage."[86]

This law is the first in the history of legislation of the State of Israel to establish a formal connection between Jewish law and the law of the State of Israel. It enables Jewish law to serve as a supplemental source of the legal system. The extent of this connection and the definition of the various terms of the law are already subjects of dispute in both

85. Palestine Order in Council 1922-1947, art. 46, *published in* III Laws of Palestine 2569 (1934) (English edition).

86. Foundations of Law 5740-1980, *Sefer Ha-Chukim* No. 978 at 163 (July 31, 1980) (official collection of statutes of the State of Israel).

the academic world and among the justices of Israel's Supreme Court.

The differences of opinion in the Israeli legal community concern to what extent courts are obliged to resort to the principles of Jewish law. There is general agreement that Jewish law must occupy, as indeed it does, an important place in the curriculum of the law schools in Israel and must serve as a source of inspiration for both the legislation of the Knesset and the decisions of the courts. Jewish law is a required subject in all Israeli law schools. The laws of the state have absorbed many Jewish legal principles. The decision of Israel's courts, particularly those of the Supreme Court, frequently cite Jewish law both for the sake of comparison with other legal systems and as a source of decision. Thus, Jewish law has, to a limited extent, returned to play a practical role in daily life and continues its creativity and development.

VI. The Teaching and Research of Jewish Law

The teaching of Jewish law and its renewed application as a legal system to everyday life must be implemented in a method that is acceptable to other legal systems. Jewish law must be interpreted according to accepted jurisprudential principles and the accepted categories of legal classifications and terminology. This approach is essential for the understanding and teaching of Jewish law as a legal system comparable to other modern legal systems. At the same time, great care must be exercised to avoid forcing Jewish law into the framework of another legal system and thereby to prevent the adoption into Jewish legal thought of alien legal principles, classifications, and terminology which have no place in the structure and basic concepts of Jewish law.

Several examples demonstrate this tension. Administrative law and conflicts of law do not exist in Jewish law as distinct branches of law. Nevertheless, these terms must be used when dealing with Jewish law as a contemporary legal system and the diverse materials of Jewish law should be arranged according to these classifications.

Great care is needed when interpreting concepts in Jewish law which are seemingly analogous to concepts of other legal systems. Thus, the concept of *dinei mamonot* (monetary issues) is not identical with all that is included in the parallel term in civil law. Similarly *dinei nefashot* (capital crimes) is more limited than the analogous concept of criminal law. Great care is also needed in applying more general concepts such as equity and public policy to their parallels in Jewish law.

Jewish law often uses concrete terminology which is derived from everyday situations. Examples include: *keren* (goring), *shen* (damage caused by consumption by animals), *regel* (damage caused by trampling by animals), and *bor* (damage caused by potholes). These terms symbolize the classic types of tort. Much care is needed when translating them into abstract accepted legal principles.

Similarly, since a term in Jewish law can often have different meanings, careful analysis is necessary to distinguish different meanings of the same term. For example, the term *hazakah* is used in Jewish law in at least four meanings: 1) to denote a form of acquisition; 2) to denote a *praesumptio juris*; 3) to denote possession; and 4) in the sense of a rule of procedure and evidence such as the *hazakah* of three years (to prove ownership of certain real property). Conversely, the term "contract", which is translated in modern legal Hebrew as *hozeh* (agreement) is designated in Jewish law by various phrases such as *hiyuv*, *kinyan*, *shetar*, and, in later periods, *hitkashrut*. These terms also have other meanings in Jewish law. Thus, the term *hiyuv* is used to denote a non-contractual obligation and the term *shetar* is used to signify an evidentiary document.[87]

In addition to great sensitivity to legal terminology, the instruction of Jewish law also demands an investigation of the development of each institution of Jewish law as it appears in the discussions which took place regarding each institution in the sources of Jewish law in all its time periods, particularly in the responsa literature. The development of a legal principle through its legal sources[88] can only be understood after an investigation of all the eras of Jewish law and the various legal sources which facilitated these changes. Only such an investigation can lead to correct conclusions regarding the position of Jewish law on each of its institutions. Such an investigation must also include study of the

87. *See* 1 M. ELON, *supra* note 8, at 132-33.
88. *See supra* note 55.

many discussions and legal deliberations in Jewish law which are found in the legal system of the State of Israel such as the laws enacted by the Knesset, the decisions of the Rabbinical Courts, and, especially, the decisions of the Supreme Court. The latter materials are particularly significant in that they set policy and deal with Jewish law in the context of legal problems arising in modern life. Fulfilling these requirements regarding the teaching and study of Jewish law is, concededly, a great and laborious task. Precisely because of this difficulty, this challenge must be met and overcome.

VII. Closing Remarks

Please allow me to express my appreciation to the New York University School of Law for establishing a Chair of Jewish Law and to Mr. and Mrs. Joseph Gruss, who established the Chair as well as the Jewish Law Library at NYU. I interpret all this as recognition of the academic status of Jewish law as a legal system worthy of study and research in the framework of a law school of such prestige as that of New York University.

I venture to suggest another consideration in the establishment of this Chair. Jewish law—on the one hand, ancient and on the other, young—has a long and illustrious history of legal thought, and of the promotion and development of principles of equity and justice, human dignity, and individual freedom. These principles have had considerable influence on the various legal systems with which Jews have had contact. The study and research of Jewish law in this distinguished law school and, I hope, in others in the United States, will enable American students and jurists to investigate the sources from which this great democracy of the United States of America derived a not inconsiderable part of its principles of freedom, equity, justice, and peace on which it stands and of which it is rightly proud. Such study and the knowledge it will generate will strengthen and intensify the mutual appreciation and respect which our two peoples feel towards each other.

[3]

Shmuel Shilo

Professor Shmuel Shilo, a distinguished scholar and author, is head of the Institute of Jewish Law of the Hebrew University in Jerusalem and editor of ***Shenaton HaMishpat HaIvri***.

THE CONTRAST BETWEEN *MISHPAT IVRI* AND HALAKHAH

INTRODUCTION

Not infrequently, when I discuss with someone in rabbinics or the yeshivah world, or with someone who is engaged in scholarly talmudic studies, my involvement in *mishpat Ivri* (or Jewish law),[1] I find that it is unclear to my companion exactly what I am doing. Are not the terms *mishpat Ivri* and halakhah interchangeable? My purpose in this essay is to delineate clearly the differences between halakhah and *mishpat Ivri*, or more precisely, the differences between scholarship in *mishpat Ivri* and halakhah—both traditional and modern.

Before going further, let me dispose of those scholars—of whom I am not one—who concentrate their endeavors in biblical law. Clearly they are doing something quite different from what is being done in yeshivot or by halakhic scholars; were *mishpat Ivri* to be equated with biblical law, there would be no need to ask how it is distinguished from halakhic scholarship. *Mishpat Ivri*, however, encompasses the entire Jewish legal tradition from biblical times to this very moment. To distinguish the *mishpat Ivri* approach from that of halakhic scholarship, therefore, requires our careful attention.

I

Halakhah and *mishpat Ivri* deal with the same substantial material. To be sure (and this has already been noted by others) those engrossed in *mishpat Ivri* are concerned primarily with those aspects of the halakhah whose equivalent is customarily covered in other contemporary legal systems, that is, matters pertaining to the relations of man and man, rather than the relation of man to God.[2] This, however, cannot be regarded as an essential distinction between *mishpat Ivri* and halakhah. Were this the only difference between the two disciplines, it would merely define

Tradition, 20(2), Summer 1982

041-0608/82/1400 0091 $02.75

mishpat Ivri as a specific province of halakhah, a part of the whole, not as something essentially different. Moreover, no one involved in the study of *mishpat Ivri* would seriously question the fact that all of halakhah is interwoven, so that it is almost impossible to delve deeply into any topic of the civil law without having recourse to some text or principle concerning matters of ritual.

Let me give you an example from a topic I am presently researching, *ha'arama*, evading the law. The question whether one is avoiding the law or evading it by using legal fictions is an important legal issue. To both layman and lawyer, the area of taxes immediately comes to mind. When is my action legal so that I can avoid paying a tax; when does it become illegal so that I become a tax evader? This is certainly a juridical topic; but anyone familiar with the question of avoidance and evasion of the law in the Jewish legal system is at once aware that the question is discussed primarily in connection with that part of the halakhah which can be described as dealing with matters of ritual, such as avoiding the payment of tithes, selling one's *hamets* before Passover, and skirting the law concerning the sanctity of the firstborn of one's cattle.[3]

If this be so, and the ritual and nonritual aspects of the halakhah are so intimately connected, what then makes *mishpat Ivri*, Jewish law, a discipline of its own?

Earlier I said that both Jewish law and halakhah deal, essentially, with the same substance; but identity of subject does not entail identity of the disciplines dealing with it. What matters is, of course, the way one looks at his subject, the purpose of one's observations and the manner in which one expresses himself. We must seek the difference between those engaged in the study of *mishpat Ivri* and those engaged in the study of halakhah in the questions that each one asks and in the methodology used. Each is engaged in a different pursuit.

As to the halakhist, we must differentiate between two paradigms: the student of the halakhah (typically incarnated by the Rosh Yeshiva) and the *poseq*. The former studies the halakhah and delves deeply into its intricacies on the theoretical and the analytic plane. His purpose is not to decide how to act in a given situation, but to understand the sources, and, if possible, to achieve their theoretical unification. He is, ideally, an analyst of halakhic concepts. The *poseq*, by contrast, is interested in determining, through study, what the law is, what should be done. The *poseq* may be a talmudic scholar who is accepted by the community as an authority on the law, or a private *poseq*, studying in order to arrive at the halakhic solution to the question of how he, personally, should act in accordance with the halakhah.

It should be noted that for either type of halakhist Jewish law is first and foremost a religious law, that is to say, a law commanded by God.

Shmuel Shilo

For the secularist, however, Jewish law is of interest because of its cultural-national components, as a part of the Jewish heritage, independent of the theonomous authority of the halakhah. The great interest in Jewish law in our century was and is undoubtedly linked with the idea of a Jewish homeland in the land of Israel and a cultural renaissance; it is similar to the type of cultural aspiration best reflected in the rebirth of the Hebrew language as a spoken, modern means of communication. That the scholar engaged in *mishpat Ivri* does not, in his work, emphasize its religious normative dimension, does not negate that dimension, just as the Hebrew language can be treated as a secular tongue without negating its sanctity, or even the land of Israel can be considered in terms of national-cultural import for the Jewish people without negating its religious importance. The orientation of *mishpat Ivri* thus does not contradict that of halakhah, but, nonetheless, serves as a basis of differentiation.

Another methodological difference between the scholar of *mishpat Ivri* and the halakhist (albeit one of lesser permanent significance) is that as the jurist views it, Jewish law is the living, practiced law; hence an emphasis on the responsa literature. (Responsa literature is equivalent to the case law which plays such a decisive role in the evolution and framing of the Anglo-American legal tradition. Without the record of cases already decided, the law has little meaning for the lawyer; its soul is missing.) In the talmudic academies, the yeshivot, it is, by way of contrast, almost unheard of to study systematically the responsa literature. I do not regard this difference as essential because I have the feeling that this emphasis on the responsa literature by *mishpat Ivri* scholars is already beginning to influence traditional talmudic academies, and that they will turn more and more frequently to this literary genre in their institutions.

Before detailing the major differences between halakhah and *mishpat Ivri*, I want to state uncategorically a view with which some people will disagree: I maintain that only someone who has had a secular, legal education can truly be a scholar in the field of *mishpat Ivri*; being a *talmid hakham* is not enough.

II

What is the approach of those engaged in *mishpat Ivri?* Or, to be more precise, what are their approaches?

Although the comprehensiveness of the following classification is debatable, it is customary to divide the methodology of legal studies into four different categories. They are:

1. a dogmatic or analytical approach;
2. a historical approach;

3. a comparative approach; and
4. an ethical or philosophical approach.[4]

Mishpat Ivri is concerned with all four approaches. The halakhah is generally interested in only two of the four; even concerning those two which are relevant to both the halakhist and the scholar of *mishpat Ivri*, the paths of halakhah and *mishpat Ivri* do not converge—although, of course, there are similarities between them. I wish to speak here about the first three of these approaches.

The dogmatic or analytical approach is probably where halakhists and scholars of Jewish law are closest to each other. The good halakhic scholar will analyze halakhic texts, or even legal institutions; at times he does succeed in making sense out of certain seemingly diffuse and contradictory halakhot. This approach is, of course, an ahistorical one, and its essence is the harmonization of halakhic rules by attempting to grasp the underlying principle behind them. One is sometimes awed by the intellectual breadth and depth of some halakhists and the outcome of these analyses, such as the *hiluq* developed so brilliantly by R. Hayim of Brisk.[5] The work of such halakhic giants is of indubitable quality and value.

Such an approach is certainly valid not only in the eyes of the halakhist, but also in the eyes of the scholar of *mishpat Ivri*. For the latter, however, it is incomplete as an analytical approach to the halakhah. Let me explain this point: it is no secret that Jewish law is predominantly casuistic. Although there have, of course, been great men like R. Hayim throughout the ages whose outstanding minds sought the general beyond the particular, most of halakhah, in the past as well as in the present, is content with the lack of systemization and with casuistry. Even the greatest of codifiers, the Rambam, did not make the leap from a casuistic formulation of the law to an analytic one.

Let us take some concrete examples. I am sure that you are familiar with the first *mishnah* of *Bava Kamma*: The four principles of tort are listed as the ox, the pit, *mave*—whose definition is debated in the Talmud,[6] and fire. The Talmud then subdivides the ox into three different categories: tooth, horn, and foot.[7] These seven physical objects which form the basis for an entire part of the law of torts—if not for all of the law of torts—are, of course, based on broad concepts when classified analytically. But it is up to the lawyer, versed in Jewish law, to translate and transform these concepts into their broader aspects—both juridical and linguistic.

Take another function of the analytic approach: systematization of the law. Here, too, the casuistic approach still reigns to the detriment of system and analysis. For example, Rambam, in his classic code, has a

Shmuel Shilo

section on the law of agency.[8] Many basic problems of agency are discussed there, but one is struck with the fact that there is no mention of the right of an agent to appoint a substitute agent. Did not the halakhah deal with this problem? If so, why is it missing from Rambam's discussion? The answer to these questions is that the halakhah did indeed discuss the substitute agent, but in the Talmud it was brought up in connection with the granting of a divorce.[9] Therefore, true to the Talmud's casuistic manner, Rambam put the law concerning a sub-agent in the book of Women in his code.[10] Maimonides was, of course, well aware that the question of a substitute agent is not limited to an agent for divorce but is a basic question in the general law of agency. His method of arrangement, however, was true to the methodology of the halakhic system, and this methodology determined the placing of this law in the book of Women. The contemporary jurist would negate such an approach to law in general, and to a code of law, in particular. It is one of the tasks of the scholar of *mishpat Ivri* to make this much needed shift in systematization by analysis and arrangement so that all the relevant pieces of the law are placed in their proper legal perspective. This is one of the pressing tasks for the scholar of *mishpat Ivri*. The halakhist can live, and live well, with matters as they are; the jurist cannot.

As we have just seen, both halakhists and Jewish law scholars are engaged in the analytical approach, despite the difference in emphasis between the schools. When we examine the next two approaches, the contrast is much more evident.

The historical approach includes two methods: external and internal. By external, I mean the factors in the society within which the Jewish people lived at any given time and place, which influenced the development of halakhah, and how this came about. Few today will debate that outside influences did affect, at least sometimes, the development of Jewish law. I am sure that there are still fundamentalists in the halakhic schools who would question this statement. What is more important, however, is that even those halakhists (whatever their number) who agree with us regard the study of this phenomenon as of little or no interest. To the jurist, of course, it is a valid and important field for research. There is no need (here) to bring examples of Jewish legal institutions and practices which were so influenced.

To me, personally, it is the internal historical approach, however, that is both intellectually gratifying as scholarship, and is more appropriately assigned to the legal scholar, as opposed to the historian, by virtue of his aptitude and training. I mean by an internal historical approach the attempt to understand and explain the law as it developed from stage to stage by formulating criteria within the Jewish legal system rather than by seeking outside influences. First, one must discover the stages in the evolution of the law and chart out when and where certain views or legal institutions were amended or changed.[11] This is not an easy task, but it is necessary before proceeding further in one's research. Let me add that the proper execution of this work, that is, establishing where and how the law developed and perhaps changed, is itself an important contribution to Jewish law scholarship. But one should, if possible, go further in a number of directions. Let me mention a few which I believe are the most important ones.

In a paper delivered some years ago[12] concerning impotence as a ground for divorce, I demonstrated, convincingly, I hope, that a seemingly sudden change of attitude on the part of the halakhic literature is connected with simultaneously changing views regarding a different halakhic problem. This question, like others, required employing both the internal and the external historical approaches. In my study of the legal problems of impotence in Jewish law, I noted that Rambam's enunciation of his view concerning impotence and sterility was probably influenced by the medical teachings of his mentor in medicine, Avicenna. It should be clear that these observations concerning this important halakhic problem are different in nature from the type of analysis done in yeshivot. The difference, at this point, lies in my use of external historical data. The scholar in *mishpat Ivri*, in his desire to grasp the internal development of the law, will attempt to observe and discover how a certain rule was formulated and later developed. He will ask, for example, if it originated in a tradition that was later expanded by exegesis or interpretation and was then amended by the logic of one of the rabbis—by a *sevara;* or if it is based on a judicial decision or conduct of an halakhic scholar in a particular concrete case which was later incorporated as a custom and then finally recorded as a *takanah* or *gezeira*, an ordinance. Again, these inquiries, which are undoubtedly a part of the halakhic system as a whole, are not directly pursued by the halakhist.

One must also note the basic difference between the legal scholar's use of variant text readings and the utilization of newly published works formerly available only in manuscript, and the traditional halakhist's attitude. Some of the leading halakhic authorities, like the Vilna Gaon, were very careful about correct readings of ancient texts, and would have been eager to partake of the textual scholarship being pursued today in Judaic studies. Many other halakhists, however, including some of the most prominent, are not interested in novel textual emendations if these conflict with a traditional reading and are not (very) impressed by the publication of heretofore unpublished works by past halakhic scholars if the contents of such treatises are liable to rock the traditional halakhic boat. As the Hazon Ish said, referring to Levin's monumental *Ozar Ha' Geonim:* The old material we have; the new we don't need. He explained:

> The sources already printed, are found in the works of the rishonim, organically within the context in which they are quoted and the way they are discussed and treated; the sources now printed for the first time from the *Geniza* manuscripts, whatever their importance may be for academic study, are irrevelant to halakhic consideration.[13]

With regard to the matter of correcting texts and publishing manuscripts, the *mishpat Ivri* scholars display an orientation different from that of the traditional halakhist, but also different from that of the university talmudic scholar. For the latter, textual work can be, and too often is, an end in itself. For the jurist, it is a means to an end.

As a final observation regarding the historical approach, I must add that Jewish law is interested in knowing both what the law was or is as *stated* in the various law books and also how the law was in fact *implemented in life*. There is not always an equation between the two, as lawyers know. The halakhist usually ignores the gap between the law and its implementation.

It is, however, in the *comparative* approach where the legal scholar can display his erudition and acumen in a manner which is unique because of his legal training. If, perhaps, the halakhist can compete with him on the analytic side, the historian in the historical approach, and the philosopher or ethicist in their respective disciplines, no one can rival the jurist when the object of one's research is to place Jewish law within the context of other legal systems.

There are three major areas where, I believe, the comparative method can be, and is, fruitful.

Two types of comparative research have been common in the past. There are scholars who have sought to investigate the influence of Jewish law on other legal systems; alternatively, there have been scholars who attempted to show where other legal systems have affected Jewish law. The former question has been pursued, for example, by the late Professor Rabinowitz of the Hebrew University, who has come up with some interesting, albeit debatable theories, such as Jewish law's very important place in the development of commercial law (especially that of bills of exchange) and Jewish law's singular influence on the development of the English mortgage.[14] Today, this type of scholarship is comparatively dormant. It remains a fascinating field for anyone inclined to such work; but it probably has more pitfalls than other avenues of scholarship in Jewish law because of the real difficulty in establishing convincingly that Jewish law did, in fact, materially influence some legal institution in another legal system in the course of the development of the law.

The second field of research I mentioned, that of foreign influences on Jewish law, has had its practitioners since Jewish law became an accepted discipline. In the past, Roman law was looked upon as the legal system most likely to have affected talmudic law,[15] but there is now an awareness that scholarly inquiry should be widened to Greek law and the legal system prevalent in the Persian empire.[16] Because of problems of language, paucity of sources and other impediments, this line of research is still in its embryonic stage. Here, too, one must be very wary before concluding that another legal system influenced Jewish law. Similarity does not prove influence.

The most important and fruitful aspect of the comparative method, however, is the in-depth study of legal institutions, both in the Jewish legal system and in other legal systems, in order to understand how universal questions of law (and let us remember that most legal problems seeking a solution, are universal in nature) are answered by Jewish law as compared with other legal systems. Often, the solutions to similar problems resemble each other in all legal systems, but many times Jewish law has its own unique approach to a question or a legal institution. Where the solutions are similar, it is important to define the precise nature of the similarity. Where they differ, it is of utmost importance and interest to the scholar of *mishpat Ivri* to be able to reveal the unique approach and structure of Jewish law and how it has developed its own, original, legal institution or solution to a question at issue.

For those who are especially interested in legal history, a most fruitful path of research is to study how well Jewish law corresponds to general theories of the development of legal institutions. For example, does the evolution of Jewish law fit into the patterns described by Maine in his classic *Ancient Law*?[17] I deliberately choose Maine because he is still the intellectual giant in this field of research although some of his theories have been strongly questioned and criticized. Maine was not well versed in Jewish law and his theories were developed by studying other legal systems. Does Jewish law follow the patterns hypothesized by Maine? Does Jewish law display development from status to contract, for example?[18] If Jewish law deviates from a pattern of development which appears to be universal, why does it?

This brief discussion of the comparative approach is sufficient to establish its absence from the halakhist's framework. Because of his special and specialized training, the scholar of *mishpat Ivri* has another significant frame of reference for his study of Jewish law not available to the traditional halakhist.

In concluding I want to note some general observations. One important contribution of the resurgence of scholarship in Jewish law over the past twenty or thirty years is the revival, if one may call it that, of certain aspects of Jewish law which were more or less moribund. Certain topics such as public law in general and *takanot kahal*—communal legislation—in particular, which are undoubtedly an integral part of Jewish law, had been neglected for many years. The renewal of interest in these topics is the product of comparatively recent scholarship. There is no doubt in my mind that the emergence of a Jewish State in the land of Israel gave impetus, conscious or subconscious, to these studies. It is to the credit of Professor Menachem Elon, now a Justice of Israel's Supreme Court, who called attention to, and wrote scholarly articles on these topics,[19] and they have consequently been dealt with by other scholars.[20]

It is my own belief that the scholarly study of *mishpat Ivri* in the State of Israel is not only of pure academic interest, but has had, and I hope will have, even more in the future, a special legal-cultural influence. The desire for such an extra-academic impact is not unusual for the jurist; any jurist is involved in a practical pursuit side-by-side with the academic one. Law is not only history, but life itself. How much more so in Israel where a young state is groping to find its way to an indigenous legal system. The product of our scholarship can, and does to some extent, influence the Israeli legal system. Some scholars of Jewish law in the past, such as Gulak, Freimann and Silberg, have advocated the preparation of a modern code of civil law, for possible incorporation in the State of Israel, based on the principles of Jewish law, but not identical with the *Shulhan Arukh*.[21] I, personally, am not a proponent of such a code, but those who are, face a major challenge for the acumen of the lawyer who is well-versed in Jewish law.

In fact, some aspects of Jewish law have been incorporated in the legislation of the State of Israel,[22] and one can find that many decisions of the Israeli Supreme Court are interspersed with precedents from Jewish law in general, and the responsa literature in particular.[23] Though the solution to a problem may be similar in American, English and Jewish law, I undoubtedly prefer a quote from the *Noda B'Yehuda* concerning Reuven and Shimon, than a precedent concerning John Doe versus Harry Smith. This, of course, may be viewed as a personal tendency, but I think that I am speaking for the vast majority of Jews who are culturally committed to the Jewish heritage. The practical application of Jewish law to a modern legal system no more derogates from the so-called scientific study of Jewish law, than Ben-Yehuda's dictionary of the Hebrew language which greatly influenced modern Hebrew, detracts from the scholarly standing of this monumental dictionary.

Not all of the above-mentioned methods of research must be employed by everyone engaged in research in *mishpat Ivri*. In fact, it is well–nigh impossible for any one individual to deal with a subject from all these angles. That is one of the most compelling attractions of scholarship in Jewish law. The field is wide open: an individual with the proper training and a personal interest in the subject can find the approach or approaches most suitable to him and can contribute to the young but growing community of lawyers engaged in *mispat Ivri*.

NOTES

1. As to the use of the term, *mishpat Ivri*, see M. Elon (ed.), *The Principles of Jewish Law* (Jerusalem, 1975), p. 5.
2. M. Elon, *The Principles of Jewish Law*, p. 5.
3. See entry *ha'arama* in *Encyclopedia Talmudit*, volume 4, p. 597.
4. See, in general, on the problematics of research in Jewish law, B. Jackson (ed.), *Modern Research in Jewish Law* (Leiden, 1980).
5. See, for example, on the *hiluq*, N. Solomon, "Hilluq and Hqirah: A Study in the Method of the Lithuanian Halakhists," *Dine Yisrael* Vol. IV, p. LXIX, (English Section).
6. *Bava Kamma* 3b.
7. *Bava Kamma* 2b.
8. *Hilkhot Sheluhin Ve'Shutfim*, chapters one and two.
9. *Gittin* 29b.
10. *Hilkhot Gerushin*, chap. 7, sec. 20-21.
11. An excellent example of this type of scholarship is M. Elon's *Herut haPerat beDine Geviyat Hov baMishpat HaIvri* (Jerusalem, 1964).
12. S. Shilo, "*Hoser Koah Gavra Kellla Le Gerushin*," *Proceedings of the Fifth Congress for Jewish Studies*, Vol. 3, p. 353. The article appeared in English translation in volume 4 of the *Jewish Law Annual pp. 127-143*.
13. Z. A. Yehuda "Hazon Ish on Textual Criticism and Halakhah", *Tradition*, 18, No. 2 (Summer 1980), 172-174.
14. J.J. Rabinowitz, *Jewish Law: Its Influence on the Development of Legal Institutions* (New York, 1956).
15. The outstanding scholar who devoted his life to the comparison of Roman law and Jewish law was Boaz Cohen. See his two volume *Jewish and Roman Law: A Comparative Study* (New York, 1966).
16. Professor Saul Leiberman has been demonstrating this for many years about Greek law, see, e.g. his *Hellenism in Jewish Palestine* (New York, 1962). The late E.S. Rosenthal has similarly been preaching the need for the study of Persian law for a proper understanding of talmudic law. See E.S. Rosenthal, "*LeMillon haTalmud—Berun Millim velyune Nusah*," in *Tarbiz* 40 (1971) pp. 178-201.
17. H.S. Maine, *Ancient Law: It's Connection With the Early History of Society and its Relation to Modern Ideas*, London, 1861 (Rev. ed. New York, 1960).
18. H. S. Maine, *Ancient Law*, p. 100. See too R.H. Graveson "The Movement From Status to Contract", *Modern Law Review*, 4 (1940/41), 261-272.
19. See, for example, M. Elon, *LeMahutan Shel Takkannot Hakahal baMishpat haIvri* in *Mehkere Mishpat Lezekher Avraham Rosenthal* (1964), pp. 1-54; M. Elon: *HaMishpat haIvri Toledotav, Mekorotav, Ekronotav* (Jerusalem 1973), pp. 367-390; 547-72.
20. See for example S. Shilo, "*Al Shetei Takkannot Kahal beSefarad*" in *Sinai*, 61 (1967), 291. A Nachalon's two articles: "*Samkhut haTsibbur Lehatkin Takkannot lefi ha–Tashbets*" in *Shenaton haMishpat haIvri*, vol. 1 p. 142 and *Idem*, 3/4, p. 271.
21. See articles by Gulak, Freimann and Silberg in *Ha Mishpat ha Ivri uMedinat Yisrael*, ed. J. Bazak (Jerusalem, 1969).
22. See, for example, Y. Goldsmith, "Jewish Law in the Legislative Activity of the Knesset," *Dine Yisrael*, vol. 5, XCIV (English Section); the references to various articles on the subject in N. Rakover, *Ozar haMishpat* (Jerusalem, 1975), p. 130.
23. See the periodic surveys in the volumes of *Dine Yisrael*, "Jewish Law in the Law Reports" compiled by S. Meron and N. Rakover, *Ozar haMisphat*, p. 132.

[4]

The Jewish Law Annual, Vol.VI

LEGAL POSITIVISM AND CONTEMPORARY *HALAKHIC* DISCOURSE

by

ALAN J. YUTER*

I Positivism and Jewish Law

Unlike natural law theories, legal sociology, or history of law, legal positivism focuses upon the legal order, its constituent norms and the hierarchy of those norms. In Hans Kelsen's formulation of legal positivism,[1] this hierarchy is abstracted from specific legal content. Ethical, political, and ideological motives are irrelevant to the evaluation of legal orders.[2] There are, however, many scholars of Jewish law who are passionately committed to the relevance, efficacy, and religious worth of their subject and, as consequence, adopt a positivist posture in their *apologia* of *Halakhah*.[3] For these scholars, changing moral climates, historical relativism, and textual criticism are "modernist" ideological concerns that are equally out of place in legal positivism as they are in theological Orthodoxy.

For the academic scholar of Jewish law, legal positivism provides an analytic tool whereby Jewish law is studied without approval [as in the cases of Orthodoxy and, until recently, American Conservatism] or disapproval [as in the cases of Reform Reconstructionism, and Secularism]. Orthodox positivists who justify their approach by appealing to the unchanging will of an eternal Lawgiver assign to the Deity the role of author of the Torah, or first constitution of the Jewish people. According to Hans Kelsen's model, *Halakhah* may be considered to be a theological positivist order, but the role

---

* Rabbi, Congregation Ohr Yisrael, Spring Valley, New York; Adjunct Faculty, Rockland Community College.

1 Hans Kelsen, *Pure Theory of Law*, trld. M. Knight (Berkeley, Los Angeles, and London: University of California Press, 1967).

2 "Uncritically the science of law has been mixed with elements of psychology, sociology, ethics and political theory. This adulteration is understandable, because the latter disciplines deal with subject matters that are closely connected with law. The Pure Theory of Law undertakes to delimit the cognition of law against these disciplines, not because it ignores or denies the connection, but because it wishes to avoid the uncritical mixture of methodologically different disciplines." - Kelsen, *supra* n.1, at1.

3 See Appendix.

of the Godhead in *Halakhah* would be formal, not theological. God merely serves as the ground, or first principle, that justifies compliance with the constitution, *without* any metaphysical assumption regarding either the personality of God or the content of His constitution.[4] Still, most halakhists fail to appreciate the difficulty in theological positivism:

> A theological ethics that regards God as the highest norm-creating authority cannot state that somebody else has ordered to obey the commands of God - because this would have to be an authority higher than God. And if the norm: "One ought to obey the commands od God" were presumed to be posited by God, it could not be the reason for the validity of God-created norms, because it would itself be a God-created norm.[5]

The unanswered question for the halakhist is "why one should obey the commands of God?" In his outstanding study of the Biblical concept of *berit*, or covenant, Professor José Faur demonstrates how Jewish law must be understood in a non-theological positivist model.[6] Significantly, no metaphysical or mystical axiom appears in Faur's halakhic positivism. Faur first shows that monotheism, as a doctrine, is independent of revelation.[7]

He then argues *against* the doctrine of natural right - "that there are certain rights that do not depend on legislation and authority, but are necessitated by the very order of the universe," and *for* the doctrine of positive right "that every right is the result of legislation, and thus depends on promulgation and authority. Fundamentally, it [legal positivism] rejects the notion of an objective criterion of right and wrong."[8] Faur's reading of the Covenant doctrine coincides with Kelsen's legal positivism, but differs with conventional Orthodox positivists. By rejecting the natural right theory that assumes an "objectively" correct morality, Faur endorses only one functional dogma: "the individual has the duty to obey the decrees of authority or society."[9] By distinguishing between law and theology, Faur finds that:

4 Kelsen, *supra* n.1, at 194-195.
5 Kelsen. *supra* n.1, at 203.
6 "Understanding the Covenant", *Tradition* 9 (1968), 33-55.
7 *Ibid.*, at 34.
8 *Ibid.*, at 37.
9 *Ibid.*, at 39.

> Although essentially Judaism means obedience to God's law, God's law is not identical to the revealed will of God. Revelation, though proceeding from God and recorded in the Bible, is not as such authoritative ... The basis of Judaism is not conformity to the revealed will of God, but conformity to the Sinaitic law.[10]

Faur's view of halakhic positivism focuses solely upon the legal norms of Jewish law. Since both man and God possess free will, any law is conditioned upon a *berit*, a covenant or pact, that would be mutually binding: only after the *berit* was ratified by Israel, during which God himself is absent, is the covenant in force. This pact is not unilateral, for Israel, at God's behest, authorized God to give the law:

> The authority of the Mosaic law does not rest on the fiat of God's will, but upon the fact that it was accepted as such by the entire people of Israel. As thus conceived, divine authority is not the effect of an Absolute Power, who dictates His will to his inferiors, but of negotiation between two parties who are equally free to assent and dissent.[11]

Faur's critique of natural law also parallels Kelsen's because both Kelsen and Faur recognize the dogmatic quality of assertions that a particular morality may be "objectively" correct or that values may be derived from nature. For Kelsen the secularist as well as Faur the religionist, positive law has no theological content and both argue that only legislated, or positive law is the content of any legal order.

II The Basic Norm in the thought of Hans Kelsen

Central to Kelsen's legal positivism is the doctrine of the basic norm. This norm is not a legal norm because (a) it is not derived from any higher norm and (b) it does not carry a sanction. This *Grundnorm*, or "ground norm", stands outside the legal order, but serves as its justification. Like Faur's dogma "that one has a duty to obey authority," Kelsen's basic norm only posits that "one ought to behave according to this specific constitution."[12] Since this basic norm is the same for any legal order, its content is derived from its function, rather than dogma. Like Faur in his treatment of the Sinaitic covenant, Kelsen argues that "the presupposition of the basic norm does approve any value transcending positive law."[13] The

10 *Ibid.*, at 41.
11 See Appendix.
12 Kelsen, *supra* n.1, at 201.
13 *Ibid.*

basic norm only authorizes the specific and general norms of the legal order; it is not itself a legal norm. It is

> the reason for the validity of all norms belonging to the same legal order, the basic norm constitutes the unity of the multiplicity of these norms. This unity is expressed also by the fact that a legal order may be described in rules of law that do not contradict each other.[14]

The theological implications that many halakhists read into the basic norm of Jewish law is consistent with the legal positivism of Kelsen's Pure Theory.

It has been argued that Kelsen's basic norm is a flawed doctrine, and cannot be used as a litmus test for legal positivism in general or halakhic positivism in particular. Actually, Kelsen's basic norm formulation not only stands the attack of its critics, it is an appropriate model for halakhic positivism as well. In his *Concept of Law*, Professor H.L.A. Hart espouses a doctrine concerning a "rule of recognition",[15] which is an alternative to Kelsen's basic norm. This rule of recognition operates in conformity with the way the legal order is viewed and accepted by the society under its rule. Hart also believes that law must have a moral minimum.[16] His insistence upon communal assent is of importance to Kelsen only insofar as legal orders, to be valid, must enjoy a modicum of compliance, and Kelsen as well as Faur reject the natural law doctrine that there exists an identifiable moral minimum in every legal order. Hart himself is unable to explain why Kelsen's basic norm has no substantive content other than that the constitution must be obeyed.[17] What troubles Hart is the "purity" of Kelsen's pure theory; Kelsen's positivism makes no assumptions concerning non-legal issues, and the basic norm, insofar as it is a non-legal norm, has no meaning whatsoever once it is separated from the legal order it serves.

Like Hart, Graham Hughes looks in vain for a specific extra-legal content in Kelsen's basic norm:

> all [that] the rules and rulings [of a legal order] have in common is common descent from the same basic set of procedures of rule making, and that this feature of legitimate descent from procedures appears to be the reason why the rules are *accepted as binding*. If the external observer now wishes to give a systematic account of the order he has observed he might well characterize it as resting on the

14 *Ibid.*, at 205.

15 H.L.A. Hart, *The Concept of Law* (Oxford: The Clarendon Press, 1961), 97.

16 *Ibid.*, at 189.

17 *Ibid.*, at 245 note 3.

> presupposition of the validity of the basic norm, by which he would mean nothing more than certain basic procedures are actually accepted in that society as authoritative rules.[18]

But for Kelsen's basic norm, itself the centerpiece of his pure theory, communal approval is irrelevant. If the legal order is effective, then the consistent normative hierarchy is valid. By appealing to a "psychological or sociological analysis of the motivations underlying acceptance", Hughes' view approaches Hart's doctrine of the rule of recognition.[19]

Professor Julius Stone is also unable to determine whether Kelsen's basic norm is intrasystemic or extrasystemic:

> The adjective "basic" is indeed itself inapt for a norm which Kelsenite theory places at the top of the pyramid of hierarchy of norms. "Apex" norm would be far more appropriate especially ... because it would still leave Kelsen's ambiguous term a residue of meaning to which that term is less sytematically incongruous.[20]

Stone focuses upon the logical connection between the basic norm and the legal order it authorizes. Kelsen's basic norm could be regarded either as intrasystemic, within the legal order, or, since it is not a legal norm, extrasystemic and, as such, the highest norm in a hierarchy of legal norms, thus an "apex" norm.

For Kelsen, the norm allows for the objective behavior of people to be assigned a normative value, and, as such, it provides the condition for the legal evaluation of behavior. This confusing metaphor is borrowed from the theory of knowledge of Immanuel Kant:

> According to Kant's epistemology, the science of law as cognition of the law, like any cognition, has constitutive character - it "creates" its object insofar as it comprehends the object as a meaningful whole. Just as the chaos of sensual perceptions become a cosmos, that is, "nature" as a unified system, through the cognition of natural science, so the multitude of general and individual legal norms .... becomes a unitary system, a legal "order", through the science of law. But this "creation" has a purely epistemological character. It is fundamentally different from

18 Graham Hughes, "Validity and the Basic Norm", *California Law Review* 29 (1971), 699, emphasis supplied.

19 *Ibid.*, at 703.

20 Julius Stone, "Mystery and Mystique in the Basic Norm", *Modern Law Review* 26 (1963), 44.

> the creation of objects by human labor or the creation of law by the legal authority.[21]

The norm is the condition for legal discourse in the same sense that, for Kant, space and time are conditions for human knowledge. Just as the sensibilities of space and time are contributed to knowledge as the *a priori* conditions of the knowing subject,[22] the basic norm is the "transcendent logical condition" of legal discourse.[23] Significantly, Kant denies that this transcendent, or non-empirical knowledge is metaphysical, even though it transcends empirical experience.[24] Just as space and time are *a priori* concepts that have no empirical content, the basic norm of a legal order contains no content because it transcends the legal order. The sensibilities of space and time apply to all knowledge in the same way that the basic norm: "obey the historically first constitution" applies to every valid legal order.

III The Basic Norm in Jewish Law: A Case Study

The recent debate between Professors Menahem Elon and Izhak Englard concerning the nature of modern halakhic research reflects two different understandings of Jewish law. Englard claims that Jewish law is a religious positivist order and assigns to the [Orthodox] rabbinate the sole authority to interpret the law. Any prescriptive judgment on the part of an academic scholar invalidates the intellectual detachment of the judgment. For Elon, objective philological and historical research into Jewish law often reveals trends, ideas, and policies that are unnoticed by contemporary [Orthodox] rabbis, and he prescriptively argues that Jewish law be integrated into Israeli

21 Kelsen, *supra* n.1, at 72. In this study, references are taken from Kelsen's *Pure Theory* rather than his *General Theory* (1945) because it is in the former that this aspect of his theory is more fully developed.

22 Immanuel Kant, *Critique of Pure Reason* (London, Macmillan, 1964), 204. See also Kelsen, *supra* n.1, at 202.

23 Kelsen, *supra* n.1, at 223.

24 For Kant, there can be no knowledge of the noumenous object, because it is not conditioned by experience. See his antinomies of pure reason, *supra* n.22, at 384f., in which the logical deduction of pure [non-experiential] reason leads to unavoidable contradictions.

law.[25] Englard, in turn, rejects Elon's "historicism" as an unscientific heresy similar to Conservative Judaism,[26] as well as his prescriptive hope that the study of Jewish law would "prepare" for its reception into the law of Israel.[27] Both Englard and Elon defend their positions with reasoned arguments, but their divergent views stem from radically different uses of positivist thought and rhetoric. Kelsen's pure theory is an appropriate analytic tool in this discussion because it alone

> describes the law and attempts to eliminate from the object of this description everything that is not strictly law: Its aim is to free the science of law from alien elements.[28]

The merits of Elon's and Englard's positions can be evaluated by examining how they treat Jewish law as a normative order, and how their descriptions of what Jewish law *is* coheres with their prescriptions of what Jewish law *ought to be*.

In his *Ha-Mishpat Ha-Ivri,* Elon devotes a chapter to a discussion of the sources of law and their application to Jewish law.[29] Although Kelsen, unlike Elon, does not consider literary and historical "sources" to be sources of law in the pure sense,[30] they focus their attention upon the specific acts of legislation which create the norms of the legal order. In Elon's scheme, historical scholarship provides the description necessary for accurate prescription; the meanings of texts must be clarified so that the norms contained therein may be understood correctly.

Although Elon acknowledges Kelsen's pure theory and its search for an ultimate principle from which other legal principles are derived,[31] he retreats into theology in his discussion of the basic norm. According to Elon, the basic norm of Jewish law is:

---

25 Menahem Elon, *Ha-Mishpat Ha-Ivri* (Jerusalem: Magnes Press, 1973) I, chapter II shows the flexibility of Jewish law to respond to changing situations, and Elon associates the lack of flexibility with the loss of national autonomy (at 70). He argues for the integration of Jewish law in the legal order of the State at I, 117-118, and "More About Research into Jewish Law", *Modern Research in Jewish Law*, ed. Bernard S. Jackson (Leiden: Brill, 1980), 85.

26 Izhak Englard, "Research in Jewish Law - Its Nature and Function", in Jackson, *supra* n.25, at 52-53.

27 *Ibid.*, at 56.

28 Kelsen, *supra* n.1, at 1.

29 Elon, *supra* n.1, at 1.

30 Kelsen, *supra* n.1, at 232.

31 Elon, *supra* n. 25, at 213f.

> that all that appears in the Pentateuch renders the legal order of Jewish law binding... [it is] the eternal legislation of Jewish law that is not given to change, addition, or diminution.[32]

The source of this "basic norm" is the word of God:

> To answer this question [concerning the source of the Torah's authority] we leave the realm of Jewish legal concepts and enter the realm of faith: it is a fundamental assumption of Judaism that the source of the authority of Torah lies in the Giver of the Torah.[33]

Unlike Faur, who recognizes that the basic norm must be an unconditioned ultimate principle, Elon's formulation of the basic norm centers upon the revealed text of the Written Torah, which is conditioned by yet another basic norm, God's will. He does not explain how God is authorized, as does Faur, to legislate. Elon's emphasis upon the written Torah, as the historically first constitution, is no less problematic. As a text, the Pentateuch is a *literary* source of law: *deoraita*, or Torah law, derives from the Divine will, and not because it is found in the Pentateuchal text. Dogmas concerning the *nature* of revelation are irrelevant to any legal discussion. In spite of Elon's imposition of a theological content upon his version of Jewish law's basic norm, Elon never allows his theology to effect his program, for "the law is not in heaven."[34] In this regard, Elon's basic norm is functional and formal, not theological. Elon's citation that the sciatic nerve rule derives from Sinai is significant because, according to the Mishnah[35] and Maimonides,[36] the

32 *Ibid.*, at 215-216.

33 *Ibid.*, at 216. This "Giver of the Torah" doctrine need not reflect a theological dogma. According to Kelsen, "the concept of God presents itself as a personification of the world order .... The state is also essentially conceived as a person, and as such is merely the personification of an order." See his "God and the State", in *Essays in Legal and Moral Philosophy* (Boston: Reidel, 1973), 70. For Kelsen, the doctrine of causality, originally assumed to be grounded in God, is a reflex of the doctrine of retribution. See "The Principle of Causality in Modern Science", in *Society and Nature* (New York: Arno, 1974), 262. These doctrines may or may not be "real", but they exist in and are created by human beings insofar as human beings try to understand their universe. Thus, the "Giver of the Torah" may be the Lord who revealed Himself at Sinai, or the personification of the Jewish world order.

34 *Deuteronomy* 30:12.

35 *Mishnah Hullin* 7:6.

36 *Commentary to the Mishnah, ad loc.* See Elon's discussion, *supra* n.25, at 216-217.

rule *is not* derived from the Pentateuch's account of Jacob's dream, but is preserved in the Oral Torah. Its normative status stems from its origins in *Torah*, or God's will, and not because it is recorded in the Pentateuch. The modern halakhic scholar examines the norms of Jewish law as a given , while the bible critic studies a literary source of law. Since the basic norm of Jewish law is that "Israelities ought to obey the words of God contained in the [Oral as well as Written] Torah," any judgment concerning the nature of God or the literary transmission of the Torah document is *legally* meaningless.

While Elon does not develop his views on the nature of revelation, he often demonstrates how halakhic norms authorize his program of the integration of Jewish law into the legal structure of an autonomous Jewish state. In his discussion of annulment of marriages where a *get*, or writ of divorce that must be initiated by the husband, is unobtainable, Elon argues that *hafkaah* [annulment] is talmudically authorized and that although the procedure has not been implemented in recent halakhic history, it is still a legitimate practice that is appropriate in an autonomous Jewish society.[37] He also prefers responsa literature and *Halakhot*, or rulings accompanied by analysis and summary, so that the current expression of Jewish legal opinion not be disconnected from its legitimating sources. In his summary of the criticism of Maimonides' *Yad*,[38] as well as subsequent efforts of codification,[39] Elon finds that Codes are treated too authoritatively. By employing the *genres* of *Halakhot* and responsa, Elon believes that the historical processes of halakhic development will be artificially inhibited by a popular acceptance of particular codes. Elon hereby implies that the rabbinate ought to exercise the authority they need to possess, and that the conservatism that developed in the Jewish Diaspora is unjustified in a modern Jewish state. While Elon does not presume to issue *pesakim*, or decisions, like the Orthodox rabbi, the program he advocates is clearly ideological, but within the historical parameters of halakhic norms.

Whereas Elon's program is defended in terms understandable to a legal positivist, Izhak Englard's rhetoric is positivist in nature, but his methodology is not. For Englard, *Halakhah* is described as a rabbinic oligarchy, not as a normative order. In place of a discussion of the relative values assigned to the norms of Jewish law, Englard emphasizes the theological basis for the law over and above the legal content:

37 Elon, *supra* n.25 at 711-712.
38 *Ibid.*, at 997.
39 See Appendix.

> The emphasis ... on substance of the legal solution is likely to blur the distinctive features of a legal system .. By open rejection of the formal basis of the normative order, a person places himself outside the original system. Thus, a judge, by declaring the American Constitution to be normatively irrelevant, would step outside the traditional American system; his declaration would signify the creation of a new normative system.[40]

For Kelsen, the term "normative order" is a system of norms that regulates human behavior.[41] Englard uses the term to signify the normative judgments of the rabbinic oligarchy. By emphasizing that the "formal basis" of Jewish law is grounded in theological-political dogma, Englard leaves the discipline of law and enters the realm of theology:

> The religious elements [of Jewish law] go to the essence of the normative order. Its validity lies ultimately in its supra-human authority; its ends are of a transcendent nature.[42]

Although Englard employs Kelsenite terms like "normative order" and "validity", his imposition of theological-political content upon the basic norm is inconsistent with Kelsen's doctrine that regards the basic norm as the *formal* assumption authorizing obedience to the historically first constitution, and to which no ideological content or approval is implied.

While Englard explicitly defines the theological content of the basic norm or the hierarchy of his so-called "normative order", he defines *Halakhah* as "the set of norms considered binding by orthodox Judaism."[43] Thus, the divinely ordained rules that are not given to change or ideological manipulation are alive and well in the sociological practice of the Orthodox community. While this observation may be empirically valid, its *legal* validity is not justified by legal norms.

In his critique of Elon's "historical" method, which he identifies with Conservative Judaism, Englard finds Elon guilty of a scientific error as well as a theological heresy:

> The assertion that Conservative Judaism is more scientific than Orthodox Judaism is as completely unfounded as the argument that the legal solution elaborated by the modern scholar is more scientific than that suggested by the Orthodox rabbi.[44]

40 Englard, *supra* n.26, at 25.
41 Kelsen, *supra* n.1, at 14.
42 Englard, *supra* n.26, at 23.
43 *Ibid.*
44 *Ibid.*, at 53.

For Englard, the scholar only engages in description, but the Orthodox rabbi is authorised to engage in prescription as well as description. Elon's adoption of historical methodology, for Englard, makes ideological assumptions that are scientifically questionable and theologically incorrect. But this normative judgment on Englard's part is justified only if *Halakhah* is viewed as a rabbinic oligarchy rather than as a Kelsenite normative order:

> If Jewish law constitutes the object of study, one has to accept it in its integral entirety. It is *totally unacceptable* that the modern scholar should reach a legal solution different from that of the [orthodox] Rabbi.[45]

Englard's term "totally unacceptable" is unacceptably ambiguous because it is not at all clear whether the "scholarly solution" referred to above is unacceptable because scholars ought not to engage in prescriptive judgments, in which case Englard bears the onus of demonstrating that halakhically committed individuals who are engaged in the study of *Halakhah* are not authorized to make normative judgments, or because Englard finds the prescription to be theologically and politically improper, in which case Englard's judgment is "normative" rather than "objective".

Englard's view that Jewish law is a rabbinic oligarchy rather than a normative order is underscored in his rejection of Justice Silberg's interpretation of the Ochnai oven legend.[46] In contrast to Silberg, who believes that the legend teaches that Judaism embodies a Rule of Law,[47] Englard argues that the Talmudic account teaches a religious rather than legal doctrine. According to the legend,[48] Rabbi Eliezer b. Hyrcanus protests to his colleagues that their ruling, reinstating a state of ritual impurity upon a defiled earthenware oven after it is shattered, is incorrect. After hearing and rejecting R. Eliezer's arguments by majority vote, the Talmud reports R. Eliezer's three miracles, none of which are accepted by the court as sources of law. Appeals to nature suggest that value, or "ought" statements, can be derived from "is" statements, or facts of nature. Convinced that his view represents an old authentic *Halakhah*, R. Eliezer summons a *bat kol*, or

45 *Ibid.*, at 52, emphasis supplied.

46 See Englard's "*Tanur shel Ochnai - Perushah shel Aggadah* ", *Shenaton Ha-Mishpat Ha-Ivri* 1 (1974), 45-46.

47 Moshe Silberg, *Kakh Darkah shel Talmud* (Jerusalem: *Mifal ha-Schichpul*, 1962), 68f.

48 *Bava Metsia* 59b.

oracle,[49] that reveals the will of God, the Giver of the historically first constitution. The sages reply that God's will is legally irrelevant because the normative order makes no provision for a "transcendent" or "supra-human authority" to intervene in legal debate. Even if one knows what God actually desires, the only *legal* criteria is the majority vote of the Talmudic court, the authorized organ of norm creation.[50]

The message of the Ochnai oven legend lies in the affirmation that *Halakhah* is foremost a normative order, and not a theological or political oligarchy. This doctrine is described most aptly by Elon:

> And even the oracle - the revelation from heaven - is not authorized to intervene in the establishment of the law because the Torah - once given - is "no longer in Heaven", and the law in that [Ochnai oven] case is established on the basis of what is written in the Torah - "the law follows the majority." .... God Himself, the Giver and Source of the law, who, as it were, by means of an oracle, made it known that R. Eliezer's view was the correct Torah truth, is forced to admit that his children [= the authorized sages] - who think differently, and who are the majority - have defeated Him [= have ruled against God legitimately].[51]

In Kelsen's terms, the doctrine *"Torah min hashamayim"*, or revelation, is a statement that the basic norm of Jewish law, like any law, transcends experience and authorizes the legal order of norms to assign legal value to human behavior. The doctrine "*Lo bashamayim Hi* ," the law is not [now] in Heaven, indicates that *Halakhah* is indeed a normative order initiated by God to be developed by and for human beings, and *any* ruling consistent with those norms is valid, but any appeal to metaphysical truth is not.

Since legal positivism, insofar as it is a scientific tool, makes no evaluation about the worth or binding quality of the legal orders it describes, positivist rhetoric cannot be mustered to defend the "unchanging" quality of Jewish law. Legal positivism can only determine whether specific decisions or norms are valid, or consistent with the principles of the legal order. If the Orthodox rabbinic oligarchy is indeed the only authorized organ of legislation, then that authorization must be demonstrated. I am *not* arguing

49 For the definition of *bat kol* as oracle, see Saul Lieberman, *Hellenism in Jewish Palestine* (New York: Jewish Theological Seminary, 1962), 194-199. The *sugya's* continuation, "My sons have bested me", indicates that the voice or echo was a Divine oracle in this context. Significantly, neither the oracle nor the fact that the old *Halakhah* was in accordance with R. Eliezer's view, as witnessed by the rule of *M. Kelim* 5:10, are of the same legal weight as a majority opinion of the court.

50 Elon, *supra* n.25, at 228.

51 See Appendix.

that Englard is wrong in his assertion that only the Orthodox rabbi can prescribe Jewish law; that assertion, however intriguing, is not within the scope of this essay. For Englard to make his case as a legal positivist, he would have to examine the authority of a State endorsed rabbinate, the authority of which is not accepted as universal, even within Orthodoxy. He also would be required to demonstrate that a halakhic argument, based on dogmatic assumptions, offered by a learned lay professional electrician, a professor of *mishpat ivri*, or a young gentleman in a *kollel* without any "official" position whatsoever, do not have halakhic validity. It is still unclear how post-talmudic rabbinates, charismatic sages, or *rashei yeshivah* (heads of Talmudic academies) are legally authorized norm creating organs in the absence of a Great Sanhedrin.

Appeals to theology, politics, history or sociology are ideological in nature, and inappropriate to a positivist study of law This too is a condition of Kelsen's positivism:

> If we do not understand by "ideology" everything that is not natural reality or its description, but nonobjective presentation of the subject influenced by subjective value judgments and glorifying or disfiguring the subject of cognition; and if we designate as "reality" not only the natural reality as the subject of natural science, but every subject of cognition including the subject of the science of law, namely positive law, as legal reality; then a presentation of positive law must keep itself free from ideology.[52]

APPENDIX

Note 3:

> For Rabbi J. David Bleich, *Contemporary Halakhic Problems* (New York: Ktav, 1977), xiii-xiv, "Judaism is fundamentally a religion of law, a law which governs every facet of the human condition. The Torah contains not merely a set of laws but also canons of interpretation as well as principles according to which possible conflicts may be resolved. He continues, at xvi, by affirming that "the methodology by which some opinions are accepted and others excluded from application to practice constitutes a highly complex aspect of Halakhah ... Decision making is also bound by rules of procedure." Perhaps the most articulate and concise formulation of Orthodox positivism is R. Moses Tendler's: "The literal interpretation of the theological doctrine of divine revelation differentiates Torah (= Orthodox) Judaism from the organized faith communities that have arisen as deviants from the traditional form ... The Pentateuch and the oral tradition are of

52 Kelsen, *supra* n.1, at 105.

equal authority, are equally obligatory on all Jews as the direct instructions of God himself to his nation, Israel ... Empathy, charity, kindness (sic) are the results of observance of the Torah commandments governing our mutual responsibilities. They are not the motivations of these observances. I feed the poor because the Torah so ordains." See *The Condition of Jewish Belief* (New York: American Jewish Committee, 1966), 236-242. According to these views, Jewish law is a divinely ordained normative order in which ethics are part of, and not transcendent to, the law.

Note 11:

Ibid., at 44. A significant distinction can be drawn between the positivist rhetoric in Bleich's thought and Faur's. Bleich never discusses any relativist, or tentative element of the covenant. *All* of Torah is binding because all the Torah is a reflection of the Divine will. For Bleich (*supra* n.3) the orthodox rabbinic intellect can understand the Torah's esoteric secrets: "To the (orthodox) scholar, a novel .... insight affords a more convincing demonstration of the Divine Presence than a multitude of philosophical arguments. It is a form of divine confrontation that must be experienced in order to be understood. Yet it is a relationship which every Jew may experience .... in miniature form, through Torah study." This experience allows the scholar to perceive "God speaking to him through the leaves of the Gemara, from the paragraphs of the Schulhan Aruch, and the words of the verses of the Bible. The Sages long ago taught 'Kudsha berich hu ve-oraita had', God and Torah are one." The Sages to whom Bleich refers is Moses De-Leon, the author of the Zohar! (See Zohar 73a, cited in Elliot M. Dorff, *Conservative Judaism: Our Anscestors to our Descendants* [New York: United Synagogue, 1979], 234). According to Bleich, the Torah content and the Divine will cannot be distinguished, and this unity, described in terms borrowed from a non-legal tradition in Judaism, merges in the mystical experience of Torah Study. While Bleich believes that the Torah scholar's correct views follow from a mystical experience, he also makes the positivist claim that Jewish law is a canon of rules, interpretation, and principles for resolving contradictions (Bleich, p. xii-xv). Faur, unlike Bleich, does not believe that man can know God from the content of the Torah or from any mundane source (Faur, at 38-39), and he cannot accept the doctrine that all that God wills is Divine law: "God's law is not identical to the revealed will of God. Revelation, though proceeding from God and recorded in the Bible, is not as such authoritative" (at 41). Bleich's "positivism" is merely authoritarian rhetoric, whereas Faur's positivism is a thoughtful examination of Jewish law as a normative order of legislation and he, like Kelsen, takes pains to distinguish the legal from the non-legal elements in Judaism.

Note 39:

For Elon, any code that presumes to be final "is not desirable, not only because the meaning of the solution and ruling may be given to dispute, but rather because this type of code is not appropriate in the world of *Halakhah*, it even endangers the capabilities and health (of *Halakhah*)" - *supra* n.25 at 1121. Elon's attitude towards codes is consistent with his treatment of the principle that "the law follows the latter day authorities (*halakhah ke-vatra'e*). In his citation of the Asheri (*Piske ha-Rosh, Sanhedrin* 4:6) and R. Joseph Kolon (*Teshuvot ha-Maharik* 84), Elon finds that the entire tradition is mediated by latter day authorities (at 235). While Elon treats this doctrine consistently, he fails to distinguish between Maimonides' Code, which claims to be a systematization of Toraitic and Rabbinic norms that are binding upon Israel, and subsequent efforts of Codification. Maimonides' Code is only a *compilation* of talmudic law, and not a *revision*, or authoritative Code. Any deflection from talmudic law that is unjustified by talmudic methodology would, for Maimonides, be unjustified, while the *Asheri* would regard just such deflections to be legitimate if the post-talmudic sages approved. By failing to distinguish between Maimonides' effort at compiling talmudic law and subsequent codifications, Elon ignores the possibility that subsequent practice may indeed be invalid according to a Halakhah that is understood as normative order. For example, current Orthodox practice ignores the prohibition against dancing on Simhat Torah because of "custom". See *Shulhan Arukh Orah Hayyim* 330:3, *Isserles, gloss ad loc.* and Kagan, *Mishneh Berurah, ad loc.*

Note 51:

After R. Eliezer offers "all the proofs in the world", which nevertheless fail to convince his colleagues, he exhausts his recourse to *legally* valid juridic activity. By appealing to Nature's miraculous intervention, which is manifest in a Carob tree uprooting itself, a creek changing its course, and the tottering of the Academy's walls, R. Eliezer claims that his opinion is confirmed by Nature's will. R. Joshua scolds the walls for tottering because Nature cannot be consulted in legal debate, for Nature's self-suspension has no legal meaning. Appeals to subjective reason or to miracles are ultimately grounded on a claim that God makes continuous legal revelations to his chosen; when a *bat kol*, or oracle, comes forth from heaven to endorse R. Eliezer's ruling, R. Joshua excommunicates R. Eliezer for persisting in a line of argument that challenges the authority of the court, the Divinely ordained norm-creating organ. This pericope rejects the claim of individuals who, in a religious society, claim religious political or legal power because *they* know God's will. The God who promulgated the Law authorized exclusive norm-creating jurisdiction to the human court, thereby disenfranchising those who arrogate to themselves the right to read God's mind. By admitting that His intrusion into legal discussion is inadmissible (*nitshu li vanai*), God actually reaffirms the authority of the court to reject all arguments, even His own, no matter how compelling and regardless of their source, when they are not grounded in legally recognized sources of law..

Part II
Noahide Law and Natural Law in Jewish Legal Theory

[5]

Jewish Law Association Studies, IV

THE "LAW" AND THE NOAHIDES*

by

NAHUM RAKOVER**

I. *The Source of the Obligation of the Seven Noahide Commandments*

Jewish tradition traces back to the Bible the obligation of all mankind to establish a judicial system, even before the Jewish people were so commanded. The Sages found the main source in the command to Adam in *Gen.* 2:16 — "And the Lord God commanded the man saying: Of every tree of the garden thou mayest eat, but of the tree of knowledge of good and evil, thou shalt not eat" — and in what is said about Abraham in *Gen.* 18:19 — "For I have known him to the end that he may command his children and his household ... that they may keep the way of the Lord to do righteousness and justice."

The Sages called the obligation to establish a court system "the commandment of '*law*'", as one of the commandments given to all mankind. The *Tosefta* (to *Avodah Zarah* 9:4) states that "the children of Noah were given seven commandments concerning law, idolatry, blasphemy, adultery, bloodshed and robbery. Just as Israel is commanded to institute courts of law ... so the children of Noah were commanded to *institute* courts. [This statement is substantially repeated in Sanhedrin 56a-b with the addition that R. Yohanan points out the similarity of phrase (*vayetsav* and *yetsaveh* — "G-D *commanded*" and "He (Abraham — the father of all nations) will *command*") in the above verses from Genesis.]

It has been emphasized that the first commandment in human history — not to eat from the tree of knowledge — is the source for the obligation to sustain a compelling judicial system.

* A fuller exploration of this topic, with source-references and comprehensive footnotes, is due to appear in the *Cardozo Law Review*.

** Deputy Attorney General, State of Israel.

It would, however, appear that the biblical source is not the basis for the commandment but merely a peg on which to hang it, as R. Yehudah Halevi writes in his *Kuzari*.

Maimonides in his *Hilkhot Melakhim* 9:1, also observes that these commandments are a tradition transmitted to Moses at Sinai. "Adam was commanded about six things: idolatry, blasphemy, bloodshed, adultery, robbery and law. Although all are of Sinaitic tradition and are intelligible to reason, it appears generally that scripture commanded them all!"

It will be noted that Maimonides adds to tradition the element of reason, and the general sense of statements in the Torah. In the last century a leading scholar, *R. Meir Dan Plotzky* (in *Ḥemdat Yisra'el* [*Ner Mitsvah* 86a]) wrote that "these remarks are obscure, and I do not know what the Master intended by them. I have given them much thought but without success."

Maimonides, parallel to tradition, reason and biblical inference, lays down in *M.T. Melakhim* 9:11 that the person who observes the Seven Commandments out of intellectual conviction is not one of the righteous of mankind but of their wise men,[1] but he who "has accepted them and acts accordingly because they were commanded by the Holy One blessed be He in the Torah and, as Moses tells us, were given to the children of Noah, he is one of the righteous of mankind and has a portion in the world to come."

II. *The Content of "Law"*

To what are the Noahides obligated? Are they required to observe the laws of the Jews, or are they simply required to enact their own laws?

If the laws of the Jews, are they to be interpreted as the Sages interpreted them in the Oral Law or are they bound only by what is actually written in the Torah? If not the laws of the Jews, is mankind free to legislate as it wishes or are there any governing principles?

In *M.T. Hilkhot Melakhim* 10:9 Maimonides writes: "A gentile who occupies himself with the Torah is liable to the death penalty.

1 The phrase "a wise man" is found in MS but not in our printed text.

He should only occupy himself with the Seven Noahide Commandments." This statement may be variously understood, either that a gentile is bound by the Seven Commandments in all their details, like a Jew, and may study these details, or that he is not so bound.

Nahmanides, in his critique of Maimonides, says with regard to the people of Shechem "but He commanded them about theft, fraud, extortion, wages, bailees, rape, seduction, torts, lender and debtor, sale and so on, like the Jews were commanded," and Shechem was killed for transgressing some of these laws. But it does not seem that one must necessarily deduce complete identity from this statement, only some similarity.

Rema (Resp. 10) makes a novel departure in his noted responsum about the infringement of the copyright held by Maharam of Padua, in the publication by a gentile of *Mishneh Torah*. According to *Rema*, the question of the identity of the laws is disputed by R. Yohanan and R. Yitshak in *Sanhedrin* 56b (as above). The former finds in the biblical sources a similarity of terms, which enables the Noahides to prescribe their own laws. R. Yitshak finds the similarity of the term "God" with that appearing in the law relating to bailees — "And the master shall be brought unto *elohim*" (= God, i.e. a judge) (*Ex*. 22:7) — which was said at Sinai to assert that Noahide law is the same as Jewish law. "It therefore appears," says Rema, "that the (Talmud) had no need to explain the difference between R. Yohanan and R. Yitshak, since it is clear as daylight: R. Yohanan thinks that the Noahides are only commanded to observe their customary law and give equitable judgment, but not in the manner of the Jews whose laws were given to them by Moses at Sinai; whereas R. Yitshak ... thinks that the Noahide Laws are those which the Jews were commanded at Sinai."

Rema adduces proof that the decided law is according to R. Yitshak — that the Noahides were commanded to obey generally and in their particulars all the laws of the Jews. *Netsiv of Volozhin* is, however, critical of this conclusion. "All would agree," he says, "that the Noahides were not given the details of the laws, but were only commanded to appoint judges as they saw necessary." He adds that taking the law into one's own hands is forbidden to the Noahides. It also the opinion of *Ḥazon Ish* that Jewish law does not apply to the Noahides, who are only obliged to act humanly and establish good government and just law.

III. *Noahide Law as Natural Law*

We might understand specifically Noahide law, as a sort of natural human law. The Talmud in *Sanhedrin* 57b tells us: "R. Yaakov b. Aha found it written in the Book of Aggada of the school of Rav that a Noahide is punished on the ruling of one judge, on the evidence of one witness and without forewarning, on the evidence of a male, not a female, and even if the witness is a relative. In the opinion of R. Ishmael, even for the killing of an embryo."

It should be noted that the rules of procedure and evidence mentioned are taken to be rules of natural human law. The laws of the Torah which apply to Jews introduce certain restrictions not essential under natural law such as that proceeding must be conducted before a bench of three judges, and in penal cases a bench of twenty three, and that judgment must be given on the evidence of two witnesses.

IV. *Laws based on Equity*

Now, if Jewish law is not identical with Noahide law, what should the latter comprise? Does the determination that a rule is a legal norm comply with the "law" obligation, or are there further requirements as to the contents of that rule?

From what was said about Abraham concerning righteousness and justice, we may infer that there is a connection between law and justice. The verse is quoted in the Talmud in association with the verse about Adam. We have already indicated that the latter is not the legal basis for the "law" obligation of the Noahides, but is quoted as part of an explanation, a quasi-*asmakhta*. Nevertheless, the observations of *Rema*, cited above, show that Noahide law must be equitable, since in explaining the view of R. Yohanan who derives the obligation from the command to Adam, *Rema* lays down that the Noahides are only commanded to observe customary law and give equitable judgment. The "law" commandment is not really concerned with *prescribing* regulations but with *implementing* just and equitable law.

This idea is a dominant theme of many Sages when dealing with the content of the "law" commandment. For instance, R. Shlomoh

Helma in *Mirkevet HaMishneh* to *M. T. Melakhim* 9:14 writes: "The commandment of "law" necessarily means the appointment of judges to uphold proper law and guard the oppressed from the oppressor. Judges must study all the laws relating to oppression and violence and apply them."

V. *The Parallel of Noahide Law and the Law of the King*

Following upon the view that Noahide law is natural human law, an interesting parallel is found between that law and the powers of the king which are also seen as upholding natural human law.

R. Meir Dan Plotzky seeks to base certain powers of the king on this parallel, for instance the rule permitting judgment on the evidence of a single witness. In *Ḥemdat Yisra'el* [*Ner Mitsvah* Commandment 248] he writes that two forms of government exist, the natural, which is Noahide, and that of the Torah given to the Jews. Thus Noah is sentenced by a single judge, on the evidence of one witness, notwithstanding the rule of the Torah which requires three Judges and two witnesses. The Rule of the King is natural human law government as explained in the Bible: "And thou shalt say: I will set a king over me, like all the nations that are around me" (*Deut.* 17:14). Hence Laws of the King are derived from the same source as Noahide law. Moreover, Plotzky seeks to restrict the authority of the king's law to matters that concern Noahide law only. "It seems," he writes, "that the laws of the King obtain in regard only to the Seven Noahide Commandments which are intended for the public good."

Reciprocally, it is possible to learn about Noahide law from what is contained in state law. *Ṣefer HaḤinukh*, Commandment 192, observes that Noahides are punished on their own confession, which scholars find surprising, but Plotzki says that the same would seem to follow from what Maimonides has to say in *M.T. Sanhedrin* 8 about David's killing of the Amalekite, who had killed King Saul. King Saul, after a military disaster, was near death and asked a young man to slay him. The lad acceded to the dying king's request and then sought out David to report Saul's death to him. Thus, David knew of the incident only from the young man's own report.

However, Maimonides does not justify David's action on the basis of the lad's being a descendant of Noah, but explains, rather, that this was an emergency measure (*hora'at sha'ah*). From here, it must be concluded that in Maimonides' opinion the death penalty may *not* be imposed on a descendant of Noah as a result of his own testimony.

R. Meir Simḥah of Dvinsk in *Or Sameaḥ* to *M.T. Melakhim* 3:10 also expresses surprise that Maimonides held that under the law of the king a person may be punished on the evidence of a single witness. And he suggests that it is only under the law of the Sanhedrin that two witnesses are required, whereas under the laws of the king, which are concerned with furthering public good, the rule is as it is in Noahide law, that is, to apply customary practice.

VI. *The Effect of the "law" obligation on the validity of acts of non-Jewish courts in the light of the rule that "the law of the King is the Law"*

Just as there is a relationship between Noahide law and Laws of the King, the "law" obligation is also important in the legal relations of Jew and non-Jew by virtue of the general rule that the law of the host state has legal effect.

VII. *Jurisdiction over Jews*

In view of the Noahide obligation to set up a judicial system, the question of the jurisdiction of gentile courts over Jews arises. The *She'iltot of R. Aha* expresses the view that this jurisdiction extends only to non-Jews and not to Jews who are commanded to maintain a judicial system of their own and are forbidden to litigate in non-Jewish courts.

The *She'iltot* commences with a discussion of the duty to settle disputes judicially and not to assert one's rights by violent action. This is in accord with R. Shimon b. Gamliel's dictum that the world is preserved by truth, by judgment and by peace (*M. Avot* 1:18). The first man, Adam, had already been commanded of the duty to apply the Law in *Gen.* 2:16, as construed by R. Yohanan, as above. For non-Jews that means that disputes should be judicially resolved by their own law, whereas Jews are governed by the laws of the Torah and may not resort to non-Jewish courts even when the applicable law is the same as Jewish law.

But how can all this be reconciled with the rule that state law prevails? If the obligation to maintain a judicial system is imposed by the Torah, a duty to submit to gentile jurisdiction should apply equally to Jews, but that might entail a displacement of laws particularly affecting Jews.

Rashbats deals with another aspect of the problem, in his well-known responsum (1:158-62) on the appointment by the state of *Ribash* as a Judge. He seeks to show that such an appointment is of no effect under the *halakhah* in spite of the rule that state law prevails, since that rule applies only to customary state practice "and it is known that the appointment of a Judge by the state to try cases between Jews is entirely unusual, and therefore to initiate such a practice is ineffective" under Jewish law. At this point *Rashbats* adds a new dimension: the appointment of judges is a religious matter lying outside state law and not involving the rule about the prevalence of state law. He also notes that *Rashba* was of a like opinion.

The last reference is to the well-known *Resp. Rashba* 6:152 dealing with a case of succession in which a man claimed return of a dowry from his son-in-law after the latter's wife had died. Although under Jewish law a husband inherits his wife's property, the father-in-law argued that it was otherwise under non-Jewish law. *Rashba* had forcefully rejected reliance on the rule that the law of the state prevails since that would mean the uprooting of the whole Torah and nothing would remain of the learning that had accumulated on the matter over the centuries.

VIII. *Explicit Differences in Noahide law*

We can now deal with some matters in which Noahide law differs from Jewish law.

We quoted above the passage from *Sanhedrin* 57b to the effect that under Noahide law punishment may be ordered by a single judge, on the evidence of a single witness, and without forewarning. A number of questions arise. First, may we conclude that these Noahide rules rest on the assumption that Noahide law is essentially the same as Jewish law, and only differs in this respect? Not necessarily. Even if Noahide law is altogether different, and not subject to Jewish law, the Noahides may not be free to make rules as they desire and go so far as not to punish a person on the evidence of the one witness; or perhaps they are free to do even that, and bound only to require some other degree of evidence, such as circumstantial evidence.

As regards circumstantial evidence under Noahide law, *Minḥat Ḥinukh* (Commandment 82) expresses some doubt. On the one hand, since a person can be convicted on the evidence of witnesses who are not qualified or of only one witness, there is nothing to exclude circumstantial evidence. On the other hand, on the view that such evidence is excluded because of the possibility of error, the same should apply to the Noahides. That is to say, even though circumstantial evidence is excluded for Jews not on the basis of scriptural decree but on grounds of reason, as explained by Maimonides in *Ṣefer Hamitsvot*, the same applies to the Noahides.

Me'iri to *Sanhedrin* 56b thinks that the Noahides do not punish on the evidence of witnesses disqualified under the Torah, but *Ṣefer HaḤinukh* (Commandments 26 and 192) thinks that they will punish even on a confession and possibly, therefore, also on circumstantial evidence. *R. Meir Arik* (in his glosses to *Ṣefer HaḤinukh*), in analyzing Maimonides' ruling which we saw above, regarding confessions (in *M.T. Sanhedrin* 18:6) suggests that David's slaying of the Amalekite was not because the latter was a Noahide but because it was a matter of emergency, and that Maimonides actually thought that the Noahides do not convict on a confession, for the reason that the person may be insane, and, so to speak, be ready to commit suicide by confessing to something he had not done. Here once more we have a rule that rests on logical reasoning, applying to the Noahides.

Me'iri to *Sanhedrin*, it may be noted, goes further, in stating that under Noahide law the evidence of a criminal, disqualified from giving testimony under the Torah, is not sufficient for conviction, which is another example of the application among the Noahides of a rule that is not explicitly laid down but is logically inferred.

Ḥazon Ish in his glosses to *Baba Kamma* 10:15 raises an interesting question about the position of a Noahide who does not observe strictly the Seven Noahide Commandments but follows civil and penal law. Is he disqualified, from acting as a witness or a judge?

Ḥazon Ish thinks not. He is not disqualified from acting as a judge or witness, since he is clearly strict about the other obligations and regards robbery, murder and false testimony as serious matters.

An interesting suggestion is made by *R. Shlomoh Yehudah Tabak* (in a gloss to *Sanhedrin* 57b) in construing the verse "At the hand of every living thing will I require it" (*Gen.* 9:5) from which he infers that credibility attaches to a single witness but imports the requirement of the witness being properly examined to show that he is telling the truth. (See *Baba Metsia* 28b regarding the restoration of lost property). To that end one credible witness is sufficient. He then raises the possibility that the single witness must be the judge himself for otherwise one person might "devour" his fellow. Here again we can see how the limits of Noahide jurisdiction are determined on grounds of reason.

IX. *Are Jews bound to enforce a Noahide Commandment?*

Is the Noahide "law" obligation linked with any obligation falling upon Jews? A link may arise in a number of situations — the appointment of judges for non-Jews, the punishment of non-Jews for not appointing judges or their punishment for offences they have committed.

In *M.T. Melakhim* 10:11, Maimonides is explicit that there is a duty to appoint judges, to try resident aliens in accordance with Noahide law, so that the world is not destroyed. As regards those who are not resident aliens, one must examine how Maimonides defines the "law" commandment (*ibid.* 1). First he lays down that "they are obliged to install Judges and Magistrates." Then by way of illustration, he refers to a Noahide who transgressed one of the Seven Commandments and "he was killed by the sword." Does that mean that a Jewish court has the duty, or is at liberty to pass sentence, or is that the duty of the Noahides themselves?

Maimonides goes on to say: "And for this reason all the people of Shechem were liable to be slain" — which seemingly means that the children of Israel were in duty bound to kill them. *Ṣefer HaḤinukh* (Commandment 192) states "It is a principle that as long as they are under our rule *we* must apply the law to them in all matters that mankind was commanded."

Nahmanides understands Maimonides to mean that Jews are

obliged to try Noahides. In his commentary to *Gen.* 34:13, dealing with the acts of Shimon and Levi regarding the people of Shechem. He writes: "Many have asked: how could the righteous sons of Ya'akov spill blood?" and he quotes Maimonides as above, but adding "this does not seem to be correct to my mind" since it involves the assumption of an obligation to punish the people of Shechem. *Nahmanides'* approach is entirely different. Contrary to Maimonides, he holds that the "law" Commandment does not mean only to install judges but to enforce the laws about robbery and fraud, which itself involves the appointment of judges. The duty to appoint judges must be distinguished from the duty of a judge to give judgment in a particular matter. However, in certain cases, where a Jewish judge must give judgment, a Noahide judge is free not to do so. Accordingly, the fact that the people of Shechem refrained from sending a prince of theirs to trial, constituted no offence on their part.

Furthermore, says *Nahmanides*, even for those offences for which the people of Shechem were liable — idolatry and adultery — the children of Israel had no jurisdiction, but since the people of Shechem were wicked people, the children of Israel wished to take revenge upon them and killed the king and all those under his rule, an act which Ya'akov said had put him in danger (see *Gen.* 34:30-31). Accordingly *Nahmanides'* view is that as long as the Noahides did no evil to Jews, the latter might not punish them.

Ḥatam Ṣofer in Resp. 6:14 suggests that Maimonides and Nahmanides do not differ over the Noahides being commanded in matters of civil law, but on the question whether this obligation comes under the "law" commandment or "robbery". As for Nahmanides' critique that the Noahides are not punishable for non-observance of a positive commandment, *Ḥatam Ṣofer* observes that though not punishable by court they are nevertheless guilty, and thus Shimon and Levi were not at fault in killing the people of Shechem.

X. *Conflict of Laws*

We have seen that a Noahide court has no jurisdiction to try Jews. Only a Jewish court can do that. When both parties are Noahides and desire to have judgment given in accordance with

Jewish law, a Jewish court, according to Maimonides, may try the case and will try the case according the Jewish law (*M.T. Melakhim* 10:12) but if they disagree as to the applicable law, Noahide law alone may be applied. As to the evidence on which the court may rely, *Ḥazon Ish* at *Baba Kamma* 10:16 takes the view that the witnesses must be Jews. *Ḥazon Ish* is here dealing with penal law and is concerned with evidence receivable under Jewish law and the protection of resident aliens who can only be condemned on the testimony of competent witnesses. In civil law, as well, he argues that Jewish law is the applicable law, following *Piṣḳe HaRosh* to *Baba Kamma* 1. *Ḥazon Ish* goes on to discuss the question whether in a Jewish court the evidence of a single Jewish witness is sufficient, as it is in Noahide law and appears to conclude that it is not. He cites *Ṣefer Haḥinukh* (Commandments 192 and 195) on the necessity of two witnesses. Some later authorities, dealing with *Ṣefer Haḥinukh*, consider that this requirement is a scribal error since it seems contrary to the rule in the Talmud and in Maimonides.

Conclusion

The present paper has discussed one of the fundamental issues of human society. We have attempted to review and clarify a number of questions on the Jewish attitude towards the obligation of maintaining a legal system.

We have seen that this obligation is incumbent upon all men and that it dates back as far as Abraham, who was expected to command his children to do righteousness and justice, and Adam, who was prohibited from eating of the tree of knowledge.

In the words of *Rav Kook*, the late chief Rabbi of Erets Yisra'el:

> Law is the concern of all humanity, as we were commanded (*Avot* 3:2), "Pray for the welfare of the state," for it is the state that establishes law in the land, "The king by justice establishes the land" (*Proverbs* 29:2). And all of this is equally true of Gentile governments, for the Noahides were also commanded concerning *dinim*.

The Noahides commandment of *dinim* establishes a point of commonality between the Jewish people and the other nations, on the most fundamental level of social existence, and with regard to the extent of this commonality and points of divergence, a number of views were presented.

Several interesting questions arise with regard to possible conflicts of legal systems, in questions of jurisdiction, both jurisdiction of non-Jewish courts over Jews and jurisdiction of Jewish courts over non-Jews and with regard to the body of law used to adjudicate such cases.

It appears that the most important aspect of the commandment of *dinim* is the commandment itself, as it emerges from the various sources — the obligation of establishing the rule of law, of natural equity, and of justice.

[6]

The Jewish Law Annual, Vol.VII

JUDAISM AND NATURAL LAW

by

J. DAVID BLEICH*

During the seventeenth and eighteenth centuries a number of Christian scholars, including the prominent Dutch scholar Hugo Grotius, sought to demonstrate that a concept of natural law might be traced to the Pentateuch. If so, the doctrine of natural law might be regarded as part of the Jewish contribution to Western thought. The Cambridge Hebraist, John Selden, developed a much more elaborate and sophisticated argument in a work entitled *De Jure Naturalis et Gentium Juxta Disciplinam Ebraeorum,* in which he advances the thesis that the Seven Noachide Commandments constitute, in effect, a highly developed doctrine of natural law. The Noachide Code, he argued, is regarded by Judaism both as predating the Sinaitic revelation and as binding upon gentile nations which did not participate in the Sinaitic experience. Accordingly, he maintained, the content of the Noachide Code must be regarded as universally binding on the basis of reason alone.[1]

On the surface, this thesis presents many features auguring in favour of acceptance. The basic proscriptions of the Noachide Code, homicide, theft, sexual licentiousness, etc., involve acts universally viewed with opprobrium.[2] Judaism teaches that all gentiles are bound by the provisions of the Noachide Code and are to be punished

* Rosh Yeshiva, Rabbi Isaac Elchanan Theological Seminary; Professor of Law, Benjamin N. Cardozo School of Law, Yeshiva University.

1 This position is also espoused by R. Chaim Hirschensohn, "Sevarah", *Otsar Yisrael,* ed. J.D. Eisenstein (New York: Hebrew Publishing Co., 1906), VII, 136; *idem, Malki ba ḳode sh* (St. Louis, 5679), I, 21; and *idem, Eleh Divre habrit* (Jerusalem, 5686), I, 5f. Cf., however, R. Eleazar Meir Preil, *Hama'or* (Jerusalem, 5689), no. 80.

2 The Roman legal system similarly contained a corpus of law, the *ius gentium,* which governed cases in which one of the litigants was not a Roman citizen or in which both litigants were resident aliens. Gaius apparently took the *ius gentium* as the model of a law practiced by all mankind and dictated to all men by natural reason as distinct from the *ius civile* or system of law which each nation gives itself. Selden apparently perceived a similar division in Jewish law.

for infractions thereof. Since the nations of the world were denied the benefit of direct divine revelation, the binding nature of these commandments can only be rooted in reason.

This thesis is, however, difficult to substantiate in terms of the legal traditions of Judaism. Nowhere in the vast corpus of rabbinic, legal or philosophical literature is there to be found a fully-developed doctrine of natural law; nor, as Marvin Fox has pointed out,[3] is the term natural law used by any Jewish philosopher or legal scholar prior to Joseph Albo in the fifteenth century. Of course, as Norman Lamm and Aaron Kirschenbaum have argued, "Ideas may be implicit in a text or body of literature, and receive their formulation in sophisticated terminology much later"[4] and undoubtedly "concepts, like people, have an existence independent of their names."[5] Nevertheless, it is remarkable that a philosophical doctrine which may be traced back as far as Cicero and which played a major role in the Latin tradition should not receive explicit reference, not to speak of detailed analysis, in Jewish philosophical or legal writings. Any *argumentum ad silencium* is weak at best, yet in the present instance silence[6] with regard to so significant a doctrine does constitute *prima facie* evidence that the notion of natural law

3 M. Fox, "Maimonides and Aquinas on Natural Law", *Diné Israel* V (1972), xi. The term is also used by a later fifteenth-century scholar, R. Shem Tov ben Shem Tov, *Derashot hatorah* (Venice: 5307), 25a, as a synonym for *mitsvot sikhliyot;* see below, note 34.

4 N. Lamm and A. Kirschenbaum, "Freedom and Constraint in the Jewish Judicial Process", *Cardozo Law Review* I/1 (Spring, 1979), 110, note 40.

5 *Ibid.*, at 112.

6 There is, to my knowledge, only one latter-day rabbinic scholar who recognizes normatively binding halakhic prescriptions based upon considerations other than revelation. R. Moses Samuel Glazner, in his commentary on *Ḥullin, Dor Revi'i* (Jerusalem, 5738), *Petiḥah Kelalit*, sec.2 and in his comments on *Ḥullin* 89b, regards, for example, public nudity, despite the absence of a direct biblical prohibition, as constituting a transgression even more severe in nature than violation of a negative commandment. Consumption of human flesh and of rancid carrion are categorized by this scholar in a similar manner. The concept invoked by *Dor Revi'i* is not, strictly speaking, that of a natural law theory but of *a priori* moral repugnance. He does, however, posit a notion closely akin to that of *obligationes naturales* of Roman law in affirming an obligation to support one's infant children that is not predicated upon biblical command or rabbinic legislation.

was not taken seriously by Judaism. It was ignored because it played no significant role in the development of Jewish philosophy or legal theory.

More devastating to Selden's contention that the Noachide Code is a reflection of a natural law position are the comments of Maimonides in his *Mishneh Torah, Hilkhot Melakhim* 8:11:

> Any person [i.e., gentile] who accepts the Seven Commandments and is meticulous in observing them is one of the pious of the nations of the world and he possesses a share in the world to come. But this is [only] if he accepts them and performs them because God commanded them in the Torah and made known to us through Moses, our teacher, that the children of Noah were previously commanded with regard to them.[7] However, if he performs them because of the determination of reason *[hekhra hada'at]* this [person] is not a *ger toshav* [resident-alien] and he is not of the pious of the nations nor of their wise men.[8]

This passage clearly expresses Maimonides' opinion[9] that non-Jews are required to accept the Noachide Code on the basis of revelation, not on the basis of reason.[10] Revelation - and not reason - is endowed with binding force. Furthermore, the perfectly moral Noachide can claim no special merit in the world to come save on the basis of prior acceptance of the Noachide Code as the revealed mandate of the Deity.[11] Moreover, when this statement is read in conjunction with Maimonides' statement in *Hilkhot Iṣure Bi'ah* 14:7, in which Maimonides equates and identifies *ḥaṣide umot ha'olam* with those who acquire the status of a *ger toshav,* it is evident that yet another condition must be satisfied in order for a gentile to achieve the status

7 See extended endnote A.

8 See extended endnote B.

9 Although, as discussed in endnote B, Maimonides' source is obscure, the only authority who explicitly postulates an opposing view is *Toṣafot Re'em,* commentary on *Ṣefer Yer'eim* 233:2.

10 Cf., Maimonides, *Hilkhot Avodat Kokhavim* 10:6 and Rabad, *ad loc.,* cf., also *Minḥat Ḥinnukh* , no. 94, and *Ḥazon Ish, Hilkhot Avodat Kokhavim* 65:3 and *Shevi'it* 24:3.

11 A similar assertion is made by Maimonides with regard to the reward of Noachides for the fulfillment of other commandments whose performance is not obligatory for non-Jews. See *Teshuvot harambam,* ed. Afred Freimann (Jerusalem: Mekize Nirdamim, 1934), no.124 and *Teshuvot harambam,* ed. Yehoshua Blau (Jerusalem, Mekize Nirdamim, 1957), I, no.148.

of "one of the pious of the nations." In *Hilkhot Avodah Zarah* 10:6 Maimonides declares that status as a *ger toshav* is conferred only upon formal acceptance before a *Bet Din*. Indeed, this condition is recorded in *Hilkhot Melakhim* 8:11 through incorporation of the phrase "who accepts" *(shekibel alav)*.[12] It is therefore evident that not only is observance of the Noachide Code on the basis of revelation a necessary condition for achieving a share in the world to come, but that such observance must be preceded by formal acknowledgment in the presence of a qualified *Bet Din* of the obligations inherent in the Seven Commandments.[13]

The demand that in order to merit eternal reward non-Jews accept the Noachide Code on the basis of revelation does not, of course, preclude acceptance of a natural law doctrine. This possibility is, however, barred by Maimonides' apparently gratuitous concluding phrase *"velo meḥakhamehem* nor of their wise men." Numerous scholars have argued that our reading is the result of a scribal or printing error and that the correct version of the passage is *"ela meḥakhamehem* - but of their scholars", which, of course has exactly the reverse import. The discrepancy involves the change of a single Hebrew letter and could have occurred quite readily. The principal support for this emendation is the reading found in the Bodleian manuscript of the *Mishneh Torah*.[14] However, most

12 See Steven S. Schwarzschild, "Do Noachites Have to Believe in Revelation?", *Jewish Quarterly Review* 53/1 (1962), 36 n.35, who questions whether the term *ger toshav* in *Hilkhot Melakhim* is used in precisely the same way as in *Hilkhot Isure Bi'ah*. See, however, *Ḥiddushe Maran Riz halevi*, p. 164, who states explicitly that formal *ḳabbalah* or acceptance of the Seven Commandments in the presence of a *Bet Din* is required and that in the absence of formal *ḳabbalah* the Noachide is not deemed to be in the category of "the pious of the nations of the world". The identical point was earlier made by R. Raphael hakohen of Hamburg, *Teshuvot veshev hakohen*, no. 38. The latter authority also endeavors to identify the talmudic source from which Maimonides' statement is derived.

13 The novel interpretation of Maimonides' statement offered somewhat tentatively by R. Abraham I. Kook, *Iggerot Re'iyah* (Jerusalem: Mosad Harav Kook, 5722), I no. 89, yields a diametrically opposite position but is contra the plain meaning of the text and the manner in which Maimonides has been understood by all previous rabbinic and philosophic scholars.

14 For early citations of the *"ela"* reading see *Encyclopedia Talmudit* VI

manuscripts and virtually all printed editions including the *editio princeps* published in Rome in 1480 contain the reading *"velo -* nor"[15] It should be noted that acceptance of the *"ela"* reading does not at all signify that in calling such persons wise men Maimonides necessarily accepted a theory of natural law. A person may be termed wise not solely because of his knowledge of transcendental truth but also, for example, by virtue of his acceptance of pragmatic[16] princi-

---

(Jerusalem, 1954), 290, n.11.

15 For a discussion of the textual problem see J. Katz, *Exclusiveness and Tolerance* (New York: Schocken Books, 1962), 175ff; Steven S. Schwarzschild, "Do Noachites Have to Believe in Revelation?" *Jewish Quarterly Review* 52/4 (1962), 301-303; Fox, *supra* n. 2, at xiv; and J. Faur, *Iyunim bemishneh Torah: Ṣefer hamadda* (Jerusalem: Mosad Harav Kook, 1978), 151 note 43. Among rabbinic scholars the reading *ela* is found twice in the citation of this passage in the responsa of the 16th-century authority R. Moses al-Ashkar, *Teshuvot Maharam alashkar,* no. 117 (on pp. 302 and 320 of the Jerusalem, 5719 edition), and more recently by R. Abraham I. Kook, *Iggerot Re'iyah, supra* n. 9, at I, 89. The text cited in R. Yosef ben Shem Tob, *Kevod Elokim* (Fürth, 1556), 29a, reads *aval* which is a synonym for *ela.* Textual considerations aside, there is one cogent reason for assuming the published text to be accurate and the Bodleian manuscript to be corrupt. It is virtually an axiom of halakhic hermeneutics that early authorities in general, and Maimonides in particular, did not employ unnecessary verbiage. The phrase *velo meḥakhamehem* serves to negate natural law doctrines and hence Maimonides would have had reason for its inclusion. The phrase *ela meḥakhamehem* has neither halakhic nor philosophical import and would constitute an irrelevant interpolation.

16 Cf., Lamm and Kirschenbaum, *supra* n. 3, at 117, who write, "it is reasonable to assume, if this reading is correct, that this indicates a natural law theory by Maimonides. The single letter in Maimonides' Code is thus of the greatest moment in deciding the question of whether Jewry's greatest jurist and most eminent philosopher advocated or rejected natural law." Quite to the contrary, Maimonides' dismissal of "some of our later sages" who speak of rational laws as suffering from the disease of the Mutakallimun (see *Eight Chapters,* VI, and *Guide,* III, 17) would appear to constitute a denial of natural law. See Munk's note to his translation of this passage in the *Guide,* III, 127 n. 1; L. Strauss, *Persecution and the Art of Writing* (Westport: Greenwood Press, 1977), 97; and R. Lerner, "Moses Maimonides", *History of Political Philosophy,* 2nd edition, eds. L. Strauss and J. Cropsey (Chicago: Rand McNally,1972), 218-219.

ples. Aristotle, after all, wrote extensively concerning *praktikos* or practical wisdom yet is not generally regarded as a natural law theorist. Although the *"ela"* reading does not conclusively establish Maimonides' position as an advocate of natural law, the *"velo"* reading does indicate rejection of a doctrine of natural law. Regardless of which version is accepted as being correct, I do not believe that Maimonides did, in fact, accept a theory of natural law in the usual sense of the notion.[17] This conclusion is based upon a statement found in his *Treatise on Logic*, as will be shown later.

Despite Maimonides' apparent rejection of any possible natural law theory in the phrase *"velo meḥakhamehem"* (assuming for the purposes of our discussion that this is the correct version) some talmudic evidence may be adduced for the existence of at least a germinal theory of natural law in rabbinic thought. It is evident that the Talmud recognized the binding legal authority not only of revelation but of *ṣevarah* or reason as well. A sharp distinction must be made between *ṣevarah* in the sense of "legal logic," i.e., the derivation of legal principles and even laws from already dogmatically accepted principles, and *ṣevarah* in the sense of a direct and independent source of law.[18] The former can hardly be assimilated to a notion of natural law; its operation is effected by application of the formal rules of logic or of common sense while ultimate authority for incorporation into law of the resultant conclusions rests upon prior acceptance, on completely different grounds, of the corpus of law upon which intellect is allowed to operate. On the other hand, *ṣevarah* as an antonomous source of law is *sui generis* in the sense that reason need not look beyond itself for authoritative validation.

Although the Talmud abounds in examples of the former applications of *ṣevarah*, at times explicitly employing the term,[19] but more often implicitly accepting the methodology of *ṣevarah* with-

17 In this I concur with Marvin Fox, *supra* n. 2, at xiv, but on entirely different grounds.

18 Cf., M. Elon, *Hamishpat Ha'ivri* (Jerusalem: Magnes Press, 1973), II, 805-828 and "Severah", *Encyclopedia Judaica* (Jerusalem: Keter, 1971), XIV, 195-1198. Cf., also, R. Eleazar Meir Preil, *Hama'or*, no. 80, who does not recognize the latter category of *severah* and fails to discuss, or even mention, the example found in *Sanhedrin* 74a.

19 E.g., *Gittin* 6b; *Shabbat* 63a; *Sukkah* 29a. See also examples cited by R. Reuben Margulies, *Margaliyot Hayam* (Jerusalem: Mosad Harav Kook, 5718), *Sanhedrin* 15a, sec.4.

out explicitly applying the label,[20] examples of the latter are rare. Instances of the latter type of *ṣevarah* appear to be, in total, no more than three in number,[21] of which two do not really bear upon a doctrine of natural law.

The Gemara, *Baba Kamma* 46b, establishes as a principle of law the rule that the burden of proof is on the claimant. Citation of a biblical verse *(Ex.* 24:14) to substantiate this principle is dismissed as superfluous and the verse in question is interpreted as establishing an entirely different rule, viz., that the plaintiff must be heard first. In declaring scriptural support to be unnecessary, the Gemara exclaims, "What need have I for a verse? - *Sevarah hu!* A person who is in pain goes to the house of a doctor," i.e., it is the patient who seeks the ministrations of the physician and not the physician who pursues potential patients to determine who is ill. Similarly, the person who has a claim against another must bring proof to substantiate his claim and the defendant need not first prove that he is liable. The appeal to *ṣevarah* in this instance does not establish the authority of reason as a source of law for several reasons. First, the matter is one of judicial procedure rather than of substantive law; no normative obligation is born of this application of *ṣevarah*. Secondly, given a dogmatic system of jurisprudence and statutory provisions for judicial adjudication, a procedural rule for the burden of proof must be established. Failure to do so would result in a legal impasse and effectively eliminate any possible judicial remedy. This would reduce the system of jurisprudence set forth in Scripture to a mere theoretical construct. Hence common sense, as reflected in the therapeutic model adduced by the Gemara, dictates that the burden of proof be upon the plaintiff. Reason is here brought to bear in developing a detail of law; it hardly functions as a forum of original jurisdiction.

The second example is somewhat less clear but upon analysis appears to be of the same genre as well. The Mishnah, *Ketubot* 22a,

20 See Rabbi Z. H. Chajes, *The Student's Guide Through the Talmud,* trans. by Jacob Schachter (New York: Feldheim Publishing Co., 1960), 29-31.

21 *Berakhot* 35a also posits *severah* as the source of the obligation to recite a blessing prior to partaking of food. However, the *severah* cited in that instance cannot be understood as compelling in an absolute sense since the obligation is rabbinic rather than biblical. For a discussion of *ṣevarah* as establishing a rabbinic obligation see R. Ḥayyim Medini, *Sede Ḥemed, Ḳuntres hakelalim, ma'arekhet hasemakh,* sec.63.

discusses the credence to be given certain types of self-serving statements. The issue in point is the liberty of a woman whose marital status is unknown to contract a marriage. In the absence of knowledge of prior marriage a woman is presumed to be free to marry. If the existence of a prior marriage has been established, the woman's own statement that the marriage has been terminated by divorce is not acceptable in the absence of corroborating evidence. However, if knowledge of prior marriage is established only on the basis of the woman's own statement, her testimony with regard to subsequent divorce is acceptable. Thus, in the absence of witnesses as to the existence of a prior marriage, the woman's statement that she was married and became divorced is accepted. The rule which is formulated is "The mouth which has rendered prohibited is the mouth which has rendered permissible." In this instance as well, the Gemara seeks scriptural justification only to reject the cited verse *(Deut.* 22:16) with the statement "What need have I for verse? *Sevarah hu!"* The selfsame testimony which is the source of any possible restriction simultaneously establishes permission to remarry. Here we are confronted not with a rule of procedure, but with a rule of evidence which effectively determines whether or not marriage shall be permitted. Nevertheless, here too, we are not confronted with a matter involving a substantive normative *halakhah* but with a question of juridical determination. *Sevarah* is here not employed to determine an actual law of marriage or adultery but merely to establish the basis of juridical determination that a state of marriage does or does not exist. Here, again, reason does not operate *sui generis* as the authority to prescribe or to proscribe but enjoys only a certain narrow latitude in determining a question of objective fact - a matter which is a far cry from endowing the intellect with legislative authority.

The third example is a matter of an entirely different nature. In general, a person confronted with a choice between transgression of a biblical prohibition or death should transgress in order to preserve life. Martyrdom is required only in face of coercion with regard to idolatry, certain forms of sexual licentiousness, including incest and adultery, and murder. Insofar as idolatry and sexual licentiousness are concerned, this principle is established on the basis of biblical exegesis. However, with regard to murder the rule is derived by the Gemara, *Sanhedrin* 74a, solely on the basis of reason: "It is a *ṣevarah...,* How do you know that your blood is sweeter? Perhaps the blood of the other person is sweeter!" Clearly, the matter at hand involves a substantive issue and establishes a prohibition against homicide which is universal in nature and admits of no exception. In effect, then, the prohibition against homicide is legislated by reason and, at least in this area, the prohibition is identical in nature to a natural law prohibition.[22] The effect of the *ṣevarah* adduced in this instance has the full force and authority of law and stands on par with dogmatic scriptural prohibitions. This becomes dramatically apparent upon examining the exegesis which yields the same rule with regard to sexual licentiousness. That exegesis is based upon the juxtaposition of homicide and adultery in the same verse *(Deut.* 22:26). The hermeneutical principle involved is that of *heḳesh,* i.e., the juxtaposition of two words or phrases. In this case Scripture explicitly compares murder and adultery: "... for as when a man rises against his neighbor and slays him, even so is this matter." As a result of the *heḳesh* between murder and adultery the already established rule with regard to murder is transposed and applied to adultery, with regard to which there exists no otherwise delineated rule. In this case the rule with regard to murder, which is derived on the basis of *ṣevarah* alone, is transposed as if it were explicit in Scripture and, accordingly, is transposed and applied to adultery. Here we find a legal prohibition derived from *ṣevarah* which is clearly regarded as having the selfsame binding authority as a divinely revealed biblical law.

The sole Jewish philosopher who explicitly assigns any role to natural law is Joseph Albo. In a short, almost cryptic passage in his *Ṣefer ha'iḳarim,* Book I, chapter 7, Albo states, "The purpose of natural law is to repress wrong and to promote right in order that

22 It would appear that, as a natural law principle, the obligation to suffer martyrdom rather than commit murder is incumbent upon non-Jews as well. This is explicitly stated by R. Judah Rosanes, *Mishneh lemelekh, Hilkhot Melakhim* 10:2 and *idem, Perashat Derakhim, Derush* 2, as well as by R. Joseph Babad, *Minḥat Ḥinnukh* , no. 296, and in a note appended by the grandson of R. Isaac Schorr to the latter's *Teshuvot Koaḥ Shor,* no. 20, p.35a. See also *Ṭevat Gom'e,* cited by *Pitḥe Teshuvah, Yoreh De'ah* 154:4. An opposing view is adopted by R. Shmuel Jaffe-Ashkenazi, in his commentary on *Bereshit Rabbah, Yefeh To'ar,* (Fürth, 5452), *Gen.* 44:5; R. Shlomoh Algazi, *Shama Shlomoh* (Amsterdam, 5470), p. 15b; *Shenot Ḥayyim* , p. 36b; R. Barzilai Baruch Ya'avets, *Leshon Arumim* (Izmir, 5516), 7; and R. Abraham Samuel Meyuchas, *Sede ha'arets* I, 55. See also Faur, *supra* n. 10, at 161.

people be kept away from theft, robbery and murder, that society may be able to exist among men and every one be safe from the wrongdoer and oppressor." Albo cites theft, robbery and murder as the sole instances in which natural law is operative. The infractions enumerated are not merely examples taken from a larger body of natural law; they are the sole areas in which Albo deemed natural law to be operative. We may presume that Albo found talmudic evidence for the authority of natural law in these areas of proscribed conduct but not in others.

The talmudic locus of a natural law prohibition against murder has been cited. A source for theft and robbery as infractions of an authoritative natural law prohibition is much less clear. I believe that Albo's source for a natural law prohibition against theft and robbery may be found in *Baba Metsia* 61b. The Gemara questions the need for a prohibition against theft, "You shall not steal" *(Lev.* 19:11) and responds with the statement that the prohibition is required in order to ban (1) theft designed for purposes of annoyance and (2) theft designed for the purpose of benefitting the victim by incurring a legal obligation to pay him the fine which is levied upon the thief. Ordinary theft, however, requires no scriptural prohibition. Rashi, undoubtedly troubled by the problem that in the absence of a formal admonition Jewish law would lack a ban against theft, explains that assumed in the Gemara's query is the presumption that a formal prohibition might be derived exegetically on the basis of *meh hatsad,* i.e., a derivation predicated upon a factor common to two other proscribed activities and present in theft as well. Since both proscribed activities share a common factor it may be assumed that the presence of that consideration constitutes the essence of the prohibition and hence any activity in which that factor is present must be considered to be banned as well. In this instance Rashi states that a prohibition against theft might be deduced from the fact that usury and fraud are both explicitly forbidden by the Torah. Both usury and fraud involve diminution of the material wealth of another (or what in contemporary legal parlance would be termed "unjust enrichment"). Since theft is the example par excellence of diminution of the material wealth of another *(meḥ aṣer mammon)* it would follow that theft is also forbidden by virtue of the fact that it is a form of *meḥ aṣer mammon.*

No part of this argumentation is, however, explicit in the words of the Gemara. Albo may well have understood the query of the

Gemara in a simple and literal way. Theft requires no scriptural admonition, not because a prohibition may be derived on the basis of hermeneutics, but because theft is known to be forbidden by virtue of natural law. If so, a scriptural admonition is required only in order to encompass within the scope of the prohibition actions which reason alone does not incontrovertibly proscribe.[23] Thus, for Albo, natural law proscribes not only murder but theft and robbery as well.

Other examples of the operation of natural law in the Jewish legal system are more obscure and their talmudic sources uncertain. Albo states that the purpose of natural law is "that society may be able to exist among men and every one be safe from the wrongdoer and oppressor." This formulation is advanced by Albo simply as a final cause or explanation of why it is that reason legislates against theft, robbery and murder. There is no evidence that preservation of society *per se* is regarded by Albo as directly mandated by natural law[24] or that any other action, whether positive or negative, is commanded or proscribed by natural law as a means of preserving society. Yet other measures designed to preserve the social structure are posited as a matter of law by other early authorities and appear to be rooted solely in natural law concepts.

Maimonides, *Hilkhot Melakhim* 10:11, following his codification of the laws pertaining to non-Jews, declares:

> [The] *Bet Din* of Israel is obligated to establish judges for these resident-aliens to judge them on the basis of these laws so that the world will not become corrupt. If [the] *Bet Din* determines to appoint judges from among them they may [so] appoint; and if they determine to appoint [judges] from among Israel they may [so] appoint.

It is, to be sure , Maimonides' position, *Hilkhot Melakhim* 9:14, that the last of the enumerated Seven Noachide Commandments, *dinin*, constitutes an obligation making it incumbent upon Noachides to sit

23 The same question may, of course, be raised with regard to the need for a scriptural prohibition against murder, which the Gemara explicitly states can be known on the basis of *ṣevarah*. It would appear to me that a formal prohibition is required for the one type of homicide in which reason does not unequivocally serve to establish a prohibition, viz., euthanasia. See R. Jacob Zevi Mecklenburg, *Haketav vehaḳabbalah*, *Gen.* 9:5. Moreover, absent a scriptural prohibition, capital punishment could not be imposed. See *Sanhedrin* 56b.

24 See extended endnote C.

in judgment and to mete out punishment for infractions of the other six commandments of the Noachide Code. The *mitsvah* of *dinin* is, however, binding only upon non-Jews. It is also the case that Maimonides, *Hilkhot Melakhim* 8:10, states that Moses was commanded by God to force all inhabitants of the world to accept the *mitsvot* which were commanded to the sons of Noah and put to death any who refuse to accept them.[25] However, that penalty, which is to be imposed by Jews, seems to be mandated only in the event of total rejection as manifest in refusal formally to accept the Seven Commandments. Indeed, mere refusal formally to accept the Seven Commandments even though no actual violation has occurred warrants the penalty described in 8:10. Punishment for actual infractions subsequent to acceptance of the Seven Commandments does not seem to be encompassed in this provision.[26] Indeed, it is presumably for precisely this reason that Maimonides found it necessary to add the explanatory phrase "lest the world become corrupt" in 10:11 but does not provide any such explanation in the codification of the earlier regulation in 8:10 which is presented simply as a divine fiat.

Incorporation of the phrase "lest the world become corrupt" would tend to indicate that while the *halakhah* recorded in 8:10 is a dogmatic obligation based on revelation, the principle reflected in 10:11 is derived by means of reason alone. 8:10 cannot be predicated upon a similar rationale since a person who does not violate any of the provisions of the Noachide Code does not endanger the social order and hence there is no readily apparent reason for punishing him simply for refusing to make a formal declaration of acceptance. Punishment of evildoers, however, is mandated, even in the absence of a revealed *mitsvah*, by reason alone; were evildoers not to be punished, the very fabric of society would be destroyed. Thus, this provision is a reflection of a natural law consideration.

Punishment for infractions of the Seven Commandments may be

25 Formal acceptance is required only by virtue of the Sinaitic revelation but was not part of the Noachide obligation prior to Sinai. This requirement was established at Sinai because observance of the Noachide Code had largely lapsed among non-Jews. See *Ḥiddushe Maran Riz halevi, loc. cit.*

26 Cf., Nahmanides, *Commentary on the Bible, Deut.* 23:18, who declares that Jews bear no responsibility vis-à-vis infractions committed by Noachides other than being obliged to prevent Noachides from engaging in idol worship.

dictated by natural law even though the content of the Noachide Code is not itself the product of natural law, i.e., the provisions of the Noachide Code cannot be viewed as binding obligations on the basis of reason alone. Yet obedience to a law whose authority is established on other grounds *is* compelled by reason alone: otherwise law would be devoid of meaning. Law can be successful in achieving its legitimate goals only if transgressors are punished; otherwise law would be honored solely in the breach with the result that the world would "become corrupt".

The same concept seems to appear in a different guise in Rashi, *Gittin* 9b. The Mishnah there cited declares that all bills and deeds executed in non-Jewish courts are valid, with the exception of bills of divorce and manumission, even if they bear the signature of gentile witnesses. The exclusion of bills of divorce and manumission is readily explainable. *Gentiles* are not *bene kritut.* The institutions of divorce and manumission are constructs of Jewish law from which non-Jews are excluded and therefore gentiles cannot execute efficacious documents of this nature. However, the validity of other documents witnessed by gentiles is problematic. It would appear that all bills and deeds of any nature should be invalid when signed by gentiles because non-Jews are not qualified to serve as witnesses in Jewish courts. Non-Jews are precluded from serving not only as testifying witnesses but also from serving as attesting witnesses. Nevertheless, the rule formulated in the Mishnah states that legal documents witnessed by non-Jews are valid for transactions between Jewish parties. The Gemara, *Gittin* 10b, questions how it is possible for such documents to effect transfer of title. In the absence of any other *ḳinyan,* or formal mode of transfer, title does not pass by deed unless the deed is properly witnessed. This problem is resolved by the Gemara in two alternative ways. The first response is that such documents are deemed valid by virtue of the principle *dina demalkhuta dina,* i.e. "the law of the land is the law." The second response is that bills which are performative rather than evidentiary are indeed invalid and are subsumed in the Mishnah under the category of bills of divorce which are ruled to be nugatory.

The first resolution is somewhat problematic. Early authorities sought to justify the principle of *dina demalkhuta dina* on a variety of grounds. Yet, it is not at all clear why the principle of *dina demalkhuta dina* should apply to jurisprudential matters between Jews in which the government has no active interest. It was obviously this difficulty which prompted Rashi, *Gittin* 9b, to comment, "... but non-Jews were commanded concerning *dinin*." Although he fails to cite explicitly the explanation advanced by the Gemara, *Gittin* 10b, Rashi is obviously advancing his own formulation of the rationale underlying the principle of *dina demalkhuta* with a view toward providing an explanation for its extension to the rule formulated by the Mishnah.

Quite obviously, Rashi rejects the analysis of *dinin* formulated by Maimonides, *Hilkhot Melakhim* 9:14, viz., that *dinin* constitutes an obligation to enforce the other provisions of the Noachide Code. Instead, he accepts a view closely paralleling that advanced by Nahmanides in his *Commentary on the Bible, Genesis* 34:13, viz., that *dinin* constitutes a commandment to Noachides to establish a comprehensive system of law to govern the manifold facets of commercial and interpersonal relationships. *Dina demalkhuta* is then no more than the actualization and implementation of such a system of law.[27] Thus the legitimacy of *dina demalkhuta* is rooted in the *mitsvah* of *dinin*.

However, the basic problem remains. The *mitsvah* of *dinin* is ostensibly solely addressed to, and binding upon, non-Jews. By what authority, then, is *dina demalkhuta* binding upon Jews? The matter is resolved if it is understood that the *mitsvah* of *dinin* is, in essence, a *mitsvah* enjoining preservation of the social order. It can be regarded as binding upon Jews only if its authority may be derived from natural law.[28] For Rashi, as well as for Maimonides, preserva-

27 If this is indeed the correct analysis of Rashi's position, Rashi then maintains that non-Jews need not necessarily comport themselves in such matters in accordance with the details of Jewish law but are free to enact any equitable system of law. This is contrary to the manner in which Nahmanides' position is understood by R. Moshe Isserles, *Teshuvot Rema*, no. 10, and R. Moshe Ṣofer, *Teshuvot Ḥatam Ṣofer*, *likḳutim*, no. 14. These authorities interpret Nahmanides as asserting that all of Jewish law pertaining to such matters is incorporated in the Noachide Code via the *mitsvah* of *dinin*. The analysis of Rashi's position here presented is, however, consistent with R. Naphtali Zevi Yehudah Berlin's understanding of Nahmanides as presented in R. Berlin's *Ha'ameḳ She'alah*, *She'ilta* 2:3. Cf., R. Iser Zalman Meltzer, *Even he'azel*, *Hilkhot Malveh veloveh* 27:1.

28 A similar position, albeit not predicated upon the notion of *dinin*, is espoused by R. Shlomo Luria, *Yam shel Shlomoh*, *Baba Kamma* 6:14. *Yam shel Shlomoh* declares, "It appears that [the king] can promulgate

tion of an ordered society is mandated by reason.[29]

It is evident that, as found in these sources, the scope of natural law is limited to say the least. In a sense it would be easier to understand a total exclusion of natural law from Jewish legal theory. Total exclusion would lead to the conclusion that reason is not legislatively autonomous and that divine sanction accompanies revealed law but not law mandated by reason. Once the authority of reason is accepted in a limited area the problem to be addressed is why Jewish thought does not accept a fully developed system of *lex naturalis*.

A solution to this vexing problem may be found in Maimonides, *Hilkhot Melakhim* 9:1. Chapter eight of *Hilkhot Melakhim* concludes with the statement that the Seven Commandments must be accepted on the basis of Sinaitic revelation and the corollary that acceptance on the basis of determination of reason does not engender the status either of one of the "pious of the nations of the world" or of one of "their wise men". The very next chapter, 9:1, begins with the statement, "Adam was commanded with regard to six matters ... even though all of them are a tradition in our hands from our teacher Moses and reason inclines toward them it may be seen from the context of the words of the Torah that he was commanded with regard to these." At first glance, Maimonides seems to have contradicted himself. In 8:11 he declares that one who accepts the Noachide Code on the basis of *hekhra hada'at* is not a wise man, whereas in 9:1 he states that indeed *hada'at noṭeh lahen*. The difficulty, however, dissipates if the terminology is examined carefully. "*Hada'at noṭeh*" means literally that reason inclines in a certain direction; *hekhra hada'at* is a final, conclusive determination of the intellect. Herein lies not only a resolution of the apparent contradiction but also an explanation of why Judaism cannot admit a

---

laws and practices in his land and punish one who violates his edict... for, if not, the world would not exist and will be destroyed."

29 Consistent with this position, Rashi, *Niddah*, 61a, s.v. *mehash leh miba'i*, may be understood as applying the identical concept in legitimization of penal sanctions for violation of criminal codes promulgated by virtue of *dina demalkhuta*. See also *Yam shel Shlomoh*, *supra* n.28. For a fuller discussion of Rashi's comment in *Niddah*, see this writer's "*Hasgarat Posh'ea shebarah le'erets yisra'el*", *Or Ham izraḥ*, Nisan-Tammuz (5747), 247-269.

fully developed system of natural law. Reason is by no means infallible. There are many matters which appear to be true by virtue of reason but which cannot be known with certainty. The propositions of logic are the best examples of *a priori* truths which are known with certainty. Those propositions commend themselves to the intellect with compelling rational force; they cannot be rejected by any rational person. Moral propositions may be commended to the intellect by reason but their binding validity cannot, in most cases,![30] be known with compelling certainty. Reason certainly "inclines" toward their acceptance but rational inclination falls short of final determination. Thus the intellect of a wise man will incline strongly toward acceptance, but the same wise man will recognize that, epistemologically, even strong inclination cannot be equated with *hekhra hada'at* or absolute certainty of determination. One who mistakenly confuses rational inclination, no matter how strong, with certainty fails to perceive a crucial epistemological distinction. Such confusion reflects ignorance of a fundamental nature; hence such an individual assuredly does not merit the encomium "wise man"

Certainly, not all propositions postulated by various natural law theorists commend themselves with equal moral force. Undoubtedly, the most compelling of such moral propositions is the admonition "thou shalt not kill." At the other extreme of the spectrum, the natural law argument against onanism, for example, is so weak that objective moralists would probably be disinclined to view it as a legitimate application of *lex naturalis*. The very fact that law theorists frequently dispute whether or not natural law is applicable with regard to a particular act or activity surely demonstrates the absence of rational compulsion of a nature similar to that which is evident in the propositions of logic.[31] Thus in Jewish legal theory the prohibition against murder is accepted by all as interdicted by *ṣevarah* or *lex naturalis*. This is because in a system of moral judgments the admonition "Thou shalt not kill" is the epistemological equivalent of the propositions of logic. With regard to proscription of theft, the force of reason is less clear, while preservation of the social order as a natural law imperative is perhaps even more debatable. The crucial question is that of determining at which point along the epistemological spectrum "inclination" is so

30 See extended endnote D.

31 *Cf.*, Thomas Aquinas, *Summa theologica* II, 2, 57.

strong that it becomes endowed with legal authority. If homicide alone is to be accepted as a legitimate application of *lex naturalis* then only the certainty which accompanies the moral equivalent of the propositions of logic and mathematics is acceptable. If other propositions are to be admitted as well, then something less than absolute certainly must be accepted as sufficient for purposes of establishing legal prohibitions. Be that as it may, failure to recognize the precise point on the spectrum which establishes legal certainty, or mistaken identification of a less compelling inclination with a more compelling inclination sufficient to establish legal certainty, reflects ignorance which is not the hallmark of a wise man.[32]

This analysis entails the acceptance of at least the prohibition against murder on the basis of natural law and, arguably, a limited number of other moral principles as well. Other moral rules may not be established with certainty but are indeed rational in the sense that it is reason which inclines toward their acceptance.

Marvin Fox argues that Maimonides consistently maintains that moral rules are not capable of demonstration.[33] Moral judgments, like aesthetic perceptions, are not subject to logical demonstration; either they are perceived or they are not. Moreover, he argues, moral rules, for Maimonides, are mere conventions. The most crucial passage in establishing this thesis occurs in Maimonides' well-known discussion of the punishment of Adam and Eve in the *Guide of the Perplexed*, Book I, chapter 2: "Through the intellect one distinguishes between truth and falsehood, and that was found in Adam in its perfection and integrity. Beautiful and ugly, on the other hand, belong to the things generally accepted as known [i.e., conventions] not to those cognized by the intellect."[34] This statement does not, however, serve to establish that moral judgments are devoid of objective validity.

The crucial point which Maimonides is intent upon establishing is a resolution of the problem of how "knowledge" can be described as punishment rather than perfection. To this he responds that when Adam was yet in a state of innocence there was no reason to judge nudity to be unbecoming to man. "After Adam's disobedience ... he began to give way to desires which had their source in the imagination and in the gratification of his bodily appetites..." With his

32 See extended endnote E.

33 *Supra* n. 2, at xv-xviii.

34 See Fox, *supra* n. 2, at xviii, note 27.

disobedience Adam became a sensual creature to whom avoidance of nakedness became a meaningful concept. Adam's punishment was metamorphosis into a sensual being. Aversion to nakedness is a meaningful judgment only when made by a sensual creature. This passage does not, therefore, serve to demonstrate that all moral judgements are subjective or matters of convention or even that aversion to nakedness is a matter of convention.

Moreover, the statement that moral rules are not capable of demonstration does not entail the conclusion that all moral judgments are mere conventions and that particular moral decisions are subjective in the sense that there exists not even a theoretical norm against which such decisions can be measured. Such a standard or norm may well exist, yet not be available to the human intellect. Nevertheless, since such norms are not perceived by means of the rational faculty, moral judgments are made on other grounds. Accordingly, Adam cannot be deemed to have been granted greater rational perceptions subsequent to his disobedience.

A statement which appears in the opening section of the eighth chapter of Maimonides' *Treatise on Logic* provides much stronger support for Fox's contention. "The propositions which are known[35] and require no proof for their truthfulness are of four kinds ... first ideas as when we know that the whole is greater than the part, that two is an even number, and things equal to the very same thing are equal to each other; conventions, as when we know that uncovering the privy parts is ugly, that compensating a benefactor generously is beautiful..." The first example of a convention is identical with Maimonides' later statement in the *Guide* and may be understood in the same way. The second example, namely that compensating a benefactor is beautiful, is another matter entirely. Maimonides here declares that the propriety of compensating a benefactor is a matter of convention and explicitly distinguishes this proposition from those which he categorizes as first ideas, i.e., those ideas immediately perceived by the intellect.

35 Fox is correct in rejecting Efros' insertion of the phrase "to be true" for two reasons: (1) The phrase is absent in the ibn Tibbon text which reads, *hamishpaṭim asher yevade'u velo yitstarekh ra'ayah al amitatam;* (2) Maimonides, in the *Guide*, explicitly rejects the adjective "true" as a categorization of aversion to nakedness. These proportions requires "no proof for their truth" because, although they are "known", they are neither true nor false. See Fox, *supra* n. 2, at xv, note 22.

Yet, one should not extrapolate from this example and universalize the statement as applying to all moral judgments. There may well be other moral perceptions which *are* in the category of first ideas, e.g., the prohibition against homicide. Hence, even for Maimonides, there remains room for a limited theory of natural law.

Marvin Fox states:

> One of the marks of a well trained mind, according to Aristotle, is that it knows how to distinguish between various types of subject-matters, and that it never expects more precision than a subject is capable of yielding.[36] Maimonides knew his Aristotle well and had great regard for the Philosopher. As a follower of the Aristotelian teaching, he quite properly would refuse to recognize a man as wise who could be so confused that he would treat matters of convention or taste as if they were capable of rational demonstration. There is, in addition, a danger to society in such an error, since it rejects authority for pseudo-reason, an error which cannot long be suppressed. Once it is clear that moral distinctions are not rational, and they are no longer accepted on the authority of sovereign or God, there is no longer any ground whatsoever for restraint in human behavior.[37]

I would recast the statement somewhat by stating that when reason "inclines" toward acceptance of a moral proposition, but is not compelling, the proposition cannot be regarded as a first principle; acceptance is therefore in the category of convention. One who confuses a convention with a first principle is hardly a wise man.

II

Two talmudic citations are frequently cited as proof texts demonstrating that Judaism accepts a much broader doctrine of natural law than has been here outlined. *Erubin* 100b teaches,"If the Torah had not been given we could have learned modesty from the cat, aversion to robbery from the ant, chastity from the dove and sexual mores from the rooster." Assumed in this passage, it has been argued, is the existence of a natural morality which, upon reflection, is apparent to the properly attuned mind. Yet, as one contemporary scholar has queried, "But what does this passage really prove?

36 Aristotle, *Nicomachean Ethics,* I, iii, 1094b, 12-28.

37 *Supra* n. 2, at xix.

How many Jews (or gentiles, for that matter) have learned modesty from the cat? And if one could learn modesty from a cat, why not promiscuity from a dog?"[38] The last question is certainly cogent. If nature is the model for a moral conduct why is chastity valued and promiscuity disparaged? Why should respect for the property of others be emulated and theft eschewed? The latter are certainly much more common than the former. Indeed, in nature, as in the human jungle, the practice of what are regarded as virtues is the exception rather than the rule. Most certainly, we cannot discern a uniform message simply by observing the conduct of members of the animal kingdom.

Properly understood, the passage does not at all establish the binding, prescriptive power of reason.[39] It does, however, eloquently demonstrate a certain "inclination" of reason. Confronted with different, diverse and conflicting models in nature some persons commit themselves to be guided by moral principles and some do not. Were reason totally autonomous it would look solely to itself, not to the cat, the ant, the dove or the rooster. The faculty of moral reason is, however, attracted by certain forms of behavior and repulsed by others. It is precisely because morality is so infrequently encountered in nature that man must seek out models of moral behavior for emulation. In the absence of a revealed corpus of law man could "learn"

38 S.Z. Leiman, "Critique of Louis Jacobs", in *Contemporary Jewish Ethics*, ed. M. Kellner (New York: Hebrew Publishing Co.,1978), 59. Similarly, M. Fox, *The Philosophical Foundations of Jewish Ethics: Some Initial Reflections* (Louis Feinberg Memorial Lecture, University of Cincinnati, 1979), 14, queries, "Might we not have decided just as readily to imitate the ferocity of the lion, the murderousness of an aroused pack of wolves, or the sexual behavior of a rabbit?" See also R Wollheim, "Natural Law", *Encyclopedia of Philosophy* (New York: MacMillan Publishing Co. and The Free Press, 1967), V, 451, who, without reference to *Erub.* 100b, asks, "Are we ... to model ourselves upon the peaceful habits of sheep or upon the internecine conflicts of ants? Is the equalitarianism of the beaver or the hierarchical life of the bee the proper example for human society? Should we imitate the widespread polygamy of the animal kingdom, or is there some higher regularity of which this is no more than a misleading instance?"

39 Fox, *supra* n. 2, at viii-ix, is quite right in rejecting a natural law interpretation of the passage. However, I do not see a reflection of pragmatism in this statement as does Fox. Cf. Aharon Lichtenstein, "Does Jewish Tradition Recognize an Ethic Independent of Halakha?", in *Contemporary Jewish Ethics, supra* n.31, at 104.

moral principles from nature in the sense that when confronted by antithetical models man would make choices on the basis of intuitive responses. Man might emulate certain models of behavior found in the animal kingdom and adopt them as the paradigms for his own conduct but could legislate them as binding law on the basis of reason alone. The product of such an endeavor would not be a system of law but an emotivist ethic. Reason could not be so certain of itself as to proclaim a universally binding law. In the absence of epistemological certainty moral decisions are essentially aesthetic judgments. Under such circumstances reason can but exclaim in the manner of C.L. Stevenson, "I do like this; do so as well." The result is a subjective morality which one recommends to others.

Yoma 67b seems at first glance to provide stronger support for a theory of natural law, but upon further examination is even less compelling. " 'You shall keep My statutes' (*Lev.* 18:5). This refers to those commandments which had they not been written [in Scripture] should properly have been written. These include the prohibitions against idolatry, adultery, bloodshed, robbery and blasphemy." The crucial phrase is "*re'uyim hayu lekotevan*" meaning "it would have been proper" or "it would have been fitting" for them to be written.[40] "Proper" or "fitting" means simply that such laws serve a necessary function. This statement implies only that in the absence of divine legislation society would find it useful to enact such laws. Indeed such legislation is found in countless societies which deny the authority of divine law. Here, then, we find not an exposition of natural law but a recognition of the need for what Albo refers to as conventional law. In context, the Gemara then proceeds to distinguish such laws from commandments which are entirely ritual in nature and which, therefore, can derive sanction only from divine law.

Saadia's distinction between *mitsvot sikhliyot* and *mitsvot shimiyot* should be understood in precisely the same manner. There are laws which *hasekhel meḥayev,* i.e., which reason mandates, not in the sense that reason serves as a sufficient and authoritative source of law, but which reason commends to us for enactment. Those are known as "rational laws" as distinct from laws which are ac-

40 The Soncino translation, "they should by right have been written" is stylistically felicitous but conveys a wrong connotation; cf. Fox, *supra* n. 2, at viii, note 8.

cepted solely on the basis of tradition, i.e., revelation.[41] In dismissing this distinction, and in asserting that all of the divine law is ultimately rational, Maimonides certainly does not imply that reason could endow all such rules with the authority of law; he means simply that were human reason capable of fathoming the purpose and benefit of every divine law it would recommend such modes of behavior in order that man might achieve the desired ends.

III

There is, however, another sense in which Jewish thought may be said to reflect natural law theory. Various forms of natural law theory have been advanced over the centuries by a host of thinkers from Zeno to John Locke. The simplest and oldest developed theory is found in the writings of the Stoics who observed that the entire universe is governed by laws which exhibit rationality. Inanimate objects adhere to such laws because they are inherent in nature itself. The laws of physics and chemistry exhibit rationality in establishing regularity and predictability. The conduct of animals is regulated by a rational pattern of behavior which we call instinct. Since the universe is a unitary whole governed by rational principles it follows that similar rational, natural laws should exist for the ordering of human conduct. Such rules or laws are readily discoverable by application of the rational faculty with which man has been endowed. Thomas Aquinas, in part as an aid in discovering the rational principles which govern the universe and hence which should be adopted by man in ordering his conduct, invoked the Aristotelian concept of nature as a teleological system. The essence of every created entity stipulates an end. Reason, and hence natural law, requires the fulfillment of those ends and militates against any form of behavior which will serve to thwart such fulfillment. Common to all formulations of natural law theory is the notion that man should seek to identify the rational principles inherent in the natural order and seek to guide himself by "the light of reason".

It is the demand that human conduct be modeled upon the rationality of the natural order which poses a formidable problem. Law, as the term is used by jurists and legal scholars, is a rule which is authoritative and binding and which, when violated, may result in

41 See extended endnote F.

imposition of sanctions against the violator. Law, as the term is used by scientists, is merely a manifestation of regularity and rationality in nature. The former is prescriptive; the latter descriptive. Reducing laws prescribed by the intellect to the rational principles manifest in the universe fails to answer the one crucial metaethical question which must be asked of any moral system: Why be moral? Granted that the universe exhibits rationality and that human conduct is part of a unitary rational mosaic of cosmic proportions, the question remains: Why must man endeavor to manifest such patterns of rationality in his moral behavior? Or as the question is put in its classic formulation: how can prescriptive laws be derived from descriptive laws?

This, in turn, is but a variant of the most crucial of all metaethical problems, viz., the bifurcation of "is" and "ought". Granted that we have successfully accomplished the task of defining and identifying the good and the moral, the question remains, "Why be moral?" The religionist who posits a theistic system of morality has a relatively simple solution to this question, viz., divine authority. One must be moral because such is the will and command of God. Any natural law theory is subject to challenge on the following grounds. Granted that the universe exhibits unitary reason, granted that such rationality was instilled in the universe by the Creator, and granted that man can govern himself by the same rationality only if he obeys the injunction "Follow nature", there is as yet no moral imperative which demands of man that he identify with the rationality of the universe and regulate his conduct accordingly.[42]

The question may be resolved only by an appeal to an antecedent metaphysical principle, viz., man ought to obey the will of the Deity insofar as he is capable of discerning His will. Since it was created by God, and since it exhibits a ubiquitous rationality, the universe testifies to God's desire that all of creation guide itself by the principles of reason. Therefore, in regulating his personal con-

42 See *Shab.* 133b which records Abba Sha'ul's exegetical interpretation of the phrase *"ve'anvehu"* which occurs in *Ex.* 15:2. Interpreting this phrase as a contraction of the words *"ani vehu"* Abba Sha'ul understands this passage as declaring "Be similar to Him. Just as He is merciful and gracious so also you be merciful and gracious." See also *Sot.* 14a and *Midrash Rabbah, Shemot* 26:2. In his codification of this *halakhah,* Maimonides, *Hilkhot De'ot* 1:6, explicitly incorporates other divine attributes as well.

duct, man is bound to pursue the dictates of natural law as discerned by reason. Recasting this explanation in the Jewish version of the doctrine of *imitatio Dei*, it is as if God were to address His creatures and to say to them, "Even as I am rational (as evidenced by the rationality of the universe which I have created), be you also rational!"[43] Only by invoking a notion such as this can prescriptive law be made to flow from its descriptive counterpart. It should be remembered that the admonition upon which the principle of *imitatio Dei* is based is regarded as a formal commandment included in the enumeration of the 613 binding precepts. The scriptural authority for regarding the doctrine of *imitatio Dei* as a formal *mitsvah* is the verse "... and you shall walk in His ways" (*Deut.* 28:9).[44]

Thus, if Judaism does attribute even limited legislative authority to the intellect, this, too, is so only because such authority is vested in reason by virtue of a direct divine command.

Of course, in a certain fundamental sense casting even a limited natural law theory in a "mitsvahitic" guise only pushes the question back one step. The question which then must be pondered is: "Why must man obey the will of God?" Fear of retribution, while it may constitute a compelling motive for many, is not a complete answer. Conceivably, a person may be willing to accept the punishment entailed in disobeying the will of God, yet no religionist would agree that morally man has a right to do so. One may park overtime at a

43 Aristotle, *supra* n.29, at VII, iii, 1146b24-1147b17, argues that the conclusion of a moral syllogism is as compelling as that of a logical syllogism. No rational person can accept the premises, "All men are mortal" and "Socrates is a man", and deny the conclusion, "Socrates is mortal." Aristotle argues that the moral syllogism, when the premises are properly perceived, compels conduct in a manner analogous to the manner in which a logical syllogism compels the assent of reason. The natural law moralist goes beyond this position in arguing, not that man is compelled in the intuitive sense, but that man is morally bound to act in conformity with the principles of reason. This leaves us with precisely the original question: Granted that the moral is to be identified with the demand of reason, by what authority is man bound to accept rational principles in regulating his conduct?

44 See Maimonides, *Sefer hamitsvot, mitsvot aseh*, no. 8; *Ba'al Halakhot Gedolot, mitsvot aseh*; *Sefer Yere'im*, no. 4; *Sefer Mitsvot Katser*, no. 46; *Sefer Mitsvot Gadol, mitsvot aseh*, no. 7; *Sefer ha hhinnukh*, no. 611. See also *Sifre* on *Deut.* 13:5: "'After the Lord your God shall you walk' - this is a positive commandment."

meter and pay the fine because the infraction does not involve moral turpitude, but no legal moralist would sanction a felony on the plea that the perpetrator is quite willing to pay the penalty exacted by society. Moreover, religious teaching demands that the moral agent strive to act out of a sense of love rather than out of a sense of fear.

The question thus formulated is a challenge not only to the acceptance of moral maxims predicated upon a natural law theory but to the entire corpus of *mitsvot*. It should be remembered that *Ba'al Halakhot Gedolot*, the earliest authority to compose a detailed enumeration of the 613 precepts of Judaism, failed to include belief in God as one of the 613 commandments. The problem for *Ba'al Halakhot Gedolot* is not only that belief cannot be commanded but that the notion of a commandment presupposes a commander. As Bertrand Russell stated in formulating his Theory of Types, a statement about a class cannot itself be a member of that class. God, the commander, stands outside the system of commandments and constitutes the authority by which commandments must be accepted. Commandments are binding because they are decreed by God. But logically prior to a system of commandment is the principle that God's decrees must be obeyed. A commandment to that effect is not self-validating. By what authority is the commandment to accept God's authority mandated?

At this point there must perforce be an appeal to some *a priori* concept. Saadia declares, "reason calls for gratitude to God for His kindness."[45] Filial devotion is common to all members of the human species. The child reacts with love and devotion to parents who have bestowed the gift of love upon him and who have showered him with concern and affection. This reaction is instinctive and intuitive; it is an *a priori* response rooted in reason. It follows, *a fortiori*, that man should respond in the same manner to his heavenly Father, the author of life itself, Who continuously exercises providential guardianship over His creatures. Such a reaction need not be commanded; it is demanded by reason. It follows, then, that obedience to the will of God is a dictate of reason and is the *a priori* assumption underlying the binding nature of the entire corpus of divine commandments.

45 *Book of Beliefs and Opinions*, Treatise III, chap. 3.

IV

The crucial notion that reason demands that man obey the will of God - even that he seek to discover the propositions mandated by divine will - is a concept for which explicit talmudic support may be found.[46] Jewish law prescribes that Noachides are to be held accountable even for transgressions committed in ignorance of the law. The Noachide is culpable, declares the Gemara, *Makkot* 9b, "because he should have learned but did not learn." This is probably the earliest formulation of the legal maxim "Ignorance of the law is no excuse," although in Jewish law this principle is restricted to violations of the Noachide Code. This dictum, which is ostensibly merely the formulation of a punitive principle, implies much more than appears on the surface. The Noachide Code applies to all gentiles, whether or not they are or were exposed to information regarding the historical phenomenon of revelation at Sinai and whether or not the Noachide tradition was transmitted to their progenitors. Judaism recognizes no doctrine of invincible ignorance. The problem of theodicy is self-apparent. How can a just God hold disadvantaged creatures who have not been the privileged recipients of revelation accountable for obedience to a law of which they have no knowledge? The answer, "He should have learned," is a cogent answer only if an underlying prior assumption is accepted, namely, that there exists an *obligation* on the part of Noachides to seek such information. By what authority is a person obliged to seek such knowledge? Indeed, in the absence of revelation, how is the uninitiated to be held responsible for (a) the discovery of the exis-

46 Of interest with regard to this point is the citation by the Gemara, *Baba Kamma* 85a, of *Ex.* 21:19 and the declaration, "From here [it is derived] that the physician is granted permission to cure." The obvious implication is that in the absence of scriptural dispensation such activity would be forbidden. Rashi comments that a biblical verse is required to teach us that we are not to say "How is it that God smites and man heals?" In much the same vein *Tosafot* and R. Solomon ben Abraham Adret state that without such sanction, "he who heals might appear as if he invalidated a divine decree." The implications of the Gemara's statement are: (1) Reason itself perceives that intervention in physiological processes in the absence of specific divine permission to do so is an attempt to thwart the will of God; and (2) man, even in the absence of a formal prohibition, ought not to act in a manner which is contrary to the will of God.

tence of God, and (b) an awareness that God has revealed a corpus of law which is binding upon all mankind? Clearly, only if both premises are known and accepted can one address the question of obligation to discover and learn the contents of that corpus of law.

It should, however, be recognized that Judaism posits that the existence of God is readily discernible to the human mind, either on the basis of an immediate *a priori* awareness or on the basis of a simple formulation of one of the classic proofs for the existence of God. Judaism must also posit that a rational mind necessarily perceives that God may well make certain demands of man and, furthermore, if He does so, God must have made His will known to mankind. Reason demands that man obey the will of God; therefore, reason demands both that man make an effort to discover God's will as expressed in revelation to man and that man obey the revealed will of God.[47] All of this must be accepted by man, not on the basis of divine command, because at this point in his intellectual inquiry man has not become aware of the content of divine commandments, but on the basis of reason alone. In this sense one may indeed speak of the presence of a natural law theory in Jewish thought, albeit the natural law here described is of a very particular and limited kind.

Extended Notes

A. Maimonides requires not merely that non-Jews accept the Noachide Code on the basis of revelation but specifically on the basis of Sinaitic revelation. Maimonides here extends to non-Jews the principle earlier formulated by him with regard to Jews. The Mishnah, *Ḥullin* 7:6, declares that the prohibition concerning the sciatic sinew does not extend to the sciatic sinew of non-kosher animals. R. Judah, in objecting to the ruling, argues that the prohibition was directed to the children of Jacob at a time when all animals were permitted. Responding to the objection, the Sages declare, "[The prohibition] was stated at Sinai but written in its proper place." Rashi, *Ḥullin* 100b, amplifies this statement and interprets it in a literal manner as meaning that the passage prohibiting the sciatic sinew, *Gen.* 32:33, was transmitted for the first time at Sinai

47 See R. Elchanan Wasserman, "*Dugma lebi'ure Aggadot al Derekh hapeshat*", no. 1; *Ḳovets He'arot* (New York, 5712); reprinted in *idem*, "Maamar al Emunah", *Ṣefer Ḳovets Ma'amarim* (Jerusalem, 5723), 11-16.

but "until Sinai they were not admonished." The verse in question "was written in its place after it was declared at Sinai; and Moses, [when] he wrote and arranged the Torah recorded this verse in association with the event...". According to Rashi, the prohibition was promulgated at Sinai for the first time but was recorded in the Torah in conjunction with the narrative concerning Jacob's strife with the angel since that incident is the reason underlying the subsequent prohibition.

Maimonides, in his *Commentary on the Mishnah,* explains the statement of the Mishnah in a quite different manner:

> Give heart to this great principle which is included in the Mishnah, viz, ... all that we disdain or perform today we do so solely by virtue of the command of the Holy One, blessed be He, through our teacher Moses, may he rest in peace, not because the Holy One, blessed be He, stated this to the prophets who preceded him. For example, we do not eat a limb torn from a live animal because God forbade [it] to Noah, but because Moses forbade to us a limb torn from a live animal by virtue of what he was commanded at Sinai to the effect that the prohibition against [eating] a limb torn from a living animal remains in effect; similarly, we do not circumcise because our father Abraham, may he rest in peace, circumcised himself and the members of his household but because the Holy One, blessed be He, commanded us through our teacher Moses, may he rest in peace, that we circumcise just as our father Abraham, may he rest in peace, circumcised; and, similarly [with regard to] the sciatic sinew, we do not follow the prohibition of our father Jacob, but the command of our teacher Moses, may he rest in peace...

[Cf., however, *Tosafot, Sanhedrin* 56b, s.v. *eser mitsvot;* R. Reuben Margulies, *Margaliyot hayam* (Jerusalem: Mosad Harav Kook, 5718), *ad locum;* and R. Shimon Moshe Diskin, *Ohel Yehoshu'a* (Jerusalem: 5738), 56ff.] Maimonides, thus, accepts the notion of binding prohibitions before Sinai, other than those of the Noachide Code, but maintains that the original command of such prohibitions lacks binding authority subsequent to Sinai. In the cited passage in the *Mishneh Torah,* Maimonides extends this principle to the Noachide Code as well. The original revelation to Adam and Noah was binding only until Sinai; the Noachide Code continues to be binding only because it was renewed at Sinai. Gentiles must accept the Noachide Code, not on the basis of the original revelation, but on the basis of Sinaitic revelation. Thus, in addition to moral conduct, a faith commitment in the form of acceptance of the validity of the Sinaitic revelation is required of all non-Jews and such acceptance is a precondition of eternal heavenly reward. See this writer's *With Perfect Faith: The Foundations of Jewish Belief* (New York: Ktav Publishing House, 1983), 15-18. *Cf.*, however, R. Yom Tov Lipman Heilprin, *Teshuvot Oneg Yom Tov* (Vilna, 5640), no.19.

B. A similar dictum occurs in a letter to R. Hasdai halevi; see *Teshuvot harambam ve'iggerotav* (Leipzig: Mekize Nirdamim, 1859), Part 2, 23b. R. Joseph Karo in his commentary on the *Mishneh Torah, Ḳesef Mishneh, loc. cit.*, states that this is Maimonides' own opinion and lacks earlier textual support, but is correct nonetheless. A number of later scholars have attempted to demonstrate that Maimonides' statement is based upon earlier authority.

R. Ezekiel Feivel, *Ṣefer Toldot Adam* (Dyhrenfurth, 1801), chapter 6, 35a, reports that an anonymous scholar from the Orient visited Vilna and, marveling at the encyclopedic knowledge of R. Zalman of Volozhin (a brother of the famed R. Chaim of Volozhin), asked him to elucidate a number of difficult passages in Maimonides' writings. When questioned with regard to the source of Maimonides' statement concerning Noachides and their obligation to accept the Seven Commandments on the basis of Sinaitic revelation, R. Zalman produced an unidentified Midrash which states:

> Rabbi Y. said, "I have heard that the pious of the nations of the world have a share in the world to come. We have, however, not been taught this with regard to the wise men of the nations of the world. Who is a pious man from among the nations of the world? He who accepts the Seven Commandments because they are written in the Torah. A wise man from among the nations of the world is one who fulfills them on the basis of the determination of his reason."

It is interesting to note that this Midrash refers to one who accepts the Seven Commandments on the basis of reason as "a wise man". See Steven S. Schwarzschild, "Do Noachites Have to Believe in Revelation?" *Jewish Quarterly Review* 52/4 (1962), 305-306.

One midrashic collection, *The Mishnah of R. Eliezer (The Midrash of Thirty-two Hermeneutic Rules)*, ed. H.G. Enelow (New York: Bloch Publishing Co., 1933), 121, contains a most interesting statement with regard to the definition of "the pious of the nations of the world". Such an appellation may be ascribed, declares the Midrash, "only when they perform [the Seven Commandments] and say 'we perform [them] because our father Noah commanded us [regarding them] by the mouth of God.' ... But if they fulfill the Seven Commandments and say, 'We have heard them from so and so' or [if they perform them] of their own accord for so does reason determine ... they receive their reward only in this world." Maimonides' central point, viz., that the Noachide Code must be accepted on the basis of revelation is certainly substantiated by this midrashic passage. Yet this Midrash could not have been Maimonides' source since Maimonides differs from the Midrash with regard to one important point. The Midrash states that Noachides may accept the Seven Commandments because they were revealed to Noah. Maimonides insists (as will be further clarified in the text) that Noachides must accept the Seven Commandments on the basis of revelation at Sinai rather than on the basis of revelation to Adam or Noah. For Maimonides, Noachides may aspire to reward in the world to come only upon acceptance of the veracity and validity of the Sinaitic revelation; see R. Abraham I. Karelitz, *Ḥazon Ish, Shevi'it* 24:2 and *Hilkhot Avodat Kokhavim* 65:2. Moreover, while the Mishnah of R. Eliezer speaks of "reward only in this world", *Teshuvot harambam*, ed. Alfred Freimann (Jerusalem: Mekize Nirdamim, 1934), no.124 and *Teshuvot harambam*, ed. Yehoshua Blau (Jerusalem: Mekize Nirdamim, 1957), I, no.148, appears to exclude any type of reward unless observance is predicated upon revelation. Nevertheless, the Midrash, precisely because it could not have been Maimonides' source, constitutes strong corroborative evidence for his contention that the Noachide Code must be accepted by non-Jews on the basis of revelation. Since the Midrash could not have been Maimonides' source it must reflect the existence of a well-established tradition with regard to this point. Cf. Schwarzschild, *supra* n. B, at 306. Although Maimonides, in his earlier noted *Teshuvot harambam* cites a work bearing the title *Beraita shel R. Eli'ezer* as a source for this position that work, because of the reasons indicated, does not seem to be identical with the extant text of the *Mishnah of R. Eli'ezer*. *Cf.*, however, *Encyclopedia Talmudit,* VI (Jerusalem, 1954), 290, n.11.

In a letter addressed to Moses Mendelssohn and published in Mendelssohn's *Gesammelte Schriften,* XVI (Berlin: Akademie-Verlag, 1929), R. Jacob Emden states that Maimonides' position is based upon *Sanh.* 105a. R. Joshua, who maintains that non-Jews may share in the world to come, interprets the verse "The wicked shall return to the nether-world, even all the nations that forget God" *(Ps.*

9:18) as follows: "'The wicked shall return to the nether-world' ... Who are they? [They are] 'all the nations who forget God.'" Maimonides, avers R. Emden, understands 'the nations who forget God' as including those who observe the Noachide Code but 'forget' that it was commanded by God.

In a posthumously published article, R. Malkiel Zvi Tennenbaum (author of *Teshuvot Divre Malki'el), Torah shebe'al Peh,* XV (5733), 164), suggests that Maimonides' position is deduced from *Baba Kamma* 38a. The Gemara cites the verse "He standeth and shaketh the earth. He beholdeth and maketh the nations to tremble" *(Hab.* 3:6), and comments, "What did He see? He saw the Seven Commandments which the sons of Noah accepted but did not observe [therefore] 'He arose and He permitted them [to the sons of Noah]." The Gemara, for exegetical purposes, renders the word "*vayater*" as "permitted" rather than "maketh to tremble". The Gemara, in the ensuing discussion, modifies this interpretation by stating that the prohibitions of the Noachide Code were not actually rescinded, but were reduced in status so that a non-Jew who observes them is rewarded "as one who is not commanded but observes", i.e., receives lesser compensation than "one who is commanded and observes". R. Tennenbaum avers that acceptance of the Noachide Code on the basis of Sinaitic revelation carries with it reward as "one who is commanded and observes". Such compensation is only just since gentiles are indeed bound by the Noachide Code as revealed at Sinai. A new revelation of the Noachide Code at Sinai became necessary because of widespread non-adherence to its provisions by gentiles. Accordingly, the original mandate was revoked at Sinai to be replaced by a new obligation. In speaking of one who observes the Noachide Code as being rewarded as "one who is not commanded", the Gemara, declares Rabbi Tennenbaum, refers solely to the non-Jew who does not accept the Seven Commandments on the basis of Sinaitic revelation but accepts them on the basis of an earlier revelation or because of some extraneous consideration. [This analysis of *Baba Kamma* 38a is also independently advanced by R. Meir Simhah hakohen of Dvinsk, *Or Sameaḥ, Hilkhot Isụre Bi'ah* 14:7, and by R. Yitshak Ze'ev Soloveitchik, *Ḥiddushe Maran Riz halevi* (Jerusalem, 5723), 164. This position is also explicitly formulated by an early authority, Ritva, in his commentary to *Makkot* 9a.] R. Tennenbaum adds that Maimonides inferred that only the gentile who observes the Noachide Code as "one who is commanded and performs" receives a share in the world to come. See also R. Yitshak Ze'ev Soloveitchik, *Ḥiddushe hagriz al hatorah (mipi hashemu'ah)* (undated), no. 152, who finds Maimonides' position reflected in the words of *II Kings* 5:8. See also R. Shlomoh ben Shimon Duran, *Teshuvot harashbash,* no. 543, who finds a source for Rambam's position in *Sanh.* 59a and R. Zevi Hirsch Chajes, *Torat hanevi'im,* chap. 11, who finds a source in *Ḥullin* 92a; see also *idem,* in R. Abraham Naphtali Jener, *Zekhuta de'avraham* (Lemberg, 1868), no. 21.

See also R. Chaim Hirschensohn, *Eleh Divre habrit,* I, 6, who advances a deductive argument in explanation of Maimonides' position predicated upon his view that prior to the Sinaitic revelation the Noachide commandments were binding solely by virtue of *ṣevarah;* see *infra* note 1.

The foregoing is merely an attempt to uncover a talmudic or midrashic source for Maimonides' view regarding Noachides and the world to come but does not address the question of why belief in Sinaitic revelation should be a necessary condition for eternal reward; see above, note A.

C Earlier, in Book One, chapter 5, Albo does state:

> It is because association and aggregation are necessary for the existence and support of the human species that the wise men have said that man is political by nature. They mean by this that it is almost necessary for a man by his nature to live in a city (state) with a large group of men that he may be able to obtain what he needs for his life and support. It is clear therefore that the whole group residing in a city, or a district, or a region, or all the human beings in the world should have some order which they follow in their conduct, maintaining justice in general and suppressing wrong, so as to keep men from quarreling in their transactions and business relations with one another. Such order would include protection against murder, theft, robbery and the like, and in general all those measures which are calculated to maintain the political group and enable the people to live in welfare. This order the wise men call natural law, meaning by natural that it is necessary for man by his nature, whether the order emanates from a wise man or a prophet.

"Association and aggregation" are "almost necessary" but not absolutely necessary. Society, to exist, requires "some order" and it is this order which "the wise men" call natural law. Such order which includes "protection against murder, theft, robbery and the like" is necessary for man by his nature. It is because such order is natural to man by virtue of his nature that Albo asserts that men can coexist within a society without difficulty. Albo does not argue that preservation of society is mandated by natural law but, rather, that natural law is logically prior to formation of society, and makes possible the existence of society.

On the other hand, it would be an error to suppose that, for Albo, natural law is manifest only in an organized society. Ralph Lerner has stated, "Albo suggests that this natural law is not absolutely necessary for man because it is not absolutely necessary for man to live in political society; moreover, he suggests that the validity of this natural law depends upon its establishment by some human individual. By pointing to the possibility of life outside the city, Albo casts some doubt on the obligatory character of natural law. By further distinguishing the purpose of this natural law from the perfection that is proper to man, Albo in effect denies that natural law is, strictly speaking, natural." See "Moses Maimonides", *History of Political Philosophy, supra* n. 11, at 221. Elsewhere, the same author writes, "We may say more generally, then, that natural law's injunctions are needed for human perfection as such, but only insofar as man is part of a city or of some kind of association." See "Natural Law in Albo's *Book of Roots*", in *Ancients and Moderns*, ed. Joseph Cropsey (New York, London: Basic Books, 1964), 141ff. However, in chapter 7, Albo does not at all present natural law as a function of political philosophy and even in chapter 5, as has been stated, natural law is cited as a logically prior concept which has the salutary effect of making society possible. The validity of natural law certainly does not "depend upon its establishment by some human individual." Albo does speak of an order which "emanates from a wise man or a prophet" but the function of such individuals is pedagogic rather than legislative. The order to which reference is made "is necessary for man by his nature" even though society itself is only "almost necessary" in contradistinction to being absolutely necessary.

D The principle "How do you know that your blood is sweeter than the blood of your fellow" which is postulated by the Gemara on the basis of *ṣevarah* is one proposition which is declared to be known with certainty on the basis of reason. Nevertheless, Maimonides, *Hilkhot Yesọde hatorah* 5:7, speaks of this principle as *"davar shehada'at noṭeh lo"*, although even stronger terminology would be in order.

It is conceivable that Maimonides used the weaker expression in order to indicate that the obligation to suffer martyrdom rather than commit an act of murder encompasses situations in which this *ṣevarah* is not applicable. In the same chapter, *Hilkhot Yeṣode hatorah* 5:5, Maimonides rules that the principle "be killed and do not transgress" applies even in a situation in which a victim is singled out and the entire group warned that, if the specific individual is not delivered, all will perish. The *ṣevarah* "How do you know that your blood is sweeter" certainly does not apply in this instance. *Ḳeṣef Mishneh, ad loc.*, states that the Sages were in possession of a tradition extending this principle even to cases in which this *ṣevarah* does not apply. R. Chaim Ozer Grodzinsky, *Teshuvot Ahiezer*, II no. 16, sec. 5, presents a formal hermeneutic derivation substantiating the extension of the rule to encompass situations in which this *ṣevarah* is not applicable. Similarly, it may cogently be argued that, according to Maimonides, the principle "be killed but do not transgress" applies even to the taking of fetal life despite the fact that fetal life is "less sweet" as evidenced by the fact that feticide does not constitute a capital crime. See J. David Bleich, "Abortion in Halakhic Literature", *Jewish Bioethics*, ed. Fred Rosner and J. David Bleich (New York: Hebrew Publishing Co., 1979), 141-142 and 173 note 71.

Maimonides' statement, *Hilkhot Yeṣode hatorah* 5:2, describing as a *mitsvah* the obligation to accept martyrdom rather than commit an act of homicide, should not be misunderstood. Maimonides means thereby only that once established as an obligation on the basis of *ṣevarah* actual fulfillment constitutes an act of sanctification of the Divine Name; in the absence of the *ṣevarah* such an obligation would not be subsumed under the *mitsvah* of sanctification of the Divine Name. Faur, *supra* n. 10, at 121, apparently misses this point.

E This analysis of Maimonides' position is at variance with the position set forth by Strauss, *Persecution, supra* n. 10, at 97, note 4. Strauss declares, "The Noahidic commandments cannot be identified with the natural law, at least not according to Maimonides. For - to say nothing of *ever min haḥai* - the prohibition against incest or unchastity which occupies the central place in his enumeration of the Noahidic commandments ... is considered by him to belong to the revealed laws as distinguished from the so-called rational laws (*Eight Chapters*, vi)... This is not contradicted by Maimonides' statement that the *da'at* inclines man toward six of the seven Noahidic commandments ... for *da'at* does not necessarily mean 'reason' or 'intelligence.'" [Strauss infers from Maimonides' statement, *Hilkhot Melakhim* 9:1, "Adam was commanded with regard to six matters ... and reason inclines toward them ... He added to Noah [the prohibition against] the limb of a living animal ..." that reason inclines only toward the first six. To be sure, the phrase "and reason inclines toward them" was used by Maimonides in association with the six commandments revealed to Adam, but there is no reason to assume that Maimonides intends to exclude the seventh from this categorization. Certainly, the *ela* reading in 8:11 which refers to all seven Noachide commandments encompasses *ever min haḥai* as well.]

It is my contention that *da'at* does indeed mean "reason" or "intelligence". Reason would indeed be inclined to abjure *ever min haḥai* as involving wanton and needless cruelty to animals.

The problem which Strauss raises with regard to *arayot* (and which was noted earlier by R. Isaiah Pik in a marginal gloss to *Yoma* 67b) does, however, require resolution. This problem may be resolved upon careful analysis of Maimonides' source. *Yoma* 67b declares:

> Our Rabbis taught: "Mine ordinances shall ye do," i.e., such commandments which, if they were not written [in Scripture], they should by right have been written and these are they: [the laws concerning] idolatry, immorality and bloodshed, robbery and blasphemy. "And My statutes shall ye keep," i.e., such commandments to which Satan objects, they are [those relating to] the putting on of *sha'atnez, halitsah* [performed] by a sister-in-law, the purification of the leper, and the he-goat-to-be-sent-away. And perhaps you might think these are vain things, therefore Scripture says: "I am the Lord," i.e., I, the Lord have made it a statute and you have no right to criticize it.

The Gemara clearly lists *giluy arayot* among the *mishpaṭim* rather than among the *ḥukim* or "revealed laws". The Gemara then proceeds to enumerate five examples of *ḥukim*. Maimonides initially gives only three examples in the passage cited but shortly thereafter adds additional ones:

> Rather they cite matters all of which are based on tradition; partaking

> of meat and milk together, wearing clothes made of wool and linen and forbidden sexual relationships *(arayot)*. These and similar commandments are what God called "My statutes *(hukkotai)* which as they [the Sages] said, are statutes which I have enacted for you, which you have no permission to question, which the nations of the world attack and which Satan denounces, such as the red heifer, the scapegoat and so forth.

If one compares the five examples listed by Maimonides with the five enumerated by the Gemara it is readily evident that the second and fifth are identical in both listings. The first example of the Gemara, *akhilat ḥazir* is replaced by *basar beḥalav* in Maimonides' enumeration; the fourth, *ṭaharat metsora*, is replaced with *parah adumah*. In both cases the substitute is of a like for a like: one dietary prohibition for another dietary prohibition and one purification ritual for another. The third in the Gemara's series, *ḥalitsat yevamot*, i.e., the rite of removing the shoe which releases the childless widow from the obligation of levirate marriage, is replaced by the term *arayot*. It is, of course, possible that the text of the Eight Chapters is corrupt. This would, however, not really resolve the problem completely for reasons which will be indicated shortly. More likely, Maimonides' reference is not to consanguineous or blood relatives but to a specific type of *ervah*, namely, to the prohibition against marrying a sister-in-law who has borne a child - and perhaps to the prohibition against marriage between the childless widow and any person save her deceased husband's brother. Such marriage is certainly not negated by reason. [See R. Abraham ibn Ezra, *Yesod Mora*, chap. 5, who declares that the prohibition against simultaneous marriage to two sisters could not have been prior to Sinai on the basis of *"shikul hada'at"* but that *arayot* are *nit'av betoladah*.] Indeed, were there a natural abhorrence militating against marrying a brother's wife, the distinction between the childless widow and a widow with children would not be readily discernible. Maimonides' reference to *arayot* is thus a reference to the laws of levirate obligation which is a paraphrase of the Gemara's *ḥalitsat yevamah* and certainly falls within the category of *ḥukim*. Reason, however, does incline against conjugal relationships with blood relatives. Prohibitions in the category of *giluy arayot* in the Noachide Code are solely of the latter nature: a widowed sister-in-law is never proscribed to Noachides.

Indeed, this distinction must be made even in the absence of

Maimonides' statement classifying *arayot* among the *ḥukim*. *Ṣifra* on *Lev.* 20:26 states:

> R. Elazar b. Azariyah said: From whence [is it known] that men should not say "I do not wish to eat the flesh of the swine; I do not wish to cohabit with an *ervah*" rather [he should say] "I wish, but what shall I do for my Father in heaven has decreed upon me thus."

Assuming, as does Maimonides, that a worthy person has no desire for that which is forbidden by the *mishpaṭim* but that the opposite is true with regard to *ḥukim*, *Ṣifra* appears to contradict *Yoma* 67b. *Arayot* are among the rational laws, declares *Yoma*, yet *Ṣifra* states that one should eschew an *ervah* only because "my Father in heaven decreed upon me." The contradiction is resolved if it is understood that *Yoma* refers to blood relatives only, whereas *Ṣifra* refers solely to other types of *ervah*. Cf., D. Rosen, *Die Ethik des Maimonides* (Breslau: 1879), 94, note 4. It should be noted that both R. Isaiah Pik, in his gloss to *Yoma* 67b, and R. David Kapah in annotations to his translation of *Maimonides' Commentary on the Mishnah, Nashim-Neziḳin* (Jerusalem: Mosad Harav Kook, 5724), 268 note 14, suggest that the phrase *giluy arayot* did not appear in Maimonides' text of *Yoma* 67b. See also *Ḥiddushe Maharasha, Yoma* 67b.

F. Fox's analysis of this point, *supra* n. 2, at x-xi, is correct, although I believe he overemphasizes the concept of "useful" as the criterion of the rational. I cannot agree with Lamm and Kirschenbaum, *supra* n.3, at 111-113, who ascribe a natural law position to Saadia. Saadia's *mitsvot sikhliyot* are quite distinct from the concept of natural law. The former, since they include many laws which are not binding upon Noachides are not at all universal in nature and hence lack the crucial determinant criterion of natural law. Cf. also, Lerner, "Natural Law", *Ancients and Moderns, supra* n. 11, at 143f. Similarly, Grotius, citing Maimonides, *Guide*, III, 26, identifies *mishpaṭim* with natural law: see I. Husik, "The Law of Nature, Hugo Grotius, and the Bible", *Hebrew Union College Annual* II (1925), 399.

Some support for identification of the term *mitsvot sikhliyot* with the concept of natural law may be found in the following passage of R. Shem Tov ben Shem Tov's *Derashot hatorah* 25:

> It should be known that of the laws and ordinances some are called nat-

> ural, some are called conventional, and some are called divine. The rational are those which nature mandates and consist of all the laws and ordinances which are identical in the entire world, such as "Thou shalt not kill" and the like. In sum, all matters which reason *(sekhel)* mandates are called in our Torah rational commandments.

Nevertheless, in context it appears that R. Shem Tov presents no more than the standard definition of *sikhliyot* and merely introduces the term *ṭeva* as a synonym for *sekhel*. It cannot be deduced from this statement that reason constitutes binding authority for natural law.

[7]

Maimonides and Natural Law Theory

Daniel B. Sinclair

One of the issues in the many-faceted debate about reason and revelation concerns the role of Natural law in Jewish thought. Is there a law discoverable by reason, a law as it were embedded in human nature? Some have attributed such a doctrine to Maimonides. Others have denied that Maimonides held such a view.

In this paper, Dr. Daniel Sinclair argues that a modified form of the doctrine can be found in Maimonides and some of his commentators, in the idea of the power of a king to punish acts which constitute a threat to the maintenance of social order.

Dr. Daniel Sinclair, LL.B. (Hons), LL.M., D. Jur., is an Associate Research Member of the Centre for Criminology and the Social and Philosophical Study of Law, Edinburgh University, and the Minister of the Edinburgh Hebrew Congregation.

Introduction

The doctrine of Natural law is one of the most powerful and persistent themes in Western jurisprudence. The essence of this doctrine is that reason rather than will is the ultimate source of law.[1] Although the term "Natural law" is hardly ever used in classical Jewish writings,[2] some modern scholars have attempted to discover the concept of Natural law in Jewish sources, especially in the writings of Moses Maimonides.[3] Others have rejected such attempts, arguing that Maimonides could not possibly have accepted the claim that human reason alone is capable of providing the basis for binding law.[4] The aim of this paper is to outline a modified form of Natural law doctrine in Maimonides' *Mishneh Torah*, which avoids the criticisms of the rejectionist school on the one hand, and satisfies the advocates of Natural law theory on the other.

The paper is divided into two parts. In the first, the main features of the classical doctrine of Natural law are sketched, and the development of the modified or modern form of Natural law theory is briefly examined. In the second part, various passages in Maimonides' *Mishneh Torah* will be analysed with a view to demonstrating that a proper understanding of them can only be achieved in the light of the modified form of Natural law doctrine referred to above. It will also be shown that such a theory is implicit in the writings of R. Meir Simha HaKohen of Dvinsk (1843-1926), a standard commentator on Maimonides' *Mishneh Torah*.

The Doctrine of Natural law

The most celebrated summary of the classical Natural law doctrine is the following extract from Cicero's *De Republica*:

> True law is right reason in agreement with Nature; it is of universal application, unchanging and everlasting; it summons to duty by its commands, and averts from wrong-doing by its prohibitions. And it does not lay its commands or prohibitions upon good men in vain, though neither have any effect on the wicked. It is a sin to try to alter this law, nor is it allowable to attempt to repeal any part of it, and it is impossible to abolish it entirely. We cannot be freed from its obligations by Senate or People, and we need not look outside ourselves for an expounder or interpreter of it. And there will not be different laws at Rome and at Athens, or different laws now and in the future, but one external and unchangeable law will be valid for all nations and for all times, and there will be one master and one ruler, that is God, over us all, for He is the author of the law, its promulgator, and its enforcing judge.[5]

Four major characteristics of the doctrine of Natural law emerge from this extract. The first is the relationship between reason and nature. Different interpretations of this relationship have been given over the centuries, although the modern view seems to be in favour of deriving the Natural law from a reflective grasp of what is good for men, rather than from observations of human or other nature.[6] It is noteworthy that according to Cicero, the rational faculties of wicked individuals are not conducive to the exercise of deriving the Natural law. Several centuries later, Thomas Aquinas spoke of the corrupt and perverted reason of the Germanic tribes who, according to Julius Caesar, saw nothing wrong in theft.[7] Clearly, the designation of the rational faculties of some people as being more equal to the task of deriving the Natural law than others, poses a logical problem for the proponents of a concent of law based solely upon human reason. The problem of deciding upon the criteria for selecting the rational conclusions of one particular individual over those of another continues to bedevil Natural law thinking down to the present day.[8]

The second characteristic to emerge from the above extract is the immutable and universal quality of the Natural law. Neither of these features have survived intact. The first was modified by Aquinas, who maintained that only the most basic principles of Natural law were immutable. Secondary principles could be altered in accordance with changes in objective circumstances and human reasoning.[9] The feature of universalism must also be qualified in the light of the need to discriminate between pure and perverted reason referred to above.[10]

The concept of the Natural law acting as a moral yardstick for the measurement of all human law is one of the most influential aspects of Natural law doctrine. It has been used by various thinkers throughout the centuries to justify both conservative and revolutionary political theories.[11] Both the French and the American Revolutions were informed by Natural law doctrines,[12] and the conservative theories of Hobbes,[13] and probably Burke[14] too, were based upon Natural law thinking. In addition to the problem raised by the chameleon-like role of Natural law doctrine in political theory, it is noteworthy that Natural law theorists disagree as to whether or not it is always necessary to disobey an immoral law. According to some thinkers, it is sometimes more immoral to disobey such a law than to obey it.[15]

The fourth and final characteristic of classical Natural law doctrine implicit in Cicero's summary is the Divine authorship of the Natural law. Although this feature played a very significant role in the development of early Christianity,[16] reason rather than Divine authorship became the hallmark of all Natural law thinking from the Middle Ages onwards. In fact, the secular approach to Natural law often associated with Hugo Grotius (1583-1645) was already implicit in Jesuit teachings of the previous century.[17]

A major crisis in Natural law thinking arose in the eighteenth century with David Hume's celebrated argument that it is not possible to derive an "ought" from an "is".[18] According to Hume, no amount of information about the facts of the world or of human nature provides proof that anything ought to be done or not done.[19] Various ways of defending the classical doctrine from Hume's objection have been explored. One of them was mentioned above, i.e. the point that Natural law is derived from a rational conception of what is good for man, not merely from brute physical or psychological facts.[20] It is nevertheless this argument of Hume's which has been regarded by many jurists as a knock-down argument against all forms of Natural law thinking.[21]

Hume himself did not, however, entirely reject the concept of Natural law. Instead, he developed what has been called "a modern theory of Natural law". According to Hume:

> Tho' the rules of justice be artificial, they are not arbitrary. Nor is the expression improper to call them Laws of Nature; if by Natural we understand what is common to any species, or even if we confine it to mean what is inseparable from the species.[22]

Natural laws, therefore, are those laws which "are as old and universal as society and human species", and are "palpable and evident, even to the most rude and uncultivated of the human race".[23] In short, Natural law is not a higher law, but merely the cement without which no society can survive. This is the modified form of Natural law mentioned in the Introduction, and it is this approach which underlies the "minimum content of Natural law" sketched out by the modern positivist H.L.A. Hart.

As a positivist, Hart denies the existence of any necessary link between law and morality.[24] He does, however, maintain that there are certain facts of the human condition which make it necessary for a society to have certain rules in order that it survive. According to Hart:

> Reflection on some very obvious generalisations – indeed truisms – concerning human nature and the world in which men live, show that as long as these hold good, there are certain rules of conduct which any social organisation must contain if it is to be viable. Such rules do, in fact, constitute a common element in the law and conventional morality of all societies which have progressed to the point where these are distinguished as different forms of social control. With them are found, both in law and morals, much that is peculiar to a particular society and much that may be seen as arbitrary or a matter of choice. Such universally recognised principles of conduct which have a basis in elementary truths concerning human beings, their natural environment and aims, may be considered the minimum content of Natural law.[25]

Hart describes these truisms as consisting of human vulnerability, approximate equality, limited altruism, limited resources, and limited understanding and strength of will. In the light of these inevitable features of the human condition, there follows a "natural necessity" for certain minimum forms of protection for persons, property and promises.[26]

This form of Natural law is not free of criticism either. Not only does Hart's list display glaring omissions,[27] but many societies have survived precisely because the "minimum content of Natural law" has been disregarded.[28] The point has also been made that in restricting Natural law to the very minimum, Hart implies that outside this area of minimum content, laws of any iniquity may stand.[29]

The merits and demerits of the approach to Natural law in the writings of Hume and Hart are, however, beyond the scope of the present paper. The aim in this part of the paper was merely to outline the classical and the modern forms of Natural law doctrine and to state the major conceptual difference between them, i.e. the former is based upon the idea of a higher law acting as a critical standard, whereas the latter is descriptive in nature, and merely attempts to provide the basic rules necessary for the preservation of civilized society. In the second part of the paper, an attempt will be made to demonstrate that it is the modern,[30] rather than classical form of Natural law doctrine which is implicit in Maimonides' *Mishneh Torah*.

Natural Law Doctrine in Maimonides' Mishneh Torah

The main source in the contemporary discussion of Maimonides' attitude to Natural law theory is the following passage from the *Laws of Kings:*

> Any gentile who accepts the Seven Noahide Commandments and is meticulous in observing them is thereby one of the righteous of the nations of the world, and he has a portion in the World-to-Come. This is only the case if he accepts them and observes them because God commanded them in the Torah, and taught us through our teacher Moses that the Noahides were commanded to observe them even before the Torah was given. But if he observes them because of his own conclusions based on reason, then he is not a resident-alien (for the purposes of dwelling in Eretz Yisrael) and is not one of the righteous of the nations of the world, nor is he one of their wise men.[31]

Those who reject any Natural law doctrine in Maimonides' teachings simply point to the fact that in the above extract, gentiles who accept the Noahide Code merely on the basis of their own rational conclusions are dismissed as being neither righteous nor wise.[32] The Noahide laws, which consist of the universal prohibitions of bloodshed, theft, forbidden sexual relations, idolatry, blasphemy, tearing a limb from a living creature, and the positive commandment to set up a judicial system, are the closest thing to a Natural law type system in Jewish law,[33] but Maimonides nevertheless rules that their acceptance on the basis of human reason alone is a relatively sterile exercise.

There is, however, a strong body of evidence to support the alternative textual reading, "but of their wise men" *(ela me-hakhameihem)*, rather than "not of their wise men" *(ve-lo me-hakhameihem*).[34] On the basis of this textual variant which is found in many manuscripts of the *Mishneh Torah* and involves the change of only a single Hebrew letter, it is argued that Maimonides does indeed accept a Natural law theory.[35] Presumably, those who adopt this view maintain that the wisdom involved in accepting the Noahide laws is of the higher law associated with classical Natural law doctrine.

Since the textual evidence is in dispute, the issue must be resolved in more theoretical terms. One powerful argument advanced by the rejectionist school[36] is that Maimonides, following Aristotle, does not recognize conventional morality as a rational category.[37] Although, as Maimonides himself admits, "reason inclines" towards the Noahide laws, reason is not conclusive regarding their truth. Hence, a gentile who accepts them as rationally binding is suffering under a logical delusion.

More significant in jurisprudential terms is the argument that it is the *halakhah* which dictates the scope of rational enquiry in the decision-making process, rather than any independent ethic.[38] In this respect, the *halakhah* reflects a powerful contemporary positivist model of legal reasoning which claims that legal conclusions must be consistent with both the rules and the principles of the existing body of law.[39] It would, therefore, be most surprising if any halakhist were to espouse the notion of a higher law implicit in classical Natural law doctrine. Such a view would be tantamount to a rejection of the normative quality of the *halakhah*.[40] In the light of Maimonides' commitment to *halakhah*, it is particularly unlikely that he would have adopted such a position.

It is, therefore, to the modified, modern version of Natural law doctrine to which the focus of this debate on Maimonides and Natural law ought to be shifted. Most significant in this context is the following extract from Maimonides' *Laws of Homicide*, in which he justifies the ruling that persons guilty of bloodshed but legally exempt from capital punishment because of defective testimony are nevertheless severely punished. According to Maimonides:

> . . . although there are worse [i.e. in the theological sense] crimes than bloodshed, none causes such destruction to civilized society as bloodshed. Not even idolatry, nor immorality, nor the desecration of the Sabbath is the equal of bloodshed.[41]

Maimonides uses the principle of the preservation of civilised society as the basis for justifying the punishment of these killers. There is a clear parallel between this principle and the idea of the cement without which no civilised society can survive characteristic of the modern doctrine of Natural law referred to above.

In another passage, Maimonides deals with murder by proxy, indirect homicide and suicide. These acts are legally exempt from capital punishment: the first two by virtue of the principle of causation[42] and the third for obvious practical reasons.[43] Maimonides, however, makes the following provisions regarding such acts of homicide:

> If, however, one hires an assassin to kill another, or sends his slave to kill him, or ties another up and leaves him in front of a lion or another animal and the animal kills him, and similarly, if one commits suicide, the rules in each of these cases is that he is a shedder of blood, has committed the crime of murder and is liable to death at the hands of Heaven, but there is no capital punishment at the hands of the court.
>
> How do we know that this is the rule? Because Scripture says, "Whoever sheds man's blood by man shall his blood be shed" (*Gen.* 9:6) referring to one who commits the murder himself and not through an agent; "And surely your blood of your lives will I require" (*Gen.* 9:5) referring to suicide; "At the hand of every beast will I require it" (*Gen.* 9:5) referring to one who places another before a wild animal for it to devour; "And at the hand of man even at the hand of every man's brother, will I require the life of man" (*Gen.* 9:5) referring to one who hires others to kill someone. In these last three cases, the verb "require" is used expressly to show that their judgment is reserved for Heaven.
>
> Regarding any of these or similar murderers who are not subject to being condemned to die by verdict of the court, if a king of Israel wishes to put them to death by royal decree and for the sake of improving society, he has a right to do so. Similarly, if the court deems it proper to put them to death as an emergency measure, it has the authority to do so as it deems fit, provided that the circumstances warrant such action.[44]

Moreover, even if circumstances are such that the needs of the time do not demand the deaths of the killers concerned, it is nevertheless the duty of the court to take the following action against them:

> . . . to flog them almost to the point of death, to imprison them in a fortress or a prison for many years, and to inflict severe punishment on them in order to frighten and terrify other wicked persons, lest such a case become a pitfall and a snare, enticing one to say, "I will arrange to kill my enemy in a roundabout way as did so-and-so, and then I will be acquitted.[45]

There are four major elements in this passage. The first is the notion that bloodshed of any form is such a grievous offence that those who perpetrate it are morally culpable, and subject to both Divine and extra-legal penalties, notwithstanding the fact that they are exempt from regular legal sanctions. It is significant that the proof verses cited by Maimonides constitute the source of the offence of bloodshed in the Noahide code.[46] In relation to bloodshed, therefore, the Noahide offence complements the halakhic prohibition on murder, and the combination of the two ensures that no act of bloodshed is without some form of sanction in Jewish law.[47]

The second point to arise from this extract is the link between the extra-legal sanctions which may be applied in this type of case and the maintenance of social order. It is primarily the king in his capacity as the custodian of public morals who exercises the right to put such killers to death. Failing that, it is up to the court to take the necessary steps, "provided that the circumstances warrant such action".[48] The operative considerations underlying this special jurisdiction of both king and court are therefore, of a social nature.[49] In this respect, there is a clear parallel with the notion of the need to preserve civilised society which constitutes the basic premise of modern Natural law theory.

Another significant point is Maimonides' invocation of Divine retribution in this passage. There is no Talmudic source for this sanction in the cases of indirect homicide and suicide.[50] Divine punishment is, however, a standard penalty in cases in which a particular act deserves condemnation but there is no legal punishment.[51] A striking instance of this role of Divine punishment is found in the *Midrash Halakhah*. According to the *Mekhilta*, an Israelite who kills a heathen is exempt from capital punishment, since the victim is not "his neighbour".[52] This rule is then subjected to the following critique:

> Issi b. Akabyah says: Before the giving of the Torah (i.e. under Noahide law) we had been warned against shedding blood. After the giving of the Torah whereby laws were made stricter, shall they be considered lighter? In truth, the Sages said: He is free from judgment by the human court but his judgment is left to Heaven.[53]

The Sages' answer to Issi b. Akabyah is to invoke th notion of Divine retribution.[54] Clearly, there is a nexu between the Noahide offence of bloodshed and Divin sanction both in the case of killing a heathen, and the form of homicide considered in the above passage from the *Law of Homicide*.

In this context, it is noteworthy that according to R. Mei

Simha HaKohen, a standard middle eighteenth and early nineteenth century commentator on Maimonides' *Mishneh Torah*, death at the hands of Heaven also applies to foeticide in Jewish law.[55] The lack of any definitive sanction on foeticide in the sources of Jewish law has given rise to an extensive body of Rabbinic literature aimed at establishing a definitive legal category for this offence.[56] In contrast to the halakhic position, foeticide is specifically classified as a capital offence in Noahide law.[57] The solution provided by R. Meir Simha is elegant in its simplicity. Since foeticide is included in the Noahide law, Issi b. Akabyah's argument applies, and the offence is immediately classified as a form of bloodshed and as such, subject to Divine retribution.

The fourth and final element is the role of the court and king in applying extra-legal sanctions to the killers in question. Now, the authority of the court to administer extra-legal penalties in order to protect religion is well established in Jewish law, and is restricted to cases involving specific and substantive threat to the religious standards of society at large, i.e. "emergency measures" and "safeguarding a cause".[58] The authority of the king, although well established with respect to rebels,[59] is not so clear in the case of criminals who are exempt from capital punishment. In fact, it would appear at first glance that the separation of powers doctrine applies to the royal and the judicial functions in Jewish law. According to the Mishnah, the king is not involved in the judicial process in any way, and Maimonides observes that the basis for this ruling lies in the inherent tension between the king's role as a judge and his authority to execute those who disobey him.[60] Penalising legally exempt shedders of blood, however, would appear to constitute an exception to this approach. Indeed, Maimonides specifically brings cases of this nature within the purview of the royal jurisdiction. In his *Laws of Kings*, Maimonides provides as follows:

> If a person kills another and there is no clear evidence, or if no warning has been given him, or there is only one witness, or if one kills accidentally a person whom he hated, the King may, if the exigency of the hour demands it, put him to death in order to ensure the stability of the social order. He may put to death many offenders in one day, hang them, and suffer them to be hanging for a long time so as to put fear in the hearts of others and break the power of the wicked.[61]

The theoretical basis for the authority of the king in this type of situation is explained by R. Meir Simha, whose view that foeticide carries a Divine penalty in Jewish law was referred to above. According to R. Meir Simha:

> . . . an Israelite king is authorised by virture of his role as the preserver of the social order to act according to the general Noahide code, and this is a rational principle.[62]

Thus, it is in his role as preserver of society, which in the case of bloodshed is synonymous with the enforcement of the Noahide code, that the king is empowered to execute killers who are legally exempt from criminal sanctions. The king is not interfering in the judicial process: he is merely carrying out the royal task of preserving the social order. In the case of bloodshed, this task cannot be properly executed as long as killers of the type under consideration escape without penalty or punishment.

The question which then arises is that of the extent to which Noahide laws other than bloodshed would also fall into this category. Although Maimonides regards bloodshed as the most serious threat to society, there would appear to be some grounds for arguing that Noahide offences such as sexual licentiousness and theft are equally dangerous. Indeed, the view that the king's jurisdiction applies to the whole range of Noahide offences is expressed in halakhic literature. According to R. Meir Dan Plotzki (1867-1928), the king's jurisdiction would also apply to offences involving sexual licentiousness and any crime against the "natural order" of society.[63] There would also appear to be sufficient grounds for extending this jurisdiction to theft, which is also forbidden under the Noahide laws.[64] This point is, however, beyond the scope of the present paper and the argument here is confined to the offence of bloodshed.

Another problem which presents itself in this context is the relationship between the extra-legal jurisdiction of the king and that of the court. Both institutions enjoy extra-legal jurisdiction with respect to killers exempt from capital punishment. The king's jurisdiction would, however, appear to be somewhat wider than that of the court.[65] It has already been observed that the court may only mete out extra-legal penalties as an "emergency measure" and in order to "safeguard a cause".[66] Moreover, with regard to killing those against whom there is defective evidence or lack of a formal warning, Maimonides specifies the king rather than the court as the relevant punitive agency.[67] Clearly, extra-legal procedures on the part of the court must be restricted to the minimum, for otherwise, the whole structure of the legal system will be threatened. Any departure from the rules of evidence by a court is bound to detract from the authority of the system as a whole. Consequently the king, rather than the court, ought to be empowered to remedy the breach in public morality by executing those against whom the evidence is inconclusive or defective.[68] The king's jurisdiction may, therefore, be of a more general nature than that of the court, which is still subject to the strictly legal forms of the *halakhah*, albeit in a somewhat flexible fashion.

The aim in this part of the paper was to demonstrate that the principle of the preservation of civilized society is a vital element in gaining a proper understanding of Maimonides' treatment of the offence of bloodshed in his *Mishneh Torah*. Only in the light of this principle can the extra-legal penalties in cases in which those guilty of bloodshed but exempt from regular criminal sanctions be properly understood.[69] Hopefully, this aim has been achieved, and therefore, it may be concluded that Maimonides does adopt the modified or modern version of Natural law doctrine in his *Mishneh Torah*.

Notes

1 See A. D'Entreves, *Natural Law* (London, 1980); J. Finnis, *Natural Law and Natural Rights* (Oxford, 1980); D. Lloyd, *Introduction to Jurisprudence* (London, 1985) ch. 3.

2 The notable exception is R. Joseph Albo, *Sefer Ikkarim* 1:7, and see R. Lerner, "Natural Law in Albo's *Book of Roots*" in *Ancients and Moderns* (ed. J. Cropsey, N.Y., 1964) 132.

3 See S. Atlas, *Netivim Bemishpat Ivri* (N.Y., 5738); N. Lamm & A. Kirschenbaum, "Freedom and Constraint in the Jewish Judicial Process", *Cardozo Law Review* (1970) 1; D. Novak, *The Image of the Non-Jew in Judaism* (N.Y., 1983) ch. 10.

4 See M. Fox, "Maimonides and Aquinas on Natural Law", *Dine Israel* 5 (1972) 1; J. Faur, *Iyunim Bemishneh Torah: Sefer Hamada* (Jerusalem, 5738) 151.

5 Bk. 3, ch. 12.
6 Finnis *op. cit.* 34.
7 *Summa Theologica*, Question 94, Article 4.
8 See J. Harris, *Legal Philosophies* (London, 1980) 21.
9 *Summa Theologica*, Question 94, Article 5.
10 *Ibid.* Question 94, Article 4; also see D. O'Connor, *Aquinas and Natural Law* (London, 1967) ch. 7.
11 See D'Entreves *op. cit.*
12 See Harris *op. cit.* 10.
13 *Leviathan* ch. 13.
14 See Lloyd *op. cit.* 125.
15 See *Summa Theologica*, Question 95, Article 2; Finnis *op. cit.* ch. 12.
16 See Fox *op. cit.* 27 ff.
17 See Finnis *op. cit.* 43 ff. Grotius' famous concession, i.e. "even if we should concede that which cannot be conceded without the utmost wickedness, that there is no God, or that the affairs of men are of no concern to Him" (*De Jure Belli ac Pacis*, Prolegomena, 11) is clearly shown by Finnis to be well known in Jesuit writings of the previous century.
18 *Treatise on Human Nature*, Bk. 3, pt. 2, p. 521.
19 cf. Finnis *op. cit.* 37ff, who attempts to ameliorate Hume's argument and attribute its more extreme form to Hume's successors.
20 See n. 6 above.
21 Harris *op. cit.* 12.
22 *Treatise on Human Nature*, Bk. 3, pt. 2, p. 236; also see D. Forbes, *Hume's Philosophical Politics* (London, 1975) ch. 2.
23 *Treatise on Human Nature*, *ibid.* p.534.
24 *The Concept of Law* (Oxford, 1961) ch. 9; N. MacCormick, *H.L.A. Hart* (London, 1981) ch. 12.
25 *The Concept of Law*, *ibid.* 188.
26 *Ibid.* 189 ff.
27 See MacCormick *op. cit.* 98.
28 See Lloyd *op. cit.* 135.
29 See D'Entreves *op. cit.* 199.
30 Similarly, the nature of the relationship between the modern form of Natural Law doctrine and the classical concept is an issue which is beyond the scope of this paper: see Lloyd *op. cit.* 134; Harris *op. cit.* 20.
31 *Laws of Kings* 8:11.
32 See Fox *op. cit.* 15.
33 On this concept in general see S. Berman, "Noahide Laws" in *The Principles of Jewish Law* (ed. M. Elon, Jerusalem, 1975) 708; Novak *op. cit.*
34 For a discussion of the textual evidence see J. Katz, *Exclusiveness and Tolerance* (N.Y., 1962) 175; S. Schwarzchild, "Do Noachites Have to Believe in Revelation?" *Jewish Quarterly Review* n.s. 52:4, 301; Lamm & Kirschenbaum *op. cit.* 117; Faur *op. cit.* 151, n. 43; Novak *op. cit.* 288. Also see *Resp. Maharam Alashkar* no. 117.
35 See Lamm & Kirschenbaum *ibid.*
36 See Fox *op. cit.* 14 ff.
37 See *Milot Hahigayon* ch. 8; *Shemonah Perakim* (Mossad Harav Kook, Jerusalem 5721) 192; *Guide for the Perplexed* 1:2. In all three sources, Maimonides indicates that moral claims such as the proposition that a benefactor should be rewarded are not amenable to rational proof but are merely matters of social convention.
38 See A. Lichtenstein, "Does Jewish Tradition Recognize an Ethic Independent of *Halakhah?*" in *Contemporary Jewish Ethics* (N.Y., 1978, ed. M. Kellner) 107 ff.
39 See N. MacCormick *Legal Reasoning and Legal Theory* (Oxford, 1978) chaps. 6-8. MacCormick's three elements of constraint in legal reasoning are the considerations of generality, consistency and coherence. All three are reflected in ordinary halakhic reasoning.
40 See I. England, "The Interaction of Law and Morality in Jewish Law", *Jewish Law Annual* 6 (as yet unpublished) according to whom "the basic question cannot be how do moral considerations affect the shaping of Jewish law, nor how does Jewish law respond to new moral problems". According to England, the only interaction between *halakhah* and morality is at a policy level. It cannot take place at a normative level since this would automatically entail loss of normative independence on the part of the *halakhah*.
41 *Laws of Homicide* 4:9.
42 *Kidd.* 43a; *Sanh.* 77a.
43 *B.K.* 91b. There is, however, the possibility that a suicide might be punished by being deprived of eternal life in the World-to-Come: see *Sem.* 2:1; *Torah Temimah Gen.* 9 no. 8.
44 *Laws of Homicide* 2:2-4.
45 *Laws of Homicide* 2:5.
46 *Gen. Rabbah* 34:14, cf. *Sanh.* 57a; Maimonides, *Laws of Kings* 9:4.
47 A clear illustration of the role of the Noahide law in complementing the *halakhah* is the ruling of the *Tosafot* that non-therapeutic abortion is not permitted on the basis of the principle that foeticide is forbidden under the Noahide code and nothing which is prohibited to a Noahide can possibly be permitted for an Israelite: see *Sanh.* 57b; *Sanh.* 59a; *Tosafot Sanh.* 59a *s.v. mi ika*; *Tosafot Hull.* 33a *s.v. ehad oved kokhavim*; R. Erusi, "Abortion – Theory and Practice in the *Halakhah*" (*Heb.*), *Dine Israel* 8 (5737) 125. Also see *Resp. Iggrot Moshe*, *Yoreh Deah* 3 no. 36 in which R. Feinstein uses the same principle in relation to the termination of the life of a person suffering from a fatal organic defect (*terefah*) in Jewish law.
48 On the role of the king and the court as the custodians of public morality and religion, see below, n. 58.
49 See below, n. 62.
50 In relation to killing by proxy, death at the hands of Heaven is mentioned in the *Talmud* (*Kidd.* 43a) and R. Joseph Karo cites this source in *Keseph Mishneh*, *Laws of Homicide* 2:2. As far as indirect homicide and suicide are concerned, however, R. Karo falls back on the Noahide offence of bloodshed as the source of Maimonides' ruling.
51 See B. Jackson, "The Concept of Religious Law in Judiasm", *Aufsteig und Neidergang der Romischen Welt* 19 (1979) 33; S. Federbush, *Hamussar Vehamishpat Beyisrael* (Jerusalem, 5739) 140.
52 *Ex.* 21:14.
53 *Mekhilta Derabbi Yishmael*, *Masekhta D'Nezikin*, 4 (ed. H. Horowitz, I. Rabin) 263.
54 This is indeed the definitive halakhic response in this case: see *Keseph Mishneh*, *Laws of Homicide* 2:1; *Yereim Hashalem* 175. Also see Maimonides, *Laws of Homicide* 4:11; *Laws of Idolatry* 11:1.
55 *Or Sameah*, *Laws of Forbidden Sexual Relations* 3:2; *Meshekh Hokhmah*, *Parashat Vayakhel s.v. shabbat shabbaton*; cf. Meiri, *Sanh.* 57b.
56 On the issue of abortion in Jewish law, see J.D.Bleich *Contemporary Halakhic Problems* (N.Y., 1977) ch. 15; *Harefuah Leor Hahalakhah* (ed. M. Stern, Jerusalem, 5740) pt. 1.
57 *Sanh.* 57b. On the historical aspects of this difference, see G. Alon, *Mehkarim B'Toldot Yisrael* (Tel. Aviv, 5727) 280: G. Weinfeld, "The Genuine Jewish Attitude Towards Abortion" (Heb.), *Zion* 42 (5737) 130.
58 See *Yeb.* 90b; Maimonides, *Laws of Rebels* 2:4; M. Elon, *Hamishpat Haivri* 2 (Jerusalem, 5733) 421; J. Ginzburg, *Mishpatim L'Yisrael* (Jerusalem, 5716); E. Quint & N. Hecht, *Jewish Jurisprudence* (N.Y., 1980) ch. 2.
59 *Sanh.* 49a; Maimonides, *Laws of Kings* 3:8.
60 Maimonides, *Laws of the Sanhedrin* 2:4-5; G. Blidstein, *Ikkronot Mediniim Bemishnat Harambam* (Bar-Ilan, 5743) ch. 5.
61 *Laws of Kings* 3:10; cf. *Guide for the Perplexed* 3:40.
62 *Or Sameah*, *Laws of Kings* 3:10; cf. Meiri, *Sanh.* 57b.
63 *Hemdat Yisrael*, *Kuntres Ner Mitzvah* no. 288, p. 75; J.D.Bleich, *Contemporary Halakhic Problems* 2 (N.Y., 1983) 351, n.11.
64 See *B.M.* 61b.
65 See J. Gershuni, *Mishpat Hamelukhah* (Jerusalem, 5740) 96.
66 *Id.*
67 *Laws of Kings* 3:10.
68 See *Resp. R. Joseph ibn Migash* no. 191; Blidstein *op. cit.*, 127 no. 25.
69 For other instances of such penalties implied by Maimonides, see *Laws of Homicide* 2:7-8.

Part III
Ethics and the Theory of Jewish Law

[8]

LAW AND MORALS IN JEWISH JURISPRUDENCE

Moshe Silberg *

WHEREIN lies the difference between the instructions of law and the precepts of morality? Law is addressed to the citizen; morality addresses man. The creator of the one is external, in the centers of government; the creator of the other is internal, in the depths of the heart; the purpose of the one is that order should reign, and of the other, peace of mind. The task of law is to save the oppressed, and of morality to save the oppressor

* Associate Justice, Supreme Court of Israel; Professor of Personal Law, Hebrew Univ.; Dr. Juris., Frankfurt-am-Mein, 1926. This paper was the Third J. L. Magnes Memorial Lecture, given at the Hebrew University in Jerusalem in 1951 and published in Hebrew by the Magnes Press in 1952.

from his own self. The one commands the payment of the debt, the other, the fulfillment of the duty. In short, law is a social creature, observing the individual in society's looking-glass. Morality is a personal experience, an individual feeling of duty, regarding even society in the individual's spectrum of colors.

I wrote the above sentences a few years ago, and I do not reject any of the thoughts expressed in them. In the present article, however, I wish to transfer the center of gravity to a different aspect of the problem. I shall not discuss the differences between law on the one hand and morality on the other, but the relationship between law and morality in the instructions of the law itself, and especially between considerations of utility and considerations of morality in the content of the law; and not of law in general, but of Jewish law.

A great difficulty arises here at once, barring the gate *in limine* before the continuance of the inquiry. The difficulty is in the very definition of the term "Jewish law." This term is not ancient; I believe it to be not more than fifty to sixty years of age, but the chaos created around it is great. Parenthetically it may here be said that this chaos is the principal cause of the confusion and conceptual unclarity prevailing with regard to one of our most important problems, the problem of the codification or "resurrection" of Jewish law.

What is Jewish law? I shall not venture to propose a general, encompassing, and exhaustive definition. I shall say only that unlike the overwhelming majority of other legal systems, Jewish law does not confine itself to relations between man and man, but in addition defines in legal categories, applies legal terms, perceives through legal concepts, the relationship between man and God — as though God Himself were a type of legal entity, enjoying rights, subject to duties, obeying and fulfilling His own laws, integrated, as it were, as a subject matter of civil law, in the system of relations between Him and His creatures. We find in the Jerusalem Talmud:[1] "Rav said to Azar . . . . 'when a king of flesh and blood decrees, if he so wishes he obeys: if he wishes otherwise, it is only for others to obey; but it is otherwise with the Holy One, Blessed be He, He decrees and is the first to keep His decrees [*i.e.*, He is not allowed as it were to will otherwise].

[1] This is a compilation of Talmudic discussion which took place in the academies in Palestine in the third through the sixth centuries. [Ed.]

Why so? "They shall keep my charge. . . . I am the Lord." (Leviticus 22:9) It is I who kept the precepts of the Law first.' "[2]

This idea of the Law's supremacy over its giver found its magnificent allegoric expression in the story of the oven of Aknai. A diversity of opinion arose among the *Tannaim* [3] regarding a dry question of the Law: whether an oven which instead of being made in one piece was made in a series of separate portions with a layer of sand between each was to be regarded as one structure of mortar liable to the laws of ritual impurity or as an earthenware utensil not subject to these laws.[4] Rabbi Eliezer was of the opinion that the oven was ritually pure, while the other Sages were of the opinion that the oven was unclean. Rabbi Eliezer looked for ways to convince his colleagues that he was right. And the *Breita* relates:

> On that day Rabbi Eliezer brought forward every imaginable argument but they [the Sages] did not accept them. Said he to them, 'If the Law agrees with me let this carob tree prove it!' Thereupon the carob tree was torn a hundred cubits out of its place — others affirm, 400 cubits. 'No proof can be brought from a carob tree,' they retorted. Again he said to them, 'If the Law agrees with me, let the stream of water prove it!' Whereupon the stream of water flowed backwards. 'No proof can be brought from a stream of water,' they rejoined. . . . Again he said to them, 'If the Law agrees with me, let it be proved from heaven!' Whereupon a Heavenly Voice cried out, 'Why do ye dispute with Rabbi Eliezer, seeing that in all matters the Law agrees with him!' But Rabbi Joshua arose and exclaimed, 'It is not in heaven' . . . (Deuteronomy 30:12) [since] the Law had already been given at Mount Sinai; we pay no attention to a Heavenly Voice, because Thou hast long since written in the Law at Mount Sinai, 'after the majority must one follow.' (Exodus 23:2).[5]

And the Talmud adds, "Rabbi Nathan met Elijah and asked him 'What did the Holy One, Blessed be He, do in that hour?' — 'He laughed (with joy),' he replied, saying, 'My sons have defeated me, my sons have defeated me!'" Here we find the Rule of Law is the absolute sense of the term: The law ruling the lawgiver; the inclusion of the legislator himself within the framework of legal

[2] Jerusalem Talmud, *Rosh Hashanah* ch. 1, 57a.

[3] Talmudic sages who lived in the years 10–220 A.D. [Ed.]

[4] *Cf. Leviticus* 11:33. [Ed.]

[5] *Baba Mezia* 59b.

and decisional relationships created by the laws given by him. He observes "the precepts of the Law," submits to the authority of the law, and furthermore submits to the authentic interpretation given by its interpreters, *i.e.*, submits himself to the jurisdiction of an authoritative body, the majority, authorized by him to determine in case of a doubt, which for him is of course no doubt at all. If the law is "After the majority must one follow," then this rule is to be applied even when the lawgiver himself is an interested party. The idea is too great to be grasped by our ordinary mind, but one conclusion certainly rises from it: that the jurisdiction of Jewish law is not confined within the boundaries of relations between man and man. Matters concerning the relationship between man and God, which are actually matters between man and himself, between him and his religious and moral feeling, are caught by the net of legal relations as well. It is obvious to any student of the Talmud that in it no line is drawn in the definition and treatment of concepts between discussions relating to pecuniary matters, ritual law, or the law of purification. No subject seems to be so remote from reality as the Law of Sacrifice — the post-Maimonides codifiers have deleted it from their codifications — and yet one finds in the Tractates relating to ritual law the typical legal techniques of the Tractates relating to the law of civil obligations and the law of family — the same dialectics, the same approach, the same conceptualism, the same classification — with but one small difference, entirely unimportant from the viewpoint of the law: the "transactions" here made are between man and God, and not between Reuben and Simon, or between Jacob and Leah.

Thus, in Jewish law it is very difficult to mark the border between the utilitarian and the moral considerations of the legislator and determine the nature of the *res* which a certain provision of the law seeks to protect. Even when the benefit from a certain provision is beyond all doubt, and even when it is impossible to imagine normal social relations without it, necessity and utility are not the identifying feature of the protected *res*. Let me pose here a seemingly naive question: Why should a man pay his debt or fulfill an obligation which he has undertaken? The Roman lawyers, as well as any modern lawyer, would be most surprised by such a question. It is clear, they would say, that the duty of payment of a debt is the correlative of the concept of ownership, and the one cannot exist without the other. No stable social regime (and not only in a capitalistic country) can exist without fulfillment of a civil-legal duty, the fulfillment of the obligation which the individual undertook. In Jewish law the question is more problematic and was regarded as such by the Sages of the Talmud.

There is a diversity of opinion among them whether the payment of a debt is a "precept" or not, *i.e.*, whether it is a religious-moral duty, requiring, like all duties of this type, a certain personal maturity (and so inapplicable, for instance, to minors), or whether it is a civil-legal duty, *i.e.*, a necessary result of the creditor's right, altogether independent of the debtor's religious-moral "capacity." "The paying of the debt is a precept," says Rabbi Papa, "and minors are not obliged to fulfill the precepts."[6] Rashi[7] elaborates: "The payment of a debt to a creditor is a precept. The debtor is religiously obliged to pay his debt and fulfill his word, for it is said, '. . . a just hin [measure] shall ye have' (Leviticus 19:36), let your 'hen' [yes] be just and your 'no' be just."[8]

It is not necessary to examine here the practical results of the problem, and the law there determined. But it is of great interest to observe one discussion, short and piquant, which took place with regard to this question: Rabbi Kahana said to Rabbi Papa, "According to the statement you made that the repayment of [a debt to] a creditor is a religious act, what happens if [a debtor] says, 'I am not disposed to perform the religious act.'" "We," the other replied, "have learned that this [administering thirty-nine lashes as punishment for a religious transgression] applies only to negative precepts, but in the case of positive precepts, as for instance when a man is told, 'build a tabernacle,' and he does not do so, or 'perform the precept of lulab' and he does not perform it, he is flogged [if he persists in his refusal] until his soul departeth."[9]

Thus, when a person refuses to pay his debt he is physically coerced to fulfill his religious obligation to pay. The concern of the court is not the creditor's debt, his damages, but the duty of the debtor, his religious-moral duty, the fulfillment of the precept by him. The creditor receives his money almost incidentally,

---

[6] *Arakin* 22a.

[7] Rabbi Solomon ben Isaac. One of the leading commentators on the Talmud and the Bible, he lived in France in the years 1040–1105 A.D. [Ed.]

[8] *Kethuboth* 86a.

[9] *Ibid.*

as a secondary result of the performance of this duty. This *problematique* is nonexistent in modern legal systems, and had already ceased to exist for the Roman lawyer. It may be said, *cum grano salis*, that modern law has no interest in duties; its sole interests are rights, and the debtor's duty to pay is only a short way of indicating the possibility of a payment coerced by the creditor. One cannot strike the words "to have a right" from the modern legal dictionary, but it is definitely possible to exist without the words "to be obliged." Instead of them one could substitute the longer phrase "may be coerced (by the courts and the marshals) into fulfillment of the creditor's right." Even with regard to the *obligationes naturales*, in so far as they exist as archaic remnants in modern legal systems — the duties fulfillment of which cannot be coerced — the word duty is no more than a fiction; their whole meaning is that the person fulfilling the duty, the payor, cannot sue for the return of the money paid. Once more we have a reflex, in this case a negative one, of a right to sue, the only criterion for the existence of a civil duty.

As we have seen, this is not true in Jewish law. It is certainly not so in the opinion of the *Amora* [10] mentioned above holding that the payment of a debt is the fulfillment of a precept; and the payment of a debt is the prototype of the whole system of legal obligations. If it is no more than a religious precept, a religious-moral obligation of the debtor, then the duty is the primary thing and the right secondary, if not less than that. But even he who does not take this extreme stand cannot disregard the great value which Jewish law attributes to the duty of fulfilling the legal obligation. Even if payment of a debt be considered not only a precept, it is universally agreed that it is *also* a precept, and this fact is prominent and influential, both directly and indirectly, on the active side of the Jewish *obligatio*.

Jewish law distinguishes between "attachment of the person" and "attachment of the property." Every debt secured by bill creates, with its inception, both attachments simultaneously, but they may be severed later. The "personal attachment" covers only the relations between the debtor and creditor, the original parties. The "attachment of the property," on the other hand, passes from person to person together with the property (immovables), or is transferable — as a right — from the creditor to the purchaser of

[10] Talmudic sages who lived in the years 220–500 A.D. [Ed.]

the debt, by lawfully determined means for transfer of debt. Many practical rules are derived from this basic distinction; for instance, "If the original holder sells a bond of indebtedness to another person, and later releases the debtor, the latter is legally [personally] released."[11] And what is this "personal," abstract attachment, if not the very same "payment of a debt" which we already know, *i.e.*, the religious-moral duty of fulfilling an undertaking, "let your 'yes' be just and your 'no' be just" in the words of Rashi. The *obligatio* in Jewish law is neither exhausted by nor limited to the possibility of civil realization of the creditor's right of action, as in other legal systems, but relies on, and to no small extent, the religious-moral duty of payment. The moral foundations of Jewish law, leaving their stamp in a diversity of ways on the special nature of the law of obligations, are here revealed.

And now to a slightly paradoxical point, one which seems to contradict the idea expressed thus far. I have in mind the stand taken in Jewish law with regard to one question, "moral" par excellence: the validity of illegal or immoral contracts. It would seem that the "morality" of a legal system should be tested by this attribute, that the more moral a legal system, the stronger would be its resistance to the recognition of the validity of illegal contracts. But as we shall soon see, this is not the case.

The problem of agreements made in contravention of the instructions of the law, or in breach of the accepted principles of morality, has occupied and still is occupying the attention of most legal systems. The answer to this question, alas, is far from being short. Various considerations come into play here: of morality, of utility, of convenience, ethical and aesthetical considerations, and considerations that involve a certain amount of the will to "show off."

I will explain by citing examples taken from the English law, which in this respect is based on Roman law. Here we find very intricate and complicated distinctions, far from clean-cut, and full of paradoxes. As a rule, the law does not recognize the validity of a prohibited contract or of an immoral contract; *i.e.*, — and this is to be stressed — it does not regard it as the basis for a cause of action. If Reuben, for instance, hires Simon to kill Levi, Simon, of course, cannot sue Reuben for his "fee."

Up to now the matter is simple. No one would propose to grant

[11] *Kethuboth* 85b; *cf.* Tossafeth and Commentaries, *ibid.*

the "agent" a right of action against his "principal." But the matter becomes more and more problematic as we descend the ladder of criminality from the grave to the slight. Let us imagine the owner of a small grocery who does not lock his shop in the hour stipulated by the law and sells his merchandise in one of the forbidden hours. Let us assume further that he does not sell his goods for cash but on credit. Will such an offender be able to sue for what is due to him from the purchaser, or will the famous maxim *ex turpi causa non oritur actio* apply here too? Or, what is the position of a producer selling his goods before obtaining the license required by the Emergency Regulations or that of the liquor seller who has not yet had the time to extend his annual license? Will the purchaser get the better part of the deal in all these cases and not be obliged to pay the consideration for the goods which he received?

Hundreds of such questions were raised in English law, and the judiciary's stand was not uniform. A baffling example was provided about one hundred and fifty years ago, when on the same day the same judge, Lord Ellenborough, tried two cases; in both the defendant claimed that the action should fail because the contract forming the basis for the claim was illegal. In the first case[12] two French *émigrés* had found refuge in London, and one of them, a priest by profession, contracted syphilis. His fellow *émigré* cured him at some expense, and sued for a £20 fee. The defendant acknowledged both the treatment and the cure; but he asserted that his fellow *émigré* had treated him in violation of a law forbidding the unlicensed practice of medicine within seven miles of the city of London and that the contract was therefore illegal. The court rejected this contention and found for the plaintiff. In the second case,[13] an action for the price of bricks, the defendant alleged that the bricks did not conform to the minimum sizes prescribed by law, that the vendor thus was forbidden to sell them, and therefore that he could not recover their price. The court accepted this contention and the plaintiff was nonsuited. A hundred and fifty years have elapsed since those two decisions, and no one yet knows what distinguishes them.

Even in more detailed and more enlightened modern opinions, we find a wealth of contradictions accompanying the search for

[12] Gremaire v. Le Clerc Bois Valon, 2 Camp. 144, 170 Eng. Rep. 1110 (N.P. 1809).

[13] Law v. Hodgson, 2 Camp. 147, 170 Eng. Rep. 1111 (N.P. 1809).

clear principles governing the problem. Two irreconcilable inclinations fight in the bosom of the judge: the wish to preserve the efficacy of the criminal prohibition; and the will to do justice to a wronged plaintiff. To effect compliance with the criminal code requires not only the punishment of an offender but also removal of the tempting flavor of sin. The purpose of every penalty is to neutralize the natural inclination towards the offense. "May the sins, and not the sinners, cease to be" goes the Talmudic expression. If one of the elements of the offense or one of its typical accompanying features is a contract or a legal bond, then one of the ways to diminish its appeal is to deny its legal validity.

But there is another consideration, also of no little weight, and that is the duty to do justice between the parties before the judge, the desire to frustrate the defendant's attempt to escape the fulfillment of his duty by an unfair allegation of illegality. Now a certain discrepancy always exists between the standard justice of the law and the individual justice suitable to all the concrete circumstances of the case at bar. There is no legislator in the world who is able to foresee all possible combinations of circumstances. Hence there does not exist a law which completely covers all cases arising within its framework; this is an evil which cannot be avoided. The justice of the law is, therefore, a "statistical" justice, an average justice, a kind of rationed goods preserving all from want but sufficient for no one. But it is not my purpose to discuss this latter shortcoming. Here, the conflict of the two inclinations is not casual, partial, or latent; it is inherent in the nature of the problem and apparent in almost every case. The crux of the matter is that very often the court must accept a completely objectionable allegation, an allegation the very reliance upon which reveals moral corruption on the side of the party advancing it. The vendor selling his goods in violation of the measures and sizes fixed in the Emergency Regulations is surely deserving of punishment. He may be sentenced to imprisonment, he may be fined, his business may be closed down; but this does not permit the purchaser — at the very least an accessory to the commission of the crime — to retain possession without paying for the merchandise.

The legal principle governing our question is *in pari delicto melior est pars possidentis*. I wish to stress that the law does *not* say: every illegal or immoral contract is a complete nullity and therefore the parties should be put in their original positions. All it says is that the possessor is in a better condition, *beati pos-*

sidentes. Possession is nine points of the law! The producer who delivered his produce on credit cannot sue for the price or for return of the goods; and if the purchaser is subject to the prohibition he cannot have restitution of his money, if he paid the price and did not get the merchandise. The court simply will not entertain such an action; dealing with it is "odious"; it does not soil its hands in such litigation. The result of all this moral indignation is punishment of the criminal-claimant and reward for the criminal-defendant; but of course in this case the reward is not given by the court's own hand; it is merely left in the hand of him who has taken it by himself. This is the unpleasant sediment left in the heart of the judge whenever he must accept the plea of "illegality" of the contract, and this is the "ill sound" of that plea referred to by Lord Mansfield in one of his famous decisions.[14] Yet it is the duty of a judge — this is what the modern legislator requires of him — to overcome this feeling, to reject his "musical sense" because of a different legal maxim, the practical, utilitarian "for they shall hear and fear."

Such, in general terms, is the response offered by the modern English legal system. This is not the place to enter into the ramifications of the rule; it need only be added that it is generally felt that the solution is unsatisfactory. In an English case a few years ago[15] the defendant had wished to send his young daughter to Italy for medical treatment, accompanied by his wife. Considering the amount of lire the postwar British government would permit them to take inadequate, he arranged to have an acquaintance provide the necessary funds in Italy. As security he was to deposit in her hands certain shares of stock. To clothe the transaction in legal dress, the husband signed a note for £150. The husband deposited the shares, the wife and daughter went to Italy, did not receive the promised money, and returned to England. The acquaintance then sued the husband on the note, and he counterclaimed for the stock, alleging the above facts. The original suit on the note was withdrawn and the sole issue became return of the shares. The acquaintance contended the counterclaim must fail because based on an illegal action, an attempt to circumvent the Exchange Control Act. The court agreed and refused to order restitution of the shares. This judgment is not of great interest,

---

[14] Holman v. Johnson, 1 Cowp. 341, 98 Eng. Rep. 1120 (K.B. 1775).

[15] Bigos v. Bousted, [1951] 1 All E.R. 92 (K.B. 1950).

legally speaking, but it is rewarding to note the tribulations which the judges must have had to undergo to reject the husband's action. For in human terms, the result seems unfair: the child received insufficient medical care, her parents lost the expenses of the trip and the shares as well, while their opponent, guilty of the most objectionable behavior, emerged with a great bounty. She did not advance any money, she received a bundle of shares, and was denied only one thing: costs in the trial.

Let us now see what stand Jewish law takes toward this question. It is clear enough that when comparing two legal systems so different and so distant from each other, in time and in spirit, we shall have to make a certain "discount" for their dissimilarities. But the nucleus of the question is essentially the same, and a comparison between them is possible in spite of the great differences.

This problem is explicitly debated in the Talmud by Abayei and Rava. Abayei said: "Any act which the Divine Law forbids, if it has been done, it *has legal effect*"; while Rava said, "the act has no legal effect at all."[16] The lively discussion which followed cites various laws and makes distinctions, but reaches no conclusion. In itself, it merely serves to raise the issue but does not advance us much toward the solution of the question on principle, and does not tell us to what extent a contract or transaction carried out in violation of a prohibition of the law has valid legal consequences. But an answer can be pieced together from other discussions in the Talmud and in the pertinent interpretations, commentaries, and *responsae*. Let us take, for example, the interesting discussion on usury between these same *Amorites*,[17] Abayei and Rava. Abayei says, "if a man had a claim of four zuz in interest upon his neighbor and he [the debtor] gave him a garment for it, when we compel repayment, we make him repay four zuz but not the garment." Rava says, "We compel him to return the garment. Why so? That people may not say, 'the garment he wears is a garment of usury.' "[18]

The Pentateuch forbids all interest as usurious. The prohibition applies to both the creditor and debtor. The receipt and *payment* of usury is forbidden.[19] Although the debtor paying the interest violates thereby an express prohibition of the Law, for

[16] *Temurah* 4b.

[17] Plural of *Amora*, note 10 *supra*. [Ed.]

[18] *Baba Mezia* 65a.

[19] *Id.* at 61a; Maimonides, *Law of Creditor & Debtor*, ch. 4, Rule 2.

the words "Thou shall not lend upon usury to thy brother"[20] were construed as applicable to him too, he may sue for a return of his money if it was of a determinate nature, in the language of the Talmud, "direct interest." "Rabbi Eleazar said: 'direct interest can be reclaimed in court, but not indirect interest.'"[21]

Although the lender may not sue for his usurious interest in court, since to compel payment would be to order an illegal act, Jewish law is not ready to accept the principle that it is not meet for a court to entertain an action based on an offense. The Hebrew legislator is not so sensitive, and he regards such abstention as exaggerated and hypocritical. After all, the courts are quite used to dealing with things which are not so clean. Since "direct interest" is retrievable in the courts, the question was raised whether a usurious debtor who undertook to pay his creditor four zuz interest, but instead gave him a garment worth four zuz, could sue for return of the *garment*, or only for its value? Abayei said: "the money is retrievable from him [the lender], the garment is not."[22] Rashi comments: "The acquisition is effective and the creditor shall return the interest to the debtor."[23] Rava, on the other hand, is of the opinion that the garment itself should be returned so "that the world should not see that the creditor is wrapped in a garment of usury and imitate his ways."[24] And the Rosh[25] writes: "It is only because we do not want people to say that he is wrapped in a garment of usury that we return the garment, for otherwise the sale would have been valid, *and we do not say that because it was made through a transgression of the law the sale is void.*"[26] There is thus no difference of opinion between Abayei and Rava on the principle in which we are interested, both holding that a transaction committed in the teeth of a prohibition is not void. The Rosh adds, citing Rav Hai Gaon:[27] "in those cases

[20] *Deuteronomy* 23:20.

[21] *Baba Mezia* 61b.

[22] *Id.* at 65a.

[23] *Ibid.*

[24] *Ibid.*

[25] Rabenu Asher Ben-Yehiel, an outstanding Talmudic authority, was born in Germany around 1250 A.D. and died in Toledo, Spain in 1328. [Ed.]

[26] *Baba Mezia* 65b.

[27] The *Geonim* were the heads of the two leading academies in Babylonia, Soura, and Pumpaditta. They were the supreme Talmudic authorities from the final completion of the Talmud to the disintegration of the Jewish center in Babylonia (609–1038 A.D.). Rav Hai Gaon (938–1038), the head of the academy at Pumpaditta, was the last of the *Geonim*. [Ed.]

where there is an illegality in the sale . . . the sale is valid nevertheless, and cannot be set aside because it was made through a transgression." [28] The transaction "cannot be set aside," whether executed or executory. The purchaser may obtain specific performance and the seller may sue for the contract price, but, of course, only as far as the law permits, *i.e.*, the principal without the interest. And in *Shulchan Aruch Choshen Mishpat*[29] it is said: "He who sells or buys on the Sabbath or on the Day of Atonement . . . his actions are [nevertheless] valid." [30]

And Maimonides rules that: "He who writes a bill of divorcement mistakenly [*i.e.*, unaware he is violating the Sabbath] on the Sabbath or on the Day of Atonement and delivers it to his wife — she is divorced . . . but if he does so willfully, she is not divorced, for the witnesses are ineligible [*i.e.*, if they knew it was the Sabbath].[31] Had the witnesses been eligible, the bill of divorcement would have been effective, even though written willfully on the Sabbath. The commentary adds significantly: "From here we infer that the teacher [Maimonides] holds that the law is with Abayei," [32] Abayei holding "any act which the Divine Law forbids, if it has been done, it has legal effect." Jewish law is not ready to accept the causal relation between the commission of an offense and the invalidity of the civil contract, or of any other legal transaction collateral to the commission of the offense. A violation of the law or of morality is separate and distinct from the question of legal validity of the contract — in so far as the performance of the contract is not itself the commission of an offense (as, for instance, payment of interest by the debtor to the creditor). Precisely because Jewish law does not distinguish between law and morality, and the fulfillment of a formal legal requirement is at the same time the fulfillment of a religious-moral precept — in the case of fiscal obligation the "precept" of paying the creditor — nonperformance of a contract entered into collaterally with the commission of an offense would be a transgression *additional* to the origi-

[28] *Baba Mezia* 65b.

[29] This was a codification of Jewish law, written by Rabbi Joseph Caro (1488–1575) in Galilee, based on an earlier codification. It covers most of Jewish law and, along with the additions of later commentators, is the most authoritative statement of Jewish law, applied by Rabbinic authorities to this day. [Ed.]

[30] *Choshen Mishpat* 235.

[31] *Law of Divorce*, ch. 3, Rule 19.

[32] *Ibid.* (*Mishna-Lamelech.*)

nal one committed by the transgressor. This is the ideological kernel for the separation between the two concepts.

In other words the separation between the criminal and the legal content of an act is the necessary outcome of the *identity* between the legal and the moral content of the law in general, and it is this rule, which at first sight contradicts the idea which I expressed earlier, which is actually an important and additional support to it.

I have dwelt on the strong relationship existing in Jewish law — "the identity" between the legal and the moral contents of the law. Truly, there is no legal system in the world, whether modern or ancient, in which the principles of morality and law are as intertwined, as interfused, as in Jewish law. Three reasons could be adduced. First, Jewish law is a *religious* law, based on the people's religious conscience. Breaches of behavior between man and man are simultaneously religious transgressions, affecting the relationship between man and God. "Thou shalt not bear the name of thy lord God in vain," and "thou shalt not steal" are both included in the Decalogue, and from a religious point of view there is no difference between them. The well-known conciliatory advice: "Render to Caesar the things that are Caesar's, and to God the things that are God's" is a novelty created in the school of Christianity. Judaism does not recognize "things of Caesar" at all. Everything is the "One Above's" — metaphorically speaking, of course — and the citizen does not owe Caesar anything which he as man does not also owe his God.

Second, Jewish law is *national* law, the principal development of which took place after the loss of national independence. The Talmud, the *Poskim* (*responsae*), the great codifications of the twelfth century (Maimonides), the fourteenth century (the *Toor*) and the sixteenth century (the *Shulchan Aruch*), the later *responsae* — have all grown on foreign soil, and their main objective was to retain and protect the national nature of the people from obliteration in the foreign cultural milieu. The exiled people willingly confined itself within the four corners of the Halacha (Law) — ritual law, civil law, and criminal law — knowing that only in this protected zone would it be able to retain its national character until it returned to the land of the fathers, until the day of redemption. This main task of the law necessarily determined its path of development. Every directive, every precept, every rule, and every regulation was primarily examined from the aspect of its usefulness for the purpose of national defense — the defense of the nation and its culture in the broadest sense of these words. And only when the matter under consideration was neutral with respect to this fundamental aspect did other considerations come to bear upon it. The Jew's mode of dress, his diet, dwelling, behavior, relation with men, his family affairs, and his business affairs were all prefixed and premolded, in a national cloak, in a set of laws that was clear, severe, strict, detailed, that accompanied him day by day, from cradle to grave.

Finally, there is a well-known historical reason, which especially influenced the *later* development of Jewish law: the lack of political or quasi-political coercive media for the execution of the binding instructions of the Law. In the end of the tenth century and the beginning of the eleventh, the Jewish autonomic center in Babylonia was shattered and the national hegemony passed to the countries of North Africa and Western Europe. After one thousand years of national, legal-cultural autonomy in the countries of pagan Rome, Christian Byzantium, Sassanide Persia, and the Arab Caliphate, the national center wandered into strange, hostile surroundings which did not grant any "legal standing" to the remnants of the exiled people. From then on there was no Jewish government anywhere in the dispersion, with the exception of a few poor, limited concessions of very little value occasionally granted by the local ruler. In this atmosphere, among the dark walls of the ghetto, without governmental coercive media, without judges and police appointed by the authorities, Jewish law developed by the force of only one authority: the free will of the people. True, this will too can impose certain sanctions, especially social sanctions. But the very exercise of these sanctions depends on the will of the individual not to leave the common spiritual soil of the people.

In these circumstances and for these reasons the definite moral nature of Jewish law crystallized, a law essentially religious, national in its objectives, and free in its means of materialization. Such law can have only one solid foundation: a common moral concept shared by all of the nation's individuals. The simple utilitarian interest of protecting the existence of a society cannot serve as its basis since this interest *ex hypothesi* conflicts with the social or antisocial interests of him who breaks the law. Society, to be sure, has an interest in the fulfillment by every individual of his obligations toward the others, but the individual debtor has no material interest in paying his debts; he is forced to do it either by the recognition of his moral obligation or by the fear of coercion. Hence every legal system functioning within a society devoid of the means of coercion and execution cannot have a foundation other than the moral consciousness of society.

The idea is very simple, but what is not so simple and well known is that these reasons determined and defined not only the essence and content of Jewish law but its form as well, its casts of thought and ways of legislation. The Talmud, and I am referring to the legal part of it, is for most people *terra incognita.* In most cases it is weighed in inappropriate scales, externally obtained from strange cultures, and the unavoidable result is distortion and discrimination, inclined toward the apologetic or slighting, all depending on the taste and inclination of the critic. Let us take one of the typical features of the Talmudic rule, its famous formalism, the well-known feature which most of the unfriendly critics of the Talmud have protested against incessantly.

What is legal formalism? Does it not mean that the act or circumstance on which the legal result depends is measured and weighed exactly to the breadth of a hair, in measurements and quantities the slightest deviation from which changes the legal result? For instance, a certain quantity of water — forty seah, and not one drop less — qualified the Mikveh [ritual bath] to remove ritual impurity; thirty days, and not "a reasonable period of time," as a modern legislature would have determined, is the time given for payment of a debt where the time for payment was not determined in an agreement; so many and so many cubits — not more and not less — differentiate between "near" and "far," for the purposes of one of the laws relating to lost objects. No legal system in the world is completely free from arbitrarily drawn boundaries, but it is true that there is a great variance in the inclination to do so, whether to coin and cast such molds indulgently or sparsely. The quantitative difference here becomes a qualitative one.

He who is able to read between the lines will find in the Talmud itself a hidden, and perhaps not so hidden, criticism of that very formalistic system. I have in mind Rabbi Jeremiah's famous question in Tractate *Baba Batra.* The issue was whether the finder of a young pigeon in the proximity of a cote, not being able to determine the ownership of the pigeon, is obliged to return it to the owner of the cote, or whether the young pigeon is to be regarded as *res nullius*, so that the finder may keep it for himself. The Mishna[33] says: "A young pigeon [*i.e.*, one incapable of flying] which is found on the ground within fifty cubits of a cote belongs to the owner of the cote; if found beyond fifty cubits from the cote, it belongs to the finder." [34] The reason given for this rule is that "a bird which can only hop does not go farther than fifty cubits." And on this rationale Rabbi Jeremiah raised the question: "If one foot is within fifty cubits and the other beyond, how do we decide?" And the Talmud adds, " 'It was for this that they turned Rabbi Jeremiah out of the academy,' says Rashi: 'Because his question was bothersome.' "

This seems to me to be no mere matter of pestering by asking foolish questions, but a frontal attack, and a very severe one, on legal formalism by *reductio ad absurdum*; but the attack failed. The formal school disregarded it; metaphorically speaking, Rabbi Jeremiah was excluded from the academy. Who was right? It will soon be clear that the question is not so simple as it appears to be and that the answer is not at all easy. Rabbi Jeremiah's question is sharp, but not very convincing. Borderline cases are to be found in abundance in any legal system and cannot be avoided even when the legislator prefers to use the most exact definitions. Rabbi Jeremiah wanted to do away with the external, formal distinction between fifty cubits and more than fifty cubits and substitute for it a more abstract, more elastic measuring yard such as proximity, distance, or a determination in a more general and more abstract way that the finder had to return the young pigeon if, in light of all the circumstances of the case, it may be presumed to belong to the owner of the cote and should not be considered *res nullius*.

But who will decide what is "proximate" and what is "distant," what circumstances are to be considered, and what is the conclusion to be drawn from them? If the matter should come to trial, the judge could, by hearing witnesses and experts, determine the facts of the case and draw from them the most reasonable conclusion. But how is the common citizen, the man in the street, who does not have this whole mechanism at his disposal, to deter-

[33] This was the first compilation of Jewish law, by Rabbi Jehuda the Nassi (d. 219 A.D.). The rules in the Mishna were the basis for discussions by the Amorites (see note 10 *supra*) in later generations. The Talmud consists of the Mishna and the Amoraitic discussion, the Gemara. [Ed.]

[34] *Baba Batra* 23b.

mine the matter? What is he to do in order to decide whether he is obliged to return the young pigeon or not? It might be answered that he does not have to do anything; he may just wait until the other party sues him, and then the matter will be fully clarified through the procedure described above. True, he may do so, but only if his sole concern is that the other person might sue him, and that he will end up having to return what he found and pay the cost of the trial in addition. This is the ordinary problem, confronting the ordinary citizen, in every ordinary state. But what if this is not the case, if the question is from the outset not one of *law* but one of *conscience*, if this particular finder wishes to maintain peace with himself and to know whether he is under the duty of fulfilling the religious-moral precept of returning a lost object? Does not this consideration demand that the legal norm should be less elegant perhaps but clearer, less elastic but more concise, so that the subject to whom the instruction of the law is addressed should be in a position to apply and fulfill it without the continuous intervention of the judge?

This, I believe, is the crucial point. Here the elastic and formalistic approaches part ways and the virtues and faults of each become clearly perceptible. The question is what is to be preferred: precision and clarity, or elasticity and greater adaptability to the concrete situation? These two things are not always compatible, and it is sometimes necessary to choose between them, to forego the one for the sake of the other. If the goal envisioned by the legislator, the ideal toward which he aspires, is not the *post factum* solution of conflict between man and man but the prospective ruling for moral behavior by each individual, then the consideration of precision and clarity prevails, and the inevitable result is legal formalism.

We find a similar though not identical idea in the framework of nonformalistic systems with relation to a certain part of the law, to its penal part. It is a matter of common knowledge that the rules for interpreting the criminal law are different from the procedures used to interpret any other law. The principle of narrow, exact interpretation is applied and the limits of a concept are not expanded beyond the exact, literal meaning of the written word. The use of an a fortiori or any similar way of reasoning is not permissible for the purpose of creating an offense not inscribed in the law. In the Talmud it is said: "punishment is not to be imposed on the basis of a logical derivative from the Law." Since the Law says (with regard to a false witness), "Then shall ye do unto him, as he had thought to have done unto his brother . . . ,"[35] it supplies a legal basis only for punishing a perjurious witness who "thought to have," but had not successfully, done harm, and does not authorize punishing a perjurer who succeeded in obtaining a judgment against his brother. By all the rules of reason the exact opposite should be the law. The principle was formulated in the paradoxical statement: "If they have not killed, they shall be put to death, but if they have killed — they are not put to death." [36]

This principle has been enthusiastically embraced by modern legal systems; *nulla poena sine lege* goes the famous classical maxim, which found its place in all enlightened legal systems. There is no punishment without law and the word "law" here means a written law, an express law, a law which does not have to be expounded and brought to completeness by external processes of reasoning. In Germany, about eighty years ago, a man was accused of having stolen electricity. The act was proved but the man acquitted. The section of the law dealing with stealing used the word "object" (*Sache*), and electricity is not an object, it is a power. It was necessary to enact a new law specifically making the stealing of electricity punishable. What is the rationale behind the rule? There are several, and they are cumulative, and one of them is that the criminal code, addressed primarily to the citizen, laying down his way of behavior, should be formulated in a manner enabling the citizen, the potential offender, to learn from it what is permissible and what prohibited, without having to resort to theories and considerations not expressly stated in the law. Thus it has been said that the criminal code is the offender's Magna Charta, because that which is written — expressly written — in it separates with precision the prohibited from the permissible, and by exhibiting the one it stresses the other.

The same holds true, *cum grano salis* of course, with regard to the question with which we are dealing now. Jewish law in its totality, in its criminal as well as its civil parts, is a legal system addressed primarily to the citizen and not to the judge. The Choshen Mishpat [37] as well as Even Haezar [38] are both "Orach

[35] *Deutoronomy* 19:19.

[36] *Makkoth* 5b.

[37] This part of the Jewish code deals with courts, evidence, contracts, and to a limited extent with criminal law. [Ed.]

[38] This part of the Jewish code deals with family law. [Ed.]

Chayim"[39] commanding the behavior of man in matters regarding relationships between man and man. It is not the right of a person to something which is the determining and determined thing, but the duty of the person under obligation — how and under what conditions he has to fulfill his religious or moral duty toward another. Therefore the measures stated in the law must be fixed and determinate, weighed and precisely evaluated, measures which every ordinary person will be able to use without the necessity of approaching the judge for interpretation.

Here we reach one question which apparently exceeds the framework of this article, but completes it from the ideal point of view, serving as its moral and conclusion. The question is, what about our modern law, how is it integrated with the moral and cultural outlook of the generation? May I say by way of introduction that the answer is not too encouraging. It looks as if the more postliberal humanity proceeds on the paths of its culture and civilization, the more the value of law, as a stabilizer, an educating moral regulator in the individual's life, will diminish. This is not because the activity of the legislator has diminished; on the contrary, it has reached unprecedented heights! Our lives are encompassed by laws from every side and direction. Not a nook exists to which the long heavy hand of the law does not extend. It could almost be said, "there is not a place free from it," and yet it always remains, as it were, on the periphery of life, grafted onto it as an alien branch, not working into the pattern of the usual cultural values of the individual.

I will explain. I have already remarked how difficult it is to interpret the term "Jewish law."[40] This difficulty increases manyfold when we come to determine the circumference of the existing law in any state, even in the most democratic state. It is very difficult for a contemporary to define the limits of the jurisdiction of the law, the *materia* subject to the orders and decrees of the legislator, because — and this is one of the identifying marks of our era — the modern legislator does not recognize any limits to his jurisdiction, except for the geographic borders of his state. I will not be exaggerating if I say that in a modern sovereign state there is not one field of life closed, as a matter of principle, to the long arm of the law and out of its reach. Even the few

[39] This part of the Jewish code deals with prayers, religious holidays, and benedictions, literally, "the way of Life." [Ed.]

[40] See p. 309 *supra*.

limitations which any liberal, decent legislator customarily recognizes, such as nonintervention in matters of religion and conscience, distribution of powers and all its resultants, are only "free" limitations which he accepts willingly, knowingly, with a certain reluctant self-restraint, as though stressing that he could set them aside without formal notice, that they do not constitute a limitation upon his authority, and that he may, if he so wishes, spread his net on those "reserves" as well.

There exists only one limitation on the intervention of the legislator, namely, a lack of interest. It may perhaps be said that this limitation is no limitation at all. It is a tautology. A lack of interest means a lack of will to intervene, and here once more we reach the unqualified statement that the legislator may do whatever he wants to do, with no limitation whatsoever. This is both correct and not correct. The restraint just mentioned is no limit in our day, but it was a limit in the ancient legal systems as in the more modern systems up to the liberal period of the nineteenth century. Every law protects something, corporeal or spiritual, deserving protection in the eyes of the creator of the laws. This is the task and essence of the law. It protects the desired, which has not yet come to the world; it protects the existing, which is subject to some kind of danger; and in every case it tries to establish or strengthen a certain condition of things, which would not have materialized or have been preserved without the intervention of the law. This definition holds true of all fields of the law, from constitutional law to criminal law, to civil law, to all the technical-regulative instructions encompassing the life of a contemporary in our times. A potential "enemy" who may attack and disrupt society's way of life lurks behind every law and every section and instruction in it, be he a murderer bent on killing or an ordinary debtor refusing to pay his debt. For the purpose of removing this social enemy the various laws of the state are promulgated. This is the modern sense of the famous Talmudic saying, "Thou hast created evil inclinations — thou hast created the Law as a medicine." "Evil inclinations" represent all those forces hostile to order and stability in society, and the law as "medicine" is a cure of or prophylaxis against those social diseases.

The protection of certain "property" — corporeal or spiritual — is, then, the main, and it may be said the only, task of the law. But who is to determine what is the individual thing to be protected, and who determines that it is worthy of protection? It is clear that the legislator has the last word. But he does not function in a vacuum, even when he is an absolute dictator. He himself is a product of social causes. Hence, "worthy of protection" means worthy according to the views — political, economic, moral, and cultural — prevailing in that society, or — to be more exact — prevailing in the circle, broad or narrow, which rules the state. And now we have reached the point of weakness. Modern legislation, especially beginning with the period after the First World War, brought with it a tremendous change in the nature and character of the "things" protected. The center of gravity of legislation, particularly in the field of criminal law, was shifted, so to speak, from public to private realms, to what was up to then considered the individual's domain, and the legislator began to include the private activities of the individual within his network. He began setting norms of "thou shalt" and "thou shalt not" with regard to matters which were up to then not included in his ambit of interest, activities and actions which the ordinary citizen did not regard as being of *public* importance at all. The inevitable result was the separation of the law from the general mentality of the people, and its frequent transformation into a "decree" coming from above, which should be accepted — if at all — with a bowing of the head before the supreme power of the state.

I do not mean to say that the new laws are less reasonable than the old ones, that there was less need for them for the purpose of protecting the justified interest of society. There were reasons for the new trends. The foundations of the state, victor or vanquished, were shaken as a result of wars and incessant revolutions; no more was there security for or in the state; a new historic phenomenon, heretofore unimaginable, arose: the existence of an external enemy which does not place itself *ante portes*, but which eats away from afar, as if telepathically, the inner life of the state, using the famous fifth column. In addition, and this is the most important thing, the economic life of the state was disrupted. It did not flow in its ordinary channel, in its traditional and accepted form, but proceeded in leaps and crises, by improvisation, from today to tomorrow, and from tomorrow to the day after, being completely dependent on the changing winds which blow on the outskirts of the state. All these joined in diminishing considerably the specific weight of private interests and in justifying, at least on principle, the intervention of the state in the individual activities of the citizen. But this is the difficulty, since the citizen himself did not grasp the inherent reason of those laws, did not see and perhaps was not able to see their *ratio legis.* The considerations involved were too complicated, their formulation too professional and learned, so that in the end they remained outside the enclosure of his understanding and did not become an integral part of his set of "may" and "may nots," of the concepts of the desired and undesired, of the ordinary citizen.

Let us not underestimate the importance of the understanding of the law or knowledge of the law. As a matter of fact this is one of the presumptions justifying in certain cases punishment of an offender. *Ignorantia juris nocet* is the famous Latin maxim, and perhaps this is what the sages of the Mishna meant when they said, "A mistake in the law is tantamount to willfullness." It does not mean that a person is punished for not having studied the law, but that his ignorance is disregarded; more correctly, his plea of ignorance is disregarded, because there exists something in the nature of a legal presumption that every person knows the prohibitions included in the criminal law. The explanation is that the official legislator in formulating the legal code does not invent prohibitions. He puts a legal stamp on inhibitions and prohibitions at least latently existent in the moral and cultural consciousness of society. He derives inspiration from the citizen and in return educates the citizen. This view requires as a presumption that the criminal code should always be a true replica of an existent philosophy of life, of the ingrained sentiments of the generation. The question is whether modern legislation in all countries of the world still maintains the high standard of that classic philosophy, whether the modern legislator does not neglect the pedagogical task of legislation because of the high degree of technicality of both the ways of life and the formulation of laws, whether he does not give up, knowingly and unknowingly, the injection of the ideas of the laws into the general consciousness of the citizens of the state.

This is in short the *problematique* of law in our day; this is at the root of the "legislative crisis" of the generation. The growth of crime all over the world should to a great extent be regarded as a result of this crisis, the crisis of faith in the law, the crisis of faith in the wisdom and understanding of the legislator. And the lesson from all this is that the law should never be merely a "decree," because "decrees are abolished" our Sages said; decrees are not saturated in the people's spirit; they do not integrate with its philosophy of life. The task facing the legislator — any legislator — is to bring the law closer to the mind (so that the people should understand it), and to bring it closer to the heart (so that the people should want to obey it). If one of the two is lacking, a surrender to the law is perhaps possible, but not its observance. The ideal is "They shall keep my charge," that the citizen should be interested in obeying the law and protecting it as a thing of great value not only from an objective aspect (as a matter of self-interest) but from a subjective aspect (as a matter of will) as well. Therefore, the admonition to study the law was regarded as the first among the precepts: therefore, it did "outweigh all the others." [41]

---

[41] *Peah Mishna* 1; *Kiddushin* 39b. [Ed.]

[9]

AHARON LICHTENSTEIN

Does Jewish Tradition Recognize An Ethic Independent of Halakha?

"DOES THE TRADITION RECOGNIZE AN ETHIC independent of Halakha?" My subject is a simple factual question presumably calling for a yes-or-no answer. But what kind of Jew responds to salient questions with unequivocal monosyllables? Certainly not the traditional kind. Moreover, as formulated, this particular query is a studded minefield, every key term an ill-defined boobytrap. Who or what represents the tradition? Is the recognition de facto or de jure? How radical is the independence? Above all, what are the referents of ethic and Halakha? A qualified reply is obviously required.

Before presenting it in detail, however, I must confess that, at one level, an unequivocal response could be easily mounted. If the issue be reduced to natural morality in general, it need hardly be in doubt. "Rabbi Yohanan stated," says the Gemara in *Erubin*, "'If the Torah had not been given, we would have learnt modesty from the cat, [aversion to] robbery from the ant, chastity from the dove, and [conjugal] manners from the cock.'"[1] The passage implies, first, that a cluster of logically ante-halakhic virtues exists; second, that these can be inferred from natural phenomena; and, probably, third—with Plato and against the Sophists—that these relate to *physis* rather than *nomos*, being not only observable through nature but inherent within it. Nor does the passage stand alone. The wide-ranging concept of *derekh eretz*[2]—roughly the equivalent of what

Coventry Patmore called "the traditions of civility"—points in the same direction. Its importance—again, not as descriptively synonymous with conventional conduct but as prescriptive *lex naturalis*—should not be underestimated. The Mishna cites Rabbi Eliezer b. Azaria's view that "without Torah, there is no *derekh eretz*, and without *derekh eretz*, there is no Torah";[3] and the Midrash goes beyond this dialectical reciprocity, stating that "*derekh eretz* preceded Torah."[4] In context, the primary reference is to chronological priority. Nevertheless, one senses that the common tendency—especially prevalent among the *mussar* masters—to include logical if not axiological precedence as well is a response to clearly present undertones; and, in this sense, the two texts are of course closely related. As the Maharal put it, "From this [i.e., the Mishna], we learn that *derekh eretz* is the basis of Torah which is," as explained by the Midrash, "'the way of the tree of life.'"[5] Their link reinforces our awareness of the Rabbis' recognition of natural morality.

There is, however, little need to adduce proof texts. Even if one assumes that the Rabbis' awareness of natural law as an explicit philosophic and historical doctrine was limited—a point that Baer and Lieberman[6] have debated—this would be, for our purposes, quite irrelevant. Indeed, even if one accepts the thesis, recently advanced by Marvin Fox,[7] that the concept of natural law, in its classical and Thomistic sense, is actually inconsistent with rabbinic and *rishonim*'s thought, our problem is very little affected. The fact remains that the existence of natural morality is clearly assumed in much that is quite central to our tradition. Discussion of theodicy is predicated upon it. As Benjamin Whichcote,[8] the seventeenth-century Cambridge Platonist pointed out, one cannot ask, "Shall, then, the judge of the whole earth not do justice?"[9] unless one assumes the existence of an unlegislated justice to which, as it were, God Himself is bound; and which, one might add, man can at least apprehend sufficiently to ask the question. Or again, any attempt at rationalizing Halakha—an endeavor already found in *Hazal*, although much more fully elaborated by *rishonim*—presupposes an axiological frame of reference, independent of Halakha, in the light of which it can be interpreted. It makes no sense to say, with Abaye, that "the whole of the Torah . . . is for the purpose of promoting peace,"[10] unless the ethical value of peace can be taken for granted. The same holds true with respect to suggesting reasons for specific *mitzvot*. The intensity of Maimonides' efforts on this front is consistent with the position—advanced by Rav Saadia Gaon[11] and, in broad outline, adopted by Rabbenu Bahya[12] and probably by Maimonides[13]—that, given sufficient time, ability, and interest, the bulk of revealed Torah could have been naturally and logically discovered.

Any supposed traditional rejection of *lex naturalis* cannot mean, therefore, that apart from Halakha—or, to put it in broader perspective, that in the absence of divine commandment—man and the world are amoral. Nor does it entail a total relativism or the view (evidently ascribed to Maimonides by Professor Fox[14]) that social convention and/or utility are the sole criteria for action. At most, the Rabbis rejected natural law, not natural morality. They may conceivably have felt one could not ground specific binding and universal rules in nature but they hardly regarded uncommanded man as ethically neutral. They could have accepted, at the natural plane, the position summarized by Whitehead: "There is no one behaviour-system belonging to the essential character of the universe, as the universal moral ideal. What is universal is the spirit which should permeate any behaviour-system in the circumstances of its adoption. . . . Whether we destroy, or whether we preserve, our action is moral if we have thereby safeguarded the importance of experience so far as it depends on that concrete instance in the world's history."[15] But they would surely have gone no further. One might contend, maximally, that natural morality is contextual rather than formal. It does, however, exist.

Inasmuch as the traditional acceptance of some form of natural morality seems to me beyond doubt, I could, were I literally minded, simply answer our original question in the affirmative and close up shop. I presume, however, that its framers had something more in mind. If I read their concern rightly, the issue is not whether the tradition accords a non-halakhic ethic some theoretical standing by acknowledging its universal validity and provenance. Rather, it is whether now that, in *Hazal*'s phrase, "Torah has been given and Halakha innovated,"[16] that standing is of any practical significance to us; whether, for the contemporary Jew, an ethic independent of Halakha can be at all legitimate and relevant at an operative level.

At this plane, the issue resolves itself, in turn, into the problem both historical and analytic, of the relation of the pre- and post-Sinai orders, something akin to the question of the relation of nature and grace that has exercised so much Christian theology. On this score, traditional thought has focused upon two complementary points. The first is that natural morality establishes a standard below which the demands of revelation could not possibly fall. Thus, in proving that the killing of a gentile constitutes proscribed murder (although the Torah at one point speaks of a man killing "his fellow" [Exod. 21:14], i.e., a Jew), the *Mekhilta* explains: "Issi b. Akiba states: Prior to the giving of the Torah, we were enjoined with respect to bloodshed. After the giving of the Torah, instead of [our obligation's] becoming more rigorous [is it conceivable] that it became less so?"[17] Moreover, this limit does not just reflect a general attitude but constitutes a definitive legal principle to be applied to specific situations. "Is there, then, anything," the Gemara asks, "which is permitted to the Jew but prohibited to the Gentile?"[18] And it uses the implicit rhetorical denial to clinch a fine point in the course of intricate discussion.

The second point is most familiarly associated with a statement—frequently quoted and never, to the best of my knowledge, seriously challenged—made by Maimonides in his *Commentary on the Mishna*. Taking his cue from a Mishna in *Hullin* concerning the prohibition against eating the sciatic nerve (*gid hanashe*), he goes on to postulate a general principle: "And pay attention to this great principle conveyed by this *mishna* as it states that it [i.e., the sciatic nerve] was 'proscribed from Sinai.' What you must know is that [as regards] anything from which we abstain or which we do today, we do this solely because of God's commandment, conveyed through Moses, not because God had commanded thus to prophets who had preceded him. For instance . . . we do not circumcise because Abraham circumcised himself and the members of his household but because God commanded us, through Moses, to become circumcised as had Abraham. . . . Take note of their [i.e., the Rabbis'] remark, '613 *mitzvot* were stated to Moses at Sinai'—and all of these are among those *mitzvot*."[19] On this view, although the substance of natural morality may have been incorporated as a floor for a halakhic ethic, it has nevertheless, as a sanction, been effectively superseded.

At another level, however, we are confronted by an issue of far wider scope. The question is not what vestiges of natural morality continue to bind the Jew or to what extent receiving the Torah abrogated any antecedent ethic. It is rather whether, quite apart from ground common to natural and halakhic morality, the demands or guidelines of Halakha are both so definitive and so comprehensive as to preclude the necessity for—and therefore, in a sense, the legitimacy of—any other ethic. In translating my assigned topic into these terms (so strikingly familiar to readers of Hooker's *Ecclesiastical Polity*[20]), I am of course taking two things for granted. I assume, first, that Halakha constitutes—or at least contains—an ethical system. This point has sometimes been challenged—most notably, in our day, by Professor Yeshayahu Leibowitz; but I do not think the challenge, albeit grounded in healthy radical monotheism, can be regarded seriously. The extent to which Halakha as a whole is pervaded by an ethical moment or the degree to which a specific *mitzva* is rooted, if at all, in moral considerations are no doubt debatable. If evidence were necessary, we need only remember conflicting interpretations of the Mishna concerning "he who says, may your mercies encompass the bird's nest"[21] and the attendant controversy[22] over the rationalization of *mitzvot* en bloc. As for the outright rejection of the ethical moment, however, I cannot find such quasi-fideistic voluntarism consonant with the main thrust of the tradition. One might cite numerous primary texts by way of rebuttal but a single verse in Jeremiah should suffice: "But let him that glorieth glory in this, that he understandeth and knoweth Me, for I am the Lord who exercise mercy, justice, and righteousness, in the earth; for these I desire, saith the Lord."[23] The ethical element is presented as the reason for seeking knowledge of God, or, at the very least—if we translate *ki ani* as "that I am" rather than "for I am"[24]—as its content. In either case, the religious and the ethical are here inextricably interwoven; and what holds true of religious knowledge holds equally true of religious, that is, halakhic, action. This fusion is central to the whole rabbinic tradition. From its perspective, the divorce of Halakha from morality not only eviscerates but falsifies it.

Second, I assume that, at most, we can only speak of a complement to Halakha, not of an alternative. Any ethic so independent of Halakha as to obviate or override it, clearly lies beyond our pale. There are of course situations in which ethical factors—the preservation of life, the enhancement of human dignity, the quest for communal or domestic peace, or the mitigation of either anxiety or pain—sanction the breach, by preemptive priority or outright violation, of specific norms. However, these factors are themselves halakhic considerations, in the most technical sense of the term, and their deployment entails no rejection of the system whatsoever. Admittedly, advocates of such rejection are no strangers to Jewish history; but they are hardly our present concern. However elastic the term *tradition* to some, it does have its limits, and antinomianism, which for our purposes includes the rejection of Torah law, lies beyond them. As a prescriptive category, the currently popular notion of *averah lishmah* (idealistic transgression) has no halakhic standing whatsoever.[25]

Essentially, then, the question is whether Halakha is self-sufficient. Its comprehensiveness and self-sufficiency are notions many of us cherish in our more pietistic or publicistic moments. For certain purposes, it would be comfortable if we could accept Professor Kahana's statement "that in Jewish civil law there is no separation of law and morals and that there is no distinction between what the law *is* and what the law *ought* to be."[26] If, however, we equate Halakha with the *din*; if we mean that everything can be looked up, every moral dilemma resolved by reference to code or canon, the notion is both palpably naive and patently false. The *Hazon Ish*, for one—and both his saintliness and his rigorous halakhic commitment are legend—had no such illusions. "Moral duties," he once wrote, "sometimes constitute one corpus with Halakhic rulings, and it is Halakha which defines the proscribed and permitted of ethical thought."[27] Sometimes—but not, evidently, always. There are moments when one must seek independent counsels. Recognition of this element rests upon both textual and practical evidence. In this setting, I presume, little need be said with reference to the latter. Which of us has not, at times, been made painfully aware of the ethical paucity of his legal resources? Who has not found that the fulfillment of explicit halakhic duty could fall well short of exhausting clearly felt moral responsibility? The point to be emphasized, however—although this too, may be obvious—is that the deficiency is not merely the result of silence or ambiguity on the part of the sources. That may of course be a factor, requiring, as it does, recourse to inference and analogy to deal with the multitude of situations that, almost a priori, have not been covered by basic texts. The critical point, however, is that even the full discharge of one's whole formal duty as defined by the *din* often appears palpably insufficient.[28]

Lest this judgment appear excessively severe, let me hasten to add that it is precisely this point that is stressed by the second source of evidence: the textual. "Rav Yohanan said," the Gemara in *Baba Mezia* cites, "'Jerusalem was but destroyed because they [i.e., its inhabitants] judged [in accordance with] Torah law within it.' Well, should they rather have followed the law of the Magians?! Say, rather, because they based their judgments solely upon Torah law and did not act *lifnim mishurat hadin* [i.e., beyond the line of the law]."[29] Nahmanides was even more outspoken. In a celebrated passage, he explains that the general command, "Ye shall be holy" was issued because, the scope of the Torah's injunctions regarding personal conduct notwithstanding, a lustful sybarite could observe them to the letter and yet remain "a scoundrel with Torah license." The same holds true, he continues, with respect to social ethics. Hence, there, too, the Torah has formulated a broad injunction: "And this is the Torah's mode: to detail and [then] to generalize in a similar vein. For after the admonition about the details of civil law and all interpersonal dealings . . . it says generally, 'And thou shalt do the right and the good,' as it includes under this positive commandment justice and accommodation and all *lifnim mishurat hadin* in order to oblige one's fellow."[30] This position is further elaborated in Nahmanides' explication of the phrase, "the right and the good." He suggests, initially, that it may refer to the collective body of specific *mitzvot*, but then presents an alternative:

> And our Rabbis[31] have a fine interpretation of this. They said: "This refers to compromise and *lifnim mishurat hadin*."[32] The intent of this is that, initially,[33] He had said that you should observe the laws and statutes which He had commanded you. Now He says that, with respect to what He has not commanded, you should likewise take heed to do the good and the right in His eyes, for He loves the good and the right. And this is a great matter. For it is impossible to mention in the Torah all of a person's actions toward his neighbors and acquaintances, all of his commercial activity, and all social and political institutions. So after He had mentioned many of them such as, "Thou shalt

> not go about as a tale-bearer," "Thou shalt not take vengeance nor bear any grudge," "Thou shalt not stand idly by the blood of thy fellow," "Thou shalt not curse the deaf," "Thou shalt rise up before age,"[34] and the like, He resumes to say generally that one should do the good and the right in all matters, to the point that there are included in this compromise, *lifnim mishurat hadin*, and [matters] similar to that which they [i.e., the Rabbis] mentioned concerning the law of the abutter[35]—even that which they said, "whose youth had been unblemished,"[36] or, "He converses with people gently,"[37] so that he is regarded as perfect and right in all matters.[38]

These passages contain strong and explicit language and they answer our question plainly enough. Or do they? Just how independent of Halakha is the ethic that ennobles us above the "scoundrel with Torah license?" If we regard *din* and Halakha as coextensive, very independent. If, however, we recognize that Halakha is multiplanar and many dimensional; that, properly conceived, it includes much more than is explicitly required or permitted by specific rules, we shall realize that the ethical moment we are seeking is itself an aspect of Halakha. The demand or, if you will, the impetus for transcending the *din* is itself part of the halakhic corpus. This point emerges quite clearly from the primary rabbinic source for the concept of *lifnim mishurat hadin:*

> "'And thou shalt show them the way'—this is the study of Torah; 'and the action they should take'—good conduct"—these are the words of Rabbi Yehoshua. Rabbi Eleazar of Modi'im says: "'And thou shalt show them'—teach them their life's course; 'the way'—this alludes to visiting the sick; 'they shall walk'—to burying the dead; 'therein'—to exercising kindness; 'and the action'—to *din* proper; 'which they shall do'—to *lifnim mishurat hadin*."[39]

Regardless of whether we accept Rabbi Yehoshua's generalization or Rabbi Eleazar's more specific catalogue, the conjunction of either "good conduct" or *lifnim mishurat hadin* with thoroughly mandatory elements clearly indicates it is no mere option.

The obligatory character of *lifnim mishurat hadin* stands revealed in the verses Nahmanides saw as related to it—"And thou shalt do the right and the good" and "Ye shall be holy." Neither was expressed in the indicative or the optative. With respect to the degree of obligation, however, *rishonim* admittedly held different views. Perhaps the most rigorous was held by one of the Tosafists, Rabbi Isaac of Corbeille. In his *Sefer Mitzvot Katan*, one of the many medieval compendia summarizing and enumerating *mitzvot*, he lists "to act *lifnim mishurat hadin*, as it is written, 'which they shall do' "[40] as one of the 613 commandments; and he goes on to cite the Gemara in *Baba Mezia* 30b as a proof text. Nahmanides did not go quite this far, as he does not classify *lifnim mishurat hadin* as an independent *mitzva*, as binding as *shofar* or *tefillin*. However, he does clearly posit it as a normative duty, incumbent upon—and expected of—every Jew as part of his basic obligation. Failure to implement "the right and the good" would obviously not be regarded as mere insensitivity to music of spiritual spheres. It is villainy—with the Torah's license—but villainy nonetheless.

Maimonides, however, does apparently treat *lifnim mishurat hadin* within a more rarefied context. After presenting his account of the golden mean in the opening chapter of *Hilkhot De'ot*, he concludes: "And the early pietists would incline their traits from the median path toward either extreme. One trait they would incline toward the farther extreme, another toward the nearer; and this is *lifnim mishurat hadin*."[41] On this view, supralegal conduct appears as the hallmark of a small coterie of *hasidim*. Postulated as an aristocratic rather than as a popular ideal, *lifnim mishurat hadin* thus represents a lofty plane whose attainment is a mark of eminence but whose neglect cannot be faulted as reprehensible.

This is, of course, drastically different from Nahmanides and may be construed as indicating—contrary to my earlier statement—that, according to Maimonides, *lifnim mishurat hadin* is purely optional: that it constitutes a kind of supererogatory extra-credit morality rather than an obligation, strictly speaking. Even if the argument is accepted, it would not render *lifnim mishurat hadin* wholly voluntary. It would merely shift it, to use Lon Fuller's[42] distinction, from the "morality of duty" to the "morality of aspiration." But a Jew is also commanded to aspire. More important, however, this point has little impact upon our present broader purposes. The semantics and substance of the term *lifnim mishurat hadin* aside, Maimonides most certainly does not regard character development, ethical sensitivity, or supralegal behavior as non-halakhic, much less as optional, elements. He simply subsumes them under a different halakhic rubric, the demand for *imitatio dei.* "And we are commanded," he writes, "to walk in these median paths, and they are the right and the good paths, as it is written, 'And ye shall walk in His ways.'"[43] The command refers, of course, to the golden mean rather than to *lifnim mishurat hadin,*[44] but we are confronted by the same normative demand for "the right and the good." The difference in terminology and source is significant, and were my present subject *lifnim mishurat hadin* per se I would discuss it in detail. For our purposes, however, Maimonides' and Nahmanides' views point in the same general direction: Halakha itself mandates that we go beyond its legal corpus. Were I to follow Fuller's[45] example and chart a spectrum running from duty to aspiration, I think that, on Maimonides' view, so-called non-halakhic ethics would be a couple of notches higher than for Nahmanides. Even after we have taken due account of the imperative of pursuing "His ways," we are still imbued with a sense of striving for an ideal rather than of satisfying basic demands. Nevertheless, the fundamental similarity remains. The ethic of *imitatio* is not just a lofty ideal but a pressing obligation. The passage previously cited from Maimonides explicitly speaks of our being "commanded" (*u'mezuvim anu*) to pursue the golden mean; and subsequent statements are in a similar vein. Thus, he asserts that Scripture ascribes certain attributes to God "in order to inform

[us] that they are good and right ways and [that] a person is obligated [*hayav*] to guide himself by them and to resemble Him to the best of his ability." Or again, he speaks of the attributes as constituting collectively "the median path which we are obligated [*hayavim*] to pursue."[46] Furthermore, it is noteworthy that in describing this ethic, Maimonides uses the very adjectives fastened upon by Nahmanides: "right and good." It can be safely assumed that, in principle, both recognize the imperative character of supralegal conduct.[47]

This exposition is admittedly partial. It rests upon two assumptions: first, that Maimonides recognizes an elitist ethic of the *hasid*, which though grounded in *din* nevertheless transcends it; second, that even the universal median ethic demands much that has not been specifically legislated and that according to Nahmanides' definition would be subsumed under *lifnim mishurat hadin*. I think both points emerge unequivocally from the account in *Mishneh Torah;* but in the earlier *Shemonah Perakim*[48] we do get a distinctly different impression. There, action *lifnim mishurat hadin* is not described as inherently superior to the golden mean but as a propaedeutic technique for attaining it. As in Aristotle's familiar example of straightening the bent stick,[49] one excess is simply used to correct another, this corresponding to standard medical practice. Second, Maimonides suggests that adherence to *din* proper produces the ideal balance so that deviation in any direction—except when dictated by the need to "cure" the opposite deficiency—becomes not only superfluous but undesirable. The brunt of this argument is directed against asceticism, and the excesses decried by Maimonides all concern material self-denial.[50] However, the list of examples adduced to prove the sufficiency of Torah law includes *mitzvot*, which relate to a whole range of virtues and vices: munificence, anger, arrogance, timidity. The net impact of the passage is therefore clearly to diminish somewhat the role of an independent ethic. Nevertheless, I am inclined to regard the later and fuller exposition in *Hilkhot De'ot* as the more definitive. The difference between

Maimonides and Nahmanides, though significant, does not therefore strike me as radical.

The variety of *rishonim*'s conceptions of a supralegal ethic may be judged from another perspective—in light of a very practical question: Is *lifnim mishurat hadin* actionable?[51] The Gemara records at least one instance in which it was enforced. It tells a story of some porters who had been working for Rabba the son of Rav Huna and who had broken a barrel of wine while handling it. Inasmuch as they had evidently been somewhat negligent, the strict letter of the law would have held them liable for the damage; and since they had been remiss in performing their assigned task, it would have allowed them no pay. By way of guaranteeing restitution, Rabba held onto their clothes—which had apparently been left in his possession—as surety; whereupon

> they came and told Rav [who in turn], told him, "Return their clothes to them." "Is this the *din?*" he asked. "Yes," he answered, "'That thou mayest walk in the way of good men.'" He then returned their clothes, whereupon they said to him, "We are poor, we have labored all day, and [now] we are hungry and left with nothing!" [So] he said to him, "Go and pay their wages!" "Is this the *din?*" he asked. "Yes," he answered, "'And keep the path of the righteous.'"[52]

Moreover, in a similar passage in the Palestinian Talmud,[53] the story is not told with reference to an *amora*—from whom a higher ethical standard could presumably be exacted—but of an ordinary potter. However, the pathetic circumstances as well as the omission of the term *lifnim mishurat hadin*[54] suggest this may have been an isolated instance. In any event, *rishonim* divided on the issue. The Rosh held that "we do not compel to act *lifnim mishurat hadin*";[55] and inferring *de silentio*, I think it is safe to assume this was the prevalent view of the Spanish school. However, a number of Tosafists—notably, Ravya and Ravan[56]—held such action could indeed by compelled. Of course, such a position could not conceivably be held with reference to all supralegal behavior. *Din* has many ethical levels; and so, of necessity, must *lifnim mishurat hadin*. Surpassing laws grounded in, say, the concept that "the Torah has but spoken vis-a-vis the evil inclination"[57] is hardly comparable to transcending those with a powerful moral thrust. Nevertheless, the fact that some *rishonim* held *lifnim mishurat hadin* to be, in principle, actionable, indicates the extent to which it is part of the fabric of Halakha.

The possibility of such compulsion arises in yet another—and possibly surprising—context. *Hazal* states that *kofin al midat Sodom*, "we coerce over a trait of Sodom."[58] As defined by most *rishonim*, the term refers to an inordinate privatism that leaves one preoccupied with personal concerns to the neglect of the concerns of others; a degree of selfishness so intense that it denies the others at no gain to oneself. There need be no actual spite. Simple indifference may suffice. Nor is *midat Sodom*—despite the severity of the term—confined to what popular morality might regard as nastiness or mindless apathy. One view in the Mishna—the definitive view according to most *rishonim*—subsumed under it the attitude that "mine is mine and yours is yours."[59] It thus broadly denotes obsession with one's private preserve and the consequent erection of excessive legal and psychological barriers between person and person.

This posture the Rabbis both condemned and rendered actionable. To the best of my knowledge, however, *Hazal* nowhere explicitly formulated the basis of this *halakha*. I would therefore conjecture that it is most likely subsumed under *lifnim mishurat hadin;* and if this be so, we have here a striking instance of its scope and force. Admittedly, most of us do not instinctively associate the two concepts. However, this is simply another manifestation of our failure to grasp the full range of supralegal obligation. So long as *lifnim mishurat hadin* is regarded as the sphere of supererogatory extracredit morality, it can hardly include rejection of actions so reprehensible as to earn the opprobrium of *midat Sodom*. However, once we appreciate its true scope—from rigorous obligation to supreme idealism—we should have little difficulty with the association.

The Maharal, at any rate, had none—precisely because he emphasized the centrality and force of *lifnim mishurat hadin.* This emphasis was clearly expressed in the course of his discussion of *gemilut hasadim* (loosely translatable as "benevolent action"). "The anitithesis of this trait," he writes, "is [a person] who does not want to do any good toward another, standing upon the *din* and refusing to act *lifnim mishurat hadin.*" This virtual equation of *hesed* and *lifnim mishurat hadin* then becomes the basis for an explanation of the Gemara's comment regarding the destruction of Jerusalem. This was not, the Maharal explains, retributive punishment. It was a natural consequence, as a wholly legalistic community simply cannot exist. Supralegal conduct is the cement of human society. Its absence thus results in disintegration: "Standing upon *din* entails ruin." Likewise, excessive commitment to law invites disaster on a broader scale, for, by correspondence, it both recognizes and enthrones natural law as cosmic sovereign, thus rejecting the providential grace of miracles that deviates from it. Finally, rejection of *lifnim mishurat hadin* is defined as the hallmark of Sodom whose evil, although it issued in corruption, nevertheless was grounded in total fealty to legal nicety: "For this was their nature, to concede nothing, as the Rabbis o.b.m. said, 'Mine is mine and yours is yours—this is the trait of Sodom.' And they have everywhere said, *kofin al midat Sodom.*"[60] Identification of *lifnim mishurat hadin* as the source of such coercion is here fairly explicit; and the conjunction of its denial with the biblical apotheosis of malice reflects the importance that the Maharal attached to supralegal conduct.

This exposition is open to two obvious objections. First, if *lifnim mishurat hadin* is indeed obligatory as an integral aspect of Halakha, in what sense is it supralegal? More specifically, on the Ravya's view, what distinguishes its compulsory elements from *din* proper? Secondly, isn't this exposition mere sham? Having conceded, in effect, the inadequacy of the halakhic ethic, it implicitly recognizes the need for a complement, only to attempt to neutralize this admission by claiming the complement had actually been a part of Halakha all along, so that the fiction of halakhic comprehensiveness could be saved after all. Yet, the upshot of this legerdemain does not differ in substance from the view that the tradition does recognize an ethic independent of Halakha—so why not state this openly?

These are sound objections; but they do not undermine the position I have developed. They only stimulate its more precise definition. As regards the first question, a comment made, interestingly, by the Ravya, points toward the solution. In explaining why Rav Nahman had not compelled the finder of a lost object whose owner had despaired of its recovery to return it—legally, he is free to retain it but the Gemara[61] notes that it is returnable, *lifnim mishurat hadin*—he suggests that, in this instance, "perhaps the finder was poor while the object's owner was well-to-do."[62] Within the framework of *din*, this would of course be a startling distinction. Powerful as is the obligation of the affluent to help the relatively disadvantaged, it is a general responsibility to a group and enforceable only through a third party, the community and its *beth din*. Although many *poskim*[63] regard charity as a legal and collectible debt rather than a mere act of grace, an individual pauper certainly has no right—except with respect to one type of *ma'aser ani* (tithe for the poor)[64]—to seize his more affluent neighbor's property. That such a point could be made with reference to *lifnim mishurat hadin* suggests its crucial distinction from *din*. It is less rigorous not only in the sense of being less exacting with respect to the degree and force of obligation—and there are times, as has been noted, when it can be equally demanding—but in the sense of being more flexible, its duty more readily definable in light of the exigencies of particular circumstances. This has nothing to do with the force of obligation. Once it has been determined that, in a given case, realization of "the right and the good" mandates a particular course, its pursuit may conceivably be as imperative as the performance of a *din*. However, the initial determination of what moral duty requires proceeds along different lines in the respective sphere. *Din* consists of a body of statutes, ultimately rooted in fundamental values but which at the moment of decision confront the individual as a set of rules. It is of course highly differentiated, numerous variables making the relevant rule very much a function of the situation. Yet the basic mode is that of formulating and defining directives to be followed in a *class* of cases—it is precisely the quality of generality that constitutes a rule—and applying them to situations marked by the proper cluster of features. Judgments are essentially grounded in deductive, primarily syllogistic reasoning. Metaphors that speak of laws as controlling or governing a case are therefore perfectly accurate.

Lifnim mishurat hadin by contrast, is the sphere of contextual morality. Its basis for decision is paradoxically both more general and more specific. The formalist is guided by a principle or a rule governing a category of cases defined by *n* number of characteristics. The more sensitive and sophisticated the system, the more individuated the categories. Whatever the degree of specificity, however, the modus operandi is the same: action grows out of the application of class rules to a particular case judged to be an instance of that class or of the interaction of several classes, there being, of course principles to govern seemingly hybrid cases as well. The contextualist, by contrast, will have nothing to do with middle-distance guidelines. He is directed, in theory, at least, only by the most universal and the most local of factors—by a minimal number, perhaps as few as one or two, of ultimate values, on the one hand, and by the unique contours of the situation at hand, on the other. Guided by his polestar(s), the contextualist employs his moral sense (to use an outdated but still useful eighteenth-century term) to evaluate and intuit the best way of eliciting maximal good from the existential predicament confronting him. A nominalist in ethics, he does not merely contend that every case is phenomenologically different. That would be a virtual truism. He argues that the differences are generally so crucial that no meaningful directives can be formulated. Only direct ad hoc judgment, usually—although this is logically a wholly separate question—his own, can serve as an operative basis for decision. Between ultimate value and immediate issue, there can be no other midwife.

It goes without saying that Judaism has rejected contextualism as a self-sufficient ethic. Nevertheless, we should recognize equally that it has embraced it as the modus operandi of large tracts of human experience. These lie in the realm of *lifnim mishurat hadin*. In this area, the halakhic norm is itself situational. It speaks in broad terms: "And thou shalt do the right and the good"; "And thou shalt walk in His ways." The metaphors employed to describe it—"the ways of the good" or "the paths of the righteous"—denote purpose and direction rather than definitively prescribed acts. And the distinction from *din* is, finally, subtly recognized in the third source we have noted: "'And the action'—this is the line of *din;* 'that they shall take'—this is *lifnim mishurat hadin*"—the reified static noun being used in relation to one and the open-ended verb in relation to the other. In observing *din*, the Jew rivets his immediate attention upon the specific command addressed to him. His primary response is to the source of his prescribed act. With respect to *lifnim mishurat hadin*, he is, "looking before and after," concerned with results as much as with origins. His focus is axiological and teleological.

Quite apart from the severity of obligation, therefore, there is a fundamental difference between *din* and *lifnim mishurat hadin*. One, at a more minimal level, imposes fixed objective standards. The demands of the other evolve from a specific situation: and, depending upon the circumstances, may vary with the agent.

This point was clearly recognized by a late *rishon*, author of a fourteenth-century commentary on the *Mishneh Torah*. In explaining why Maimonides both expanded and differentiated the concept of *dina debar mezra*, making it legally enforceable in some cases but only obligatory *ante facto* in others,[65] the *Mag-*

gid Mishneh both echoes Nahmanides and goes beyond him. "The point of *dina debar mezra,*" he comments,

> is that our perfect Torah has laid down [general] principles concerning the development of man's character and his conduct in the world; as, in stating, "Ye shall be holy,"[66] meaning, as they [i.e., the Rabbis] said, "Sanctify yourself with respect to that which is permitted you"[67]—that one should not be swept away by the pursuit of lusts. Likewise, it said "And thou shalt do the right and the good," meaning that one's interpersonal conduct should be good and just. With regard to all this, it would not have been proper to command [about] details. For the Torah's commands apply at all times, in every period, and under all circumstances, whereas man's characteristics and his behavior vary, depending upon the time and the individual. The Rabbis [therefore] set down some relevant details subsumed under these principles, some of which they made [the equivalent of] absolute *din* and others [only] *ante facto* and by way of *hasidut*[68]—all [however] ordained by them. And it is with reference to this that they said, "The words of consorts [i.e., the Rabbis] are more beloved than the wine of Torah, as stated, 'For thy love is better than wine.'"[69]

The *Maggid Mishneh* is certainly not espousing an exclusively relativistic or situational ethic. No conscientious halakhist could even countenance the possibility. He is, rather, defining the character of *dina debar mezra,* specifically, and of "the right and the good," generally; and, beyond this, noting that, from a certain perspective, the greater flexibility and latitude that characterize this class of rabbinic legislation gives it an edge, as it were, over the Torah's absolutely rigorous law. The concluding remark is of considerable interest in its own right. Comparisons aside, however, the passage clearly reveals the respective characters of *din* and *lifnim mishurat hadin.*

The second objection—that I am either playing games or stalking a Trojan horse, and possibly both—can likewise be parried. Whether supralegal behavior is regarded as an aspect of—

and in relation to—Halakha does matter considerably. The difference, moreover, concerns not so much the prestige of Halakha as the substance of that behavior. And this in three respects. First, integration within Halakha helps define the specifics of supralegal conduct. One of its principal modes entails the extension of individual *dinim* by (1) refusal to avail oneself of personal exemptions; (2) disregard of technicalities when they exclude from a law situations that morally and substantively are clearly governed by it; and (3) enlarging the scope of a law by applying it to circumstances beyond its legal pale but nevertheless sufficiently similar to share a specific telos. All three, however, constitute, in effect, the penumbra of *mitzvot*. To this end, relation to a fundamental law, which posits frontiers and points a direction, is obviously essential.

Not all supralegal conduct bears this character, however. It may, alternatively, either fill in a moral lacuna at a lower level—*kofin al midat Sodom* is an excellent example—or, at a higher plane, aspire to attainments discontinuous with any specific practical norm. Even within these nether and upper reaches, however, relation to the overall halakhic system is important both for the definition of general goals and by way of molding orientation, context, and motivation. Even while closing an interstice or reaching for the stars, one does not move in a vacuum. The legal corpus is here, to adapt Ben Jonson's remark about the ancients, more guide than commander; but it is vital nonetheless.

Finally, the halakhic connection is relevant at a third level, when we are concerned with an ethic neither as decisor of specific actions nor as determinant of a field of values but as the polestar of life in its totality. Halakhic commitment orients a Jew's whole being around his relation to God. It is not content with the realization of a number of specific goals but demands personal dedication—and not only dedication but consecration. To the achievement of this end, supralegal conduct is indispensable. Integration of the whole self within a halakhic framework becomes substantive rather than semantic insofar as it is reflected within the full range of personal activity. Reciprocally, however, that conduct is itself stimulated by fundamental halakhic commitment.

Let me emphasize that in speaking of the investiture of an independent ethic with a halakhic mantle, I hold no brief for terminology per se. I would readily concede that we can, if we wish, confine the term *halakha* to *din* and find some other term to cover what lies beyond. Moreover, such limitation would probably be consonant with the use of the term *halakha* by *Hazal.* In classical usage, the term *halakha*—properly lowercase and commonly used without the definite article—generally denotes a specific rule (hence, the frequent appearance of the plural, *halakhot*) or, in broader terms, the body of knowledge comprising Torah law. It does not convey the common contemporary sense in which it is roughly the equivalent of halakhic Judaism—the *unum necessarium* of the Jew committed to tradition, in which, as a commanding presence, magisterial to the point of personification, it is regarded as prescribing a way of life; in which, as with the term *Torah* in *Hazal*, Halakha and its Giver frequently become interchangeable. Hence, we ought not be surprised if we find that *Hazal* did differentiate between *halakhot* and other normative elements. Thus, in commenting upon the verse, "If thou wilt diligently hearken to the voice of the Lord thy God, and wilt do that which is right in His eyes, and wilt give ear to His commandments, and keep all his statutes,"[70] the *Mekhilta* notes:

> "'And wilt do that which is right in His eyes'—these are wonderful *agadot* which hold every one's ear; 'and wilt give ear to His commandments'—these are orders; 'and keep all His statutes' these are *halakhot.*" . . . These are the words of Rabbi Yehoshua. Rabbi Eleazar of Modi'im says . . . "'And wilt do that which is right in His eyes'—this is commercial dealing. [The verse thus] teaches [us] that whoever deals honestly and enjoys good relations with people is regarded as having realized the whole Torah. 'And wilt give ear to His commandments'—these

> are *halakhot* 'and keep all His statutes'—these are [prohibitions concerning] forbidden sexual relations."[71]

This exposition I understand readily and, semantics apart, find fully consistent with the view I have outlined above. At most, it requires that we adjust our customary terminology somewhat and then issue with the thesis that traditional halakhic Judaism demands of the Jew both adherence to Halakha and commitment to an ethical moment that though different from Halakha is nevertheless of a piece with it and in its own way fully imperative.[72] What I reject emphatically is the position that, on the one hand, defines the function and scope of Halakha in terms of the latitude implicit in current usage and yet identifies its content with the more restricted sense of the term. The resulting equation of duty and *din* and the designation of supralegal conduct as purely optional or pietistic is a disservice to Halakha and ethics alike.

In dealing with this subject, I have, in effect, addressed myself both to those who, misconstruing the breadth of its horizons, find the halakhic ethic inadequate, and to those who smugly regard even its narrower confines as sufficient. In doing so, I hope I have presented my thinking clearly. But for those who prefer definitive answers, let me conclude by saying: Does the tradition recognize an ethic independent of Halakha? You define your terms and take your choice.

1. *Erubin* 100b. Soncino translates "we could have learnt," but I think "would" is more accurate. Rabbenu Hananel, it might be noted, has *lamadnu*.

2. In the passage cited from the Gemara in *Erubin*, the term has a rather narrow meaning, referring, in context, to proper conjugal gallantry. Elsewhere, however, it clearly denotes far more, sometimes civility or culture generally. The *Mahzor Vitry*, commenting on *Abot*, 3:17 (ed. Horowitz, p. 517), renders it as *nourriture*, and the Maharal of Prague spells out its latitude quite clearly: "The things that are *derekh eretz* are all ethical matters included in *Abot*, those mentioned in the Talmud, and all other ethical matters. It is that conduct which is right and fitting toward (possibly, "in the eyes of") people; and failure to pursue some of its elements is sinful and a great

transgression" (*Netivot Olam*, "*Netiv Derekh Eretz*," chap. 1). See also N. S. Greenspan, *Mishpat Am Haaretz* (Jerusalem, 1946), pp. 1–5; the references cited in Boaz Cohen, *Law and Tradition in Judaism* (New York, 1959), p. 183n.; and *Encyclopedia Talmudit*, Vol. 7, pp. 672–706. One might add that the flexible range of *derekh eretz* parallels those of curteisie and manners in their Middle English and Elizabethan senses.

3. *Abot*, 3:17. Cf. also ibid., 2:2, and *Tosafot Yeshanim*, *Yoma* 85b, s.v. *teshuva*.

4. *Vayikra Rabba*, 9:3 (*Tzav*); cf. *Tanna Debei Eliyahu Rabba*, chap. 1.

5. *Netivot Olam*, "*Netiv Derekh Eretz*," chap. 1.

6. See Saul Lieberman, "How Much Greek in Jewish Palestine?," in *Biblical and Other Studies*, ed. A. Altmann (Cambridge, Mass., 1963), pp. 128–29.

7. M. Fox, "Maimonides and Aquinas on Natural Law," *Dine' Israel* 3 (1972): 5–27. Cf. also Ralph Lerner, "Natural Law in Albo's *Book of Roots*," in *Ancients and Moderns*, ed. Joseph Cropsey (New York, 1964), pp. 132–44.

8. The statement appears in one of his *Discourses* but the exact reference eludes me at present.

9. Gen. 18:25.

10. *Gittin* 59b. This passage was cited by Maimonides in the concluding lines of *Sefer Zemanim*: "Great is peace as the whole Torah was given in order to promote peace in the world, as it was stated: 'Her ways are the ways of pleasantness and all her paths are peace'" (*MT*, *Hannuka*, 4:14). There may be a shift in focus, however, as Maimonides dwells upon the reason for giving the Torah while the Gemara may conceivably refer to its content and the telos to which its inner logic leads. In either case, Torah is regarded as serving the interests of peace and therefore, presumably, as axiologically ancillary to it. In the *Guide* (III: 27; and cf. III: 52), this nexus is reversed. Peace and social stability are subsumed under the welfare of the body that is merely a condition for attaining man's ultimate perfection via the soul's intellectual apprehension. There is no contradiction, however, as the passage in *Mishneh Torah* probably refers to the specific corpus of revealed Torah and the regimen prescribed by it rather than, as in other contexts, to the full range of spiritual perception.

11. See *Ha'emunot Vehadeot*, "Introduction," sec. vi; and cf. III: iii.

12. See *Hovot Halevavot*, III: i–iii.

13. This point is not explicitly developed in Maimonides' discussions of prophecy, which focus upon its nature rather than upon the need for it. However, it is implicit in the substance and tone of numerous passages concerning the Torah's revelation and dovetails with Maimonides' faith in the spiritual capacity of singular individuals, on the one hand, and his conviction about the average person's indolence, on the other.

14. See Fox, "Maimonides and Aquinas on Natural Law," pp. 15–17.

15. Alfred North Whitehead, *Modes of Thought* (New York, 1938), p. 20.

16. *Shabbat* 135b.

17. *Mishpatim, Massekhta Dinezikin*, iv (ed. Horowitz-Rabin), p. 263.

18. *Hullin* 33a; cf. *Sanhedrin* 59a.

19. *Perush Ha-Mishnayot, Hullin*, 7:6. The talmudic citation is from *Makkot* 23b.

20. See, especially, Book 2.

21. *Berakhot* 5:3 and *Megilla* 4:9.

22. See Maimonides, *Guide*, III:26, III:31, and III:48; Nahmanides' comment on Deut. 22:7; and Maharal, *Tiferet Israel*, chaps. 5–7. See also Yitzhak Heinemann, *Taamei Ha-Mitzvot Besafrut Yisrael* (Jerusalem, 1954), Vol. 1, pp. 46–128.

23. Jer. 9:23.

24. The J.P.S. translation, following A.V., has "that I am," an interpretation implicitly supported by *Ikkarim*, 3:5. However, Radak is closer to "for I am," which I am more inclined to accept. The Septuagint's *hoti* is inconclusive but the Vulgate's *quia* parallels "for." For a discussion of the verse, see Maimonides, *Guide*, III: 54.

25. The term *avera lishma* does, of course, appear in the Gemara that cites a statement by Rabbi Nahman b. Yitzhak that "an *avera lishma* is greater than a *mitzva* performed with an ulterior motive" (*Nazir* 23b and *Horayot* 10b). However, this apparent priority of telos and motivation over formal law has no prescriptive or prospective implications. At most, it means that, after the fact, we can sometimes see that a nominal violation was superior to a licit or even required act; but it gives no license for making the jump. Moreover, in the case at hand—Yael's sexual relations with Sisera—most likely there was no formal violation. Most *rishonim* assume that a woman, inasmuch as she can be regarded as passive during coitus, is not obligated to undergo martyrdom rather than engage in incest or adultery (see *Sanhedrin* 74b). This is true even when she is threatened but not assaulted, as it is the element of willful involvement that defines her sexual participation as a human action. Hence, when motivated by the need to save her people, Yael's relations with Sisera, even though she may have initially seduced him, may very well be regarded as passive and therefore no formal violation whatsoever; see *Tosafot*, *Yebamot* 103a, s.v. *veha* and *Yoma* 82b, s.v. *ma*. The term *avera* refers, then, to an act which is proscribed under ordinary circumstances and yet, its usual sinful character notwithstanding, here becomes superior to a *mitzva*. Likewise, Raba's remark that the verse, "In all thy ways know Him and He will direct thy paths" (Prov. 3:6), is to be understood "even with regard to a matter of *avera*" (*Berakhot* 63a), may refer to acts that are ordinarily forbidden but in certain cases have formal dispensation. See, however, Maimonides, *Shemonah Perakim*, chap. 5.

26. K. Kahana, *The Case for Jewish Civil Law in the Jewish State* (London, 1960), p. 28n (his italics).

27. *Hazon Ish: Emunah Uvitahon* (Jerusalem, 1954), p. 21. The point is

illustrated by a discussion of economic competition, aspects of which are very differently evaluated, depending upon their being regarded as aggressive or defensive; and this, in turn, is a function of legal right. Of course, in such a case, the moral duties include many outright *dinim*. However, the implication of the sentence stands and is clearly accepted in the following chapter, pp. 44–46. Cf., however, p. 49.

28. Many of the leaders of the *mussar* movement, who criticized what they regarded as the ethical shortcomings of their contemporary Torah community, often ascribed many of these failings to the fact that the relevant halakhot had been insufficiently developed. They therefore urged the fuller analysis and exposition of these categories as a remedy; see J. D. Epstein, *Mitzvot Ha-bayit* (New York, 1966), pp. 34–57. I am inclined to think that while such neglect could be a factor in causing the alleged failings, its importance—and the potential for resolution via fuller halakhic exposition—has been exaggerated by the *mussar* movement.

29. *Baba Mezia* 30b.

30. Lev. 19:2.

31. In his edition of Nahmanides' commentary, *Perush Ha-Ramban al Ha-Torah* (Jerusalem, 1960), II, 376n., C. B. Chavel notes that no extant source of this comment is known.

32. Rashi, Deut. 6:18, comments, "This is compromise *lifnim mishurat hadin*." This reading—he is presumably quoting the same source as Nahmanides—narrows the scope of the remark considerably.

33. In the preceding verse, 6:17.

34. The verses cited are from Lev. 19:16, 18, 16, 14, and 32, respectively.

35. A Rabbinic ordinance that requires a seller to give first option to any prospective customer who already owns property adjacent to that to be sold; see *Baba Mezia* 108.

36. *Ta'anit* 16a.

37. *Yoma* 86a.

38. Deut. 6:18.

39. *Mekhilta, Yithro, Massekhta D'Amalek*, ii (ed. Horowitz-Rabin), p. 198. The phrase I have rendered as "their life's course" is *bet hayehem*. Rashi interprets it variously as "the study of Torah" (*Baba Kama* 100a, s.v. *bet*) and as "a trade from which to derive a livelihood" (*Baba Mezia* 30b. s.v. *zeh*).

40. *Semak*, 49.

41. *MT, Hilkhot De'ot*, 1:5.

42. See his *The Morality of Law* (New Haven, 1964), pp. 5–9; cf. also A. D. Lindsay, *The Two Moralities* (London, 1940), passim.

43. *De'ot*, 1:5.

44. Maimonides thus distinguishes here between "the right and the good" and *lifnim mishurat hadin*. Elsewhere, however, he seems to identify them.

See Rabbi M. Krakowski's commentary, *Avodat Hamelekh* (Vilna, 1931), *ad loc.*, and S. Rawidowicz, *Iyyunim Bemahashevet Yisrael* (Jerusalem, 1969), I, 430–31.

45. See Fuller, *The Morality of Law*, pp. 9–13.

46. *De'ot*, 1:6 and 1:7, respectively.

47. See, however, *Avodat Hamelekh, De'ot* 1:5, who expresses some uncertainty on this point.

48. See chap. 4; cf. also *Perush Ha-Mishnayot Abot* 4:4.

49. See *Nic. Eth.*, 1109b.

50. Most involve actual physical deprivation so that the passage largely anticipates *MT, De'ot*, 3:1. However, it also criticizes excessive munificence; cf. *MT, Arakhin* 8:13.

51. There is of course no question about practices such as *dina debar mezia* (i.e., "the law of the abutter") that were instituted by Hazal on the basis of the principle of "the right and the good;" see *Baba Mezia* 108. The question concerns situations that have not been singled out for rabbinic prescription.

52. *Baba Mezia* 83a. The citations are from Prov. 2:20.

53. *P.T., Baba Mezia* 6:6

54. However, Rashi, *ad loc.*, does use the term.

55. *Pesakim, Baba Mezia* 2:7.

56. This view was advanced by the author of the *Mordecai, Baba Mezra*, sec. 327, who cites his predecessors, the Ravan and the Ravya as support, but it is usually associated with the latter and cited in his name by *Hagahot Maimuniyot, Hilkhot Gezela*, 11:3. The Ravya's original text is no longer extant, however. The reference to the Ravan is presumably to *Sefer Ravan* (ed. Ehrenreich), II: 198, but that passage, while it unequivocally states that the finder, in the case in question, is fully obligated to return the lost object, says nothing of juridic coercion. Perhaps the *Mordecai* drew upon another, more explicit source. See also Z. Y. Meltzer, "*Lifnim Mishurath Hadin*," in *Mizkeret: In Memory of Rabbi I. H. Herzog* (Jerusalem, 1962), pp. 310–15.

57. *Kiddushin* 21b.

58. *Ketubot* 103a. For an analysis of this *halakha*, see my "*Leverur kofin al midat Sodom*," in *Hagut Ivrit Be'Amerika*, ed. M. Zohori et al. (Tel Aviv, 1972), Vol. 1, pp. 362–82.

59. *Abot* 5:10

60. *Netivot Olam*, "*Netiv Gemilut Hasadim*," chap. 5.

61. See *Baba Mezia* 24b.

62. Quoted in *Mordecai, Baba Mezia*, sec. 327.

63. See *Ketzot Ha-Hoshen*, 290:3.

64. See *Tosafot, Yebamot* 100a, s.v. *ma'aser* and Maimonides, *Matnot Aniyim*, 1:8.

65. The *halakha* in question concerns criteria for assignment of priorities

among various prospective purchasers, none of whom is an abutter. In such cases, Maimonides states that while "this, too, is included within the good and the right," the priority is not enforceable, "for the Rabbis only commanded regarding this by way of *hasidut*, and it is a virtuous soul which acts thus" (*Shekhenim*, 14:5).

66. Lev. 19:2.

67. *Yebamot* 20a.

68. I know of no satisfactory English equivalent for this term. It suggests a blend of spiritual elevation and refinement with scrupulousness and pietism. Perhaps "saintliness" comes closest, though more in the Jamesian than in the popular sense, of total selflessness or other-worldiness; but that too, has too ethereal a ring.

69. *Shekhenim* 14:5. The concluding talmudic quotation is from *Avoda Zara* 34a, the verse from Cant. 1:3.

70. Exod. 15:26.

71. *Beshalah, Massekhta D'Vayissa*, i (ed. Horowitz-Rabin), pp. 157–58; see also the notes there.

72. This is pointed up by the fact that Nahmanides (Exod. 15:26) quotes Rabbi Eleazar's statement and yet, in the same passage, refers the reader to his subsequent discussions of "the right and the good."

[10]

Can a Religious Law be Immoral?

David Weiss Halivni

Jewish Theological Seminary
New York, N.Y.

It is commonplace to say that whenever a conflict arose between morality and law, the Rabbis of the Talmud resorted to interpretation, interpreting the law out of existence. The assumption being that the Rabbis were aware of the conflict and, siding as they did with morality, they abrogated the offensive law. In short, they favored morality over the law.

If this were so, our present religious predicament would be of less magnitude, for we, too, like the Rabbis of old, could resolve our religious versus moral conflicts in favor of the moral. Unfortunately, the picture is much more complicated. The notion that the Rabbis of the Talmud were aware of a possible conflict between morality and religious law, and consciously resolved in favor of morality, cannot be defended historically. Historically, they gave other reasons for their interpretation. They did not, as we would have expected if the above notion is correct, pose moral problems before they resorted to interpretation. Interpretation usually followed exegetical inconsistencies rather than moral dilemmas. Unless one is willing to say that the loquacious Rabbis hid this important factor from us (an unlikely supposition), one is forced to conclude that, although subconsciously the conflict with morality undoubtedly played a major if not a decisive role in interpretation, consciously they sought, and to their satisfaction found, other reasons. Indeed, the one instance where they allowed the conflict with morality to enter into their consciousness, in the case of ממזרות, the case of a child born out of an illicit relationship, they became so paralyzed that no substantial change of the law was enacted. I am referring to the famous passage in *Leviticus Rabba*, chapter 32, section 8: ושבתי אני ואראה את כל העשוקים דניאל חייטא פתר קרייה בממזרים. והנה דמעת העשוקים, אבותם של אלו עוברי עבירות, ואילן עלוביא מה איכפת להון. כך אביו של זה בא על הערוה, זה מה חטא ומה איכפת לו. ואין לה מנחם אלא מיד עושקיהם כח־מיד סנהדרי גדולה של ישראל שבאה עליהם מכחה של תורה ומרחקתן על שום לא יבא ממזר בקהל ה׳. ואין להם מנחם אמר הקב״ה עלי לנחמן.

> "But I returned and considered all the oppressions" [Eccles. 4:1]—Daniel the Tailor interpreted the verses as applying to bastards. And behold the tears of such as were oppressed—If the parents of these bastards committed transgression, what concern is it of these poor sufferers? So also if this man's father cohabited with a forbidden woman, what sin has he himself committed and what concern is it of his? And they had no comforter but on the side of their oppressors there was power. This means, on the side of Israel's great Sanhedrin which comes to them with the power derived from the Torah and removes them from the fold in virtue of the commandment. "A bastard shall not enter into the assembly of the Lord" [Deut. 23:3]. But they had no comforter, says the Holy One, blessed be He: It shall be my task to comfort them. [Soncino trans.]

I need not mention the recent crisis in Israel concerning the marriageability of a brother and sister who were branded as bastards to impress how little was done to modify this ancient law. I suspect that by declaring bastardy, ממזרות, immoral, causing an open conflict between morality and the law, it closed the possible avenues of adjustment. The point being that even when the Rabbis altered a law, they never abrogated it. They retained *the integrity of the law*. By integrity I mean partial applicability. They did not totally eliminate the law. It still remained valid and pertinent to an extreme and rare situation.[1] That was

1. Cf. B. Talmud *Nazir* 51b: א״ל רב שמואל בר אבא לרב פפא: ואי ס״ד כל הני דקאמר הוי גלגלין, רקב דמטמא היכי משכחת להו? דאשקייה מי דקלים וסכיא נשא ושלקו במי טבריא.

R. Samuel b. Aha said to R. Papa: If now you assume that all these mentioned act as Gilgelin, how can there be corpse-mould which defiles? If he was given to drink water from the well of the palm tree, depilated with nasha and was steeped in the hot springs of Tiberias.

For reasons unknown to us today, the Rabbis in the late Tannaitic period tried to limit the defilement of רקב. By the time of רב פפא—the end of the fourth century—it was practically out of existence. Yet he was not satisfied until he had found at least one instance—

necessary in order not to impugn the *Lawgiver* with a lack of moral sensitivity which may undermine not only this law, but laws in general. Once one has formulated, as in the case of bastardy, ממזרות, the need for changing the law because of moral exigency, any subsequent change will be interpreted as an admission that initially there was no moral sensitivity, imputing to the Lawgiver a defective moral awareness. The Rabbis instinctively shied away from such a formulation.

Instead, they created objections to the law other than moral ones, foreclosing thereby a possible later accusation that their predecessors were morally weak. A case at hand is capital punishment. As is known, some Rabbis of the Mishnah, R. Tarfon and R. Akiba in particular, did away with capital punishment, saying: אלו היינו בסנהדרין לא נהרג אדם מעולם—"Had we been in the Sanhedrin, none would ever have been put to death." They did not say that capital punishment is immoral per se. That would have meant that the Bible too is immoral, for not only does the Bible frequently employ the phrase "he shall surely be put to death." It also reports at least two instances where capital punishment was actually carried out. I am referring to the מקלל and מקושש עצים, the blasphemer of the Name, in Leviticus 24:10–15, and to the stick-gatherer in Numbers 15:32–37. Instead, the Rabbis retained capital punishment in principle but hedged around the carrying out of capital punishment with so many prerequisites that for all practical purposes it became nigh impossible to execute anyone. They particularly insisted on complete proof that the perpetrator, while committing the act, was fully in command of his senses and realized the enormity of his act. This they claimed could be ascertained only if a pre-warning, התראה, was administered to the defendant immediately prior to the committing of the act and the defendant duly acknowledged it by saying על מנת כן—"because of that." Short of that there looms the possibility that the

irrespective of its most impossible occurrence—where the law of רקב may apply. That single instance preserved the integrity of the law.

Similarly, according to Rabbi Eliezer, an early second century Palestinian scholar, the biblical requirement in Exodus 22:2: ואם אין לו ונמכר בגנבתו—"If he has nothing, then he shall be sold for his theft," applies only when the worth of the thief is exactly equal to the value of the theft: היה גנובו כנגד ממכרו נמכר. ואם לאו אינו נמכר (T. B. Kidushin, 18a and Parallels)—a very unlikely occurrence. For all practical purposes, Rabbi Eliezer did away with the biblical requirement to sell a thief into slavery if he could not repay the theft. The law, however, was not abrogated. It was reserved for that rare instance when the sum of his worth equaled exactly the sum of the theft. That was necessary in order to preserve the integrity of the law.

defendant did not know what he was doing. For a person to fulfill all these requirements, he would have to be in a state of mind wanting to commit suicide, which the court should not help him carry out.[2]

By retaining capital punishment in principle, and by not overtly saying that capital punishment is offensive to morality, the Rabbis obliquely tell us that their opposition to capital punishment was not based on moral grounds. (Consciously that is, for subconsciously I am convinced morality was uppermost in their mind.)[3] How could it be morally offensive if the Bible sanctions it? They objected to capital punishment because of lack of confidence in human justice. They were obsessed with an ever-lurking suspicion that most capital punishment cases are frame-ups. They went so far as to declare a unanimous guilty decision as in-

2. I am saying this fully aware that the Babylonian Talmud, *Makkoth* 7a, gives another reason why they did away with capital punishment—they feared דלמא במקום סייף נקב הוה, "maybe the sword only severed an internal lesion." I find our explanation more plausible in light of the fact that the first name in the Talmud associated with the requisite of התראה, pre-warning is ר׳ יוסי, R. Josi, a disciple of R. Akiba whom we quoted above as saying that had he been in the Sanhedrin none would ever have been put to death. Their historical proximity suggests a relationship between the two.

3. I realize the difficulty in stating, let alone in proving, anything that exists only in the subconscious. Nevertheless I believe it best accounts for the rabbis' seeming inconsistency in the use of morality in Halacha. Morality played a role in halachic deliberations as attested by referring to such biblical phrases as ועשית הישר והטוב—"And you shall do what is upright and good" (Deut. 6:18); למען תלך בדרך טובים—"That thou mayest walk in the way of good man" (Prov. 2:20); דרכיה דרכי נועם—"her ways are ways of pleasantness" (Prov. 3:17). Except that it served only to circumscribe the law, delineate it, sometimes even to limit it, but not to abrogate it. Morality was never allowed to assume a course that might lead to a "head-on collision" with a law. The Rabbis could not bring themselves to consciously admit that a divine law could be immoral. The closest they got to it was putting in the mouth of Saul the king a protest on moral grounds against God's command to him to destroy the whole tribe of Amalek including the animals. בשעה שאמר לו הקב״ה לשאול לך והכית את עמלק, אמר ומה נפש אחת אמרה תורה הבא עגלה ערופה, כל הנפשות הללו על אחת כמה וכמה; ואם אדם חטא בהמה מה חטאה ואם גדולים חטאו קטנים מה חטאו. יצאה בת קול ואמרה לו אל תהי צדיק הרבה.—Said Saul: "If on account of one person the Torah said: perform the ceremony of the heifer whose neck is to be broken; how much more consideration ought to be given to these persons! And if a human being sinned, what have the cattle committed; and if the adults have sinned, what have the little ones done?" A divine voice came forth and said: "Be not righteous overmuch" (B. Talmud *Yoma* 22b). In a parallel source in *Ecclesiastes Rabah* 7:16, the version is that God told Saul: אל תהי צדיק הרבה יותר מבוראך—"Don't be more just than your creator!" Since it was a "once upon a time" commandment given to a single person at a particular point in history, it constituted no danger that someone might draw an analogy to existing laws. And even there God clamped down on Saul saying "Don't be more just than your Creator!"

valid. If none of the judges could find something favorable in behalf of the defendant, they reasoned, then the judges must have been prejudiced against him. Death being as irrevocable as it is, and human propensity for error as great as it is, one must be absolutely certain of the defendant's guilt—as in the two cases mentioned above where God was the Judge,[4] or theoretically when the Bible uses the phrase מות יומת—"He shall surely be put to death"—before an actual execution can take place. That is rarely the case (except when an Eichmann is on trial).

In brief, a Divine commandment cannot be branded as immoral. Even *Lex talionis*, עין תחת עין, an eye for an eye, which the Rabbis totally eliminated to the extent that when they thought that R. Eliezer, an early-second-century Palestinian scholar, may have said something to the contrary, they expressed amazement, סלקא דעתך—"is it possible?," even that was not formulated as a moral problem, though subconsciously that was undoubtedly the major cause for its elimination. Morality (our sense of morality) recedes before a Divine commandment.[5] Unless one first satisfies the Divine commandment, as in capital punishment, where it was reduced to a situation where no doubt persisted, or in *Lex talionis*, where the text in the Bible is not specific and lends itself to interpretation,[6] one cannot change a religious law. Invoking morality against it may cause it to become an insoluble dilemma. We are today still plagued by the problem of ממזרות, bastardy. Who knows—had the Rabbis of the Talmud not made it a moral issue some fifteen hundred years ago, it might have been solved long ago. Capital punishment and *Lex talionis* found their solution, but they were never presented by the Rabbis of the Talmud as a moral problem.[7]

4. Cf. B. Talmud *Sanhedrin* 78b: מקלל הוראת שעה היתה. The blasphemer's case was a special case (literally "an instruction of the hour" which cannot be duplicated), and ibid. 80b: מקושש הוראת שעה היתה. The stick gatherer's case was a special case.

5. Cf. Tosefta *Sanhedri* 14.3.

6. Cf. J. J. Finkelstein, "Ammisaduqa's Edict and the Babylonian 'Law Codes,'" *Journal of Cuneiform Studies*, vol. 15 (1961), p. 98–99, and Judah Goldin, "Of Change and Adaptation in Judaism," *History of Religions*, vol. 4 (1964–65), pp. 272–73.

7. Most revealing in this regard is the statement in the B. Talmud (*Sanhedrin* 71a and parallels) by R. Simeon: אמר ר׳ שמעון וכי מפני שאכל זה תרטימר בשר ושתה חצי לוג יין האיטלקי, אביו ואמו מוציאן אותו לסקלו. אלא לא היה ולא עתיד להיות. ולמה נכתב? דרוש וקבל שכר.

> Said R. Simeon: Because one eats a tartamar of meat and drinks a half a log of Italian wine, shall his father and mother have him stoned? But it [the stubborn and rebellious son] never happened and never will happen, why was the law

The above is a précis of a work in progress which will deal with the topic in much greater detail.

written? That you may study it and receive reward. (The latter point is also said about עיר הנידחת, an apostate city.)

On the surface it looks as if R. Simeon was voicing a moral objection to the law of the stubborn and rebellious son. "What has he done to deserve such a severe punishment?" R. Simeon seems to be saying, he only ate a tartamar of meat and drank a half a log of wine. The law is immoral. Yet R. Simeon ends up saying, "Study it and receive reward." One is not being exhorted to study immoral laws, and certainly one doesn't receive a reward for doing so. R. Simeon is not objecting to the law of the stubborn and rebellious son on moral grounds. No law in the Torah is immoral! Theoretically he was confident that the law is moral. Practically, however, he had misgivings and was torn by doubts. Can one be sure that the case before him is an exact replica of the case the Torah is talking about? May not there be differences which can radically alter the outcome of the law? Is eating a tartamar of meat and drinking a half a log of Italian wine all there is to the guilt of a stubborn and rebellious son? There must be more to it, reasoned R. Simeon. But what is that more? Since he was not sure, he did away with the execution of the punishment the Torah meted out to the stubborn and rebellious son but left the law on the statutes in order to impress us with the severity of the sin of stubbornness and rebelliousness, especially of a young person—a lesson that we have to study and for which we will receive reward.

Cf. also the statement by R. Josi the Galilean, quoted in ibid. 72a.

[11]

The Jewish Law Annual, Vol. VII

THE INTERACTION OF MORALITY AND JEWISH LAW*

by

IZHAK ENGLARD**

A meaningful and productive discussion of law and morality has always proven itself an extremely difficult enterprise, given the variety of meanings in which these terms have been employed. It is not only a problem of semantics, which probably could be solved with relative ease, but unfortunately one of basic philosophical and methodological assumptions. The definitional differences are founded upon divergent ideologies which often cannot be bridged. Furthermore, similar problems beset the notion of Judaism and to some degree even the term "interaction" is ambiguous. I shall try to overcome these indeed formidable obstacles to fruitful discussion by stating some of my assumptions.

First the notions of law and morality in general, their relationship and interaction will be treated. Only then shall I proceed to the specific problem concerning Jewish law.

I

Both *law* and *morality* are concerned with establishing rules of human behavior. They actually constitute sets of such rules, normative orders.

The essential difference between a legal and a moral norm resides in the nature of the respective sanction imposed for a violation. Whereas behind a legal rule stands the threat of a predetermined and organized societal sanction (generally physically executed by a State organ), moral sanctions are of a different kind. The notion of *morality*, however, is used in different meanings: in one sense, it denotes what can be called *positive morality*, a set of rules of behavior generally accepted by society. It comprises rules of etiquette, and

* This paper is based on a lecture given in 1976 in the framework of a theological conference in California, U.S.A. A completely revised, updated and fully referenced version is to be published by the Princeton University Press.

** Professor of Law, Hebrew University, Jerusalem.

general standards of human behavior. Very often it is used in relation to sexual behavior. Society enforces its rules of positive morality by imposing a variety of sanctions (ranging from derision to ostracism) but none of them by way of predetermined organized physical force.

In another sense, morality means what can be called personal ethics, a normative order created by the individual for his own behavior. It is the individual's decision on the ideal conduct sanctioned by internal feelings of remorse or gratification.

Formally, every normative system is by its very nature self-sufficient. It possesses all the necessary criteria for evaluating the human behavior with which it is concerned. In other words, a normative order is unitary and exclusive. According to Kelsen's school, the unitary test of validity of the single norm is to be found in the so-called *basic norm*, the fundamental hypothesis of any given normative order.[1] In the United States the basic norm of the legal system would accordingly be the hypothesis that one ought to abide by the provisions of the U.S. Constitution. Thus, no legal norm is valid in the United States which cannot be shown to derive its validity from the same Constitution.

Hence, from a purely normative and formal point of view no interaction is possible between law and morality, both constituting separate and exclusive normative systems.[2] The validity of a specific legal system is completely independent from morality or ethics, and *vice-versa*. In more concrete terms: a law may be considered immoral, but remain valid under its own legal criteria; an act judged moral may nevertheless constitute a violation of the law.

A relationship between law and morality can be created on the normative level only by formal incorporation. A law may refer explicitly to moral rules and standards, but normatively this would signify the transformation of these rules and standards into legal norms by providing them with legal sanctions. Conversely, positive morality or personal ethics may stipulate obedience to a law, not only because of its specific content but merely because of its being law

1 H. Kelsen, *Pure Theory of Law* (Berkeley: University of California Press, 1967).

2 On this problem in general see I. Englard, *Religious Law in the Israel Legal System* (Jerusalem: Harry Sacher Institute for Legislative Research and Comparative Law, 1975).

enacted by society. Thus, in the famous trial of Socrates, the latter considered himself morally bound to submit to judicial decision.[3]

The normative aspect of law and morality is of course not the only possible one. Psychology, sociology, history and other sciences will provide a different vantage point. But all these other outlooks are what can be called *"external"* to the system, whereas the normative one is *internal*, i.e. the system is seen from within. The "validity" and "legitimacy" of the norms must be based on the internal rules of the system itself.

II

Besides the formal distinction between law and morality, there exists another important difference concerning their substance. Morality and Ethics tend to base themselves on the content of normative principles considered "just", "good", "right", "moral", an expression of absolute values. The desirable human behavior in a given concrete situation is the application of these principles. Hence, moral behavior is the one in conformity to the substantive principle. In Kelsen's terminology[4] a moral system in this sense is a *static* normative order, since the validity of every moral rule can be traced back to a permanent substantive principle. For example, from the general principle "love your neighbor as yourself" one could derive rules such as: "do not harm him" or "help him in need", etc. The validity of these specific rules would be tested against the static content of the general principle. Moreover, from the general rule an indefinite number of concrete rules could be deduced.

Systems of positive law on the other hand are essentially of a *dynamic* character, in the sense that the presupposed basic norm does not supply any specific content to the norms constituting the system.

The basic norm determines only the authorization of a norm-creating authority. It is a formal test devoid of substance: one ought to behave according to the commands of the highest norm-creating authority or according to the norms created by custom. In the context of

3 See recently A. D'Amato, "Obligation to Obey the Law: A Study of the Death of Socrates", *Southern California Law Review* 49 (1976), 1079-1108.

4 *Pure Theory of Law, supra* n. 1, at 195-198.

the United States it states as above mentioned: one ought to behave as the Constitution prescribes, i.e., whatever the Constitution prescribes is legally binding. But once given this supreme dynamic principle, the Constitution by its concrete substantive content imposes upon the lower norms, including the laws of Congress, a static principle. Laws which contradict the *tenor* of the Constitution are (declared) void. Thus a supreme dynamic principle can be combined with static principles.

The substance of moral rules raises the fundamental problem of values. We limit ourselves to a simple and simplistic statement of our personal assumptions. There is no way to determine objectively *absolute* values. Neither reason nor nature can establish absolute human values. We do not deny the existence of values, but we consider them of an inherent relative nature.

We prefer therefore to define the problem of morality as one of *moral decision* which is the required value judgment in a given situation.[5] Moral problems are the result of conflicting values, the choice between which is a moral decision. These problems and their resolution demonstrate the relative nature of the values involved. In other words there is no human value which will prevail in all situations. For instance, human life itself, certainly a most important value in any moral system, has to yield in all societies before the country's survival (war) and in most of them before the aims of punishment (death penalty). The act of preferring one value over another, the essence of the moral decision, is therefore a *subjective* value judgment. It is precisely the basic legitimacy of all relevant values that renders in practice the moral decision so difficult. Indeed, very often each of the values involved in the conflict is, when separately considered, legitimate. It is their mutual inconsistency which requires a choice, a rejection of some of them in the given circumstances.

If we consider now the problem of morality and ethics as one of value judgment, of moral decision, the relationship between them and the law receives a further dimension, beyond the formal normative one.

Any specific law is the result of a moral decision made by the legislator. By imposing a certain behavior it necessarily restricts

5 See the excellent discussion in E. Goldman, "Religion, Morality, and Halakha", *De'ot* 20 (1962), 47-61; 21 (1962), 59-72; 22 (1963), 65-76.

the individual's freedom of action, preferring a collective aim over personal autonomy. By requiring obedience to the legislator's will, the law constitutes an institutionalized normative context (value) with a highly standardized solution of a moral problem.[6] In other words, the individual, faced with the problem of how to behave in the situation envisaged by the law, is required to forgo a renewed and independent weighing of the relevant values involved. He is asked to accept the law's solution of the moral problem.

But in reality most legal norms cannot provide a clear-cut solution. The reasons for this uncertainty of the law are manifold and we will mention some of them in discussing the application of Jewish law. It suffices to mention here that as a result, the judge, when applying the rules of law, has to make new moral decisions. This flow of value judgments during the judicial process is the well-known phenomenon of judicial creativity.

In conclusion, the interaction of law and morality, excluded on the pure normative level, is most significant in the legal and judicial process which determines the specific content of a legal norm.

Any actual conflict between legal and moral norms takes place only in the mind of the individual who considers himself initially bound by the two sets of norms. The resolution of this conflict requires individual moral decision, implying preference of one norm over the other and endurance of the rejected norm's sanction.

III

To what extent is our general discussion on the relationship between law and morality relevant to the specific problem of interaction between morality and Jewish Law? The concept of Jewish Law introduces the element of religion. Jewish Law, the *Halakhah*, is a religious law, which means that it assumes a supra-human lawgiver. Furthermore, it threatens the violator of its norms with additional transcendent sanctions which are beyond human control.

From a pure formal normative point of view, Jewish Law is an exclusive and unitary set of rules, exactly like any other normative order. Hence, its normative validity cannot logically be subordinated contemporaneously to another test besides its own basic norm, namely that one has to abide by the precepts of the divine legisla-

6 In Goldman's terminology, *ibid.*, a "closed moral context".

tor.

But this formal answer does not solve the actually experienced problem of the relationship and interaction between Jewish law and morality.

There is the primary and indisputable fact that we often experience a real conflict between positive morality and personal ethics on the one hand and specific religious rules on the other. Even if the norms of social or personal morality cannot claim to be of an absolute nature, we conceive them psychologically as binding or at least desirable in ordering human life.

In the context of Jewish Law this conflict is actually quite common in relation to the discriminatory rules against Gentiles, women, bastards *(mamzerim)* and in connection with the ideas of religious coercion implying a basically intolerant attitude towards non-believers and members of other religions.

This situation creates a deeply felt theological problem. The issue is by no means novel, witness the medieval discussions between rationalists and voluntarists. But it seems that these ancient speculations were of a more theoretical nature. In the modern context the fundamental question of the significance of religious experience and of the aims and functions of religious law is raised. This question is of crucial importance when the individual stands before the dilemma of a religious precept which contradicts his deeply felt own convictions, both norms being conceived as essentially binding. The easy intellectual escape of denying the very possibility of such a conflict does not exist. Hence the solution which presupposes the necessary rationality (morality) of *true* religion - as Kant assumed - is of no avail to the believer who accepts the authentic nature of the specific religious command.[7] In these cases there is a genuine conflict between the moral and religious experience of a person.

Morality as a normative order is necessarily anthropocentric, directed at the fulfillment of human interests. The human being is the end object of all moral rules. In traditional halakhic Judaism, however, the problem clearly requires a theocentric answer. Religion transcends human interest, its ultimate end is not human happiness but service of the Creator. This is probably true in many religions, but the specific Jewish idea is its implementation by

7 See for a criticism of Kant's position towards the religious experience, P. Haezrahi, *The Price of Morality* (London: Allen & Unwin, 1961), ch. 8.

means of detailed rules of behavior of a predominantly legal nature *(Halakhah)*. Service of the Creator is the absolute value in face of which no contrary human value system can be considered legitimate. An extreme formulation of this idea would be that the greater the sacrifice of human values (morality, ethics), the greater the religious significance of obedience to the law. The sacrifice of human values is an act of faith.

An illustration of the idea can be found in the Talmud in relation to King Saul's conduct towards the Amalekites: "When the Holy One, blessed be He, said to Saul: Now go and smite Amalek, he said: If on account of one person the Torah said: Perform the ceremony of the heifer whose neck is to be broken, how much more ought consideration to be given to all these persons. And if human beings sinned, what has the cattle committed; and if the adults have sinned, what have the little ones done? A divine voice came forth and said: Be not righteous overmuch."[8]

The parallel passage in *Midrash Rabbah* adds: "Don't be more just than your Creator."[9]

The basic attitude of modern orthodox Judaism has found its extreme formulation in the influential writings of Y. Leibovitch: "Ethics has only one of two meanings: (1) Ethics is the direction of man's volition according to his perception of the truth of reality - this is the ethic of Socrates, Plato and Aristotle, of the Epicureans and Stoics, especially of the latter, and in modern philosophy - of Spinoza. (2) Ethics is the direction of human volition according to his perception of duty - this is the ethics of Kant and German Idealism. But in the *Shema* prayer it reads *(Num.* 1.39): '... and that ye seek not after your own heart and your own eyes': 'seek not after your own heart' - this is the rejection of Kant; 'seek not after your own eyes' - this is the rejection of Socrates. Hence, there are no moral precepts based on perception of reality or perception of duty: there is only the command of the Creator."[10]

In the same line of reasoning Leibovitch rejects every attempt to base religious precepts on purely utilitarian grounds. In his customary incisive language he stigmatizes the moral approach: "Only one who considers the human being the ultimate end and supreme value,

8 *Yoma* 22b.

9 *Midrash Ḳohelet*, 7.33.

10 *De'ot* 9 (1959),15-22, at 20.

i.e., man in the place of God, can be a moral person."[11]

IV

Even if this direct opposition between the moral and the religious experience may be unexceptionable in principle under the neo-orthodox conception, the inevitable pre-legal and meta-legal dimensions of Jewish religion create a further level of interaction between morality and Jewish law. This relationship does not concern head-on conflicts between personal convictions and *halakhic* precepts, where the latter take absolute precedence. A possible positive interaction relates first to personal motivation in the fulfillment of religious precept. Judaism attaches considerable importance to the mental attitude of the individual abiding by the rule of behavior. He is required to act under the conscious acceptance of the obligatory nature of the precept *qua* religious command. A few Talmudic and rabbinic sources will illustrate this central point. First, the fundamental principle mentioned in the name of R. Hanina: "He who is commanded and does fulfill the law, stands higher than he who is not commanded and fulfills it."[12]

The required motivation is therefore not one of personal conviction but the conscious acceptance of the external character of God's command.

The same idea is articulated in the Midrash in relation to the prohibition of pork: "Don't say: 'I have no desire for it,' but 'I want it, but what can I do, God has ordered it to be prohibited.'[13]

We encounter this idea throughout rabbinic literature. Maimonides denies gentiles who abide by the seven Noahide laws, by virtue of their own reasoned conviction, the status of the "pious"; they have to acknowledge the obligatory character of the rules as *religious laws given on Sinai.* [14]

Further examples can be found in connection with universally accepted rules of behavior, which men tend to base on reason or "natural law." Many Rabbis underline the importance of bestowing on these acts a religious dimension, by accepting the obligatory

11 *Ibid.*

12 *Avoda Zara,* 3a and elsewhere.

13 *Ḳohelet, Ḳedoshim,* 11, 22, in the name of R. Elazar b. Azaria.

14 Maimonides, *Hilkhot Melakhim,* 8:11.

character of the divine command.

The idea is further developed in the classic problem, who is greater, the man who in order to behave well has to overcome his evil inclinations, or the one who by nature is good. It is of no surprise that in principle the former is considered greater in Judaism.[15]

It is true that an identical approach can be found in Kant's concept of moral *duty*. In his view, a man acting "good" out of natural inclination, does not perform a "moral act". But Kant's moral duty relates to an imperative based on human reason, not to a supra-human law.

Finally, the Talmudic distinction of serving God out of fear or out of pure love[16] stresses again the importance of the motivational aspect of human behavior in relation to religious law.

A second area of interaction between religious law and morality is to be found where the strict legal standards established by religious law are considered too permissive. In practice this situation does not constitute a very serious problem, since the possibility of forbearance is a satisfactory solution.

Interestingly, the *Halakhah* itself recognizes various grades of behavior - the requirements of a *Ḥaṣid* (just) are stricter than that of an ordinary man. A series of concepts introduces norms of a moral character (in the sense of being non legally-enforceable, but recommended to the pious). Mention should be made of such Talmudic notions as: "And you shall do what is upright and good (in the sight of the Lord)" *(Deut.* 6:18); "Beyond the strict law";[17] "Standard of Saintliness".[18]

One further, and possibly the most important aspect of interaction relates to the legal and judicial process of religious law.

Given the open texture of the *halakhic* system, a characteristic of all legal systems, moral decisions, in the sense of value judgments,

15 Compare Maimonides, *Shemone Peraḳim*, ch. 6, and see Yaabez, *ad loc.*, who rejects the distinction made by Maimonides between two kinds of prohibitions.

16 On Fear of Heaven, Awe and Love in relation to human conduct, see generally, E.E. Urbach, *The Sages, their Concepts and Beliefs* (Jerusalem: Magnes Press, 1969), ch. 14.

17 *Baba Mezia* 24b, 30b; *Baba Kamma* 99b.

18 *Baba Mezia* 51b-52b, *Shabbat* 120a, *Ḥullin* 130b. See Silberg, *Talmudic Law and Modern State* (New York: Burning Bush Press, 1973), 93-130.

must be made during the judicial and legislative process.

Beyond the inherent flexibility of legal language - which is partly the result of the ambiguity of language in general - the *Halakhah* has evolved principles which can serve as a vehicle for the infusion of human values. A few examples will illustrate the point.

Thus, the talmudic principle of "avoidance of hostility"[19] has been employed *inter alia* to implement norms of positive morality in relation to Gentiles. A similar role is played by the maxim: "Her [Tora's] ways are ways of pleasantness and all her paths are peace" (*Prov.* 3:17)[20] - the notions of pleasantness and peace having clear moral and utilitarian undertones.

Moreover, even if it is assumed that the ultimate and overriding aim of Judaism is "service of the Creator", the welfare of the individual and of society are important - albeit mediate - goal of religious law. They are not conceived as ends in themselves, but their realization is often a prerequisite for the achievement of the ultimate calling.

There can be no doubt that Jewish law has adapted to historical circumstances in order to maintain a proper social framework.

Any external historical assessment of the development of Jewish law will stress the reality of a multitude of moral decisions reflecting then current views and beliefs. But contrary to widespread belief, no normative conclusions can be drawn from the historical fact of legal changes. Historic reality by itself cannot determine or create a rule of behavior. It is the underlying ideology which is able to provide rules of conduct. From an internal halakhic point of view, the problem is one of legitimacy, namely, what are the legitimate considerations which may be taken into account when creating a new norm?

There exists, no doubt, a considerable freedom of choice in legislation and adjudication. The ubiquity of dissent in Rabbinic literature bears witness to the "leeways" of decision. Halakhic Judaism was always well aware of the central place personal value judgments occupy in the judicial process. As a result it has always required the personal commitment of the scholar and judge to the basic

19 *Avoda Zara*, 26a.

20 *Yebamot* 87b.

tenets of religion: the fear of God precedes wisdom.[21]

The legitimating factor of all norm-creating activity is to be found in the ideological assumptions of the individual decider. In *halakhic* Judaism they center around the theocentricity of all human concerns. The decisive element in the human condition is man's position before his Creator.

In conclusion: the basic question cannot be how do moral considerations affect the shaping of Jewish law, nor how does Jewish law respond to new moral problems.

The fundamental issue is normative: *should* current moral considerations affect the shaping of Jewish Law? *Should* Jewish law respond in an affirmative sense to new moral attitudes?

Any attempt to answer these crucial questions puts the believing Jew to his ultimate test. It requires from him to determine his position before the Creator in the light of a binding tradition. He will have to ask himself if his striving for the adaptation of religious law to his personal convictions and feelings of morality is not an act of human conceit and insubordination, manifesting an oblivion to his real position before God. No measure of intellectual knowledge and sophistication can relieve him from seeking an honest and humble answer.

21 *Psalms* 111:10; *E Avot* 3:9. Compare I. Englard, "The Problem of Jewish Law in a Jewish State", *Israel Law Review* 3 (1968), 254-278, at 270.

Part IV
Ethical Concepts in Substantive Law

[12]

MORAL RIGHTS AND DUTIES IN JEWISH LAW

IT is not my object to discuss the relation between law and ethics in terms of Jewish law, nor to compare the relative ethical standards of Jewish law and other legal systems, ancient or modern.

What I wish to present to the general student of jurisprudence, in as lucid a form as I can, is the manner in which the moral or ethical, as distinct from the strictly legal, element is thrown into bold relief in Jewish law as embodied and systematised in the Mishnah, in the Talmud, and in the Rabbinic codes.[1]

In every civilised society governed by a definite legal system there is the consciousness of a certain gap, more or less wide, sometimes existing between the law as actually enforced by the courts and the categoric imperative of ethical duty. The most advanced systems of law and legislation are ever striving to fill this gap, but it is not always found possible or practicable to fill it completely. Owing to certain causes and factors inherent in the law as an agency compelling obedience to duty, it sometimes cannot help falling short of the highest ethical standard. This inevitable shortcoming is tacitly recognised, but, generally speaking, legal codes and rules pass over in silence the ethical aspect when it might be introduced to supplement the law as enforced by the courts. This is regarded as outside of their province. And here Jewish law, to an

[1] The principal sources of Jewish law are: (1) the Pentateuch; (2) the *Mishnah* (third century); (3) the Palestinian Talmud (fourth century); (4) the Babylonian Talmud (sixth century); (5) Maimonides' Code, *Mishne Torah* (1180); (6) Jacob ben Asher's Code, *Tur* (1340); (7) Joseph Caros' Code, *Shulhan Arukh*, (sixteenth century).

appreciable extent, offers an exception. This peculiarity of Jewish law is due, in no small measure, to its specifically religious character. In Judaism what would generally be described as civil law is an integral part of the Jewish religion. It is not, by any means, of so rigid a nature as the religious law in the stricter sense—including, for instance, the law of marriage and divorce—and it admits of a much greater flexibility and elasticity than the latter, but it is none the less part and parcel of the Jewish religion. Jewish law, even in the sense in which the term law is generally understood, is therefore bound to advert to the ethical or higher aspect oftener and with greater emphasis than purely secular legal systems. We must also note this important difference. Other sources of law are chiefly intended for the lawyer and the judge, but Jewish law addresses itself to the people as much as to the judge. It is part of the *Torah*, in the widest signification of that term, and the *Torah* is meant to be read and studied by the entire people of Israel. Its scope is therefore not limited by what the courts, for one reason or other, will or will not enforce, but by what is intrinsically right or wrong. Like any other legal system it cannot sometimes make the law coincide with the ruling of ethics, but, in such instances, it takes care to point out the ruling of the higher law, as it were, which although not invested with the ordinary legal sanctions is none the less binding from the ethical standpoint.

Moral Claims in Jewish and in English Law Compared

English law in its later stages of development presents in the direction of moral claims and obligations, or moral rights and duties, a striking parallelism with Jewish law. It does not, as a rule, for reasons already indicated, expressly concern itself with the ethical standpoint when the actual law necessarily falls short of the latter, but it sometimes recognises a moral claim to the extent of investing it with legal effects. "A perfect right is one which corresponds to a perfect duty; and a perfect duty is a right not only recognised by the law, but enforced."[1] An imperfect right, on the other hand, is one which is recognised by the law, but whose correlative duty is not enforced. Such recognition on the part of the law is, however, of practical legal importance, for it may carry with it legal effects. A leading example of this class of imperfect rights in English law is a debt barred by the Statute of Limitations.[2] No action can be brought for the recovery of the debt, but the debt is not extinct. The law recognises the claim though it will not enforce it. Such an imperfect right "may be good as a ground of defence though not of action."[3] The nearest approach in Jewish law to imperfect rights in this sense is offered by those instances in which the law while dismissing the plaintiff's claim, expressly declares that the defendant is liable under what I may term "the higher law," *dinei shamaim*, or that he ought to satisfy the plaintiff's demand "in order to discharge his duty towards Heaven"—*laseth Yedei Shamaim*. Should the plaintiff take, *even* by force, money or goods of the defendant covering the amount to which he is entitled on moral grounds, he can successfully defend any claim for recovery. According to some authorities all rights coming within the above categories carry with them such legal effects. Others restrict the entailing of legal effects in the sense just indicated to a particular class within those categories.[4] A comparison with English law may not be without interest. "He from whom a chattel is taken wrongfully and detained for six years loses all right to sue the *taker* for its recovery: but he does not cease to be the owner of it." This is one of the examples cited by Salmond of an imperfect right entailing legal effects. If the true owner peaceably retakes the goods after being out of possession for however long a

[1] Salmond, *Jurisprudence*, p. 197. [2] *Ibid.*, p. 198.
[3] *Ibid.*, p. 199. [4] *Hoshen Mishpat*, 28. See Commentaries.

period, he can successfully defend any claim for recovery, but although he has a moral right to the goods, the effect of a recapture by force "seems open to doubt." [1]

The case of an informal contract is another example by which Salmond illustrates the principle attaching legal effects to an imperfect right. "I cannot sue on an informal contract, but if money is paid or goods delivered to me in pursuance of it, I can successfully defend any claim for its recovery." [2] Although there are differences of opinion, one may say that where a contract is binding in the forum of conscience, or, in other words, where its performance is enjoined as a duty "to be discharged towards Heaven," Jewish law would agree with English law where money has been paid or goods delivered in pursuance of that contract.[3]

There are several other aspects under which Jewish law offers interesting parallels with English law in connection with imperfect rights, but an attempt to deal with them would take us beyond the limits of this article.

Principal Types of Moral Duties or Rights emphasised in Jewish Law

A comprehensive review of the entire field of Jewish law enables us to distinguish a certain grading of the ethical standard now and again brought in to supplement or fulfil the law. The tone and emphasis vary within a range beginning at a point very close to enforceable law and ending in the highest degree of virtue. It would be impossible to give within the present compass anything like a complete analysis of the various grades and shades. I shall only try to indicate the leading types. The order which my analysis will follow is based upon the principle that the nearer a moral duty is to legal or enforceable duty, or, in other words, to use Kantian phraseology, the more binding a

[1] Pollock and Wright, *Possession*, p. 114.

[2] Salmond, *Jurisprudence*, p. 199.

[3] See *Kṣoth Haḥoshen* on *Hoshen Mishpat*, 75, and cf. *ibid.*, 209.

duty is from the point of view of the categoric imperative of ethical duty, the lower it ranks in the scale of ethical merit. I am, of course, envisaging the matter from the positive aspect, from the angle of the merit or credit achieved by the performance of the duty. Starting from this premise, I would designate lowest in the scale the type covered by the technical term, *dinei shamaim*, or Judgments of Heaven, to which reference has already been made. This type is exemplified in Jewish law by cases of certain tortious acts of commission or omission, where the plaintiff's claim is dismissed, but where the defendant is at the same time warned by the law that he is liable under a higher law to make due reparation to the aggrieved party. The *locus classicus* is *Baba Kama*, 55b–56a. Numerous examples are cited in the Talmud in illustration of that category, but two will suffice for our purpose. *A* refrained from giving evidence in *B* v. *C*. *B* would probably have succeeded in his claim but for the delinquency of *A*. The circumstances are such that recovery from *C* is not possible. *B* therefore sues *A* for the recovery of the loss indirectly caused by him. *B*'s claim is dismissed, but *A* is informed that the higher law—the *dinei shamaim*—demands that he shall make good *B*'s loss. *A* broke a weak fence and thereby released an animal belonging to *B*, which went out and damaged the property of *C*. *A* is liable under the *dinei shamaim* to pay for the damage. A great many torts committed in an indirect way (*grama b'nizakin*) come within the scope of *dinei shamaim*.

Akin to this type are certain wrongs for which the law provides no remedy, but which it expressly stigmatises as "wicked acts." Thus if *A* was on the point of buying certain property from *B*, the parties having agreed about the price and all other details, the only element required for closing the bargain being the formal mode of transfer, and *C* intervened and bought the property, the law cannot interfere, but it denounces *C* as a wicked person, *rasha'*.[1]

[1] *Kiddushin*, 59a; *Hoshen Mishpat*, section 237.

The later authorities add that it was customary to denounce publicly in the synagogue the perpetrator of such an act as a *rasha'*.[1]

Of a similar character is the severe censure administered by the court in certain civil cases, and which took the form of a fixed formula beginning with the words *mi shepara'*. This censure, to which great prominence attaches in Jewish commercial law, is technically known as *mi shepara'*. In the case of moveables (*metaltelin*), the payment of the price does not, generally speaking, in the absence of certain formal modes, operate a legal transfer. But once the price had been paid and accepted, the transaction was deemed binding in the forum of conscience upon both vendor and vendee, and the party taking advantage of the rule of the law had to submit to an imprecation pronounced by the court invoking divine retribution against the man "who does not stand by his word." Whether a given trade between buyer and seller did, or did not, come within the scope of application of *mi shepara'* was a matter for the decision of the judge.[2]

Of a somewhat lighter nature, perhaps, and therefore of a higher ethical order than a moral duty enjoined in the name of *dinei shamaim*, is a moral claim for which the law demands satisfaction by the defendant "in order that he may be acquitted by Heaven"—*laṣeth yedei shamaim.*[3] To this, too, allusion has already been made. Needless to say, the law does not actually enforce such a claim.

A duty of a higher ethical grade than those hitherto dealt with is one whose non-performance only entails the relatively milder censure of *meḥusar amanah*, *i.e.* lacking in honesty.[4] A mere verbal promise to buy or sell is not binding, but the law takes care in such cases, and under

[1] *Hoshen Mishpat, loc. cit.*

[2] *Baba Mesi'a*, 44a, etc.; *Hoshen Mogpah*, 204, etc.

[3] *Baba Mesi'a*, 37a, etc.; *Hoshen Mishpat*, 365; cf. *Hoshen Mishpat*, 75, 9, and section 76, 1.

[4] *Baba Mesi'a*, 49a.

certain circumstances, even in the case of a promise to give, to point out that failure to keep one's word amounts to a lack of honesty, Another form of censure by the law, and perhaps a shade milder, is the intimation that such and such action "is not pleasing to the sages of Israel." Of this we have an interesting illustration in the case of one who disinherits his children in favour of others. The act is recognised as legally valid, but the above intimation is embodied in the law.[1] Sometimes this is conveyed in a positive form. Thus the *Mishnah* states that he who repays a debt cancelled by the Sabbatical year[2] performs an action which pleases the sages of Israel.[3] One is reminded in this connection of the payment of a debt barred by the Statute of Limitations.

A somewhat analogous note of disapproval, though of a more tenuous character, is the remark made by the law in the case of certain voidable contracts that the plaintiff can only entertain a grievance (*taru'moth*) against the defendant.[4] It is understood that a man of very high character (*a ḥasid*) would do his best in such a case to remove the cause of the grievance.[5]

Jewish law sometimes takes cognisance of a claim or right which the ordinary man would hardly regard as even a moral claim. In such instances the law aims at laying down a line of conduct for those who strive after the highest degree of ethical perfection (*middath hasiduth*).[6] It appears that there existed in early times a species of code or body of rules (*Mishnah*) particularly designed for the guidance of men of piety and virtue (*ḥasidim*) in their commercial or contractual relations with men of the average ethical standard. This would seem to have borne the title of *Mishnath Ḥasidim* the "*Mishnah* of the Pious" or "Virtuous."[7] "The *Mishnah* incorporated in the Talmud

---

1 *Baba Bathra*, 134b.
2 Deuteronomy xv. 1, etc.
3 *Shebii'th*, chap. 10, 9.
4 *Baba Mesi'a*, 75b, etc.
5 *Ibid.*, 52b.
6 E.g. *Baba Mesi'a*, 52b; *Hullin*, 130b.
7 See *Yerushalmi Terumoth*, chap. 8, 4.

exhibits many a trace of that pre-eminently ethico-legal collection. We may perceive an echo of the tendency of that body of teaching exemplifying the "higher law" in the distinction often drawn in the Talmud between the "law," *din*, and that "'which goes beyond the boundaries of the law"—*lifnim mishurath hadin.*[1] It is thus accentuated that the spirit of the law at times demands from man to conform to a loftier norm and standard than that which its letter can enforce. Men to whom the masses looked up for example and leading were, in particular, expected to rise to that higher standard, and failure on their part to do so would be regarded as an actual infringement of the law. The following illustration is of some interest. A noted teacher of the law, Rabbah bar bar Hanah (flourished in the third century), hired labourers to transport a barrel of wine. The men, while not guilty of actual negligence, failed to exercise that care which the law requires from a bailee for pay, and the barrel was broken in the carriage. Rabbah seized their cloaks to cover his loss. The carriers summoned him before Rab (Abba-Arika), the great regenerator of Babylonian Judaism. Rab ordered Rabbah to return the cloaks. In answer to Rabbah, who questioned whether this was the law, Rab said "'Yes,' for it is written 'That thou shalt walk in the way of the good.'" The men hereupon pleaded that they were poor, they had worked a whole day and had earned nothing. "Go then," said Rab to Rabbah, "and pay them their day's wages!" "Is this the law?" Rabbah wondered. "Yes," came the answer, "for it is written, 'And the paths of the just shalt thou keep.'"[2]

Only considerations of practicability prevented, in general, the "higher law" from crystallising into actual enforceable law. But here and there, after some struggle, the spirit of the law, by which the post-Biblical authorities, the scribes (*soferim*) and the rabbis, were as much swayed as the prophets of old, forced its way into the body of forensic law. Thus, to quote a typical example, a pious

[1] E.g. *Baba Kama*, 100a.

[2] *Baba Mesi'a*, 83b.

aspiration to facilitate repentant sinners to return to the path of duty resulted in fixing the law on a point long debated between the two great juristic schools of Shammai and Hillel. Suppose *A* stole a beam from *B*, and made it the support of his house. Can *B* insist upon the return of the beam itself, or must he be satisfied with its value? The school of Shammai held that *A* can be made to restore the beam, although this might entail the ruin of his mansion. The school of Hillel, on the other hand, ruled that the plaintiff can only recover its value, and they grounded this upon the moral duty to facilitate repentant sinners—*takanath hashabim.* A man desirous of returning to the right path might be deterred from giving effect to the promptings of his reawakening conscience, if the law, in a case like this, were to be literally applied. The law was finally fixed in accordance with the Hillelite opinion.[1]

In some instances a moral duty or right virtually coming under what Scripture calls *hesed* (loving-kindness), and the rabbis more often designate by the term *gemiluth ḥasadim,* only obtained full legal recognition at a comparatively late date. The abutter's right of pre-emption is nowhere mentioned in the Mishnah, to say nothing of the Bible, but it became enforceable Jewish law in the later Talmudic period.'[2] From the fact that it does not occur in the Palestinian Talmud it has been inferred that the Jewish judges in Babylonia probably derived the right from some custom of the new Persian Kingdom. But there is nothing to warrant the inference. The silence of the Palestinian Talmud is of no consequence. For the greater part during the period which stretches between the revolt of Bar-Cochba and the final redaction of the Palestinian Talmud the Jewish Courts in Palestine were deprived by the Roman power of their jurisdiction.[3] In Babylonia, on the other hand, the

---

[1] Gittin, 55a, etc. [2] *Baba Mesi'a,* 108a; *Hoshen Mishpat,* 175.

[3] See *Codex Theodosianus,* 11, 11, 10; *Corpus Juris. Codex Justinianus,* vol. xi., liber 1, lx. 8. See *Yerushalmi,* Sanhedrin, chap. i. 1. Jewish courts functioned, of course, in Palestine despite the lack of Government recognition. Under

Jewish Courts were invested with full powers by the State government. It was, therefore, natural for Jewish law to attain a much higher stage of development in Babylonia. The right of redemption by the debtor of landed property juridically forfeited to his creditor is another example of this kind.[1] In such instances the rabbis usually quote as their authority the Pentateuchal injunction, "Thou shalt do that which is right and good in the eyes of the Lord" (Deuteronomy vi. 18).

The way in which the ancient masters amplified and developed the Pentateuchal law offers in many respects an interesting parallel to the development of Equity in English law. But this is a subject with which I hope to deal (*D.V.*) somewhat fully on another occasion.

On the whole, we can see that the spirit of modern legislation at its best, seeking to bring the law as much as possible into line with the highest ethical norms, already presided over the growth and development of Jewish law, of that law which alone, among all the other early legal systems, embodied charity and benevolence to the poor and the needy—Poor Law—in its code, and which alone, among all the other early legal systems, commanded, "Love thy neighbour as thyself" and "Love the stranger as thyself" (Leviticus xix. 19 and 33–34).

NOTE.

In my reference to "informal contracts" I have followed Salmond, but I really fail to see what connection this has with imperfect rights in the sense defined by Salmond. Under the Statute of Frauds a partial delivery of goods with reference to the contract of sale as a whole raises an informal contract into a valid contract, or, rather, proves the contract.[2]

---

the Patriarchate of Rabbi Judah Hanasi (third century) the Jews in Palestine would seem to have enjoyed a considerable measure of legal autonomy, *cf.* also Origen, *Epistola ad Africanum*, 14.

[1] *Baba Mesi'a*, 35a; *Hoshen Mishpat*, 103, 9.

[2] Pollock, *Possession in the Common Law*, p. 75.

Before the modern Statute of Limitations one might perhaps speak of the imperfect right of the owner who had been dispossessed for twenty years. His right would revive if he came into possession again. But this would appear to have been altered by the Statute of Limitations, though, in a certain measure, it is still the rule in the case of chattels.[1]

Rabbi Isaac Herzog.

[1] Pollock, *Possession in the Common Law*, p. 99.

[13]

JEWISH LAW AND THE ABUSE OF RIGHTS*

*By Aaron Kirschenbaum***

> "The possibility that a legal right may be exercised with impunity in a spirit of malevolence or selfishness is one of the unsatisfactory features of our law... A rule of law should not be transformed into an instrument for the gratification of private spite or the promotion of chicanery",
> wrote a professor of English law in 1933.[1]

Let us ennumerate some examples illustrating the abuse of rights.[2]

1. A erects a structure on his property which has no purpose other than to annoy his neighbour B (see below re "spite fences").
2. A's tree produces branches that extend over into B's property. B enjoys the shade thereby produced. A cuts off the branches and throws them away.
3. A has a plot of land of which he makes no use: neither to cultivate nor to rent nor to build thereon. He refuses to allow B passage.
4. A seeks a court order to restrain B from harmless, non-sustained and inobtrusive trespass.
5. A possesses a right of way which is of great advantage to B and of insignificant value to C. A prefers to sell to C in order to wreak revenge upon B.
6. A owns a plot of land and refuses to renew B's lease thereon for reasons of revenge or caprice; there are no other customers.
7. A destroys produce, water or natural resources needed by others.

* The abbreviations used in the notes to this article are as follows:
B. — Babylonian Talmud; b — ben (son of); E.H. — Even Ha-ezer;
H.M. — Hoshen Mishpat; M. — Mishnah; P. — Palestinian Talmud;
R. — Rabbi; T. — Tosefta.
Unless otherwise indicated, all sources are cited from standard editions.

** Ph.D.; D.H.L.; Professor of Jurisprudence and Jewish Law, Tel Aviv University.

1. H.C. Gutteridge, "Abuse of Right", 5 *Cambridge L.J.* (1933-1935) 22-32.
2. Based upon: A. Rozen-Zvi, "Abuse of Rights in Immovable Property", 4 *Iyunei Mishpat* (1975, Hebrew) 653-654.

In the course of expressing his criticism of the decision of Anglo-American courts in this area, Professor Gutteridge makes the following remarks:

> The absolutist view of right which is a feature of the Common Law was summed up by Lord Macnaghten in trenchant language when he said in *Mayor of Bradford v. Pickles*[3] that although Mr. Pickles' conduct in wilfully depriving his fellow townsmen of part of their water supply might be "shocking to a moral philosopher", there was nothing in the law of England which could stop him from being as "churlish, selfish and grasping" as it was possible for a man to be. In other words, our law has not hesitated to place the seal of its approval upon a theory of the extent of individual rights which can only be described as the consecration of the spirit of unrestricted egoism.[4]

Roman law, or at least some of the Roman jurists, may have recognized the possibility that a right might be abused. Thus, a person intercepting underground water would be liable if the purpose of his action was to injure his neighbour.[5] Similarly, having bought land which did not belong to the vendor, the *bona fide* purchaser, who must now remove himself, is entitled to fair compensation for improvements he made on the land. The jurists then proceed to make the following remarks regarding the opposite possibility:

> However, we lay down that if the owner is prepared to give you an amount equivalent to whatever you, the possessor, would have in your hands if you took away the things referred to, he shall be allowed to do so; and you are not to be at liberty to act spitefully;[6] you might, for instance, be disposed to scrape off plaster which you had put on, or efface pictures, though this should serve no object but that of giving annoyance.[7]

These, however, are isolated instances. Citing the absolutist doctrine, "No one who is exercising his right is regarded as acting wrongfully",[8] [9]

3. [1895] A.C. 587, at 600; *see* text below at n. 43.
4. Gutteridge, *ibid.*
5. Ulpian, D. 39.3.1.12, citing Marcellus: *si non animo vicini nocendi.*
6. *Neque malitiis est indulgendum.*
7. Celsus, D. 6.1.38.
8. *dolo facere,* doing something fraudulently.
9. Gaius, D. 50.17.55: *Nullus videtur dolo facere qui suo iure utitur.* Cf. Wills J. in *Allen v. Flood* [1898] A.C. 1, at 46: "Any right given by contract may be exercised against the giver by the person to whom it is granted, no matter how wicked, cruel or mean the motive may be which determines the enforcement of

Professor Gutteridge declares that the Roman law possessed no general theory of the abuse of right.[10]

English law continues to follow the principle that a person can do with his property whatever he wishes. There have been, however, isolated decisions in nuisance cases which have prevented the unsocial use of one's right to private property. In America, the well-known problem of "spite fences", where a farmer builds a fence maliciously, i.e. for the sole purpose of annoying, punishing or taking revenge upon his neighbour, has evoked a positive response from the courts; and the farmer is restrained from doing so in the great majority of jurisdictions. Continental legal systems, such as the French, German and Swiss, make the abuse of property rights a good defence where the predominant objective of the exercise of the right has been chicanery or the intent to do injury to another party.[11]

What is the position of Jewish law regarding the problem of abuse of rights? Emanating from a radically different universe of discourse, Jewish legal literature nevertheless yields some surprisingly positive results. Since, however, the problematics, concepts and terminology are strange to Western ears, we find it necessary to expound upon the subject in a manner emphasizing pedagogic clarity.

Deuteronomy 25:5-10 requires a man to take to wife his brother's widow if his brother died childless. The union is referred to as *yibbum*, "levirate marriage" (*levir*, Latin, "brother-in-law"). If he refuses to do so, he must submit to the ceremony of *halizah*, "the drawing-off" of the shoe. The purpose of the *halizah* ceremony is ostensibly to subject the recalcitrant brother to public humiliation.[12] Its legal effect, however, is to release the woman from her bond to the family of her deceased husband and to permit her to remarry. A woman who has received *halizah* is free to marry anyone except a priest (*kohen*); this prohibition is based upon the talmudic interpretation of Leviticus 21:7.

If a man died childless leaving a number of widows, the *halizah*

the right. It is hardly too much to say that some of the most cruel things that come under the notice of a judge are mere exercises of a right given by contract"; Gutteridge, *ibid.*, 22, n. 2.

10. Gutteridge, *ibid.*, 31-32.

11. Gutteridge, *ibid.*; W. Friedmann, *Law in Changing Society* (Berkeley, 1959) 76-7

12. It should be noted that *Yibbum* is the biblical form of adoption, whereby some form of continuity for childless people was provided for. The public humiliation of a surviving brother "that doth not build up his brother's house" should be understood accordingly.

ceremony of one of them releases them all. In this connection, a *mishnah* declares:

> If one of the widows was eligible [for marriage with a priest] and the other [*e.g.*, having once been divorced] is ineligible; if the brother-in-law submitted to *halizah*, it must be from her that was ineligible.[13]

The Babylonian Talmud[14] reports that when Rabbi Judah the Prince (*ca.* 200 C.E.) taught this *mishnah*, he decared in explanation:

> One may not throw away the waters of one's well when others are in need of them.

In other words, why perform a *halizah* ceremony with the widow who would otherwise be eligible to marry a *kohen*, disqualifying her to do so henceforth and forever more, when the same thing could be accomplished by performing the ceremony with the other widow who in any event is already disqualified from ever marrying a *kohen?*

But what is there in the law to prevent a person from abusing his right of ownership and from throwing away the waters of his well which others need? Apparently none. Rabbi Judah's declaration bears all the marking of a moral, not a legal admonition.

Yet the Palestinian Talmud[15] finds that the *mishnah's* moral exhortation as to which widow the brother-in-law was to submit to *halizah* should influence court practice.

> Shall we create a fiction? [Commentary: If the brother-in-law expresses the intention of performing the *halizah* ceremony with the widow who would otherwise be eligible to marry a *kohen*, may the court deceive him by fabricating a legal prohibition to prevent him from doing so?]
>
> Did not Rabbi Tarphon, the father of all Israel, act on the basis of a fiction when he married three hundred women in a famine year for the purpose of feeding them *terumah?*[16] [Commentary: So, too, in our case, it should be permitted to act on the basis

13. M. Yevamot 4:11.
14. B. Yevamot 44a. R. Joseph the *Amora* is the reporter.
15. P. Yevamot 4:12, on the basis of the interpretation of *Korban-Ha-edah*. Other commentaries offer alternative interpretations of the passage.
16. R. Tarphon (2nd cent. C.E.) was a priest (*kohen*) and the law permits a *kohen's* wife to partake of *terumah*, sanctified food, otherwise forbidden to the laity.

> of a fiction, so that the widow should not be deprived of the potential right of eating *terumah*, as the possible wife of a *kohen*]...
>
> R. Judan of the school of R. Ishmael [or, R. Judan said that the school of R. Ishmael] actually did so [i.e. fabricated the prohibition and deceived a brother-in-law, so that he should perform the *halizah* ceremony with the widow who was ineligible to marry a *kohen* and not with the other widow of the deceased who was eligible to marry a *kohen*].

But whereas the school of R. Ishmael resorted to a strategem, and the Palestinian *Amoraim* would do so as well, in order to prevent the abuse of the right of *halizah*, there is medieval precedent for the employment of *coercive* measures to prevent such abuse. R. Meir Todros Halevi Abulafia ruled that a brother-in-law may actually be compelled to perform the *halizah* ceremony with the widow who is already ineligible to marry a *kohen* rather than with her eligible co-wife. Anyone violating the court's directive to do so was to be placed under the ban of excommunication. Nay more. If he had been forewarned accordingly, he could be put to the lash.[17]

Rabbi Meir Halevi's ruling was accepted as the definitive law by the latter day authorities.[18]

We thus have arrived at a clear instance wherein the *halakhah* legislates against the abuse of one's rights, in this case the right to choose which sister-in-law should undergo the *halizah* ceremony. Does this indicate that Jewish law recognises a general legally enforceable prohibition of the abuse of rights? We are inclined to think so. In order to expound the basis of this opinion, we propose to analyze the very prohibition cited by Rabbi Judah the Prince in explanation of the *mishnah* regarding *halizah*.

> One may not throw away the water of one's well when others are in need of them.

What is there in the law to prevent someone from throwing away the waters of his well? At first blush, we would assume from the general silence of the sources that there is no generalized restriction of the abuse of rights. We could argue in behalf of this first impression on the basis of the general rule that

17. *Bet Yosef* E.H. 161, citing *Rabbenu* Yeroham as the reporter of R. Meir Halevi's ruling.

18. *E.g., Turei Zahav, Bet Shmuel, Arukh Hashulhan, ad* Even Ha-ezer 161:2.

> something that may be used by its "owner" neither for food nor for any other useful purpose (indeed, its "owner" does not retain even the discretionary decision as to its disposition) may not be viewed as his property. Thus, our teachers have taught that if one takes upon himself a vow whereby he renders [*e.g.*] a loaf of bread [totally] forbidden to himself, anyone who takes it from him has not committed an act of theft; for he has deprived the "owner" of nothing since the latter could do nothing with it – neither eat it, nor sell it, nor give it away as a gift...[19]

The thrust of this rule is that there is a point at which ownership becomes so tenuous that the law removes the restrictions of theft with which it ordinarily protects private property. Similar is the case where an owner treats his property in a manner which indicates the abdication of ownership, *i.e.* when he deliberately or knowingly leaves it in a place where he is most likely to lose it (*avedah mida'at*, "intentional loss"). Such property is treated as *hefker*, property whose ownership has been officially renounced by its owner; and it is no longer forbidden for anyone to appropriate it.[20]

But the thrust of this general view of *hefker*-property carries with it no limitation on the owner's treatment of the property, no restriction regarding the abuse of his rights in the property. In other words, the waters he is spilling out may be permitted to anyone who wishes to take them – the laws of theft no longer apply to them – but there is nothing in the rules of *hefker* to prevent the owner from spilling them out in the first place.

Although it would appear that the owner of the well could not be restrained by a general theoretic interdiction against abuse of rights, he could and would be prevented from throwing the waters away by a specific practical prohibition known as *bal tash-hit* ("Thou shalt not destroy"). Basing itself upon the scriptural injunction against destroying the fruitbearing trees of the enemy in a besieged town,[21] Jewish law in its developed form extended the prohibition to the unjustifiable destruction of anything that could be put to constructive use, widened the application from a time and place of war to all times and all places,

19. R. Joseph Habiba, *Nimmukei Yosef*, Nedarim 85a, *s.v.* "*shanei terumah*"; *cf.* R. Nissim b. Reuben Gerondi *(Ran) ibid.*
20. *Cf. Talmudic Encyclopedia* (Hebrew), *s.v.* "hefker" and "avedah mi-da'at".
21. Deuteronomy 20:19-20.

and incorporated the interdict as a criminal one subjecting the violator to corporal punishment.[22]

We have thus arrived at a source of law, *bal tash-hit*, whereby the courts could prevent someone from spilling out the waters of his well when others are in need of them.[23] But following this line of interpretation, the reference made by R. Judah the Prince to the throwing away of waters in explanation of the restriction placed upon the brother of the deceased in performing the *halizah* ceremony would be somewhat inaccurate, for the latter is clearly motivated by intolerance toward the abuse of one's rights, whereas the former appears to be forbidden under the *bal tash-hit* clause.

Thus, although both limitations are of rabbinic (*derabbanan*) and not biblical (*de'oraita*) force,[24] the limitation placed on the brother-in-law (disregarding for the moment the medieval innovation of R. Meir Halevi Abulafia) was essentially unenforceable — and last resort could be had to a stratagem invented by the school of R. Ishmael and adopted by the Palestinian Talmud. The limitation placed upon the owner of a well, on the other hand, was enforceable in the same manner that all rabbinic interdicts were enforced; any citizen showing the need he had for the waters could prevent the owner from destroying them.[25] The latter, however, could be commanded to desist not because of any generalized rule concerning abuse of rights, but because of the transgression of the specific *bal tash-hit* law.

It is at this point that we can appreciate the development in Jewish legal thinking, a product of certain medieval rabbinic authorities, which led to a generalized view regarding the abuse of rights.

The first of these authorities whom we have been able to discover was R. Menahem b. Solomon Meiri (1249—1316) of the Provence; the second was R. Simeon b. Zemah Duran (1361—1444) of Algiers.

R. Menahem Meiri takes the analogy made by Rabbi Judah the Prince between the restriction on the *halizah* ceremony and the restriction on spilling out one's well water seriously. If the former represents

22. The various talmudic passages relevant to this matter are summarized in Maimonides *Judges*, "Kings" 6:8-9. Full details may be found in *Talmudic Encyclopedia* (Hebrew), *s.v.* "bal tash-hit".
23. R. Moses Coucy, *Semag*, Neg. Comm. 229.
24. Maimonides, *supra* n. 22 at 6:10.
25. Cf. R. David Zvi Hoffman, *Melamed Le'ho'il* (Frankfurt A.M., 1926; reprinted: New York, 1954), II, 148.

legislation against abuse of rights, so does the latter. For us, his language is of even greater significance.

> ...If he wishes to perform the *halizah* ceremony, he should perform it with the widow who is already disqualified from marrying a *kohen*.
>
> On the basis of this ruling, it has been declared that one may not throw away the waters of one's well when others are in need of them, for in such cases *we coerce people not to act in a Sodomite manner.* If he wishes to throw them away, we prevent him from doing so.[26]

The italicized words, "We coerce people not to act in a Sodomite manner", are the translation of a talmudic dictum, *Kofin al middat Sodom*,[27] which R. Meiri is citing as the theoretic basis for the very rabbinic restrictions we are examining. What is meant by behaviour "in a Sodomite manner"?

A passage in the talmudic tractate known as *The Ethics of the Fathers* reads as follows:

> There are four types of men. One who says, "Mine is mine and thine is thine" — this is the average person. Some say: This is the Sodomite manner (*middat Sodom*). "Mine is thine, and thine is mine" — the boor. "Mine is thine, and thine is thine" — the saintly person (*hassid*). "Mine is mine, and thine is mine" —the wicked.[28]

The second opinion, the condemnatory one, regarding the "Mine is mine, and thine is thine" mentality, saw in it more than a summary of the right to private property and private living — values which, in and of themselves, are certainly acceptable to the author of the second opinion. After all, Sodom[29] was no band of outlaws — neither bandits nor cavemen. Seeking to explain the existence of a city, an organized body politic, that was inherently wicked and corrupt, the author of the second opinion saw in the "Mine is mine, and thine is thine" attitude the seeds of a civic state of mind inordinately obsessed with a privatism that left its citizenry preoccupied with personal concerns to the neglect

26. *Bet Ha-behirah*, Yevamot 44a; italics added. The same position is taken by R. Simeon b. Zemah Duran, *Tashbez IV*: 1, resp. 27.
27. Hereinafter referred to as "The *Kofin* rule".
28. M. Avot 5:10.
29. Cf. Genesis 19:13 and Ezekiel 16:45-56.

of the concern of others. Nay more, he saw the roots of Sodomite society in a degree of selfishness so intense that citizens could, in theory, suffer no one's gain, not even when accomplished through no loss of their own (*zeh neheneh ve-zeh lo hasser*). Grounded in fealty to legal nicety, the Sodomite character of "Mine is mine..." broadly denotes obsession with one's private preserve and the consequent erection of excessive legal and psychological barriers between person and person – the necessary prerequisite for the systematic cultivation of barbarism.[30]

Rashi,[31] the classical commentator of the Middle Ages, summarizes "the Sodomite manner" succinctly: It is the refusal to benefit one's fellow even when one incurs no loss thereby.

The psychological inability or deliberate refusal of a citizen to allow his fellow to derive some benefit or advantage from him or from his property – despite the fact that the citizen himself incurs no loss thereby – is regarded in Judaism as reprehensible and morally defective. The citizen may actually be coerced into allowing his fellow to enjoy the advantage free of charge. Thus,

> If one takes residence in another's courtyard without his knowledge, the rule is that if the courtyard is not usually rented, the tenant need not pay the owner any rent even though he does usually rent a place for himself. For one has benefited without the other having lost anything (*zeh neheneh ve-zeh lo hasser*).[32] [33]

Indeed, the insistence upon one's rights where one has suffered neither harm nor disadvantage is viewed as inordinate and unseemly, and is branded as "Sodomite" in character. A person who is denied a possible benefit because of a citizen's Sodomite behaviour is afforded recourse to the courts where his petition will be heard and a remedy provided. Thus,

> When brothers or partners wish to divide a field in order that each may take his share of it, then if it is all of equal quality, *i.e.*

30. A. Lichtenstein, "Does Jewish Tradition Recognize an Ethic Independent of Halakha ?" in Marvin Fox (ed.) *Modern Jewish Ethics: Theory and Practice* (Ohio State University Press, 1975), 75-76.

31. *Rashi*, Eruvin 49a, *s.v.* "middat sodom".

32. Hereinafter referred to as "The *Zeh neheneh* rule". In basing the *Zeh neheneh* rule upon the *Kofin* rule, I follow R. Joshua Falk, *Pnei Yehoshua*, Bava Kamma 20a to Tosafot *s.v.* "zeh eino".

33. Maimonides *Torts*, "Robbery and Lost Property" 3:9, summarizing the talmudic discussion in B. Bava Kamma 20a-21a.

> all of one grade and there are no good and poor sections in it, they divide it by measurement.
>
> If one says, "Give me my share on this side of the field so that it be adjacent to another field that I have and become as one field with it", we listen to him and oblige the other to consent, because raising objection in a case like this is acting in the manner of the people of Sodom.
>
> If, however, one part of it is better or nearer to a river or nearer to the road, and they appraise the good and the bad, and then one says, "Give me my share on this side, with proper financial settlement",[34] we do not listen to him but let him take his share by lot...
>
> A square piece of land that is bordered by a river on its east and north sides and by a road on its south and west sides should be divided diagonally in order that each of the two (brothers or partners) should have on his border a river and a road.
> If one says, "Give me the half that is on this side because it is adjacent to my field", we listen to him.
>
> The principle of the thing is that whenever the arrangement is an advantage to one while the other does not suffer thereby, we oblige the other to comply.[35]

The first four paragraphs of this Maimonidean citation make it abundantly clear that this example of talmudic legislation is limited to those instances in which the citizen himself would be placed at no disadvantage. Beneficent legislation at the expense of another is explicitly eschewed in all discussions of the *Kofin* and *Zeh neheneh* rules.

It is in the hands of the medieval rabbis that this talmudic provision received its complete explanation in both theory and practice. Modest beginnings may already be discerned earlier in the extant literature of the post-talmudic (*ca.* 600—1000 C.E.) authorities of Babylonia (the *Geonim*). Its full theoretic interpretation as well as its definitive prac-

34. The Anglo-American expression for unequal partition which is equalized by payment is "owelty".

35. Maimonides *Acquisition*, "Neighbours" 12:1,3, summarizing the talmudic discussion in Bava Batra 12b. In the Anglo-American legal tradition, such requests for preferential allotment to one co-owner of an otherwise equal share adjoining other property owned by that co-owner appear to be generally acceded to favourably. This may also be assumed regarding Israeli law on the basis of paragraphs 41 (a), 43 and 47 of the Land Law, 1969.

tical application, however, are chiefly the work of the "earlier" (*ca.* 1000–1500) authorities (*Rishonim*) of Spain (*Sepharad*) and Franco-Germany (*Ashkenaz*). The "later" (*ca.* 1500–1850) medieval authorities (*Aharonim*), and their modern counterparts, are the faithful repositories of the traditions of their predecessors, and have produced nothing that is essentially new in this area of Jewish law.[36]

The *Rishonim* examined all the relevant talmudic terms and concepts; worked through the exegesis of the various talmudic passages fully; defined the meanings of "benefit", "loss", and the rule, "Whenever an arrangement is of benefit to one while the other suffers no loss thereby we oblige the other to comply"; and resolved any doubts that had lingered on in the Talmud itself.

Unanimity is most rare among the *Rishonim*. As in most questions, differences of opinion abound.

"Whenever an arrangement is of benefit to one while the other suffers no loss thereby, we oblige the other to comply". The obligation to comply may be enforced in two ways. If the petitioner is not impinging seriously on the defendant's rights, the latter may be obliged to comply *ab initio*. If, however, there is a clear infringement upon the defendant's private property — without causing him harm or loss — the obligation is generally limited to a *de facto* situation; the owner of the property cannot collect rent for past occupancy. He does retain, however, the legal right of preventing future or continued intrusion. Some commentators view this latter right as absolute; others require justification for its exercise (*e.g.* the owner wishes to rent out the premises, or at least is present — personally or represented by an agent — so that there exists the possibility of converting the premises into a "For Rent" status). A minority view would coerce the owner of private property to yield it *ab initio* to occupation as long as he cannot show that he is sustaining harm, damage or some recognizable disadvantage.

The owner is compelled to accede to the request of the beneficiary — whether it be *ab initio* or *de facto* — only if the benefit or the enrichment is unidentifiable and unrecognized as such. (On the contrary, positive enrichment would serve as an enforceable cause of action on the part of the owner). Again, he is compelled to accede only if he

36. Documentation for these and the following remarks will be published in a monograph the author is preparing on the Jewish law of equity. In the meantime, *see* the excellent treatment in Sh. Shilo, "Kofin Al Midat S'dom: Jewish Law's Concept of Abuse of Rights", 15 *Is. L. R.* (1980) 49-78.

incurs no loss. There is wide disagreement in the Talmud and in the commentaries as to how this loss is to be understood. Some take it to be a quantitative loss calculable, not in terms of qualitative preferences, but in terms of dollars and cents; other interpret it as a qualitative deprivation, not measurable in dollars and cents, but in terms of individual preferences; still others explain that even if the benefactor sustains no loss at present but reasonably fears some possible future loss, he may not be coerced; a fourth opinion maintains that even if the loss is nothing more than the deprivation of the possibility of cashing in on the increased value of one's property engendered by the needs and desires of the petitioner himself, the benefactor may not be compelled to accede.

As to the juridic basis for compelling a citizen to act the benefactor where he sustains no loss — however defined — the early medieval interpreters again present conflicting opinions. With varying emphasis on benefit derived or cost incurred as the source of *obligato stricti juris*, some would regard scriptural law (rabbinically understood) as the "strict law" which would have theoretically allowed a citizen to insist upon his rights — proprietary or otherwise; these interpreters identify the coercion compelling the citizen to comply and *not* to stand on his rights as a rabbinic enactment (*takkanah de rabbanan*). Others regard the "strict law" as itself the theoretic prerogative inherent in *dominium*, and its antidote — coercion to act above and beyond the prerogatives of one's rights of ownership — as a product of biblical legislation (rabbinically reported, i.e. *de'oraita*).

"Whenever an arrangement is of benefit to one while the other suffers no loss thereby, we oblige the other to comply". In the application of this principle, Jewish law, as enunciated by the early medieval authorities, appears to have taken two divergent paths.

The talmudic precedent which applied the principle to cases where the rights of private property were invaded (B. *Bava Kamma* 20a—21a) was construed narrowly. It was limited to fields and farms and generally viewed as inapplicable to houses and apartments. It is similarly inapplicable where the owner registers his protest or where the occupier indicates his readiness to pay. Where the owner incurs a loss, the Sodomite character of this insistence upon asserting his rights vanishes, and he may sue successfully not only for restitution of the loss incurred but even for compensation for the benefit conferred.

As evidenced by the last sentence, wherever the principle was found to be inapplicable, rational grounds always lay at the bottom of such a finding. Nevertheless the net result is a pervading narrow construction placed upon the principle itself.

Not so where a citizen's rights of private property are *not* involved completely or substantially. With the talmudic passages which applied the principle to non-proprietary situations (B. *Bava Batra* 12b B. *Ketubot* 103a, B. *Eruvin* 49a, *et al.*) as precedent, the principle was converted into a legal maxim, extended by analogy and given the widest possible application in adjudication and in the solution of new problems. Hundreds of responsa ranging from *ca.* 1000 to *ca.* 1850 and representing communities geographically far and wide bear eloquent testimony to the fruitfulness of the principle in everyday Jewish life.

One area of life where this is true is that of the abuse of rights with which we are presently concerned. By definition, the abuse of rights does not involve a citizen's rights of private property in the sense that he is being deprived of the right to exercise legitimate use thereof. The question rather is whether ownership *per se* gives the owner the right to use his property for the sole purpose of malevolence or selfishness. In other words, may he, for example, "throw away the waters of his well when others are in need of them"?

Jewish law declares that he may not, and R. Menahem Meiri, followed by R. Simeon b. Zemah Duran, invoked the rule, "We coerce people not to act in a Sodomite manner", as the basis for the *halakhic* restriction.

This application of the *Kofin* rule is crucial.[37] It is true that the *bal tash-hit* clause would have served our purposes regarding the throwing away of well water. Indeed, many of the *halakhic* rules governing relations between neighbours would cover most of the situations envisaged at the beginning of our presentation. Nevertheless, there are cases — notably these involving "spite fences" — which are beyond the scope of *bal tash-hit* specifically and beyond the control of the Jewish law of nuisance generally. It is in these cases that the rule, *Kofin al middat Sodom*, comes to the rescue. The erection of a spite fence constitutes a case of *Zeh lo neheneh ve-zeh hasser*, "the one [the owner of the fence] derives no benefit whilst the other [his neighbour] is being harmed". When the neighbour, as plaintiff comes to court petitioning the

37. It is also novel; for, it should be noted, both the talmudic discussions of the *Kofin* rule and the *Zeh neheneh* rule cite neither the *mishnah* in Yevamot 4:11 regarding *halizah* nor the dictum of R. Judah the Prince in Yevamot 44a regarding throwing away water, which preceded them in time.

removal of the fence, the action he is calling for is in the category of *Zeh neheneh ve-zeh lo hasser.* "The one [the neighbour] benefits from removal whereas the other [the owner] sustains no loss". Hence, the petition is granted, for we coerce people not to act true to Sodomite character.

The principle opposing the abuse of rights, of course, represents a restriction on individual freedom of action; it is in a sense a manifestation of the legislation coercing *lifnim mishurat hadin* conduct, *i.e.* conduct beyond the requirements of strict law, where *din* ("strict law") stands for one's rights under law or by contract. The application therefore of this principle must be accompanied by great caution — as is evidenced from the following decision rendered by one of the greatest of the latter-day authorities.

A number of gardens situated along a downgrade are supplied with water from a spring at the top. According to the Talmud, should the spring be ruined at the source, all the lower owners must join the topmost one in its repair. Should the water flow be ruined at any point along the downgrade, all the lower owners must join the owner at the point at which the waterflow has been hindered. The upper owners, however, cannot be compelled to contribute to its repair, for they derive no benefit from the waterflow beneath them. Thus, the owner of the very lowest garden must join all the other owners in repairing the waterflow, but should the flow be ruined near his garden, the upper owners cannot be compelled to join him in its repair.[38]

Examining these talmudic stipulations governing neighbouring gardens in the light of the rules of *Kofin* and *Zeh neheneh*, R. Ezekiel Landau (Prague, d. 1793)[39] makes the following observations:

(1) The *Zeh neheneh* exemption is a *de facto* one. Thus, compulsion of the lower owners to contribute to the repair of the waterflow above them or to the repair of the spring at its source applies to owners who, at the time of the disrepair, are in need of and are making use of the spring's water supply. If, however, at the time of the repair, the owner of a lower plot of land had no garden and was in no need of the water supply, he need not participate in the expenses involved in its repair. Should the lower owner *subsequently* convert his plot into a garden and desire to draw from the waterflow, the upper owner cannot charge

38. B. Bava Mezia 108a; Maimonides *Acquisition*, "Neighbours" 3:9; *Tur* and *Shulhan Arukh*, H.M. 170:1.

39. *Responsa Noda Bihudah* II (Orig. Prague 1811; Vilna ed. reprinted: Jerusalem, 1960), H.M. 24.

him for the earlier digging-and-repair project. After the fact, the former is deriving a benefit whereas the latter incurs no loss thereby.

(2) R. Landau extends the non-liabiilty even to a lower owner who, in converting his plot to a garden, goes to the added expense of widening and deepening the spring at the source. Although such action on the part of the lower owner might be construed as implying his readiness to be considered a partner and to contribute to the digging-and-repair project, the original exemption is maintained, for the conversion has caused no added expense to the uppermost owner whose digging-and-repair work has by now been completed.

(3) The *de facto* exemption is to be interpreted strictly. Although the upper owner has no legal claim on the lower owner to participate in the expenditures involved in the past digging-and-repair work, he cannot be prevented from threatening the latter, "Should you persist in your refusal to contribute to the expenses entailed, I shall undo the repair work and fill with earth that which I have dug. Indeed, if you refuse to contribute, it shall be neither mine nor thine";[40] nor can he be restrained from carrying out his threat. For the upper owner is within his legal rights. The need that the lower owner has of the water supply converts the situation to one of *hasser;* the upper owner is losing the very money he can charge for the needed water.[41] Moreover, even following Maimonides,[42] we cannot apply the rule of *Kofin* to our situation. The Talmudic rule of *Kofin* referred to a field held in partnership wherein each party had equal rights, individual shares were as yet undefined, and neither party had incurred any expense therein. In our situation, however, the upper owner had made an appreciable investment of money and effort – for which he could demand a compensatory contribution from others who reap benefits therefrom. Although R. Landau does not state it explicitly, his thinking may have been influenced by the idea that by undoing the repair work, the upper owner will have converted the *de facto* situation he was discussing into the *de jure* situation to which the Talmud had addressed itself. It will be recalled that, according to the Talmud, when the various owners are in need of and making use of the spring's water supply, *ab initio* the law

40. The heartless words of the spurious mother in the judgment of Solomon (I Kings 3:26). Thus, although the law can issue no restraining order against the upper owner, R. Landau's moral derogation of such behaviour is clear.

41. *Rosh, Bava Batra* 1:46, interpretating *Rabbenu Tam, Tosafot s.v.* "ma'alinon", Bava Batra 12b.

42. *Acquisition*, "Neighbours" 12:1, who adopts an interpretation of the talmudic rule of *Kofin* which differs from that of *Rabenu Tam* (previous note).

could be invoked whereby all may be compelled to contribute to the digging-and-repair work around the spring. It is doubtful whether R. Landau would require the upper owner to actually undo the repair work he had done. The legal right to do so is probably sufficient to render actionable his present demand for participation on the part of the lower owners in the original expenses.

The significance of R. Landau's decision is to be found in the observation that, despite the existence of the rules of *Kofin* and *Zeh neheneh* in Jewish law which promote restrictions on the abuse of rights, R. Landau's findings are remarkably similar to those of the judges in *Mayor of Bradford v. Pickles.*[43] Mr. Pickles had dug a hole in his ground so as to abstract water from a neighbouring property in order to raise the purchasing price of his own property which was wanted by a local authority. In a legal system whose primary orientation is toward private property, economic objectives are legitimate, and their pursuit, though somewhat ruthless, may not be regarded as an abuse of rights. Thus, the very case that aroused Professor Gutteridge's ire and motivated him to express his criticism of Anglo-American law may not necessarily have been decided otherwise if a law against the abuse of rights were on the books.[44] Not every act that arouses one's moral indignation can be countered by legislation.[45] Moreover, enlightened systems may resort to other areas of the law to cope with the abuse of rights. After all, spite fences are a rather rare phenomenon.

Thus, the following remarks by a leading legal analyst are well taken:

> The practical significance of the whole doctrine is very much smaller than its theoretical interest. In the practice of American, French, German or Swiss courts, it means little more than that the very unusual kind of landowner who creates obstacles out of spite for his neighbour, or who prefers to leave a piece of land unused rather than grant a right of passage, may be restrained by the courts.[46]

43. See above, p. 99.
44. I write the word "necessarily" advisedly, for my friend, Dr. Uriel Reichman of the Tel Aviv University Law School, points out a distinction between R. Landau's decision and the case of Mr. Pickles. The latter's spite work had no direct connection with the possible "benefit" he hoped to derive therefrom. Thus, a law against the abuse of rights would have been effective against Mr. Pickles, although it was irrelevant with regard to the upper owner.
45. Compare Lord Macnaghten's remarks on p. 99 to the veiled condemnation of R. Landau on p. 112 n. 40.
46. Friedman, *op. cit.,* 77.

Indeed, the theoretical interest in the doctrine of the abuse of rights should not be taken lightly. Although its practical application may be limited, the principle preventing such abuse helps restore one's faith in the law as an instrumentality of justice.

Thus, here too the contrast between Jewish law and Anglo-American law is also a marked one. It comes therefore as no surprise that adherents to Jewish law welcomed the passage of Section 14 of the Land Law of Israel 5729—1969, as a step in the right direction. It reads:

> Ownership and other rights in immovable property shall not by themselves justify the doing of anything that causes damage or inconvenience to another.

The restriction entitles every citizen to the correlative right not to be injured or inconvenienced by an abuse of rights. From the *halakhic* point of view, however, it does not go far enough; for although it prevents a property owner from acting in a manner otherwise legal, it does not provide for coercion *to act* in a certain way. Moreover, it is limited to residual rights; it does not apply to rights intrinsic to ownership. On the other hand, to be commended are a number of features that are characteristic of Jewish law, such as: (1) It does not demand positive proof of ill-motive or malice. The objective facts that one's action causes damage or inconvenience and that it is of no benefit to the owner suffice to bring it under the provisions of the law; (2) It does not limit the beneficiaries of the law to owners of neighbouring property. Any citizen harmed is thereby protected.

In sum, then, in the area of the abuse of rights, Jewish law appears to be closer to the continental systems of law than to the general Anglo-American orientation, inasmuch as it regards the law as a legitimate instrument to enforce what may be regarded as essentially a moral norm — the prohibition of exercising a legal right out of spite or selfishness, in a spirit denying benefit to others although incurring no loss or injury to oneself. The basis for this position may be found in the *Kofin* and *Zeh neheneh* rules that were formulated already in the Talmud. The legal development came to its fullest fruition when R. Menahem Meiri and R. Simeon b. Zemah Duran went beyond the specific *bal tash-hit* ("thou shalt not destroy") injunction as well as beyond the various laws of nuisance, and, basing themselves on the *Kofin* and *Zeh neheneh* rules, formulated a generalized prohibition of the abuse of rights.

[14]

ON ONE ASPECT OF LAW AND MORALS IN JEWISH LAW: *LIFNIM MISHURAT HADIN*

*By Shmuel Shilo**

Introduction

In Talmudic literature the term *lifnim mishurat hadin* (i.e., beyond the line of the law) is mentioned a number of times.[1] Before analyzing the various Talmudic passages where this concept is found, we will ask a number of questions, some of which we will answer in this article. Not all of the answers will be unequivocal and some questions will remain, in the end, provocative and open. Hopefully, the paper will encourage further discussion of the concept *lifnim mishurat hadin.*

Is *lifnim mishurat hadin* a specific norm of behaviour which can be precisely defined, or is it rather a concept referring to recommended ethical behaviour, similar to general moral values and examples of ethical behaviour which abound in the Talmud but which have no clearly definable characteristics? If we conclude that *lifnim mishurat hadin* is indeed a precisely defined norm of behaviour does it stand on its own as a specific type of moral behaviour, or is it synonymous with certain other moral norms, *dinei shamayim* (the Laws of Heaven), *midat hassidut* (the degree of ethical perfection of men of piety and virtue) or one of the other ethical norms found in the Talmudic sources? If *lifnim mishurat hadin* is not just another term for some other moral norm, what is the difference between them? (A reasoned answer to this question cannot be given without a full discussion of all the other moral norms in the Talmud; therefore in this article we will only suggest approaches to answering this question). Are there differences of degree within the norm of *lifnim mishurat hadin* itself? Are there types of behaviour recorded in the Talmud, about which the phrase *lifnim mishurat hadin* is not used, but which are in fact examples of behaviour *lifnim mishurat hadin?* If so, is there a reason why such actions were not explicitly described as *lifnim mishurat hadin?*

Is this demand or request to act *lifnim mishurat hadin* directed towards everyone or only to certain special individuals? Is this conduct *lifnim mi-*

* Dr. Jur. (Jerusalem), Head of the Institute for Research in Jewish Law, Faculty of Law, The Hebrew University of Jerusalem.

1 *Mekhilta, Yitro, Massekhta D'Amalek, Parsha* II; *Mekhilta* of R. Simon b. Yohai, Exodus 18:20; *Ber.* 7a; *ibid.,* 45 b; *Ket.* 97a; *B.K.* 99b–100a; *B.M.* 24b; *ibid.,* 30b; *A. Zar* 4b; *Deut. Rabbah, Re'eh* 4:3.

shurat hadin left entirely to the free will of the doer, or is there a moral or even a legal imperative so to act? If there is a legal duty to act *lifnim mishurat hadin* can one be compelled by the courts so to act just as one can be compelled to fulfil other legal duties? Furthermore, if one can be compelled to act *lifnim mishurat hadin* — what type of coercion may be used?

Is the duty or request directed to an individual *per se,* or to the court who is to decide a case *lifnim mishurat hadin?* Or, perhaps, the court is enjoined to influence a litigant to waive a legal right in favour of the ethical norm of *lifnim mishurat hadin?* If the side to a dispute is adamant, may the court, on its own, stray from the strict law and decide according to *lifnim mishurat hadin?*

When this request or duty concerns monetary matters — which is at the heart of *lifnim mishurat hadin* — does the financial position of the parties involved influence, alter or even annul the request or duty to act *lifnim mishurat hadin?*

Is the word *lifnim* to be understood *"within"* or *"beyond"?* What are the implications of these two different senses? We find both translations by those who discuss the maxim.[2]

The Talmudic Sources

The behaviour of *lifnim mishurat hadin* is attributed not only to man but to God himself. In the two places in the Talmud where it is stated that God acted *lifnim mishurat hadin,* it is clear that God is acting out of compassion — *midat harahamim,*[3] or out of ethical perfection and virtue — *midat*

2 "Beyond" — e.g., I. Herzog, *The Main Institutions of Jewish Law* (2nd ed., London, 1965) vol. 1, p. 385; A. Lichtenstein, "Does Jewish Tradition Recognize an Ethic Independent of Halakha" in M. Fox, ed., *Modern Jewish Ethics* (Ohio, 1975) 62 at 69; "Within" — e.g., B. Cohen, *Jewish and Roman Law — A Comparative Study* (New York, 1966) vol. 1 p. 52; S. Berman, "Lifnim Mishurat Hadin" (1975) 26 Journal of Jewish Studies 86; (1977) 28 *ibid.*, 181. In the Soncino translation of the Talmud, sometimes *lifnim* is translated "beyond" and sometimes "within".

3 *Ber.* 7a: "The Holy One, blessed be He, says prayers. What does He pray? — R. Zutra b. Tobi said in the name of Rab: May it be My will that My mercy may suppress My anger, and that My mercy may prevail over My [other] attributes, so that I may deal wtih My children in the attribute of mercy and, on their behalf, *lifnim mishurat hadin.* It was taught: R. Ishmael b. Elisha says: I once entered into the innermost part (of the Sanctuary) to offer incense and saw Akathriel Jah, the Lord of Hosts, seated upon a high and exalted throne. He said to me: Ishmael, My son, bless Me, I replied: May it be Thy will that Thy mercy may suppress Thy anger and Thy mercy may prevail over Thy other attributes, so that Thou mayest deal with Thy children according to the attribute of mercy and mayest, on their behalf, act *lifnim mishurat hadin.* And He nodded to me with His head".

hahesed.[4] In spite of the conceptual proximity of *midat harahamim* and *midat hahesed* to what is described as man's conduct *lifnim mishurat hadin,* analysis of the passages brought below where it is stated that a mortal acted *lifnim mishurat hadin* demonstrates that such actions cannot be described as referring either to *midat harahamim* or *midat hahesed.*

Another passage where God's behaviour is described as *lifnim mishurat hadin* is in Midrash Rabbah. "R. Haggai said [God said]: 'And what is more, not only have I set two paths before you, but I have dealt with you *lifnim mishurat hadin* and I have said to you, Therefore choose life" (Deut. 30:19).[5] In this passage God did something which He did not have to do, i.e., He did more than what was expected of him.

It appears then that in Talmudic literature there is more than one sense to this phrase, and the aggadic passages describing God's behaviour use the term in a different sense than do those that refer to man's acting *lifnim mishurat hadin.* In its human, legal context, the phrase *lifnim mishurat hadin* undoubtedly refers to action above and beyond what one is expected to do according to strict legal rights and duties. In the aggadic use of the term, the phrase is used for actions above and beyond what is expected of anyone (in this instance God himself) in various situations that are not necessarily legal in nature.

We will now cite the three major passages where the phrase *lifnim mishurat hadin* occurs. (Two other passages — less important for us — will be discussed later). Henceforth we shall refer to the three passages as a) the unloading case; b) the moneychanger case, and c) the lost property case.

a) *The unloading case:*[6] The Talmud concludes that under certain circumstances an elder is exempted from the obligations of returning a lost article or of helping with the unloading of a neighbour's animal, when it is inconsistent with his dignity. The Talmud also informs us that "Rabbi Ishmael, son of R. Jose was walking on a road when he met a man carrying a bag of faggots. The latter put them down, rested and then said to him 'help me to take them up'. 'What is it worth'? he enquired. 'Half a zuz' was the answer. So he gave him the half zuz and declared it ownerless. Thereupon he (the carrier) reaquired it. He gave him another half zuz and again declared it ownerless. Seeing that he was about to reaquire it, he said to him 'I have declared it ownerless for all but for you' . . . R. Ishmael son of R. Jose did in fact render it ownerless for all and he stopped the other

4 *A. Zar.* 4b: "[While occupied with] the Torah, which Scripture designates as 'truth'; as it is written *buy the truth and sell it not,* (Proverbs 23:23) The Holy One, blessed be He, will not act *lifnim mishurat hadin* (but when sitting in) judgment, which is not designed by Scripture as 'truth', the Holy One, blessed be He, will act *lifnim mishurat hadin*".

5 *Deut. Rabbah, Re'eh* 4:3. See S. Federbush, *Ha'Mussar Ve'Hamishpat Beyisrael* (New York, 1944) 44-45.

6 *B.M.* 30b.

(from taking possession again) by mere words. Yet, was not R. Ishmael son of R. Jose an elder for whom it was undignified (to help one take up a load)? He acted *lifnim mishurat hadin*. For R. Joseph learnt: 'And thou shalt show them'[7] means their house of life; 'the way'[7] means the practice of deeds of lovingkindness; 'they must walk' — means visiting the sick; 'therein'[7] — means burial; 'and the work'[7] — means strict law; 'that they shall do'[7] — means *lifnim mishurat hadin*... R. Johanan said: Jerusalem was destroyed only because they gave judgment[8] therein in accordance with the law of the Torah... and did not act *lifnim mishurat hadin*."

b) *The money-changer case:*[9] The Talmud (R. Papa) concludes that a moneychanger, even if he is an expert, is responsible for loss due to his erroneous advice. However, an *exceptional* expert is exempt — such as the two exceptional expert moneychangers, Dankho and Issur. We are then told that: "There was a certain woman who showed a dinar to R. Hiyya and he told her that it was good. Later she came again to him and said to him, 'I afterwards showed it (to others) and they said to me that it was bad, and in fact I could not pass it'. He therefore said to Rav: 'Go forth and change it for a good one and write down in my register that it was a bad business'. But why should he be different from Dankho and Issur who would be exempt because they needed no instruction? Surely R. Hiyya also needed no instruction? — R. Hiyya acted *lifnim mishurat hadin*, on the principle learnt by R. Joseph: 'And thou shalt show them' — means the source of their livelihood; 'the way' — means the practice of deeds of lovingkindness; 'they must walk' — means visiting the sick; 'therein' — means burial; 'and the work' — means strict law; 'that they shall do' — means *lifnim mishurat hadin*".

c) *The lost property case:*[10] "Rab Judah once followed Mar Samuel into a street[11] of whole-meal vendors and asked him: 'What if one found here a purse? — Mar Samuel answered: It would belong to the finder. What if an Israelite came and indicated an identification mark? (Mar Samuel) answered: He would have to return it. Both? (Mar Samuel) answered: *Lifnim mishurat hadin*. Thus the father of Samuel found some asses in a desert, and he returned them to their owner after a year of twelve months: *Lifnim mishurat hadin*".[12]

7 Exodus 18:20. A similar but somewhat different exegesis was already made in Tannaitic times. See text *infra* at n. 99.

8 This is the Soncino translation, according to the reading "*dineihem*". But see *Dikdukei Soferim*. The correct reading should more probably be "*divreihem*" which then should be translated differently.

9 *B.K.* 99b–100a.

10 *B.M.* 24b.

11 This Soncino translation of "*shuka*" as street and not marketplace is probably correct. See M. Ber, *Amoraei Bavel* (Ramat Gan, 1975) 223–224.

12 The Talmud continues: "Raba once followed R. Nahman into a street of skin-

The other two instances recorded in the Talmud of action *lifnim mishurat hadin* are of much less importance for us. R. Papa agreed to rescinding a sale of property which he bought, since the seller eventually did not need the money. The Talmud says that R. Papa acted *lifnim mishurat hadin.* However, the final conclusion of the Talmud is that R. Papa acted according to the strict law and there is no need to explain R. Papa's action as an example of *lifnim mishurat hadin.*[13] The last specific Talmudic example of *lifnim mishurat hadin* refers to ritual and not monetary matters. R. Papa agreed to interrupt his meal and say grace together with a person with whom he ate, even though according to the law if one of three people eating together wants to say grace and leave, the other two are not obliged to interrupt their meal in order to join in the saying of grace. It is explained that R. Papa acted *lifnim mishurat hadin.*[14]

Defining Lifnim Mishurat Hadin

Is there a common denominator behind the actions of those who acted *lifnim mishurat hadin?* If so, we may conclude that there are certain specificable characteristics of *lifnim mishurat hadin.* If not, we must conclude that *lifnim mishurat hadin* is a catch phrase for moral and ethical conduct beyond what strict law requires.

Four of the five instances of *lifnim mishurat hadin* are to be understood as a waiver of a right where such waiver does not cause an actual monetary loss but, at most, a possible loss of profits. Those four cases are the unloading case (R. Ishmael could have acted *lifnim mishurat hadin* by helping the man unload. He did not have to pay him in lieu of the help he could have physically given), the lost property case, the rescission of sale and the saying of grace case (which is a waiver of privilege, but does not entail any monetary loss). In the fifth case which does entail a loss, that of the moneychanger, the situation is unique. Here, R. Hiyya, the unusually expert moneychanger caused the loss to the other party. Only in such a case, does *lifnim mishurat hadin* require a real monetary loss. Hence we have discovered a major common characteristic.

ners — some say into a street of scholars — and asked him: "What if one found here a purse? — (R. Nahman) answered: It would belong to the finder. What if an Israelite came and indicated its identification mark? (R. Nahman) answered: It would (still) belong to the finder. But that one keeps protesting! It is as if one protested against his house collapsing or against his ship sinking in the sea". It seems that R. Nahman disagrees with Mar Samuel's view concerning the duty to return the lost article *lifnim mishurat hadin.* For a short discussion of the phrase "a street of skinners, some say a street of scholars" see M. Rubinstein, "Ha'Melakhtiut Ba'Talmud" in *Mehkarim U'Mevo'ot La'Talmudim* (Jerusalem, 1971) 56.

13 *Ket.* 97a.

14 *Ber.* 45b.

Upon analysis of the three cases which are undoubtedly examples of *lifnim mishurat hadin* in civil matters, it appears that *lifnim mishurat hadin* refers to cases where 1) the general rule is that people must act in a certain manner, 2) the person involved is exempt from the general legal obligation for some specific reason, e.g., it is beyond his dignity to follow the general legal rule, and 3) he is to act according to the general rule not because the law commands him to so act, but *lifnim mishurat hadin.*[15] *Lifnim mishurat hadin* requests him to waive his special right and act according to the general legal principle. Therefore, a) the sage has to help with another's unloading *lifnim mishurat hadin,* b) a finder must return a lost article *lifnim mishurat hadin* even though according to strict law, the special circumstances of the loss, i.e., constructive abandonment, exempts the finder from returning the property and c) the unusually expert moneychanger is responsible for the damage he caused *lifnim mishurat hadin.* In other words, in all three cases, the individual is told to act according to the general legal principles respectively of a) the duty to help your neighbour unload, b) the duty to return lost property, c) the duty to pay damages for a loss caused by wrong advice — *lifnim mishurat hadin* — in spite of the strict law — *shurat hadin* — which exempts him.

This analysis of one's duty to act *lifnim mishurat hadin* seems, at first glance, to be at odds with the exegesis of the verse which was brought to teach us that one should act *lifnim mishurat hadin.* From that exegesis[16] it appears that *lifnim mishurat hadin* is a broad principle and does not seem to be referring exclusively to the special circumstances of someone exempted from a general rule. Furthermore, the statement of R. Yohanan that Jerusalem was destroyed because the people acted according to strict law and not *lifnim mishurat hadin,* seems to bear this out. However, the latter Amoraic interpretation of the exegesis on the verse from Exodus, may be hinting to an interpretation based upon the general rule. exemption, return to the general rule analysis.

As cited above, a number of duties were derived from the exegesis of the Scriptural verse, which included visiting the sick. the practice of deeds of lovingkindness, the burial of the dead and *lifnim mishurat hadin.* In a more developed analysis of the exegesis of the verse, in Baba Mezia, the Talmud states: "The Master said: 'they must walk' — means visiting the sick. But that is the practice of deeds of lovingkindness? — That is necessary only in respect of one's affinity (a person born at the same hour and under the same planetary influence). For a Master said: A man's affinity takes away a sixtieth of his illness, yet even so he must visit him. 'Therein' — means

15 *Cf. Tosafot, B.K.* 100a s.v. *lifnim, Tosafot B.M.* 24b s.v. *lifnim* with Berman, *ibid.* Our interpretation is similar to that of the Tosafists and Berman, but is different in some respects and broader in certain explanations.

16 See text at nn. 6 and 9.

burial. But that (too) is identical with the practice of deeds of lovingkindness? — That is necessary only in respect of an elder for whom it is undignified. (Yet even he must take part in burial)".[17] This Amoraic interpretation suggests that the entire verse is referring to instances where there is a general duty, a possible exemption from the duty and a final statement that there is no exemption even in a special case and for the special individual, and so that part of the exegesis which refers to *lifnim mishurat hadin* is to be construed in a similar sense.

Coercing Compliance

Is there a moral or legal duty to act *lifnim mishurat hadin,* or only a request or suggestion that one do so? If there is a duty so to act, is there a sanction against someone who fails to do so? Can one be compelled to act *lifnim mishurat hadin?*

From close scrutiny of the writings of the Rishonim, it appears that there was a strong German view that a court could or should compel compliance with *lifnim mishurat hadin.* On the other hand, in the Sephardic sources it appears that acting *lifnim mishurat hadin* was left completely to the person's conscience. Within the German school there are also differences of opinion as to the scope of compulsion and the type of compulsion, as we shall see below. In spite of the Ashkenazi stand, we shall see that even they did not look upon *lifnim mishurat hadin* as a legal imperative equal to other legal imperatives, but that the imperative was somewhat softened in a manner not consistent with legal imperatives in general. Our personal view is that the Sephardic school's understanding of the Talmudic sources is the more plausible, and, in Talmudic time *lifnim mishurat hadin* was a concept in the realm of morals and ethics.

Among the Sephardic scholars, R. Hananel wrote, in explaining the passage concerning the lost property "if an Israelite came and indicated an identification mark what is the law? He answered: '*If he wants* to act *lifnim mishurat hadin* he returns (the lost property)".[18] In other words, the decision is up to the finder, if he does or does not want to act *lifnim mishurat hadin.* So, it seems does the Ritba explain this Talmudic passage[19] and the Provençal R. Jonathan categorically states that one cannot be compelled to act *lifnim mishurat hadin,*[20] as does Asheri.[21] (We shall discuss Maimonides' view below together with our discussion of the question who is obliged to act *lifnim mishurat hadin*).[22] A detailed discussion of our question and a strong refutation of the view that one can be forced to act *lifnim*

17 *B.M.* 30b.

18 R. Hananel to *B.M.* 24b.

19 Ritba to *B.M.* 24b.

20 R. Jonathan of Lunel, brought in *Shita Mekubetzet* to *B.K.* 115a s.v. *matnei.*

21 *Piskei Ha'Rosh B.M.* chap. 2 sec. 7.

22 See text *infra* at nn. 55–63.

mishurat hadin, is found in the writings of Rabbi A.I. Hakohen Kook. Rabbi Kook[23] agrees with Karo's statement that after carefully scrutinizing the arguments of the pro-compulsion school he, (Karo), could come to but one conclusion which is: "R. Yeruham wrote in the name of Asheri that one does not compel action *lifnim mishurat hadin*, and this is self-evident in my view. And I am amazed with what the Mordekhai wrote in Chap. two of *Mezia* that one is compelled to act *lifnim mishurat hadin;* from the Talmudic cases he cites as proof (for this view), there is no mention of compulsion".[24]

The first scholar who ventured the view that one can be compelled to act *lifnim mishurat hadin* was R. Eliezer b. Nathan (Ravan). Ravan decided[25] that if the individual is a man of sufficient means who can afford to act *lifnim mishurat hadin*, the court will compel him to do so. Other Ashkenazi scholars followed Ravan's lead including R. Eliezer b. Yoel Halevi (Raviah),[26] R. Samson of Chinon,[27] Mordekhai b. Hillel Hakohen,[28] R. Meir Hakohen MiRitenberg, author of *Hagahot Maimoniot*,[29] and R. Alexander Zuslin Hakohen, author of the *Agudah*.[30] This classification of what seems to be a moral imperative, as a legal one, which can be enforced by the court, is not a purely legal norm but even according to this German school, only a quasi-legal one. The legal imperative of *lifnim mishurat hadin* is different from other legal imperatives in that another factor, usually extraneous when discussing strict law, is brought into direct play — namely, the relative financial position of the sides to the dispute. A legal system will almost never take into consideration the financial situation of a claimant or respondent when having to decide if a claim will be accepted or rejected.[31] The Jewish legal system in particular adheres to very strict standards in this respect. The Torah states that "neither shalt thou favour a poor man in his cause",[32] "ye shall do no unrighteousness in judgment: thou shalt not respect the person of the poor"[33] and the like. Even those halakhic scholars who dress the maxim

23 *Be'er Eliahu, Hoshen Mishpat* sec. 12, 2 notes 8–9.

24 *Beit Yosef* to *Tur Hoshen Mishpat* sec. 12, 8 (newer notes).

25 Brought in *Mordekhai, B.M.* sec. 327, In the *Sefer Ravan* II, 198 the question of *lifnim mishurat hadin* is discussed, but Ravan does not specifically state that one can be coerced to act *lifnim mishurat hadin*. See too, *Hagahot Maimoniot* M.T. *Gezela* 11:3, *Agudah, B.M.* sec. 34.

26 *Mordekhai, ibid. Hagahot Maimoniot, ibid.*

27 *Hagahot Maimoniot, ibid.*

28 *Mordekhai, ibid.*

29 *Hagahot Maimoniot, ibid.*

30 *Agudah, ibid.*

31 But, see R.A. Newman (ed.), *Equity in the World's Legal Systems* (Brussels, 1973) 404, 468–470, 604.

32 Exodus 23:3.

33 Lev. 19:15.

lifnim mishurat hadin in legal clothes are also aware of the fact that, in contrast to a usual legal norm, here extra-legal considerations must be taken into account. A claim *lifnim mishurat hadin* is legally actionable only under certain exceptional circumstances. Here is a new type of norm which falls somewhere between legality and morality. A legal right arises, i.e., the right to coerce compliance, only if an external non-legal situation is present, i.e., a certain relationship between the capacity of the defendant to pay and the monetary needs of the claimant.[34]

The two most prominent later authorities who subscribe to the coercion view and who attempt to explain its basis, are R. Joel Sirkes and his disciple R. Menahem Mendel Krochmal.

Agreeing with the view of the early Ashkenazi schools, Sirkes[35] relates their arguments based on their understanding of the Talmudic passages involved. They base their view on the following: 1) In a passage which we will analyze below[36] — a passage which does not use the term *lifnim mishurat hadin* but it is understood by many as an example of *lifnim mishurat hadin*—a certain Amora asked if the duty to act in a certain manner (which is explained by others and Sirkes as *lifnim mishurat hadin*), is a legal duty, and he was answered by the Amora Rav that it was. From here, it can be deduced that *lifnim mishurat hadin* is actionable and coercion may be used in order to implement *lifnim mishurat hadin*. 2) From the lost property case one can deduce from the language of the Talmud that there is a legal duty to return the lost article *lifnim mishurat hadin*, since the phrase "*hayav*" is used — "one *must* return (the object)". This is so even though R. Joel Sirkes himself observes that the use of "must" is also common when discussing a discharge of a duty toward Heaven — *Lazet yedei shamayim*. Not only does Sirkes agree in theory with this early Ashkenazi view, but he relates that in practice, in his time, the Jewish courts do, in fact, compel wealthy individuals to pay less prosperous claimants if the court thinks that it is right to do so even though, according to strict law, they are exempt. R. Sirkes

34 In this article we use the accepted classification of a legal right, as one which can be enforced in law. We are aware, however, that for Jewish law the usual classification of a legal right or duty as against a solely moral right or duty, as based on enforceability, is not valid. In Jewish law there are duties which one must comply with according to the law, even though there is no human sanction for non-compliance. These duties at times also give rise to rights against those who are commanded to fulfill the duties. As Silberg has pointed out (*Talmudic Law and the Modern State* (New York, 1973), English translation of *Kakh Darko shel Talmud* (*Principia Talmudica*) (Jerusalem, 1961) 68–69), the thrust of halakhic norms is in one's duties, not in one's rights. Moreover, for practical purposes, we shall continue to refer to enforceability and non-enforceability as legal and moral, respectively.

35 *Bayit Hadash* to *Tur Hoshen Mishpat* sec. 12, 4.

36 Text beginning at n. 76.

tries—unsuccessfully in our opinion—to explain away those scholarly opinions which categorically stated that one may not coerce compliance with *lifnim mishurat hadin,* as only referring to cases where the defendant is not wealthy. If he is wealthy, Sirkes adds, all halakhic scholars would agree that he can be compelled to act *lifnim mishurat hadin.*

Sirkes goes even further. He adds that even though the individual is not wealthy, if acting *lifnim mishurat hadin* does not cause him a monetary loss, he must comply with the duty of *lifnim mishrat hadin,* since non-compliance under such circumstances would be looked upon as *midat Sodom* — a trait of Sodom and an example of "one reaps enjoyment and the other does not lose" — a situation where Jewish law uses coercion.[37]

R. Menahem Mendel Krochmal further develops the coercion view in one of his responsa concerning the return of a lost article. He, too, as his teacher R. Joel Sirkes, quotes the Ashkenazi view at length and personally agrees with their statement of the law that a rich man can be compelled to act *lifnim mishurat hadin.* However, he is very much aware of the school of thought which disagrees with the coercion view and he attempts to harmonize both views, as his teacher tried to do in his *Bayit Hadash.* The harmonization is attempted as follows: Those who negate compulsion, negate physical brute compulsion, i.e., by lashes. But, he argues, those scholars would look upon other types of coercion, favourably. Examples of such acceptable coercions are actual execution against the property of an individual, or at least putting under a ban an individual who refuses to act *lifnim mishurat hadin.* Here, too, Krochmal's explanation is based on his understanding of the phrase "*must* return (the lost article)" used in the Talmud as implying compulsion. Krochmal, too, cites the case to be discussed in detail below[38] where Rav is asked if the conduct which Rav demands is conduct according to the law, and an affirmative reply is given. R. Krochmal, explicitly approves of the line of thinking and decision of his teacher R .Joel Sirkes, and expounds and adds to his interpretation of the Talmudic lost property case. R. Menahem Mendel concludes that on principle, one may be coerced to act *lifnim mishurat hadin.* The only time that one need not act *lifnim mishurat hadin* is (using the example of the constructive abandonment of lost property case), where the finder is poor and the loser is rich. If, however, the finder is poor but the loser is not rich, the finder is compelled to act *lifnim mishurat hadin,* and return the lost article.[39]

37 See A. Lichtenstein, "Kofin al Midat Sodom (Sdom)" *Hagut Ivrit Be'America,* vol. 1, p. 368.

38 Text at nn. 77–82.

39 Resp. *Zemah Zedek* No. 89. See *Arukh Ha'shulkhan Hoshen Mishpat* 12, 2 who, similar to Krochmal's statement, decides that at least some type of non-physical coercion is allowed according to the view of all scholars — even those who make general statements negating coercion.

With all due respect to the Ashkenazi view concerning coercion, upon analysis of the relevant Talmudic passages, one must conclude that R. Joseph Karo and others are correct; there is no real evidence in the sources to substantiate the view that *lifnim mishurat hadin* is enforceable by compulsion. True to his unequivocal statement of the law in his *Beit Yosef*, R. Joseph Karo does not even mention the possibility of coercion when he refers to *lifnim mishurat hadin* in his *Shulhan Arukh*. Isserles, in his glosses follows R. Joseph Karo in that he too does not allow for coercion, but he also mentions the other view of the Ashkenazi school, but as the view to be rejected.[40] In any event, as we have already pointed out, even those halakhic scholars who subscribe to the coercion view are aware of the quasi-legal status of *lifnim mishurat hadin* and decide that *lifnim mishurat hadin* is acted upon by the court only when certain subjective criteria are present, i.e., a certain comparative financial position of the parties involved.[41]

A Duty Upon Whom?

Another basic question in connection with *lifnim mishurat hadin* is — to whom is this duty or moral imperative addressed? In the halakhic sources two views emerge, with variations on these two major outlooks in the works of some halakhists. One stand has as its most eloquent proponent Nahmanides, and the other, Maimonides. The Nahmanidean position is that the imperative (whether it be legal or ethical), is addressed to Everyman, while the Maimonidean position is that it is addressed to specific élitist individuals but not to each and every member of the Jewish community.

Let Nahmanides speak in his own words: "And our Rabbis have a fine interpretation of this ('And thou shalt do the right and the good'). They said: This refers to compromise and *lifnim mishurat hadin*. The intent of this is that, initially, He had said that you should observe the laws and statutes which He had commanded you. Now He says that, with respect to what He has not commanded, you should likewise take heed to do the good and the right in His eyes for He loves the good and the right. And this is a great matter. For it is impossible to mention in the Torah all of a person's actions toward his neighbours and acquaintances, all of his commercial activity, and all social and political institutions. So, after He had mentioned many of them such as 'Thou shalt not go about as a talebearer',[42] 'Thou shalt not take vengeance nor bear any grudge'[43] 'Thou shalt not stand idly by the blood of thy fellow',[42] 'Thou shalt not curse the

40 *Sh.Ar. Hoshen Mishpat* sec. 12, 2. See too *Resp. Shev Yaacov, Even Haezer* No. 29 who disagrees with Sirkes and agrees with the first view brought by Isserles in his gloss.

41 For a further analysis of the question about rich-poor in the context of *lifnim mishurat hadin*, and other contexts, see S. Shilo, *Dina De'Malkhuta Dina (The Law of the State is Law)* (Jerusalem, 1974) 177–183.

42 Lev. 19:16.

43 *Ibid.* 19:18.

deaf',[44] 'Thou shalt rise up before age',[45] and the like, He resumes to say generally that one should do the good and the right in all matters, so that there are included in this compromise, *lifnim mishurat hadin* and (matters) similar to that which they (i.e., the Rabbis) mentioned concerning the law of the abutter[46] — even that which they said, 'whose youth had been unblemished'[47] or 'He converses gently'[48] so that he is regarded as perfect and right in all matters".[49] The above complements what Nahmanides writes in explaining the verse in Leviticus "Holy shall you be"[50] and R. Vidal the author of *Maggid Mishna* follows Nahmanides' lead without specifically referring to his commentary of the Torah.[51]

Nahmanides and the author of *Maggid Mishna* explain general Biblical and Talmudic commands as not specifically referring to one or another given duty, but as referring to conduct in general, i.e., whatever one does during his lifetime, he must act in a manner compatible with the general moral or legal principle. He who takes into account only the strict law itself is considered "a scoundred with Torah license". Similarly, as R. Yohanan said "Jerusalem was but destroyed because they (i.e., its inhabitants)

44 *Ibid.* 19:14.

45 *Ibid.* 19:32.

46 *B.M.* 108.

47 *Ta'anit* 16a.

48 *Yoma* 86a.

49 Nahmanides, Commentary to the Torah, Deut. 6:18. See appendix *infra* p. 388.

50 *Ibid.*, Lev. 19:2. Here Nahmanides explains that the command "Ye shall be holy" comes to bar conduct which is technically within the permissive ground of the law, but can be abused and one who so acts is referred to in the Talmud as "a scoundrel with Torah licence". Nahmanides goes on to state: "And this is the Torah's mode to detail and (then) to generalize in a similar vein. For after the admonition about the details of civil law and all impersonal dealings... it says generally "And thou shalt do the right and the good", as it includes under this positive command justice and accomodation and all *lifnim mishurat hadin* in order to oblige one's fellow".

51 "Our perfect Torah sets forth general principles for the cultivation of human virtue and for (ethical) behaviour in the world, in the statement: 'Holy shall you be...' This means, as the Rabbis said, 'Sanctify yourself in what is permitted' — that one should not be drawn after lusts. Similarly the Torah says: 'You shall do that which is right and good' meaning that one should deal well and uprightly with men. It was not appropriate in all this to command details, for the commandments of the Torah are obligatory for every period and all time and in every circumstance, but the virtues of man and his conduct vary according to the time and the people. The Sages of blessed memory specified some useful particulars under these principles, some of which they made binding law and others only rules recommended before the fact, but not binding or actionable after the fact, still other rules for those who seek the way of special piety". *Maggid Mishneh, Hilkhot Shekhenim,* 14:5. See also appendix *infra* p. 388.

judged (in accordance with) Torah law. Well, should they rather have followed the law of the Magians? Say, rather, because they based their judgments solely upon Torah law and did not act *lifnim mishurat hadin*".[52]

An argument in favour of this point of view can be based on the nature of the rabbinic source for *lifnim mishurat hadin*. We have seen[53] that other duties are derived from the Pentateuchal verse together with the duty to act *lifnim mishurat hadin*. These duties include the visiting of the sick, and the burial of the dead. Just as these two duties are incumbent upon every Jew, so, we can strongly argue, is the duty mentioned in the continuation of the exegesis — to act *lifnim mishurat hadin*. In fact, perhaps even going further than Nahmanides and the author of *Maggid Mishna*, Rabbi Isaac of Corbeile, in *Sefer Mizvot Katan*, enumerates *lifnim mishurat hadin* as one of the 613 commandments.[54]

Upon analysis of Maimonides' statements of the law in his *Mishne Torah*, we are confronted with a completely different view. According to Maimonides, only the ethical élite are duty bound to act *lifnim mishurat hadin*. It is not incumbent upon every individual Jew to act *lifnim mishurat hadin* — one is duty bound to act so only if one wishes to be a man of piety and virtue — a *hassid*. Maimonides uses the phrase *lifnim mishurat hadin* not only for those quasi-legal acts which the Talmud refers to in the specific context of *lifnim mishurat hadin* but — in this Nahmanides and Maimonides use similar terminology — for behaviour in general (e.g. conversing gently); while Nahmanides refers to the general comportment of Everyman, Maimonides talks about the conduct of the ethical elite. It is the man of piety and virtue — the *hassid*, as against the scholar — the *hakham*, who acts *lifnim mishurat hadin*. What God *requires* of us is not to be a *hassid* or to act *lifnim mishurat hadin*, but to "walk in His ways" — meaning, the middle way, not the extremes even in piety and goodness. This view is clearly enunciated in his opening sections of his *Mishne Torah*, in those sections where Maimonides discusses the basics of Judaism, and is elaborated upon later in his work when he discusses specific cases of *lifnim mishurat hadin* which are brought in the Talmud.

Maimonides writes in *Hilhot De'ot*:[55] "Whoever is particularly scrupulous and deviates somewhat from the exact mean, in disposition, in one direction or the other, is called a saint (*hassid*). For example, if one avoids haughtiness

52 *B.M.* 30b. See above, text at nn. 6–8.

53 See text at nn. 6–8, 17.

54 *Semak*, 49.

55 *M.T. De'ot* 1:5. *Cf., ibid. Yesodei Ha'torah* 5:11. Here Maimonides uses the phrase *lifnim mishurat hadin* in connection with the actions of the *hakham* — which seems to contradict his statement in *Hilkhot De'ot*. However, it seems, that in *Hilkhot Yesodei Ha'Torah* Maimonides' use of the term refers only to those qualities such as general comportment and not to the more specific use of the maxim.

to the utmost extent, and is exceedingly humble, he is termed a *hassid* and this is the standard of saintliness *(midat hassidut)*. If one only departs from haughtiness as far as the mean, and is humble he is called wise *(hakham)* — and this is the standard of wisdom. And so with all other dispositions. The ancient saints trained their dispositions away from the exact mean toward the extreme in regard to one disposition in one direction, and in regard to another, in the opposite direction. This was *lifnim mishurat hadin*. We are bid to walk in the middle paths which are right and proper ways, as it is said 'and thou shalt walk in His ways'[56]."

This general attitude of Maimonides is given its clear demonstration in his phrasing of the law based on the Talmudic cases which we brought above. Concerning the lost property case, Maimonides writes that because of the constructive abandonment by the loser, the finder does not have to return the lost article. But, he adds, "He who wants to take the good and the straight road and act *lifnim mishurat hadin* should return the lost article".[57] In other words, it is up to the finder to decide whether he wants to act *lifnim mishurat hadin*. Similarly, when Maimonides brings the case of the exemption given an elder from returning lost property where it would be embarrassing to do so, he adds that "he who follows the good and straight road" should return the lost article.[58] Here, too, we see, that Maimonides subscribes to the position that acting *lifnim mishurat hadin* is designed for the ethical élite — he who takes the good and straight path and usually acts *lifnim mishurat hadin*. Exactly the same phraseology is used when Maimonides discusses the law of unloading and the exemption given to the elder because of his dignity.[59]

We can conclude from Maimonides' phraseology that not only is the ordinary individual free from having to act *lifnim mishurat hadin* but even those persons — *including sages and scholars* — who are exempted from returning a lost article under certain circumstances, and from helping with loading and unloading, are not duty-bound to act *lifnim mishurat hadin*.

56 Deut. 28:9.

57 *M.T. Gezelah ve'Avedah* 11:7.

58 *Ibid.* 11:17.

59 *M.T. Rozeah u'Shemirat Ha'Nefesh,* 13:4. Maimonides consistently refers to the phrase of doing the good and the right, a phrase which reminds one of the verse in Deut. 6:18. "Thou shalt do what is right and good in the eyes of the Lord". We have seen that Nahmanides in his commentary to the Torah on this verse brings the maxim of *lifnim mishurat hadin* as something to be deduced from this verse, and although this verse serves as the basis for another similar but different concept in the Talmud (See *B.M.* 15b, *ibid.* 35a; *ibid.* 108a) perhaps there is a lost exegesis of this verse which states that *lifnim mishurat hadin* stems from this verse. So it seems too from the phraseology in the commentary of Rashi to Deut. 6:18 and in *Sefer Hassidim* (Wistinetzki) No. 1899.

Furthermore, one can deduce from Maimonides' omissions in his Code, that if acting *lifnim mishurat hadin* would cause one a monetary loss, even the man of special piety and virtue, the *hassid,* is exempt from so acting. The previously cited *halakhot* from the *Mishne Torah* are the only ones mentioned by Maimonides in the context of *lifnim mishurat hadin.* Two other Talmudic cases are omitted in his Code. One is that of the moneychanger where R. Hiyya gave the woman a zuz and asked Rav to record a loss in his ledger. The second is that of the employees' breaking their employer's wine barrels,[60] which is considered by many halakhic scholars to be an additional example of *lifnim mishurat hadin.* It is reasonable to conclude that Maimonides did not cite these two cases since both of them entail a direct monetary loss to the person who acts beyond the demands of the strict law and compensates the other party out of his own pocket. Maimonides does not require such action even from the *hassid.* This is so even though the *hassid* caused the loss to the other party, as R. Hiyya did in the moneychanger case.

We can now explain why Maimonides' statement of the law concerning the unloading based on the story concerning R. Ishmael b. R. Jose, is not strictly in accordance with the tale told in the Gemara. As the reader will recall, R. Ishmael did not help with the unloading but instead paid the man — more than once — the worth of the bundle. Asheri, for example, deduces from this tale that a scholar is not permitted to unload a load which would be embarrassing for him but he should, instead — if he acts *lifnim mishurat hadin* — pay its worth as R. Ishmael in fact did.[61] Maimonides, however, states: "If one is an elder unaccustomed to loading or unloading, he is exempt, seeing that the act is not in keeping with his dignity".[62]

Why did Maimonides refer only to actual helping in the unloading? We submit that Maimonides in fact does not prescribe, even for the *hassid,* any action which would cause him a monetary loss. Therefore, Maimonides strays from the original story and explains the case as one concerning only the indignity of the elder that would be involved in his actual unloading of the bundle.[63]

A strong argument in favour of the Maimonidean view is the fact that in

60 See text *infra* at nn. 55–63.

61 *Piskei Ha'Rosh B.M.* chap. 2, sec. 21.

62 *M.T., Rozeah u'Shemirat Ha'Nefesh, ibid.*

63 There is another difference between the original story and Maimonides' wording. The Talmud relates that R. Ishmael helped the man unload the bundle from himself. Maimonides is speaking — in the context of the 13th chapter of *Hilkhot Rozeah u'Shemirat Ha'Nefesh* — of the Biblical unloading a burden from an *animal.* Perhaps Maimonides holds that the law of loading and unloading refers only to animals and not to man who should know better than to overburden himself. And see *Ozar Mefarshe Ha'Talmud B.M.* 381, s.v. *R. Ishmael.*

all the Talmudic discussions of *lifnim mishurat hadin,* the person who so acts is a sage and it appears that certain sages were more likely to act beyond the strict dictates of the law than were others.[64] This strengthens the contention that *lifnim mishurat hadin* is attuned to the morals of exceptional individuals.[65]

One may even discern a third view — midway between those of Maimonides and Nahmanides. This view was enunciated by R. Azaria Figo and answers the questions one can pose to both. According to R. Figo, especially righteous people usually act *lifnim mishurat hadin.* Therefore, that which is called

64 See n. 120.

65 It would seem obvious that even though acting *lifnim mishurat hadin* is not incumbent upon everyone according to the elitist theory, he who wants to act *lifnim mishurat hadin* may certainly do so and should even be commended for it. This is the view of several halakhists and scholars (e.g. E.E. Urbach, *The Sages, Their Concepts and Beliefs* (trans. from Hebrew, Jerusalem, 1975) 333. However, S. Albeck, according to his general overall conception of Jewish civil law in Talmudic times, disagrees. According to Albeck (*Dinei Ha'Mamonot ba'Talmud,* (Tel Aviv, 1976) 230–231) the *hassid* and he who acts *lifnim mishurat hadin* follow standards of conduct different from the ordinary individual's standard. Such an individual consciously does not want to act like the ordinary man. He acts as he does because he is someone of greater stature than the majority of people and he measures himself according to this higher standard. The ordinary halakhic demands are based on the expectations of the ordinary individual's behaviour. Equality means, then, that the greater the man the greater is the expectation of a higher degree of conduct on his part. As the expectation level is raised, so is the demand from him. The higher standard demanded of him is similar to the lower standard expected from and demanded of the ordinary individual. Up to this point S. Albeck's view is both logical, incisive and in accordance with one of the main streams of halakhic thought, and similar to the view presently to be discussed in the text. Albeck goes even further, and it is here, we submit, that his stand is wrong. Albeck adds that the ordinary man *should not* act like the greater individual, and in his own words: "An ordinary individual is not permitted to act according to the standard of a great man or to do an act of greatness, for, by so doing, he causes damage to the strict law". Albeck goes on to explain that a certain type of behaviour is expected from a certain type of individual, and if his behaviour is in fact different from what is expected of him — be it *more noble or less noble* — he who so acts is *deceiving society* and his conduct is therefore wrongful. With all due respect to Albeck, it seems to us that pure logic has led him astray and Urbach's statement that in interpersonal relationships it is commendable for all to act *lifnim mishurat hadin* is the correct enunciation of the position of the *halakha.* Albeck's view reminds one of Ihering who wrote — albeit on a different question — that he who waives a legal right is acting immorally, for he who stands on his legal rights is, at the same time, defending the Rule of Law in general. See Ihering, *Der Kampf um's Recht,* (Vienna, 1889).

lifnim mishurat hadin for ordinary people is *din* — law, for these élites, since that is the way they usually behave. The *halakha* has a double standard of demands with respect to ethical behaviour: One is for the ordinary and the other for the exceptional individuals.[66]

R. Shlomo Ha'Kohen of Vilna (who was apparently unaware of R. Azaria Figo's view), presents the same analysis in the name of R. Shlomo Ze'ev, who relies on the reply which Rav gave to Rabbah b. Bar Hannan in a case which we will fuly analyze below.[67] There, Rav demanded of Rabbah b. Bar Hannan action beyond what the strict law demanded of him. Rav quotes to him the verse from Proverbs: "So that thou mayest walk in the way of good men and keep the path of the righteous".[68] What Rav meant to say, explains R. Shlomo Ze'ev, was that those who are good, go their own way, they have a special *derekh tovim* — way of good men, a way different from the way of other ordinary people. From the latter half of the verse which Rav quoted to Rabba b. Bar Hannan "and keep the path of the righteous" one can deduce that the righteous have their own *orhot* — paths which too are at variance with the manners of the common man. Therefore, concludes R. Shlomo Ze'ev, the ordinary people should try to emulate the good and the righteous and walk in their paths, as is written in Proverbs, but the righteous themselves, the *Zadikim,* are duty bound so to act.

R. Shlomo Ha'Kohen of Vilna supports this view with another argument. There is an halakhic view that although one does not have to make the blessing "to sit in the *sukka*" when eating fruit in a *sukka* during the feast of Tabernacles, since according to the *halakha* one is permitted to eat fruit outside the *sukka,* a person who is very stringent in his observance and eats fruit only in a *sukka,* must make the blessing "to sit in the *sukka*" even when eating fruit. R. Shlomo Ha'Kohen explains this law thus: since the sages look favourably upon someone who is so strict on himself that he will not even eat fruit outside of the *sukka,* for him eating fruit only in the *sukka* becomes a legal requirement. Therefore, he must make the blessing "to sit in the *sukka*" when he eats fruit there, whereas others, need not, even though they may be eating fruit in the *sukka* together with him. Similarly, the righteous individual who regularly acts *lifnim mishurat hadin, must* act *lifnim mishurat hadin.*[69]

66 *Bina Le'Itim,* No. 12.

67 See text *infra* beginning at n. 76.

68 Proverbs 2:20.

69 *Azei Broshim, Hilkhot Nedarim,* sec. 53.
Be it as it may, whether *lifnim mishurat hadin* is a legal or a moral imperative, and whether it is referring to an ordinary individual or to. a special one, it is quite clear that R. Ishmael b. Jose in the unloading case, felt that it was his duty — probably legal duty — to help with the unloading. The person carrying the bundle, who attempted to get more and more money from R. Ishmael, was certainly acting in a manner which would cause any normal individual to

Lifnim Mishurat Hadin and Similar Concepts

Is *lifnim mishurat hadin* a concept *sui generis,* or is it known under another name as well, in Talmudic literature? On the one hand it seems from the Tosafits and from Berman's structural analysis of the passages which specifically use the phrase *lifnim mishurat hadin,* that the concept is unique.[70] On the other hand, many modern scholars equate *lifnim mishurat hadin* with other concepts. The discussion of this question is so difficult because commentators throughout the ages frequently used the phrase *lifnim mishurat hadin* in a broad non-technical sense when describing good conduct beyond what the strict law decrees. The concepts to which *lifnim mishurat hadin* have most frequently been equated are *midat hassidut* — the standard of men of piety and virtue,[71] *gemilut hessed*—deeds of lovingkindness[72] and *dinei*

stop paying him — unless the individual was of the opinion that he had an halakhic duty to help with the unloading no matter what the circumstances were. So, it seems, R. Ishmael felt halakhically *obliged* to act, time and time again, *lifnim mishurat hadin.*

70 Text at nn. 15–17.

71 Rashi *B.M.* 83a s.v. *b'derekh; B.K.* 108a s.v. *tavuhu be'alim; ibid,* 108b, s.v. *at avdat;* cf. Rashi, *R.H.* 17b s.v. *hassid.* Here Rashi is explaining the verse "The Lord is righteous in all His ways and gracious (= *hassid*) in all His works" (Psalms 145:17)and the Talmud's comment that "at first righteous and at the end gracious". Rashi comments on the word *hassid* — *lifnim min hashura,* i.e. within (or beyond) the line (of the law). Perhaps Rashi decided to use a phrase almost identical with *lifnim mishurat hadin,* i.e. *lifnim min hashura* to explain the Talmud's exegesis of this verse, because of the use of the word *ma'aseh* (= works) both here — *hasid bekhol ma'asav* — "gracious in all his works" and the verse which teaches us *lifnim mishurat hadin* — *ha'ma'ase asher ya'asun* — and the *works* that they shall do; Tosafot, *Ketuvot* 89a s.v. *shema mina;* R. David Kimhi (Radak) to Psalms 4:4.

72 Rashi *B.M.* 33a s.v. *kol; Sh. Ar. Hoshen Mishpat,* 264:1, based verbatim on Rashi (an unusual phenomenon). Perhaps the most developed discussion and equation of the maxim *lifnim mishurat hadin* with the idea of *gemilut hessed* is found in the writing of Maharal of Prague. To him *hessed* — lovingkindness, and *lifnim mishurat hadin* are one. The exegesis on the verse "And thou shalt show them the way they must walk therein and the work that they shall do:" refers to different aspects of *hessed* or *gemilut hessed* — including the last exegesis wherein *lifnim mishurat hadin* is adduced. R. Yohanan's statement that Jerusalem was destroyed only because the people stood adament in their rights according to the strict law is explained in the following manner: Just as the people desired *midat hadin* — strict law, so God judged them according to *midat hadin* and not according to *midat harahamim* — the degree of compassion. If they would have acted according to *lifnim mishurat hadin,* so would God have acted toward them according to *hessed,* as it is written *olam hessed yibaneh* — "the world shall be built up by Mercy" (Psalms 89:2). Just as the world is built on mercy so also the opposite is true, — it will be

shamayim—the Laws of Heaven (or *Lazet yedei shamayim*) — in order to discharge his duty toward Heaven.[73] Urbach[74] equates *lifnim mishurat hadin* with *midat hassidut*—the standard of men of piety and virtue, and disagrees with Silberg's equating *midat hassidut* with *"ein ruah hakhamim noha heimenu"*—"the spirit of the sages is not pleased with him". Urbach is undoubtedly closer to the truth than is Silberg.[75] But, if one accepts the non-élitist view of *lifnim mishurat hadin,* even Urbach is wrong: *middat hassidut* and *lifnim mishurat hadin* according to this view, are not interchangeable. One cannot do justice to the question of the relationship of these other concepts to *lifnim mishurat hadin* without a comprehensive analysis of them which is beyond the scope of this paper.

"That thou Mayest Walk in the Path of Good Men"

A proper discussion of *lifnim mishurat hadin* necessitates comparative analysis of an important passage in the Babylonian Talmud and its parallel in the Palestinian Talmud, even though, in both sources, the words *lifnim mishurat hadin* are not explicitly mentioned. Many, if not most, halakhists and modern scholars explain the passage as another illustration of *lifnim mishurat hadin*. For example, Rashi, in his commentary states as a matter of fact, that what one Amora answered to another, in the following episode, is that he should act *lifnim mishurat hadin.*[76] Here is the episode—as related in the Babylonian Talmud: "Some porters broke a barrel of wine belonging to Rabbah b. Bar Hannan.[77] Thereupon he seized their garment; so they

destroyed, as was Jerusalem, when there is no *hessed* i.e., no *lifnim mishurat hadin* (*Netivot Olam, Netiv Gemilut Hassadim,* chap. 5).

73 Responsa of Maharil (*Hahadashot*) No. 137.

74 Urbach, *ibid.,* 332.

75 Silberg, *ibid.,* 94–95, 115.

76 Rashi, *B.M.* 83a s.v. *b'derekh.*

77 Other readings are Rabbah b. R. Huna, Rabbah B. Hanna, Rabbah b. Hannan. If the reading of the next name brought in this passage, Rav, is correct, then it would be difficult to accept the printed editions' Rabbah b. Bar-Hannan since Rav flourished during the first generation of Babylonian Amoraim, and Rabbah b. Bar-Hannan flourished during the third generation. Therefore, it is most likely, as Ch. Albeck conjectures (see Albeck, *Mavo La'Talmudim* (Tel Aviv, 1969) that the correct reading should be Rabbah b. Hanna, Rav's contemporary and kin. Albeck shows that interpolations between Rabbah b. Bar Hannan and Rabbah b. Hanna are common. However, if the correct reading in the continuation of the passage is Raba, as is found in some texts, then Rabbah bar Hannan seems more appropriate. Silberg (*ibid.,* 121) prefers the reading Rabbah bar Rav Huna. He explains that we are witnessing a special rabbi-disciple relationship. Rav Huna was Rav's disciple and Rav Huna's son, Rabbah also studied under Rav. From this Silberg asserts that Rav is not giving a legal decision but is only explaining to his disciple how one should ethically behave in such a situation. The passage, according to Silberg, is describing a unique situation of a rabbi-disciple relationship.

went and complained to Rav.[78] 'Return them their garments', he ordered. 'Is that the law?' he enquired. 'Yes',[79] he rejoined: 'That thou mayest walk in the way of good men'.[80] Their garments having been returned, they observed, 'We are poor men, have worked all day, and are hungry, are we to get nothing?' 'Go and pay them' he ordered. 'Is that the law?' he asked. 'Yes', he rejoined, 'and keep the path of the righteous'."[81]

A similar story, though differing in some very important details, is brought in the Palestinian Talmud.

"R. Nehemia taught: A potter handed over his pots to a certain individual. They broke. He (the potter) took off his (the individual's) garment. He went before R. Jose b. Hanina. He (R. Jose b. Hanina) said to him 'Go and tell him 'That thou mayest walk in the way of good men'. He went and told him so, and he returned his garment. He (R. Jose b. Hanina) said to him: 'Will he (the potter) pay you your wages?' He rejoined: 'No', he said to him, 'Go and tell him 'and keep the path of the righteous'. He went and told him so, and he gave him his wages."[82]

It cannot be stated with certainty whether these are two separate incidents or parallel versions of one incident.[83] In any event, before analyzing the cases we will first point out the major differences between the Palestinian and Babylonian Talmudic versions. We will then discuss, *inter alia,* the significance of these differences.

1. In the Palestinian Talmud the story is introduced by R. Nehemia.[84] There is no such introduction in the Babylonian Talmud.

2. The Babylonian Talmud gives us the name of the employer, he is one of the Amoraim, a sage; in the Palestinian Talmud the employer is an anonymous individual.

3. In the Babylonian Talmud the workers broke a barrel of wine; in the Palestinian Talmud—the employee broke the pots of his employer, a potter.

4. In the Babylonian Talmud the workers came before Rav with their complaint, and the employer was also present before Rav. In the Palestinian Talmud the employer is not present when the employee complains before R.

78 See preceding note.

79 Most readings omit this reply "yes"—of Rav's and only bring the quote from Proverbs as Rav's reply.

80 Proverbs 2:20.

81 *B.M.* 83a.

82 *Yer. B.M.* chap. 6, 6 (27a-b).

83 E.g., Silberg, *ibid.*, 119–120.

84 Some scholars argue that something is missing in the text of the Palestinian Talmud, since the phrase used — *tania* — (*"Tania R. Nehemia"* (= R. Nehemia taught) is usual when introducing something Tannaitic and not Amoraic, as is the case here. But Ch. Albeck has already shown that the phrase *tania* can also be found prefacing an Amoraic source (See Ch. Albeck "Le'Ofyan shel Ha'Halakhot b'Seder Nezikin", in *Torah She-B'al Peh,* vol. 4, pp. 24–25, n. 20).

Jose b. Hanina. The worker related R. Jose's decision back to his employer, the potter.

5. In the Babylonian Talmud the Rabbi before whom the complaint came was Rav.[85] In the Palestinian Talmud, it is R. Jose b. Hanina.

6. In the Babylonian Talmud Rav was asked if this is the law. In the Palestinian Talmud such a query is absent. Furthermore, according to some readings of the text, Rav gave an affirmative answer to the question.

7. In the Babylonian Talmud the workers complain that they are poor, worked all day and are hungry. This is missing in the Palestinian version.

8. In the Babylonian Talmud it is the workers who ask for their wages. In the Palestinian Talmud they do not bring up the topic of their wages; it is R. Jose b. Hanina, on his own initiative who asks of them if they were paid.

9. In the Babylonian Talmud it is specifically stated that the Rabbi told the employer to return the garments and to pay their wages. In the Palestinian Talmud such specifics are missing, although from the context of the story it is clear that the Rabbi meant to tell the employer that he should so act.

It is obvious that the Babylonian version is a more developed one—if we are talking about the same case—and, according to Silberg,[86] is the more "authentic" one. Of course one can argue against such a view, and Talmudic scholars could certainly put up a forceful argument against choosing the Babylonian text here as the one closer to historic certainty. But, as already mentioned, these may well be two different but similar stories; there is no need to discuss which of the two texts is to be preferred. In terms of the development of halakhic thought, the Babylonian Talmud's version is the more important one, since most halakhists refer only to it and not to the Palestinian source in their discussions—(a well known phenomenon concerning the Palestinian Talmud). We shall see, though, that there are very significant differences to be deduced by comparing the two versions.

Why are the workers liable according to strict law? The most obvious explanation is that they were negligent. This view is espoused by some of the most authoritative commentators.[87] Others, however, explain the situation differently.[88] The difficulty with the "negligence" explanation is that if the workers were indeed proven to have been negligent, they would not have a moral claim against their employer. Furthermore, if one understands the answer of Rav as his stating that the law itself is on the workers' side, they could not have been negligent.

85 See n. 77.

86 Silberg, *ibid.*

87 Rashi, *B.M.* 83a s.v. *shkulei; Tur Hoshen Mishpat*, 304.

88 Rashi, *ibid.*, second explanation; *Shita Mekubetzet B.M.* 83a; Meiri, *B.M.* 83a; *Shitat Hakadmonim, Talmid Ha'Rashba B.M.* 83a; *Hidushei Haramban B.M.* 83a; *Maharsha, Hidushei Aggadot, B.M.* 83a; *Or Zarua B.M.* 278. *Cf.* Ch. Albeck, *ibid.*, who has a novel explanation of this passage, but upon closer scrutiny, it is not free from flaws.

As mentioned above, there are two different readings of the text concerning Rav's answer. It seems that the correct reading is the one which omits the affirmative reply to the question "is this the law"? (it is omitted in most of the more reliable Talmudic and halakhic texts and manuscripts), and we agree with those halakhists and scholars who explain the passage as one of a moral duty but not a legal one. Furthermore, even if the text would read 'yes' as Rav's answer, we would still be very hesitant to explain this passage as one concerned with a statement of law. Even those who explain this passage on the basis of the printed text, can explain Rav's answer as referring to the realm of morals and ethics rather than strict law.[89]

Even without taking a stand on the question of whether Rav gave a legal or only an ethical judgment, we can discuss the reason behind Rav's choice of this verse from Proverbs as appropriate for the situation which was presented to him. While only a few of the traditional commentators attempt to explain why Rav chose this particular verse, many contemporary scholars do so. The following is a representative sampling of interpretations.

Maharsha explains Rav's choice of the verse from Proverbs as a play on words. Rav told Rabbah b. Bar Hannan that since he sent the labourers down an incline (as it appears from the preceding Talmudic passage) the labourers were not at fault. Therefore, the verse "that thou mayst *walk* in the *way* of *good* men" is a hint that he should have sent them to walk on a good, straight way (road = *derech*).[90] Although the explanation is not very plausible it is most ingenious.[91]

Ch. Albeck, who explains the passage in a novel manner[92] says that our case refers to a *takkanah*—legislation by the Sages—for the good of the worker, which, as a result, is in the long run, for the benefit of employers as well. This *takkanah* stated that even if the worker was negligent and broke the barrel, he is not liable and is even entitled to his wages. The *takkanah* is based on the general halakhic position of legislating in favour of the poor worker.[93] The logic behind the legislation in our case is that if a worker would be held liable and also lose his wages for breaking barrels while transporting them, labourers would not take upon themselves the transportation of barrels, and employers would be at a loss to find labourers. Therefore, such legislation is beneficial both to worker and employer. On the basis of the above theory, Ch. Albeck explains that Rav told Rabbah b. Hanna, his close friend and relative, that he should walk in the ways of the good, i.e., the good Sages who enact such *takkanot* in favour of the

89 See Silberg, *ibid.*, 118–123; Urbach, *ibid.*, 330–331; S.H. Kook, *Iyunim u'Mehkarim*, vol. 1, pp. 188–89.

90 *Hiddushei Aggadot, Maharsha, B.M.* 83a.

91 Resp. *Heshiv Moshe Yoreh Deah* No. 48, who disagrees with this interpretation.

92 Ch. Albeck, *ibid.* But compare *Maharsha, Hiddushei Halakhot B.M.* 83a who explains the passage in a similar, but slightly different manner.

93 See, S. Warhaftig, *Dinei Avodah Ba'Mishpat Haivri* (Tel Aviv, 1969) 2–10.

poor labourer, and that he should "keep the path of the righteous". The latter part of the verse is connected, according to Ch. Albeck, with what the Sages taught: "Be liberal with what is yours and give it to him".[94] Even though, according to strict law, the labourers are entitled to their wages, you should give them their wages from what is legally yours. This, explains Ch. Albeck, is similar to the well-known *takkanah* where the labourer swears he has not received his wages and on the basis of his oath, the employer must pay him even though according to strict law the employee would have had to bring real evidence against his employer who claims that his wages were already paid.[95] A reason given for the enactment of this *takkanah* was that employers too, in general, are satisfied with such a *takkanah* since, if not for the *takkanah,* it would be difficult for an employer to find labourers willing to work for him.

Silberg points out[96] that the reason a verse from Proverbs was brought, rather than the usual Pentateuchal verse quoted in connection with *lifnim mishurat hadin,* was to emphasize the ethical, non-legal aspect of Rav's statement. It is a well known halakhic principle that "Law is not derived from Prophets and Hagiographia".[97]

According to E.E. Urbach, who also asks why was the verse from Proverbs brought instead of the Pentateuchal verse, Rav agrees with R. Joshua's exegesis of the verse from Exodus, and not R. Elazar Ha'Moda'i's, both of which are found in the *Mekhilta* which predated the Amora R. Joseph whose interpretation was brought twice in the Talmud.[98] The *Mekhilta* states: "And Shalt show them the way etc.' meaning the study of the Torah; 'And the Work that They Must Do' meaning good deeds. These are the words of R. Joshua. R. Elazar of Modi'im says: 'And Shalt Show Them' means show them how to live; 'The Way' refers to visiting the sick; 'They Must Walk' refers to burying the dead. 'In' refers to bestowal of kindness. 'And the Work' meaning along the line of strict justice; 'That They Must Do', *lifnim mishurat hadin*".[99] Urbach adds that the verse from Proverbs was brought to teach us that the good and the righteous arrive at such conduct by their own understanding. Rav wanted to emphasize that the employer is *not* enjoined by law so to act, but that he should arrive at such a conclusion basing himself on his own conscience.[100]

94 *B.B.* 88b; *Hullin* 134a. 95 *Shevuot* 45a. 96 Silberg, *ibid.*, 122.

97 This rule is really not a hard and fast rule, and we find many exceptions to it. It seems that the statement that *"divrei Torah midivrei Kabbalah lo yalfinan"* i.e., the rule just mentioned, was not accepted by all the Talmudic Sages. See, E.E. Urbach, "Halakha U'Nevuah" (1958) 18 *Tarbiz* 1–22, at 12.

98 See text at nn. 7 and 9.

99 *Mekhilta, ibid.* Translation by Lauterbach, in Jewish Publication Society edition, vol. 2, p. 182. Cf., *Mekhilta* of R. Simon b. Yohai, Exodus 18:20.

100 Urbach, *ibid.* See too, Y. Muriel, "Hayashar ve'Hatov" (1972) 70 Sinai 92, at 97–99.

As already mentioned, the view of many commentators and scholars is that the case under discussion is another example of *lifnim mishurat hadin* even though this phrase is not explicitly mentioned in the two Talmudic sources. This is the view held by Rashi,[101] R. Jacob b. Asher,[102] R. Joel Sirkes,[103] R. Menahem Mendel Krochmal,[104] R. Moshe Teitelbaum,[105] and in our times, Rabbi Z.Y. Meltzer[106] and Y. Muriel.[107] We think, along with others,[108] that the case before us is different from *lifnim mishurat hadin* since the employer is asked to pay money out of his own pocket, and waive his right to damages, even though there was no fault on his part. Rav is demanding more than *lifnim mishurat hadin*. Some halakhists and scholars compare Rav's ruling to other halakhic concepts, such as one who is God-fearing,[109] or one who acts according to *midat hassidut*,[110] which is according to some authorities, interchangeable with *lifnim mishurat hadin*.[111]

The case of the porters served as the basis for a number of conclusions, some of which are directly concerned with *lifnim mishurat hadin*. For example, one of the arguments in favour of the view that an individual can be compelled to act *lifnim mishurat hadin* is based on an analysis of the porter passage.[112]

101 Rashi, *B.M.* 83a, s.v. *b'derekh*.

102 *Tur Hoshen Mishpat* sec. 304.

103 *Bayit Hadash*, to *Tur, ibid.*

104 *Responsa, Zemah Zedek*, No. 89.

105 *Responsa, Heshiv Moshe, Yoreh Deah*, No. 48.

106 Z.Y. Meltzer, "Lifnim Mishurat Hadin" in *Mizkeret* (Jerusalem, 1962) 310–315.

107 *Ibid.*

108 *Tosafot, B.M.* 24b s.v. *lifnim;* S.H. Kook, *ibid.* The Tosafists graded *lifnim mishurat hadin* into three different levels. 1. Those cases where the verse whence *lifnim mishurat hadin* is adduced is brought, are the examples *par excellence* of the maxim. These are the cases where others are duty-bound, a privileged individual is exempt, and *lifnim mishurat hadin* requires the exempt person to waive his right. These are, for example, the cases of R. Hiyya — the money-changer case — and R. Ishmael b. Jose, the unloading case. 2. Cases of *lifnim mishurat hadin* where the verse is not brought in the Talmud. These are cases where, under the circumstances no one is duty-bound to so act, but an individual is requested to act *lifnim mishurat hadin*. An example of this type is the lost property case. 3. As opposed to cases 1 and 2, the third case is not an example of *lifnim mishurat hadin*. This last case is where someone caused a great loss to another, and nevertheless Jewish law advises the one damaged to waive his right. An example of such a case is the porters breaking the wine barrels; such a situation is *not* considered one where *lifnim mishurat hadin* applies. That is why Rav brought the verse from Proverbs. See too, Meltzer, *op. cit.*, at 312–314 who discusses this *Tosafot.*

109 *Shitat Hakadmonim, Talmid Ha'Rashba, ibid.*

110 *Me'iri, ibid.; Hiddushei Ha'Rashba, B.M.* 83a; S.H. Kook, *ibid.; Be'er Eliahu, Hoshen Mishpat*, sec. 12, 2, n. 9.

111 See above and Y. Muriel, *ibid.*

112 See above text at nn. 18–41, and especially Resp. *Zemah Zedek, ibid.*

The passage in the Babylonian Talmud where, according to the printed text and some other readings, the workers claim that they are poor and have nothing to eat, explains why Rav acted as he did. According to this theory, the circumstances of the porters was mentioned not only to embellish the tale, but to teach us that one does not have to act the way Rev prescribed in all circumstances where workers caused damage to their employers, but only where the workers are in comparatively dire straits. For example, R. Jacob b. Asher writes in his code, the *Turim,* that, in a case such as the one described, the employer should pay his worker's wages "if he has nothing to eat".[113] R. Joel Sirkes, in his commentary on the *Turim,* adds that according to this view, if workers have at least enough for a day's sustenance, they do not have a claim for their wages; but, on the other hand, even if they do have enough to eat, they still are not responsible for the damage they caused.[114] We see quite clearly that the state of the workers is taken into account when deciding to what they are entitled. In another commentary to the *Turim,* the author of the *Perisha* states[115] that we learn from the Talmudic passage under discussion that even if it is not clear that the labourers are poor, they do not have to pay for the damage they caused. His proof is as follows: Rav freed the labourers from responsibility for the damage they caused, even before he knew of their financial situation. He became aware of the porter's being destitute only later, and this information influenced his decision on their claim for wages.[116]

From the Babylonian passage, some halakhists and scholars try to prove that the duty to act the way Rav ordered, is a duty only for special individuals—such as the Amora Rabbah b. Bar Hannan.[117] Others develop this theme, declaring that the moral duty turns into a legal one for these special people.[118] Still others bring evidence for the opposite view, from the story as told in the Palestinian Talmud. There, as against the Babylonian Talmud's tale, the employer is an ordinary individual, not a Sage; nevertheless R.

113 *Tur Hoshen Mishpat* 304, 1.

114 *Bayit Hadash,* to *Tur, ibid.*

115 *Perisha* to *Tur, ibid.*

116 Silberg (*ibid.* 122) puts much emphasis on the fact that the labourers were destitute and were it not for this fact Rav would not have ordered Rava bar Rav Huna to pay them their wages. One can answer these types of arguments by quoting the text of the Palestinian Talmud, where no mention is made of the worker being poor and hungry, proving that the workers' financial situation plays no role in deciding such a question. However, one can rebut by arguing that it was a known fact that such workers were poor; for Silberg, the question from the Palestinian Talmud is not valid since he is of the opinion that the Babylonian story is a more authentic and fuller version of the same tale. See above text at n. 86.

117 S. Federbush, *ibid.*, 81; S.H. Kook, *ibid.*

118 See above, text at nn. 66–69.

Jose b. Hanina ordered him to act beyond the scope of the strict law.[119] These differences of opinion are relevant to the problem described above concerning the identity of the person to whom *lifnim mishurat hadin* is addressed, and we have already discussed them in detail.[120]

R. Sa'adia Gaon, in explaining the passage under discussion[121] expresses a view which seems to be based on a correct interpretation of the passage

119 Z.Y. Meltzer, *ibid.*, 312.

120 See text at nn. 41–69. From the texts we have discussed in this article, and from some other texts which we shall presently bring, we become aware of the fact that certain Sages were especially prone to act beyond the demands of the law. One may even be inclined to submit this as evidence supporting the view that *lifnim mishurat hadin* is addressed to the élite and not to the common man. For example, we have seen that R. Papa's conduct was twice referred to as *lifnim mishrat hadin* (see *supra* text at nn. 13–14). R. Hiyya acted *lifnim mishurat hadin* in the moneychanger case, and also in another situation it is reported that he paid labourers, even though he did not have to do so according to strict law, and he made a point of this fact by stating that according to strict law he owes nothing to the workers, but since he is R. Hiyya, he will pay them nevertheless (Jer. Talmud *B.M.* 6, 1(25a). It is perhaps Rav who is most frequently associated with conduct beyond the dictates of the strict law. It is Rav who makes the statement concerning the return of a lost article that even though according to the law precedence is given to efforts made in order to return one's own lost article before returning another's lost article, he who constantly acts so will in the end become destitute and fall upon the mercy of others (*B.M.* 33a and Rashi, *ibid.*). It is Rav who gave the zuz to the woman in the moneychanger case at the request of his uncle R. Hiyya, and it is Rav who tells R. Hiyya to pay the above-mentioned labourers even though R. Hiyya was not duty-bound to do so under the circumstances. If the correct reading of the text in *Yoma* 87b is Rav (See *Dikdukei Soferim*) then we probably have a further example of Rav's acting beyond the line of the law, e.g., Rav's asking forgiveness for a slight he caused to another, more than the limit of three times prescribed by law. (See Rashi, *Yoma, ibid.*, s.v. *Rav.* Even if the text is *"Rav"* and not *"rabbo"*, not all the commentators agree with Rashi's explanation that Rav acted beyond the strict law, but they, too, explain that R. Hanina was Rav's teacher and concerning one's teacher the law is more stringent as to the process of asking for his pardon). It was Rav, according to most readings of the text, who told the employer in the porter case to act beyond the strict law and to return their garments and pay their wages. Again it is Rav who, according to the Palestinian Talmud, acted stringently with himself in that although he decided for others that a certain promise to give a gift was not legally binding, he felt himself bound to give such a gift and commanded members of his own household to make good such a promise, acting in accordance with *midat hassidut* (Yer. *Shevi'it* end of chap. 10).

121 Brought in S.Y. Cohen, "Lifnim Mishurat Hadin" in *The Adam Noah Braun Memorial Volume* (Jerusalem, 1969) 166.

and its ramifications. The duty to act in the manner that Rav advised is a personal duty of an individual. It is not, however, the duty of a court to judge in this manner. R. Sa'adia adds that a judge is not permitted to decide in this manner, for if he would do so, he would be iniquitous — acting contrary to the Biblical commandments "Ye shall do no unrighteousness in judgment; thou shalt not respect the person of the poor. . ."[122] Without being aware of R. Sa'adia Gaon's view, Ch. Albeck comes to the same conclusion.[123] Rabbi Meltzer on the other hand, comes to a completely different conclusion.[124] He emphasizes the text of the Palestinian Talmud and learns from this text that it is incumbent on the court to act beyond the limits of strict law. Recall that in the Yerushalmi story R. Jose b. Hanina took the initiative; although the worker did not demand his wages, R. Jose b. Hanina asked him if he was paid and when he discovered that he was not, ordered the employer to pay, basing himself on the verse from Proverbs. Rabbi Meltzer equates this case with *lifnim mishurat hadin* and learns from here that the court itself must decide according to that maxim.[125]

In concluding our discussion of the porter passage, we would like to submit a novel explanation. Our case may be related to two other Talmudic sources and legal problems. One of these concerns a debtor's property that is exempt from execution, and the other, the question of whether or not one may be compelled to give charity.

122 Lev. 19:15.

123 Ch. Albeck, *ibid.*, 23–25. But here, we submit, one must be careful about his conclusions. Both Albeck and S.Y. Cohen (*ibid.*, 176–177) automatically equate the barrels of wine case with *lifnim mishurat hadin*. Rabbi Cohen goes so far as to state that R. Sa'adia Gaon is discussing *lifnim mishurat hadin* — although R. Sa'adia is only explaining the passage under discussion which does not mention *lifnim mishurat hadin*. One cannot prove from R. Sa'adia Gaon's explanation whether that is his stand concerning *lifnim mishurat hadin* in general.

124 Z.Y.Meltzer, *ibid.*, 312.

125 Perhaps an argument in favour of R. Sa'adia Gaon's view can be deduced from what is related in the Talmud about R. Yohanan. As the reader will recall, it was R. Yohanan who related that Jerusalem was destroyed because *lifnim mishurat hadin* was not followed. (As mentioned above, it is not clear whether R. Yohanan is referring to court judgments or to people's individual action). It seems, though, that when a case came before him, he decided according to the strict law even though in similar circumstances R. Hiyya, in the moneychanger case, acted *lifnim mishurat hadin*. A *shohet* caused an animal to be *terefa* and R. Yohanan was asked if the *shohet* is liable for damages. He answered that if the *shohet* was an expert (and did not receive remuneration for his *shehita*), he is not liable. One may perhaps, deduce from here that since R. Yohanan did not decide that the expert *shohet* should be liable, as R. Hiyya the exceptionally expert moneychanger decided concerning himself, a judge should not compel a side to the proceedings to act *lifnim mishurat hadin*. *Cf. Biur Ha'Gra, Hoshen Mishpat* Sec. 12, 2 and *Biur Eliahu, ibid.*

The law of civil execution, as finally decided in Talmudic times, protected the debtor from having certain basic property taken from him by his creditors. One of the obvious examples of this rule is that a debtor is left with his basic garments which the creditor has no right to take in lieu of the debt. But, as I have pointed out elsewhere,[126] during the Amoraic period the law was unclear. It appears that at one time during that period the law was that a creditor was permitted to take all of the debtor's property to satisfy his debt. With this in mind, we can reconstruct the first part of our broken barrels story thus: Rabbah b. Bar Hannan took the garments since he was of the opinion — which was prevalent at the time — that the law concerning the exemption of the debtor's basic property did not apply. Rav answered that although such is the strict law, I tell you that you should return the garments to them on the basis of the ethical imperative as enunciated in Proverbs.[127]

Having explained the first of Rav's answers to Rabbah b. Bar Hannan, we turn to his second decision. Rabbah b. Bar Hannan did not pay the porters their wages. Legally, he was within his rights, since the workers caused him such great damage. However, we have seen from the Babylonian Talmud that the workers were extremely poor and even lacked food. Rav told Rabbah b. Bar Hannan that at least as a charitable duty he should pay them. But Rabbah b. Bar Hannan was aware of Rav's view — albeit a minority view — that one may not compel another to give charity.[128] Therefore, Rabbah b. Bar Hannan asked Rav "is this the law"? — knowing all too well that Rav would have to answer in the negative. To which Rav answered, that although it is true that this is not the strict law, one should act generously and take the good and the righteous path.

126 S. Shilo, "Debtor's Property Exempt from Execution in Jewish Law" (1970) 2 *Mishpatim* 67–82.

127 Another possible explanation in this same context of the debtor's rights against execution, may be the following: Even when the law was accepted that certain property of the debtor was exempt from execution — including his clothing — it applied only to debts arising from a loan but not to debts from another cause e.g. a tort, which in fact is the view of one halakhic school of thought. (See *Sefer Ha'Trumot*, Gate 1, part 2, sce. 3; *Tur Hoshen Mishpat* sec. 97, 24; *cf. Tur, ibid.*, 97, 25, where a dissenting view of R. Meir Halevi Abulafia is brought. See too, *Levush Ir Shushan*, 97, 29; *Sh.Ar. Hoshen Mishpat*, sec. 97, 29, and *Biur Ha'Gra, ibid.*, sub-sec. 101; *Arukh Ha'shulhan, Hoshen Mishpat* 97, 35; *Avnei Nezer, Hoshen Mishpat*, 39). If so, then perhaps, Rabbah b. Bar Hannan took the garments according to his strictly legal rights since the debt to him was one based on a tort. Rav, when asked about this case, agreed that this is the strict law, but told the creditor to return the clothing to them on the basis of the above-mentioned ethical imperative.

128 *Baba Batra* 8b; and, see Rashi, *ibid.*, s.v. *u'pakadeti*.

Concluding Remarks

Having studied in depth the halakhic concept of *lifnim mishurat hadin,* it seems appropriate to classify it, according to Lord Moulton's system of law and manners,[129] as the domain of Obedience to the Unenforceable. Lord Moulton has pointed out "the dangers that threaten the maintenance of this domain" by the "countless supporters of the movement to enlarge the sphere of Positive Law", and we have seen this threat in the Jewish legal system by those who attempt to make *lifnim mishurat hadin* actionable and enforceable even by coercion. We feel that in spite of some voices to the contrary in the later development of the *halakha, lifnim mishurat hadin* is an excellent example of what Lord Moulton is discussing, when he writes: "In that domain there is no law which inexorably determines our course of action, and yet we feel that we are not free to choose as we would... The obedience is the obedience of a man to that which he cannot be forced to obey. He is the enforcer of the law upon himself... This is the land in which all those whom the law cannot reach take refuge... The infinite variety of circumstances surrounding the individual and rightly influencing his action make it impossible to subject him in all things to rules rigidly prescribed and duly enforced. Thus there was wisely left the intermediate domain which, so far as Positive Law is concerned, is a land of freedom of action, but in which the individual should feel that he was not wholly free... But there is a widespread tendency to regard the fact that they can do a thing as meaning that they may do it. There can be no more fatal error than this. Between 'can do' and 'may do' ought to exist the whole realm which recognizes the sway of duty, fairness, sympathy, taste, and all the other things that make life beautiful and society possible".

Lord Moulton has given expression to much of what we have learnt from the halakhic Sages. However, there are at times different emphases in Lord Moulton and in the halakhists, which are only natural when considering that the two were moulded by such different cultures and legal systems.

In conclusion, may we suggest that the reader reflect upon the following question: Does the Jewish system of values and law agree with Lord Moulton that "the true greatness of a nation, its true civilization, is measured by this land of Obedience to the Unenforceable"?

129 J.F. Moulton, "Law and Manners" (July, 1924) The Atlantic Monthly 1–5.

APPENDIX

There are many examples in the Jewish legal system of what is universally recognized as "equity". The universal striving for equitable solutions within any given legal system, and the development of legal, quasi-legal and moral imperatives as a result of such human striving, is all too well known. The Roman *aequitas* and the Greek *epeukeia* which greatly influenced the former, immediately come to mind. It would be of great interest to compare equitable developments in both ancient and modern legal systems with similar developments in Jewish law. It would go very much beyond the scope of an appendix or even an article, to do so. However, to arouse a comparative jurist's curiosity, a few equitable developments and rules of equity in some legal systems, which have their counterparts in Jewish law, will be briefly alluded to.

The Bible is replete with equitable and moral commands. It is questionable, however, whether in Biblical times such admonitions were fully integrated into the legal system of the Hebrews. Be it as it may, there is no doubt that during the classical period in the development of Jewish law — Talmudic times — equitable principles akin to those classified as such by modern jurists and philosophers, had already become part of its legal system.

For example, the Pentateuch tells us to "do that which is right and good in the sight of the Lord". This command is repeated twice in the Pentateuch. On the basis of these verses, Jewish law arrived at two equitable principles, which, already in Talmudic times, had become law. One is an equity of redemption — a rule of equity whose counterpart in English law has been described by Professor David M. Walker, a leading modern British jurist as Chancery's "greatest contribution" to the law of mortgages. The other one, the right of pre-emption of an abutter, for historical reasons, does not find its parallel in English law. However, it is found in many other legal systems, and is recognized as an example of a legal right which developed from equitable principles.

Upon reading the Biblical command to do "what is right and good", one is immediately struck by its similarity to the Roman rule of equity, of *aequum et bonum* — "right and good". It is not our purpose here to discuss the vexing question whether Roman law was influenced by Jewish law or if the early English judges and jurists who referred to *aequum et bonum* were basing themselves on Roman precedents or on the Bible.

In addition to the already mentioned equity of redemption and the right of pre-emption, the Roman *actio negotiorum gestio* which has found its way into many modern legal systems, is based on Roman equitable principles and has its parallel in Jewish law. Similarly, the Roman view that a will may be automatically revoked by the birth of a child subsequent to the date of the will, by an implied condition *si testator sine libres decesserit,* a rule which has been accepted by various modern legal systems, is akin to the Talmudic case of nullifying a gift in contemplation of death where the donor excluded his son as a beneficiary since he believed that his son had already died while, in fact, his son was living. A third example is that of decisions of courts reducing professional fees or rewards promised by a person in danger, decisions based — at least according to the French judiciary and jurists — in equity. Here, too, the Talmud arrives at the very same conclusion. In all three examples non-Jewish law bases itself on principles of equity: Jewish law developed these equitable rules within the strict law itself.

Perhaps the most fruitful field for comparison is the concept of abuse of rights — a highly developed principle of law in the civil law, but not developed in English law. In Jewish law there is a conceptual similarity leading to the same legal conclusions arrived at by the civil law systems. Here, as opposed to the aforementioned examples, the development of the principle akin to abuse of rights, in Jewish law, is clearly based on equity. This Talmudic rule is known as *kofin al midat Sodom* "we coerce over a trait of Sodom". This trait of Sodom is one of selfishness which denies others where there is no gain to oneself. The application of this principle in Jewish law is much wider in scope than what is accepted by modern legal systems which recognize the equitable principle of abuse of rights. In both modern and Jewish law, the law will, under certain circumstances, compel an individual to waive his legal right where exercising such a right is not especially beneficial to the possessor of the right and damaging to another. Jewish law has taken that giant step forward where the modern juridical developers of the abuse of rights principle fear to tread. In Jewish law, not only possible damage to another can lead to the legal coercion of the holder of the right to refrain from exercising his right. Where the holder of the right would gain nothing in its exercise and by not exercising his right another would benefit (i.e., not merely sustain a loss), the former can, under certain circumstances, be compelled to refrain from using his right so that his fellow man could profit.

Finally, much is to be gained by comparing the legal and moral reasoning behind the universal need and striving for equity in a given legal system. For instance, a discussion of the views of that great jurist of Jewish law, Nahmanides, and those of Rabbi Vidal of Toulouse together with those of that greatest of England's jurists, Blackstone, enlarging on Grotius, would be stimulating indeed. Comparing what those Jewish jurists wrote[130] with the following words of Blackstone, one can readily see the universality of many aspects of legal theory: "From this method of interpreting laws by the

130 See *supra* nn. 49-51 and accompanying text.

reason of them, arise what we call *equity;* which is thus defined by Grotius, the correction of that, wherein the law is deficient. For since in laws all cases cannot be foreseen or expressed, it is necessary, that when the general decrees of the law come to be applied to particular cases, there should be somewhere a power vested of defining those circumstances (which had they been foreseen) the legislator himself would have expressed. And these are the cases which, according to Grotius, *lex non exacte definit, sed arbitrio boni viri permittit*". [131]

It is hoped that this appendix will whet the intellectual appetite both of scholars of Jewish law and jurists concerned with comparative law, and encourage them to deal with this neglected area of jurisprudence, i.e., the comparative study of Jewish law with other legal systems. Such study could yield a rich mine of provocative thought.

131 *Blackstone's Commentaries,* Book I, sec. 2.

Part V
The Juristic Process in Jewish Legal Theory

[15]

FREEDOM AND CONSTRAINT IN THE JEWISH JUDICIAL PROCESS*

NORMAN LAMM**
AARON KIRSCHENBAUM***

Benjamin Nathan Cardozo, in his small but influential volume, *The Nature of the Judicial Process*,[1] made a major effort to separate and describe the subjective elements that operate in the judge's decision-making process and in the body of objective law which he

---

*ED. NOTE: To aid the uninitiated reader in following Dr. Lamm's and Professor Kirschenbaum's discussion, we offer a brief chronological overview of the basic rabbinical texts employed in the article.

The oral interpretation of biblical law, passed down from Moses through the sages of each generation, was first redacted by R. Judah ha-Nasi (d. 219 C.E.) in the topical compendium known as the *Mishnah*. The *Mishnah* is subdivided into six Orders, each of which deals with a broad self-contained area of the law (*e.g.*, *Nezikin* (Torts)). The six Orders are further subdivided into a total of sixty-three tractates, each of which explores a circumscribed topic (*e.g.*, *Sanhedrin* (Judges)) within the more general Order. Scholars in the *Mishnahic* era were known as *Tannaim*. The *Gemara*, a large body of commentary to and expansion upon the *Mishnah*, was developed over the next four centuries. There are two *Gemarot* (plural of *Gemara*), one that was composed in the Babylonian academies and another that represented the contributions of the Palestinian scholars. The former is the more exhaustive and authoritative of the two *Gemarot;* citations to any of the tractates refer to the Babylonian *Gemara* unless prefaced with the notation T.J. (Talmud Jerusalem). Scholars cited in the *Gemara* were known as *Amoraim*. The *Mishnah* and the *Gemara* form the component parts of the Talmud, the basic text of rabbinic learning.

The post-talmudic history of Jewish scholarship is divided into three eras: the era of the *Geonic* (roughly 600-1050), the era of the *Rishonim* (early scholars—roughly 1050-1550), and the era of the *Acharonim* (latter-day scholars—roughly 1550 until the present). Outstanding among the *geonim* was Saadia Gaon, whose philosophical works are considered classics to this very day. Prominent among the numerous *Rishonim* whose works are cited by Dr. Lamm and Professor Kirschenbaum is Maimonides (1135-1204), who contributed a formal Code of Jewish Law (*Mishneh Torah),* as well as numerous commentaries and philosophical writings. R. Joseph Karo's *Shulchan Arukh*, composed during the middle of the sixteenth century, serves as the authoritative Code of Jewish Law, and is often viewed as demarcating the era of the *Rishonim* from that of the *Acharonim*. Aside from commentaries and codes, rabbinic writings include a vast body of responsa literature that provide great insight into the decision-making process of the Jewish judge.

For an elaborate discussion of the chronology and structure of Jewish Law, *see*, *e.g.*, D. FELDMAN, MARITAL RELATIONS, BIRTH CONTROL, AND ABORTION IN JEWISH LAW 3-18 (paperback ed. 1974); M. MARGOLIS & A. MARX, A HISTORY OF THE JEWISH PEOPLE 216-76, 321-64 (1938).

** President and Erna and Jakob Michael Professor of Jewish Philosophy, Yeshiva University. B.A., Yeshiva College, 1949; Ph.D., Bernard Revel Graduate School, 1966.

*** Professor of Law, Tel Aviv University. B.A., Brooklyn College, 1946; M.H.L., Jewish Theological Seminary, 1950; D.H.L., Jewish Theological Seminary, 1967; Ph.D., Columbia University, 1969.

[1] B. CARDOZO, THE NATURE OF THE JUDICIAL PROCESS (1921).

must consult and whose loyal interpreter he must be in reaching a judicial decision. The four "methods"[2] he elaborates offer a structure by which to probe the degree of freedom of and restraint upon the judge in his judicial role.

It is appropriate to pursue the same theme in other forms and traditions of law. This essay is devoted to a preliminary exploration of the question of freedom and constraint in the Jewish judicial process. Because of certain basic dissimilarities between Jewish law (*Halakhah*) and Anglo-Saxon and American law, the problem will have to be posed in different form and begin with more fundamental philosophic issues. Hence, we shall first investigate the theoretical underpinnings of the question, and we shall then proceed to a *halakhic* survey and analysis.

I. The Halakhic System: Monistic or Pluralistic?

The *Halakhah* claims for itself divine origin: the Written Law (or *Torah*—*i.e.*, the Scriptures, especially the Pentateuch) and the Oral Law (later reduced into writing in the Talmud) were revealed to Moses at Mount Sinai, and contained a warrant for the judges of each succeeding generation to decide, in each case brought before them, all doubts and disputes in the light of the revealed legislation. This assumption of divine provenance must, of course, be accepted at face value and on its own terms if any investigation into the nature of the *halakhic* judicial process is to be valid in assessing the role of the judge who must, a priori, accept this assumption in order to qualify as a judge.

The problem, then, may be stated as follows: Is the *Halakhah*, which has undergone massive development and elaboration through the centuries, always assumed to be in consonance with the absolute, divinely revealed will; or is it, despite its transcendent origin, open to a plurality of judgments, all of which retain divine sanction? If we choose the first option, then there is only one valid solution to every legal problem, and the judge is thus denied any significant latitude. Under this approach, judicial error (in the sense of non-conformity with the Absolute, rather than technical error) represents a major catastrophe: the falsification of the single unequivocal divine will. The conscientious judge who is aware of this potential catastrophe will obviously approach his task with great trepidation and is likely to con-

---

[2] They are more accurately described as classification devices. *See* G.E. White, The American Judicial Tradition 259 (1976).

sider his range of discretion severely constrained. If we accept the second thesis, we assume a plurality of valid solutions, at least theoretically, and we broaden the scope of the judge and allow him significant freedom in coming to a decision. In pursuing this issue, it must be borne in mind that the sources are mostly indirect, and that we do not find this formulation explicitly in them. The great *halakhists* were, for the most part, practitioners rather than philosophers of the law.

Some of the renowned medieval talmudists (*Rishonim*) incline to a monistic view of the *Halakhah*: there is only one correct decision, and that is presumed to accord with the divine will. The laws of the *Halakhah*, like the moral qualities of right and wrong, are intrinsic. As the revealed will of God, the *Halakhah* presents us with norms that are ontological and hence not subject to qualification. The judge's role, in this case, is solely that of the transmitter of the law, and his creativity is limited to the discovery, transmission, and promulgation of the true law which, though previously unknown, is indeed the authentic will of the divine legislator.

The author of *Sefer ha-Chinnukh*, commenting on the principle of majority rule,[3] holds that it is not only a legal procedure for adjudication, but also a desirable means for arriving at the truth:

> When [the two sides] are equal or approximately equal in wisdom, the *Torah* informed us that the majority views always accord with the truth, more so than the minority; and whether or not it indeed accords with the truth according to the opinion of the observer, the law is that we may not depart from the way of the majority.[4]

Yehudah Halevi, referring to the Biblical injunction against adding to or detracting from the Law, coupled with the grant of the right to interpret doubtful issues to the priests or judges of each generation,[5] maintains that they have divine assistance and would never concur in anything which contradicts the *Torah*.[6] The infallibility of

---

[3] This principle is derived from the accepted talmudic interpretation of *Exodus* 23:2. *See generally Mishnayot Sanhedrin* 1:1; *Bava Metzia* 59b; *Chullin* 11a; T.J. *Moed Katan* 3:1; *Sanhedrin* 29a, *Rashi s.v. shenayim*. Although the plain meaning (*peshat*) of the scriptural text is quite different, the Oral Law—as recorded in the above sources—does attach the principle of majority rule in a divided court to the last three words of this verse; hence it is accorded the authority of Biblical Law.

[4] SEFER HA-CHINNUKH, Commandment 78.

[5] *Deuteronomy* 13:1, 17:8-11.

[6] Y. HALEVI, KUZARI 3:41. But this may be more an expression of faith than an assertion that the doctrine of infallibility is necessary to a valid conception of the *halakhic* process.

the authorized courts, in the sense that their decisions accord with the original intention of the law, is also mentioned by Nachmanides.[7]

Despite the views of these influential *halakhists*, the greater weight of authority may be cited for what might be termed the pluralistic view of the *Halakhah*, namely, that it is possible to have more than one valid solution to a legal problem; that "*halakhic* truth" is not and need not necessarily be identical with absolute or divine truth. This is so because the revealed law is, in its nature, not necessarily unequivocal or absolute; it is extrinsic and existential rather than intrinsic and ontological, and more than one judgment may therefore claim equal validity.

The source for this pluralistic view is a fascinating passage in the Talmud.[8] The Rabbis were debating a *halakhic* issue: the ritual purity or impurity of an oven (the "oven of *Akhnai*") made of rings with sand as filler. R. Eliezer ruled that it was levitically pure, while his colleagues held it impure. Despite all of R. Eliezer's arguments in favor of his opinion, the Rabbis persisted in their decision. Having failed to succeed through the forces of logic, R. Eliezer invoked a number of miracles in an attempt to persuade the Rabbis. "If the *Halakhah* (law) is according to my opinion, let this carob tree offer testimony." The tree was uprooted and moved a hundred or four hundred ells. But the Rabbis said, "We adduce no evidence from carob trees." R. Eliezer then tried another miracle: the waters of a nearby brook reversed their direction. The Rabbis persisted, maintaining that this proved nothing. A third miracle was then produced by R. Eliezer, and still the Rabbis refused to yield. Whereupon R. Eliezer exclaimed: "If the *Halakhah* accords with my view, let it be demonstrated from Heaven." Thereupon, a Heavenly Voice (*bat kol*) issued forth, saying, "Why do you disagree with R. Eliezer; *Halakhah* is always as he says it is." R. Joshua responded by citing the Biblical verse: "It [the *Torah*] is not in heaven."[9] The Talmud here parenthetically inserts R. Jeremiah's explanation of R. Joshua's response: Once the *Torah* was revealed at Sinai, we pay no attention to a

---

[7] M. NACHMANIDES, PERUSH AL HA-TORAH (COMMENTARY TO THE PENTATEUCH), *Deuteronomy* 17:11. However, it is doubtful if this theory of infallibility because of divine grace is fully accepted by Nachmanides. He mentions it in what seems to be an afterthought ("certainly you ought to think that. . . .") after he tells us that the authority of the courts as authentic interpreters of the divine will must be accepted because the Law was given to us as they decide it "even if they are in error." Moreover, in his HASAGOT HA-RAMBAN LE'SEFER HA-MITZVOT (CRITIQUE ON THE BOOK OF COMMANDMENTS), Root I, Nachmanides omits any mention of the infallibility theme.

[8] *Bava Metzia* 59a-b.

[9] *Deuteronomy* 30:12.

Heavenly Voice,[10] because the law is decided by the majority.[11] Furthermore, we are told, R. Nathan encountered the prophet Elijah and asked him: "What did the Holy One do at that time?" Elijah answered, "He laughed [with joy], and said, 'My children have defeated Me, My children have defeated Me!'" Returning to the debate itself, the Talmud informs us that the Rabbis resolved to excommunicate R. Eliezer.

What may appear to the modern reader as a strange mixture of fact and fancy, law (*halakhah*) and legend (*aggadah*), is nevertheless an accepted method of the Talmud. The *aggadah* in this passage teaches us something about the conception of the law itself:[12] what we have called "*halakhic* truth" is independent of the original revealed law, even if the latter is confirmed by a fresh revelation.

R. Nissim Gerondi turns to this passage on the oven of Akhnai as the *locus classicus* of thinking on this problem:

> Now, all of them saw that R. Eliezer came closer to the truth than they . . . and Heaven decided according to his view, and yet they acted on their own opinion; for since their reason inclined them to declare [the oven] impure, though they knew that this opinion was the opposite of the truth, they did not wish to declare it pure. Had they declared it pure, they would have violated the words of the *Torah* because their reason told them [the oven] was impure. The [power of] decision was given over to the Sages of each generation, and what they agree to—that is what God commanded.[13]

---

[10] There is a considerable literature on the validity of prophecy and visions as a source of legislation or judicial decision. Such mystical intrusions into the *halakhic* process continued well into modern times. *See, e.g.*, Heschel, *Al Ruach ha-Kodesh Be'yemei ha-Benayim (On the Divine Spirit in the Middle Ages)*, in SEFER HA-YOVEL LI'KHEVOD ALEXANDER MARX (ALEXANDER MARX JUBILEE VOLUME) 175 (1950); Urbach, *Halakhah u-Nevuah (Halakhah and Prophecy)*, 18 TARBITZ 1 (1947); note 19 *infra*. If one accepts such supra-rational visions as a legitimate source of Jewish law, one might then refer to a fifth or "mystical method" in addition to the four adumbrated by Cardozo in his THE NATURE OF THE JUDICIAL PROCESS, *supra* note 1, except that one can hardly call a spiritual-charismatic event a "method"; at most it can be termed an alternative "classification." *See* note 2 *supra*.

[11] We may have here one of two explanations. *See* Englard, *Majority Decision vs. Individual Truth*, 15 TRADITION 137, 150 n.6 (1975).

[12] Englard, *supra* note 11, is skeptical as to whether this talmudic passage may be used to adduce any general views on Jewish law. Although he is undoubtedly right in cautioning about the problematical nature of generalizing from single remarks or passages, and while he correctly points to a variety of interpretations of this very passage, this much is certain—that all agree that what we have here is a statement of the difference between *halakhic* truth and original truth.

[13] NISSIM OF GERONDI, DERASHOT HA-RAN (EXPOSITIONS), *Derashah* VII. *See also id.*, *Derashot* III & V. R. Nissim comments on another talmudic tale, *see Bava Metzia* 86a (concerning Rabbah bar Nachmeni) which, while providing less dramatic force, offers a similar melange of *halakhah* and *aggadah* leading to the same conclusion.

More explicitly, the notion of divine sanction for competing judicial opinions is evident in the following talmudic exegesis of a verse from *Ecclesiastes* (12:11):

> The disciples of the wise (*i.e.*, scholars of the Law) sit in manifold assemblies and occupy themselves with the *Torah*, some pronouncing unclean and others pronouncing clean, some prohibiting and others permitting, some disqualifying [witnesses] and others declaring [them] fit. Should a man say: how [in view of these contradictory opinions] shall I learn the *Torah*? Therefore [*Ecclesiastes*] says, "all of them are given from one Shepherd." One God gave them; one leader [Moses] uttered them from the mouth of the Lord of all creation.[14]

Rav maintains that in order to qualify for membership in the *Sanhedrin* (the highest *halakhic* court) a candidate had to be able to prove, from Biblical sources, the ritual purity of *sheretz* ("swarming" or "creeping" creatures, explicitly declared impure by the *Torah*).[15] Rav, and according to another version, Ravina, attempted to do just that, but without success.[16] Before them, R. Meir was praised for his ability to demonstrate the ambivalence in the law; he was so profound that his colleagues could not follow him, and the *halakhic* decision therefore usually went against him.[17] The Palestinian Rabbis were less tolerant of what they considered casuistry than were their Babylonian colleagues.[18] But what motivated these Rabbis to recommend extraordinary intellectual agility was not a preference for casuistry or a liking for virtuosity per se, but an awareness of the nominalist character of the law and the consequent need for the judge to be prepared with a variety of solutions.[19]

The sixteenth century *halakhic* judge and commentator, R. Solomon Luria, affirms the theory of *halakhic* pluralism and its con-

---

[14] *Chagigah* 3b.

[15] *Sanhedrin* 17a.

[16] *Eruvin* 13b; *Sanhedrin* 17a.

[17] *Eruvin* 13b.

[18] *See* T.J. *Sanhedrin* 15b.

[19] *See* N. LAMM, FAITH AND DOUBT 253-58 & 257 n.30 (1971). Mention should also be made of the various references to divine assistance to the judge in his *halakhic* deliberations. Some scholars take these references to the supernatural quite literally. *See* I. TWERSKY, RABAD OF POSQUIERES 291-300 (1962) (concludes that such *kabbalistic* references in the works of *Rabad* and other medieval *halakhists* are literary flourishes and not descriptive of actual mystical experiences). Twersky's arguments are convincing. One might add, however, the observation that the very fact that their *personal* evaluations (as opposed to tradition and precedent) were couched in these powerful metaphors indicates the importance they attached to such instances of independent and intuitive judicial interpretations and decisions.

comitant idea of the freedom of interpretation. He offers a mystical basis for the role of the individual personality of the judge: all souls were present at Mount Sinai when the *Torah* was given, and each received the revelation through his own specific "channel," according to his own powers of perception, so that a variety of mutually incompatible opinions on a given question may result, and yet "all are true."[20]

Similar sentiments are voiced by a renowned eighteenth century talmudist, R. Aryeh Leib ha-Kohen:

> *Torah* was . . . given to man, endowed with human reason. The Holy One gave us the *Torah* . . . in accordance with the dictates of human reason, even if it be not true according to the Separate Intelligences (*i.e.*, absolute truth).[21]

An illustrious contemporary talmudic scholar, Rabbi Moshe Feinstein, echoes this view. Decisions must be made:

> as the sage sees it, after proper research to clarify the *Halakhah* [as it emerges from] the Talmud and Commentaries to the best of his ability, in seriousness and with piety. What appears to him as the [correct] verdict is the truth for decision-making, and he is obligated so to decide, even if in fact Heaven knows that this is not the [correct] interpretation.[22]

Natural Law and Positive Law

A question that has serious consequences for Jewish thought in general and the conception of Jewish law in particular is that of natural law. Legal positivists will naturally tend towards a pluralistic conception of the *Halakhah*, while advocates of natural law will in-

---

[20] S. LURIA, *Introduction* to YAM SHEL SHELOMOH, *Bava Kama*. On the role of the judge's individual value-judgments in his judicial decision-making, *see* Goldman, *Ha-Musar, ha-Dat, Ve' ha-Halakhah (ethics, Religion, and Halakhah)* (pt. 4), 22 DEIOT 65, 71 (1962). In a debate with Eugene Borowitz, *see* Borowitz, *Subjectivity and the Halachic Process*, 13 JUDAISM 211 (1964), Immanuel Jakobovits defends the presence of objectivity in the *halakhic* process. *See* Jakobovits, *Jewish Law Faces Modern Problems*, in STUDIES IN TORAH JUDAISM 335-38 (1969). What should be added is that there obviously are subjective elements that come into play in the decision-making process, but never does the decision-maker *consciously* intrude his extraneous ideological or value judgments into his *halakhic* verdicts. Paradoxically, the judge's subjectivity is most acceptable when he is least aware of it. Otherwise, the integrity of the *Halakhah* is at the mercy of influences that derive from axiological structures that may be most inimical to its most cherished fundamentals. *See* Kirschenbaum, *Rabbi Moshe Feinstein's Responsa: A Major Halakhic Event*, 15 JUDAISM 364, 366-67 (1966).

[21] ARYEH L. HA-KOHEN, *Introduction* to KETZOT HA-CHOSHEN.

[22] M. FEINSTEIN, *Introduction* to IGGEROT MOSHEH, *Orach Chayyim* (1959).

cline to a monistic view. As will be seen, it is not at all clear whether or not Jewish law as such can rightly be said to accommodate a natural law theory or whether, indeed, there ever was a major *halakhic* jurist, as opposed to a Jewish philosopher, who ever advocated natural law in the *Halakhah*.

Some definition of the terms "natural law" and "legal positivism" are necessary in order to determine whether they apply to Jewish law. By positivism we mean the view that the law is what the divine Sovereign commands;[23] it is the will of God which He revealed to man. There are no immanent qualities in the nature of man or the world which constitute moral criteria that need to complement or can supplant the Law which was transcendentally legislated. Such extraneous notions as right/wrong, good/evil, just/unjust can be considered only when the law specifically makes room for them. Hence, great emphasis is placed on the judge's use of logical deduction and interpretation in order to reach decisions. This does not necessarily lead, however, to a "slot-machine" conception of the judicial process. On the contrary, because positive laws can never cover the whole gamut of life and its almost unlimited possibilities, and because moral judgments are not considered as absolutes, the judge is comparatively free in his decision-making.

The theory of natural law holds that the universe is governed by laws which exhibit rationality.[24] They issue from a primordial and eternal order and govern even inanimate nature.[25] Hence, certain moral notions are indigenous to man and nature and discoverable by unaided reason. Because such natural law is ontological and intrinsic, it constitutes a form of obligation that preceded the promulgation of positive law[26] (in the case of Jewish law, revelation), and that now complements positive law in those areas where the latter does not legislate. It stands as a criterion for the judge in his interpretation of positive, revealed law, because it is unthinkable that the two should be in conflict. In his deliberations, therefore, the judge must be guided not only by the body of positive law which he seeks to interpret and apply, but by his reason or moral intuition as well. Moreover, because natural law is identified as the core and essence of revealed law, the judge must be exceedingly careful to discover the

---

[23] *See* M. GOLDING, PHILOSOPHY OF LAW 25 (1975).
[24] *See* A.P. d'ENTRÈVES, NATURAL LAW 37-50 (1970).
[25] AQUINAS, SUMMA THEOLOGICA.
[26] *See* A.P. d'ENTRÈVES, *supra* note 24.

correct decision which is the one, true answer to the question before him.[27]

Some fifty years before Plato, a notion of natural law had already appeared in Euripides. It received its most active development among the Stoic philosophers. Roman philosophy, in its classical period, accepted the legal authority of this *jus naturale*[28] as one of the major foundations of jurisprudence. Cicero held that natural law is identical with the divine mind, and with the *ratio summa* which was impressed in nature and which is the divine understanding.[29] Natural law, which is thus fixed in the essence of both God and man, is not limited in either time or space—it is universal and eternal and is discoverable by man's use of *recta ratio*[30] or *sana ratio*. The various "natural laws" constitute a common element in a large variety of codes and conventions, referred to by some Roman jurists as *ius gentium*,[31] and this became the basis for the modern conception of international law.[32]

The principle of natural law was accepted by the Church Fathers and the Scholastics as a major feature of their ethical and religious philosophy. The *lex naturalis* is the source of other laws; when derived by human reason, it is called natural law, and when revealed by prophecy, it is termed *lex divina*. Unlike man-made, positive laws, natural law does not require proclamation or *promulgatio*. Natural law is related to natural morality—the idea that the values of good and evil are inherent in the human mind,—and to natural religion—that there exists a natural bond (*religatio*) between God and man, and man can, therefore, by himself discover the nature of true religion.[33]

To resolve the question of natural law in the Jewish legal system, however, one must concentrate more on the development of the theme in Islam than in Christianity. To the extent that the great Jewish jurists and philosophers in the Middle Ages were influenced at all by the environing culture, that influence was much greater and much more direct in the case of Islamic thought and jurisprudence.

---

[27] *See generally* Dworkin, *Hard Cases*, 88 HARV. L. REV. 1057 (1975), *reprinted in* R. DWORKIN, TAKING RIGHTS SERIOUSLY 82, 82-90 (1977); R. SARTORIUS, INDIVIDUAL CONDUCT AND SOCIAL NORMS 181-210 (1975).

[28] *See generally* A.P. d'ENTRÈVES, *supra* note 24, at 26-35; C. J. FRIEDRICH, THE PHILOSOPHY OF THE LAW IN HISTORICAL PERSPECTIVE 32-34 (1958).

[29] C.J. FRIEDRICH, *supra* note 28, at 29.

[30] *Id.* at 30.

[31] *Id.* at 32.

[32] *See* H.S. MAINE, INTERNATIONAL LAW 20-25 (J. Murray publ. 1890).

[33] A.P. d'ENTRÈVES, *supra* note 24, at 43-46.

José Faur shows that two great opposing schools in Islamic thought correspond to the schools of natural law and positive law in Western philosophy and law.[34] The rationalistic *Mu'tazila* (part of the *Kalam*—the two names are often used interchangeably) held that there is an absolute category of good and evil which is inherent in the nature of things and which is cognizable by any rational being by his own intuition and without the assistance of divine revelations. This moral concept is primordial and eternal in the mind of God and obligates even God Himself.

The Traditionalists (variously: *Ash'ariya*, *ahl al-haq*, *ahl al-faqqah*) maintained that good and evil are subjective ideas, not established in the nature of man, and what is good or evil for one is not necessarily so for another. Because man's obligations flow from the free will of the Deity (rather than from His supernal reason), God may forbid what man considers good, and command him to do that which he regards as evil. Revelation not only informs us what is good and what is evil, but establishes their content. Justice is what God commands, injustice what He forbids. There are no values or principles that obligate God, because He supersedes all and is not subservient to any order of good and evil. By means of reason one can differentiate between good and evil, but they do not obligate man before God. This controversy was not limited to theology, but encompassed law as well. The *Mu'tazilites* placed a much greater emphasis on reason than did the Traditionalists, and the latter were far more insistent upon the inviolability of the *Kuran* and the *Sunnah* (the Moslem oral law, equivalent to the Jewish *Halakhah*).

Most important for our own consideration of freedom and constraint in the Jewish judicial process is how the two Islamic schools related their views on natural law to their conceptions of the role of the judge. What is the authority of the judge in the interpretation of laws, especially those not directly dealt with in revelation? According to the *Mu'tazila*, justice precedes, and is obligatory even before, revelation by prophecy. The judge's systematic reasoning, his interpretive-judicial exercises (*ijtihad*), merely disclose this primordial justice; they do not establish the law *ab initio*. The Traditionalists, however, held that whatever was not explicitly revealed does not obligate man. The judicial *ijtihad* is actual legislation and not merely revelation of what was previously valid but concealed; it is an act of *promulgatio* of law established by the judge. Hence, the form that

[34] J. FAUR, INYUNIM BE'MISHNEH TORAH: SEFER HA-MADDA (STUDIES IN THE MISHNEH TORAH: THE BOOK OF KNOWLEDGE) 66-73 (1978).

the law takes depends on the judge's decision. The obligatory nature of laws defined by *ijtihad* is not uniform for all times and places. The judge has the right to make differentiations and to redefine the law. Even though one judge may forbid and one may permit, both are the will of God.[35]

Can *Halakhah* support a natural law theory? Does Judaism, especially Jewish law, lend itself to a belief in the ontological quality of laws? If the answer is affirmative, we have the philosophical underpinnings for a restrictive and highly limited view of the autonomy of the judge. If negative, we have room, at least theoretically, for a broader conception of the role of the judge and his freedom in the exercise of his judicial functions.

No simple answers to this question are available. They range from a blanket statement by one historian of the Jewish law that the Rabbis believed that religion, ethics, and *Halakhah* flow from natural law and that the *Torah* is in its entirety rational,[36] to a contemporary writer who argues strongly against a natural law conception in the *Halakhah*.[37] A nineteenth century Italian scholar argues that the identification of the *Torah*'s laws for man with natural law is one of the most characteristic teachings of the *Kabbalah*, and that the laws of the *Torah* have cosmic and ontological significance.[38] A contemporary scholar, in contrast, sees in the attitude to natural law a major difference between Judaism and Christianity, declaring unqualifiedly that "[i]n Judaism there is no natural law doctrine and, in principle, there cannot be,"[39] and, "there is nothing in the Hebrew Bible

---

[35] *Id.* at 79-80.

[36] *See* I.C. TCHERNOWITZ, TOLDOT HA-HALAKHAH (HISTORY OF THE HALAKHAH) 151-63 *passim* (1934). Less sweeping is the contention of the late Samuel Atlas that natural law constitutes an inner and suppressed layer of much of talmudic law. *See* S. ATLAS, NETIVIM BE'MISHPAT HA-IVRI (PATHWAYS IN HEBREW LAW) 17-20 (1978).

[37] *See* Goldman, (pts. 1-2), *supra* note 20; 20 DEIOT 47, 49 (1962); (pt. 3) 21 DEIOT 59 (1962); (pt. 4) 22 DEIOT 65 (1962).

[38] *See* E. BENAMOZEGH, ISRAEL ET L'HUMANITÉ 179 (Heb. trans. 1967). Benamozegh supports his arguments by referring, *inter alia*, to statements in the Talmud and in the *kabbalistic* literature referring to God observing the commandments—both the social-ethical and the ritual or cultic. This recalls the idea of the *Mu'tatzilites*, that natural law implies that God too is obligated by these laws. However, these sayings of the Sages may be nothing more than *aggadic* or didactic statements illustrating the importance of being law-abiding by averring that even the Lawgiver abides by His norms; they need not be invested with philosophic significance leading to a conclusion that the Sages considered the law intrinsic and ontological. Benamozegh, in this section, tends to rely more on *kabbalistic* approaches to the *Halakhah* than on what the *halakhists* thought about the *Halakhah*. However, he is on more solid ground in citing both *kabbalistic* and talmudic texts referring to the preexistence of the *Torah* which, by suggesting the independence of the law from the act of revelation, imply their ontological quality, and hence natural law.

[39] Fox, *Maimonides and Aquinas on Natural Law*, 3 DINÉ ISRAEL v, v (1972).

which even approaches the Ciceronian idea of natural law."[40] While this article is not the place for a full exposition of the natural law question in Jewish law, it may be worth pursuing the matter briefly by testing a limited number of talmudic sources and medieval authorities.

First, a brief historical note: An identifiable and explicit concept of natural law came into Jewish thought from Muhammedan philosophy of law via the Karaites, a fundamentalist heretical Jewish sect which was quite powerful in the medieval period and now has all but vanished. Karaism followed the *Mu'tazila* in advocating natural law, in holding that good and evil are inherent in nature; in attacking the authority of the oral tradition; and in upholding the Islamic notion of *Qiyas*[41]—the use of reason and analogic argumentation in formulating the law.[42]

The major talmudic passage which may serve as a source for a theory of natural law expounds upon a verse in *Leviticus* (18:4):

> Our Rabbis taught: "Mine ordinances shall ye do," *i.e.*, such commandments which, if they were not written [in Scripture], they should by right have been written, and they are: [the laws concerning] idolatry, immorality, bloodshed, robbery, and blasphemy. "And My statutes shall ye keep," *i.e.*, such commandments to which Satan objects, [such as] . . . the prohibition against wearing a mixture of wool and linen, the ceremony performed by a childless widow in the event her brother-in-law refuses to marry her, the purification of lepers, and the scape-goat. Perhaps you might think that these are vain things [because these latter laws cannot be explained rationally]? Therefore Scripture says, "I am the Lord," *i.e.*, I the Lord have made it a statute and you have no right to question it.[43]

---

[40] *Id.* at vii. Fox's argument against natural law in the Bible on the grounds that there is no word for "nature" in biblical Hebrew is poor etymological support for his thesis. Ideas may be implicit in a text or body of literature, and receive their formulation in sophisticated terminology much later; the absence of specific terms cannot prove the openness to, or exclusion of, a theory explicated much later without risking an etymological anachronism. Moreover, his assertion that in ancient Hebrew thought there is only one source for the knowledge of good and evil, namely revelation, leaves unanswered the question of why punishment was meted out, according to the Bible, for moral infractions of laws for which no revelation is recorded. Thus, if there is not some form of natural law, how does one explain the punishment of Cain for slaying Abel, or the deluge in the days of Noah? Some universally valid moral code seems presupposed by these narratives.

[41] *Qiyas* is derived from the talmudic exegetical term *hekkesh* (or *heqqesh*). *See* J. SCHACHT, THE ORIGINS OF MUHAMMADAN JURISPRUDENCE 99 (1950).

[42] *See* J. FAUR, *supra* note 34, at 64-65, 99-107, 115.

[43] *Yoma* 67b.

On the face of it, the Talmud is distinguishing between rational laws and those which defy rational explanation (and hence "to which Satan objects" because they require an act of faith), with the former constituting the core of what might be called "natural law." Yet Faur insists that natural law has no *halakhic* basis in all talmudic literature, that according to the Rabbis all obligation flows from divine command in the *Torah*, and that the concept of natural law is in direct contradiction to the basis of Judaism.[44] Similarly Fox concludes that "there is no suggestion here that human reason could have known by itself that these acts are evil" and that the words "should by right have been written" (the Soncino translation of *din hu she'yikatvu*) asserts only that, "having been commanded to avoid these prohibited acts, we can now see, after the fact, that these prohibitions are useful and desirable."[45] There is sufficient ambiguity in the passage to warrant caution against reading a natural law doctrine into the Talmud. However, the same ambiguity, on the other side, should caution against the categorical denial of natural law in Jewish law. On balance, the passage does tend more to favor an autonomous moral-rational criterion independent of revelation, *i.e.*, one that could have been operative had the Law not been revealed, but which is now subsumed under the Law as a totality. In the absence of proof to the contrary, we must at least reserve the possibility that some talmudic Rabbis were aware of a notion of natural law.

The tenth century Saadia Gaon (along with Joseph Albo of the fifteenth century), is most prominent in his espousal of natural law in Judaism. Guttmann pointed out some one hundred years ago that Saadia's famous distinction between rational laws (*sikhliot*) and religious or revelational laws (*shim'iyot*), which is the methodological foundation of his entire religious philosophy, represents a compromise between the *Mu'tazila* and the *Ash'ariya*.[46] While the revelational commandments are a species of Aristotle's "legal religion" or positive law, the laws that can be independently formulated by reason (*'aql*) are based on the *Kalam* and are in direct descent from the Stoics' identification of reason (*logos*) with nature. The classical instance of a rational law for Saadia is that proposed by the *Mu'tazila* writers: gratitude.[47] While Saadia may have consciously taken over

---

[44] *See* J. FAUR, *supra* note 34, at 63, 174, 175. Faur qualifies his position somewhat at 65 n.51.

[45] Fox, *supra* note 39, at viii.

[46] *See* J. GUTTMANN, DIE RELIGIONSPHILOSOPHIE DES SAADIA 133 (1882).

[47] *See* Altmann, *Chalukat ha-Mitzvot Le' Rasag (The Division of the Commandments by R. Saadia Gaon)*, in RAV SAADIA GAON 658, 661 (1943).

the theory of natural law from the Karaites in order the better to do battle against Karaism,[48] he "followed a tradition which was not entirely alien to the Jewish heritage,"[49] and indeed the talmudic passage cited above was unquestionably a major source of influence on Saadia.[50] Saadia, drawing upon both Jewish and Islamic sources, bequeathed his formulation of natural law—without, however, calling it by that name—to Joseph Albo and, through him, influenced Hugo Grotius and thus, the entire school of natural law.[51]

Marvin Fox, who adamantly rules out any possibility of natural law in Jewish thought, applies to the exegesis of Saadia, the same form of criticism that he did to the Bible and Talmud: since Saadia does not use the term "natural law," as did Albo some five or six hundred years later, one may not attribute a natural law theory to him.[52] This argument is weak indeed; concepts, like people, have an existence independent of their names.[53]

Fox further argues that Saadia means by "rational commandments" those laws for which, *after* their legislation by revelation, good reasons can be found; this is the interpretation he gives to the Talmud's "by right they should have been written."[54] He asserts that this is not, however, "equivalent to saying that reason knows them independently, or that reason alone can determine what is proper behavior for man."[55] But this interpretation is clearly contradicted throughout Saadia's writings on the subject. Thus, when Saadia lays down his first rational principle, from which a number of laws flow, that of gratitude, he writes that "reason demands that whoever does something good be compensated either by means of a favor shown to him, if he is in need of it, or by means of thanks if he does not require any reward."[56] In the next sentence, Saadia tells

---

[48] *See* J. FAUR, *supra* note 34, at 65.

[49] *See* Altmann, *Saadya's Conception of the Law*, 28 BULL. JOHN RYLANDS LIB. 320, 337 (1944).

[50] *See* D. NEUMARK, *Saadya's Philosophy*, in ESSAYS IN JEWISH PHILOSOPHY 145 (1929). *See generally* Neumark, *Musar ha-Yahadut (The Ethics of Judaism)*, 6 HA-SHILOACH 65, 70-72 (1899).

[51] *See* Altmann, *supra* note 49, at 334.

[52] Fox, *supra* note 39, at x. Albo's writings on the subject may be found in SEFER HA-IKKARIM (THE BOOK OF PRINCIPLES) ch. 7 (I. Husik trans. 1929).

[53] *See* note 40 *supra*.

[54] *See* Fox, *supra* note 39, at x.

[55] *Id.*

[56] SAADIA GAON, THE BOOK OF BELIEFS AND OPINIONS 139 (S. Rosenblatt trans. 1948). Rosenblatt translates the first word in the cited passage as "logic," and later uses "reason." While this variation may make for more literary grace, it is more accurate to follow Saadia's words with greater fealty. The word Saadia uses throughout is the Arabic *'aql*, reason.

us that since reason demands this it would not have been seemly for the Creator to neglect it in His own case, and then:

> It was, on the contrary, *necessary for Him* to command His creatures to serve Him and thank Him for having created them. Reason also demands that he who is wise not permit himself to be treated with contempt or be insulted. It was, therefore, likewise *necessary for the Creator* to forbid His servants to conduct themselves in such a way toward Him.[57]

Clearly, the "necessity" for the Creator to legislate what "reason demands"[58] goes far beyond an after-the-fact search for good reasons for the laws. Moreover, in Chapter III of his *magnum opus*, Saadia proceeds to explain why, if reason can independently attain the rational laws, it was necessary for revelation to ordain them. He answers that reason could derive only the general principles, but revelation was necessary to provide the practical details.[59] The question is irrelevant, and the answer superfluous, if Saadia did not intend the ability of autonomous reason to formulate the moral laws. It requires but a change in terminology to say that natural law provides us with the general principles of law, and positive law with the details.

Of even greater moment to the determination of the role, if any, of natural law in the history of the Jewish philosophy of law, but less certain than the case of Saadia, is the view of the greatest of all Jewish philosophers and jurists, the twelfth century Maimonides.[60]

Did Maimonides espouse the theory of natural law?[61] Faur, in his recent book on the first volume of the Maimonidic *Code*, maintains that Maimonides denies that there are any natural obligations and disagrees with those of the *Geonim*, particularly Saadia, who held that good and evil (*i.e.*, the "rational commandments") are engraved in the nature of man. The laws of the *Torah* are positive, in that they are the command of the Deity. The *Torah* is "created," not primor-

---

[57] *Id.* (emphasis added).

[58] The Arabic for "reason *demands*" and "*necessary*" is the same root, *wajab*.

[59] SAADIA GAON, *supra* note 56, at 145.

[60] Maimonides is widely known as the greatest of medieval Jewish rationalists. The extent to which this is true, and to which this judgment must be qualified, is beyond the scope of this paper. He certainly accorded reason a very high role, especially in his MOREH NEVUKHIM (GUIDE FOR THE PERPLEXED), yet he was contemptuous of the *Kalam*. We shall confine our remarks here to his conception of reason insofar as it affects his philosophy of law.

[61] On the philosophic question of whether morality is considered by Maimonides "conventional," in the same category with aesthetic judgments, or as part of the rational order, *see* N. LAMM, *supra* note 19, at 268 n.35.

dial.[62] Maimonides sees a need for laws in order to regulate society. Such laws, however, do not exist in nature, and one of the purposes of *Torah* is to compensate for this lack. Hence, one may regard as "natural" any law the purpose of which is the ordering of society. The adjective "natural" thus describes the *telos* of the law, not its source. But Maimonides does not recognize natural law in its classical or Aristotelian interpretation.[63]

While Faur and Fox[64] make a strong case against a theory of natural moral law in Maimonides, the sixteenth century R. Judah Loewe, known as the *Maharal* of Prague, held that Maimonides did indeed base his philosophy of law on the principle of natural law. He devoted a good part of one of his major works, *Tiferet Yisrael*, to a polemic against Maimonides for this. He faults Maimonides for advocating a pre-existent criterion of right and wrong that issues from the nature of man and that is discoverable by reason. Maimonidean rationalism leads to a preference for the *via contemplativa* over the *via activa*, and hence is injurious to the *Halakhah*, which is theonomous.[65]

---

[62] *See* J. FAUR, *supra* note 34, at 147-48. Faur cites a passage from Maimonides' MOREH NEVUKHIM 3:17, to prove his point. Maimonides, adumbrating five theories of providence, attributes to the Sages of the Talmud the concept of divine providence as distributive justice. God's reward and punishment are determined by man's conduct. Here Maimonides adds, in what seems a casual comment, that the Rabbis held that "an obedient individual receives compensation for all the pious and righteous actions he has accomplished, even if he was not ordered by a prophet to do them, and that he is punished for all evil acts committed by him, even if he was not forbidden by a prophet to do them." M. MAIMONIDES, GUIDE FOR THE PERPLEXED 470 (S. Pines trans. 1963). In the paragraph following, Maimonides presents his own theory of providence which is at variance with that of the Sages. An argument can be made for the thesis that Maimonides disagrees with the view in the above quotation, *see* J. FAUR, *supra* note 34, at 147 n.20, although this is not at all certain. Yet it is clear that Maimonides attributed to the talmudic sages a view of obligation—deserving of reward and punishment, albeit in a different measure for the reward and punishment for revealed law—that is independent of revelation. Surely this is sufficient to challenge the sweeping statements of Faur himself, *id.* at 174-75, and others that the Talmud knew of no theory resembling natural law.

[63] J. FAUR, *supra* note 34, at 164.

[64] *See* Fox, *supra* note 39, at xii-xix.

[65] *Maharal* substitutes for what he takes as Maimonides' natural law a supernatural essence of man to which the *Halakhah* corresponds by virtue of a metaphysical order of its own as a divinely revealed *logos*. Hence, the observance of the *Halakhah* is an accommodation to the absolute order of existence. *See* Shatz [Uffenheimer], *Ha-Tefisah ha-Mishpatit shel ha-Maharal: Antitezah Le'chok ha-Tiv'i (The Judicial Conception of Maharal: Antithesis to Natural Law)*, 9 DINÉ ISRAEL (to be published in 1979). *Maharal's* own thesis cannot, however, serve as an example of that kind of philosophy of the *Halakhah* which would lead to a pluralistic view of judicial decision-making and hence greater freedom for the judge, for instead of a natural law conception we have what might be called a "supernatural law" theory which, like natural law, presupposes an immutable body of preexistent law to which the judge must conform in deciding on open questions in his interpretation of positive or revealed law.

The determination of whether or not Maimonides advocated natural law turns on two issues: how Maimonides related to the Saadianic bifurcation of the law into rational and revelational commandments, and how he formulated the *halakhic* doctrine of the "Noahide Laws."

In Chapter VI of his *Eight Chapters*,[66] Maimonides essays a reconciliation between two opposing ethical theories—whether a saint, *i.e.*, a naturally moral and benevolent man, is the highest type of personality, or whether one who struggles against his base instincts and overcomes them is superior—and utilizes the distinction between rational and revelational commandments: The "saint" is preferable in the case of the rational laws; the man who exercises self-control, in the case of the revelational laws. In describing the rational commandments, such as the prohibition of bloodshed, theft, robbery, fraud, etc., he says,

> The prescriptions against these are called "commandments" (*mitzvot*), about which the Rabbis said, "If they had not already been written in the Law, it would be proper to add them." Some of our later Sages, who were infected with the unsound principles of the *Mutakallimun* [*i.e.*, the *Mu'tazilates*] called these *rational laws*.[67]

Here Maimonides accepts the distinction made by Saadia (whose name he respectfully does not mention) between the two categories of law, and acknowledges that it had precedents in the Talmud. Yet he is harsh in referring to the philosophy of the *Kalam* as a sickness or disease.

It is obvious that Maimonides accepts the methodological dichotomy between *sikhliot* (rational laws) and *shim'iyot* (revelational laws) and that he yet disagrees with the *Mu'tazila*. Faur goes too far in asserting that Maimonides rejected any notion that the rational commandments have some relation to the nature of things and that his doctrine of "reasons for the commandments" is based upon his opposition to the rational/revelational dichotomy.[68] It is equally evi-

---

[66] M. MAIMONIDES, THE EIGHT CHAPTERS 75-78 (J. Gorfinkle trans. 1912).

[67] *Id.* at 76-77. The quoted talmudic portion appears in *Yoma* 67b. *See* text accompanying notes 43-45 *supra*.

[68] J. FAUR, *supra* note 34, at 169-74. However, he does make a trenchant point in distinguishing between the source and the practical utility of the commandments: "[R]ational" for Maimonides describes a commandment the practice of which results in socially, morally, or politically beneficial results. This point was made by Dr. Samuel Belkin, who distinguished between "reason" (or motivation, source) and "purpose" (practical beneficial effect). *See* S. BELKIN, THE PHILOSOPHY OF PURPOSE (1958).

dent that Maimonides does not accept this analysis in the way that Saadia intended it.[69] The term "rational" (*'aql*) is reserved by Maimonides for the cognitive commandments, not the moral laws.[70] Fox is probably correct in saying that Maimonides regards certain moral laws as "rational" not in the sense of being demonstrable, but in the sense that man can give good reasons for them.[71] Hence, this one passage in Maimonides would seem to indicate a non-acceptance of a theory of natural law; but one passage is not enough to establish the matter definitively.

The question of the Noahide laws is more complex. The Talmud teaches that there are seven commandments that are obligatory on "the sons of Noah," *i.e.*, all mankind.[72] These include the prohibitions against idolatry, bloodshed, immorality, blasphemy, robbery, the eating of a limb torn from a living animal, and the positive commandment to establish courts of justice. This apparently constitutes a prima facie case for a doctrine of natural law in classical Jewish sources: the laws are universal, they allow for no exceptions and, unlike other laws, do not consider ignorance of the law as an excuse—they require no explicit warning in order for the violator to be punished. Are these, indeed, the core of natural law, rationally discoverable, or are they, too, positive divine commandments given to all humanity and not only, as are the other commandments, to the Children of Israel?

The interpretation of Maimonides' view revolves about this crucial text towards the end of his monumental Code of Jewish Law, the *Mishneh Torah*:

> Anyone [*i.e.*, any non-Jew] who accepts the seven commandments and is meticulous in observing them is considered one of the righteous (*chasidei*—pious, saintly) of the nations of the world and he has a share in the world-to-come. But this is so only if he accepts and observes them because the Holy One commanded them in the Torah, and informed us through our teacher Moses that the children of Noah were commanded [to observe] them from before [*i.e.*, before the Torah was given]. But if he observed them because of his own rational decisions, he is not a resident-alien and is not one of the righteous (*chasidei*) of the nations of the world, and not one of their wise men (*chakhamehem*).[73]

---

[69] *See* Fox, *supra* note 39, at xvi-xvii.

[70] *See* Editor's Notes, in 18 RAMBAM L'AM 193 (M. Rabinowitz ed. 1960); N. LAMM, *supra* note 19, at 268 n.31.

[71] Fox, *supra* note 39, at xxvi.

[72] *Sanhedrin* 56a.

[73] M. MAIMONIDES, MISHNEH TORAH (CODE OF LAW), *Hilkhot Melakhim* 8:11.

Maimonides presents us with two categories of universal law: the Noahide law accepted as revealed and hence of divine origin, and the Noahide law accepted on the basis of rational-moral values. Unquestionably the former is preferable.

That Maimonides recommends acceptance of the Noahide legislation because of its divine origin does not argue against his conception of the Noahide commandments as a type of natural law. The Noahide laws may well represent universal moral principles, but they become more significant—and entitle one to the encomium of a gentile *chasid* or saint—if what already exists "in nature" is consciously accepted and deliberately adopted for one's self as a code of personal and societal conduct.

What is most significant is the last category—those who accept Noahism not because of revelation but because of rational considerations or moral intuition. If Maimonides regards such a person as neither a saint (*chasid*) nor a wise man (*chakham*), then he obviously holds no brief for natural law.

But this issue is compounded by a textual problem. The standard printed editions read as above—"not one of the righteous of the nations of the world, *and not* one of their wise men." The emphasized words are represented in the Hebrew by the three-letter word *ve'lo*. However, the manuscript of the *Mishneh Torah* in the Bodleian Library changes the first of the three letters and reads *ela*, "but"; hence, "not one of the righteous of the nations of the world, *but* one of their wise men." If this variant reading is correct, Maimonides is distinguishing between *chasid* and *chakham*, saint and sage: one who follows the Noahide code because of moral considerations is a *chakham*, sage; if because of revelation, or religious reasons, he attains the status of *chasid*, saint. It is reasonable to assume, if this reading is correct, that this indicates a natural law theory by Maimonides. The single letter in Maimonides' *Code* is thus of the greatest moment in deciding the question of whether Jewry's greatest jurist and most eminent philosopher advocated or rejected natural law.[74]

In the absence of an autograph manuscript, and because of the large number of manuscripts containing one variant or the other, the

---

[74] For an elaborate discussion of the textual problem and citation of the various sources, as well as a history of the exegesis of this passage, *see* Schwarzschild, *Do Noachites Have to Believe in Revelation?* (pt. 1), 52 JEWISH Q. REV. 297 (1962); (pt. 2), 53 JEWISH Q. REV. 30 (1962). *See also* J. FAUR, *supra* note 34, at 151 n.43. Schwarzschild, among others, accepts the Bodleian reading "*ela*," while Faur and others prefer "*ve'lo*." A remarkable, but questionable, interpretation of our text is offered in A. KOOK, IGGEROT REIYAH 99 (1943).

matter must be decided on other than textual grounds—preferably, on a contextual basis. The following points are offered to support the reading of *ela*, "but."

1. The term *chasidei umot ha-olam*, righteous gentiles, is widely used in talmudic literature. The term *chakhmei umot ha-olam* is all but unknown. Had Maimonides meant to discount completely those who embraced Noahism purely out of moral or rational considerations, he would have said simply that such people are not qualified as *chasidei umot ha-olam*, and would have dispensed with the phrase *ve'lo mi-chakhamehem*, "and not of their wise men." It adds nothing but confusion, and Maimonides was too gifted a stylist to permit that. Moreover, he would have taken the effort of defining positively what constitutes a wise gentile, before denying that honorific to those whose moral conduct is independent of revelation. If, however, the correct reading is *ela*, then Maimonides is making a distinction that his readers were probably unaware of before, and the concluding phrase is indeed meaningful.

2. The juxtaposition of the two terms, *chasid* and *chakham*, appears fully developed in Maimonides' *Code*, in his *Hilkhot Deiot*, or *Laws of Character*. This typology must be considered in the light of Maimonides' use of the relevant terms in his *Guide* and in his *Eight Chapters*.[75] In general, the *chasid* and the *chakham* are, for Maimonides, different but not antipodal types: The *chasid* must first have been a *chakham* and then surpassed him; saintliness includes and transcends wisdom. The *chakham* is one whose intellectual deliberations lead him to a functional morality, while the *chasid* embodies the element of holiness which leads him beyond moderation to a higher degree of virtue. Thus, for instance, in his *Commentary to the Mishnah*, Maimonides writes that the *chasid* is a *chakham* who acts morally in a supererogatory manner.[76] Maimonides is consistent in his treatment of this theme.[77] This typology articulates well with our passage if we accept the *ela* reading: the gentile whose morality is autonomous, and does not include the element of holiness, is a wise man; the one whose acceptance of the Noahide laws is predicated upon divine revelation is a *chasid*.[78]

---

[75] For an analysis of Maimonides' typology of character, *see* Lamm, *He-chakham Ve'ha-chassid Be'mishnat ha-Rambam (The Sage and the Saint in the Thought of Maimonides)*, in SEFER HA-ZIKARON (DR. SAMUEL BELKIN MEMORIAL VOLUME) (to be published in 1979).

[76] M. MAIMONIDES, PERUSH MISHNAYOT (COMMENTARY TO THE MISHNAH), *Avot* 5:7.

[77] *See* Lamm, *supra* note 75.

[78] An additional point may be made which, while less cogent, is still supportive of the *ela* reading. The immediately preceding *halakhah*, 8:10, informs us that the *Torah* and commandments were given only to Israel and the proselytes, and that no gentile may be forced to accept

We may conclude this discussion of Maimonides by saying that we have no indisputable proof one way or the other, but that the weight of the evidence would imply that Maimonides sees in the Noahide code the core of a natural law. Yet, even if this be so, it is clear that natural law by no means played as important a role in the thought of Maimonides as it did in the Muhammedan *Kalam* or in Christian Scholasticism.

Other Jewish thinkers dealt with the problem, some directly and some by implication. Natural law theory was favored by many of the *Geonim* and found its most articulate spokesman in the beginning of the Middle Ages, in Moslem Spain, in the person of Bachya *ibn* Pakudah.[79] Others who may be mentioned in this respect are Shem b. Shem Tov and possibly David Kimchi;[80] and, toward the end of the medieval period, the previously mentioned Joseph Albo. Yehudah Halevi was opposed to natural law and most insistent upon revelation as the exclusive source of Jewish law.[81] *Kabbalists* would normally tend toward a conception of natural law, if only because of the correspondence they posited between creation and revelation, and the conception of *Torah* as the mystical Name of God. Lurianic *Kabbalah* saw in the observance of the commandments an act of *tikkun* or repair of flaws in the cosmos. R. Chayyim of Volozhin (1749-1821) was aware of the tension between this mystical conception of *Torah* and the *Halakhah*;[82] he clearly opted for *Halakhah* over mystical *tikkun*.[83] Translated into exoteric terms, he is eager to preserve the *Halakhah* and the positive *halakhic* process from interference by a corpus of norms independent of revelation.

---

or observe them. God commanded through Moses, however, that the Noahide be forced to observe the seven Noahide commandments; one who accepts them is called a *ger toshav*, a resident-alien. The next *halakhah* begins at this point—after having codified the requirement for coercion. *Halakhah* 11 is therefore concerned with those gentiles whose acceptance of the Noahide laws is voluntary. If the acceptance is formal (before a court of three scholars), one is considered a *ger toshav*; if not formalized, but predicated on religious belief in the Mosaic revelation, a gentile is considered as one of the *chasidei umot ha-olam*. It stands to reason that Maimonides now lists another category, beneath that of *ger toshav* and *chasidei umot ha-olam*, and yet higher than one whose moral observance is forced upon him, and this is the *chakham*, the wise but unsaintly gentile who observes the Noahide code neither out of coercion nor out of religious conviction, but because of rational-moral persuasion.

[79] *See* J. FAUR, *supra* note 34, at 115-26.

[80] *See id.* at 65 n.50.

[81] Y. HALEVI, KUZARI 1:89; *see* J. FAUR, *supra* note 34, at 127.

[82] An example of this tension is provided by those actions performed by the Patriarchs, presumably to effect *tikkun*, which were illegal in terms of the Revelation at Sinai, *e.g.*, Jacob marrying two sisters. CHAYYIM OF VOLOZHIN, NEFESH HA-CHAYYIM 1:21.

[83] *Id.* at 1:22. *See* N. LAMM, TORAH LISHMAN BEMISHNAT RABBI CHAYYIM MI'VOLOZHIN U-VE'MACHSHEVET HA-DOR (THE STUDY OF TORAH FOR ITS OWN SAKE IN THE WORKS OF R. CHAYYIM OF VOLOZHIN AND HIS CONTEMPORARIES) 65 (1972).

To sum up this section, we have seen that some *halakhists* favor a monistic conception of the law, making for a more restrictive view of judicial function, while others tend towards a pluralistic conception. Assuming that the relationship we found in Muhammedan jurisprudence—namely, a natural law theory limits the judge's freedom whereas a positivist view expands it—applies to Jewish law, we have found a considerable lack of consensus. The key talmudic passage does lend itself to a natural law interpretation. Saadia, along with other *Geonim*, and followed by Bachya, Albo, and others, espoused natural law. Yehuda Halevi opposed it, and certain *kabbalistically* inclined *halakhists* attempted to isolate the *Halakhah* from a natural-law of type structure. Maimonides presents a special problem. In some passages he seems to deny natural law, in others to be receptive to it; but even then, natural law does not at all assume for him the significance it does in other traditions.

II. A Halakhic Survey

The underlying philosophical principles of Judaism regarding freedom and constraint as well as their inner dialectic are reflected in the formal *halakhic* rules governing the Jewish judicial process. Here, too, we meet the paradox of a system of thought in which the appearance of underpinnings of divine fiat, theocratic authority, and the sovereignty of tradition—with all their creedal significance—nevertheless allows, fosters, and even encourages wide parameters of freedom. No monolithic, one-party-line mentality here. Rather, controversy and disagreement, flexibility and discretion are regularly prevalent in a legal system based on Holy Scripture and its authoritative interpretation in the Oral Tradition as recorded in talmudic literature and its medieval development in commentaries, codes, and responsa. These characteristics of dispute and development, modification and adaptation which inhere in Jewish law have already been described as far as the legislative process is concerned.[84] We propose to describe these very characteristics as they

[84] *See* 2 M. ELON, HA-MISHPAT HA-IVRI 239-828 (1973). The *grundnorm* of Jewish law has been defined as the Five Books of Moses with their authorized-received interpretation as formulated in the Oral Tradition. *See* note 87 *infra* and accompanying text. What are the inner dynamics of a legal system which is accepted as of divine origin? How are the laws subsequently developed, modified, abrogated, or adapted to new situations? Elon describes the five methods whereby *Torah* law *(de'oraita)* is derived, formulated, modified, amended, or even annulled: interpretation *(midrash)*, legislation *(takkanah u-gezerah)*, custom and usage *(minhag)*, case and precedent *(ma'aseh)*, and legal logic *(sevara)*. A 19th century scholar, Rabbi Zvi Hirsch Chajes, was perhaps the first to undertake a systematic analysis of the topic. *See* Z. CHAJES, THE STUDENT'S GUIDE THROUGH THE TALMUD (2d ed. J. Schacter trans. 1960).

inform the judicial process. Because an exhaustive, fully documented treatment would carry us far beyond the confines of an article, we have limited ourselves to a broad outline of the subject, merely alluding to its major highlights—with the hope that experts and future students will take up our suggestions and subject them to full scientific scrutiny.

Three major constraints limit the freedom of a judge: the body of substantive law, the rules of civil and criminal procedure, and the rulings and decisions of his predecessors ("precedent") and superiors. It is in the light of these constraining factors that we approach our survey of the Jewish judicial process.

The Body of Substantive Law

In *The Nature of the Judicial Process,* Cardozo produced a classical formulation of his subjective awareness of those factors that are at work in the rendering of a judicial decision and in the creation of judge-made law.[85] Early in his work, Justice Cardozo points to the formulated statute, if clear and if appropriate, as the obvious source of the law and the obvious determinant of the decision.[86] This is, of course, equally true of Jewish law, as it is for almost all systems of law known to man once society reached the level of statutory legislation. We may say the same thing for all these systems in negative terms as well, namely, that the body of normative law serves as the greatest constraint on the judge; deviation therefrom renders the judicial decision null and void. Systems might vary as to how this deviation is determined and how the nullity is declared; the principle nevertheless remains constant.

Maimonides describes the sum total of Jewish law as being comprised of the Written Law of Moses and the Oral Tradition.[87] Al-

---

[85] B. CARDOZO, *supra* note 1.

[86] *Id.* at 14.

[87] M. MAIMONIDES, HAKDAMAH LE'PERUSH HA-MISHNAYOT (INTRODUCTION TO COMMENTARY ON THE MISHNAH). Maimonides describes the oral tradition as being comprised of the following five elements: (a) interpretations of the Written Law that have been received from Moses himself and that have been unanimously accepted as authentic from time immemorial; (b) oral traditions of similar antiquity and authenticity but having no relationship to the Written Law literally, through allusion or hermeneutically; (c) rabbinic interpretations of the Written Law which have been derived through the accepted hermeneutical rules but which have been the subject of disagreement among the rabbinic interpreters and, therefore, lack the unanimity which is the hallmark of Mosaic origin; (d) precautionary measures taken by the Rabbis to guard against infringement upon or erosion of Mosaic provisions; (e) institutions, conventions, usages and customs ordained or ratified by the Rabbis, the legal authorities of each generation. These five elements are divided into two categories: those that have Biblical status similar to the Written Law *(de'oraita),* and those having Rabbinic status *(de'rabbanan).* Oral interpretations of the Written Law and oral traditions (items (a) and (b)) clearly attain Biblical status; precaution-

though the highest courts—in their judicial-legislative role[88]—are empowered to make certain limited changes in the body of substantive law,[89] the regular courts are bound by the entire body of Written and Oral Law. For them, the governing rule regarding deviation from the law reads, "If the judge errs in a law cited in the *Mishnah*, the decision is reversed; if he erred in the weighing of [conflicting] opinions, the decision may not be reversed."[90] Indeed, a judge could be held personally liable for monetary damage he caused by a faulty decision.[91]

Whether and to what extent "a law cited in the *Mishnah*" should be given an ever-widening construction has been a matter of controversy throughout the generations. Maimonides defines the class as those laws that are widely known, "such as laws that are explicit in the *Mishnah* or *Gemara*."[92] Some early medieval opinions included *geonic* decisions;[93] others excluded them.[94] Later medieval Sephar-

---

ary measures and institutions, etc., (items (d) and (e)) are clearly of Rabbinical status. Disputed hermeneutical derivations (item (c)) are, in Maimonides' view, Rabbinic unless the Talmud explicitly labels them Biblical. *See* M. MAIMONIDES, HAKDAMAH LE'SEFER HA-MITZVOT (INTRODUCTION TO THE BOOK OF COMMANDMENTS). Nachmanides, however, considers them Biblical unless the Talmud declares them to be Rabbinic, either explicitly or by identifying the biblical source as merely an external support *(asmakhta)*. *See* M. NACHMANIDES, HASAGOT HA-RAMBAN LE'SEFER HA-MITZVOT (CRITIQUE ON THE BOOK OF COMMANDMENTS), Rule 2. *See generally* Elon, *Introduction* to THE PRINCIPLES OF JEWISH LAW 10 (M. Elon ed. 1975) [hereinafter cited as PRINCIPLES]; J. FAUR, *supra* note 34, at 19-32.

[88] Jewish legal tradition knows no strict separation of powers. The biblical king was both chief executive and chief justice possessing also legislative prerogatives. With Moses—who was simultaneously the chief legislative officer and chief judicial officer of the Israelites—as its model (*see Sanhedrin* 16b, *Rashi s.v. de'oki)*, the Great *Sanhedrin* functions both as the highest house of *halakhic* legislation and as the supreme judicial body. *See* MISHNEH TORAH, *Hilkhot Mamrim* 1:1. The Hebrew term *Bet Din* (Court) is used indiscriminately throughout the legal literature to describe this judicial-legislative body.

[89] As a general rule, the high court can neither augment nor diminish laws that attain Biblical status *(de'oraita; see* note 87 *supra)*, but is freer to add to or subtract from law of Rabbinic stature *(de'rabbanan; see* note 87 *supra)*. *See generally* M. MAIMONIDES, MISHNEH TORAH, *Hilkhot Mamrim* 2.

[90] *Sanhedrin* 33a. The developed *halakhic* doctrine contains a number of additional factors: the source of the judge's authority *(e.g.*, the agreement of the parties or the license of the state); the manner of execution (*e.g.*, by judicial fiat or by physical intervention). *See generally* M. MAIMONIDES, MISHNEH TORAH, *Hilkhot Sanhedrin* 6. Although the resultant combinations and permutations have important practical consequences, they are tangential to our thesis.

[91] *Sanhedrin* 33a. *See generally* 4 A. GULAK, YESODEI HA-MISHPAT HA-IVRI (1967); Mechlowitz, *Finality of Judgments in Jewish Law*, 1 DINÉ ISRAEL 7 (1969). *Contra*, Stump v. Sparkman, 435 U.S. 349 (1978) where the United States Supreme Court, in a case involving a state judge who approved the sterilization of a fifteen-year-old girl and had been sued for damages, declared: "A judge will not be deprived of immunity because the action he took was in error, was done maliciously or was in excess of his authority." *Id.* at 356.

[92] M. MAIMONIDES, MISHNEH TORAH, *Hilkhot Sanhedrin* 6:1.

[93] *Rabad, cited in* TUR, *Choshen Mishpat* 25.

[94] *See* J. FAUR, *supra* note 34, at 45-46 & nn.85-92.

dic scholars tended to consider Maimonides' *Code* itself as so authoritative that they viewed a decision that contravened a Maimonidean restatement of law as tantamount to an error in "a law cited in the *Mishnah*."[95] Late medieval authorities declared that contravening a law of the *Shulchan Arukh* which had been accepted without dispute by its classical successors is to be regarded as an error in "a law cited in the *Mishnah*"; and for Ashkenazic Jewry, whenever R. Moses Isserles cites with approval an opinion that disagrees with the *Shulchan Arukh*, that opinion achieves the status of "a law cited in the *Mishnah*."[96] Yet R. Moses Isserles himself—with all due respect to earlier accepted authorities—asserts in no uncertain terms that the authorities of each generation have the right consciously to overturn any provision found in the Codes if they are convinced otherwise—as long as they do not abrogate a law of the Talmud.[97]

Error "in the weighing of [conflicting] opinions," the second clause in the governing rule of the Talmud, is defined by the Talmud itself narrowly:

> If, for example, two *Tannaim* or *Amoraim* opposed each other's views in a certain matter, and it was not clear with whom the true decision lay, but the general trend of practice followed the opinion of one of them, and yet he decided according to the opinion of the other, that is termed "an error of judgment in the weighing of [conflicting] opinions."[98]

The overwhelming body of legal literature has retained this narrow interpretation. This is significant, for the definitive law did hold errors in the weighing of conflicting opinions sometimes reversible, and, sometimes, even to be remedied by compensation on the part of the judge.[99]

Thus the substantive law itself, in its fullest formulation, is the first major constraint on the judge.

Yet the rabbinic interpretation of *Deuteronomy* 17:11, whereby judicial decisions are regarded as binding upon the citizen even if the

---

[95] J. KARO, BET YOSEIF, *Choshen Mishpat* 25, *Bedek ha-Bayyit*.

[96] *See* A. EISENSTADT, PITCHEI TESHUVAH, *Choshen Mishpat* 25:1 (citing a responsum of R. Ya'ir Bachrach).

[97] M. ISSERLES, HAGAHOT [GLOSS TO] SHULCHAN ARUKH, *Choshen Mishpat* 25:1 (following the opinion of R. Asher b. Yechiel *(Rosh), cited in* TUR, *Choshen Mishpat* 25).

[98] *Sanhedrin* 6a, 33a.

[99] *See* text accompanying note 91 *supra*. However, errors in judicial discretion were rarely interfered with. *See* 4 A. GULAK, *supra* note 91, at 179-83; Mechlowitz, *supra* note 91, at 39-47.

judges have declared "left" to be "right" and "right" to be "left,"[100] would appear to grant the judges extraordinary freedom to overrule legislation or authorized interpretations thereof that define what is "right" and what is "left."

This is not so. The overwhelming majority of authoritative teachers read the rabbinic interpretation as referring to the subjective frame of the citizen's mind.[101] In effect, it says to the citizen: "Even though you sincerely believe that you are being told that left is right, you are mistaken, and you must obey the judges." A minority opinion does hold the rabbinic interpretation valid even if the judicial tribunal is in fact mistaken: better that discipline be maintained and a bad judgment obeyed than that civil chaos prevail where any member of society can arrogate to himself the authority to decide what is the "right" decision.[102]

In reaction to this last opinion, Don Isaac Abarbanel offers a novel understanding of the rabbinic interpretation. In his *Commentary to the Pentateuch*,[103] Abarbanel refuses to acknowledge the fallibility of pious, devout judges administering the divine law. Yet the purport of the biblical verse as interpreted by the Rabbis indeed does indicate that the "correct" or "true" law is being distorted. He therefore expounds the intent of the rabbinic interpreters in the following manner. Divine law, *i.e.*, the *Torah*, is formulated in objectively true, just, and equitable *generalizations*, which of necessity disregard individual circumstances. Pious and devout judges, however, are duty-bound to find the just decision in the *particular* case before them. Hence in the individual case they are judging, factors may enter which demand that the solution, to be just, must deviate from the general law. Thus, if we think of the generalization as being "right," their decision emerges as "left." Nevertheless, their decision must be obeyed "even" if they have declared "right" to be "left."[104]

---

[100] SIFRE, *Deuteronomy* 17:11, *cited in* RASHI, PERUSH AL HA-TORAH (COMMENTARY TO THE PENTATEUCH), *Deuteronomy* 17:11.

[101] *See, e.g.*, M. NACHMANIDES, PERUSH AL HA-TORAH (COMMENTARY TO THE PENTATEUCH), *Deuteronomy* 17:11.

[102] This opinion is cited in I. ABARBANEL, PERUSH AL HA-TORAH (COMMENTARY TO THE PENTATEUCH), *Deuteronomy* 17:11.

[103] *Id.*

[104] Abarbanel's discussion is reminiscent of Plato's struggle—and development—regarding the superiority of an individualized rendering of judgment (THE REPUBLIC) and the (second best) generalized formulation of rules (THE LAWS, with THE STATESMAN somewhat intermediate). *See* H. CAIRNS, LEGAL PHILOSOPHY FROM PLATO TO HEGEL 39-40 (1949). For an alternate interpretation of Plato, *see* J. HALL, STUDIES IN JURISPRUDENCE AND CRIMINAL LAW 48 (1958).

But not only do the courts have wide latitude in applying laws, no matter how clearly and authoritatively formulated; they have equally wide latitude in arriving at a specific decision—no matter how profuse the regulations are regarding judicial procedure.

Judicial Procedure

The Jewish law of judicial practice and procedure contains fully developed provisions concerning the conduct of a case and the taking and weighing of the pleadings of the parties and of the evidence of the witnesses. The two-witness rule[105] is of great probative value: qualifications and disqualifications of witnesses and documentary evidence are carefully detailed; the place of oaths is carefully circumscribed; in relatively rare instances, courts must cope with common repute, rumor, and hearsay. Under the rubric of judicial notice, there is an elaborate structure of presumptions and quasi-presumptions of conduct, or credibility, of common sense, and of conditions.[106]

Despite,[107] or because of,[108] all these rules, regulations and guidelines, the judicial theory of the Talmud—as understood by the authoritative interpreters of the Middle Ages (*Rishonim*)—left it for the mind and heart of the individual tribunal to decide between truth and falsehood and to dispense justice.

Thus, on the basis of the Judicial Certitude Rule (*kim li*), Maimonides viewed the judge as the pillar upon which the entire judicial structure rests.[109] This rule emerges from the talmudic account (with approbation) of a judge who modified the prescribed administration of an oath (placing it upon the plaintiff instead of upon the defendant as provided by law) on the lone testimony of his (the judge's!) wife, whose honesty and accuracy he trusted implicitly.[110]

---

[105] *See Deuteronomy* 19:15.

[106] *See generally Umdana*, 1 ENCYCLOPEDIA TALMUDIT 137 (1947); *Anan Sahadei*, 2 ENCYCLOPEDIA TALMUDIT 70 (1949); *Ha-Peh she-Osar*, 9 ENCYCLOPEDIA TALMUDIT 722 (1959); *Chazakah*, 13 ENCYCLOPEDIA TALMUDIT 453 (1970); *Chezkat*, 14 ENCYCLOPEDIA TALMUDIT 1 (1973). Other summaries appear in the writings of Haim H. Cohn in PRINCIPLES, *supra* note 87, at 574-620; 4 A. GULAK, *supra* note 91, at 72-174; G. HOROWITZ, THE SPIRIT OF JEWISH LAW 673-97 (1953).

[107] *See* Cohn, *Evidence*, in PRINCIPLES, *supra* note 87, at 603; G. HOROWITZ, *supra* note 106, at 652-53.

[108] *See* 4 A. GULAK, *supra* note 91, at 108-09.

[109] The following account of Maimonides' position is drawn from C. Heifetz, Circumstantial Evidence in Jewish Law 50-64 (Hebrew); 10-12 (English summary) (1974) (unpublished dissertation in Hebrew University).

[110] *Ketubot* 85a.

A contemporary scholar has described Maimonides' view:

> It is the judge's absolute prerogative and duty to decide between truth and falsehood and to dispense justice. His decisions in all civil matters ultimately rest solely on his deepest inner subjective convictions as to where the truth of the matter lies. All the forms of evidence, including the two-witness rule, merely serve as instruments to aid him in reaching his convictions concerning the truth. Therefore, if he feels secure in his convictions in a particular civil matter, all the evidence and all the witnesses to the contrary need not deter him from deciding the truth as he sincerely believes he knows it. The judge's knowledge and conviction constitute thus the highest norm of the laws of evidence in civil matters. In criminal matters, public legal policy rules come into play which place certain restrictions on the judge's wide inherent powers, but not stifling them entirely.[111]

The two-witness rule is of great persuasive value, of course; but only when the judge otherwise has little if any conviction in the matter does the two-witness rule achieve the crucial and ultimate probative value usually attributed to it. The judge's broad discretion in this area is evidenced by two of his judicial powers. First, the testimony of the two witnesses must be a faithful, objective rendering of what they saw. Conjecture, conclusions based upon approximations, or deductions made from reasoning upon circumstances are not in the domain of the witnesses—they are the function of the judge. Second, under the Fraud on the Court rule (*din merummeh*), if a judge has scruples about a case, suspecting dishonesty, or has no confidence in the witnesses, although he has no valid ground on which to disqualify

---

[111] C. Heifetz, *supra* note 109, at 11 (English summary), based on M. MAIMONIDES, MISHNEH TORAH, *Hilkhot Sanhedrin* 24:1. Maimonides' position is of greater theoretical than practical significance, for in the subsequent paragraph he states that inasmuch as the rabbinic judiciary has suffered a deterioration in the caliber of its members, the majority of judges reached a common consensus to refrain from wielding their wide discretionary powers and to abide closely to the formal rules of procedure as laid down in the legal sources. One should not, however, dismiss the Maimonidean position as *mere* theory. Time and again we read of the refusal of the great legal authorities to be unduly submissive to the formal rules of the Talmud.

> Know ye that in all matters, the truth of which is known to the *Bet Din*, even though the litigants may be turned from the path of truth by their own arguments and even though the rightful party may be unable to bring clear testimony and valid proof, it is incumbent upon the court to render a verdict which should be in accordance with what it knows to be true. Let no judge say, 'I base my decision only on the direct testimony of witnesses and, for the rest, the responsibility rests on the litigant . . .' For we have been commanded to render judgments of truth and nothing else.

2 SHELOMOH B. ADERET, SHE'ELOT U-TESHUVOT HA-RASHBA (RESPONSA), *Teshuvah* 148, *translated in* G. HOROWITZ, *supra* note 106, at 653.

them, he is forbidden to render a decision.[112] He either should withdraw from the case and let it be handled by another judge who can without qualms of conscience pronounce judgment;[113] or he should reject the suit outright.[114]

Admittedly, not all interpreters would go to the exact lengths Maimonides went in the totality of the discretion granted to the judicial tribunal.[115] Nevertheless, his doctrine serves as a representative sample which illuminates our thesis.

Judicial Precedent

Even greater freedom is granted the judge with regard to judicial precedent, for the simple reason that the *Halakhah* never adopted the doctrine of *stare decisis*.[116] As a modern authority on Jewish law has pointed out,[117] there are two reasons for this.

First, in *halakhic* theory, no case is ever closed, even with respect to the instant parties themselves. A case can always be reheard if new facts are introduced; thus, there always exists the possibility that a judgment will be set aside. Moreover, error "in a law cited in the *Mishnah*" also nullified the judgment given.[118] Although the value of putting an end to litigation once and for all inspired some practical counter-measures, this theoretical view of judgments as never being closed militated against the adoption of a doctrine of binding precedent.[119]

Second, the pervasiveness and legitimacy of differing points of view, coupled with the premium placed upon incisive thinking and humane application of principle, nurtured an abiding faith that, just as God's Word may have more than one meaning, a human problem may have more than one just solution.

> This conception of a flexible and dynamic legal order naturally left no room for the doctrine that especially a conclusion springing from a practical decision should impose itself on the judicial process. If . . . the judge should, in reasonable manner and in reliance

---

[112] *See* M. MAIMONIDES, MISHNEH TORAH, *Hilkhot Sanhedrin* 24:3; SHE'ELOT U-TESHUVOT HA-RASHBA, *supra* note 111.

[113] *See* M. MAIMONIDES, MISHNEH TORAH, *Hilkhot Sanhedrin* 24:3.

[114] *See* ASHER B. YECHIEL, TESHUVOT HA-ROSH (RESPONSA) 68:20; 107:6; J. KARO, SHULCHAN ARUKH, *Choshen Mishpat* 15:3.

[115] *See* C. Heifetz, *supra* note 109, *passim*.

[116] *See* Elon, *Ma'aseh and Precedent*, in PRINCIPLES, *supra* note 87, at 115-16.

[117] *Id.*

[118] *See* notes 90-97 *supra* and accompanying text.

[119] *See* 4 A. GULAK, *supra* note 91, at 114.

> on the *halakhic* system itself, come to a different legal conclusion from that reached by earlier scholars, he will have not only the right but also the duty to decide as he sees fit; such decision will take precedence over an earlier decision in a like matter, since the judge will also have known the legal thinking of earlier scholars and have decided as he did by going to the root of the matter.[120]

License for judicial independence, granting ultimate authority in a particular case to the judges immediately involved therein, was found in this talmudic dictum quoted time and time again: "A judge has nothing but (*i.e.*, must be guided only by) that which his eyes see."[121] Thus from fourteenth century Barcelona we read: "If another case comes before him, even if it be a like case in all respects, he may deal with it as he sees fit, since a judge must be guided only by that which his eyes see."[122] Similarly, a sixteenth century Polish authority in Lublin refused to reduce his decisions to writing:

> I know that [once I do so] people, following the rule of *hilkheta ke-ratra'ei*,[123] will decide on the basis of what I shall have written. I do not wish people to depend upon me. . . . A judge must be guided only by that which his eyes see. Let each one decide according to the promptings of his heart regarding the exigencies of the moment.[124]

Indeed, the idea that the entirety of the law of Scripture was given *ab initio* with the intention of the divine Legislator that the scholars and sages of Israel, its legal authorities and judges, be entrusted with defining its ultimate content—by interpretation, construction, and decision[125]—is the key to an understanding of the roles of freedom and constraint in all the areas of Jewish law.

---

[120] Elon, *supra* note 116, in PRINCIPLES, *supra* note 87, at 117.

[121] *E.g.*, *Bava Batra* 131a; *Sanhedrin* 6a.

[122] R. Nissim of Gerondi, *quoted in* SHITAH MEKUBETZET, *Bava Batra* 130b.

[123] Literally, "the law is according to the later scholars," a rule dating from the period of the *Geonim*, whereby from the time of Abbaye and Rava (Babylonia, mid-fourth century C.E.). "The statements of later scholars carry primary authority because they knew the reasoning of earlier scholars as well as their own, and took it into consideration in making their decision." ASHER B. YECHIEL, PISKEI HA-ROSH (RULINGS), Sanhedrin 4:6. *See* Elon, *The Rule of "Hilkheta Ke-vatra'ei"*, in PRINCIPLES, *supra* note 87, at 55.

[124] M. ISSERLES, TESHUVOT HA-RAMA (RESPONSA), *Teshuvah* 25, quoting a sixteenth century Polish authority (footnote added).

[125] *E.g.*, in defining the laws of *Chol ha-Moed*, *see Chagigah* 18a; in defining the afflictions obligatory on *Yom Kippur*, *see* M. MAIMONIDES, MISHNEH TORAH, *Hilkhot Shevitat Asor* 1:5, as interpreted by R. Nissim of Gerondi, in PERUSH HA-RAN AL HA-RIF (COMMENTARY TO ALFASI), *Yoma* 8; in defining *Torah* generally, *see* ARYEH L. HA-KOHEN, *supra* note 21; in judicial decisions, *see* I. SPEKTOR, *Introduction* to NACHAL ITZCHAK at ¶ 4.

Exercise of Judicial Discretion in Practice

But the broad discretionary powers granted rabbinical judges in the application of substantive laws (read, with Abarbanel: generalizations[126]) to particular cases, the essential freedom to be master of and not subservient to the mass of rules governing practice and procedure in deciding cases (read, with Maimonides: in pursuing truth and justice[127]), and the lack of a doctrine of binding precedent, never led to a chaotic hodge-podge of ad hoc awards or to an idiosyncratic maze of judge-made laws. Even a superficial perusal of the vast responsa literature, the case law of the Jewish legal system,[128] leads to the conclusion that Jewish judicial decisions reveal a remarkable loyalty to the body of codified law, a steadfast adherence to the rules of judicial procedure, and a most respectful attitude to precedent as being extremely persuasive though not formally binding.[129]

Why is this so? How did this come about?

Beyond a doubt, we behold before us the manifestation of a most powerful force in the Jewish religious psychology—and rabbinical judges throughout history were most pious and devout—namely, the awe with which former generations were regarded, the esteem in which earlier authorities were held, and the concomitant humility felt by later teachers in comparison. Something of the spirit of these feelings is conveyed by the following statements which are found in the Talmud and which became the refrain of each and every subsequent generation—indeed among the traditional God-fearing unto this very day.

> If the earlier [scholars] were sons of angels, we are sons of men; and if the earlier [scholars] were sons of men, we are like asses . . . .[130]
>
> The hearts [*i.e.*, intellectual powers] of the ancients were like the door of the *Ulam* [a Temple chamber whose door was twenty

---

[126] *See* text accompanying notes 103-04 *supra*.

[127] *See* text accompanying note 111 *supra*.

[128] *See* S. FREEHOF, *Preface* to THE RESPONSA LITERATURE AND A TREASURY OF RESPONSA (2d ed. 1973).

[129] It has similarly been pointed out, for example, that Lord Atkin in the landmark case of Donoghue v. Stevenson, [1932] A.C. 562, was not bound by precedent since all the important decisions which he discussed were those of courts inferior to the House of Lords. He was therefore permitted to overrule outright or simply not to follow the authorities who could be cited as being opposed to the doctrine he was advocating. Nevertheless, Lord Atkin used a variety of techniques to distinguish, explain away, or refute the opposing authorities. *See* W. TWINING, KARL LLEWELYN AND THE REALIST MOVEMENT 239 (1973).

[130] *Shabbat* 112b.

> cubits wide], and that of the later generations was like the door of the *Hekhal* [of the Temple which was ten cubits wide]; but ours is like the eye of a fine needle.[131]

Thus, in all the dynamism of Jewish law alluded to above,[132] and despite the broad freedom that Jewish law grants its jurists, we have here a most potent source of constraint upon them: their great reverence for their predecessors.

The *halakhic* attitude towards precedent may be depicted as one of extreme reverence but not absolute allegiance. Rabbinical decisions have constantly coped with new situations and have often been innovative—more or less, depending upon the times, the generations, the scholarship, and the self-reliance of the authorities. *Halakhists* have often avoided the impact of precedent in much the same fashion as have secular legal scholars faced with changing social conditions: by distinguishing, by reinterpreting, by modifying, or by simply ignoring them.

To what extent has this happened? How has it been done? What were the lines of thinking that accomplished it? How was the interplay of freedom and constraint enacted? To answer these questions, we await a Jewish treatment of the problem that will imitate Karl Llewellyn's *The Leeways of Precedent*,[133] making proper allowances for the differences in history, spirit, and nuances between the common law and the Jewish tradition.

In the meantime, Cardozo's *The Nature of the Judicial Process* has a significant contribution to make to the understanding of the operation of Jewish law.

The Four Methods and the Halakhic System

Cardozo sets out to identify and describe those factors that are at work in the rendering of a judicial decision and in the creation of judge-made law *after* the law as formulated has been examined and been found indeterminant or after apparently contradictory provisions or conflicting precedents have been pondered. He delineates four "methods" whereby the judge resolves the problem before him: the

---

[131] *Eruvin* 53a. A judge lacking either reverence for earlier authorities or knowledge of a talmudic provision would be subject to great communal pressure. It has been pointed out that the appearance of the Maimonidean Code, which was understandable to the laity because of its clarity of language and simplicity of formulation, was disturbing to some rabbinical judges. *See* J. FAUR, *supra* note 34, at 57-60; Marx, *Texts by and about Maimonides*, 25 JEWISH Q. REV. 371, 426-27 (1934-35).

[132] *See* note 84 *supra* and accompanying text.

[133] K. LLEWELYN, THE COMMON LAW TRADITION: DECIDING APPEALS 62 (1960).

methods of philosophy, of history, of tradition, and of sociology.[134] It may prove illuminating to examine the Jewish judicial process, with its analogous duty of resolving conflicts and deciding cases in the face of unclear guidelines, using Cardozo's "methods." An examination, cursory by necessity, but pregnant with suggestion, is all we may allow ourselves in the present context.

(1) *"The Method of Philosophy," Which Follows the Rule of Analogy along the Line of Logical Progression.*[135] Here the inner logic of the law reigns supreme. Every judgment has a generative power; hence by comparing the case before him to the precedents available, the judge generally will decide a case on the basis of logical analogies.[136] "The method of philosophy," thus defined, is the very air the Jewish judge breathes. *Medameh milta le'milta* (literally, "comparing one thing to another") or logical analogy, is the basic exercise of logical reasoning that is the legal thinker's primary tool.[137]

(2) *"The Method of History," or of Evolution, Whereby a Principle, rather than Expand Itself to the Limit of its Logic, may Tend to Confine Itself within the Limits of its History.*[138] On the one hand, the historical reluctance of medieval courts to utilize their powers to annul a marriage, despite their theoretical right to do so, has had a strong influence on judicial behavior to this very day.[139] On the other hand, the impact of the changed position of women in society upon practice and procedure in the rabbinical courts of Israel may prove substantial.[140]

(3) *"The Method of Tradition," that is, the Great Influence the Customs of the Community Exert on the Judicial Mind.*[141] Allusion has already been made to custom as a source of Jewish law and as a factor in its development.[142] *Minhag mevattel halakhah*, "custom

---

[134] B. CARDOZO, *supra* note 1, at 30-31; *see* notes 1-2 and accompanying text *supra*.

[135] B. CARDOZO, *supra* note 1, at 31-50.

[136] *Id.* at 19-20.

[137] *See, e.g.*, L. JACOBS, STUDIES IN TALMUDIC LOGIC AND METHODOLOGY (1961); Solomon, *Chilluq and Chaqira: A Study in the Method of the Lithuanian Halakhists*, 4 DINÉ ISRAEL at lxix (1973); Solomon, *Definition and Classification in the Works of the Lithuanian Halakhists*, 6 DINÉ ISRAEL at lxxiii (1975).

[138] B. CARDOZO, *supra* note 1, at 51-58.

[139] *See* ISAAC B. SHESHET, TESHUVOT RIVASH (RESPONSA), *Teshuvah* 399. On the broad historical development, *see* 2 M. ELON, *supra* note 84, at 686-712.

[140] *See* Holzer, *Edut Ishah Be'mishpat ha-Ivri (The Testimony of a Woman in Jewish Law)*, 67 SINAI 94 (1970); Rubinstein, *Kabbalat Edut Nashim, Kerovim, U'shear Pesulim Be'halakha (Accepting the Testimony of Women, Relatives, and Other Disqualified Persons in the Halakhah)*, 10 TORAH SHE-BE'AL PEH 99 (1968).

[141] B. CARDOZO, *supra* note 1, at 58-64.

[142] *See* note 84, *supra*. *See also* Z. CHAJES, DARKHEI HA-HORA'AH (pt. I), chs. 3-7. Although Rabbi Chajes refers only to ritual law, many of his observations are equally valid with regard to Jewish civil law.

overrides the law," may be a much-abused maxim; it nevertheless has a significant role in assisting the rabbinical judge in deciding an issue before him.[143] Thus, for example, acquisitions and conveyances in consonance with the Law Merchant have been accorded recognition as legitimate by rabbinic jurists.[144] Similarly, financial settlements arranged by the rabbinic courts between divorcing couples have indicated an increased recognition of the woman as an economic partner to her husband in present-day society.[145]

(4) *"The Method of Sociology" Along the Lines of Justice, Morals, and Social Welfare, i.e., the Mores of the Day.*[146] To paraphrase Cardozo in a Jewish context: "The final cause of law is the welfare of society under God and in accordance with His *Torah*." The Jewish tradition is replete with values and ideals which serve as constant antidotes to excessive formalism and which guard against *summum ius* leading to *summa iniuria*. Full description of these antidotes and the functions they fulfill in the Jewish legislative and judicial processes are prime desiderata in modern Jewish legal research.

(a) *Kedoshim tiheyu*, "And ye shall be holy."[147]

(b) *Ve'asita ha-yashar ve'ha-tov*, "And thou shalt do that which is upright and good."[148]

(c) *Darkhei no'am*, "Ways of pleasantness."[149]

(d) *Dinei shamayyim*, "Laws of heaven."[150]

(e) *Middat chasidut*, "An act of piety."[151]

(f) *Kofin al middat Sedom*, "We coerce people not to act true to Sodomite character."[152]

(g) *Le'migdar milta, Seyag*, "As a precautionary or protective measure."[153]

(h) *Tikkun ha-olam*, "For the welfare of society."[154]

(i) *Mi'pnei darkhei shalom*, "To promote peace and goodwill."[155]

---

[143] *See* Elon, *Minhag*, in PRINCIPLES, *supra* note 87, at 97-103.

[144] *See* Katz, *The Acquisition by Situmta in the Decisions of the Rabbinical Courts of Israel*, 1 MORASHAH 79 (1971).

[145] *See* Elon, *The Sources and Nature of Jewish Law and its Application in the State of Israel* (pt. 3), 3 ISRAEL L. REV. 416, 432-33 (1968).

[146] B. CARDOZO, *supra* note 1, at 64-114.

[147] *Leviticus* 19:2. *See* M. NACHMANIDES, PERUSH AL HA-TORAH (COMMENTARY TO THE PENTATEUCH), *Leviticus* 19:2.

[148] *Deuteronomy* 6:18. *See, e.g.*, *Bava Metzia* 35a, 108a.

[149] *Proverbs* 3:17. *See, e.g.*, *Sukkah* 32a; *Yevamot* 15a.

[150] *See Dinei Shamayim*, 7 ENCYCLOPEDIA TALMUDIT 382 (1956).

[151] *See, e.g.*, *Shabbat* 120a; *Bava Metzia* 52b; T.J. *Shevitt* 33a.

[152] *See, e.g.*, *Bava Kama* 20b-21a; *Bava Batra* 12b.

[153] *See, e.g.*, *Mishnayot Avot* 1:1; M. MAIMONIDES, MISHNEH TORAH, *Hilkhot Mamrim* 2:4.

[154] *See, e.g.*, *Mishnayot Gittin* 4:2-5:3.

[155] *See, e.g.*, *Mishnayot Gittin* 5:8-9.

(j) *Mi'shum eivah*, "To avoid hostility."[156]

(k) *Li'fnim mi'shurat ha-din*, "Above and beyond the requirements of the law."[157]

(l) *Mi'pnei Chillul Ha-shem*, "To prevent the desecration of God's Name."[158]

(m) *Gemilat chassadim*, "Acts of loving kindness."[159]

Moreover, result-orientation in rabbinic decisions may be discovered in numerous instances that go beyond the maxims we have listed.[160] Clearly, Cardozo's "method of sociology" as a tool of analysis of the Jewish judicial process gives us an insight into the wealth of values that abound therein.

Constraints on a rabbinical judge abound: the substantive law, the rules of procedure, and the awesome reverence for the previous generations of scholars and authorities and for their rulings and decisions. Yet it is in the context of these very constraints that a true freedom of action and of resolution prevails: a freedom tempered by thoughtful responsibility, by the dutiful pursuit of justice, by the passion of fostering a Kingdom of God here on earth.

---

[156] *See Eyvah*, 1 ENCYCLOPEDIA TALMUDIT 228 (1947).

[157] *See, e.g.*, *Bava Metzia* 24b, 30b; *Bava Kama* 99b.

[158] *See Chillul ha-Shem*, 15 ENCYCLOPEDIA TALMUDIT 340 (1976).

[159] *See* M. MAIMONIDES, MISHNEH TORAH, *Hilkhot Evel* 14. A somewhat different listing of terms and phrases in Jewish law that represents values and ideals that are within the legal framework, yet not formally enforceable, appears in Septimus, *Obligation and Supererogation in Halakha*, 7 YAVNEH REV. 30 (1969).

[160] Thus, Z. CHAJES, *supra* note 142, at (pt. I) ch. 2, explains a number of *halakhic* relaxations and dispensations granted by the early medieval authorities (*Rishonim*) of Franco-Germany (*Ashkenaz*) in commerce and moneylending as being motivated by the economic plight of the Jewish population and the dire need it had for relief. In a similar vein, a recently published responsum of Rabbi Moshe Feinstein of New York, *see* 9 AM HA-TORAH 8 (1978), prohibits the use of electrical gadgets to accomplish prohibited labors on the Sabbath. Although formally within the letter of the law, such use—if allowed—would in effect destroy the traditional Jewish day of rest. In the course of his argument, Rabbi Feinstein cites the talmudic prohibition of the employment of non-Jews to perform tasks forbidden to Jews on the Sabbath as having been similarly result-oriented, namely, to prevent the destruction of the traditional Jewish Sabbath by subterfuge. *Id.* at 10.

[16]

The Justification for Controversy Under Jewish Law

Jeffrey I. Roth

This article evaluates the role of dissent in a system of sacred law. The author demonstrates that Jewish law accommodates expression of minority positions, although controversy and dissent challenge its notion of an ancient and unbroken oral law tradition. Professor Roth exposes the shortcomings of explanations for controversy that condemn dissent or treat it as an aberration. He proposes a multifaceted justification for controversy that affirms the dissenter's indispensable contribution to Jewish law. Professor Roth concludes with a survey of the valuable functions dissent performs in the Jewish legal system.

INTRODUCTION: THE NATURE OF THE PROBLEM

Controversy is a fact of Jewish law[1] and a challenge for Jewish legal

---

‡ B.A. 1968, Yeshiva University; M.A. 1969, Columbia University; J.D. 1974, Yale Law School.

The author would like to express his appreciation to Professors David Chang, Ben Zion Eliash, Neil S. Hecht, and David Schoenbrod for their helpful comments on drafts of this article.

Unless otherwise noted, translations are by the author. Published English translations of sources are cited where available for the convenience of the reader, although original Hebrew sources were consulted in the preparation of this Article. Citations to the Babylonian Talmud [hereinafter also Talmud Bavli] refer to the multivolume English translation edited by I. Epstein and published by the Soncino Press from 1935 to 1948. The Soncino translation has been reprinted many times in a variety of formats. Citations will note specific tractates, page numbers, and translators as necessary. References to other Hebrew sources adhere to title pages, using transliterated spelling that may differ among sources. Where useful for locating sources, citations include first and last names of authors, Hebrew and English versions of titles, and other necessary information. Where publication is dated according to the Hebrew calendar only, the Hebrew year is given. The Hebrew year runs from fall to fall; for comparison purposes, Hebrew year 5748 runs from September 1987 through September 1988.

1. "Jewish law" is a translation for the Hebrew term *halakhah*.

The term halakhah is used to designate both the system of Jewish law in its broadest sense, and also, a statement of a single rule of law. It is derived from the Hebrew word meaning "to go." Thus, the term connotes the way in which Israel goes, the path it follows. M. ELON, 1 HA-MISHPAT HA-IVRI 143 (1973). It encompasses the entire subject matter of Jewish law, including public and private law—civil, criminal, administrative, religious, ritual, and moral law.

More limited in their meanings are the terms Biblical law, Talmudic law and rabbinic law. Each designates a successive historical phase in the evolution of Jewish law. The result is an amalgam of all three with its own characteristics; it cannot be identified with any single one of them.

The modern Hebrew term *mishpat ivri* ("Hebrew law") also has a more limited connotation, being confined to those areas of Jewish law that correspond to the subject matter of modern legal systems. *Id.* at 146.

The state of Israel has incorporated into its legal system miscellaneous elements of Jewish law theory. The authorities of Jewish law often disagree among themselves. Support for contradictory legal positions, all justified by citations to the same legal sources, is common. The "controversy among authorities"[2] is the central unit in the study of Jewish law. Even after ruling on a disputed legal point, the authorities preserve dissenting opinions in their works for future study.

Yet differences of opinion about law challenge a basic tenet regarding the origin and authenticity of Jewish law: the belief that God's revelation of law to Moses at Sinai was two-fold in nature, written and oral. In this view, God revealed a written law, the Five Books of Moses, together with an oral law, explanations necessary for the proper performance of the written commandments.[3] This oral law constitutes the corpus of Jewish legal teaching which has been transmitted from master to disciple in an unbroken chain reaching back to the original revelation.[4] But if the initial, two-part revelation was *complete*, and the chain of transmission *unbroken*, then how is it possible for the legal sages—the links in the chain—to disagree about the law? The pedigree of the oral law and the authority of the sages as its interpreters are at stake in answering this question.

Scholars who respond to the question make undesirable concessions too often. They typically argue either that controversy grew out of errors that distorted the oral law in the process of transmission,[5] or that controversy originated in historical events that prevented the Jewish legal system from operating normally.[6] However, by conceding that legal controversy is a sign that something has gone wrong and needs to be corrected, they undermine the legitimacy of dissent in Jewish law. The suggestion that, ideally, authorities should not disagree about the law provides a handy rationale for suppressing the expression of dissenting points of view. This rationale for suppression can be combined with other arguments against dissent—including its potential for causing sch-

as a matter of legislative or judicial policy, but Israeli law is the law of a modern, secular nation state, and not Jewish law. For a discussion of the relationship between Jewish law and Israeli law, see I. ENGLARD, RELIGIOUS LAW IN THE ISRAEL LEGAL SYSTEM (1975). Roth, *Responding to Dissent in Jewish Law: Suppression versus Self-Restraint*, 40 RUTGERS L. REV. 31, 32 n.1 (1987).

2. In Hebrew, *mahaloket*; in Aramaic, *pelugta*. On these terms, see Daube, *Dissent in the Bible and Talmud*, 59 CALIF. L. REV. 784, 786-87 (1971).

3. *See, e.g.*, M. MAIMONIDES (1135-1204), MISHNEH TORAH: THE BOOK OF KNOWLEDGE 1b (M. Hyamson trans. 1965).

4. *See id.* at 1b-3a. Maimonides provides a list of outstanding scholars "who received the Oral Law each from his predecessors in unbroken succession." *Id.* at 3a. These authorities comprise the major links in a chain of transmission that spanned forty generations, commencing with the original revelation of the oral law to Moses and continuing until the death of Rav Ashi, one of the editors of the Babylonian Talmud, early in the fifth century.

5. *See infra* notes 59-78 and accompanying text.

6. *See infra* notes 79-91 and accompanying text.

isms, confusing the public and weakening their respect for authority and tradition—to jeopardize freedom of debate under Jewish law.

This Article presents legal controversy as an inherent and desirable feature of the Jewish legal process. It reconciles the existence of such controversy with the oral law tradition without impairing confidence in the authenticity of the oral law. It explains the origins of halakhic controversy in a manner that accommodates dissent by the authorities of Jewish law and legitimates the conduct of the dissenters among them. In addition, the Article identifies the valuable functions controversy and dissent perform in the Jewish legal system to demonstrate why the authorities of Jewish law should actively promote the expression of dissenting opinions by their colleagues.

The Article is divided into four parts. Part I illustrates the Jewish legal process in operation with a case study of a controversy. Part II critically examines explanations for the origins of halakhic controversy that undermine the value of dissent. Part III argues from Jewish legal theory that the expression of nonconforming legal positions is both legitimate and desirable. Part IV buttresses the theoretical conclusion by providing a functional justification for dissent in Jewish law, showing the beneficial role that dissent plays in the study, development and application of Jewish law.

I
A Case Study in Controversy and Dissent: Release From Combat Duty

Jewish partisan forces were defeated by Roman legions, first in the year 70 and again in 135, ending two prolonged military challenges to the supremacy of Rome.[7] A Jewish army took the field again eighteen centuries later, in 1948, upon the establishment of the state of Israel. In the interim, the authorities of Jewish law debated the issue of release from military combat duty.

A verse in Deuteronomy charges that prior to battle, the officers address their troops in the following words: "What man is there that is fearful and faint-hearted? let him go and return unto his house, lest his brethren's heart melt as his heart."[8] The soldiers released pursuant to this provision return home for noncombatant duties, such as repairing roads and supplying food and water for the frontline troops.[9]

---

7. After the destruction of Jerusalem and the Second Temple in the year 70, a small group of Jewish partisans held out against the Romans in the desert fortress of Masada until the year 73. *See* Y. Yadin, Masada 11 (1966). For a history of the second revolt, the Bar Kokhba War, see 2 G. Alon, The Jews in their Land in the Talmudic Age 570-637 (G. Levi trans. 1984).

8. *Deuteronomy* 20:8 (Jewish Publication Society 1917).

9. Mishnah, *Sotah* 8:2 (H. Danby trans. 1933); *see also* 3 The Code of Maimonides

Three sages of Jewish law who lived during the second century disagreed over the interpretation of the verse. Their opinions are recorded in the Mishnah.[10] The first, Akiva, understood the words "fearful and fainthearted" literally to mean a conscript is entitled to release if "he cannot endure the armies joined in battle or bear to see a drawn sword."[11] His contemporary, Jose Hagalili, construed the words with reference to sins. In his view, exemption is available to the recruit who is afraid that he will be harmed in battle as punishment for having sinned.[12] The third sage, Jose ben Halafta, citing examples of persons who have violated *Biblical* laws, stated: "such a one it is that is fearful and fainthearted."[13]

The study of the Mishnah recorded in the Talmud supplies a useful elaboration of these positions.[14] Jose Hagalili agrees with Akiva that a

(MISHNEH TORAH): BOOK FOURTEEN, THE BOOK OF JUDGES, *Kings and Wars* 7:9, at 226 (A. Hershman trans. 1949) [hereinafter M. MAIMONIDES, MISHNEH TORAH].

The Mishnah is a compilation of concise statements about Jewish law, edited and arranged by Rabbi Judah Hanasi around the end of the second century. It reflects the development of Jewish law by sages (Heb. *Tanna'im*) active mainly in the land of Israel during the preceding two centuries. Danby's translation contains a useful introduction at xiii-xxxiii.

The MISHNEH TORAH, a code of Jewish law, is divided into fourteen books, including the Book of Judges. Each book is subdivided into treatises, such as "King and Wars." The treatises are further subdivided into chapters and *halakhot* ("laws"). Unless otherwise indicated, subsequent references to MISHNEH TORAH cite a specific treatise, chapter, and law within Hershman's translation of the Book of Judges. On the codes of Jewish law generally, see *infra* note 22 and accompanying text.

10. MISHNAH, *Sotah* 8:5 (H. Danby trans. 1933). On the Mishna, see *supra* note 9.

11. MISHNAH *Sotah* 8:5. Akiva was the spiritual mainstay of the second revolt against Rome; many of his students enlisted in the military ranks, and he was martyred at its unsuccessful conclusion. For brief biographical notes on Akiva, Jose Hagalili, and Jose ben Halafta, see M. MIELZINER, INTRODUCTION TO THE TALMUD 29-30, 33 (5th ed. 1968).

12. MISHNAH, *Sotah* 8:5. Jose Hagalili is "Jose the Galilean" in English.

13. *Id.* The Mishnah refers to Jose ben Halafta as Rabbi Jose.

14. The Talmud, an encyclopedic compendium of the oral law, reflects the study and development of Jewish law by sages (Heb. *Amora'im*) who were active for three centuries after the Mishnah was compiled around the year 200. The Talmud is essentially silent on the process of its own composition. According to the traditional account, Rav Ashi (d. 427), principal of the school at Sura in Mesopotamia (Heb. *Bav'l*, hence Babylonia) for 60 years, began the editorial process. A successor, Ravina (d. 499), continued the editing, and after his death, a group of scholarly redactors (Heb. *Savora'im*) polished the work for the next century and a half. *See* 6 S. BARON, SOCIAL AND RELIGIOUS HISTORY OF THE JEWS 19-21 (1958) (by 650, the editing of the Talmud was complete, but copies were scarce for another century). For surveys of theories of modern researchers explaining how, why, and by whom oral debates in the Babylonian academies of Jewish law were transformed into a literary work, see, e.g., J. KAPLAN, REDACTION OF THE BABYLONIAN TALMUD (1933); FORMATION OF THE BABYLONIAN TALMUD (J. Neusner ed. 1970).

The Talmud is composed of two strata, the Mishnah and the Gemara. For an explanation of the Mishnah, see *supra* note 9. The Gemara, by far the bulk of the Talmud's contents, is an extensive running commentary on 37 of the 63 tractates of the Mishnah, along with discussion of many related and tangential matters.

Although the Babylonian Talmud (Heb. *Talmud Bavli*) is usually referred to as "the Talmud," legal sages in Israel by the end of the fourth century had compiled an earlier Talmud known as the Jerusalem or Palestinian Talmud (Heb. *Talmud Yerushalmi*). For a comparison of the two

soldier who is literally scared of battle may return home for noncombatant duty. However, unlike Akiva, he derives this law from the last words of verse, "lest his brethren's heart melt as his heart." In addition, Jose Hagalili draws the exemption more broadly than Akiva, holding that a soldier who is afraid on account of his transgressions also may return home.[15]

The Talmud also reveals a difference in the positions of Jose ben Halafta and Jose Hagalili. By confining his examples to Biblical laws, Jose ben Halafta meant that release was available only to a soldier who was afraid for having transgressed Biblical laws, but not *rabbinic* enactments. By contrast, Jose Hagalili, who refers to fear of sins generally, holds the exemption is equally available to one afraid for having violated either rabbinic enactments or Biblical laws.[16]

The positions can be summarized as follows, based on the Talmud's report of the study of the Mishnah:

(1) Two sages concur that release is available to the soldier who is literally afraid:

(a) Akiva, who derives it from the words, "What man is there that is fearful and fainthearted?"

(b) Jose Hagalili, who derives it from the words, "lest his brethren's heart melt as his heart."

(2) Two sages, Jose Hagalili and Jose ben Halafta, concur that release is available to someone who is afraid on account of Biblical transgressions.

(3) One sage, Jose Hagalili, holds that someone who is afraid on account of rabbinic transgressions may return home.

Who then is entitled to exemption from combat duty as "fearful and fainthearted?" Neither the Mishnah nor the Talmud states a conclusion. After the destruction of Jerusalem in the year 70, inquiring sages could no longer refer a disputed legal question to the High Court of Jerusalem, the Great Sanhedrin, for a ruling. The High Court of seventy-one members, which met on the Temple Mount to debate unsettled questions of Jewish law, had authority to decide the law by consensus or majority vote and issue final, binding rulings.[17] The destruction of Jerusalem

---

Talmuds, see L. GINZBERG, ON JEWISH LAW AND LORE 3-57 (1955). The Jerusalem Talmud is an ancillary source of law used to explain the contents of the Babylonian or fill lacunae in its coverage.

On the authority of the Talmud as a source of Jewish law, see Roth, *supra* note 1, at 42-49.

15. TALMUD BAVLI, *Sotah* 44b, at 223-24 (A. Cohen trans. 1936)

16. *Id.*, *Sotah* 44b, at 223.

The duties imposed by Jewish law fall into two categories based on their derivation: (i) Biblical laws, arising from verses in the Five Books of Moses, and (ii) rabbinic laws, originating in the legal activities of post-Mosaic authorities. Halakhic authorities dispute the criteria for distributing laws between the two classes. *See* 1 I. HERZOG, THE MAIN INSTITUTIONS OF JEWISH LAW 2-11 (2d ed. 1965); THE PRINCIPLES OF JEWISH LAW 9-10 (M. Elon ed. 1975).

17. MISHNAH, *Sanhedrin* 1:6, 11:2 (H. Danby trans. 1933); TOSEPHTA, *Sanhedrin* 7:1, at 425 (M. Zuckermandel ed. 1970) (in Hebrew); TALMUD BAVLI, *Sanhedrin* 88b at 586 (J. Shachter & H.

destroyed the national legal center on the Temple Mount and the locus of final authority in Jewish law. Thereafter, the sages of the law, in the land of Israel and in the diaspora, continued to exercise a localized authority in their communities, but no individual or assembly succeeded to the undisputed authority of the High Court to settle controversial questions of Jewish law for the legal system as a whole.[18]

The existence of an unsettled controversy among the sages creates a need to extract, from the variety of their opinions, a rule to govern conduct. This is the calling of the halakhic authority (Heb. *posek*) of each community, a legal scholar recognized by the community as possessing the expertise and other qualities that enable him to decide cases and answer unsettled questions of Jewish law for them.[19] Canons of decisionmaking, which the legal sages developed over the course of time, govern the process of deciding the law.[20] The canons are not applied mechanically; rather, authorities must make many subjective judgments, including an assessment of the relative merits of the halakhic authorities whose positions are under review.[21]

In addition to deciding individual cases, some halakhic authorities perform an additional function by composing codes of Jewish law. From the give and take of legal debate, the authors of the codes extract normative rulings, which they present to the reader in concise, unembellished form, free of distracting polemics.[22] These works are not codes in the continental, civil law sense because they do not supersede preexisting law

Freedman trans. 1935); *see also* M. MAIMONIDES, MISHNEH TORAH, *Rebels* 1:3, *supra* note 9, at 139.

18. *See* Roth, *supra* note 1, at 38-42 (discussing role of High Court of Jerusalem and loss of final authority in Jewish law).

19. These qualities ideally include demonstrated mastery of the sources of Jewish law and the ability to apply them sympathetically to contemporary local conditions, along with impeccable religious piety in conduct and beliefs and a personality that is self-effacing when being offered an honor, but courageous when a question of principle is involved. On the problems that are involved in identifying authorities of Jewish law, see Roth, *supra* note 1, at 34-35.

20. For a collection of canons of decision, see Sperber, *Conflict of Opinions*, in 5 ENCYCLOPEADIA JUDAICA 890 (1972) (for example, in a controversy between a majority of the sages and a minority, the majority view is preferred; in a controversy over a biblical law, the stricter position is adopted; over a rabbinic enactment, the more lenient position is adopted; when earlier and later authorities conflict, opinion of a later authority takes precedence over that of an earlier authority; and many others).

21. See 1 J. BLEICH, CONTEMPORARY HALAKHIC PROBLEMS xvii (1977), describing halakhic decisionmaking as follows:

> [Deciding the law is] the product of highly specialized skills. It is in choosing between conflicting precedents and opinions that the consummate expertise of the decisor becomes apparent . . . . He must carefully weigh and balance opinions and decisions, assigning weight not merely on the basis of sheer number but also on the relative stature of the scholars whose opinions are under consideration, and must at the same time assess the complexities and relative importance of any number of component factors.

A specific enumeration of the "component factors" halakhic authorities take into account remains a scholarly desideratum.

22. The earliest attempts at codification date from the centuries following the completion of

nor do they become the exclusive source of law.[23] A Jewish code of law resembles a restatement of the law.[24] It sets forth the author's view of the law, arranged systematically, stated concisely, and striving for completeness. The author's conclusions are based on a thorough review of prior authorities, filtered and refined by his legal insight, especially in doubtful or unresolved cases. The author aims to make access to the law easier, to guide practioners of the law, and to promote greater uniformity in practice among widely scattered Jewish communities. Acceptance of

---

the Talmud. For a survey of the history of efforts to codify Jewish law and descriptions of the major works, see THE PRINCIPLES OF JEWISH LAW, *supra* note 16, at 120-46.

A major achievement in codification is the Mishneh Torah of Rabbi Moses Maimonides (1135-1204). For a detailed analysis of the work, see I. TWERSKY, INTRODUCTION TO THE CODE OF MAIMONIDES (*Mishneh Torah*) (1980). On the structure of the code, see *supra* note 9.

The more recent, comprehensive code, SHULHAN ARUKH ("The Set Table"), is the work of Rabbi Joseph Caro (1488-1575), a Spanish authority who settled in Safed, Israel. For his biography, see R. WERBLOWSKY, JOSEPH KARO: LAWYER AND MYSTIC (1963). A Polish authority, Rabbi Moses Isserles ("Rema," 1520-1572), wrote critical glosses known as *Mappah* ("The Tablecloth") to cover the omission from Caro's code of Ashkenazic laws and customs. Publishers incorporated the glosses into the text of Caro's code and published the work of both authors as a single book known as the SHULHAN ARUKH. For a discussion of the composite work and its legal impact, see I. TWERSKY, *The Shulhan Aruk: Enduring Code of Jewish Law*, in STUDIES IN JEWISH LAW AND PHILOSOPHY 130 (1982).

Caro's code distributes Jewish law into four divisions: *Orah Hayyim*—prayer, Sabbaths, and festivals; *Yoreh De'ah*—dietary, ritual, and moral law; *Even Ha-Ezer*—family law and divorce; and *Hoshen Ha-Mishpat*—courts, property law, and torts. For a list of the topics treated in each division, see G. HOROWITZ, THE SPIRIT OF JEWISH LAW 738-40 (1953). Each division is subdivided into chapters and paragraphs. Subsequent references to provisions in the SHULHAN ARUKH will note whether the author is Caro or Isserles and cite the relevant division, chapter, and paragraph. For an English translation of a few chapters in the fourth division and a synopsis of selected commentaries, see J. CARO, CODE OF HEBREW LAW: SHULHAN 'ARUK, HOSEN HAMISHPAT (C. Denburg trans. 1955).

23. *Cf.* J. MERRYMAN, THE CIVIL LAW TRADITION 27 (1985) (distinguishing role of codification in civil law states and common law states); R. SCHLESINGER, COMPARATIVE LAW: CASES, TEXT, MATERIALS 269-93 (4th ed. 1980) (discussing the impact of codes in civil law countries); A. WATSON, THE MAKING OF THE CIVIL LAW 131 (1981) (existing law ceases to have force upon adoption of civil code).

24. *See* Kirschenbaum, *Towards a Restatement Of Jewish Law*, in JEWISH LAW IN LEGAL HISTORY AND THE MODERN WORLD 97, 115-16 (B. Jackson ed. 1980); *cf.* Friedmann, *Problems of Codification of Civil Law in Israel*, in 2 JEWISH LAW ANNUAL 88, 90 n.13 (1979) (observing that codes Mishneh Torah and Shulhan Arukh resemble nonbinding private restatements, which from frequent usage and tradition, may come to represent the true law). For a useful comparison of codes and the American Law Institute's restatements of the law, see Fleming, *The Restatements and Codification*, in 2 JEWISH LAW ANNUAL 108 (1979).

Justice Elon's characterization of Jewish codes as "compilations" is less helpful. M. ELON, HA-MISHPAT HA-IVRI 946-47 (1973); *see also* THE PRINCIPLES OF JEWISH LAW, *supra* note 16, at 122. While a compilation presents the texts of statutes arranged according to subject matter and provides prima facie evidence of the texts, Jewish codes are not based on statutory law and make no effort to present the original texts of the underlying sources. Their concern is to articulate the substance of the final rulings, and halakhic authorities regard them as providing more than merely prima facie evidence of the law. *See id.* at 122 ("from the standpoint of the validity attaching to such compilatory work and the possibility of deciding in terms of it, it has been regarded *not merely as constituting presumptive evidence, but as carrying also the authority of a proper codex*") (emphasis added).

the code depends on the personal authority and stature of the author and the quality of his work.[25]

The twelfth century codifier, Moses Maimonides, who devoted four chapters in the final treatise of his code to the laws of warfare,[26] offers his resolution of the dispute regarding exemption from military combat duty. He states: "Who is the man that is fearful and fainthearted? To be understood literally, that he does not have in his heart the ability to stand in the military ranks."[27] In keeping with the purpose and form of his code, Maimonides does not cite any source for the rule, nor does he mention any contrary points of view.[28]

The task of identifying the sources of a codifier and reconstructing his probable *ratio decidendi* is performed by later commentators, known as "arms bearers."[29] The chief arms-bearer for Maimonides, Joseph Caro, cites Akiva as the authority upon whom Maimonides relied for his ruling.[30] Caro attempts to explain why Maimonides adopted Akiva's position over the others. Since, according to the Talmud, Jose Hagalili agrees with Akiva that someone who is literally afraid of battle is entitled to the exemption, then two of the three sages, a majority, adhere to that

25. No single code has ever been accepted as authoritative by all Jewish communities. Sephardic Jewry adheres to Caro's rulings in his Shulhan Arukh, Ashkenazic Jewry follows the glosses of Isserles when they run counter to Caro's rulings, and Yemenite Jewry regards Maimonides' code as their primary post-Talmudic authority. The situation guarantees a certain measure of pluralism in legal usage. *See* THE PRINCIPLES OF JEWISH LAW, *supra* note 16, at 130-32, 140-44 (discussing reasons for the initial, general opposition to the codes and its eventual dissipation); H. ZIMMELS, ASHKENAZIM AND SEPHARDIM 1-58 (1976) (discussing the origins of the split between Ashkenazic and Sephardic Jewries, and the role played by allegiance to different codes); Eliash, *Ethnic Pluralism or Melting Pot? The Dilemma of Rabbinical Adjudication in Israeli Family Law*, 18 ISRAEL L. REV. 348 (1983) (discussing the state of Israel's problems in the administration of Jewish family law to a diverse population of Ashkenazim and Sephardim).

26. M. MAIMONIDES, MISHNEH TORAH, *Kings and Wars* chs. 5-8, *supra* note 9, at 217-30.

27. M. MAIMONIDES, MISHNEH TORAH, *Kings and Wars* 7:15 (author's translation); *cf.* MISHNEH TORAH, *supra* note 9, at 227 (A. Hershman trans.) ("who is not *physically fit* to join the ranks in battle") (emphasis added). The Hershman translation suggests some physical impairment for military service, rather than incapacitating psychological terror. The Hebrew is *eyn b'lebo koah*, literally, "does not have strength in his heart."

28. Other halakhic authorities criticized Maimonides for omission of his sources and alternative legal positions. *See, e.g.*, BOOK OF MISHNAH TORAH: WITH RABD'S CRITICISM AND REFERENCES 18 (S. Glazer trans. 1927) (criticism of Rabbi Abraham ben David ("Rabad," 1125-1198) that Maimonides aimed to improve but did not; he "abandoned the path of all authors who preceded him," who quoted the authorities on whom they relied, permitting their sources to be weighed in assessing their positions); RABBI SOLOMON LURIA ("Maharshal," 1510-1574), YAM SHEL SHLOMO, *Bava Kama*, Introduction (Hebrew year 5720) (in Hebrew) (Maimonides' code is like a dream without an interpretation, since he does not bring any proof to support his views; further, how can his positions be refuted, if one cannot determine what sources he relied on in reaching his conclusions?); *see also* I. TWERSKY, INTRODUCTION TO THE CODE OF MAIMONIDES, *supra* note 22, at 61-81, 97-175 (discussing Maimonides' purpose in adopting the abbreviated form of his work).

29. In Hebrew, *nosei kelim*. *See* THE PRINCIPLES OF JEWISH LAW, *supra* note 16, at 132.

30. Caro, *Kesef Mishnah*, in M. MAIMONIDES, MISHNEH TORAH, *Hilkhot Melakhim* 7:15 (in Hebrew). Caro was himself the author of a code; *see supra* note 22.

view. Only Jose ben Halafta disagrees. In taking Akiva's position, Maimonides resolved the legal controversy by applying the primary canon of decision—the position agreed to by a majority of sages prevails over the position of the minority.[31] In short, Maimonides shaped the disputants into a three judge panel to consider the issue of release from combat duty. Akiva spoke for the majority, Jose Hagalili concurred in part and dissented in part, and Jose ben Halafta dissented.

Maimonides' ruling in favor of Akiva's position has a double impact. First, he endorses Akiva's position as authoritative, and second, he marks the other positions as dissents. A reading of the Mishnah without Maimonides' ruling reveals the conflict of opinions but does not disclose who was dissenting from whom. While controversy is a necessary precondition for dissent, the mere existence of a difference of opinion does not by itself permit any position to be characterized as a dissent. Only after a halakhic authority determines "the law" can the positions he rejected be denominated "dissents" according to his view.

The initial question—who is entitled to release from combat duty under the cited verse from Deuteronomy?—can be answered with a much greater degree of certainty if Maimonides' ruling is taken into account. Yet, given the nature of authority and the lack of finality in Jewish law in the absence of a functioning High Court,[32] even Maimonides' ruling does not settle the issue. Not every subsequent authority of Jewish law felt bound to accept Maimonides' conclusion. His determination of the law generated its own line of dissents and concurrences.

In the thirteenth century, a learned scholar wrote a manual of instruction for youth which listed the 613 commandments contained in the Five Books of Moses and surveyed the additional laws associated with each commandment.[33] Commandment Number 526, "the priest

31. Majority rule is the only canon of decision derived from interpretation of a Biblical verse, *Exodus* 23:2. *See* M. MIELZINER, *supra* note 11, at 121-22 (explaining derivation). On the canons of decision, see *supra* note 20 and accompanying text.

32. *See supra* notes 17-18 and accompanying text.

33. SEFER HA-HINUKH (E. Hacohen ed., Hebrew year 5718) (in Hebrew). Although some scholars attribute the book to Rabbi Aaron Halevi of Barcelona (13th century), it appeared anonymously, and other scholars doubt the attribution. *See id.* at 1-2.

The notion that the Five Books of Moses contain 613 commandments (248 positive, 365 negative) finds its first literary expression in the Talmud, where it is attributed to a third century sage, Rabbi Simlai. TALMUD BAVLI, *Makkot* 23b, at 169 (H. Lazarus trans. 1935). No enumeration is given in the Talmud, but in post-Talmudic times, an extensive iiterature sought to identify the commandments and pinpoint their source verses in the Bible. *See* L. JACOBS, A TREE OF LIFE: DIVERSITY, FLEXIBILITY AND CREATIVITY IN JEWISH LAW 16-17 (1984) (referring to the literature). An official list cannot be said to exist; authors dispute some particulars in each other's lists. Maimonides' *Sefer Ha-Mitzvot* is an important exemplar of the genre. He prepared it as a checklist in anticipation of writing his code. Often printed as a forward to the code, it contains a statement of the author's criteria for inclusion and exclusion of commandments from his list. For an

annointed for battle,"[34] provided the anonymous author with his occasion to discuss the laws of warfare and the exemptions from combat duty. He writes that the man who is afraid on account of his sins returns home from the front.[35] He does not mention any release for the recruit who is literally afraid. The author does not cite any authorities who support or contradict his position nor does he give any explanation for his view. Acting as our own arms-bearers for the author, we can identify the authority on whom he relied as Jose Hagalili.

The author's departure from Maimonides' position is striking. It is more than likely that he was aware of the latter's ruling which had appeared at the end of the twelfth century. Maimonides' code forms the very basis of the author's enumeration of the 613 commandments, and many of the associated laws that he cites are taken verbatim from Maimonides' code.[36] While according Maimonides his due rank as a foremost authority and codifier, the author displays a measure of independence from the latter's views. On this issue, he dissents from Maimonides' ruling, without opinion.

Some six centuries after Maimonides' ruling, a Lithuanian Talmudist of the first rank, Rabbi Aryeh Loeb ben Asher, wrote a full-fledged dissent, with opinion.[37] In his view, the positions of Akiva and Jose Hagalili cannot be combined to form a majority. While these sages agree that the exemption is available to someone who literally is frightened of combat, each derives the rule from a separate phrase in the verse. Since they do not agree on the source of the exemption, their positions cannot be combined to form a majority,[38] as Caro suggested Maimonides had done.[39] Loeb holds that the more justifiable combination consists of Jose Hagalili and Jose ben Halafta. Both agree on release for fear of *Biblical* sins, and both derive the rule from the *same words* in the same verse. Akiva's view, then, is the view of a single individual. Under the canons of decision, the view of Akiva prevails against a single colleague,

---

English translation, see THE COMMANDMENTS: SEFER HA-MITZVOTH OF MAIMONIDES (C. Chavel trans. 1967).

34. See *Deuteronomy* 20:1-4 for the Scriptural verses that form the basis of the duties imposed on the "priest annointed for battle."

35. SEFER HA-HINUKH, *supra* note 33, at 318.

36. The author of *Sefer Ha-Hinukh* acknowledges his debt to Maimonides in the introduction to his work. *Id.* at 7. For a discussion of the relationship between the contents of *Sefer Ha-Hinukh* and Maimonides' code, see *id.*, Introduction, at 4-5.

37. RABBI ARYEH LOEB BEN ASHER (c. 1695-1785), SHA'AGAT ARYEH, New Series, No. 14, § 2, at 48 (Warsaw, Hebrew year 5634) [hereinafter SHA'AGAT ARYEH], *noted in* S. ZEVIN, L'OR HA-HALAKHAH 31 n.39 (2d ed., Hebrew year 5717) (in Hebrew).

38. *See* Shilo, *Majority Rule*, in THE PRINCIPLES OF JEWISH LAW, *supra* note 16, at 163-64 (discussing the role of majority rule in the determination of halakhah: "If a majority of scholars should arrive at the same conclusion but each for a different reason, some scholars hold this to be a majority opinion which is binding while other scholars hold the contrary view . . . .").

39. *See supra* text accompanying notes 30-31.

but not against two,[40] as here. Thus, Loeb concludes, Caro's explanation "does not say anything," and Maimonides' ruling "requires further study."[41]

Rabbi Moses Margaliot, a contemporary of Rabbi Aryeh Loeb, evaluated Maimonides' ruling further in his commentary on the Jerusalem Talmud. Margaliot objects to Maimonides' ruling for the same reason that Loeb did—Akiva's view should not prevail against two colleagues holding a contrary opinion.[42] But Margaliot offers a possible justification for Maimonides' ruling. He notes that Jose ben Halafta was a student of Akiva's. Accordingly, in weighing the three authorities in the Mishnah, Maimonides may have declined to treat the student on par with the teacher and thus did not count Jose ben Halafta's opposition to Akiva.[43] Having eliminated Jose ben Halafta from the equation and leaving only Jose Hagalili to oppose Akiva, Maimonides properly applied the canon of decision that Akiva prevails over the view of a *single* colleague. Akiva therefore prevails without the need to combine the partially congruent views of Akiva and Jose Hagalili to form a majority, as Caro suggested.

The reception Maimonides' ruling received may be summarized as follows:

(1) Two authorities concur with Maimonides and hold that he was right to rule in accordance with Akiva's position:

(a) Caro.

(b) Margaliot but only after raising an objection and answering it.

(2) Two authorities dissent from Maimonides' ruling:

(a) The author of *Sefer Ha-Hinukh*, without opinion; he adopts the position of Jose Hagalili.

(b) Rabbi Aryeh Loeb, with opinion; he argues in favor of the position of Jose ben Halafta.

Rabbi Aryeh Loeb would surely deny that he has "dissented" from Maimonides' ruling; he would insist that he has merely "raised a question" about it.[44] Loeb is a "latter-day" authority and, as such, displays a marked deference toward an "early" authority such as Maimonides.[45]

40. Talmud Bavli, *Erubin* 46b, at 323 (I. Slotki trans. 1938).

41. Sha'agat Aryeh, *supra* note 37, at 48.

42. M. Margaliot (d. 1780), Mareh Ha-Panim, *Sotah* 8:9, *noted in* S. Zevin, *supra* note 37, at 31 n.39. Was this a case of two independent researchers making the same discovery simultaneously, as often happens in the natural sciences, or did Margaliot know of Rabbi Aryeh Loeb's difficulty with Maimonides' ruling?

For a biographical sketch of Margaliot, see L. Ginzberg, *supra* note 14, at 42-43 (at the age of 70, he enrolled as a university student in botany, in order to understand better the laws of agriculture contained in the Jerusalem Talmud).

43. *See* Roth, *supra* note 1, at 75-86 (discussing reasons why a halakhic authority might discount the opinion of a student that contradicts the views of his teacher).

44. This is the distinction, in Hebrew, between *holek* (literally, dissent), which Loeb would deny that he has done, and *maksheh* (literally, question), which he would acknowledge he did.

45. The appearance in 1565-1566 of Caro's *Shulhan Arukh* marks the temporal dividing line

Avoiding a direct contradiction of an early authority, Loeb never says Maimonides is "wrong" but tepidly concludes that Maimonides' ruling "requires further study."[46]

Rabbi Aryeh Loeb's probable characterization of his position should not obscure the fact that he has written a dissent. His words certainly read like a dissent from Maimonides' position.[47] He disagrees with Maimonides' reasoning, his application of the canons of decision, and his conclusion, and he provides a rationale for adopting the view of Jose ben Halafta which Maimonides rejected. His criticism is no less a dissent because he implicitly acknowledges that Maimonides may have had other reasons for ruling as he did, although Loeb is unable to fathom those reasons. In view of his stature relative to Maimonides, the fact that he dissents without directly negating the latter's position does not render Loeb's tract any less of a dissent, albeit a respectful one. Indeed, his deferential attitude toward the early authorities in general only emphasizes the element of dissent in this case.

If Rabbi Aryeh Loeb refuted Maimonides' ruling, then it appears that we have come full circle. The original question—who is entitled to release from combat duty under Jewish law as "fearful and fainthearted?"—remains unanswered. Each of the three positions recorded in the Mishnah is endorsed by one or more of the later authorities. If the issue were not academic but had urgent practical importance—for example, if a combat unit governed by Jewish law presently required an answer in order to administer properly the system of Biblical exemptions from combat duty—the army's command would inquire of the halakhic authority in its jurisdiction. The authority would issue a practical ruling based on careful review of the sources just discussed, weighing the sources in light of contemporary local conditions.

between the two categories. On the Shulhan Arukh, see *supra* note 22. Thus, the "early authorities" (Heb. *Rishonim*) were active from about the year 1050, when the academies in Babylonia closed and the Gaonate ceased, until about the year 1550. The "latter-day authorities" (Heb. *Aharonim*) include scholars from about the year 1550 until the present. See Roth, *supra* note 1, at 74-91 (discussing reasons why later authorities tend to defer to the views of their predecessors).

46. SHA'AGAT ARYEH, *supra* note 37, at 48.

47. A full statement of Rabbi Aryeh Loeb's objections reads as follows:

> But what shall I do, for Maimonides wrote in *The Laws of Kings*, chapter 7, "Who is the man that is fearful and fainthearted?—to be understood literally . . . ." Hence he decided according to R. Akiva and not according to R. Jose Hagalili and R. Jose [ben Halafta]. This itself is questionable—how could he have abandoned the position of the two and decided according to the one? For it is established, the view of R. Akiva does not prevail as a matter of law against two colleagues. Now I have seen [the explanation for Maimonides' ruling suggested by Joseph Caro in his work] *Kesef Mishnah* . . . and it does not say anything. For even so, it would be appropriate to decide according to R. Jose Hagalili and R. Jose [ben Halafta] who both interpret the verse as referring to a man who is afraid on account of his [Biblical] sins; for as to [R. Jose Hagalili's agreement that] "fearful" is to be understood literally, he derives that from different words [than R. Akiva, namely,] "lest his brethren's heart melt like his." The words of Maimonides require further study.

SHA'AGAT ARYEH, *supra* note 37, at 48.

The case of exemption from combat duty is a good example of controversy in Jewish law. The number of conflicting positions is not excessively large, nor is the time frame, spanning two millenia, uncharacteristically long. A question of law that does not elicit differences of opinion among the sages in the Mishnah and Talmud, that finds early and latter-day authorities in agreement, or that is settled definitively by a ruling in a code that satisfies everyone, is the exception, rather than the rule.

Further, "Jewish law" is not found in any single position, but rather in the complete picture in which all the positions are represented, with their gradations of disagreement and shadings of controversy. Jewish law is not a fixed body of set rules with a ready answer to every question. Instead, Jewish law consists of a variety of opinions from which a ruling can be derived by competent authority. For this reason, teachers of Jewish law do not attempt to gloss over the disputes in order to convey a harmonious whole to their students. In the preceding case study, a person who had been taught only Akiva's position or Maimonides' ruling but was unaware of the other views in the Mishnah or the controversy over the ruling, would be an unreliable source of answers to legal questions and would not qualify as a halakhic authority in any community.

The case study suggests the following lines of inquiry. Akiva, Jose Hagalili, and Jose ben Halafta were links in the chain of transmission of the oral law. They received from their teachers traditions regarding the interpretation of Scripture and the laws to be derived from it, and in turn they passed on these traditions to their students. In light of this common foundation, what is the origin of their controversy? If they are faithfully reporting what they heard from their teachers, then how did the teachers' difference of opinion develop? Is it possible that one or more of them, or their teachers, did *not* transmit an accurate rendition of the oral law but an erroneous version? If so, how is one to determine which is the true law?

Can the continuation of the controversy from Maimonides to Rabbi Aryeh Loeb be attributed to the system's inability, following the abolition of the High Court, to produce a final ruling on a disputed point of law? If the normal institutions of Jewish law, including the High Court, were restored, then would controversy and dissent be eliminated? If the persistence of controversy is nothing more than a sign that Jewish law is operating under abnormal conditions, then does controversy serve any legitimate functions in Jewish law, or is it an undesirable by-product of the legal process that must be tolerated under current conditions but should not be encouraged? The remainder of this Article addresses these questions.

II
Explanations for Controversy That Undermine The Value of Dissent

The authorities of Jewish law diligently study their predecessors' differences of opinion and generate disputes of their own. They cannot help noticing the pervasiveness of controversy as a feature of the halakhic process. In addition, opponents of the oral law tradition point to the multiplicity of halakhic disputes as proof of their position that the oral law did not originate in revelation at Sinai but was created later by the halakhic sages themselves.[48]

Despite this attack, the authorities of Jewish law are not overly self-conscious about the number of their differences of opinion, nor are they preoccupied by the need to reconcile controversy with the oral law tradition. They seldom regard the existence of controversy as a problem to be solved. For instance, the Talmud, a veritable storehouse of legal disputes, contains a few brief passages that treat controversy as a phenomenon,[49] but it does not record a sustained effort by the sages to explain or justify it. For later authorities who attempted to explain the existence of controversy, the Talmudic passages suggested a variety of approaches to the problem but not fully articulated solutions. Using the passages as springboards, these authorities selected themes from the Talmud and elaborated upon them to arrive at their own explanations. They did not all reach the same conclusion.

It is not surprising that halakhic authorities disagree over the correct explanation for disagreements in Jewish law. However, what is needed is not so much a uniform explanation for controversy as a convincing justification of it. Any explanation that does not legitimate the authorities of Jewish law and the procedures they use to accomplish their mission—particularly the halakhic controversy with its expression of a variety of dissenting points of view—creates as many problems for Jewish law as it solves, calling into question the conduct of the very individu-

48. *See, e.g.*, Salmon ben Jeroham (10th century), Book of the Wars of the Lord (original Hebrew title: Sefer Milhamot Ha-Shem), in Karaite Anthology: Excerpts from the Early Literature 71, 75-77, quatrains 2, 7, 9, 10-11, 13 (L. Nemoy trans. 1952):

> I have looked again into the six divisions of the Mishnah/ and behold, they represent the words of modern men. . . . I have set the six divisions of the Mishnah before me. . . . And I saw that they are very contradictory in content,/ This one Mishnaic scholar declares a thing to be forbidden to the people of Israel, while that one declares it to be permitted. . . . I said, Perhaps one of the two did not know the right way . . . . While anon the scholars issue a decision,/ Agreeing neither with the one nor with the other, but contradicting both./ Had I been among them . . . I would not have accepted the words of these 'others' and 'scholars.'/ Rather would I have weighed the word of the Lord with them,/ And I would have judged accordingly every word which they had contrived. . . . Thine escape has been cut off by this argument, else answer me, if thou canst.

49. *See, e.g.*, *infra* notes 66, 80, 105, 114 and accompanying text.

als who are responsible for the development, application and transmission of the law.

Parts II and III of this Article analyze the various proposed explanations from this perspective, in reverse order of acceptability. The solutions surveyed in Part II are unsatisfactory explanations for halakhic controversy because they disparage the performance of halakhic authorities and undermine the value of controversy and dissent in Jewish law. The minimizing approach is the worst offender in this regard, followed by explanations that attribute controversy to errors in the transmission of the oral law or historical events that befell the Jewish nation. Maimonides explained the origins of halakhic controversy without justifying its persistence. By contrast, the explanations presented in Part III defend controversy and dissent as legitimate phenomena and justify the conduct of authorities who generate halakhic disputes when they advocate dissenting legal positions. Part III will show why these are satisfactory solutions for the problem of controversy in Jewish law.

A. The Minimizing Approach

An attempt is sometimes made to minimize the importance of controversy in Jewish law. The purpose is to deflate the strength of the challenge to the oral law tradition that is posed by the multiplicity of halakhic disputes. The minimizers characterize halakhic controversies as nothing more than arguments over incidental details of the performance of the commandments.[50] They view these arguments as minor matters when compared with the fundamentals of Jewish law about which consensus exists. Instead, they argue that the wide areas of agreement about fundamentals of the law prove the reliability of the oral law tradition, while the areas of conflict over small details are insufficient to prove the reverse.

Some minimizers argue that halakhic controversies are more apparent than real and evaporate upon a correct understanding of the subject matter.[51] Others dismiss the disputes as trivial matters, extrinsic to

50. *See, e.g.*, ABRAHAM IBN DAUD (1110-c.1180), THE BOOK OF TRADITION (SEFER HA-QABALLAH) 3-4 (G. Cohen trans. 1967); DAVID NIETO (1654-1728), MATEH DAN: KUZARI SHENI 3, 5, 55-67 (1958) (in Hebrew); *see also* BENJAMIN DE VRIES, MEVO LA'TALMUD U'L'HALAKHAH 14-16 (1965) (adopting minimizing approach to explain halakhic controversies in Israeli textbook for high school students).

51. SAADIA BEN JOSEPH GAON (c. 882-942), PERUSH RAV SAADIA GAON L'VERESHIT 187-88 (M. Zucker trans. 1984) (Hebrew translation from Arabic of part of SAADIA BEN JOSEPH GAON, PERUSH AL HA-TORAH (["Commentary to the Torah"]) (citing apparent controversies arising when, for purposes of debate, one sage contradicts another only to provoke him to clarify his position; or when two sages cite separate aspects of the same rule, so that one appears to permit in a case where the other would prohibit; or when two sages, each of whom has heard only part of a rule, recite that part as if it were the complete rule).

humanity's ultimate search for religious knowledge.[52] Some denigrate the halakhic process by charging that halakhic authorities deliberately manufacture disputes to serve their own dialectical ends.[53] In this view, the authorities generate controversies to demonstrate their cleverness to each other while creating a body of law so complex and so arcane that their services become indispensable to the nation, since they are the only ones who can decipher the law and apply it.

The minimizing approach is not a satisfactory solution to the problem of controversy in Jewish law. Depicting the legal sages as quibblers over details, players of mind games, or pedants who intentionally make things difficult does not contribute to their stature. Nor does charging that they are preoccupied with matters that are incidental to humanity's ultimate quest for religious knowledge lead to an appreciation of their work.

The minimizing approach misrepresents the character and concerns of the halakhic process by focusing on consensus and slighting conflict. While there are areas of agreement among halakhic authorities, they tend to take them for granted. Instead, halakhic authorities direct their attention to the areas of controversy, the unsettled legal questions which comprise the essential focus of the halakhic process.

The minimizing approach makes a questionable distinction between fundamentals of the commandments, on the one hand, and incidental details, on the other. This distinction is a necessary prelude to characterizing the details as unimportant. But "details" are not unimportant in Jewish law, since fulfillment of halakhic duties generally requires as an initial matter observance of the details of performing the commandments. Details are so vigorously and often debated precisely because

---

52. *E.g.*, PROFIAT DURAN (c. 1350-1415), MA'ASEH EFOD 6 (J. Friedlander ed. Hebrew year 5625) (arguing that those who claim humanity's highest objective is striving to know the Lord through an inquiry into His commandments do not have in mind the controversies recorded in the Talmud; in terms of attaining humanity's ultimate purpose, such controversies are a small matter).

I am indebted to I. TWERSKY, INTRODUCTION TO THE CODE OF MAIMONIDES, *supra* note 22, at 99 n.5, for suggesting the relevance to our topic of Duran's work and the other works that Professor Twersky lists in the cited note.

53. For example, Isaac Samuel Reggio made a characteristic statement of the charge:

> And anyone who has eyes to see can see that the purpose [of the post-Talmudic legal commentators] was not to get at the essentials of the law, but to initiate controversies, and to make points regarding disputes found in the Talmud, to contradict one of the parties and support the other. If you ask, who led them to trod this path? you will find the Talmud itself the reason for this, for what the Talmud did to the Mishnah, they sought to do to the Talmud. They worked day and night, not to answer questions raised by predecessors and to arrive at the legal conclusion, but to investigate [trivial matters, such as] what so-and-so's objection is based on and how he could have posed it in another manner, and why he posed his question in this language, and why he didn't utilize some other passage for support . . . . All of the foregoing is called sophistry [Heb. *pilpul*] and many have already declaimed against this practice.

I. Reggio ("Yashar," 1784-1855), *Behinat Ha-Dat: Perush Ve-He'arot*, commentary and notes in ELIJAH BEN MOSES DEL MEDIGO (1460-1497), BEHINAT HA-DAT 34-35 (1833) (in Hebrew).

they are so important.[54]

One proponent of the minimizing approach recognized that details are important and in doing so, inadvertently demonstrated the untenability of his own position. In the introduction to his book, David Nieto quoted with approval a passage from Abraham Ibn Daud, stating that the sages never disputed the fundamentals of the commandments, but only the incidental details.[55] Nieto also presents an example given by Ibn Daud to illustrate this point: The Mishnah opens with a dispute over the correct time for reciting the *Shema*[56] in the evening, but it records no controversy concerning the underlying duty to recite the *Shema*, so complete was agreement on that fundamental point.[57] Later in his book, however, Nieto uses the same example to prove the *necessity* of the oral law to provide details of the commandments and to defend the sages who argue over such details against the charge of hair-splitting:

> We are obligated to read the *Shema* morning and evening, as it is written, 'You shall speak of them . . . when you lie down and when you rise up.' [Deut. 6:7] Now since the Torah has defined the time, we naturally must consider when morning and evening start and finish. We must know if morning begins when the morning star rises or at sunrise, and similarly if evening begins when the sun sets or when the stars come out. If so, this question is not extraneous but *necessary and fundamental* for [performing] the command of reading the *Shema*. On the contrary, without [answers to these questions] we would not know what to do.[58]

If "details" are necessary and fundamental to performance, then the premise of the minimizing approach to controversy—that details do not matter much—is invalid.

Even if details were unimportant, it does not necessarily follow that controversy over details is itself a trivial matter. Controversy would be unimportant only if it occurred rarely and concerned few details. But in the actual state of affairs, halakhic sages have subjected to controversy virtually every "detail" of the law. These disputes over details occur despite the fact that *the function of the oral law was to supply the details.* The sheer weight of the number of controversies makes it impossible to

54. *See, e.g.*, Wurzburger, *The Oral Law and the Conservative Dilemma*, 3 TRADITION 82, 86-87 (1960) (emphasis added):

> Because Traditional Judaism is committed to the divinely revealed law *in its totality*, it must object to the cavalier treatment accorded to the minutiae of the law. Alterations cannot be condoned on the ground that they allegedly affect not the essence but only relatively trivial details. Traditional Judaism cannot brook *any* departure from the divine will.

55. D. NIETO, *supra* note 50, at 3-4 (quoting A. IBN DAUD, *supra* note 50, at 3-4).

56. This prayer consists of the Biblical verses *Deuteronomy* 6:4-9, 11:13-21 and *Numbers* 15:37-41. *See* DAILY PRAYER BOOK 75-78 (P. Birnbaum trans. 1949). For the dispute in the Mishnah, see MISHNAH, *Berakoth* 1:1, at 2 (H. Danby trans. 1933).

57. D. NIETO, *supra* note 50, at 3-4 (quoting A. IBN DAUD, *supra* note 50, at 3-4).

58. D. NIETO, *supra* note 50, at 59 (emphasis added).

sidestep the issue by minimizing the significance of controversy as a phenomenon in Jewish law.

Finally, the minimizers' arguments implicitly threaten freedom of debate. If controversy is not important, then there is no reason to encourage it. If debating the "details" distracts attention from fundamental concerns, such debates ought to be limited. If dissenters are quibbling over incidental matters, then whether they are prevented or inhibited from speaking will not matter much. Arguments of this sort, if used to justify the imposition of limits on debate, endanger the vitality of the halakhic process.

In sum, the minimizers offer an unacceptable approach to controversy in Jewish law. Their arguments impair the stature of halakhic sages, underestimate the importance of details to the practice of Jewish law, and jeopardize freedom of debate. The weaknesses of the minimizers' positions require that a different approach be taken to explain controversy and justify the expression of dissent in Jewish law.

B. *Faults in the Chain of Transmission*

The most frequently suggested explanation of the phenomenon of halakhic controversy blames errors in the transmission of the oral law. An examination of the premises underlying this approach reveals its fundamental flaws.

1. *Blaming Weak Links in the Chain for Inadvertent Errors*

A legal system that is dependent upon oral transmission from one generation to the next is vulnerable to faults in the chain of transmission. An error may slip into the tradition, or an omission may cause a gap, and the effect may be compounded over the course of time. As a result, two or more alternative versions of the tradition may enter into circulation. In an extreme case, the original teachings may be lost completely and replaced by a debased and inauthentic substitute. The shortcomings of the weakest links in the chain of transmission jeopardize both the uniformity and the reliability of an oral tradition.[59]

---

59. The discussion is limited to inadvertent errors, although an oral tradition may also be compromised by deliberately falsifying reports of what has been heard. The classical sources of Jewish law naturally stress the extreme fidelity of the teachers of the oral law to the formulations of their predecessors. *See, e.g.*, TALMUD BAVLI, *Sukkah* 28a, at 122-23 (I. Slotki trans. 1938) (Rabbi Johanan ben Zakkai "never in his life said anything which he had not heard from his teacher . . . and so did his disciple R. Eliezer conduct himself after him."). The suggestion that intentional tampering may have occurred in the transmission of the oral law cannot be made from within the confines of the halakhic system, because such a possibility contradicts a constitutional principle on which the system is based—the trustworthiness of the rabbinic sages as witnesses to the contents of the oral law. *See* Cohen, *Introduction*, in A. IBN DAUD, *supra* note 50, at lviii (probity of oral tradition depends on probity of its bearers). When a critic levels such a charge from outside the halakhic system, there are two strong responses. First, the public nature of the transmission process

The difficulties of committing an entire body of knowledge to memory and then transmitting it intact over the course of centuries appear so obvious that the very notion of the oral law tradition may seem like a fable. But transmission errors should not be assumed merely because of modern skepticism about a person's capacity to memorize large quantities of data. The ancients engaged in learning by rote and actively cultivated the faculty of memory.[60]

The earliest rabbinic sages, who were teachers as well as legal authorities, nevertheless recognized the vulnerability of the oral law tradition. They regarded forgetfulness as an obvious and serious source of potential problems. Each succeeding generation seemed capable of remembering less than its predecessors.[61] Even a student with a good memory might be responsible for introducing an error into the chain of transmission. The student may simply misunderstand what the teacher said.[62] Absence from the lecture hall or inattention to the lecture may cause a student to miss important points of law.[63] In addition, a national tragedy that distracts legal scholars from their labors may result in forgetting important laws. In a dramatic example, three thousand laws were forgotten during the period of mourning for Moses.[64]

---

serves as a check against deliberate distortion. Second, the principle of majority rule reduces the risk of distortion, at least to the extent that the possibility of a conspiracy among a majority of the sages to falsify the tradition is deemed untenable. *See, e.g.*, SAADIA BEN JOSEPH GAON, THE BOOK OF BELIEFS AND OPINIONS 157 (S. Rosenblatt trans. 1948); Zucker, *Le-Ba'ayat Ha-Mahaloket B'Masoret (The Problem of Controversy in Tradition)*, in 3 SALO WITTMAYER BARON JUBILEE VOLUME 319, 322-23 (1974) (in Hebrew).

60. *See* B. GERHARDSSON, MEMORY AND MANUSCRIPT 71-170 (E. Sharpe trans. 1961). He elaborates:

> Knowing the basic text material in the oral Torah by heart is an elementary accomplishment, presupposed of every teacher and pupil at the more advanced stage [during the period of the Mishnah and Talmud]. . . .
>
> To have the wording of the most important collections of texts at one's disposal [by heart] is in fact regarded by the Rabbis [of that period] as being nothing more than *elementary knowledge*.

Id. at 101, 106.

Where vestiges of the traditional system of learning persist, prodigious feats of memory are possible even today, and these evoke a sense of how the system might have operated in ancient times. See, for example, the report of a celebration that was held in Brooklyn, New York, on March 19, 1979, to honor 12-year-old Aron Bursztyn, winner of a national competition for the memorization of the Mishnah. Aron successfully committed to memory 1335 paragraphs of that work. The runner-up, Shalom Perl, also 12 years old, was reported to have "1,200 Mishnayos [paragraphs of the Mishnah] under his belt . . . ." 13 Jewish Observer 39 (1979).

61. TALMUD BAVLI, *Erubin* 53a, at 370 (I. Slotki trans. 1938) ("We, said R. Ashi, are like a finger in a pit as regards forgetfulness.").

62. *E.g.*, TALMUD BAVLI, *Shebu'oth* 26a, at 140 (A. Silverstone trans. 1935). For discussion of this passage, see *infra* note 72.

63. *E.g.*, TALMUD BAVLI, *Bezah* 24b, at 126 (M. Ginsberg trans. 1938) (reporting that Levi was absent from a lecture when Rabbi Judah retracted a point of law he taught the previous day, causing Levi later to state the law incorrectly and maintain the position that his teacher had retracted).

64. TALMUD BAVLI, *Temurah* 15b-16a, at 107, 109 (L. Miller trans. 1948); *see also id.* 16a, at

The question is whether the pitfalls of the oral tradition, which may have plagued individual students, also beset the system as a whole, persisting over time and impairing the uniformity of the oral law itself. Some authorities say the answer must be yes,[65] based on their interpretation of a report in the Talmud concerning the students of Hillel and Shammai in the first century. The report, attributed to Rabbi Jose, states: "When there increased the students of Shammai and Hillel who did not sufficiently attend [upon their teachers], controversies increased in Israel and the Torah became like two Torahs."[66]

The report completely lacks details. It does not identify the students of Hillel and Shammai by name, state how their attendance on their teachers was insufficient, describe how this led to a multiplication of controversies, or give any examples of the controversies that resulted. The authorities who cite the report to explain the origins of controversy in Jewish law therefore must combine the report with the general pedagogic concerns expressed by the rabbinic sages in *other* contexts.[67] Based on this synthesis, they allege a nexus between insufficiently attending upon teachers and the origins of halakhic controversy. Impatient students leave the tutelage of their rabbis before having mastered their lessons. They are prone to forgetfulness. Their formulations tend to be inexact. They may have remained long enough to hear the fundamentals of the laws but not the details. They may have been present when general rules were expounded but left before the exceptions were stated. They will mistake their partial knowledge of the oral law for complete knowledge. If they recognize gaps in their learning, they may fill them in from unreliable second-hand sources. Naturally they will engage in disputes with each other and with their better trained colleagues who attended longer

---

110 (listing other conclusions, analogies, and specifications forgotten during the period of mourning for Moses).

65. *E.g.*, RABBI JAIR HAYYIM BACHARACH (1639-1702), HAVVOT YA'IR, Responsum No. 192, at 103a, (1894); D. NIETO, *supra* note 50, at 62-63; Zucker, *supra* note 59, at 319 (citing fragment of a medieval manuscript that author attributes to the 10th century authority, Rabbi Jacob ben Ephraim).

66. TALMUD BAVLI, *Sanhedrin* 88b (author's translation); *see also* TALMUD BAVLI, *Sanhedrin*, at 586 (H. Freedman trans. 1935) ("But when the disciples of Shammai and Hillel, who [the disciples] had insufficiently studied, increased [in number], disputes multiplied in Israel, and the Torah became as two Toroth.").

The sentence concerning the students appears in the body of a larger report by Rabbi Jose concerning the resolution of conflicts by the High Court of Jerusalem. *See also* TOSEPHTA, *Sanhedrin* 7:1, *Hagigah* 2:9, *supra* note 17, at 425, 235 TALMUD YERUSHALMI, *Sanhedrin* 1:4, at 8b (alternative versions of Rabbi Jose's report containing small variations in language). The sentence concerning the students also appears in Talmudic literature as an independent passage, separately from Rabbi Jose's report. TOSEPHTA, *Sotah* 47b, at 321; TALMUD YERUSHALMI, *Hagigah* 2:2, at 10b; TALMUD BAVLI, *Sotah* 47b, at 253 (A. Cohen trans. 1936). On the Talmud Yerushalmi (Jerusalem Talmud), see *supra* note 14.

67. *See supra* notes 61-64 and accompanying text.

upon their teachers, heard more, and retained what they heard.[68]

Under this explanation for the origins of controversy in Jewish law, the aim of the halakhic process is to sift through the mass of opinions, sort out the erroneous viewpoints from the authentic ones, and attempt to reconstruct the laws that have been distorted or lost in the process of transmission. The archetypal sage is Othniel ben Kenaz, who through the strength of his dialectical powers was able to restore 1,700 *a fortiori* arguments, linguistic analogies, and scribal tabulations that were forgotten during the period of mourning for Moses.[69] His work serves as a model for all subsequent scholars of Jewish law, for their primary function, in this view, is to restore the oral law to its original, pristine condition.

2. *Shortcomings of the Weak Link Theory*

While highlighting the very real difficulties of preserving an oral tradition intact, the theory that weak links in the chain of transmission are responsible for controversy in Jewish law has fundamental shortcomings. First, it assumes that the rabbinic sages either took no steps to remedy the situation or that their actions were ineffectual. Yet the same sources that reveal the sages' awareness of the problems also disclose their ways for overcoming these problems. The Talmud recommends strong measures to combat forgetfulness.[70] Instruction in the oral law was conducted publicly, in small groups or larger assemblies, and a painstaking, repetitious procedure for transmitting the oral law was instituted in earliest times.[71] Students and teachers engaged in a considerable amount of give and take which afforded many opportunities to uncover problems, clarify ambiguous points, and resolve contradictions.[72] When conditions finally

---

68. *See supra* note 65 for citations to the authorities whose arguments are summarized in this paragraph.

69. TALMUD BAVLI, *Temurah* 16a, at 110 (L. Miller trans. 1960); *see also* E. DEL MEDIGO, *supra* note 53, at 37-38 (Del Medigo's text and Reggio's accompanying commentary).

70. *E.g.*, TALMUD BAVLI, *Erubin* 53a, 54a, 54b, at 370, 374, 383 (I. Slotki trans. 1938) (recommending students use exact language in their formulations of the oral law, employ mnemonic devices, and repeat lessons four hundred times, if necessary, in a loud, clear voice and not in an undertone).

71. *See* TALMUD BAVLI, *Erubin* 54b, at 381-82 (I. Slotki trans. 1938) (describing laborious procedure employed to transmit oral law from Moses to Aaron, the elders and the people); *see also* Baumgarten, *Form Criticism and the Oral Law*, 5 J. STUDY OF JUDAISM IN PERSIAN, HELLENISTIC & ROMAN PERIOD 34, 36-37 (1974) (suggesting that procedure for transmitting the oral law attributed to Moses reflects method of teaching oral law that rabbinic sages used in Mishnaic times).

72. A proponent of the weak-link theory cites the following incident, reported at TALMUD BAVLI, *Shebu'oth* 26a, at 140 (A. Silverstone trans. 1935), to illustrate misunderstanding as a cause of controversy:

> As the case of R. Kahana and R. Assi: when they rose from [the lecture of] Rab, one said, "I swear that thus said Rab," and the other said, "I swear that thus said Rab." When they came [again] before Rab, he would agree with one of them; then the other would say to him, "Did I, then, swear falsely?" He would reply to him, "Your heart deceived you."

threatened to break the chain of transmission, the sages committed the oral law to writing.[73]

Second, if serious and widespread forgetfulness went unchecked, the probable result would have been the disappearance of the oral law tradition, not the scrupulous maintenance of a debased version of the tradition. It seems unlikely that those students who were forgetful, inattentive or frequently absent were the ones who went on to become teachers of the oral law and to occupy important positions as links in the chain of transmission. On the contrary, the ideal teacher was praised for being the first to arrive at the academy in the morning and the last to leave at night and for never sleeping or even dozing at his post.[74] Absent direct evidence that students' problems in mastering the oral law went unchecked and pervaded the system, impairing the body of the oral tradition itself, the weak link theory fails to account adequately for the pervasiveness of controversy in Jewish law.

Third, attributing controversy to faults in the chain of transmission is objectionable because it injures the reputation of the rabbinic sages.[75]

Zucker, *supra* note 59, at 322. In fact, the incident demonstrates the reverse—how students sought and received immediate clarification from their teacher to dispel an error and eliminate a controversy *before* it could cause a problem in the transmission of the oral law. *See also* TALMUD BAVLI, *Berakoth* 27b, at 166-67 (M. Simon trans. 1958) (reporting case of student who approached two teachers privately to seek an answer on a point of law and received contradictory answers; he was told by the second to wait until the scholars gathered in their assembly when the question would be discussed and resolved publicly).

73. When the sages committed the oral law to writing is a subject of controversy. *See* H. STRACK, INTRODUCTION TO THE TALMUD AND MIDRASH 18-20 (1931) (listing one group of authorities, including Maimonides, who maintain the commission of the oral law to writing occurred at the end of the 2nd century, when Rabbi Judah Hanasi compiled the Mishnah and reduced it to writing, and a second group of authorities, including Rashi, who hold the oral law remained oral until the 6th century when the Talmud was redacted by the scholars known as *Savora'im*). In addition, some authorities believe the learning process was not completely oral, *even before* the compilation of the Mishnah. *E.g.*, M. MAIMONIDES, MISHNEH TORAH: THE BOOK OF KNOWLEDGE 2b (M. Hyamson trans. 1965) (teachers and students of the oral law transcribed personal notes which they consulted in private as an aid to retention); *see also* H. STRACK, *supra*, at 12-20; B. GERHARDSSON, *supra* note 60, at 157-63.

74. TALMUD BAVLI, *Sukkah* 28a, at 122 (I. Slotki trans. 1938) (referring to Rabbi Johanan ben Zakkai).

75. Maimonides rejected the explanation for this reason. M. MAIMONIDES, MISHNAH IM PERUSH RABBENU MOSHE BEN MAIMON (J. Kafah ed. 1963) (in Hebrew) (explanation which attributes controversies of the sages to their errors, forgetfulness, or inattendance upon their teachers "is debased, exceedingly strange and absolutely incorrect; it does not accord with general principles; it casts aspersions on the men from whom we received the Torah; and it is a complete nullity"). For Maimonides' explanation, see *infra* notes 92-104 and accompanying text.

In his monumental Responsum Number 192, Jair Hayyim Bacharach marshalled an extraordinary number of arguments and texts from rabbinic sources to refute Maimonides' position and to show that forgetfulness did play a role in the transmission of the oral law. Bacharach was not enamored of forgetfulness, but he felt compelled by the sources he cited to acknowledge its role:

> It was Maimonides' intention to place a fence around forgetfulness . . . . Would that we could strengthen it and establish it! . . . But in my humble opinion, it is impossible to escape from saying that forgetting did occur, whether in the explanation of Scriptural

Although the halakhic authorities of each generation have the important task of restoring the oral law to its initial condition, their predecessors are claimed to be the weak links in the chain who made the arduous labor necessary. Arguing that the earlier sages were only human and that a certain amount of slippage was to be expected does not avoid the negative implications. The rabbinic sages should have used whatever extra degree of care was necessary to safeguard intact the oral law that was placed in their charge. Further, the quantum of controversy would indicate a vast amount of forgetting, inattentiveness, and neglect, and not a small measure of slippage.

In addition, the explanation undermines confidence in the reliability of the oral law. If controversies originate in faults in the chain of transmission, then at least one party to each halakhic controversy must be proposing a rule that does not accord with the original contents of the oral law. It is also possible that the original rule has been lost so that all sides to the dispute are defending corrupt rules. For controversy to exist, these corrupt rules must be indistinguishable in appearance from authentic rules and equally supportable by proofs from Scripture. What certainty, then, is there that the controversy will be resolved by restoring the authentic rule? Some reassurance is possible if the majority of the sages are a party to the dispute and their position prevails, as a majority is less likely to have fallen into error than an individual. But on occasion an individual's view prevails over that of the majority;[76] on other occasions, a controversy is between only two individuals. Arguments against reliability are especially strong in these cases. The halakhic authority who adopts the weak link theory while maintaining the reliability of the oral law tradition advocates positions that are internally inconsistent.

Finally, the weak link explanation jeopardizes the legitimacy of dissent in Jewish law. In general, when a party to a halakhic controversy argues that an opponent's position is "wrong," he means either that it is

---

> verses, or in the application of rules of interpretation, whether in matters referred to by our sages as "laws received by Moses from Sinai" or in all the other details of the laws recorded in all six orders [of the Mishnah and Talmud.]

J. BACHARACH, *supra* note 65, at 102a-b.

In viewing the issue from within the four corners of the rabbinic texts that discuss forgetfulness, Bacharach failed to address Maimonides' basic point—that we *cannot* accept faults in the chain of transmission as an explanation for controversy because the explanation shakes the foundations for allegiance to the oral law. The explanation cannot be reconciled with faith in the excellence and trustworthiness of the sages nor with submission to the halakhah as reliable, authentic, and authoritative. Hence, Maimonides' criticism that the explanation attributing controversies of the sages to their errors, forgetfulness, or inattendance upon their teachers "does not accord with general principles; it casts aspersions on the men from whom we received the Torah . . . ." M. MAIMONIDES, *supra*, at 11.

76. *E.g.*, TALMUD BAVLI, *Abodah Zarah* 7a, at 29-30 (A. Mishcon trans. 1935); *id.*, *Yebamoth* 108a, at 748 (I. Slotki trans. 1936); *see also* 9 ENCYCLOPEDIA TALMUDIT, *Halakhah* 241, 259-60 & nn. 258-64 (1959) (in Hebrew).

unpersuasive in its reasoning (Heb. *sevarah*) or unsupported by prooftexts (Heb. *ra'ayot*). But if faults in the chain of transmission are responsible for differences of opinion, then the range of permissible counterarguments is expanded. One may charge that an opponent's position is "wrong" because it is debased, inauthentic, or corrupt, while maintaining that one's own position is the "true" one, correct and authentic. The frame of reference for halakhic controversy has been altered in a subtle but important way. Authoritativeness has become a question of pedigree and authenticity rather than logic and persuasiveness, with predictably negative consequences for the position that is rejected as "corrupt."[77] Arguments of this sort do not create an environment tolerant of vigorous expression of dissenting points of view.

Thus, attributing controversy to faults in the chain of transmission is an explanation that undermines the esteem of the sages, the reliability of the oral law, and the legitimacy of dissent. It does a great deal more harm than good and must be rejected.[78]

---

77. Jewish law has a genuine antipathy to characterizing the legal position of any halakhic authority as corrupt or incorrect, preferring to explain halakhic controversies in a manner that permits all the positions to be right, depending on the circumstances. *See, e.g.*, TALMUD BAVLI, *Ketuboth* 57a, at 336 (S. Daiches and I. Slotki trans. 1936) ("[It is preferable to assume] that two Amoraim [legal sages of the Talmud] differ in their own opinions rather than that two Amoraim should differ as to what was the view of another Amora.") and Rashi's accompanying commentary in Hebrew editions of the Talmud, beginning with the words *Ha Kamashma Lan:*

> When two authorities disagree about what another authority said, one of them saying, "Thus said so-and-so," while the other claims, "Thus said so-and-so," one of them must be incorrect. But when the two authorities disagree in their own opinions about a decision or about whether a matter is prohibited or permitted, each one saying for himself "This reasoning seems more logical," neither of them is necessarily incorrect. Each one gives his own reasons, one finding a reason to permit, the other finding a reason to prohibit. The first authority reasons by analogy this way, the other reasons by analogy in a different way. [In such cases] it can be said that both [views] are the words of the living God. On some occasions, the reasoning of the first will apply; on other occasions, the reasoning of the second will apply; for the [appropriate] reasoning changes with small changes in external circumstances.

78. To explain Rabbi Jose's report concerning the students of Shammai and Hillel, *see supra* note 66 and accompanying text, one does not have to concede the existence of errors in the chain of transmission. The report does not expressly mention forgetting, inattentiveness, or any other fault in the chain of transmission as the reason for the multiplication of legal disputes. Rather, the students are said to have "insufficiently attended on" their teachers (Heb. *lo shimshu kol tzarkhan*). The meaning of the phrase is best understood in light of the fact that Jewish law has never been treated as a purely academic discipline. In the times of the Mishnah and Talmud, Torah studies included a sort of apprenticeship. In addition to listening to his lectures, students spent time outside the academy in their teacher's presence, observing his behavior, learning customs, manners and deportment, and rendering personal services to him. In its primary meaning, attending on a teacher refers to these apprenticeship aspects of the process. As a secondary meaning, "attendance" came to encompass the entire educational process, academics as well as apprenticeship. *See* L. GINZBERG, *supra* note 14, at 247-48 n.13 (discussing two meanings of "attendance on the sages"); G. ALON, *supra* note 7, at 476-78; M. AUERBACH, HA-HINUKH HA-YEHUDI BI-TEKUFAT HA-MISHNAH VEHA-TALMUD 96-110 (1982) (in Hebrew) (describing attendance on the sages).

The students of Shammai and Hillel who attended insufficiently on their teachers were not deficient in *learning* or in their ability to retain the oral law. *See* TALMUD BAVLI, *Sukkah* 28a, at

C. *Controversy as a Historical Phenomenon*

Although the development of Jewish law is intertwined with the course of Jewish history, halakhic authorities seldom seek historical explanations for the origin and evolution of a rule of law. Their approach to the principles of Jewish law is conceptual, dogmatic, and analytical, rather than historical.[79] Yet in their attempts to explain the origins of controversy, some have focused on historical circumstances to an uncommon degree and display a willingness to cite them as the causes of controversy or as contributing factors.

There are two reasons for this unusual attention to history. First, the period of the proliferation of controversy, roughly the first century, coincides with three of the most important events in Jewish history: the destruction of the Jewish state, the abolition of the High Court in Jerusalem, and the destruction of the Second Temple. These historical events had enduring significance for the nation. They preoccupied halakhic authorities who made discovering their meaning a central con-

---

123 (I. Slotki trans. 1938) (Hillel had eighty students—thirty who were as worthy as Moses, thirty who were as worthy as Joshua, and only twenty who were ordinary). Rather, their shortcomings were in the realm of *conduct and deportment*. Their great teachers knew when it was appropriate to make a concession to end a legal controversy:

> And why do they record the opinions of Shammai and Hillel when these do not prevail? To teach the generations that come after that none should persist in his opinion, for lo, "the fathers of the world" [i.e. Shammai and Hillel] did not persist in their opinion.

MISHNAH, *Eduyoth* 1:4 (H. Danby trans. 1933). In addition, Hillel and Shammai were men who loved peace. *Id.*, *Aboth* 1:12, 1:15 (Hillel taught, "Be of the disciples of Aaron, loving peace and pursuing peace," and Shammai taught, "[R]eceive all men with a cheerful countenance"). By contrast, their students failed to absorb the peace-loving attitudes of their teachers and carried scholarly disputes to the point of bloodshed. TALMUD YERUSHALMI, *Sabbath* 1:7, at 3c. Their intransigence was a character fault they should have overcome in the course of attending on their teachers by emulating their conciliatory conduct.

The result of the students' failure was the creation of two distinct factions. (The version of the report in TALMUD YERUSHALMI, *Hagigah* 2:2, at 10b, states this expressly—the students of Shammai and Hillel divided into two factions [Heb. *kitot*].) Previously, the sages had coalesced into ad hoc blocs regarding each legal controversy as it arose, and the blocs dissipated once the controversy was resolved. After Hillel and Shammai, however, their students formed enduring parties that had an institutional life and took a position on every controversial point of law. A chasm of unresolved legal issues divided them. With neither side willing to yield and each side maneuvering to prevent unfavorable votes, the issues remained unresolved for several generations, until the assembly of sages met in Yavneh after the destruction of the Jewish state. TOSEPHTA, *Eduyoth* 1:1, *supra* note 17, at 454. Understood in this light, Rabbi Jose's report is not an explanation for the origins of halakhic *controversy*, as proponents of the weak-link theory argue, but rather an explanation for the appearance of *factions* in Jewish law. *See* J. BACHARACH, *supra* note 65, at 102a-b (interpreting the term "controversy" in the report to mean "factional strife"); for a further discussion of his view, see *infra* note 89.

79. *See* Rackman, *Halakhah: Orthodox Approaches*, in ENCYCLOPAEDIA JUDAICA YEARBOOK 134, 142 (1976) (suggesting historical approach as alternative to analytical approach typical of halakhic authorities); Jackson, *History, Dogmatics, and Halakhah*, in JEWISH L. ANN. 1 (Supp. II 1980) (suggesting historical approach to study of Jewish law).

cern. The quest naturally included attempts to relate these events to the contemporaneous emergence of controversy in Jewish law.

Second, the classical sources of Jewish law, such as the Talmud, depict controversy itself as a historical phenomenon. They do not suggest it always existed in its present form but instead portray its emergence and evolution over time. For example, the Jerusalem Talmud contains a capsule history of controversy in Jewish law.[80] In olden times, it relates, just one legal controversy existed in Israel, and it concerned a rule of ritual procedure—whether one performed the ceremony of laying on of hands on the festival sacrifice in the Temple. Judging from the parties to the controversy, who are identified in the Mishnah,[81] one can infer that the controversy was both early, starting around 140 B.C.E., and longstanding, remaining unresolved for at least five generations. Hillel and Shammai introduced the next phase in the history of controversy; they increased the number of halakhic disputes to four. In addition to continuing the conflict over the laying on of hands, they added three additional disputes.[82] The students of Hillel and Shammai initiated the third phase in the history of controversy with over three hundred legal disputes between their respective schools. This phase, characterized by the vast increase in the incidence of halakhic conflicts, continues at the present time. The Talmud anticipates a fourth and final phase when the Son of David will come to restore the legal harmony that existed in olden times. Because the Talmud thus recognizes controversy as a historical phenomenon, halakhic authorities feel free to seek explanations in the political and social environment in which the legal system operates.

Historical circumstances may be included in an explanation for controversy in one of two ways. First, they may serve as an adjunct to the theory that faults in the chain of transmission are responsible for differences of opinion.[83] Difficult times, persecution, and exile decrease the number of legal scholars, explain their inability to remain for extended periods at their studies, account for inattentiveness, and act as a catalyst for forgetfulness.[84] This approach not only *explains* why faults occurred

80. TALMUD YERUSHALMI, *Hagigah* 2:2, at 10b; *see also* MENAHEM BEN SOLOMON LE-BEIT MEIR ("Meiri," 1249-1306), BEIT HA-BEHIRAH, *Avot* 20-27 (B. Pereg ed., Hebrew year 5724) (surveying history of transmission of the oral law in an account that closely tracks the Jerusalem Talmud's account).

81. MISHNAH, *Hagigah 2:2* (H. Danby trans. 1933).

82. *See id., Eduyot* 1:1-3; TALMUD BAVLI, *Shabbath* 15a, 17a, at 60-63, 69-71 (H. Freedman trans. 1938).

83. *See supra* notes 59-78 and accompanying text.

84. *See* RABBI ISAIAH BEN MALI DI TRANI ("Tosafot Rid," c. 1180-1250), SEFER TOSAFOT RID, *Shabbath* 138b, at 9b (1861), *cited in* D. HALIVNI, MIDRASH, MISHNAH, AND GEMARA: THE JEWISH PREDILECTION FOR JUSTIFIED LAW 45-46 (1986) (when persecutions increased, students were unable to remain at their studies as required, and legal doubts and controversies proliferated); J. BACHARACH, *supra* note 65, at 103a (after Hillel and Shammai, exiles and troubles increased and

in the chain of transmission, but to a large extent *excuses* the legal scholars who allowed them to occur. The scholars' deficiencies become understandable in light of the conditions they had to endure. Their personal shortcomings were not responsible for the resulting problems.

Alternatively, historical factors may provide a complete explanation for the origins of controversy, without any reference to faults in the chain of transmission. In this view, there is nothing inherent in the study of the commandments or in the oral form of the tradition that predisposes the halakhic process to generate legal disputes. However, ever since the destruction of the Jewish state, and occasionally even earlier,[85] the Jewish legal system has been compelled by external forces to operate under abnormal conditions. These conditions, which include exile from the land and the loss of political independence, make controversy inevitable. The dispersion of the people and their legal sages to the many centers of the diaspora makes communication difficult and militates against consensus. In addition, each diaspora center has developed its own approach to the study of the Talmud, and each scholar charts his own path. With the style of analysis varying so radically from place to place, it is not surprising that contradictory conclusions of law develop.[86]

Historical circumstances are responsible for another aberration in the Jewish legal system which has left a legacy of halakhic controversy: the decision to commit the oral law to writing to protect it from being forgotten during harsh times. Originally, when a difference of opinion arose, either the sages worked toward a consensus or the High Court resolved the issue by a vote and that was the end of the conflict. The final decision was added to the body of the oral law and transmitted, but the arguments of the parties to the dispute were not preserved. When, however, the sages reduced the oral law to writing in the Talmud, they transcribed the arguments of all sides for posterity. In this sense, writing

so did controversy caused by forgetting); D. NIETO, *supra* note 50, at 63-65 (harsh conditions created by two unsuccessful revolts against the Romans during the first two centuries prevented students from spending a long time at their studies; they concentrated on mastering the fundamentals, never having the time to learn the details; subsequent attempts to derive the details through logic or reasoning led to controversies).

85. *See, e.g.*, Z. CHAJES (1805-1855), THE STUDENT'S GUIDE THROUGH THE TALMUD 114 (J. Shachter trans. 2d ed. 1960) (Hebrew title, MEVO HA-TALMUD) (exile of legal scholars around 140 B.C.E., pursuant to decrees of Syrian king Antiochus IV, prevented High Court from assembling to ascertain majority's view, resulting in continuance of controversy over the laying on of hands on the heads of sacrifices). Chajes acknowledges here a major problem confronting the historical explanation: the fact that some legal disputes, although few in number, existed earlier than the abolition of the Jewish state in the year 70. These include the four disputes between Hillel and Shammai, *see supra* note 82 and accompanying text, and several others. *See* Z. CHAJES, *supra*, at 115-16. His solution is to identify a distinct historical cause for the early disputes: the "exile of scholars" two centuries before the loss of political independence.

86. E. DEL MEDIGO, *supra* note 53, at 36 (text by Del Medigo and accompanying commentary by Reggio).

perpetuated the controversy indefinitely into the future. Further study and dissection of the recorded arguments by future generations of scholars led to even more controversies. This snowball effect is plainly evident in the commentaries and supercommentaries on the Talmud.[87]

The disintegrative effects of the exile are compounded by the absence of the central organs of Jewish sovereignty, particularly the High Court of Jerusalem. Without an acknowledged authority to decide legal questions with finality, not only are disputes more likely to arise, but they are more likely to remain unresolved over time. In this vein, Maimonides wrote in his code:

> So long as the Supreme Court was in existence, there were no controversies in Israel . . . .
>
> After the Supreme Court ceased to exist, disputes multiplied in Israel: one declaring "unclean," [sic] giving a reason for his ruling; another declaring it "clean," giving a reason for his ruling; one forbidding, the other permitting.[88]

However profound the impact of history on the development of Jewish legal institutions, the historical approach must be rejected as an unsatisfactory method of explaining the origins of controversy in Jewish law. Because the historical approach necessarily entails a consideration of beginnings and ends, its proponents cannot avoid arriving at an unduly harsh comparison between an idealized past and future, on the one hand, and the current state of affairs, on the other. Such a comparison undermines the value of dissent in Jewish law. If controversy commenced at a certain point in Jewish history, then it must have been

87. *Id.* at 35-36; *see also* M. MAIMONIDES, THE GUIDE FOR THE PERPLEXED, Part I, ch. 71, at 108 (M. Friedlander trans. 2d ed. 1956) (keeping the oral law unwritten "averted the evils which happened subsequently, viz., great diversity of opinions, doubts as to the meaning of written words, slips of the pen, dissensions among the people, formation of new sects, and confused notions about practical subjects."); 3 JOSEPH ALBO (c. 1380-1444), SEFER HA-IKKARIM, ch. 23, at 202-03 (I. Husik trans. 1946) (written word is inherently subject to divergent interpretations; writing of Mishnah and Talmud created doubts and controversies, requiring many commentaries to resolve them).

88. M. MAIMONIDES, MISHNEH TORAH, *Rebels* 1:4, *supra* note 9, at 139-40. According to the commentaries of Joseph Caro, David Ibn Abi Zimra, Abraham Di Boton, and Nahum Ash, which are printed in standard Hebrew editions of Mishneh Torah alongside Maimonides' text, Maimonides' source is the report of Rabbi Jose. That report attributes the increase in controversies to students of Shammai and Hillel. *See supra* notes 65-66, 78. Yet the substance of Maimonides' account differs from all four versions of Rabbi Jose's report. Maimonides does not mention these students but instead cites the abolition of the Supreme Court. He thus substituted a neutral historical explanation for one that blames controversy on weak links in the chain of transmission. *See* D. HOFFMAN, THE FIRST MISHNAH AND THE CONTROVERSIES OF THE TANNAIM 79-82 (P. Forchheimer trans. 1977) (suggesting that sentence regarding students of Shammai and Hillel is an interpolation in Rabbi Jose's report from another source, in which case Maimonides, by eliminating the sentence, restored both the original version of R. Jose's report and its internal consistency.) On Maimonides' reasons for rejecting an explanation premised on faults in the chain of transmission, see *supra* note 75.

preceded by a primeval epoch in which the legal system operated without differences of opinion.[89] Similarly, if the emergence of halakhic disputes was a consequence of the tumultuous events that led to the loss of political independence and the abolition of the High Court, then the promised restoration of the state and the Court, when realized, will be accompanied by a return to the original state of affairs, including the elimination of controversy as a phenomenon in Jewish law.[90]

But to posit a controversy-free past, and to hope for a future free of legal disputes, disparages the disputatious operation of the halakhic process in the interim. The historical approach depicts halakhic controversy and dissent as undesirable aftereffects of the national catastrophe, in the same lamentable class of events as the destruction of the Temple and the exile of the people from their land. In addition, the historical explanation provides a basis for disparaging the entire subsequent course of development of Jewish law in the period of the exile. The proliferation of

---

89. It is difficult to imagine any legal system without controversy, however simple the society and whatever the degree of consensus. *Cf.* BENJAMIN DE VRIES, MEHKARIM BE-SIFRUT HA-TALMUD 172-78 (1968) (interpreting Rabbi Jose's report and concluding that, while controversy may have been kept to a minimum in certain periods, it was never completely absent).

Not all proponents of the historical approach believe that the Jewish legal system once operated without controversy. *See, e.g.*, Z. CHAJES, *supra* note 85, at 114-16 (finding references in the Talmud to ancient legal disputes that predated the destruction of the state; interpreting the term "controversy," as used in Rabbi Jose's report, to mean a dispute that persisted unresolved from generation to generation, thus allowing for any number of early disputes that were quickly resolved but whose details have not been preserved); J. BACHARACH, *supra* note 65, at 102a-b (concluding that legal disputes were present almost from the beginning of Jewish history, at least as early as the period of mourning for Moses when some laws were forgotten). Bacharach reconciles his view with Rabbi Jose's report of "controversy" by interpreting the report to describe the origins of factions in Jewish law. Thus, he concludes, while legal disputes were present almost from the beginning of Jewish history, factional strife—the existence of organized parties arrayed against each other and preventing final rulings on disputed points of law—was a late development.

The version of Rabbi Jose's report in the Babylonian Talmud acknowledges the existence of *some* conflicts of opinion in early times: "Originally there were *not many* disputes in Israel . . . ." TALMUD BAVLI, *Sanhedrin* 88b, at 585 (J. Shachter & H. Freedman trans. 1935) (emphasis added). But the three other versions of his report posit unanimity prior to the students of Shammai and Hillel: "In olden times, there were *no* controversies in Israel . . . ." TOSEPHTA, *Hagigah* 2:9, *Sanhedrin* 7:1, *supra* note 17, at 235, 425; TALMUD YERUSHALMI, *Sanhedrin* 1:4, at 8b (emphasis added). For a possible explanation of this discrepancy, see Weiss, *L'She'elat Tiv Ha-Bet Din shel Shivim Ve-Ehad*, in LOUIS GINZBERG JUBILEE VOLUME 189 (1946) (Hebrew volume) (suggesting that version in Babylonian Talmud reading "not many disputes" is an emendation of an earlier version which read "no disputes" to allow for the ancient dispute over the laying on of hands on the heads of sacrifices). The fact that Maimonides, in his code, adopted the Jerusalem Talmud's version of no previous controversy may indicate that he had reservations regarding the wording in the Babylonian Talmud. *See supra* text accompanying note 88; *see also* NAHUM ASH, TSIYUNEI MAHARAN, *Mishneh Torah: Mamrim* 1:4.

90. MISHNAH, *Eduyoth* 8:7 (H. Danby trans. 1933) (statement of Rabbi Simeon that Elijah the Prophet will come "to bring agreement where there is matter for dispute"); TALMUD YERUSHALMI, *Hagigah* 2:2, at 10b (situation prior to proliferation of controversies will be restored "when the Son of David comes"). *But see* MISHNAH, *Aboth* 5:17 ("Any controversy that is for God's sake shall in the end be of lasting worth . . . . Which controversy was for God's sake? Such was the controversy of Hillel and Shammai.").

halakhic disputes in the centuries after the destruction, in this view, is not evidence of a flourishing legal culture. Rather, it indicates that the deterioration of the legal system that followed the loss of statehood was never stanched in the diaspora but continued at a rapid pace. Treating controversy as a historical phenomenon clearly fails to supply the justification for halakhic controversy and dissent that an adequate explanation should provide for law that sustains Jewish people.

Whether the exile in fact caused a "deterioration" in the study of Jewish law or the development of its institutions cannot be answered definitively. Since there is no way to know how the institutions of Jewish law would have evolved in an independent state, it is impossible to compare empirically the actual development of Jewish law in the diaspora with the course it would have taken if the loss of political independence had not occurred. Any purported comparison is no more than a subjective evaluation of what did develop against an ideal and speculative standard. It is certain that *specific* periods of *intense* persecution in the exile, whether the Crusades, the expulsion from Spain in 1492, or the Holocaust, severely inhibited the study of Jewish law in certain places for limited periods. But apart from instances of this type, the long expanse of history since the loss of statehood in the year 70 yields little evidence of the forgetting, lack of concentration, and inattendance upon teachers that the historical approach posits as inevitable consequences of exile, harsh conditions and troubled times. Instead, most evidence suggests a remarkable devotion to the study of Jewish law which sustains the people. A wide variety of diaspora centers, from Babylonia to Europe, from North Africa to North America, support intensive legal activity and produce a prodigious literary output that includes the Talmud, codes, responsa and their commentaries. Z. H. Chajes, in the first half of the nineteenth century, could write, with justice, that "although we have been subject to constant persecutions and wanderings for almost 1,800 years, we have, thank God, only increased our knowledge of His Torah, so that it adorns us like a crown."[91] The premise underlying the historical approach, that the study of Jewish law has deteriorated as a result of harsh historical events that befell the nation, is an unnecessary price to pay for an explanation of the origins of controversy.

D. *Controversy as Inevitable but Regrettable*

The two preceding explanations share a common feature. Each believes Jewish law without dissent is possible and preferable to the current state of affairs. If faults in the chain of transmission are responsible for controversy, then to the extent the chain of transmission can be

91. Z. CHAJES, *supra* note 85, at 46.

improved, differences of opinion will decrease. If weak links could be eliminated entirely, then controversy and dissent would disappear. Similarly, if historical or political factors are responsible, then reinstitution of central halakhic authority would end the dissension that has characterized the halakhic process since the abolition of the High Court. Explanations of this type delegitimize the operation of the halakhic process by repudiating the value of its major component, the halakhic controversy. A satisfactory explanation would recognize, first, that the halakhic process cannot operate without generating dissent, and second, that even if the elimination of dissent were possible, it would not be desirable.

Maimonides offers an explanation that fulfills the first requirement, but not the second.[92] In the introduction to his commentary on the Mishnah, he classifies the contents of the oral law into five categories[93] which, for our purposes, represent two groups. The first consists of the laws revealed orally to Moses at Sinai, whether or not hinted at in the text of the written Torah.[94] These laws comprise the whole of the initial, original contents of the oral law. The second group consists of laws that originated, subsequent to the initial revelation, in the efforts of halakhic authorities.[95] The authorities either derive these laws through the interpretation of Biblical verses or create them by legislative enactment.

According to Maimonides, halakhic controversy can exist in the second group of laws only, but not in the first, because Sinaitic revelation and controversy are mutually exclusive concepts.[96] The laws Moses received orally at Sinai have been transmitted unchanged and complete over the course of time. They were not forgotten and never generated

92. M. Maimonides, Mishnah Im Perush Rabennu Moshe ben Maimon 8-12 (J. Kafah ed. 1963) (in Hebrew).

93. Maimonides' five categories are the following:

(1.) Laws revealed orally to Moses at Sinai that are alluded to or hinted at in the written Torah;

(2.) Laws revealed orally to Moses at Sinai that are not evidenced by any hint in the written Torah (Heb. *halakhot l'Moshe mi'Sinai*);

(3.) Laws the sages derived from the written Torah by applying the recognized principles of interpretation (Heb. *midot*); *see infra* note 99;

(4.) Decrees enacted by the sages as preventive measures (Heb. *gezerot*); and

(5.) Ordinances the sages adopted to improve the social or religious order of mankind (Heb. *takkanot*). *Id. See also* J. B. Soloveitchik, *Two Types of Tradition*, in Shiurim Le-Zekhar Avi Mori Zal 220, 224-31 (Hebrew year 5743) (in hebrew) (discussing the categories and their bearing on controversy in Jewish law).

94. Maimonides' first and second categories; *see supra* note 93.

95. Maimonides' third, fourth and fifth categories; see *supra* note 93.

96. *See also* E. Del Medigo, *supra* note 53, at 30 (text by Del Medigo and Reggio's accompanying commentary). *But cf.* J. B. Soloveitchik, *supra* note 93, at 231-34 (certain rabbinic enactments in the second group also are *not* subject to controversy, namely, those rabbinic enactments that resemble in form "laws received orally by Moses at Sinai," in that they were transmitted from one generation of legal sages to next without a statement of their underlying reasons, *id.* at 233).

any disputes. In fact, if a rule elicits a difference of opinion among the sages, that proves that it was not part of the original contents of the oral law. In this manner, Maimonides totally vitiates the arguments against the authenticity of the oral law that are based on the prevalence of halakhic disputes.[97] The presence of disputes cannot disprove that the oral law stretches back in an unbroken chain to Sinai because halakhic disputes do not involve laws that were revealed at Sinai in the first place.[98]

The second group of laws originates in the activities of legal sages of later generations. These scholars apply and adapt the laws originally revealed at Sinai to the contemporary conditions that confront them. To accomplish this, they engage in two activities—interpretation of the Torah and legislation.[99]

In the course of these activities, differences of opinion occur. How disputes regarding the interpretation of biblical verses arise is perplexing at first blush because each halakhic authority begins with the same verses and the same rules of interpretation, yet some reach different conclusions. According to Maimonides, disputes are caused by differences in the sages' knowledge and understanding of the rules of interpretation and in their ability to apply them. If all of the sages possessed equal knowledge and ability, few, if any, disputes would arise regarding the correct interpretation of verses.[100]

Disputes about proposed legislation are much easier to explain. These are policy differences over the desirability of suggested courses of action.[101] Unanimity in the legislative sphere is exceedingly rare.

It is virtually impossible for the halakhic process, as Maimonides depicts it, to operate without controversy and dissent. Controversy would be absent only if two unlikely conditions were met. First, all of the participants would have to possess equal reasoning ability and knowledge of general principles. Second, all of the participants would have to be of one mind in their evaluation of policy alternatives. Yet despite

97. For an example of such an argument against the authenticity of the oral law, see, *supra* note 48 and accompanying text.

98. In view of the great number of halakhic controversies, the price Maimonides pays for his mutually exclusive groups is a great reduction in the number of laws originally revealed at Sinai. *See* Blidstein, *Maimonides on "Oral Law"*, in 1 JEWISH L. ANN. 108, 109-12 (1978). Bacharach soundly took him to task for this. J. BACHARACH, *supra* note 65, at 103a (criticizing Maimonides because if laws revealed at Sinai are not subject to disputes, then "the majority, nay, virtually all, of the Oral Torah did not originate at Sinai!").

99. For a discussion of interpretation as a source of Jewish law and a description of the principles of interpretation that are utilized to derive laws from the text of the Bible, see THE PRINCIPLES OF JEWISH LAW, *supra* note 16, at 58-70. For a survey of the role of legislation by halakhic authorities in the development of Jewish law, see *id.* at 74-91.

100. M. MAIMONIDES, *supra* note 92, at 11-12.

101. *Id.* at 12.

Maimonides' acknowledgement of these facts, one detects something of a wistful quality in his analysis. He expresses no predilection for the vigorous give and take that characterizes halakhic debate. On the contrary, his models are Hillel and Shammai who agreed on almost everything.[102] What accounts for their harmony, in his view, is the fact that they were very similar in their intellectual abilities and knowledge of general principles. Hence, they tended to derive the same conclusions from the same premises by applying the same rules of interpretation. Their students' intellectual attainments did not match those of their great teachers. However, the students are not to be blamed for this; not everyone is capable of ranking among the foremost intellectual lights of his era.[103]

Given that halakhic authorities will naturally differ in knowledge, reasoning ability, and policy preferences, Maimonides concedes that controversy is a virtually inevitable consequence of the operation of the halakhic process.[104] But he falls far short of endorsing controversy and dissent as desirable features of the process, let alone articulating any rationale that justifies creating conditions that tend to promote them.

III
The Justification for Controversy In Jewish Law: Controversy as Inherent and Desirable

A satisfactory explanation for the origins of controversy in Jewish law would reconcile legal disputes and the oral law tradition without belittling halakhic authorities or undermining the reliability of the oral law. This explanation would disclose why controversy is a natural and inherent feature of the halakhic process, and why the authorities should encourage their colleagues to express their dissenting opinions. Viewed from within the confines of the Jewish legal system, explanations that bolster confidence in the authenticity of the oral law and buttress the esteem of its interpreters and transmitters, the argumentative legal sages, are preferable to approaches that minimize the importance of halakhic controversy or blame transmission errors and tragic historical circumstances.

Three satisfactory explanations for controversy are presented in this Part. Each takes, as its point of departure, a report in the Talmud that

102. *See supra* note 82 and accompanying text.

103. M. Maimonides, *supra* note 92, at 12 (explaining Rabbi Jose's report: Hillel's and Shammai's students who caused controversy to proliferate were not deficient in their attainments in any absolute sense, and certainly not because they forgot their lessons or erred in repeating the tradition, but only in comparison to their illustrious teachers); *see also* D. Hartman, Maimonides: Torah and Philosophical Quest 112-13 (1976).

104. *See* I. Twersky, Introduction to the Code of Maimonides, *supra* note 22, at 99 & n.5.

describes a controversy between the schools of Hillel and Shammai.[105] The dispute lasted for three years as the parties wrestled inconclusively with an unresolved legal point, each side steadfastly maintaining the correctness of its position. Finally, a Heavenly Voice was heard declaring, "[The utterances of] both are the words of the living God, but the *halachah* is in agreement with the rulings of Beth Hillel."[106]

The report addresses two aspects of the halakhic process. The first is the possibility of direct divine intervention in the determination of law. This feature of the report must be evaluated against other sources which deny that miracles, voices, or signs have any role in the halakhic process.[107] The weight of authority discounts the possibility of divine intervention in legal debate.[108] At Sinai, God entrusted the further development and application of Jewish law to the legal sages of each generation. They must rely on their human faculties to determine the law and must not allow miracles or prophetic signs to influence their deliberations.

Second, the Heavenly Voice in the report characterizes the positions of both schools as equally constituting "the words of the living God." As seen from within the confines of the Jewish legal system, this part of the story deserves a broad construction because of the way it casts halakhic debate in a favorable light. From this perspective, the report should not be read narrowly to limit the characterization to the facts of the case, so that it applies only to the schools of Hillel and Shammai or to the controversy in question. The fact that the report does not disclose the legal issue which elicited the Heavenly Voice indicates that the subject of the report is the halakhic process itself and not the specific dispute that engaged the two schools. To bolster the respect due to halakhic authorities, the characterization should be read broadly to encompass all author-

105. TALMUD BAVLI, *Erubin* 13b, at 85-86 (I. Slotki trans. 1938). The schools are known as Beth Hillel and Beth Shammai.

106. *Id.* For an epilogue to the report, see *infra* note 118.

107. *See, e.g.*, TALMUD BAVLI, *Erubin* 7a, at 35 (Rabbi Joshua does not recognize the authority of a divine voice in deciding legal disputes); M. MAIMONIDES, COMMENTARY ON THE MISHNAH 57-62 (F. Rosner trans. 1975) (prophet may participate in deciding halakhah like other sages, through argumentation, deduction, and reasoning, but not by performing signs). *See also* TALMUD BAVLI, *Baba Mezi'a* 59b, at 352-54 (S. Daiches & H. Freedman trans. 1935) (miracles performed on behalf of dissenter Rabbi Eliezer, and presumably indicating the "correctness" of his position, failed to sway majority of sages); Englard, *Majority Decision Vs. Individual Truth: The Interpretations of the "Oven of Achnai" Aggadah*, 15 TRADITION 137 (1975) (surveying rabbinic explanations of why the miracles performed for R. Eliezer did not influence the outcome of the debate).

108. *See* Elon, *The Sources and Nature of Jewish Law and its Application in the State of Israel*, 2 ISRAEL L. REV. 515, 555 (1967) (view that attributes to suprahuman authority certain influence in determination of halakhah "must be regarded as the opinion of individual scholars and it is clear that the dominant view was that of R. Yehoshuah [Joshua] who said that we do not pay regard to a Heavenly Voice"); E. BERKOVITS, NOT IN HEAVEN: THE NATURE AND FUNCTION OF HALAKHA 47-53, 73, 78-79 (1983) ("One pays no attention to the voice from heaven in matters of Torah-realization on earth." *Id.*, at 73.)

ities and all of the legal positions they advocate in their many disputes down through the ages.

Both the broad and the narrow interpretation of the report are achieved only with some difficulty, although the narrow constructionist needs to offer an explanation for only the single case. The broad constructionist must explain generally how two or more contradictory legal positions can all equally constitute "the words of the living God." Some commentators doubted whether the endeavor was possible or worthwhile.[109] Other authorities, however, met the challenge and provided answers that are much more than skillful exercises in logic and interpretation.[110] Each answer provides a satisfactory explanation for controversy in Jewish law and a complete justification for halakhic dissent. The following sections of this Part outline three of the answers.

A. *The Choice Among Options*

In one view,[111] the initial revelation of the oral law to Moses did not consist of the communication of precisely formulated legal rules. Instead, the law was communicated as a series of options, allowing a range of permissible outcomes for every case that requires a decision. The halakhic process consists of selecting the most appropriate option. The final decision in any case is not preordained but left to the sages of each generation to decide as questions arise.[112] They must determine the law for their times, using their best judgment to select the most suitable

109. *E.g.* Reggio, *supra* note 53, at 37, 93 (attributing two contradictory positions to a Divine source results in one law canceling out the other, so that logically nothing remains); J. Bacharach, *supra* note 65, at 102a-103a (finding it unlikely God would reveal His will as a range of alternatives, a pro and a con for every future legal issue with decisionmaking delegated to the legal sages of each era; rather, as God knew there would be uncertainty in the future, it is more likely that He revealed clear-cut laws to cover every possible contingency but that some laws were forgotten, leading to disputes among the sages).

110. *E.g.* Rabbi Yom Tov ben Abraham Ishbili ("Ritva," c. 1250-1330), Hidushei Ha-Ritva: Eruvin 13b, at 107-08 (M. Goldstein ed., Hebrew year 5740) (broad construction); Rabbi Meir ben Ezekiel Ibn Gabbai (c. 1480-1540), Avodat Ha-Kodesh 169-71 (1901) (translated in part in G. Scholem, The Messianic Idea in Judaism 298-300 1971) (broad construction); Rabbi Judah ben Bezalel Loew ("Maharal of Prague," c. 1520-1609), Be'er Ha-Golah 19-21 (1964) (narrow construction).

111. Y.T. ben Abraham Ishbili, *supra* note 110, at 107-08.

112. A midrashic interpretation of a verse in the book of Psalms similarly depicts law as consisting of options, with final decisions delegated to the majority of legal sages:

> *The words of the Lord are . . . silver tried in the open before all men refined seven times seven.* [Psalms 12:7] R. Yannai said: The words of the Torah were not given as clear-cut decisions. For with every word which the Holy One, blessed be He, spoke to Moses, He offered him forty-nine arguments by which a thing may be proved clean, and forty-nine other arguments by which it may be proved unclean. When Moses asked: Master of the universe, in what way shall we know the sense of a law? God replied: The majority is to be followed: when a majority says it is unclean, it is unclean; when a majority says it is clean, it is clean.

1 The Midrash on Psalms, *Psalm* 12, § 4, at 173 (W. Braude trans. 1959) (footnotes omitted; emphasis in original).

legal option for their generation. In passing judgment, they are not creating new laws but are selecting among options included in the initial revelation.

Controversy and dissent are thus inherent parts of the halakhic process because God did not communicate, nor even contemplate, single, "correct" rules as part of the initial revelation. Disputes naturally occur because the sages differ over which option to adopt as the most suitable in any given case. Their robust debates, including the vigorous advocacy of dissenting points of view, serve the critical function of ensuring that they sift through all of the possible alternatives carefully, rather than in a perfunctory manner, so that the best one is finally selected. Nevertheless, all of the positions advocated in the course of the debate equally constitute "the words of the living God," since all were included as options in the initial revelation.

B. The Continuing Revelation

In a second view,[113] all Jewish souls were present at Sinai, and each witnessed the revelation. While Moses, on the mountain top, heard God reveal the details of the law, the Israelites, assembled at the base of the mountain, heard God's will in a more general way. Each individual experienced the revelation from a unique position; hence, each received but a portion of the total.

The voice that thundered at Sinai did not cease after a single day but continues to speak across the ages. Revelation is a spring that flows continuously. Revelation is necessary because the human mind, relying solely on its own capacity to reason, cannot fathom the will of the infinite God. The teachers of Israel, its prophets and sages, partake in this ongoing revelation. The sages are the direct successors of the Biblical prophets, for their enactments, like the prophets' visions, originate in revelation and are not the products of logic or intellect.

Just like the initial Sinaitic revelation, the continuing revelation through the generations is received in a fragmented way. Each prophet or sage, depending on his or her unique perspective, receives an individual portion. This fragmented perception accounts for differences of opinion among halakhic authorities; each has a different perspective regarding the continuing revelation. All of their positions, however, reside within the great and continuing voice of revelation, because one God gave them all.[114] This common source is proven by the fact that all

113. M. BEN EZEKIEL IBN GABBAI, *supra* note 110, at 169-71; *see also* R. SOLOMON LURIA, *supra* note 28, *Bava Kama*, Introduction.

114. An interpretation of a verse from *Ecclesiastes* affirms one divine source as the origin of all the conflicting positions advocated in halakhic disputes, and advises scholars to become conversant with all viewpoints:

the parties to a controversy, no matter how seemingly contradictory their positions, are able to find and to cite support in the same place: the Torah. All future teachings of the prophets and sages are implicit in the Torah given to Moses. The purpose of the halakhic process and the function of the prophets and sages are to transform what is potential in the Torah into something actual, to render explicit for their time and place what was implicit in the Torah at Sinai.

Expression of the variety of viewpoints therefore is necessary to disclose revelation in its fullness, since no one individual perceives it all. A sense of the complete revelation, in all its aspects, appears only in the give and take of halakhic debate. Unceasing revelation courses in the ebb and flow of the halakhic controversy—the arguments and counterarguments, proofs and refutations. The totality of such viewpoints comprises the complete revelation, which would be incomplete if any one were missing. For this reason, the editors of the Talmud not only recorded legal conclusions but also transcribed the debates. The Talmud is a record of the ongoing process of revelation and not just a code of law.

The various points of view appear contradictory because people lack the ability, with their finite reasoning, to integrate all the viewpoints into a unitary whole. Similarly, an individual cannot possibly perform at the same time two commandments that contradict each other. In order to know how to act in cases of halakhic dispute, therefore, people have a practical need for a final decision, one that authoritatively adopts one point of view and rejects the others. From the point of view of the Divine Lawgiver, however, all of the positions are part of a unitary whole without contradiction. All sides in halakhic controversy are "the words of the living God."

C. *The Complex Reality*

In a third view,[115] controversy in Jewish law mirrors two aspects of a complex reality—the physical reality of concrete objects and the psy-

---

> "*The masters of assemblies*" [*Ecclesiastes* 12:11]: these are the disciples of the wise, who sit in manifold assemblies and occupy themselves with the Torah, some pronouncing unclean and others pronouncing clean, some prohibiting and others permitting, some disqualifying and others declaring fit.
>
> Should a man say: How in these circumstances shall I learn Torah? Therefore the text says: "*All of them are given from one Shepherd*" [*Ecclesiastes* 12:11]. One God gave them; one leader [Moses] uttered them from the mouth of the Lord of all creation, blessed be He; for it is written: "*And God spoke all these words*" [*Exodus* 20:1]. Also do thou make thine ear like the hopper [funnel] and get thee a perceptive heart to understand the words of those who pronounce unclean and the words of those who pronounce clean, the words of those who prohibit and the words of those who permit, the words of those who disqualify and the words of those who declare fit.

TALMUD BAVLI, *Hagigah* 3b, at 10 (I. Abrahams trans. 1938) (emphasis in original; footnotes omitted).

115. J. BEN BEZALEL LOEW, *supra* note 110, at 19-21.

chological reality of the human intellect. Concrete objects in the real world are not simple and one dimensional, composed of a single element. Rather, they are multifaceted hybrids composed of a combination of often contradictory elements. Consequently, no matter is completely fit or unfit, pure or impure, permitted or prohibited; each object contains some measure of each quality and its opposite.

At the same time, every individual possesses a unique capacity to perceive this complicated real world. Some individuals will naturally perceive and focus on one aspect of reality, while others will perceive and focus on other, perhaps contradictory, aspects of the same reality.

The inherent complexity of matter combines with the varieties of human perception to shape the operation of the halakhic process. Jewish law reflects this complex, hybrid reality, both in the substance of its laws and in the operation of the halakhic process. The laws themselves are multifaceted. A law that proclaims a matter fit for use contains a basis for declaring the matter unfit; a law that prohibits an action contains a basis for permitting it.

The sages applying the laws will naturally differ in their opinions because they differ in their perceptions of the matter under consideration. One will perceive that aspect of an object that warrants prohibiting its use under Jewish law while another will perceive that aspect that tends to render its use permissible.[116] Each will give reasons and support his views from the sources of Jewish law, resulting in halakhic controversy.

However, although the object under consideration is a hybrid, the elements which comprise its nature are not usually present in exactly equal measure. One feature will predominate. One aspect will be more fundamental to its nature than the others. The outcome of the halakhic controversy—the final ruling of clean or unclean, permitted or prohibited, fit or unfit—is based on this most fundamental aspect.[117]

The accuracy of the final decision is guaranteed by the collective nature of the halakhic process. The sages deliberate in assemblies in which all viewpoints are represented, freely expressed, and seriously con-

116. According to Rabbi Moses ben Noah Isaac Lipschutz (16th century), some halakhic authorities are by their nature strict, harsh, and severe, while others are merciful, easy-going, and lax. In approaching halakhic questions, the former are predisposed to find a reason to prohibit or condemn, while the latter tend to find reasons to permit and acquit. For Rabbi Lipschutz, then, halakhic controversy is a question not just of differing perceptions of the real world, but of fundamental psychological predispositions that shape and define individual personalities. *See* CHAIM HILLEL BEN-SASSON, HAGUT VE-HANHAGAH 29 (1959) (quoting RABBI MOSES BEN NOAH ISAAC LIPSCHUTZ, LEHEM MISHNAH 33b (Lublin, Hebrew year 5402)) (in Hebrew).

117. It is also possible that the elements are present in precisely equal measure, with none predominating. Such was the case debated by the schools of Hillel and Shammai that elicited the Heavenly voice. It is only in cases of this type that one may say that *both* positions represent "the words of the living God." J. BEN BEZALEL LOEW, *supra* note 110, at 20-21.

sidered.[118] Each participant states his perception of the matter, disclosing, over the course of the debate, the full nature of the object in all its aspects. Through this collaboration, the sages come to recognize the most fundamental aspect of the matter under consideration, and they make the final halakhic determination accordingly.

Operating in this physical, intellectual, and legal environment, it is inconceivable that all of the sages should be of one mind. Hence, their differences of opinion are an inherent part of the process, and freely expressing them is essential to arriving at the correct halakhic outcome.

D. *Hallmarks of a Satisfactory Explanation for Halakhic Controversy*

There is no need to choose among the three preceding views of the halakhic process. A phenomenon characterized by so much diversity ought to be susceptible to a variety of equally valid depictions. But the three views do share a number of features that are essential to any satisfactory explanation for controversy in Jewish law. First, each reconciles the existence of legal disputes with the oral law tradition. Such disputes do not negate the unbroken chain of transmission if: (a) the oral law was initially communicated as a series of options; or (b) the oral law is conveyed along a continuing stream of revelation that began at Sinai and each sage perceives and expresses but a part of the whole; or (c) if the oral laws are multifaceted hybrids, containing within themselves both a basis for permitting and for prohibiting the disputed conduct.

Second, for the very same reasons, it is inconceivable that controversy will disappear as a result of improvements in the chain of transmission or in the historical conditions that confront the nation. Controversy is inherent in the nature of Jewish law; neither the personal deficiencies of the sages nor the external circumstances of the nation cause it to occur.

Third, each of the explanations contributes to the esteem of the legal sages and to an appreciation of the importance of their work. The expla-

118. If the sages restrict membership in their councils to colleagues they agree with, or if they divide into factions and create separate schools where contrary viewpoints are not represented, the halakhic process cannot operate properly. The report of the Heavenly Voice, *supra* notes 105-6 and accompanying text, is followed by an epilogue that explains why Hillel's school deserved to have its ruling endorsed as authoritative:

> Since, however, "both are the words of the living God" what was it that entitled Beth Hillel to have the *halachah* fixed in agreement with their rulings?—Because they were kindly and modest, *they studied their own rulings and those of Beth Shammai*, and were even so [humble] as to mention the actions of Beth Shammai before theirs . . . .

TALMUD BAVLI, *Erubin* 13b, at 86 (I. Slotki trans. 1938) (emphasis added; footnotes omitted). The law was fixed according to Beth Hillel's rulings, not as a reward for their kindness, modesty, and humility, but because better law emanated from Hillel's school, where the disciples were trained to consider carefully both their own rulings and the dissenting opinions of the rival school before reaching a conclusion. The program of instruction at Hillel's school thus counteracted, to some extent, the negative consequences of the rift in Jewish law.

nations portray the sages as engaging in a task of the greatest significance, no matter whether it is described as: (a) clarifying and selecting among options; (b) expressing the revelation in its fullness; or (c) dealing with a reality that is so complex that it requires their collective efforts. The fact that their labors generate multiple points of view is not a demonstration of mere cleverness on their part but an indication of the effectiveness of their performance—a job well done.

Most importantly, each of these views of the halakhic process provides a rationale for arguing not just that the expression of dissenting viewpoints should be expected or tolerated, but also that it should be actively encouraged. Such encouragement is desirable because free expression of alternative legal positions is necessary to: (a) ensure selection of the best course of action; (b) provide a well-rounded picture of the continuing revelation with all of its nuances; or (c) guarantee an accurate halakhic outcome in the context of the complex reality that each sage confronts with his finite perception. Suppression of dissent is undesirable because it would impede the halakhic process from accomplishing these results.[119]

These explanations leave us with no reason to doubt the reliability of the oral law, no cause to disparage the sages or their performance, and no expectation that a change in the historical fortunes of the nation will or should cause any change in the operation of the halakhic process. Together, the explanations justify the actual operation of the halakhic process governed by the argumentative authorities who have been responsible for the study, development, and transmission of the oral law since its revelation at Sinai.

IV
The Functions of Dissent in Jewish Law

Once the origins of controversy have been satisfactorily explained, a functional justification for controversy and dissent may seem unnecessary. Viewed from within the confines of the Jewish legal system, controversy and dissent appear as natural components of the system, together with a constellation of other features that include the revelation at Sinai, the oral law tradition, and the authority of the legal sages of each generation. From this perspective, as features that define the halakhic process, they require no further justification.

Even so, the attempt to identify the functions that controversy and dissent perform in the Jewish legal system is a worthwhile undertaking. If one can demonstrate that controversy and dissent foster the study, development, and application of Jewish law, then controversy and dis-

119. For discussion of suppression of dissent under Jewish law, see generally Roth, *supra* note 1.

sent receive additional justification in terms of the valuable benefits they provide the Jewish legal system. Further, a recognition of their positive role may serve as a benchmark for policy. Halakhic authorities should encourage their colleagues to express their dissenting opinions if controversy and dissent contribute positively to the development of Jewish law.

The following sections of this Part set forth the functional justifications for controversy and dissent in Jewish law.

A. Issue-Sharpening

Dissent directs attention to weaknesses in the majority position, forcing a careful scrutiny of its premises. The results are a more fully articulated justification for the majority position and a better understanding of the law. Justice William J. Brennan, Jr. highlighted this function of dissent when he wrote:

> [T]he dissent demonstrates flaws the author perceives in the majority's legal analysis . . . . keeping the majority accountable for the rationale and consequences of its decision . . . . [V]igorous debate improves the final product by forcing the prevailing side to deal with the hardest questions urged by the losing side.[120]

A story in the Talmud makes the same point. Rabbi Johanan, a third century scholar of Jewish law, was mourning the death of his colleague and study partner, Rabbi Simeon ben Lakish. The other sages devised a way to console him by sending him a capable replacement, Rabbi Eliezer ben Pedath. Thereafter, for every legal point that R. Johanan made, R. Eliezer cited additional authority that supported his position. But R. Johanan was not consoled; on the contrary, he felt his grief even more. He complained:

> Are you as the son of Lakisha? . . . [W]hen I stated a law, the son of Lakisha used to raise twenty-four objections, to which I gave twenty-four answers, *which consequently led to a fuller comprehension of the law*; whilst you say, "A Baraitha [oral teaching] has been taught which supports you:" do I not know myself that my [legal] dicta are right?[121]

Rabbi Johanan welcomed objections and shunned facile support for his

---

120. Brennan, *In Defense of Dissents*, 37 HASTINGS L.J. 427, 430 (1986).

121. TALMUD BAVLI, *Baba Metzia* 84a, at 482 (S. Daiches and H. Freedman trans. 1935).

The same recognition that a consideration of dissenting opinions is essential for a complete understanding of Jewish law is expressed in the introduction to the ENCYCLOPEDIA TALMUDICA, a multivolume work designed to distill and present the corpus of Talmudic jurisprudence, where the editors give the following justification for their decision to include dissenting opinions together with authoritative rules in the projected articles:

> In order to gain a comprehensive knowledge of the Torah, it is insufficient for one to know the Halakhah as it is actually applied in Jewry; he must also gain an insight into the various opinions expressed over the generations in relation to the Law or subject matter in question, even though in actual practice such opinions have been rejected. For purposes of study, reflection, and comprehension, both are of equal weight. Although the ruling may not have been accepted, the reasoning may remain valid.

conclusions because he shared, with Justice Brennan, the recognition that animated dissent, by sharpening the debate, contributes to the clarity of the law.

B. Meeting the Needs of Hard Cases

Every legal system must confront the hard case—the set of facts to which application of a law will work an unusual hardship or impose an extraordinary loss, and for which an exception appears warranted to prevent an unjust or inequitable result. When encountering cases of this type, authorities of Jewish law have no central authority to which they can turn to obtain dispensations from the law. But halakhic authorities may themselves find the solution to the problem in a prior dissent. To cope with an emergency or to prevent an extraordinary loss, halakhic authorities are authorized to adopt the dissent as the rule of the case and to render a decision according to the dissent in order to mitigate the severity of the outcome.[122]

The responsa of Rabbi Moses Isserles of Cracow provide an example.[123] Isserles was scheduled to perform the marriage ceremony of an orphan girl on Friday afternoon, before the commencement of the Sabbath at sundown. Jewish law prohibits performing marriages on the Sabbath.[124] In this case, the guests had assembled, the festive meal was prepared, and the bride had taken her ritual bath in preparation for the ceremony. But a snag in negotiations over the bride's dowry caused a delay and the groom reneged. He did not consent until after sunset to go through with the match. Isserles had to decide whether to send the guests home and postpone the wedding until Saturday night or to conduct the marriage then and there, on the Sabbath. The prospect of sending the guests home threatened to embarrass the bride and permanently blemish her reputation. Isserles decided to act according to the minority position of a twelfth century authority, Rabbenu Jacob Tam, who held

---

1 ENCYCLOPEDIA TALMUDICA xviii (M. Berlin & S. Zevin eds. 1959) (I. Epstein & H. Freedman trans. 1969).

122. MISHNAH, *Eduyoth* 1:5 (H. Danby trans. 1933); TOSEPHTA, *Eduyot* 1:4, *supra* note 17, at 455; TALMUD BAVLI, *Erubin* 46a, at 320 (I. Slotki trans. 1938); TALMUD BAVLI, *Niddah* 6a, 9b, at 33-34, 61-62 (I. Slotki trans. 1948). Authorities prior to the close of the Talmud could rule according to a minority position in an emergency so long as there had been no express ruling that the majority position was the *halakhah*; authorities after the close of the Talmud can rule according to a minority position only where the conflict between the majority and the minority is a conflict among post-Talmudic authorities and not a dispute among authorities recorded in the Talmud itself. See 9 ENCYCLOPEDIA TALMUDIT, *Halakhah* 241, 260-61 (1959) (in Hebrew) (discussion of these and other limitations on the principle).

123. MOSES ISSERLES ("Rema," 1520-1572), RESPONSA, NUMBER 125, at 488-95 (A. Ziv ed. 1970). For a synopsis and partial translation of the responsum, see S. FREEHOF, A TREASURY OF RESPONSA 113-17 (1973).

124. J. CARO, SHULHAN ARUKH, *Orah Hayyim* 339:4.

that a wedding may be performed on the Sabbath in the case of a childless man. Isserles justified relying on a dissent in this case because it was an emergency; he had to avoid an affront to the dignity of an orphan girl who had been waiting all day to become a bride.[125]

C. Responding to the Challenge of Hard Times

While hard cases create problems for individuals, hard times confront the entire community, disrupting the normal operation of Jewish life and Jewish law. Halakhic authorities possess "emergency jurisdiction" (Heb. *hora'at sha'ah*) to deal with these situations.[126] Under extreme conditions characterized by a general breakdown in observance of law, habitual and widespread transgressions,[127] halakhic authorities are authorized to suspend regular laws, adopt temporary emergency measures, and impose extralegal sanctions.[128] The decision whether or

125. M. ISSERLES, *supra* note 123, at 491 ("It was an emergency, the girl was embarrassed, and [the dissenting view of] Rabbenu Tam is adequate to rely on in the case of an emergency. You have no greater emergency than this, [the threat of] an orphan girl, already of age, embarrassed and disgraced all her days."). *See also* Isserles, *Mappah*, *Orah Hayyim* 339:4 ("There are those who permit performing a marriage [on the Sabbath] where he has no wife and children [Rabbenu Tam] . . . and even though the law is not fixed so, still we rely on this in an emergency . . . ."). *See supra* note 22 for an explanation of Isserles' glosses to Caro's code.

126. The Talmudic source for emergency jurisdiction and remedies is the dictum of Rabbi Eliezer ben Jacob: "I have heard that the Beth din [the court] may, [when necessary,] impose flagellation and pronounce [capital] sentences even where not [warranted] by the Torah; yet not with the intention of disregarding the Torah but [on the contrary] in order to safeguard it." TALMUD BAVLI, *Sanhedrin* 46a, at 303 (J. Shachter & H. Freedman trans. 1935). Maimonides, himself a physician, offers the following justification for such power:

> Even as a physician will amputate the hand or the foot of a patient in order to save his life, so the court may advocate, when an emergency arises, the temporary disregard of some of the commandments, that the commandments as a whole may be preserved. This is in keeping with what the early Sages said: *Desecrate on his account one Sabbath that he be able to observe many Sabbaths.*

M. MAIMONIDES, MISHNEH TORAH, *Rebels* 2:4, *supra* note 9, at 141; (emphasis in original).

127. Maimonides and Caro posited widespread lawlessness as a precondition to the imposition of extralegal sanctions. M. MAIMONIDES, MISHNEH TORAH, *supra* note 9 *Sanhedrin* 24:4, at 73, *Rebels* 2:4, at 141; J. CARO, Shulhan Aruhk, *Hoshen Hamishpat* 2:1. But see 1 E. QUINT & N. HECHT, JEWISH JURISPRUDENCE: ITS SOURCES AND MODERN APPLICATIONS 172-78 (1980) (summarizing view of some halakhic authorities that extralegal sanctions can be imposed on an individual, even apart from any such general state of emergency, when the individual is a habitual offender or when his unpunished conduct might encourage others to violate the law).

128. The identity of the halakhic authorities authorized to exercise emergency jurisdiction is subject to dispute. *Compare* M. MAIMONIDES, MISHNEH TORAH, *Sanhedrin* 24:4-10, *supra* note 9, at 73-75 *and* J. CARO, Shulhan Arukh, *Hoshen Hamishpat* 2:1 (all Jewish courts possess emergency jurisdiction) *with* ISSAC ABRAVANEL (1437-1509), PERUSH AL HA-TORAH, *Deuteronomy* 17:8, at 159, 166 (Hebrew year 5724) *and* Denburg, *supra* note 22, at 21, n.6 (citing J. HABIB, NIMMUKEI YOSEF, *Sanhedrin* ch. 7, at 52b) (emergency jurisdiction is vested exclusively in Jerusalem High Court; local courts may not impose extralegal sanctions). In addition, according to Maimonides, the king has an executive prerogative to deal summarily with offenders when the needs of the hour demand it. M. MAIMONIDES, MISHNEH TORAH, *Kings and Wars* 3:10, *supra* note 9, at 214. On the "king's law," see A. SCHREIBER, JEWISH LAW AND DECISION-MAKING 236-37 (1979); THE PRINCIPLES OF JEWISH LAW, *supra* note 16, at 30-31. *But see* I. ABRAVANEL, *supra*, *Deuteronomy*

not to utilize this emergency jurisdiction is wholly within the discretion of the halakhic authorities of each age. The measures taken must respond to the needs of the hour,[129] and their purpose must be the ultimate strengthening of observance of the law.[130] The measures adopted are not binding precedents once the emergency passes.[131] Notwithstanding the emergency, ethical restraints on the conduct of officials remain in effect to circumscribe their actions; the authorities must preserve individual self-respect and take no action that will impair human dignity.[132]

Once halakhic authorities determine that contemporary conditions warrant an exercise of emergency jurisdiction, what should be the source of the temporary rules they implement to govern during the crisis? According to Rabbi Ephraim Luntshitz, halakhic authorities should draw temporary rules from the dissenting positions articulated in previously settled halakhic disputes.[133] The dissents constitute a pool of alternative rules, available to be pressed into service when hard times require temporary legal solutions.

Rabbi Luntshitz shares the view, mentioned earlier, that controversy and dissent are inherent parts of a multifaceted reality in which halakhic authorities arrive at a ruling in each case by weighing the component factors to determine which predominates.[134] Thus, for Rabbi Luntshitz, it follows that if circumstances change radically, an element previously in the minority might come to play the major role. This is what has happened when a halakhic authority exercises his emergency jurisdiction, suspending a law and substituting another. The authority

---

16:18, 17:8, at 154, 159 (king may not impose extralegal sanctions). Finally, a prophet, as part of his mission commanded by God, may temporarily suspend ordinary laws because of special circumstances. MOSES MAIMONIDES' COMMENTARY ON THE MISHNAH 57-59 (F. Rosner trans. 1975); *see also* 8 ENCYCLOPEDIA TALMUDIT, *Hora'at Sha'ah* 512 (1957) (in Hebrew); *infra* note 132.

129. Isserles, MAPPAH, *Hoshen Ha-Mishpat* 2:1.

130. *See* TALMUD BAVLI, *Sanhedrin* 46a, at 303 (J. Shachter & H. Freedman trans. 1935) (extralegal sanctions may be imposed, not with intention to disregard Torah, but to strengthen it); M. MAIMONIDES, MISHNEH TORAH, *Sanhedrin* 24:4, *supra* note 9, at 73 (extralegal sanctions may be imposed to build a fence around the law); *id.*, *Rebels* 2:4, at 141 (emergency measures may be adopted to bring the multitudes back to religion or save them from general religious laxity); J. CARO, Shulhan Arukh, *Hoshen Ha-Mishpat* 2:1. (exercise of emergency powers must be for the sake of Heaven).

131. M. MAIMONIDES, MISHNEH TORAH, *supra* note 9, *Sanhedrin* 24:4, *Rebels* 2:4, at 73, 141.

132. *Id.*, *Sanhedrin* 24:10, at 75. Halakhic authorities clearly understood the potential for abuse in the exercise of extralegal power. For this reason, they tended to restrict its exercise to a limited class of individuals, such as the outstanding personalities of each generation, who would possess personal qualities that reduced the possiblity of abuse. *See* E. QUINT & N. HECHT, *supra* note 127, at 183-204.

133. RABBI EPHRAIM SOLOMON BEN AARON OF LENCZYCZA ("Ish Luntshitz," 1550-1619) [hereinafter E. LUNTSHITZ]. KELI YEKAR, *Deuteronomy* 17:11, printed in standard editions of the rabbinic Bible known as MIKRAOT GEDOLOT. For an evaluation of Luntshitz's career, see Bettan, *The Sermons of Ephraim Luntshitz*, in 8 HEB. UNION C. ANN. 443 (1931-32); see also CHAIM HILLEL BEN-SASSON, HAGUT VE-HANHAGAH 25-29 (1959).

134. *See supra* notes 115-18 and accompanying text.

has determined that under present abnormal conditions, the element formerly in the minority has come to predominate, and he must temporarily administer the law in a manner that recognizes this fact. The dissent becomes law for the duration of the emergency, that is, until conditions revert back to normal.[135]

This view of emergency jurisdiction has important implications for the position of dissent in Jewish law. If the expression of dissenting points of view is inhibited, the number of options available to meet emergency conditions will be artificially restricted. If authorities entertain alternative positions until a disputed point of law is resolved but forget them once the halakhah has been finally determined, they will be less able to deal effectively with crisis. To prevent this, halakhic authorities should encourage the expression of dissenting points of view, and they should teach Jewish law in a manner that always conveys the dissenting positions as well as the final rules. Future halakhic authorities must be as conversant with dissenting positions as they are with authoritative rules, because in an unforeseen emergency, they may need to implement a temporary solution based on a dissent to meet the needs of the hour.[136]

D. Providing Partial Self-Justification for Nonconforming Conduct

The variety of positions halakhic authorities advance in their legal debates provides a de facto measure of flexibility for the individual deciding on a course of action. A person should conform his or her conduct to the halakhah as finally determined rather than act according to a dissenting viewpoint. If the issue is still open to debate by the authorities, then a person should consult an authority in his or her jurisdiction for advice on how to act. One should not engage in halakhic forum-shopping, first deciding what to do and then attempting to locate an authority who agrees that the desired action is permitted.[137] But individuals sometimes

135. See E. LUNTSHITZ, *supra* note 133; *cf.* E. BERKOVITS, *supra* note 108, at 49 ("The minority view is kept in abeyance; it has been overruled conditionally, till such time [as] valid arguments would be found for its acceptance. The teaching of the minority is not suppressed; it may retain its theoretical validity.").

136. If the sage or prophet is unaware of any reasoning contrary [to the established ruling], then he will never declare pure [something which has previously been declared impure], even to meet the needs of the hour when he is obligated to do so. . . . Our rabbis correctly advised, "Make your ear like a funnel to acquire the words of those who render pure and those who render impure" [TALMUD BAVLI, *Hagigah* 3b], because in truth, *each individual has need to know all of the positions.*

E. LUNTSHITZ, *supra* note 133 (emphasis added); *see supra* note 114.

137. The Talmud addresses the necessity of adopting a principled and consistent approach to disputed questions of halakhah:

> One who adopts the view of Beth Shammai only when they incline to leniency, and likewise the view of Beth Hillel only when they incline to leniency, is a wicked person. One who adopts the view of Beth Shammai only when they incline to strictness and likewise the view of Beth Hillel only when they incline to strictness, [is a fool] . . . . But one must either adopt the view of Beth Shammai in all cases . . . or the view of Beth Hillel in all cases.

fall short of this ideal standard. When they do, they may find solace and some measure of self-justification in the fact that a great halakhic authority, although in dissent, holds the view that their conduct is permitted.

This function of dissent operates *sub rosa,* in the mind and conscience of the individual who engages in nonconforming conduct, and normally does not leave a trace in the literature of the halakhic system. Occasionally, however, halakhic authorities express a view that seems to acknowledge its operation. Two examples follow:

(1) Reading "everyday documents" is prohibited on the Sabbath.[138] The prohibition covers business-related materials, such as promissory notes and account books, but authorities disagree whether it also covers ordinary letters such as friends send to each other.[139] Although a number of impressive authorities, including Maimonides and Nachmanides, held that the prohibition did not extend to letters, the codifiers, Jacob ben Asher and Joseph Caro, held otherwise.[140] Rabbi Solomon ben Abraham Adret (the *Rashba*) also held that such letters may not be read on the Sabbath, but he wrote that it was wrong to scold those who do read them since they are relying on the position of Nachmanides who held it is permitted.[141]

(2) At the *seder*, the festive meal that inaugurates the celebration of Passover, the nation's freedom is demonstrated in a variety of tangible ways. Slaves eat perched at the edge of their seats waiting to be recalled to work, while free persons eat at a leisurely pace and recline in comfort on pillows. Hence the participants in the *seder* must recline like free persons to demonstrate their freedom. But one medieval authority, Rabbi Eliezer Halevi, reasoned that however common it was in antiquity for princes and free persons to recline at their meals, it is not customary today, and the law ought to recognize this change at the contemporary

---

TALMUD BAVLI, *Hullin* 43b-44a, at 235 (E. Cashdan trans. 1960) (bracket in original). *See also, e.g.*, Isserles, MAPPAH, Hoshen Ha-Mishpat 25:2 ("In a case where there is controversy among authorities, a person [i.e., the judge] must not say, 'I will decide as I please,' and if he does, he renders a false judgment.").

138. THE CODE OF MAIMONIDES (MISHNEH TORAH): BOOK THREE, THE BOOK OF SEASONS, *Sabbath* 23:19, at 154 (S. Gandz & H. Klein trans. 1961); *see also* TALMUD BAVLI, *Shabbath* 116b, at 572 (H. Freedman trans. 1938).

139. *See* J. CARO, BEIT YOSEF, *Orah Hayyim* 307.

140. JACOB BEN ASHER, ARBA'AH TURIM, *Orah Hayyim* 307; J. CARO, SHULHAN ARUKH, *Orah Hayyim* 307:13.

141. RABBI DAVID BEN SAMUEL HA-LEVI ("Taz"), TUREI ZAHAV, *Orah Hayyim* 307:13 (citing Rabbi Solomon ben Abraham Adret); *see also* J. CARO, BEIT YOSEF, *Orah Hayyim* 307 ("The *Rashba* wrote in a responsum, 'As to reading friendship letters on the Sabbath, you have already seen my view that it is prohibited. But as to one who is inclined to the view of Nachmanides [that it is permitted], we are not able to refute him . . . . Therefore, if one conducts himself according to one of the great sages of Jewish law, where we have no convincing proof [against his view], we have no power to prevent it.' ").

Passover feast.[142] Hence, he held that in modern times, no one is obligated to recline at the *seder*. Caro, in his code, rules otherwise.[143] He also rules, however, that a woman does not need to recline unless she is "notable."[144] On this point, Isserles comments, "All of our women are considered notable, but they customarily do not recline because they rely on the *Ravyah* [Rabbi Eliezer Halevi]."[145] Isserles does not explain why women are *entitled* to rely on Halevi's view, which is a dissenting opinion, but he cites Halevi's position as a partial justification of their nonconforming practice not to recline.

E. *Accommodating Social and Cultural Diversity*

Wherever Jews live, they are subject to the diverse social and cultural influences of their host countries. If Jewish law were unable to acknowledge this diversity, the Jews would become increasingly divorced from their environment. Dissent in Jewish law provides one way to accommodate the diversity. Since halakhic authority is divided along territorial lines, a dissenting position that the halakhic authorities of one jurisdiction reject may be adopted as the rule in another jurisdiction. The availability of both the majority rule and its converse and perhaps intermediate positions as well, maximizes the number of options for local adaptations. To the extent they have discretion, the authorities of each jurisdiction will naturally tend to select the position that is best suited to the social and cultural conditions of their community and its surroundings.

The controversy between Caro and Isserles regarding the obligation of women to recline at the Passover table is again illustrative.[146] They disagree whether Jewish law, for this purpose, recognizes two categories of women—"notable women" who are obligated to recline, and women who are not notable and who are not required to recline. It was not happenstance that Caro affirmed the distinction and Isserles disavowed it. Caro wrote for Sephardic and oriental Jewry in Islamic lands where polygamy was allowed.[147] He was comfortable with a distinction between important and inferior wives. For Isserles, writing for the Jews of Christian Europe where polygamy was prohibited, such a distinction

---

142. RABBI ELIEZER BEN JOEL HALEVI ("Ravyah," c. 1160-1235), SEFER RAVYAH, § 525, at 154 (A. Aptowitzer 2d ed., Hebrew year 5724); *see also* M. KASHER, HAGADAH SHELEMAH 211-16 (3d ed. 1967) (in Hebrew) (suggesting that Halevi's opinion was shared by many of the legal sages of his era).

143. J. CARO, SHULHAN ARUKH, *Orah Hayyim* 472:2.

144. *Id.*, 472:4. The word for "notable" in Hebrew is *hashuva*, literally "important."

145. Isserles, *Mappah*, *Orah Hayyim* 472:4.

146. *See supra* notes 142-45 and accompanying text.

147. *See* Schereschewsky, *Bigamy and Polygamy*, in THE PRINCIPLES OF JEWISH LAW, *supra* note 16, at 366-71.

had no resonance.[148] His freedom to register a dissent from Caro's position allowed him to accommodate the sensibilities of European Jewry and to adapt this detail of Jewish law to their social and cultural environment.

F. *Preventing Recovery in Civil Suits Where the Law is Unsettled*

In a civil suit under Jewish law, the plaintiff has the burden of proving the facts he claims entitle him to recover. However, once the plaintiff satisfies this burden, the defendant may plead the unsettled state of the law as an affirmative defense. Conceding that the plaintiff is entitled to recover on the facts under the majority position, the defendant may counterpose his own reliance (Heb. *kim li*) on the contrary legal position of the minority of authorities. The defendant's plea requires the plaintiff to satisfy an additional burden of proof, this time regarding the law: the plaintiff must now convince the court that the minority line of authority which supports the defendant is wrong. If the plaintiff fails to persuade the court that the minority is in error, he cannot recover.[149]

Some halakhic authorities disfavor this affirmative defense, regarding it as a dysfunction of dissent under Jewish law rather than a legitimate function. Because conflicts of opinion regarding the law are so common, they believe reliance on the plea might prevent recovery in virtually every civil case. For this reason, these authorities restrict the right to assert it.[150]

The plea may be viewed in a more favorable light as a manifestation of pluralism in Jewish law.[151] The legal theories the parties advocate to support their respective claims each represent "the words of the living God,"[152] and some factual settings may find the component factors on which the court's decision should be based equally balanced. In such cases, when the defendant pleads *kim li*, a stalemate results that prevents the plaintiff from recovering. Thus, the plea embodies the recognition that, given the pluralistic nature of Jewish law, some legal problems will

148. Isserles, *Mappah*, *Orah Hayyim* 472:4 ("But all of our women are considered notable.").

149. *See* 3 M. ELON, HA-MISHPAT HA-IVRI 1062-63 (1973) (in Hebrew); 1 I. HERZOG, MAIN INSTITUTIONS OF JEWISH LAW 271-72 (1980); THE PRINCIPLES OF JEWISH LAW, *supra* note 16, at 134-35.

150. *See, e.g.*, RABBI MOSES IBN HABIB (1654-1696), GET PASHUT, *Kelal Beth* 282-86 (A. Shalem ed., Hebrew year 5740) (defendant's plea of *kim li* will not be entertained if (1) defendant cannot cite more than one authority in his favor against all the other authorities who expressed an opinion on the point; or (2) if the authorities on which he relies are minor in comparison to the authorities in the majority that support the plaintiff's position; or (3) if the authors of the Shulhan Arukh, *see supra* note 22, are among the authorities whose position supports the plaintiff's recovery).

151. *See* H. Ben Menahem, *Towards a Jurisprudential Analysis of the Kim-li Argument*, in 6-7 SHENATON HA-MISHPAT HA-IVRI 45 (1979-80) (in Hebrew).

152. *See supra* notes 105-18 and accompanying text.

have two equally valid halakhic solutions, one favoring the plaintiff, the other favoring the defendant, denying the court any basis on which to modify the status quo.

G. *Making the Torah Great and Glorious*

Whatever the functional role of law in society, scholars of Jewish law never divorce it from its ultimate source, the Torah, the word of God. Their dissatisfaction with simple explanations and their attempt to extract from legal texts every nuance of meaning are rooted in a respect for the word of God and a desire to know it completely. They view the study of Jewish law as the study of God's word and will.

From a verse in the Book of Isaiah, the rabbis learned that "The Lord was pleased, for His righteousness' sake, to make the teaching [in Hebrew, *Torah*] great and glorious."[153] "Making the Torah great" involves making it larger, adding to its content. "Making the Torah glorious" entails honoring the Torah, embellishing it and adorning it. The give and take of halakhic authorities regarding disputed points of law accomplishes both of these functions. Each position in a legal dispute, along with its rationales, proofs, and contrary arguments, add to the edifice of the Torah—increasing the quantum of the material and its complexity. At the same time, the legal arguments of halakhic authorities adorn the Torah as much as brocade wrappers and silver ornaments.[154] The edifice that the legal sages build to honor God is not constructed out of stone and mortar but out of knowledge of the Torah. Knowledge grows with each generation, and the dissenter's contribution to this enterprise is pivotal to making the Torah great and glorious.

H. *Sustaining Interest in the Study of Jewish Law*

Most creative people probably find that participating in a debate is more interesting and more challenging than acting as a passive conduit to transmit a settled body of rules. A large measure of the intrinsic interest and satisfaction derived from studying Jewish law comes from the right to formulate and express innovative ideas—even when they run counter to the views of other authorities—and from the challenge of studying the resulting mass of conflicting opinions. The study of Jewish law is a creative process, affording many opportunities for self-fulfillment and for developing individual potential. It seems unlikely that the intense study

153. *Isaiah* 42:21 (Jewish Publication Society 1917); *see* TALMUD BAVLI, *Niddah* 51b, at 357 (I. Slotki trans. 1959).

154. *See, e.g.*, RABBI MOSES CORDOVERO ("Ramak," 1522-1570), THE PALM TREE OF DEBORAH 108 (L. Jacobs trans. 1960) (scholar "should further accustom himself, when he debates words of Torah, to have the intention of adorning the *Shekhinah* [Divine Presence], to adorn and decorate Her for Beauty, and this is the meaning of *Halakhah* for Truth").

of Jewish law could have flourished over the centuries and engaged the attention of the best minds, in good times and bad, in friendly and hostile environments, if it had not allowed for the self-expression that comes from the right to challenge authority by articulating and defending novel legal positions.

Conclusion

In any legal system, dissent will sharpen the issues in legal debate, and skillful judicial craftsmen who take pride in their work will view their dissenting opinions as important and interesting additions to legal literature. But an extraordinary degree of legitimacy must attach to dissent in a legal system in which a rejected legal position may govern in a hard case or in hard times, justify nonconforming practices, or even prevent recovery in a suit where the plaintiff has satisfied the burden of proof as to the facts.

Dissent in Jewish law can perform so many important functions because of the belief that all the legal positions expressed by halakhic authorities, no matter how seemingly contradictory, emanate from the same divine source. For this reason, dissenting viewpoints are not "wrong" in any absolute sense; they are "also right." This element of rightness permits the dissent to replace the law on occasion, imparting to Jewish law a measure of flexibility and suppleness necessary to respond to the changing social and cultural conditions of the Jews, in all the countries where they reside and in all eras of their history.

[17]

Izhak Englard

Professor Englard is a member of the faculty of law at the Hebrew University in Jerusalem.

MAJORITY DECISION VS. INDIVIDUAL TRUTH

The Interpretations of the "Oven of Achnai" Aggadah

INTRODUCTION

The story of Achnai's oven[1] opens with a *Mishnah* in Tractate *Kelim*.[2] There Rabbi Eliezer and the rabbis debate the "purity" of an oven made of rings in between which is filled with sand. Rabbi Eliezer ruled that it was pure while the rabbis held it was impure. Although Rabbi Eliezer advanced every possible argument in his favor, the rabbis refused to rule his way. Thereupon he tried to convince them by invoking a number of miracles. First he stated:

> If the law is in accord with my views, let this carob tree offer testimony.

The carob tree was uprooted from its place and moved one hundred ells; others say four hundred ells. But the rabbis replied:

> We adduce no evidence from a carob tree.

Then Rabbi Eliezer said:

> If the law is in accordance with my views, let this water brook testify.

The water of the brook flowed in a reverse direction. Again the rabbis said:

> We adduce no evidence from a water brook.

Rabbi Eliezer said:

> If the law accords with my views, let the walls of the academy bear witness.

The walls of the academy began coming together and were about to fall. Rabbi Yehoshuah rebuked them, saying:

> If scholars debate an issue of law, what business is it of yours to intervene?

They did not collapse out of deference to Rabbi Yehoshuah, and they did not resume their straight position out of deference to Rabbi Eliezer; they remained in a bent position. Finally Rabbi Eliezer cried out in desperation:

> If the Halakhah is as I say, let it be demonstrated from Heaven.

At that, a Divine Voice (*bat kol*) gave utterance:

> Why do you disagree with Rabbi Eliezer. The Halakhah is always as he says it is.

Rabbi Yehoshuah then rose to his feet and exclaimed:

> It is not in Heaven.[3]

The story continues with Rabbi Yirmiyah's answer to the question put by the Talmud[4] as to the real meaning of Rabbi Yehoshuah's exclamation. His answer is two-fold: since the Torah has already been revealed at Sinai, no regard is to be paid to any Divine Voice: the Torah[5] has already prescribed that one must abide by the majority.[6] The story proceeds to relate the meeting of Rabbi Nathan with the prophet Elijah. Rabbi Nathan asked "What did the Holy One do at the time" and Elijah replied "He laughed and said: "My sons have defeated Me, My sons have defeated Me".

Reverting to the events of the day, the Talmud continues:

> All objects which Rabbi Eliezer had ruled to be clean were brought and burnt, and then they resolved to excommunicate him.

Rabbi Akiba volunteered to go and inform Rabbi Eliezer of his excommunication, and the entire natural world was profoundly shaken by Rabbi Eliezer's anguish. Rabbi Gamaliel, however, was saved from the sea's rage by vindicating the excommunication — "So that strife shall not multiply in Israel" — although in the end he died because of Rabbi Eliezer's grief. The story concludes with the moral uttered by Rabbi Eliezer's wife (a sister of Rabbi Gamaliel's):

> I have it as a family tradition that all gates are locked except the gate of grievously wounded feelings.

This concluding note links the whole story with the theme of denigrating another, in the course of which it figures in the Babylonian Talmud.[7] This interweaving of the story leaves the impression that the editor wished to emphasize the wrong done to Rabbi Eliezer and the serious consequences of so hurting a person's feelings.[8]

II

In his *Talmudic Law and the Modern State,*[9] Mr. Justice Silberg has observed that whilst this story has long impressed scholars and literary people with its beauty, it possesses more than literary elegance. He writes:

> Here in this legend, as well as in the statement from the Palestinian Talmud quoted earlier, is disclosed to us the singular characteristic of Jewish jurisprudence. We have here the rule of law in its absolute sense, the rule of law over the one who decrees the law, the introduction of the lawgiver into the hierachy of relationships, juridical and administrative, which were created by the law which He himself ordained. He heeds "the commandments of the Torah," that is to say, He takes on himself the discipline of the law and He submits to the authentic interpretation of the authorized interpreters. In other words, He accepts the discipline of the judgment pronounced by an authoritative body—the majority—which was empowered by Him for deciding doubtful cases, even though in this instance the doubtful case is for Him not doubtful at all. If the law is to follow a majority, one must act in accordance with this law, even if the one involved in litigation is the giver of the Torah Himself.[10]

The modern concept of the Rule of Law which Mr. Justice

Silberg has discovered is, as he says: "A mighty conception, mightier than can be grasped by our simple common sense."

Those engaged in philosophical speculation will almost inevitably select the complex of sources which will lend support to their own value judgments. And rabbinical legend is a fertile field for harvesting the most varied of crops. There are those students of the law of our own time, (most of them Jewish) who cite the legend of Achnai's oven to support their own views about jurisprudence. Edmond Cahn, for instance, describes the bitter and ultimately tragic dissension between Rabbi Eliezer and his colleagues as a joyful event when the sounds of hearty laughter echoed from Heaven,[11] because he believes that the story points out the moral that the individual has the right and duty to bear personal responsibility for his decisions. The judge must interpret the law as best as he can and no miraculous act can relieve him of the attendant responsibility.[12] By contrast, the Italian scholar, Ascarelli,[13] finds in the story, and, in particular in the stand taken by Rabbi Yehoshuah and the others, support for his view that it is in the nature of statutory formulations not to be unequivocal: hence his conclusions that the task of the interpreter is always creative.[14]

Very frequently scholars directly engaged in Jewish studies in general and Jewish law in particular have drawn broad conclusions about the character of Judaism and Jewish law from *aggadic* material. This approach is very problematical, for to lay down general principles in these fields of study which involve selecting one or another source is not a satisfactory procedure. The entire range of the sources must be reviewed to establish convincingly that the source actually cited representatively exemplifies what is intended. And in this regard the historical and philological aspects of the material must not be overlooked.[15]

All this applies with equal force to the story of Achnai's oven. It furnishes no ground for any far-ranging conclusions regarding the existence of the democratic idea in Judaism. Nor does it provide certain and sufficient foundation for the view of Mr. Justice Silberg about the prevalence of the rule of law in the Jewish legal system.[16] Characteristically, it has also

Majority Decision Vs. Individual Truth

been said, that the story in fact clearly manifests an anti-authoritarian stream in Jewish thought.[17] Even if "a stream in Jewish thought" is very cautious of expression, not presuming to lay down any general proposition, the conclusion itself is not to be accepted as determinative unless it rests on foundations which are secure and firm in point of history and philology.[18]

These misgivings as to methodology, elementary though they may sound, are only intended to suggest the purpose of this note. It is not to examine the substance of the story from the historical, philological or any other aspect. Nor is it to deduce or to stress any philosophical idea. Quite another end is in mind. The tale, as reported in the Talmud, is replete with tension. It is profoundly thought provoking and cries out for exegesis. Not unexpectedly, Jewish scholars through the ages have responded to the challenge which it presents. And it is this response which concerns us here. The pluralism in matters of faith and doctrine which has prevailed in halakhic Judaism renders the varying and often inconsistent interpretations of the story a matter of no very great surprise. But common to them all is the premise that the Halakhah is a living law and the Talmud in all its variety the authentic expression of Judaism. Professor Urbach has observed that

> the sayings of the sages were accepted by following generations as a supreme authoritative source not to be questioned, but the freedom to expound the truth contained therein lent itself to a variety of possibilities. The philosophers of medieval times, the Kabbalists and the Hasidim, all base themselves on the sayings of the sages in expounding their own systems of thought. But because for them the system of thought was primary, they dimmed and detracted from the original import of these sayings, especially because the modes of expression and the literary form of the sayings made them like a tree of abundant fruit.[19]

While sayings of the sages were regarded as an authoritative and binding expression of Jewish thinking different interpretations were made in future generations as the sayings were retold. The story of Achnai's oven is an example. The group of interpreters who addressed themselves to the story grew. Not only those who found in it support for their own views but also those — and perhaps particularly those — who found it difficult to reconcile the story with their personal outlook have felt the need to interpret the story, each in his own fashion. Very clearly individual values turned the story into statements of personal philosophy. The starting point, historically, should have been the personality of the interpreter in the context of his time and place. But the opposite course will be taken here. We shall examine the different views of the story taken by Jewish scholars. In so doing we shall not only have displayed before us the varying approaches to a number of problems which the story presents but shall also be able to gauge the vast range of meaning which words embrace and learn something of the manner in which the rabbis have regarded *Aggadah*.

Obviously, the present investigation is not exhaustive of all the views. We have endeavored to collect most of the printed sources and extract the more important ones.[20] Many of the details of the story served as texts for commentary in succeeding generations. Three aspects, however, have gained particular attention:

> 1. the conflict between a Divine Voice and a majority decision of the rabbis in halakhic matters; 2. the occurrence of miracles, and 3. the victory of the rabbis over the Divinity.

III

The relationship between rabbinical opinion and an opposing Divine Voice in favor of the view of an individual is essentially a normative problem: which of the two should, in principle, prevail. In our story the problem is posed in a particularly acute form since doctrinally a Divine command stands at the apex of the religious normative hierarchy from which the rabbis themselves derive their whole authority. If a Divine Voice is the expression of the Lawgiver's will, how can any contrary decision, even of a majority of rabbis, prevail normatively? Many of the commentators, as we shall see, have not been prepared to put the problem in this fashion and their understanding of the story is directed to avoiding the creation of such a profound normative conflict in the religious sphere.

Majority Decision Vs. Individual Truth

The attempts to resolve the problem lend themselves to a classification. The first, which may be termed *monistic*, regards all religious norms as belonging to one order in which any inconsistency is to be composed. The other, *dualistic*, mediates the conflict by creating two normative orders, each valid at a different level.

To deal with the monistic approach, if the order is unitary, it must follow logically that one norm is rejected in favor of another. In principle, the rejection can rest either on substantive grounds or on formal grounds. The Divine Voice in the story of Achnai's oven, could be either true or false in substance or valid or invalid in form. The same holds for the rabbis's decision.

A review of the different monistic interpretations shows that the rejection on formal grounds of the Divine Voice is part of a rationalistic current in Jewish thought of which Rabbi Nissim Gerondi is an outstanding representative. The sory is mentioned by him a number of times.[21] He cites it as proof his general standpoint that all halakhic decisions must be based on the human intellect.

> Thus, although all of the rabbis saw that Rabbi Eliezer had put the matter more correctly and that all the signs he gave Divinely authenticated his decision, nevertheless in the end the final word was with them because the decision they had arrived at was dictated by their human reasoning. They were conscious of the fact that in the circumstances that decision was wrong but they could not hold otherwise, for that would have meant going against their religious conviction, when their intellect told them that the oven was unclean, the determination being entrusted to the rabbis at all times.[22]

Here the reason is formal. Although the final decision of the majority was erroneous, it nevertheless took effect because "whatever they agreed upon, the Lord had commanded."[23]

A similar approach is taken by the author of *Sefer HaHinuch*,[24] who gives a practical reason for preferring the majority view to the absolute truth, which is the privilege of the individual.

> It is better to suffer one error and all bend to the good understanding

> of the rabbis rather than each of us should act as he thinks, for in that direction lies the destruction of religion, the rupture of the people and the complex disarray of the nation.

This outlook accords well with the general theory of Maimonides[25] — that prophecy has no function in interpreting the law.[26] And the observations of Rabbi Nissim Gerondi also serve as a conceptual basis for later opinion, such as that of the author of *Kezot HaHoshen*,[27] regarding the creative function of those who decide the law. Doctrinal recognition of the possibility of error strengthens them, for otherwise they might hold back from accepting judicial office in view of the serious responsibilities which attach.[28]

But the formal approach was not acceptable to others who tried to explain the rejection of the Divine Voice on material grounds. The Divine Voice, it was urged, was not accepted because it was not authentic in the broad sense and because it was not intended originally to be binding in its normative essence. It is in this spirit that Rabbi Nissim Gaon[29] dwells on the language in which the story is couched.

> The Divine Voice did not proclaim that the law on the specific matter was as he said it was but that in general it was "always" so, and it can be said that "always" meant other than in the present case.

Another interpretation, which he suggests, is that the Divine Voice went forth to try the rabbis and see whether they would yield a legal tradition of theirs in the face of the challenge of a Divine Voice. According to both interpretations, the Divine Voice was not meant to decide the law in this instance and *ipso facto* did not create any normative conflict.[30]

The Tosefot[31] adopt a similar approach, suggesting the possibility that the Divine Voice only issued to render honor to Rabbi Eliezer who had asserted that Heaven would prove the matter.

Despite their varying points of departure, these interpretations[32] are akin in their solutions of the problem in affirming that a Divine Voice possesses no normative significance and, accordingly, the decision of the rabbis is both correct in essence and binding.

An opposite view — and perhaps most far-reaching, having regard to the plain meaning of the story — is offered by Rabbi Moses of Bisencz in his *Darash Moshe.*[33]

> The reason why they paid no heed to the Divine Voice is simple. So is the reason why the Holy One Blessed Be He burst out in laughter. It is known that the Torah and equally the sages speak in the language of ordinary people. Thus it would seem as if the Holy One made of Rabbi Yehoshuah's reply a matter of laughter since he erred greatly. The Torah only says that the majority must be followed in respect of human beings who do not understand the real truth of a matter but that does not pertain with regard to the Glorious One who knows the truth of all things. The Holy One laughed when He contemplated His children wishing to defeat him with fantasies and baseless argument.[34]

According to this commentator there the Divine Voice is expressive of the truth and normatively binding: the decision of the rabbis is in error and not binding. The Divine Voice reacted with ironic amusement at the attitude of Rabbi Yehoshuah and his companions who, so to speak, wished to score a victory over Him.

Very many of the commentators offer a dualistic construction, in the sense that "both are the words of the Living God": both decisions are correct and each is binding but at different levels, although views differ as to the nature of these levels.

Rabbi Moses ben Yitzhak Bonems, the author of *Mahadura Batra l'HaMarsha,*[35] distinguished between the study of the Torah in Heaven and deciding the law on earth. The majority rule applies only to the latter. In Heaven, learning is pursued for its own sake without any other aim or motive. Thus the opinion of the majority need not necessarily prevail, provided that the individual is rightly disposed towards the Halakhah. It is for this reason that Rabbi Yehoshuah said to the Divine Voice "It is not in Heaven," that is, our dispute is not being conducted in Heaven and You have already proclaimed at Sinai which is of this world that the majority must be followed. The Divine Voice is authentic in stating that in Heaven the law is as Rabbi Eliezer, one against the many. But here on earth we pay no regard to that but follow the majority.[36] Hence, Rabbi Eliezer was right in the contemplation of Heaven, even if it was condemned in the world below.[37]

Two different appraisals are found in the commentary of Rabbi Yosef's Delmedigo of Candia in his *Ta'alumot Hochmah,*[38] where he deals generally with the relationship between Kabbalist theory and the Halakhah. For him Rabbi Eliezer was right from the individual viewpoint but the law was nevertheless with Rabbi Yehoshuah and his fellow rabbis. He wrote:

> Even if the true law is according to the possessors of the mysteries we cannot but follow the modalities laid down in the Torah and at Sinai for resolving doubts. Even if we err, we incur no penalty. But, he whom the Lord has graciously distinguished from among the other sages in discovering the essential truth of things from another source has no need to go along the ordinary path. Thus Rabbi Eliezer was so steadfast in his views in the disputation and could not accept the reply of Rabbi Yehoshuah to follow the majority.[39]

According to this individualist approach, the person who knows the absolute truth may, perhaps even must, adhere to it in contrast to others who are subject to majority rule.[40]

A parallel to this difference between the individual and the majority is to be found in *Be'er Hagolah* by Maharal of Prague.[41] Here the matter is viewed more abstractly. The story is explained by a qualitative distinction between minority and majority opinions. In the process of reaching the generality of the majority, the limitations of the individual are transcended and we approach more closely to the Supreme Intellect. Once again both of the opposing views are authentic but that of the majority is to be preferred.[42]

IV

Apart from the Divine Voice, the other main theme discussed by Jewish scholars concerned the miracles which manifested themselves at the instance of Rabbi Eliezer. Two basic trends can, it seems, be discerned in the commentaries. Neither accepted the miracles in a literal sense. According to Rabbi Hananel, as quoted in *Shitah HaMekubezet,*[43] the miracles did not actually take place — one of the scholars present dozed off and saw them all in a dream. This is but another version of the well-known view which generally denies miracles and seeks to explain those which are said to have occurred to the rabbis as visions seen in a dream.[44]

This view, itself in dispute, is subject to severe criticism, particularly in the present context from the author of *Sefer Ha-Kanah*.[45] Indeed he hurled abuse at those who maintain that the miracles only occurred in a dream, and urges rather that it all actually happened while awake. Rabbi Ashkenazi in *Y'fei Mareh*[46] also observes

> For myself I understand these things only in their literal sense, for the sages were not incapable of such great deeds.

The proponents of the other trend do not address themselves directly to the possibility of miracles, either generally or on that particular occasion, but they suggest an allegorical interpretation which aims to attach to each incident its own specific meaning relative to the dispute. Somewhat in like fashion, each of the miracles has been seen as a symbol of the qualities and character of Rabbi Eliezer himself and their recital as intended to convince the rabbis that he was right. Thus the carob tree symbolizes his being satisfied with little,[47] or his venerable age or his having acquired learning arduously.[48] The stream of water is remindful of his possession of the oral traditions of the past,[49] or his humility and meakness of spirit[50] or his profound scholarship.[51] The walls of the school house are indicative of his assiduity, his tirelessness and abundant diligence in the study of the Torah.[52] And the refusal of the rabbis to accept his opinion is explained on the ground that the high qualities of an individual are not evidence of his rightness in Halakhic disputes.

Another similar explanation attributes to the miracles a symbolism which goes not to Rabbi Eliezer but to those rabbis who were inclined to agree with him. Thus,[53] the carob tree suggests Rabbi Hanina ben Dosa, whom a peck of carobs sufficed from one week's end to another. The stream of water represents Rabbi Elazar ben Arach, who is described as an ever-swelling fountain, and the walls of the schoolhouse the young scholars studying there.

Still another interpretation, that of Maharsha,[54] links the evidence of the miracles not with the personality of any individual but with the essential argument put by Rabbi Eliezer. The carob tree represents his reason for not holding with the majority.

> The decision of the majority of you who oppose me is like the carob tree that bear no fruit . . . your words are as the carob . . .

A substantive connection between the miracles and the dispute is also pointed out in *Rosh Yosef* by Yosef ben Ya'akov,[55] who, with scholastic dialectic, associates them with the question of the impurity of the oven.

An outstanding allegorical exegesis is presented by Rabbi Efrayim of Luntschitz in Poland in his *Ollelot Efrayim*. He likens the oven to the offense of defamation which cannot be atoned either by repentance or by good deeds unless the person sinned against has been truly conciliated. The miracles symbolize certain other serious transgressions for which repentance is atonement, but they do not persuade the rabbis.

V

A largely theological theme which has engaged the attention of the commentators is that of Divine admission or Divine defeat. A legal scholar of our day[56] finds an interesting contrast between this victory of man over the Divinity and the reaction of Zeus to the success of Prometheus in circumventing him and bestowing fire upon mankind. In the one case, a laughing admission of defeat, in others, rage and awesomely brutal punishment.

Some commentaries[57] mention in this connection the *aggadic* passage in Tractate *Pesakhim*.

> Rabbi Kahana said on the authority of Rabbi Yishmael ben Rabbi Yose: What is meant by "*La-menazeah David?*" (a common super-

> scription to a number of Psalms, the first word deriving from *nazeah*, to be victorious), Sing praises to Him who rejoices when they prevail over Him. See how the character of the Holy One Blessed Be He is unlike that of mortal man. Mortal man is saddened[58] when he suffers defeat but the Holy One rejoices, for it is said, "Therefore He said He would destroy them, had not Moses His chosen stood before Him in the breach" (Psalm 106:23).[59]

Others, however, have explained differently "my sons have defeated me." Maharal of Prague[60] deals at length with the difficulty that it is not possible for the ordinary man to score a victory over his rabbi in a matter of Halakhah. Nor is it proper to say that the Divinity has retracted from his own commandment, for that would involve His changeability. Maharal explains the "defeat" by propounding a theory about the relationship between God the giver and Israel the receiver. The will of the child is the will of the Father.

> Since they received the Torah at Sinai together with the rule that the majority is to be followed, the latter cannot be set aside. And in this regard the Holy One Blessed Be He said "They have defeated Me." I say that they were right to do so and I agree with them although I have said that the Law is with Rabbi Eliezer. Just as a father whose sons "defeat" him will do what they wish until he also desires what they do.

That the Sages themselves carried out the eternal will of God in abiding by the original prescript of the Torah to follow the majority is also expressed by Z. H. Chajes.[61] What is involved, he says, was not a defeat in the sense of prevailing over an opponent but "the moment The Holy One Blessed He heard that the Sages would pay no attention to the miraculous supernatural happenings evoked by Rabbi Eliezer but instead said: 'it is not in Heaven,' that was evidence how deeply implanted in their minds was the concept of God's eternity, i.e., it was not subject to chance or change." That is what "My sons have defeated Me" really meant — the profound belief in His unchangeable over-lastingness (*Nezah*).[62]

The author of *Sefer HaKanah*[63] also does not find any victory of the Sages in the halakhic story. *Nitzhuni* here possesses the meaning of "reinforcing Me and doing My wish, of honoring Me."

TRADITION: *A Journal of Orthodox Thought*

NOTES

1. *Baba Meziah* 59. In the Jerusalem Talmud the story is found in *Moed Katan*, III, 1. Important differences exist between the two sources. For a comparative study see A. Guttmann, "The Significance of Miracles for Talmudic Judaism," (1947) 20 *H.U.C.A.* 363.

2. V, 10 and also *Eduyot* VII, 7.

3. Deuteronomy 30:12.

4. *Y. Moed Katan* III, 1 reports this explanation as of Rabbi Haninah. The printed text is somewhat garbled. See *Dikduke Sofrim ad locum.*

5. Exodus 23:2.

6. Between these two explanations there is no necessary connection. The view of the majority need not prevail when a problem is of a kind which merits a revelation from Heaven. "It is not in Heaven" and "no regard is paid to any Divine Voice" are much broader conceptions. They deny categorically the necessity of paying any attention to a halakhic decision which issues from Heaven, even when no opinion at all exists on a particular matter or it is unanimously held that the matter is in doubt. "One must abide by the majority" adds a dramatic touch to the story by setting a Divine Voice against human opinion.

7. In *Y. Moed Katan* the story appears in discussion of excommunication. See also *B. Berakhot* 19a.

8. For the historical background, see M. Aberbach, "Did Rabban Gamliel II impose the Ban on Rabbi Eliezer ben Hyrcanus?" (1964) 54 *J.Q.R.* 201; Guttmann, *op. et loc. cit.*

9. New York, 1973.

10. *Ibid.*, p. 64.

11. Edmund Cahn, "Authority and Responsibility," 5 *Columbia Law Review* 838.

12. See the criticism of Stone, *Human Law and Human Justice* (1965) p. 27, n. 89.

13. Ascarelli, *Problemi Giuridici*, (1959) pp. 14, 157-58. Cf. Ch. Perelman, "L'interprétation dans le droit," *Archives de Philosophie du droit*, tome XVII (1972) pp. 29, 34-35.

14. But see G. Tedeschi, "Insufficiency of the Legal Norm and Loyalty of the Interpreter," *Proceedings of the Israel National Academy*, vol. 1 (1964).

15. E. E. Urbach, *The Sages — Their Concepts and Beliefs* (1969) p. 3. (Hebrew).

16. Cf. the general criticism of A. Levontin in (1962) *HaPraklit*, p. 182, n. 3.

17. E. Fromm, *Psychoanalysis and Religion*, (1950) pp. 54 et seq. Cf. W. Kaufman, *Critique of Religion and Philosophy* (1958), pp. 238-40; Stone, *op. et loc. cit.*

18. See Y. Baer, *Israel Among the Nations* (Hebrew), (1955), pp. 108-9: "It was ultimately found necessary to restrain the magic power of the individual scholar so as to arrive at a decision binding upon all. Typical in this regard is the story of the Oven of Achnai and the excommunication of Rabbi Eliezer ben Hyrcanos, particularly in the Babylonian version." But contrast Urbach, *op. cit.*,

p. 99.

19. *Ibid.*, p. 3.

20. Most of the later sources were brought to my attention by Rabbi Joseph Buchsbaum, Director of the Jerusalem Institute, *The Treasury of Talmudic Commentators.*

21. *Derashot HaRan,* III, V, VII.

22. *Ibid.*, III, at end.

23. *Ibid.*, V.

24. *Sefer Hahinuch* (Mosad HaRav Kook, 1963, 5th ed.) Commandment 408. See also Rabbi Bahya on Deuteronomy 13:5.

25. *Mishneh Torah, Yesode Hatorah,* IX, 4. So also in his *Introduction to the Mishnah, Zeraim.* Cf. E. E. Urbach, *"Halachah U'Nevuah,"* (1947) 6 *Tarbitz,* 20-21.

26. On this problem, see generally *ibid.*, and the sources cited by Z. H. Chayes, *Torat HaNeviim.*

27. Introduction.

28. See Englard, "The Problem of Jewish Law in a Jewish State," (1968) 3 *Israel Law Review* 254, 256-58, nn. 9, 10.

29. On *Berakhot* 19b.

30. See the criticism of Urbach, *op. cit.*, p. 11.

31. *Baba Meziah* 59b. s.v. *"Lo Bashamayim Hi."*

32. It is an attempt to reconcile the *Gemara* here with *Eruvin* 13b and *Yevamot* 14a, where a Divine Voice was accepted in a dispute between Bet Hillel and Bet Shammai.

33. Cracow, 158-9, p. 59.

34. This interpretation also appears in *Hidushe Geonim* noted in *Ein Yaakov* on *Baba Meziah* 59.

34a. *Gittin* 6b.

35. The author was a son-in-law of Maharsha. (Rabbi Shmuel Edels). In the introduction to his book, he indicates that the novellae on the *aggadot* mentioned are his own.

36. This is the version according to the text published in Altona, 1734. A somewhat different version is given in *Ohel Yosef* by Rabbi Yosef Molcho (Salonica, 1756) p. 87, apparently in reliance on one of two earlier editions.

37. An interpretation along similar lines is given by Rabbi Yosef ben Yaakkov in his *Rosh Yosef* (1717) on *Baba Meziah,* 86.

38. (1629) pp. 22 *et seq.*

39. *Ibid.*, p. 23. Continuing, the author explains in this manner the fact that the *poskim* differ from Rabbi Shimon bar Yohai.

40. Compare also the approach of the Kabbalist Rabbi Menahem Azariah of Fano in *Asarah Mamarot, Hikur Hadin,* Part 2, ch. 18: "Thus Rabbi Yehoshuah well said that *in practice* it is not in Heaven, although dialectic truly justified Rabbi Eliezer. Yet the Divine Voice which said the Halakhah was with Rabbi Eliezer also spoke truly for he never said anything unless he had received from his teachers." See *Yad Yehudah, ibid.*

41. *Be'er* 4.

42. Not all have agreed that Rabbi Eliezer might continue to maintain his view in face of that of the majority. See *Sefer HaKanah* (1784) pp. 79 *et seq.* according to which the Divine Presence inclined to Rabbi Eliezer's view out of love for purity and therefore agreed to everything which he did although he was in a minority of one. But when the rabbis did not concede to him, it was for him to have retracted and accepted the decision of the majority.

43. On *Baba Meziah*, 59.

44. See Z. H. Chayes, *Mevo HaTalmud*, ch. 28 (English Translation, London 1952) and the sources cited there, and particularly in the present context *Hakotev, Ein Ya'akov, Berakhot* and the Novellae of Ritba to *Baba Batra* 73. See also Rabbi Nissim on *Berakhot* 19.

45. See note 42. The author of the book is unknown. For the date of this book (14th cent.) its historical significance and its tendency, see G. Sholem, *Major Trends in Jewish Mysticism*, 2nd ed., (1946) p. 211, 292: Y. Baer, *History of the Jews in Christian Spain*, (1961-66), vol. 1, p. 369 *et seq.*

46. Rabbi Samuel ben Rabbi Yitzhak Yafeh Ashkenazi on the legends in the Jerusalem Talmud (Venice, 1590) *Moed Katan*, III.

47. *Toledot Adam*, Biography of Rabbi Shlomo Zalman of Volozin, by Y. Feivel, p. 108. So also *Orah Yesharim*, on *Baba Mezia*, 59.

48. *Y'fei Mareh*, n. 46 above.

49. *Ibid.*

50. *Ibid.; Toledot Adam* and *Orah Yesharim, ubi supra.*

51. *Darash Moshe*, as above.

52. See the sources cited in n. 50.

53. This interpretation is given by *Maharam Schiff* in his commentary on *Baba Mezia*, 59, but he has reservations about the allegorical method in concluding "and all this is far fetched."

54. On *Baba Mezia*, 59.

55. See n. 37.

56. Tammelo cited in Stone, *op. cit.*, p. 28 n. 89a.

57. *Shita Mekubetzet, ibid.; Mitzpeh Eitan*, on *Baba Mezia*, 59; *Ahavat Eitan*, to *Ein Yaakov, ibid.*

58. See the sharper reaction of a human king recited in *Avodah Zarah*, 10a: "Anyone who defeats a king in argument is to be cast into a furnace."

59. *Pesakhim*, 119a. For further parallel sources, see Heschel, *Theology of Ancient Judaism* (Hebrew) vol. 2, p. 309.

60. *Be'er Hagolah, Be'er* 4.

61. In his Novellae to *Baba Mezia* 59.

62. In the same spirit, *Orah Yesharim*, as above, as well as *Toledot Adam*: "In my view the word of *nizhuni* has the connotation of continuous existence, persistence, that is to say, after my children have reached the stage where all signs and miracles contrary even to a minor principle basic to the Torah are treated as null and void, I am assured that My children have made Me eternal. I shall be their Father and their God for time everlasting."

63. See notes 42 and 45.

[18]

Legal Reasoning in Maimonidean Jurisprudence

Daniel B. Sinclair

Maimonides and Nachmanides held different views as to which elements of the Oral Law had Biblical, and which merely rabbinic status. Maimonides held a narrow view. Those traditions about which there is no argument are Biblical. The others are rabbinic. Nachmanides took a broader position. Laws derived from the Torah through interpretation, even when there is argument, are also Biblical.

In this article, Dr. Daniel Sinclair argues that the difference between them can be explained in terms of their differing approaches to legal reasoning, differences which persist in contemporary jurisprudence.

Dr. Sinclair is the author of the recently published ***Tradition and the Biological Revolution.***

The Nature of Analogical Reasoning and Maimonides' Definitions of Scriptural and Rabbinic Law

In his *Introduction to the Mishnah*, Maimonides distinguishes between two types of Oral law. The first consists of Divinely revealed explanations of the Written law given to Moses and passed on by him during his lifetime. The second comprises laws derived from Scripture by means of principles of interpretation such as analogy and *a fortiori*. The first type of Oral law never became the subject of controversy, whereas the second type is inherently controversial in nature. The only way to resolve such controversies is to follow the opinion of the majority in accordance with the Biblical dictum "to incline after the majority".[1]

In his *Book of the Commandments*, Maimonides grants scriptural status to the first type of Oral law mentioned above. The second type of Oral law is rabbinic. In order to explain the fact that the Talmud derives some scriptural laws on the basis of the principles of interpretation, Maimonides observes that the "wisdom of the text of Scripture" is such that these laws may be learned through exegesis. Nevertheless, the sole normative criterion for differentiating between scriptural and rabbinic law is tradition. Only those laws in relation to which there exists a talmudic tradition that they were communicated to Moses on Sinai are to be defined as scriptural laws. All others are rabbinic in nature.[2]

An important feature of Maimonides' classification of the two types of Oral law is the issue of controversy. According to Maimonides, textual interpretation is incapable of yielding results of an apodictic nature. Only tradition is capable of serving as a source of certainty. This idea is expressed by Maimonides in the following terms:

> And of the laws which they derived [on the basis of the principles of interpretation], some . . . became the subject of a dispute, with each side merely seeking to fortify its own position [rather than attempting to arrive at a definitive conclusion]. This is often the case when interpretation by analogy[3] is involved.[4]

In order to grasp the full significance of this statement, it is necessary to refer to Maimonides' concept of a logically demonstrative argument. In an early work on logical terms, Maimonides, following Aristotle, explains that a demonstrative syllogism is one in which both premises are apodictic, i.e. they consist of propositions the truth of which is known by means of physical perception, primary and secondary ideas, or experience.[5] Such a syllogism is logically demonstrative because the truth of its premises may be readily ascertained.[6] This is not the case with regard to the analogical syllogism employed in the interpretation of the Written law. The premises of these syllogisms consist of scriptural texts and oral traditions. The syllogisms constructed on this basis belong to the art of rhetoric rather than that of demonstration.[7] Since rhetorical logic proceeds upon the basis of shared fundamental assumptions rather than strict deductive reasoning, it is clear that there is plenty of room for controversy in the process of interpreting the Written law.[8]

Only in those rare cases in which the interpreters share identical traditions and intellectual ability is there likely to be agreement with regard to a particular interpretation. This is a result of the fact that human intelligences "differ from each other by nature".[9] This point is made by Maimonides in his explanation of the talmudic statement that "when the disciples of Shammai and Hillel, who had insufficiently studied, increased, disputes multiplied in Israel and the Law became as two Laws".[10] Maimonides observes that the great sages Shammai and Hillel disagreed only rarely, since they were equal in their knowledge of received principles and intellectual acumen. Their students, on the other hand, fell short of the erudition and intelligence of their teachers, and hence, disputes proliferated.[11] Interestingly enough, modern criticism of the application of the "new rhetorics" to legal reasoning also emphasises the fact that the conditions for the establishment of the shared fundamental assumptions required for the rhetorical argument to proceed to its conclusions are generally lacking in contemporary society.[12]

Maimonides' definition of scriptural law therefore, is strongly informed by his appreciation of the logical shortcomings of legal argumentation. In this respect, Maimonides reflects one of the major concerns of medieval Islamic jurists i.e. the logical validity of conclusions derived on the basis of analogy or *qiyas*.[13]

According to one view, any form of reasoning which falls below the logical standards set by the Aristotelian syllogism is invalid. As a result, all legal argumentation must be forced into the syllogistic mode.[14] Another view regards the traditional *giyas* as being a sufficiently valid tool for arriving at conclusions of a legally binding nature, notwithstanding any logical shortcomings which may be inherent in analogical reasoning.[15] In the course of time, the second view prevailed, and eventually Greek logic was completely banned from the field of religious law.[16]

Maimonides is clearly in sympathy with the first of the two above-mentioned approaches in Islamic jurisprudence, and he resolves the conflict between the Aristotelian syllogism and the *giyas* by relegating all derived Oral law to the rabbinic category. This solution preserves the absolute truth of a small kernel of scriptural law whilst at the same time admitting the relative nature of the bulk of the halakhah which falls into the category of rabbinic law.

It is noteworthy that Maimonides' distinction between the two types of Oral law constitutes a significant departure from the views of some of his Gaonic predecessors. According to a widely-held Gaonic view, genuine disputes over interpretation did not exist amongst the talmudic sages. All differences over interpretation are explained as attempts to clarify a law which was already known by tradition, or to reconstruct a part of the tradition which had been forgotten.[17] This monolithic view of halakhah according to which all Oral law stems from Moses on Sinai is supported by the Talmud[18] in the same way that Maimonides finds talmudic support for his approach.[19] There is however, little doubt that it was shaped in no small way by the struggle between the Gaonim and the Karaites. In order to defend themselves against the Karaite charge that the Oral law was not authentic, the Gaonim painted a picture of a monolithic tradition stemming from Moses on Sinai and continuing through to talmudic times.[20] Maimonides was obviously not constrained by the struggle with Karaism even though it still constituted a serious threat to rabbinic Judaism in his time. Presumably, he was more concerned with the threat posed to his intellectual integrity by the monolithic approach to the Oral law, than he was with the writing of anti-Karaite polemics.

Maimonides' appreciation of the relativist nature of analogical argumentation is nicely illustrated in his ruling on the issue of reversing the decisions of earlier courts. In his *Mishnah Torah*, Maimonides rules that a decision based upon the application of the principles of interpretation to the Written Law may be reversed by a later court if it has good reason to disagree with the grounds of the original decision.[21] This is not the case with respect to rabbinic legislation, which may only be abolished if the later court is greater in "wisdom and numbers" than the earlier one.[22] Presumably, the reason for the distinction is the logical imperfection of the reasoning upon which the derived Oral Law is based. Since there is no logically demonstrative solution to disputes concerning the interpretation of Scripture, the only way of establishing the law at any particular time is to follow the most convincing argument. Hence, Maimonides cites the Biblical injunction to go to "the judge that shall be in those days"[23] and the talmudic exegesis that "you must be content to go to the judge who is in your days" in this context. Rabbinic legislation, however, draws its authority from the formal authority of the rabbis to enact laws. Consequently, only a court possessing greater formal authority can abolish such legislation. In this area, too, the logical imperfection of the reasoning involved in deriving laws from Scripture renders them inferior to legislation based upon criteria of a purely formal nature.

Criticism of Maimonides' Theory of the Development of the Oral Law

Maimonides' definition of scriptural law is widely criticised. In his critical notes to the *Book of the Commandments*, Nachmanides raises numerous objections to Maimonides' definition, most of which are aimed at demonstrating that the sages of the Talmud do include derived laws in the category of scriptural law. He also points out that Maimonides contradicts himself in the sense that he claims both that the principles of interpretation were given to Moses on Mount Sinai and that laws derived on this basis are rabbinic in nature. According to Nachmanides, all derived laws are scriptural unless there is an explicit talmudic statement to the effect that the derivation is merely a literary flourish. In his concluding sentence, Nachmanides sums up his opposition to Maimonides' approach as follows:

> "And there are many more statements in the *gemara* which I could cite in opposition to Maimonides' view. . . . For his position uproots great mountains in the *Talmud* and destroys mighty walls in the *gemara*. It is evil and bitter for the students of *gemara* and may it be erased from memory."[24]

It would appear on the surface that Nachmanides is mainly concerned with the conflict between Maimonides' definitions of scriptural and rabbinic law, and the talmudic position on this issue. Now, although it is possible that this is indeed the sole grounds for the disagreement,[25] it is arguable that the root of the dispute lies in a difference of opinion with regard to the role of logic in legal reasoning. In the introduction to his glosses on the *Sefer Halakhot* of R. Isaac Alfasi, Nachmanides makes the following observation regarding the role of logic in establishing the law:

> . . . there is no such thing as absolute proof in this wisdom as there is in mathematics or astronomy . . . therefore we devote all our energies to the rejection of one of the opinions in a dispute . . . and strengthen the case for adopting the other. This is the best we can hope to achieve.[26]

Clearly, Nachmanides does not share Maimonides' rigorous approach to legal reasoning. He rejects the Maimonidean view according to which there can be no other rationally convincing claim in legal interpretation than a logically demonstrative one. Indeed, according to Nachmanides, marshalling arguments with a view to bolstering one side to a dispute and rejecting the other is the ultimate goal in legal reasoning. In his view, rhetoric is a virtue, not a shortcoming. There is therefore, no reason according to Nachmanides to downgrade derived Oral law from scriptural to rabbinic status. Consequently, all derived law is scriptural unless there is a specific talmudic directive to the contrary.[27]

The majority of rabbinic commentators and scholars attempted to blunt Nachmanides' critique by distinguishing between Maimonides' definition of the Divine Commandments and his concept of scriptural law. Maimonides only intended to exclude derived Oral law from the Sinaitic Commandments, he did not mean to exclude them from the category of scriptural law.[28] Although there are indications in the *Mishnah Torah* that Maimonides did not strictly adhere to his clarification of scriptural and rabbinic law,[29] his theoretical position certainly did not change in any of his works. In theoretical terms therefore, Maimonides' position is clear and unambiguous, and the consistent attempts to harmonise it with that of Nachmanides mainly reflect the concern felt by rabbinic authorities for the deeper implications of the Maimonidean position for the theology of halakhah. In this context, it is noteworthy that the seventeenth century authority, R. Yair Bachrach, wrote that Maimonides' theory was more dangerous than it was beneficial "since it leads to the conclusion that of all the Orders of the *Mishnah*, only a fraction originated from Sinai."[30] In R. Bachrach's period, if not earlier, the plain interpretation of Maimonides' classification of law was seen as a threat to the theology of the halakhah and hence, had to be modified. As was the case in Islamic law, the view of the traditionalists prevailed.

The Relationship between Legal Reasoning and the Scope of the Halakhah in Maimonidean Jurisprudence

Clearly, there is a link between Maimonides' view of legal reasoning and the unique blend of philosophy and law characteristic of his halakhic writings.[31] Free of the shackles of the notion of a deductively valid reasoning process, Maimonides could legitimately include ethical and pragmatic elements in his presentation and resolution of Jewish law. It is therefore no wonder that of all the codifiers of Jewish law, Maimonides has generated the most interest in relation to the search for concepts and values in the halakhic system. In this respect, Maimonides's position would appear to be close to that of the modern philosopher, R. Dworkin who argues that law must include the moral and philosophical values of the society although their inclusion must be carried out in a "principled" fashion.[32] The position adopted by Nachmanides and the majority of rabbinic authorities might resemble that of N. MacCormick, who argues that there is a strong deductive element in legal reasoning which covers all but the most difficult of cases. These so-called "hard-cases" constitute the grist for appellate and academic mills, but even with respect to such cases a model may be established which provides a rigorously rational basis for the decision. According to this view, the distinction between morality and law is still a valid one.[33] The debate between these two schools of thought persists in modern jurisprudential circles as it does amongst contemporary scholars of halakhah, although the link between reasoning and the scope of the law has not received a great deal of attention in halakhic circles.

The parallel between Maimonides and Dworkin is obviously not an exact one on any but the most general of levels. It might however, be observed that whereas Dworkin has reservations with regard to the incorporation of policy considerations i.e. considerations based upon general social consequences into the law,[34] Maimonides is fully prepared to incorporate such considerations into the halakhah. A fine example of Maimonidean policy is the invocation of Divine and extra-legal sanctions in cases where murderers are exempt from capital punishment because of technical defects such as indirectness and lack of sufficient witnesses.[35] In relation to all of these cases, Maimonides stresses the morally debilitating effects upon society of leaving such killers unpunished, and cites Biblical sources in which they are subject to intense criticism. He also invokes Divine penalties and calls upon the King and the court to use their extra-legal powers to subject these murderers to various punitive measures including death. It is noteworthy that a similar problem was encountered in Islamic law. In this system, it was resolved by the creation of a new category of laws which could be administered by the Caliph on the basis of his general role as the preserver of Islamic society.[36] Maimonides' approach to the development of Jewish law however, enabled him to incorporate policy considerations into his formulation of the halakhah in a smooth and integrated fashion.

Notes

1. *Introduction to the Mishnah*, translated by J. Kapah, Jerusalem, 1964, 3.
2. *Book of the Commandments*, ed. H. Chavel, Jerusalem, 1981, Second Principle, 29ff.
3. Maimonides uses the term *giyas*, which is a loan-word in Arabic, and is derived from the Hebrew word *hekesh*, see J. Schacht, *Introduction to Islamic Law* (Oxford, 1984) 21; R. Brunschvig, "Logic and Law in Classical Islam" in *Logic and Islamic Culture* (ed. G. von Grunebaum, Wiesbaden, 1970) 15. The term *hekesh* has two main connotations in Jewish law. The first is a general one, i.e. any interpretation based upon an analogy. The second is more restrictive, and refers to the principle that whenever two laws are present in the same scriptural verse, it may be inferred that whatever is true of one is true of the other: see *Encyclopaedia Talmudit* 10, 557 *s.v. Hekesh; Encyclopaedia Judaica* 8, 368. Since Maimonides refers to all thirteen standard principles of interpretation in his description of the derived laws, it is clear that he is using the term in its general sense. Maimonides uses the same term to designate the Aristotelian syllogism in his work on logical terms (see no. 5 below).
4. *Introduction. ibid.*
5. On Maimonides' logic and its sources, see I. Efros, "Maimonides' Treatise on Logic", *Proceedings of the American Academy for Jewish Research* 8 (1937-1938) 19.
6. Efros, *ibid.*, 48. The knowledge that the whole is greater than the part, that two is an even number, and that things equal to the very same thing equal each other are primary ideas. Secondary ideas are derived from primary ones, e.g. geometric theorems and astronomic calculations.
7. "When one or both premises of the syllogism belong to traditions, we call it a rhetorical syllogism" *id.* Aristotle defines rhetoric as "the faculty of observing in any case the available means of persuasion" (*Rhetorica*, Bk.1, Ch.2). As in dialectics, the rhetorical syllogism yields probabilities of truth only. In this context, it is noteworthy that principles such as *a fortiori* and *a maiore ad minus* which are used by the rabbis in their interpretation of the Written law, were well-known to the Greek rhetors, and are cited by Cicero in his *Topica*, Bk.4, Chs.15 and 23. The question of Greek influence on rabbinic hermeneutics is still an open one: see S. Lieberman, *Hellenism in Jewish Palestine* (New York, 1950) 54; D. Daube, "Rabbinic Methods of Interpretation and Hellenic Rhetoric", *Hebrew Union College Annual* 22 (1949) 239. It would appear, however, that with regard to terminology as distinct from method, the rabbis were influenced by Greek rhetoric: see Lieberman, *loc. cit.*, 61. Interest in rhetorics in the field of legal reasoning has been rekindled in recent years with the elaboration of the "new rhetorics" as opposed to those of the ancient world: see Ch. Perelman and L. Olbrechts-Tyteca, *The New Rhetoric: A Treatise on Argumentation*, translated by J. Wilkinson and P. Weaver, Notre Dame, 1969: Ch. Perelman, *The New Rhetoric and the Humanities*, translated by W. Kluback, Dordrecht, 1979: Ch. Perelman, *The Idea of Justice and the Problem of Argumentation* translated by J. Petrie, London, 1963; J. Stone, "Reasoning in Judicial and Juristic Argument" in *Legal Essays, A Tribute to Frede Castberg*, Scandinavian University Books, 1963, 185.

Also see: P. Goodrich, *Reading the Law*, Oxford, 1986, Ch.6.

8. The difficulty of establishing shared fundamental assumptions with regard to many of the questions preoccupying contemporary law is one of the major criticisms of the application of the "new rhetorics" to legal reasoning: see Stone, *ibid.*, 195.
9. *Introduction*.
10. *Sanhedrin* 88b.
11. *Introduction*, 11.
12. See no. 8 above. One way of overcoming this difficulty would be to narrow down the group of people whose fundamental assumptions are to be taken into consideration: see Aristotle, *Topica*, Bk.1, Ch.1; Stone, *op. cit.*, 195. Such a solution would, however, reduce the attractiveness of the whole idea of rhetorical argumentation in the context of legal reasoning.
13. See no. 3 above.
14. See e.g. the *at-Taqrib* of Ibn Hazm, and Brunschvig *ibid.*, 19.
15. See especially the *Mi'yar al-Ilm* of I. Ghazali, and Brunschvig *ibid*, 19. Also see : J. van Ess, "The Logical Structure of Islamic Theology" in *Logic and Islamic Culture*, ed. G. von Grunebaum, Wiesbaden, 1970, 49.
16. See Brunschvig, *ibid.*, 19.
17. A. Halkin, "R. Saadyah Gaon's Introduction to the *Torah*" in the *Levi Ginzberg Memorial Volume*, New York, 1956, Hebrew Section, 153; S. Abramson, "From the Fifth Chapter of R. Samuel b. Hofni's Introduction to the *Talmud*", *Sinai* 88, 1918, 214. Also see: Rashi, *Eruvin* 21b, *s.v. veyoter* and Tosafot *ad. loc. s.v. mipnei*; J. Blidstein, "Transmission and Institutional Authority in the Concept of the Oral Law in Maimonidean Thought", *Da'at* 16, 1986, 15.
18. See e.g. *Berakhot* 5a. *s.v. amar R. Shimon b. Lakish*.
19. See *Introduction, ibid*, 1-4; Blidstein *ibid*, 19.
20. Blidstein *id.*
21. *Laws of Rebels* 2:1.
22. *Laws of Rebels* 2:2. "Wisdom" in this context refers to the wisdom of the President of the Court, and "numbers" refers to the number of disciples in the court: see Maimonides, *Commentary to the Mishnah, Eduyot* 1:5, *c.f.* Rabad *ad. loc.* Also see Elon, *op. cit.*, 2. 443.
23. Deuteronomy 17:9.
24. *Book of the Commandments, ibid.*, 51. R. Yom Tov Ishvilli following in Nachmanides' footsteps writes that the whole of the Oral law is contained in Scripture and nothing is derived by the Sages *de novo*. They do however, have discretion with regard to the formal validation of Oral Law (Ritva, *Rosh Hashanah* 16a, *s.v. umalkhuyot*).
25. See Blidstein *ibid.*, 21.
26. *Milkhamot Hashem*, Introduction.
27. *Book of the Commandments, ibid.* 33.
28. *Marganita Tava*, Second Principle, *Maimonides' Book of the Commandments; Siftei Kohen, Shulchan Arukh, Choshen Mishpat* 33:1; *Or Sameakh, Laws of Rebels* 1:1; *Book of the Commandments, ibid.*, Notes on p.33, *s.v. ukra asmakhta*.
29. As indicated by his many references to the "*Shemuah*" "that which was heard" i.e. a Sinaitic tradition, see: Blidstein, *ibid.*, 17.
30. *Responsa Havot Yair*, no.162.
31. See I. Twersky, *Introduction to the Code of Maimonides*, New Haven, 1980 Ch.6; D. Hartman, *Maimonides: Torah and Philosophic Quest* J.P.S., 1976.
32. See R. Dworkin, *Taking Rights Seriously* (London, 1977); *A Matter of Principle*, Oxford, 1986. Dworkin's theory of interpretation is incisively presented in his most recent work, *Law's Empire*, London, 1986. For a collection of critical comments on his position, see: *Ronald Dworkin and Contemporary Jurisprudence*, ed. M. Cohen, New Jersey, 1984.
33. See N. MacCormick, *Legal Reasoning and Legal Theory* (Oxford, 1978). The deductive thrust of MacCormick's position is criticised by A. Wilson, "The Nature of Legal Reasoning: A Commentary with Reference to Prof. MacCormick's Theory", *Legal Studies* 2 (1982) pp. 269-287, *c.f.* MacCormick's reply, *ibid.*, pp. 286-290. Also see: N. Simmonds, *The Decline of Juridicial Reason*, Manchester, 1984, for a strong critique of the deductivist tradition in legal reasoning today.
34. *Taking Rights Seriously, ibid.*, 82ff.
35. Maimonides, *Hil. Rozeah* Chs. 2 and 4.
36. See N. Coulson, *A History of Islamic Law*, Edinburgh, 1964, pp. 132-133; E. Rosenthal, "Some Aspects of Islamic Political Thought", *Islamic Culture* 22, 1984, 1; J. Schacht, "The Law" in *Unity and Variety in Islamic Civilization*, ed. G. von Grunebaum, Chicago, 1985, 71. ■

Part VI
Selected Topics in Jewish Jurisprudence

Public Law

[19]

The Jewish Law Annual, Vol. I

MAIMONIDES ON "DINA DE-MALKHUTA DINA (THE LAW OF THE STATE IS LAW)"

by

SHMUEL SHILO *

The purpose of this article is to collate and incisively analyze what Maimonides has to say concerning "the ramified problems of the 'law of the kingdom' so crucial for the entire history of Judeo-Gentile symbiosis in the dispersion." [1] We will discuss, dogmatically, Maimonides' many-sided conception of the legal maxim *dina de-malkhuta dina* (the law of the State is law), and, where possible, the application of the maxim in actual practice. It is hoped that Maimonides' contribution to the development of the *halakha* on this crucial subject will be more fully appreciated. It is, of course, preferable to view Maimonides' views within the wider context of the whole scope of *halakhic* opinion on this topic which evolved from one generation to the next and from century to century, but this would be too lengthy a task for an article such as this. Therefore, although we are aware of the need for such perspective when writing an essay such as this, and we will occasionally point out Maimonides' view within the general *halakhic* context, in order for the reader to get a complete picture of the general question of *dina de-malkhuta dina* and, consequently, Maimonides' place within the legal development of this Talmudic maxim, one must also refer to my book on *dina de-malkhuta dina.* [2]

The Legal Basis of Dina De-Malkhuta Dina

Although the legal maxim *dina de-malkhuta dina* appears in the Talmud four times [3] the legal basis of the principle is unclear. It is only in Maimonides' time that a general theory behind the legal maxim was clearly enunciated. We do find, here and there, before Maimonides' time, attempts to explain the principle's legal basis—but it is only with Maimonides in the east and his contemporary in the west R.

---

* Senior Lecturer in Jewish Law, Hebrew University of Jerusalem.

[1] S. Baron, *A Social and Religious History of the Jews*, 2nd ed. (New York, 1952-1967), vol. 5, 324, note 93.

[2] S. Shilo, *Dina De-Malkhuta Dina* (*The Law of the State is Law*) (Jerusalem Academic Press, Jerusalem, 1974).

[3] *Nedarim* 28a; *Gittin* 10b; *B.K.* 113a-b; *B.B.* 44b-45a.

Samuel b. Meir (Rashbam), that we find the principle's legal basis analyzed. Maimonides' explanation became, perhaps, the most basic legal source for the *halakhic* scholars in later generations when they discussed this problem.

After describing the king's rights, Maimonides sums up the basic rule as follows: "All the above rules apply only to a king whose coins circulate in the localities concerned, *for then the inhabitants of the country have accepted him and definitely regard him as their master and themselves as his servants.*" [4] This view is similar to but not identical with Rashbam's view that the basis for accepting the king's laws is "for all the citizens accept the king's statutes and laws of their own free will." [5] According to Maimonides the people agree to accept the king's dominion over them, and according to Rashbam they accept his laws. In other words, the will of the people is what gives the king's laws effect. Therefore, it follows, if the people do not accept the ruler and his laws, such laws are invalid and not within the scope of *dina de-malkhuta dina.*

During most of the middle ages a ruler could not be considered ruling legally unless it was postulated that he was ruling as a result of the people's will. It is only after medieval times that the theory of the divine right of kings fully developed. During the Middle Ages the ruler's right to rule had to be based on the fact or fiction of the people's will. In the late Middle Ages a similar but different view began to develop which was based on Roman classical law, which postulated that the basis of government is a contract between ruler and ruled. [6]

One of the sources which Christian jurists expounded as a basis for the contractual view between the ruler and ruled, was the covenant between the king and the people in Hebron, when the people accepted David as their king. [7] What is puzzling is that the Jewish *halakhists,* when they discuss the contractual basis of accepting the Gentile king's dominion and laws, or when elaborating on the theme that the king rules because of the people's will, a view initiated by Maimonides, or when

4 *M.T. Gezelah* 5:18.

5 Rashbam, *B.B.* 54b.

6 See F. J. C. Hearnshaw, *The Social and Political Ideas of Some Great Mediaeval Thinkers* (London, 1923), 21-22; O. Gierke, *Political Theories of the Middle Ages* (trans.) (Cambridge, 1927), 40-41; W. Ullmann, *A History of Political Thought, The Middle Ages* (Harmondsworth, 1965), 12-13, 16; E. Lewis, *Medieval Political Ideas*, vol. 1 (New York, 1954), 158-162.

7 *2 Sam.* 5:3. See H. O. Taylor, *The Medieval Mind—A History of the Development of Thought and Emotion in the Middle Ages*, 4th ed. (London, 1957), 307.

certain rabbis parallel the kingdom of Israel to non-Jewish kingdoms as a basis for the acceptance of *dina de-malkhuta dina,* they never refer to this historical precedent in the book of Samuel.

Conditions Precedent to Applying Dina De-Malkhuta Dina

Jewish law did not, of course, accept as binding every "law" promulgated by every ruler; a number of conditions precedent were established without which such law was not binding. Perhaps first and foremost of these rules is the description of the form of government which is to be recognized. The first *halakhist* to describe the nature of such government was Maimonides.

> "All the above rules apply only to a king whose coins circulate in the localities concerned, for then the inhabitants of the country have accepted him as their master and themselves as his servants. But if his coins do not circulate in the localities in question, he is regarded as a robber who uses force, and as a troop of armed bandits, whose laws are not binding. Moreover such a king and all his servants are deemed robbers in every respect." [8]

From this one can conclude that Maimonides would recognize only a strong—usually central [9]—government, the test of which is the circulation of its own coins. It appears that Maimonides would not apply *dina de-malkhuta dina* to a local fief which did not circulate its own coins. The actions of such rulers may nevertheless be recognized as acts of the king's agents. [10] This view of Maimonides that the circulation of his own coins is a sine qua non for recognition was followed by some rabbis, [11] but the majority of *halakhic* scholars who discuss this problem do not advance the circulation of coins as a condition precedent for the application of the legal maxim *dina de-malkhuta dina.*

Does *dina de-malkhuta dina* apply to Jewish kings in the land of Israel—or is this legal maxim purely a diaspora concept? Elsewhere I have discussed this question at length. [12] Maimonides' views on the subject are unclear. Although the majority opinion of *halakhic* scholars who flourished around Maimonides' times was that the principle did not apply to the land of Israel and the kingdom of Israel, it may well

---

8 M.T., *ibid.*

9 Mr. Jacob J. Schacter has pointed out to me that the right to mint coins was not limited only to the king or to a central government. The city of Barcelona, for example, enjoyed this power in the thirteenth century. See C. E. Chapman, *A History of Spain* (New York, 1918), 99.

10 *B.K.* 113b; *M.T. Gezelah* 8:11.

11 See S. Shilo, *ibid.*, 88.

12 *Ibid.*, 99-108.

be that Maimonides was the earliest of the rabbis to hold the opinion that *dina de-malkhuta dina* can also be applied to a Jewish government in the land of Israel—a view that began to gain acceptance at a much later period.

In his commentary to the Mishnah, Maimonides states that if a tax collector was duly appointed by the government and he does not demand illegal or exorbitant taxes, one must pay him the tax demanded —because "*dina de-malkhuta dina* ... and there is no difference concerning this between a Gentile king and a king of Israel."[13] The question we pose is—what is Maimonides referring to when he writes "concerning this"? Is he referring to the collection of taxes, or to the maxim *dina de-malkhuta dina*? If we explain "concerning this" as referring to the tax payment, we cannot conclude that Maimonides is of the opinion that *dina de-malkhuta dina* also encompasses "a king of Israel". What Maimonides is saying, according to this interpretation, is only that one may not evade payment of taxes under either Gentile or Jewish rule. This does not necessarily mean that the principle *dina de-malkhuta dina* is to be applied—generally—to both. On the other hand, it may well be that "concerning this" refers to the legal maxim *dina de-malkhuta dina* which was referred to in his earlier remarks in his commentary to the Mishnah. If so, then we may conclude that Maimonides explicitly applies *dina de-malkhuta dina* to both Gentile governments in the diaspora and Jewish governments in Israel.

Between the two possible interpretations, we tend to accept the narrower one mainly on the basis of comparing Maimonides' commentary to the Mishnah to what Maimonides stated in his *Mishneh Torah*. In the latter book, where Maimonides refers to a king of Israel, he writes that tax evasion from the king is prohibited, but he does not mention the principle of *dina de-malkhuta dina*.[14] In other words, there is a prohibition against tax evasion both under Israeli and Gentile rule, but the basis for this prohibition is different in each of the situations. The prohibition in connection with a Jewish king is based on that specific branch of the law concerning kings of Israel— a whole section of the *Mishneh Torah* is devoted to the kings of Israel —Israel's constitutional law. Tax evasion under a Gentile king in the diaspora is illegal because of the principle *dina de-malkhuta dina*.[15]

---

[13] Commentary to the *Mishnah*, *Nedarim*, 3:4.

[14] *M.T. Melakhim* 4:1.

[15] *Migdol Oz* to *M.T.*, *ibid.*, explains the rule of Maimonides concerning evading the taxes a king of Israel as based on *dina de-malkhuta dina*. We are

Equality under the law is another condition precedent for its acceptance. This principle was first clearly enunciated by Ibn Migash, [16] who was revered by Maimonides, [17] and Maimonides follows his view and even his wording. It is Maimonides that the later authorities quote most often, when they too enunciate and apply this principle of equality under the law. Thus writes Maimonides: "The general rule is: any law promulgated by the king to apply to everyone and not to one person alone is not deemed robbery. But whatever he takes from one particular person only, not in accordance with a law known to everyone but by doing violence to this person, is deemed robbery." [18]

It is undisputed that *dina de-malkhuta dina* does not apply to religious or ritual observance but only to civil matters. Interestingly, this obvious rule is almost never clearly enunciated. Maimonides does not write, when discussing *dina de-malkhuta dina* in Chapter Five of *hilkhot gezelah,* that this principle only encompasses monetary matters. However we can discern this basic rule from another section of Maimonides' code, albeit in passing. In his opening chapter dealing with the laws of original acquisition and gifts, he writes: "... where the law of the state is an established law to the effect that ... we follow the law of the state because *in all monetary matters* we abide by the law of the state." [19]

One of the cardinal questions concerning the range of recognized laws is whether, in principle, all the laws of the state must be kept or only those which are "in the king's interest"—namely, those laws which are promulgated in order to further the needs of the king or kingdom, and not those laws which arrange purely private matters between people. Such a question seems very strange to the modern jurist, but it is better understood in the light of medieval society and legal thought. I have discussed this *halakhic* question in depth elsewhere and I pointed out the differences of opinion between the *halakhic* scholars on this point. [20] What interests us here is Maimonides' view, but upon analysis of his position, we are left with a huge question mark.

---

of the opinion that this is not the correct interpretation of Maimonides' statement. Maimonides specifically refers to and bases his view on scripture and on laws discussed in the context of the laws of the king of Israel. See also responsa of *Rivash Ha-Hadashot,* No. 9, who also adduces Maimonides' *Mishnah* commentary.

16 See S. Shilo, *ibid.,* 109.

17 See Maimonides' introduction to his commentary to the *Mishnah.*

18 *M.T. Gezelah* 5:14.

19 *M.T. Zekhia* 1:15.

20 S. Shilo, *ibid.,* 131-184.

Some medieval rabbis are of the opinion that Maimonides accepts only those laws which are in the king's interest. This interpretation of Maimonides is based on Maimonides' voiding of gifts in writing drawn up in a Gentile court.[21] From this these *halakhists* conclude that Maimonides limits the scope of application of *dina de-malkhuta dina* by denying the legal maxim validity, concerning private law transactions between individuals, and, therefore, Maimonides accepts *dina de-malkhuta dina* only in the context of the king's interest.[22] We are of the opinion that Maimonides' statement of the law concerning documents of gifts drawn up in a Gentile court is in accordance with the view of the Geonim who explained the Talmudic source for this law —a discussion in the tractate Gittin[23]—according to a strict technical rule of interpretation[24], and therefore one can learn little, if anything, from that decision of Maimonides concerning the question we posed.

It is submitted that a strong case against the aforementioned view can be made on the basis of Maimonides' statement of the law in a different section of his code. Maimonides writes: "... but where there is an established law to the effect that only he who writes a deed or pays the price or does anything similar acquires title to real property, we follow the law of the state *because we abide by all the king's laws* in monetary matters."[25]

On the other hand, if one looks for a Maimonidean source which can be interpreted as restricting *dina de-malkhuta dina* to the king's interest, it is to the law of sales that one should turn. Concerning a vendor's warranty and responsibility if the property sold is seized by a Gentile third party, Maimonides writes: "This rule applies only if the vendee is deprived of the purchased article through a Jewish court, as when the articles purchased are movables that were stolen or robbed, or when it is land held adversely or when a creditor of the vendor has

---

21 *M.T. Malveh ve-Loveh* 27:1.

22 *Maggid Mishneh* to *M.T.*, *ibid.*; resp. of Rivash, no. 203.

23 *Gittin* 10b.

24 This rule concerning how one decides the *halakha* cannot be discussed in this article. See S. Shilo, *ibid.*, 47-52.

25 *M.T. Zekhia ibid.*; cp. *Tashbez* p. 1, no. 158; *M.T. Gezelah* 5:14, where Maimonides states that Jewish law recognizes "every law promulgated by the king." Rabbi Herzog in *The Main Institutions of Jewish Law* (London, 1936-1939), vol. 1, p. 29, writes that Maimonides constricts *dina de-malkhuta dina* to the king's interests. Only at the end of his volume, in a note, does he adduce the above-mentioned *halakhah* of Maimonides from *M.T. Zekhia*, and writes that perhaps from here one may conclude that Maimonides in fact gives *dina de-malkhuta dina* a much wider scope (*ibid.*, p. 376).

come and seized the article from the vendee for his debt—all through a Jewish court. However, if it is a Gentile who has seized the article from the vendor, whether *through the king's law* or through Gentile courts, then the vendor is not responsible. Even if the Gentile claims that the vendor has stolen or robbed the article from him and brings Gentile witnesses to testify, the vendor is nevertheless not answerable inasmuch as this is considered duress."[26] Here Maimonides ruled that if a Gentile seizes the property according to Jewish law, the seller is responsible. If, however, the property is seized according to "the king's law", the seller is not responsible, for such a seizure is deemed duress and a vendor is not responsible for seizure under duress. It is clear that this statement of Maimonides is incompatible with what Maimonides wrote in *hilkhot gezelah.*[27] Therefore there is an argument in favour of the view that Maimonides limits *dina de-malkhuta dina* to the king's interests.

Most medieval halakhists held that *dina de-malkhuta dina* does not apply to laws promulgated by the king himself but only to well-known ancient laws of the kingdom.[28] This view is better understood in the light of the prevailing opinion in medieval jurisprudence which recognized only ancient law as valid.[29] Fritz Kern writes: "For us law needs only one attribute in order to give it validity—it must directly or indirectly be sanctioned by the State. But in the Middle Ages, different attributes altogether were essential; mediaeval law must be 'old' law and must be 'good' law ... If law were not old and good law it was not law at all, even though it were formally enacted by the State ... For us law, from the time of its promulgation to that of its repeal, is neither old nor new, but simply exists. In the Middle Ages, it was a different matter altogether; age was then the most important quality even of objective law ... Law is old; new law is a contradiction for either new law is derived explicitly or implicitly from the old, or it conflicts with the old, in which case it is not lawful. The fundamental idea remains the same: the old law is the true law, and true law is the old law.

---

26 *M.T. Mekhirah,* 19:4.

27 Cp. *Kessef Mishneh* to *M.T. Mekhirah, ibid.*

28 Resp. *Bacalei ha-Tosafot* no. 12; Nov. Rashba B.B. 55a; Nov. Ritva B.B. 55a.

29 See F. Kern, *Kingship and Law in the Middle Ages* (trans.) (Oxford 1939), 149-151; H.O. Taylor, *ibid.*, vol. 2, 308; E. Lewis, *Medieval Political Ideas* (New York, 1954), vol. 1, 4, 243-244; S. Albeck, "Dina DeMalkhuta Dina be-Kehilot Sefarad", *Abraham Weiss Jubilee Volume* (New York, 1964), 115-116.

According to mediaeval ideas, therefore, the enactment of new law is not possible at all." [30] Maimonides' view on this question is unclear, although we submit that Maimonides probably disagrees with the aforementioned legal theory.

Maimonides does not deal directly with this question, but we may surmise from his writings—and some *halakhic* scholars do so surmise [31] —that Maimonides does not limit the application of *dina de-malkhuta dina* to "old law" only but he is willing to confer validity to "new law" as well. We can arrive at this conclusion, it is submitted, from Maimonides' phraseology concerning taxation and by carefully comparing Maimonides' position with his Talmudic source.

In his code, Maimonides writes: "The general rule is: any law *promulgated by the king* to apply to everyone and not to one person alone is not deemed robbery. But whatever he takes from one particular person only, not in accordance with a law known to everyone but by doing violence to this person, is deemed robbery. Consequently, when the king's treasurers or officers sell fields for the fixed tax due on such fields, their sale is valid. But the tax imposed on each individual may not be collected except from the person himself, and so, if they sell his field to recover the poll tax, it is not a legal sale *unless the king's law permits such action.*" [32] From this quote it appears that the king does have a right to promulgate new laws. This can readily be seen by Maimonides' opening words of his general rule—"any law promulgated by the king". Furthermore, the Talmudic precedent for Maimonides' aforementioned statement of the law is the Babylonian Talmud, *Bava Batra*, 55a. The Talmud states at the conclusion of a discussion concerning *dina de-malkhuta dina* that the king has a legal right to confiscate land for default of payment of the land tax but he has no right to do so when the poll tax is in default. Maimonides, in his usual casuistic manner of stating the law, seems to be following the Talmudic decision—until we come to his closing words, which, in fact, reverse the law, for "it is not a legal sale *unless the king's law permits such action*". In other words, if the king's law does permit such action, the sale is valid notwithstanding the change in the law from the accepted old law as found in the Talmud that the sale of a field for non-payment of the poll tax is invalid. If this ancient law is changed by the king such

---

30 F. Kern, *ibid.*

31 See *Maggid Mishneh* to *M.T. Gezelah,* 5:13.

32 *M.T. Gezelah,* 5:14.

change is accepted by the *halakhah* as valid—even if it is diametrically opposed to what was decided in the Talmud. [33]

Taxes

The king's right to tax his subjects was recognized in the Talmud and in all subsequent *halakhic* literature. However, both in the Talmud and subsequently in post-Talmudic *halakhic* sources, Jewish law differentiates between taxation which is legal and illegal taxation. [34] Maimonides, too, differentiates between recognized and illegal taxation. [35]

One specific question dealt with in the Talmud and later in diverse *halakhic* sources, which we have already alluded to, concerns the collection of taxes from someone who is not a tax-debtor, for the debts of another who cannot be reached at the time of collection. What are the rights of this innocent bystander against the tax debtor? Does he have a valid claim for reimbursement against the debtor for the amount taken from him by the authorities in every case or only in certain specific circumstances—or has he no right at all against the debtor? The law is clear that there is a valid claim against the debtor when the seizure was made for payment of certain specific taxes. But is this right against the debtor recognized in all cases of seizure by the government for another's debt due the king, or is such a legal right recognized only when the innocent bystander was forced to pay for certain specific well-known taxes but not for other claims of the government? We shall presently see that the answer to our query is not a simple one.

Maimonides decides that a right to compensation arises where "A is seized on account of a fixed tax payable annually by each individual or if he is seized on account of a requisition payable by each individual when the king or his army passes through". [36] It is not clear whether Maimonides limits the right to repayment to the two examples mentioned by him, or whether these two levies are but examples and there

---

[33] Cp. *M.T. Gezelah*, 5:12, which is based on *B.K.* 113b. The Talmud states that the king may force anyone found in the field to pay the owner's arrears of the land tax—except for a sharecropper who may not be compelled to pay such back taxes. When Maimonides codifies this law, he does not mention the Talmudic exception, i.e. the sharecropper. We submit that Maimonides excluded the exception because the law had changed and in his day the new law that everyone could be seized if found in the field, superseded the old law which excepted the sharecropper.

[34] *B.K.* 113a; *Nedarim* 28a.

[35] *M.T. Gezelah*, 5:11-12.

[36] *M.T. Hovel u-Mazik*, 8:6.

exists a right to reimbursement in all cases where the authorities seize A's property for the payment of a debt due from B.

There are valid arguments for and against both these possible interpretations of Maimonides' opinion. In chapter five of the laws of robbery, Maimonides recognizes all types of taxes and makes no distinction between the numerous varieties of taxes and levies—except of course for the blatantly illegal levies which are deemed robbery. Maimonides' recognition is based on *dina de-malkhuta dina*. If, when writing about the basic recognition of the king's taxes Maimonides makes no distinction between the various taxes, why should we assume that he makes distinctions when we come to the right of compensating one who was forced to pay such tax for another? On the other hand, it can be argued that since the general legal principle is that one does not have to reimburse another who paid his debt for him without having been asked to do so by the debtor [37] (we are aware of the fact that there although the payer was not asked to pay for the debtor, he did not pay of his free will), one must give a narrow interpretation to the exception to this rule—debts due the government—only to the two cases which Maimonides specifically mentions—cases which were adduced in the Talmud. It seems that R. Jacob b. Asher, author of the *Turim*, understood Maimonides' view as being a restrictive one—and R. Jacob disagrees with Maimonides' opinion. [38]

For a proper understanding of the next question—subjugation of the tax defaulter to the payer of the defaulter's debts—one must be very much aware of the Talmudic sources. In the Talmudic period a poll tax defaulter would be subjugated to one who paid the tax for him. It is still a moot question whether the Talmud was referring to Jewish or Gentile debtors, or to both. We are of the opinion that the Talmud referred to both. It is respectfully submitted that E. E. Urbach is correct

[37] *M.T. Malveh ve-Loveh*, 26:6; Sh. Ar. *H.M.* 128:1.

[38] *Tur* H.M., 128. A comparison between where this law is brought in the *Mishneh Torah* and where it is brought in the *Turim* is enlightening. Maimonides brings it in the middle of a chapter dealing with informers. In this chapter Maimonides brings a number of examples of decrees of the king which are not recognized by Jewish law for they are—in the eyes of Jewish law—illegal expropriations. It is here that Maimonides brings the law concerning one who is seized for another's debt, and he declares the right to reimbursement in the two specific cases which we brought in the text. This law is not brought again anywhere in his code. On the other hand, the author of the *Turim* brings this law in the chapter dealing with *ma^camad sheloshtan*, i.e. the laws of assignment of debts, that is, within the general framework of the problem of the payment of another's debt without having been asked to do so by the debtor.

when he writes [39] that the Talmud refers to Jewish tax defaulters. This, it appears, is also the Maimonidean view. Our position is based on the context around which this statement concerning subjugation of the tax defaulter is brought. One source is in the Babylonian Talmud, *Bava Mezia* [40]—in the context of a discussion of the laws of interest between Jews. It follows that the reference sandwiched in between two clear discussions of interest between Jews, and which is connected with the discussion of the laws of interest, is also referring to a Jewish tax defaulter. The other basic Talmudic source [41] brings up the question whether such a slave—the tax defaulter who was subjugated—needs a bill of manumission in order to be freed. This source may very well be referring to both Jews and Gentiles who were subjugated.

It would seem that Maimonides differentiates between these two Talmudic sources and would probably explain the former Talmudic passage (*Bava Mezia*) as referring to Jews, and the latter (*Yevamot*)—to Gentiles. A complete picture of Maimonides' conception can be arrived at only by carefully analyzing all four different places where Maimonides discusses this *halakhah* in his code. [42]

In the laws of robbery Maimonides writes: "Similarly if a king decrees that whoever pays the fixed tax due from any individual may compel the one delinquent to be subjugated to him, and then an Israelite comes and pays the tax due from some other impoverished Israelite, he may make him work more than would be usual, for the king's law is binding. But he must not make him work like a slave". [43] Ra^cavad does not add a gloss here, and, prima facie, he agrees with Maimonides' statement of the law. However, upon turning to the laws of slaves in Maimonides' code, we find that although the aforementioned statement of the law is repeated almost verbatim, here Ra^cavad vehemently disagrees with Maimonides.

The following is Maimonides' wording in the laws of slaves: "If the king decrees that whoever does not pay the fixed tax due from any individual may compel the one delinquent to be subjugated to him who has paid the tax for him, it is permitted to use such person more than

39 E. E. Urbach, "Hilkhot Avadim ke-Mekor Le-Historia Ha-Hevratit Biyemai ha-Bayit ha-Sheni u-Betkufat ha-Mishna ve-ha-Talmud", *Zion* 25 (1960), 141-189. And see M. Elon's dissenting view in his *Herut ha-Perat be-Darkhei Geviat Hov ba-Mishpat ha-Ivri* (Jerusalem, 1964), 16, note 31.

40 *B.M.* 73b.

41 *Yevamot* 46a.

42 *M.T. Gezelah* 5:16; *Malveh ve-Loveh* 5:17; *Avadim* 1:8 and 9:4.

43 *M.T. Gezelah, ibid.*

is usual but not so much as a slave."[44] In spite of the fact that the decision and even the wording are identical, here, and only here, does Raᶜavad write a gloss stating, in very strong language, that Maimonides' interpretation of the relevant Talmudic passage is errroneous. Raᶜavad explains the Talmudic passage, which undoubtedly was the source for Maimonides' statement, as referring to the following position: if one paid another's taxes for him and as a result the debtor labors for the payer-creditor and works more than is needed to cover the debt—is this considered interest and therefore illegal, or not? The Talmud concluded that this is not *halakhically* considered a loan situation but is classified as a sale since the king has a right to sell his subjects as slaves if they default in the payment of their taxes.[45]

It is submitted that both Maimonides and Raᶜavad agree in principle, but that Raᶜavad misunderstood Maimonides' meaning. It appears that Raᶜavad understood Maimonides' phrase "to use such a person more than is usual" to mean that such a person was considered almost enslaved. Secondly, the placing of this law within the law of slaves also tends to lead one to interpret Maimonides' words in such a light. That explains, somewhat, why Raᶜavad wrote his gloss here and not in the other section of Maimonides' code where it is also included, in the laws of robbery. In our opinion Maimonides, too, agrees that the subjugation that is permitted is not quasi-slavery, and the phrase "to use such person more than is usual" means the same type of subjugation that Raᶜavad refers to—the duty to work for another until the debt paid by the latter is repaid fully by the debtor's labor. This can be deduced from Maimonides' third statement concerning this law—in the section dealing with creditors and debtors. He writes: "Where the law of the king is that he who has paid the head tax for a person in default may subjugate the person whose tax he has paid, it is permissible to do so even if the value of the man's service is greater than the tax paid for him. And so it is in all similar cases."[46] It appears that this is what Maimonides means when he writes, in the other sections, about using such a person more than is usual. If so, there is no difference of opinion between Maimonides and Raᶜavad.[47]

---

44 *M.T. Avadim* 1:8.

45 Raʾavad to *M.T.*, *ibid.*

46 *M.T. Malveh ve-Loveh*, *ibid.*

47 It seems quite clear that Maimonides explains the discussion in *Yevamot* concerning manumission as referring to Gentile debtors only. Apparently basing himself on the discussion in *Yevamot*, Maimonides writes: "If a Gentile king . . .

The next question under discussion—the payment of taxes by *halakhic* scholars—is an example of a problem discussed in theory and demanding a solution in practice not only in Talmudic times but throughout the ages—Maimonides' time and place being no exception. The Talmud explicitly exempts the *halakhic* scholars from payment of various taxes. Does the scholar have to pay taxes to the king's agents or can he demand that the Jewish community itself pay his taxes for him?

In countries under Moslem rule, both Jewish and Christian clergy were usually not exempted from the poll tax. [48] Not all Moslems who performed religious functions on behalf of the community were exempt: holders of certain positions in the Moslem religious hierarchy were exempted while holders of other positions were not. [49] In western Europe, it was not uncommon for Jewish scholars to receive governmental exemptions from paying taxes. The reason for this policy seems to be that since the times of the Roman Empire secular scholars were exempted from payment of taxes. Afterwards, a similar exemption was given to the Catholic clergy and so the Jewish "clergy" were also exempted. [50]

---

if his law is that he who does not pay the tax should be sold or that anyone who does such and such or fail to do so shall be sold, then his law is law and a slave who is bought according to that law has the status of a heathen slave in every respect," *M.T. Avadim*, 9:4. If such a slave has the status of a heathen slave in every respect, he must surely need a writ of manumission to be freed—as stated in *Yevamot*. See, also, *Kessef Mishneh* to *Avadim*, 9:4; *Bet Hadash* to *Tur* Y.D., *sec.* 267 s.v. *eved ivri*; *Giddulei Terumah*, 46, 4:16.

48 See S. Baron, *ibid.*, 76.

49 See the very informative responsum on this question, *Tashbez* Sec. 3, no. 254, where Simon b. Zemah Duran discusses the situation in his time both under Moslem and Christian rule.

50 This exemption for scholars dates back to before the second century C.E., and was expanded by Constantine the Great. It was widened by Charlemagne in 800 and enlarged even further by Kaiser Frederick Barbarosa in 1158. During the thirteenth and fourteenth centuries these rights were discussed at length by the jurists and in the years 1295 and 1297 Philip the Fourth of France greatly widened their scope. In defending this move against his critics, Philip the Fourth eloquently described the life of the scholars and university students, a description which bears a remarkable resemblance to the life of their Jewish counterparts studying in the European *Yeshivot.* Philip argued that "we believe it right to have great concern for the hardships, exertions, the sleepless nights, the drudgery, the deprivation, the tribulations and the perils which the scholars undergo to seek the precious pearl of knowledge, and to consider how they have left their friends, their kinsmen and their native lands, how they have abandoned worldly goods and family fortunes, to come from distant parts to drink of the waters flowing from the fountain of life...". See S. Baron, *ibid.*; S. Baron, *The*

Returning to Jewish law, the Talmud exempts *halakhic* scholars from paying taxes.[51] It appears that this exemption is very wide and covers all types of taxes and levies. However, near the end of the Geonic period, R. Hananel b. Hushiel explained the Talmudic source restrictively. R. Hananel explains that the Talmud refers only to those types of taxes and levies which were levied on the community as a whole. In such circumstances, when the communal leaders divide the lump sum demanded between the community's individual members, the scholars are not to be included. It follows—although R. Hananel did not say so explicitly but later *halakhic* authorities explained his view in the following manner—that if the authorities specifically name who is to pay a tax, and a scholar is included in the list, he must pay the tax himself and may not demand that the Jewish community pay his tax for him, since the law of the land is law.[52] This stand is followed by many *halakhic* authorities.[53]

A dissenting view—which also had many followers—was first enunciated by Maimonides. In three different sources—and types of sources—in his commentary to the *Mishnah,* in his code and in a responsum, Maimonides takes a different view than that of R. Hananel. According to Maimonides a scholar is exempt from paying all taxes, even if the governmental authorities explicitly declared that a particular scholar must pay a tax. The Jewish community, declares Maimonides, must pay the tax for the scholar. In fact, it seems that in Maimonides' day, at least in the Moslem countries around the Mediterranean, the Jewish community usually did pay the scholars' taxes, including the poll tax.[54]

Early in his life, Maimonides wrote: "The Torah also exempted all halakhic scholars from *all governmental levies* such as levies, anona, taxes *specifically placed on the person* which is known as a head tax, and *the community must pay them for him* ... and this is the law of our Torah just as the Torah exempted the priests from [paying] the

---

Jewish Community (Philadelphia, 1942), vol. 2, 14-15, 274; P. Kibre, "Scholarly Privileges: Their Roman Origins and Medieval Expression", *A.H.R.* 59 (1953-54), 543-567; G. J. Campbell, "Clerical Immunities in France During the Reign of Philip III," *Speculum,* 39 (1964), 404.

[51] *B.B.* 8a.

[52] See Novella of Nahmanides, *B.B.* 8a; *Bet Yosef* to *Tur H.M.* section 163, 11.

[53] See S. Shilo, *ibid.,* 253-257.

[54] See S. D. Goitein, *A Mediterranean Society,* vol. 2, *The Community* (Los Angeles, London, 1971), 121, 386.

half-shekel."[55] The same decision, although based on a different Biblical verse, is given in his code,[56] and this principle served as the basis for one of Maimonides' responsa where he wrote very harshly of those who took tax payments from the scholars. Maimonides writes to the *halakhic* scholar who was forced by the community to pay a tax, that their action is tantamount to robbery and that the money in the hands of the community is the take of thieves.[57] These two views, that of R. Hananel and that of Maimonides, served as the basis for further discussions for centuries afterwards, and even in our times the question is still moot—some present day rabbis favoring Rabbi Hananel's view and others Maimonides'.[58]

Penalties and Expropriations

Linked closely to the question of taxation are two other problems—the right of the king to punish his subjects and his right to expropriate their property.

The king's right to punish his subjects is mentioned in the Talmud. All post-Talmudic rabbinic authorities agree that under certain circumstances Jewish law will recognize such a right;[59] problems arise because of the differences of opinion concerning the correct application of this principle and the different shades of opinion surrounding this question.

Maimonides states: "... a king ... decrees that if one breaks a specified law, he shall forfeit all his property to the palace ... none of these cases is deemed robbery ... Similarly, if a king becomes angry with one of his servants or ministers among his subjects and con-

---

55 Commentary to the *Mishnah, Avot* 4:7. The reason or analogy given by Maimonides—the half-shekel—is not the one given in the Talmud. Here we have a very good example of Maimonides' failure to rely on his basic Talmudic sources for explaining a legal rule. Cp. J. Levinger, *Darkhei ha-Mahashava ha-Hilkhatit shel haRambam* (Jerusalem, 1965), 88-116.

56 See the previous note. Here in the Code Maimonides cites the same proof-text, Hosea 8:10, as is adduced in the Talmud, even though another verse also cited in the Talmud, from Deuteronomy, might have been preferable, since a verse from the Five Books of Moses is stronger proof than a verse from the later scriptures. Maimonides' choice seems to have been made on the grounds that the Talmudic explanation of the passage from Hosea is much closer to its simple meaning than the explanation given to the verse from Deuteronomy. See *B.B.* 8a; *M.T. Talmud Torah*, 6:10.

57 Resp. Maimonides, no. 325.

58 See S. Shilo, *ibid.*

59 See *ibid.*, 38-41. As to Maimonides' explanation and codification of these sources, which will not be discussed in this article, see *ibid.*, 270-271.

fiscates his field or his courtyard, this is not deemed robbery and one is permitted to benefit from it for the law of all kings permits them to confiscate all property of those ministers with whom they are displeased, and the king has therefore cancelled the owner's original right to it so that the courtyard or field in question is regarded as ownerless, and if one buys it from the king he becomes its lawful owner. But if a king takes the courtyard or field of one of the citizens contrary to the laws he has promulgated, he is deemed a robber and the original owner may recover it from anyone who buys it from the king." [60]

Maimonides recognizes the king's right to punish, but with certain restrictions. In the above text Maimonides speaks only of the punishment of expropriation, but it would seem that this is only an example and other types of punishment would also be recognized by him. The principles here enunciated by Maimonides are constantly quoted by later authorities as a precedent when they discuss the king's right, in general, to punish his subjects and to expropriate their property.

An example of a confiscation which took place during Maimonides' life, and about which he gave *halakhic* approval, is found in one of his responsa. Sacred books were plundered from a synagogue and the question arose as to the legal rights of one who bought the books from the plunderers. Maimonides answers that if the spoils were taken "without the Sultan's permission", then the purchaser of the spoils is deemed a buyer of stolen property from a thief. But "if this plunder was ordered by the Sultan, the buyer becomes the legal owner and the laws of sacred property are nullified". [61]

It appears, however, from another responsum of Maimonides, that Maimonides does not recognize such a right of confiscation. This latter responsum, on the face of it, is not in accord with the former responsum and with Maimonides' statement of the law in his code.

Maimonides was asked concerning property which was willed to charity by a testator who had no legal heirs. The sultan got word of the will and since the deceased had no heirs he decided to expropriate the deceased's property, which was willed for the upkeep of scholars in their Torah study. The question posed to Maimonides was: "is the

---

[60] *M.T. Gezelah* 5:12-13.

[61] Resp. Maimonides, no. 209. Also noted in *Shitah Mekubetzet* to *B.M.* 24b. In explaining the source of this law, Maimonides quotes the words of the Talmud (*B.T. Nedarim* 62a; *B.T. Bekhorot* 50a; *B.T.A.Z.* 52b) that from the verse in Ezekiel 7:22: "... and robbers shall enter into it and profane it" the holiness of sacred articles is nullified when they are plundered.

person in charge of the *hekdesh* permitted to swear falsely to the authorities to the effect that the property is in fact his own private property"? Maimonides' answer is a very ringing yes. [62]

Much can be deduced from this responsum. The sultan has no right to confiscate the property of one who dies without leaving any heirs—at least not if the property was willed to another. The legal maxim *dina de-malkhuta dina* does not apply here. Further, one may even swear falsely in order to defeat a possible expropriation even though swearing falsely is a cardinal sin according to Jewish law and by doing so one transgresses against one of the Ten Commandments. Maimonides not only permits such action—he orders it. In so doing he clearly enunciates an important rule concerning the Jewish people and their attitude toward the government. The rule is that it is a *religious duty* of each and every Jew to combat any attempt made by the authorities to cause damage to another Jew, where such action on the part of the authorities is not recognized by Jewish law. A Jew who swears falsely to save even a *peruta* of another's property "is performing a *mitzvah* and is complying with the words of the Sages of Blessed Memory."

Why did Maimonides decide as he did? To answer this question one must be familiar with the historical background of the place and period referred to. In Moslem North Africa, although the individual religious communities were allowed judicial autonomy, their right was constantly encroached upon when dealing with estates. Such encroachment was in fact illegal and was an easy way of filling the coffers of those in power. S. D. Goitein writes, as part of a lengthy discussion of the problem, that "next to the poll tax the appropriation of estates by the government caused constant concern to the people speaking to us through the Geniza records". [63] Surely we have here an example of what Maimonides discussed in his code—"if a king takes the courtyard or field of one of the citizens, contrary to the law he has promulgated, he is deemed a robber ... whatever he takes from one particular person only, not in accordance with a law known to everyone but by doing violence to this person, is deemed robbery." [64] One may add another explanation for the *halakhic* opposition to interference with the Jewish law of inheritance: the laws of inheritance are sometimes classified as

[62] Resp. Maimonides, no. 210.

[63] S. D. Goitein, *ibid.*, 394. The question of confiscation of estates is extensively dealt with on pages 394-398.

[64] *M.T. Gezelah*, 5:13-14.

belonging to the realm of purely religious law and, therefore, the maxim *dina de-malkhuta dina* would not apply to them. [65, 66]

Documents of a Gentile Court

The recognition of documents of a Gentile court, as specifically stated in the *Mishnah* [67], was explained in the Talmud as based on *dina de-malkhuta dina.* The Talmud records two views as to the scope of the *Mishnah's* ruling. One view is that all documents (except for bills of divorce and writs of manumission) are recognized. The other is that only documents which attest to a transaction—such as a bill of sale—are valid, but documents which in themselves effect a transfer—such as a deed of gift—are not valid. [68] Maimonides, in accordance with the Geonim who preceded him [69], accepts the second view, thus limiting the scope of recognition to declaratory documents and not to constitutive documents.

Maimonides' view concerning documents of a Gentile court was formulated in his early years and hardly changed at all throughout his

---

[65] See B. Lipkin, "Hatnaᶜat ha-Gormim be-Devarim she-be-Mamon, (ius dispositivum) ba-Mishpat haᶜIvri", *Sinai* 35 (1954), 111-126.

The facts of the case as discussed in the responsum of Maimonides show that the authorities knew of the situation as the result of information given to them by an informer. Perhaps Maimonides took this too into account when he responded, for we find a similar view of his concerning the acts of a king as the result of the information supplied by an informer in the *Mishneh Torah.* Although it seems that in the situation he discusses the king's act is legal because of *dina deᵓmalkhuta dina,* we find that Maimonides does not accept the legality of the action. He writes: "Thus if a king decrees that wine or fodder or the like must be brought to him, and an informer comes forward and says that a certain person has a store of wine or fodder at a specified place, and the king's men go and take it, he must pay compensation," *M.T. Hovel u-Mazik,* 8:3.

[66] The problem of government interference with estates was one which plagued the Jews in many places, and other halakhic authorities were also of the opinion that one could or should evade such governmental interference. See H. Z. Hirschberg, *Toldot HaYehudim bᵓAfrika ha-Zefonit* (Jerusalem, 1965), vol. 1, 147. Hirschberg, in discussing the question, does not cite this responsum of Maimonides nor another one from a North African rabbi, R. Simon b. Zemach Duran, *Tashbez* sec. 3, no. 5. We find a similar situation in Christian Spain—see resp. of R. Asher b. Yehiel, 66:9—and also in Ashkenaz—see resp. of R. Haim Or Zarua, no. 111. These, obviously, are from later periods than that under discussion but it seems that this was the situation in general both in the early and the late Middle Ages, with fluctuations in the governments' attitudes from time to time.

[67] *M. Gittin* 1:5.

[68] *Gittin* 10b.

[69] For the view of the Geonim, see S. Shilo, *ibid.,* 47-52, 54-56.

lifetime. In his early *Mishnah* commentary, Maimonides expounded a number of principles: (a) Both the Gentile witnesses which appear before the Gentile court, and the judges must be known to be honest and not amenable to bribes. This condition precedent concerning witnesses (not judges) seems to be an innovation of Maimonides; (b) In the document itself, there must be a statement that the witnesses themselves saw the transfer of payment; (c) Jewish law recognizes only probative documents and not constitutive documents.

In his code,[70] Maimonides adds—against the views of his teachers—that bills of indebtedness are also recognized. However, he adds, in order to be recognized the witnesses must write in the bill that they saw the making of the loan itself. Maimonides then proceeds to give us a list of different types of documents not recognized by Jewish law—a list which includes admissions, gifts, compromises, waivers, and also bills of indebtedness which do not include the phrase attesting to the witnesses' own observance of the loan being made.

Concerning the evidence needed to prove that the witnesses and judge do not accept bribes, it may be that Maimonides took a less stringent view in his code than in his Mishnah commentary. It would appear that in his commentary Maimonides demanded positive proof that the Gentiles concerned did not take bribes—or at least positive proof of an honest reputation. However, in the *Mishneh Torah,* Maimonides is willing to accept negative proof, i.e. evidence that it is not known that these Gentiles do take bribes.

Another decision of Maimonides is that collection on such an instrument may be made only out of free property (*nekhasim benei horin*) and not from property in the hands of a third party (*nekhasim meshubadim*), since deeds in Gentile courts are "not accompanied by publicity and the obligor's vendees are not presumed to have known what was done by the Gentile". It also appears from this lengthy *halakhah* in the section dealing with debtors and creditors, that a deed in a Gentile court, too, must be "prepared in accordance with the formal requirements of instruments used in Israel, which cannot be forged or added to or diminished from". If the deed is not so drawn up, even though it complies with all other conditions precedent to its recognition by Jewish law, such a deed is deemed invalid.

Even though Maimonides agrees that, theoretically, one can recognize sundry documents of a Gentile court, it seems that this was so in theory

---

[70] *M.T. Malveh ve-Loveh,* 27:1.

but not in practice. In one of his responsa [71] which, we submit, was written after Maimonides completed writing his *Mishneh Torah*, i.e. after 1180, [72] Maimonides discusses a lease written in a Gentile court. [73] Maimonides invalidates the lease and explains that "all that was done in the laws of the Gentiles concerning this matter is invalid and a lease according to the Gentiles is like a sale witnessed by them and is not valid ***unless certain conditions are fulfilled which are now not found ...***". What conditions is Maimonides referring to which are not found in his day? We submit, on the basis of the historical sources which we have, that Maimonides was hinting at the rampant bribery given to the Moslem judges, which was notorious during Maimonides' time. Not only was it an open secret that bribery was part and parcel of the Moslem judiciary; often the official witnesses who were carefully screened and chosen for their uprightness—the *udul*—would also frequently give false testimony. [74]

A more technical point to be gleaned from this responsum is that Maimonides classified a written lease as a declaratory document, akin to a bill of sale. Therefore, in principle, such a document would be recognized by Jewish law if all the other conditions precedent for recognition were present. However, such a position is a difficult one to take if one carefully compares the document mentioned in the responsum with Maimonides' statement of the law in his code. True, if the instrument of lease is drawn up so that the witnesses to the lease state in the document that they witnessed the payment of the rent, such a document could certainly be classified as similar to a bill of sale or an instrument of debt which are both declaratory and which Maimonides recognizes in principle. However, from the responsum itself, it appears that payment of the rent was not witnessed by the witnesses to the document and, therefore, according to Maimonides' narrow view which validates only declaratory documents, such a lease should be automatically disqualified by Maimonides.

In spite of the state of affairs in the Moslem courts, the Jews

---

[71] Resp. of Maimonides, no. 408.

[72] This is the more or less accepted date of completion, although there is a good argument in favor of 1178. See I. Twersky, "The Beginnings of Mishneh Torah Criticism", in *Biblical and Other Studies*, ed. A. Altmann (Cambridge, Mass., 1963), 161-182.

[73] The reason for dating this responsum as after 1180 is based on the following. In 1180 a certain *takkanah* was instituted by Maimonides and his court—see notes of Blau to responsa nos. 27 and 347—and in the responsum under discussion the questioner refers to this *takkanah*.

[74] See S. D. Goitein, *ibid.*, 365, 368.

would nevertheless occasionally, or perhaps even frequently, draw up their documents in Gentile courts [75] or draw up their deeds in accordance with Jewish law and then go to the Gentile courts to have a similar document drawn up. [76] The reason for such a course of action can be understood from another responsum of Maimonides. He writes: "Everyone who owes a debt according to Jewish law is obliged, if his creditor so desires, to write a note of indebtedness in the laws of the Gentiles. Then the Arabic instrument is deposited in escrow and if the debtor does not comply with what he is obliged to do according to Jewish law he can then be sued according to the laws of the Gentiles." [77]

Conclusions

Most of the basic principles concerning the interpretation, conditions precedent and scope of the legal maxim *dina de-malkhuta dina* are found in Maimonides' works—mainly in his *Mishneh Torah*. Concerning some of these principles, Maimonides follows the *halakhah* as it developed until his time, but concerning others, we find Maimonides an innovator. His original contribution had a lasting influence on the *halakhic* scholars who came after him. Here, in conclusion, we will point out a few of the major contributions of Maimonides to a better understanding of the Amora Samuel's dictum that *dina de-malkhuta dina.*

It was Maimonides who laid the foundations for a theoretical conception of the basis for this far-reaching legal maxim. It is the people who accept the king, *therefore* the law of the state is law. The logical next step to be deduced from this outlook, is—where there is no acceptance by the people, the law of the state is not law in the eyes of Jewish law. The type of government to which *dina de-malkhuta dina* applies is described by Maimonides, and here too he is the first rabbinic scholar clearly to enunciate what qualities of the king or kingdom are a sine qua non for their recognition. It is not clear whether Maimonides is of the opinion that *dina de-malkhuta dina* applies to Jewish kings in the land of Israel or only to Gentile kings in the diaspora. If Mai-

---

75 See, e.g., resp. of Maimonides, no. 27; S. D. Goitein, *ibid.*, 400.

76 See, e.g., resp. of Maimonides, no. 26.

77 Resp. of Maimonides, no. 193. Cp. *M.T. Sanhedrin*, 26:7: "... If the hand of the Gentiles is powerful and his opponent is a man of violence and the claimant is unable to recover what is due to him through the Jewish court, he must first summon him to appear before Jewish judges; if his opponent refuses to appear, the plaintiff obtains permission from the court to recover his claim through the Gentile court."

monides does hold that *dina de-malkhuta dina* applies to both, then he is breaking new ground, since it is only after his times that this view was clearly aired and eventually became predominant and perhaps even prevailing. It seems that Maimonides also accepted "new law" and not only "old law"—a view which was contrary to the opinion of many medieval *halakhic* scholars. Maimonides took a very strong stand in favor of scholars who claimed tax exemptions on the basis of Talmudic precedent, and even if the government would levy taxes specifically on scholars, Maimonides orders the Jewish community to pay taxes for the scholars. This view was not in accord with his *halakhic* predecessors' view and Maimonides' stand is undoubtedly novel.

In discussing Maimonides and his *halakhic* writings, we have an excellent opportunity to see the interplay of theory and practice. Although the most important source is his *Mishneh Torah,* we have also referred to his *Mishnah* Commentary and, of special interest, his responsa. Through his responsa we had an excellent opportunity to see some of his codified views put into actual practice. Although there is usually no conflict between the two, at times we did point out some diversity and at times we were able to explain away a seeming contradiction. Keen analysis of the sources is both imperative and fruitful. We have seen that in a number of instances only after close scrutiny of both his code and his responsa can we arrive at a correct understanding of Maimonides' view. This is especially so in connection with problems of taxation, expropriations and documents drawn up in a Gentile court.

What is most important for the jurist is the law itself. However, one must also be very much aware—especially when dealing with a topic such as ours—of both the general political and legal theory of the period under discussion, and the actual historical setting of the times. The two latter played an important role in the development of the former. The Gentile jurists' conception of the foundation upon which the king's right to rule rests, and the concept of old law and new law are just two examples of extrinsic legal concepts which helped shape the *halakhah.* Without our knowledge of day to day life of the Jews under Moslem rule during Maimonides' lifetime, Maimonides' discussions of expropriations and of documents executed in a non-Jewish court would remain puzzling to us. Ecclesiastes would undoubtedly agree that this triple cord too—dogmatic *halakhah,* secular political and legal theory, and the historical background—will not quickly be severed.

[20]

8

Power And Authority
Halachic Stance of the Traditional Community and its Contemporary Implications

Menachem Elon

On the face of it, a discussion of the Jewish Political tradition should focus on such examples as the history of the kingdoms of David and Solomon, the Hasmonean period, or at least the days of the *Nesiim* (Patriarchs) in Israel, or the *Roshei Golah* (Exilarchs) in Babylonia. Indeed, one might ask, what does the Jewish community of the Middle Ages—a period when Israel had no King or *Nasi*, a period repudiated by the architects of modern Jewish attitudes—have to do with our political tradition? But the concept on which this perplexity is founded—a concept which is deeply rooted and commonly accepted by many—is both erroneous and misleading. On the contrary, Jewish internal rule, as embodied by the *Kehillah*, the characteristics of such Jewish autonomy, the problems encountered, and the tremendous creative vitality revealed in the establishment of the framework and content of this autonomy—all these are of special, far-reaching significance today.

The Autonomy Of The Jewish Community (Kehillah)

When we speak of the *Kehillah* as an autonomous body which fulfilled internal political functions in all areas of communal life—legal, social and economic—and which imposed its rules and regulations upon its members, we are speaking of the *kehillah* as it began to emerge in the middle of the tenth century, continuing until the period of the emancipation at the end of the eighteenth century. Indeed, Yitzhak Baer has already pointed out that "the foundations of the *kehillah*, which remained in existence until the Enlightenment, were laid mainly in the first generations of the Second Temple period."[1] and it is to this early period that we must ascribe several Tannaic sources which discuss the laws governing *bnei ha'ir* (the citizens, literally "the children of the city") and *anshei ha'ir* ("the people of the city").[2] But, for this long period of history, there remain no records of the special autonomous powers of the community in the sphere of local and judicial rule.

Towards the end of the Gaonic period, a basic change occurred in Jewish life, giving rise to a change in the status and role of the *kehillah*. Until then, there had generally been one center with spiritual hegemony over the scattered Jewish communities. This center was originally been Eretz Israel; later it was Babylonia. In the tenth century, a fundamental change took place in this situation. As a result of various external and internal factors, the Babylonian center declined and, with its decline, the hegemony of a single Jewish center ceased to exist. A series of centers arose, functioning alongside one another, none of which was recognized to have spiritual hegemony over the others. In addition to the centers in Babylonia, North Africa and Italy, in the course of time other centers arose in Germany, Spain, France, Eretz Israel, Turkey, the Balkan countries, Poland, Lithuania and elsewhere. Although there were occasionally great spiritual leaders whose authority was recognized by the various communities, as a rule, each center was autonomous in most matters of law and justice, and looked for guidance to its own halakhic scholars. There was no center which issued decisions binding on all the communities of the diaspora.

This great historic change led to a modification in the character and status of the *kehillah*. The scope of the *kehillah's* jurisdiction and control was extended to cover the entire range of its members' activity, shaping their social life and spiritual image. It enjoyed a large measure of autonomy: it had its own internal governing bodies, on which both elected and appointed representatives served; it fulfilled the educational and social needs of its members; it had its own courts with the authority to deal with civil, administrative and, to a certain extent, even criminal cases; it levied and collected taxes in order to pay the tax imposed on the community by the non-Jewish rulers, as well as to finance communal services. Often a federation of several *kehillot* whould perform a large number of these functions, including the maintenance of governing bodies and the collection of taxes.

In order to exercise this autonomy, two prerequisites—one external and one internal—had to be met. The external factor was the *opportunity* granted to a group of people living as a minority under foreign rule to exercise autonomy, and the *readiness* of the foreign regime to grant this autonomy. As this is not the major concern of our discussion,[3] let us note briefly that both opportunity and readiness existed. The reason for this was rooted in the political-legal understanding of the concepts of government and jurisdiction which prevailed until the eighteenth century, as well as in the fiscal and social relationships existing between the regime and the various classes—including aliens—living within its jurisdiction. The state was not interested in centralization. It was a corporate state made up of various autonomous bodies—the aristocracy, the burghers, the guilds, etc.—which often vied with one another or with the central authority. At times, the Jewish community served as a point of controversy between the various groups and the central regime. The judicial system was based on personal-group identification, and the state recognized the legal systems of the various groups living within it. In this political-legal environment, a legally autonomous Jewish entity was able to exist. The willingness of the central regime to grant the Jews such autonomy stemmed from various considerations: a certain degree of tolerance towards other religions, varying according to time and place; religious and ideological considerations; and, finally and most importantly, fiscal considerations. The government felt that it was both its duty and its "right" to levy heavy taxes on the Jews—"tolerance money"—for the privilege of being allowed to live on its land. In order to collect these taxes, the government found it more convenient to demand the entire tax from the Jewish community as a whole. For this purpose, the community was allowed to exist as a cohesive, autonomous unit with leaders responsible for delivering the taxes collected by each communal organization from its members.

The second factor accounting for the existence of Jewish autonomy—and, in the last analysis, the primary factor—was the desire of the Jews themselves to maintain their own internal authority. They had the necessary intellectual capacity and practical ability to create the framework and organs for their self-government, both of which were suited to the prevailing historio-social conditions in the diaspora.

The Authority of Communal Government—Legal Problems

It is clear that internal Jewish rule during this period did not mean the rule of the individual—as embodied by a king, *nasi*, or *rosh golah*—but rather communal rule, either in the early, simple meaning of rule by the entire community or by representatives chosen or appointed to represent the community and constituting its political system. Of course, since this was a society whose members and leaders both recognized the Torah and the *halakhah* (Jewish law) as the supreme authority, communal government, in the form of the *kehillah*, had to be based on *halakhah*. This brings us to the following question: what was the place of such communal rule in the world of *halakhat* ?

Let us clarify the problem. A basic component of the concept of government is the principle of authority, the power of government to compel the individual to obey the law; hence government is classified under public as opposed to private law. The commonly accepted definition of these two branches of law, applicable to Jewish law as well, is worth noting here. Public law includes "a large number of norms issued by public institutions intended to be binding upon the individual.... This power to compel is what constitutes the *authoritative* character of these norms; the sum total of the authoritative norms of the state is known as the *public law* of that state."[4] On the other hand, where the norms of the private law are concerned, we find that: "What is common to these norms or transactions is the lack of con pulsive power over the individual without his consent; that is to say, they lack an authoritative quality., This set of norms or transactions is called *private law*."[5]

This principle—the right to compel someone to act in a certain way without his consent—is also found in Jewish public law, in the authority of the king, and later of the *nasi* or the *rosh golah* who, from an historical and halakhic point of view, were regarded as continuations of the monarchy and its authority. But the community, or its representatives, did not, at that time, possess this authoritative power. In fact, according to the *halakhah*, the community—or the *kehillah*—had no such power. According to the Talmud, ten, twenty or even a hundred Jews living in a community are considered partners and the laws of partnership—or private law in general—does not provide for compulsion; rather, any decision requires the consent of each and every individual. To quote Rabbi Asher ben Jehiel (Rosh), "One individual restricts the actions of another, and the individual restricts the actions of the majority."[6]

Because of this, the scholars and communal leaders were faced with a basic problem: can a community, or its representatives, exercise authority without possessing compulsive power over the individual; that is to say, is the decision of the majority binding upon the minority, and is such a decision enforceable. Although the Torah states, "By a majority you are to decide," this rule was interpreted by the scholars of the Talmud as referring to halakhic decisions or legal judgments which must, according to law, be made by the majority, or regarding the majority as a legal presumption (*Praesumptio Juris*), but not to the right of a majority of the community to impose its will on the minority. (It should be noted here that, during the twelfth century, the prevailing legal view in Europe—unlike that of Roman law—was that decisions of the public were valid only if they were taken unanimously. In controversies between the majority and a minority, the majority had to win the consent of the minority through negotiation or by force. Thus, according to a few halakhic scholars, the foremost of them Rabbenu Tam, the decision of the majority was not binding upon the minority. But this solution was unacceptable to the majority of halakhic scholars, for it did not provide a basis for the establishment and maintenance of orderly communal government.[7])

This problem was only one among many. The social, economic and commercial life of the Jews, different in every country of their dispersion, and the relations of each Jewish community with the non-Jewish environment and the general government, created many new problems in the areas of civil and criminal law. Other problems arose as a result of the new character of the *kehillah*, its representative and elective bodies: what should be the network of relations between the individual citizen and the community, between the communal government and its employees? How should the communal institutions be organized and legally administered? How were elections and appointments to communal institutions and other public positions to be carried out? How were taxes to be levied and collected? In addition to these questions, the scholars were faced with a long list of other problems related to the legal aspects of the economic and fiscal relations of the *kehillah*. Some of these were solved through the accepted methods of the *halakhah*: rabbinical decisions and ordinances (*takkanot*), custom, etc. But these methods did not always meet the dynamic needs of the community, and a significant number of them called for new *takkanot* to be enacted by the *kehillah* and its representatives, or by the federations of *kehillot* and statewide councils. This phenomenon of communal ordinances (*takkanot ha-kahal*) was an innovation stemming directly from the new reality—the authority of the *kehillah*. Indeed, as we have noted, even in the days of the *Tannaim*, the community had established a system of weights and measures, wages, etc., but this activity was marginal and most major decisions stemmed from the central halakhic authority. In the Middle Ages, however, the legislative activity of the *kehillah* was extended to many areas of Jewish law, both civil and public, and, to a certain extent, even criminal.

These far reaching changes in the scope of communal legislation raised many fundamental legal questions which could not be answered by the existing *halakhah*. Thus, for example, we find no discussion in the Talmud on the source of the community's authority to issue *takkanot*, and hence the degree and scope of this authority were not clear. This was true of many fundamental questions concerning legislative procedures and the scope of their application. For example, do decisions on communal *takkanot* have to be made by the entire community with all members present, or can they be made by their representatives?

Similarly, with the question already raised: is a decision passed by the majority binding upon a dissenting minority? Finally, are decisions binding on a person who was outside the community or who was not yet born at the time the decision was taken, and if so, to what extent? These questions and their solutions are, by their very nature, in the realm of public law, but the Talmud does not deal with these problems and they cannot be solved through analogies to private law (for example, laws of partnership). The solution required by public law is in opposition to the very essence of private law which, by definition, cannot be binding upon an individual without his consent.[8]

The Authority of Communal Government A Solution Based on Jewish Law

The solution which the halakhic scholars found in order to grant authority to the new political reality of the *kehillah* was both simple and revolutionary: simple in its conclusion that the community, when acting as a community, is subject to the regulations of Jewish public law, and all that this implies; revolutionary in the extensive use made by the scholars of those days of the accepted methods of creation in the world of *halakah–midrash* (interpretation), *takkanah* (ordinance), *minhag* (custom), and *ma'aseh* (case and precedent). The basis of all these methods was a bold and far-reaching use of the creative source of legal logic (*sevarah*), that is, the reasoning and logic of the scholars, based on a penetrating insight of the halakhic world against the background of the practical realities of daily life.[9] Different rabbis cite various Talmudic sources to prove that the rules concerning public law differ from those concerning the individual,[10] but this was no more than an attempt to find some support for their decision. From all these sources we can conclude only that the Talmud viewed public and private acts differently (for example, the laws governing vows made with public consent), but this distinction had no further legal significance.[11] Certain scholars found a solution to some of the problems cited above, such as the right of the majority to impose its will and decisions on the minority, through expansive interpretation. Thus, they extended the meaning of the precept that the residents of a city can compel their fellow townsmen to build a synagogue or to purchase a Torah scroll[12] to mean provision for all the needs of the community.[13] Similarly, the scope of "By a majority you are to decide" was extended to include not only legal decisions and judgments, but also "matters which concern the public."[14] Others solved this problem by referring to the *midrash aggadah* which relates that "The tribes decided (by threat of ban) amongst themselves that they would not reveal the sale of Joseph, and when Reuben, who had been absent, returned and said, 'The boy is gone! Now, what am I to do? The brothers told him what they had done and he was silent."[15] But even these solutions did not solve all the problems which arose in the governing of the community.

A general solution to these problems was found in the decision of the halakhic scholars to consider the community, from a legal point of view, as equivalent to those bodies included within the scope of Jewish public law, such as the King or *Nasi* and, most importantly, the Court, or even the High Court. "In each community, the individuals are subject to the authority of the majority and they must act according to the majority in all matters. They are to their fellow townsmen as Israel is to the High Court or to the King."[16] "No one can exclude himself from the enactments of the community and its ordinances; because the individuals are subservient to the community, and just as all the communities are subservient to the High Court or to the *Nasi*, so is each and every individual subservient to the community in his city."[17] "For the power of the community over the individuals is like the power of the *Nasi* over all of Israel."[18] Thus, the parallel can be stated as follows: the relation of every community to the individuals comprising it is like that of the King, the Nasi, or the High Court to Israel as a whole.

The parallel between the townspeople and the *Nasi* is vaguely alluded to in the Mishnah: "He who is banned from his city, is banned from all other cities; he who is banned from the presence of the *Nasi*, is banned from the presence of all Israel."[19] The parallel between the *kehillah* and the court, however, is both revolutionary and far-reaching, appearing for the first time in the tenth century, with no precedent in Talmudic *halakhah* or *aggadah*. Furthermore, the rabbis did more than draw a parallel between them—they affirmed, in fact, that the community functions as a court, with each and every member a judge. To quote Rabbi Elijah Mizrahi, one of the great scholars of Turkey in the second half of the fifteenth and early sixteenth centuries:

> The community as a whole is like a court in these [communal] matters. They are like judges to assemble in court and are not free to leave although there are differences of opinion between them: pure or impure; innocent or guilty; rather, they must be counted and must follow the majority decision, as it is written in our holy Torah: "By a majority you are to decide"; and he who opposes the majority is considered a sinner. It makes no difference whether the majority be wealthy or poor, wise men or ordinary people, because the entire community is considered a court in matters concerning its members.[20]

As previously noted, no basis for such a parallel between the authority and status of the *kehillah* and those of the court was to be found in the *halakhah* of the Talmud. The scholars of the post-Talmudic period simply stated that the authority of the community, or of the majority, was comparable to that of the court, but they did not give any legal-halakhic argument to support this far-reaching conclusion. At a later period, the halakhic scholars did cite arguments in support of this parallel, two of which are given here.

Rabbi Elijah Mizrahi, quoted above, based his argument on the fact that the power and authority of the court and the communal leaders are both derived from the same source—the community as a whole. He stated:[21]

> For the power which was granted to the High Court in Jerusalem and to every court in every generation—as our sages interpreted the passage (from Deuteronomy), and appear before the heretical priests, etc., whether he be Jephthat or Samuel, although one cannot be compared with the other—was granted because the decrees, ordinances and customs of the High Court in every generation were and are recognized by all members of that generation, and for this reason the High Court was granted greater power than the other courts of that generation to issue decrees and ordinances and to establish customs. And although it was not explicitly chosen and no specific conditions were agreed upon, it is well-known that all its decisions were recognized by everyone as conclusive; and although someone may object, it is as if he explicitly gave his consent and then changed his mind. Therefore, wherever this principle applies, the authority in question has the power which was granted to the High Court in Jerusalem without reservation. This also applies to the leaders of the city, for all the townspeople recognize their authority in matters related to the improvement of communal life, and they, the townspeople, all rely on them. Thus, it is as if the leaders were explicitly chosen, and all their decisions stand. And although some may object to their decrees and ordinances, it is as if they explicitly gave their consent and then changed their minds.[22]

The argument put forward by one of the great contemporary halakhic scholars, Rabbi Avraham Yeshayahu Karelitz, the "*Hazon Ish*," is interesting. He stated: "This may have been a *takkanah* of the sages, designed to grant the townsmen the authority of a court."[23] That is to say, this was a special *takkanah* of the halakhic scholars, the purpose of which was to grant the communal leaders the status and authority of a court,[24] in order to establish Jewish autonomous rule.

If the question is asked: why was it not sufficient to compare the status of the community to that of the King or *Nasi*—a logical comparison, for the rule of the *Kehillah* was a continuation of the internal rule exercised after that of the King and the *Nasi*?[25] Why did they find it necessary to compare its status to that of the court? The answer is simple: Drawing a parallel to the King or *Nasi* was not sufficient to solve all the problems with which the halakhic scholars were faced. For example, the *takkanot* of a community would often be in conflict with a particular ruling of the *halakhah*. One such case was the *takkanah* allowing witnesses to testify, and judges to sit in judgment, in cases involving their own families or personal considerations, when the case involved communal matters, such as taxation, charitable trusts, etc. The reasoning was that otherwise there would not be a single witness who could testify, or judge who could sit, in matters concerning his own community. This was true of many *takkanot* in various civil matters and in criminal law which prescribed punishments for criminal acts which, while harmful to the community, could not be punished under halakhic law. This community authority was based on the Talmudic principle which granted the sages the authority to issue *takkanot*, even when they were in opposition to established *halakhah*—in civil matters, by virtue of the principle that the court has the power to revoke private ownership (*hefker bet din hefker*); and in criminal cases, by virtue of the principle that the court may mete out punishments not prescribed by law. Thus, because of the parallel between the community and the court, it was established that the community, like the court, has the power to revoke private ownership and to inflict punishments not specified by law.[26]

To cite another example: Jewish law generally requires a *kinyan* (an act whereby a person voluntarily obtains proprietary or contractual rights) to make a legal transaction valid. This formal requirement hampered legal relationships between the community as a public authority, with its network of affairs, and anyone needing to negotiate with it. Thus, beginning in the twelfth and thirteenth centuries, we find a new legal principle that any legal transaction by the community is valid even without a *kinyan*. And, after a short time, it became an accepted custom and rule that "All public matters are valid even without a *kinyan* and the laws of *kinyan* are not applicable in these cases."[27] Here, too, there is no basis in Talmudic law for exempting the community from the *kinyan*. This innovation was based on the parallel between the community and the court, the actions of which are valid without a *kinyan*.[28] Using this same principle, other far-reaching allowances were made for the community, such as the right to purchase and sell articles which did not yet exist; in addition, it was decided that the defect of *asmakhta* does not apply to the conduct of transactions made by the community.[29]

Basic Principles in Administrative Law and Public-Private Relations

The authority of the Jewish communal government—the *kehillah*—was founded on several basic principles set down by the halakhic scholars which endowed the *kehillah* with great power. This power did not depend upon physical forces but, on the contrary, on spiritual strength, resulting in fact from the limitation and supervision of such physical forces. It is difficult to say which was more important—the granting of physical power or its limitation—but it is clear that only both these factors together can create a governing authority with practical and spiritual stability.

In the public life of the Jews in the *kehillah*, as in every community, there were social tensions between the various classes which often brought them into sharp conflict. There were also cases of criminal offenses against property, morality, and family life; there were forgeries, assaults, and sometimes, though quite rarely, even murders. These pathological phenomena, though relatively few in number, can also be found in the responsa literature, which reveals how the *halakhah* succeeded in dealing with them, either by means of existing laws or new rulings. At times, the actions of the community leadership were called into question, whether in the form of simple offenses on the part of a communal leader, or of questions of a socio-constitutional nature. These required the intervention of halakhic scholars in order to protect the basic rights of the minority and the weak, to establish norms for relations between the different classes in the community, and so on. This complex of problems resulted in the creation of many new fundamental principles in Jewish public law. Some examples follow.

"Clean Hands" as a Condition for Public Office

Certain problems were solved by virtue of the principle which drew a parallel between the community and the court. In a particular case, a man made a false statement in declaring his taxes; he was fined by the appropriate authority, and then an agreement was reached with the *Kehillah* as to the sum he was to pay in tax. After a while, this same man sought to be appointed as a leader of the community. Rabbi Israel Isserlein—a scholar living in Germany in the fifteenth century—was asked[30] whether "this man could sit with the elders of the community for the purpose of tending to the public good . . .and of supervising public and private matters," since it was clear that he had previously sworn falsely. Rabbi Israel answered that he could not serve as a leader of the community, having sworn falsely out of lust for money; because of this act, he was comparable to a thief or robber and was therefore disqualified from being a judge—and "the elders of the community, when supervising public and private affairs, act in the place of a court." This principle served as a guideline for determining who was qualified for publc service, and was accepted as *halakhah*: "The elders of the community, who are appointed to deal with public or private matters, are viewed as judges, and he who is disqualified from judging because of wrong-doing cannot be appointed to sit among them."[31]

A Community Cannot Claim: "We Were Wrong."

This same principle of the existence of a parallel between the community and the court implies that the community cannot argue that it did not seriously consider a certain matter, or that it misunderstood it and had arrived at an erroneous decision. Rabbi Solomon ben Simeon Duran (Rashbash), son of the author of the *Tashbetz* and, during the fifteenth century, spiritual leader of the Jewish community in North Africa, stated: "Observe how this is done in all the holy communities; a decision is never rescinded.... For it is a disgrace for a community to say: 'We were mistaken'...The power of the community is like the power of the court, and if we invalidate a sale made by the community, what is the power of the court?"[32]

Principles Of Justice And Equity

Restrictions on the arbitrary authority of the communal leaders can be found in the control which the halakhic scholars maintained over the content of communal *takkanot*. As stated above, a communal *takkanah* could contradict the content of a specific ruling or *halakhah*, and the rabbis generally accepted this. But communal *takkanot* could not contradict essential principles which were basic to the framework of Jewish law—for example: equality before the law, protecting the rights of the minority or the weak, improving the social order, etc. Thus, a framework of general principles of justice and equity was created in Jewish law.

Controlling the Management Of Public Affairs

In a certain community there was a functionary whose duty it was "to strive to eradicate crime and punish transgressors"—in modern terms, a kind of state or city comptroller. One day, by a *takkanah* issued by the majority, it was decided to discontinue this position. The minority turned to Rabbi Solomon ben Aderet (Rashba)—the halakhic authority of Spanish Jewry in the late thirteenth century—and asked him whether such a *takkanah* was valid, since it would lead to an increase in immoral behavior. He replied unequivocally that such a decision was indeed null and void. "And although it was implemented by the people responsible for most of the community's needs, laws are made by them to maintain order and not to disturb it, and they cannot violate the lines on which the Torah is based."[33] Rashba added that one comptroller may be replaced by another if he is considered to be better, but a decision discontinuing the function as such cannot improve a situation but only aggravate it and hence is void.

Restrictions On The Power To Levy Taxes: The Case of a Person Who is Unable to Pay

In a question addressed to three scholars in Mainz early in the thirteenth century, we read of a *takkanah* enacted in a community obligating every person to pay a minimal tax. One man refused, arguing that he was poor and could not afford the tax, and he was willing so to swear. The community representative (referred to as the "*apotropa*"), on the other hand, argued that the community had decided "not to allow anyone to swear; rather they would be required to pay a certain amount according to the sum paid the previous year . . . .It was not in the public interest for the members of the community to take an oath . . . .The community can take action in order to meet the needs of the moment, so as not to take an oath from any member of the cmmunity. And I do not wish to cite any further argument, since the community may issue any *takkanot* it wishes."[34]

The "utilitarian" arguments of the community representative were rejected, and the scholars of Mainz unequivocally declared the decision null and void on the grounds that the validity of a law rests on the ability of people to comply with it. How could the man be required to give what he does not possess?It is an important principle that God exempts those who, for reasons beyond their control, cannot comply with His laws. Thus, "If the man is really unable to pay, he should be exempt from payment. Can the majority be rogues (*gazlanim*)?" That is to say, the majority, merely by virtue of the fact that it is a majority, cannot unjustly deprive anyone of his money and deny him his basic rights; for no one can require a poor man to pay taxes he cannot afford.

Protecting the Basic Rights of the Minority

In this same response, the scholars of Mainz established another principle. The principle that the majority can exert its will on the minority applies only when the majority and the minority are on an equal footing—for example, when both have the ability to pay, but the minority objects to the tax as such. But when the economic situation of the minority is such that, were the majority to be in a similar situation, it too could not comply with the law, the principle of majority rule does not apply. Finally, the following principle of public law is stated in this responsa: "if a man is not financially capable of paying, why should he be harassed and fined for lack of means? According to the law, if he has no financial means the community must support him and his family; hence, how can the community demand payment from him? And if his oath is not suspect, why should he not be allowed to swear and be exempt, since he protested the tax from the very beginning?"

Prohibition Against Double Taxation

This fundamental principle of Jewish public law—the majority cannot be rogues[35]—applies not only when the majority acts in such a way as to deprive the underprivileged, but also when the majority unlawfully deprives anyone, even if he is a man of means. This is revealed in the following example: a certain man lived in Community A, while part of his property was in Community B. The leaders of Community A wanted to tax him for the property which was located in Community B, but he protested, arguing that the tax was levied on the property and not on the individual. Community B had already taxed the property owned there, so that were he also to pay taxes on this property in the community in which he lived, he would be paying a double tax on the same property. The leaders of the community, on the other hand, argued that "the community has the power to enact laws which apply to and are binding on everyone." Here, too, Rashba rejected the community's argument: "The argument that the community can enact laws in such matters seems to me to be no more than robbery, and unjust enactments are not valid. . . .It is not within the power of the community unjustly to deprive anyone of his money and appropriate it for communal use."[36] The community cannot use the legislative authority granted to it and obligate anyone by law—even with the consent of the majority—if such action involves an infringement of justice or law, or involves some form of swindling.

Payment of Taxes which are under Dispute—When?

Rabbi Meir (Maharam) of Rothenburg, the greatest halakhic scholar in thirteenth century Germany, established this same principle in another matter. A number of responsa by various scholars dealt with the fairly common case of disputes between an individual and the community as to the amount of taxes to be paid, where the individual appeals to the court. According to the law, were it to be strictly applied, the person who demands payment must show due cause; thus, the community would be able to collect only that amount on which there was agreement, while the remainder, which was under dispute, could not be collected until a court decision had been reached. Nevertheless, the rabbis ruled—whether on the basis of a special *takkanah* or otherwise—that the individual must pay the entire sum, and only after a court decision in his favor will the money be refunded to him. This decision was based on the following argument: "People cannot be left free to say, 'I will not pay until after litigation,' for then everyone would do so, the tax could never be collected, and cheating would be encouraged."[37] "Whenever the community has a claim against anyone, it is assumed that it is in possession of the claim, for otherwise public affairs could not be conducted. Everyone would act dishonestly, thinking: 'Who will challenge me in court?'"[38] Therefore, the public good is to be upheld over the letter of the law, for this enables the community to maintain services and to pay the sums demanded of it by the government. However, Maharam ruled, the public good is to be upheld over that of the individual only in cases in which there is reasonable doubt as to the amount of tax to be paid. But, "Where it is clear that the public authority is not in the right, it must not be permitted to wrong the individual, for its status as a public authority does not entitle it to be unjust to anyone." The law, then, is as follows: "every person must pay tax on all his property, apart from cases clearly exempted; but if there is some doubt as to exemption and the community claims that he must pay, he must do so and then go to law."[39]

Elections to Public Bodies—Who Can Vote, and What is the Weight of Each Vote?

Problems in the realm of public law often reflect the social environment of a community. A clear example of this was the preoccupation of the Rabbis, at different times and in different Jewish communities, with the nature of the majority. As we have seen, one of the greatest problems in determining the framework of Jewish internal rule was the problem of the majority versus the minority. After the principle of majority rule was established, a fundamental question arose: how is the majority to be composed? Should the vote of every person have equal weight, whether he be rich or poor, educated or ignorant? Perhaps the majority ought to be determind by a combination of these factors? These problems were dealt with extensively within various legal frameworks. Different usages were common under different legal systems, in different eras, and under different forms of government. It is reasonable to say that there was interaction—both positive and negative—between the non-Jewish and Jewish environments. Thus, what emerged from the halakhic discussions on this question is a spectrum of solutions, all guided by the realities of life and all, in turn, regulating life.

At one end of this spectrum, we find, for example, the opinion of Rabbi Elijah Mizrahi, the foremost scholar of Constantinople in the late fifteenth century and early sixteenth, already cited above: "It makes no difference whether the majority are wealthy or poor, men of learning or common people, since each community acts as a court in dealing with its own affairs."[40] A view diametrically opposed to this is that of Rabbi Samuel de Medina, the Maharashdam, one of the great rabbis of sixteenth century Salonika. He argued that:

> The Torah speaks of "By a majority you are to decide" only when both parties are equal; then the opinion of the majority is decisive. But when the two groups are not equal, one man may have the weight of a thousand .... When they are equal, the majority is determined by number; when they are unequal, the majority is determined by personal standing. Accepting the will of the majority, when that majority is composed of ignorant men, could lead to a perversion of justice. For if there were one hundred men in a city, ten of whom were wealthy, respected men, and ninety of whom were poor, and the ninety wanted to appoint a leader approved by them, would the ten prominent men have to submit to him regardless of who he was? Heaven forbid—this is not the accepted way ("the way of pleasantness").[41]

Complete equality, irrespective of wealth or knowledge, according to the Maharshdam, stands in contradiction to both law and the "ways of pleasantness." Hence, when the members of the community are not on an equal footing, the majority is determined not by number but by prestige, by the specific weight of each vote. Between these diametrically opposed positions, there are many shades of meaning and nuance. These include those expressed by: Rabbi Isaac Adarbi of sixteenth century Salonika, who believed that decisions on fiscal matters should follow the "economic majority" while the "simple majority"—with every vote having equal weight—should decide in all other matters[42]; and Rabbi Abraham di Boton, also of sixteenth century Salonika, who gave a broad definition of the concept "fiscal matters" in which the "economic majority" was to rule, while only those matters which were in no way related to finance, such as laws determining prohibited behavior, should be decided by a simple majority.[43]

How did the halakhic scholars determine their positions on this issue? Here, too, various analogies, legends (*aggadot*), etc., were used as sources in the formation of definite halakhic positions on this fundamental question. For example, the following question was posed to Rabbi Menachem Mendel Krochmal, one of the great German scholars of the mid-seventeenth century: in a particular case, several of the notables of the town wished to establish the rule that only those "who paid high taxes or who were learned in the Torah should have the right to vote . . . .since most public matters require an outlay of money; therefore, how could the opinion of the poor be equal to that of the wealthy? Similarly, how could the opinion of the ignorant be equal to that of the scholar?" However, "The masses of the poor cried out: why should our rights be limited if we, too, are taxpayers and give our share. Although the wealthy pay more, it is more difficult for the poor to give their small share than it is for the wealthy to pay much more."[44] Rabbi Menachem Mendel Krochmal decided in favor of the poor, ruling that the majority should be determined by a combination of both factors—wealth and numbers. He based his decision on the last *mishnah* of the tractate *Menahot*[45]: "Concerning the burnt-offering of an animal or a fowl and the meal-offering (*minha*) it is written: 'A sweet-smelling sacrifice' (i.e., all three sacrifices are equally pleasing although they differ in intrinsic value). From this we learn that although there are those who spend much and those who spend little, what is important is that they direct their thoughts to heaven." From this *mishnah*, Rabbi Krochmal concludes: "Therefore, clearly the small sum which the poor contribute is equal to the large sum which the rich contribute....The little that the poor man contributes is worth more than the greater amount given by the wealthy." This, too, is derived from the tractate *Menahot*[46] dealing with the meal-offering: "Rabbi Isaac said, 'Why does the word *nefesh* (soul) appear in relation to the *minha* sacrifice?'[47] God said: 'Who generally brings a meal-offering? A poor man (who owns no animals). I therefore regard his sacrifice as though he had offered his very soul.'" Thus the sacrifice offered by the poor is greater than that offered by the rich, "for the poor man must give of himself in order to obtain what he brings...whereas the rich man brings that which he already possesses without labor."[48] On the basis of this—and other similar references in the *Aggadah*—Rabbi Menachem Mendel Krochmal concludes that "the argument of the poor is to be accepted, for it is harder for them to give their small share than it is for the rich to give their larger share."[49]

Equally original is the proof that Rabbi Krochmal adduces refuting the argument that sought to distinguish between the weight of the scholar's vote and that of the unlearned. The source cited is the tractate *Hagigah*[50]. "Rabbi Papa said: On what basis do we today accept the testimony of the unlearned (as opposed to the opinion of the sages in the *baraita* cited in the Babylonian Talmud, *Pesahim* 49, 2, that the testimony of the unlearned is unacceptable)? This is the opinion of Rabbi Yose, who held that: 'We should trust everyone as to the purity of wine and oil, for otherwise they will set themselves apart from the community.'" From this, Rabbi Krochmal concludes:

> It is clear that even the testimony of ignorant men is to be accepted for fear of animosity—if they are afraid that they are being kept apart they will set

up their own forum. This is even more true in the matter under discussion. If we isolate the ignorant to such an extent that we do not include them in the community consensus, they will surely feel animosity towards us and will set up their own forum and separate themselves from the community, leading to dissention among the Jews, heaven forbid! Therefore this is to be avoided.

The manner by which an eminent scholar such as Rabbi Menachem Mendel Krochmal established such a basic principle of election law, within the framework of Jewish law, serves as an additional example of the broad-mindedness and initiative displayed in the formation of fundam. ntal principles of *halakhah*. For, from a logical, formal point of view, the legends telling of the sacrifices offered by the poor have little to do with the fundamental and controversial question of assigning greater weight to the votes of the wealthy members of the community in elections to the communal government. Moreover, it was argued, it was the wealthy citizens who, in the last analysis, financed the public services. What answer could be found to this argument—which is by no means simple—in the Talmudic discussion on the *minha* sacrifice offered by the poor? But this was the method adopted by the rabbis, whose responsibility was proportional to their greatness, when called upon to solve new problems, immersed as they were in the world of the *halakhah*, its aims and its spirit. After they had established a new principle, it was incorporated into the existing *halakhah*, and if there was no appropriate *halakhah*, into an existing *aggadah* in one way or another.

The Creative Power of the Sevarah (Reasoning) in the Development of Jewish Public Law

The concept of the *sevarah*, that is, the logic on which the reasoning of the halakhic scholars was based, has been discussed at length elsewhere.[51] The *sevarah* served as a special tool for creation in the world of the *halakhah* and as one of its important sources. As a source for the formation of a particular *halakhah*, it is fostered by a logical penetration of the essence of halakhic and legal principles, an understanding of man's behavior in his social relationships, and an examination of the realities of life. An important place was assigned to this creative tool in the development of Jewish public law.

The great changes which occurred in the social-economic-political environment on the one hand, and the lack of real precedents in the existing Talmudic law which could be used to solve the new problems arising from this environment on the other hand, led the rabbis to make extensive use of the creative power of the *sevarah*. Many examples of this can be found in the matters dealt with here. For example, when Rabbenu Asher Ben Jehiel, the Rosh (a leading halakhic scholar, both in Germany and in Spain, towards the end of the thirteenth century) sought to establish the principle that the majority of a community can compel a dissenting minority to comply with a *takkanah* enacted by the majority, his overriding motives were logic and practical necessity. As Rabbenu Asher states, "Were it not so, the community would never agree on any subject, if individuals were able to revoke the consent of the majority," or, as he states elsewhere, "Were it not so, the community would never have any hope of real order, for when is the community ever of one mind?"[52]

Conversely, when it is necessary to revoke an existing *takkanah*, logic demands that the majority be free to do so. Thus, Rabbi Simeon ben Zemah Duran, the leading scholar of Algiers in the fifteenth century, states: "It is unreasonable to say that a single opinion can outweigh the opinion of many, forcing them to consent against their will . . .for if this were so, the majority would be subject to the individual and might be compelled to act in a manner contrary to the law. This would be a surprising state of affairs."[53]

Another question which arose within the framework of the majority-minority issue is the following: in a court judgment, the minority must be present—they debate with one another[54]—during both the discussion and the decision. If only the majority is present, the decisions of the court are invalid. Were we to apply this ruling to communal decision, the minority, by purposely absenting themselves at the time of the vote, could thwart a decision accepted by the majority. However, the rabbis ruled that the decision of the majority is valid even if the minority is absent from the meeting: "[The minority] brought it upon themselves, and they must, however reluctantly, accept the decision, for otherwise the maxim 'By a majority you are to decide' would be meaningless. Those who object to the majority decision would set themselves apart and refrain from attending meetings and being present at voting, and thus be exempt from the ruling. Such a situation is clearly unacceptable."[55]

The solutions found to other questions of community law were similar. When Rabbi Joseph Colon, one of the foremost halakhic scholars in fifteenth century Italy, sought to explain why a *kinyan* is not required in order to grant validity to a public agreement—in contradistinction to a private agreement, which is invalid without a *kinyan*—he stated the following: "An agreement made by the public follows in 'the path of pleasantness and all these are paths of peace.' Therefore it was said that the decisions of the public are valid when made in agreement and unity, and no one will be able to change his mind and disturb the confidence in, and peace of, the community."[56] This explanation is based on a *sevarah*—on Rabbi Joseph Colon's view of the meaning of "the paths of pleasantness.[57]

When Rabbi Isaac ben Sheshet Perfet (Ribash), a leading halakhic scholar, both in Spain and Algiers towards the end of the fourteenth century, considered the problem of how to make the enactments of the community binding on those categories of people who, according to the fundamental principles of private law, could not be held legally responsible, such as minors, he did so using the following *sevarah*: "Minors must abide by existing enactments when they come of age, for otherwise the people of the city would have to reestablish their enactments daily as the minors came of age. This is unreasonable, hence the enactments are binding on all residents of the city.[58] This decision, too, is based not on any halakhic proof but rather on practical necessity, rooted in logic and reality: if the ruling were otherwise, enactments would have to be re-enacted every time a minor came of age—a situation which would be both irrational and untenable. In such cases where the amount of taxes levied on an individual by the community was disputed, this same approach was adopted by Rabbi Solomon ben Adret (Rashba) and by Rabbi Meir of Rothenburg. The individual who lodged the appeal was to pay the entire sum and would be reimbursed if and when the court decided in his favor. This view contradicts the basic principle that "He who demands payment has the burden of proof." Yet, although here it is the community which is demanding payment, this ruling regarding payment by the individual can be justified on the basis of logic: if the rabbis ruled in favor of the appelant, everyone would argue that he was exempt from payment of taxes, or had already paid his taxes and therefore taxes could never be collected; cheating would be encouraged, and the community would suffer.[59]

In this same way, the Maharshdam, previously quoted, solved one of the most difficult and troublesome problems—also of an outstanding social-communal nature—facing the halakhic scholars after the expulsion of the Jews from Spain. With the increase in the number of Marranos, as they began to return openly to Judaism in Turkey and elsewhere, the question arose as to the validity of legal transactions carried out by them before they returned to Judaism, as these transactions had not been made according to halakhic law—with a proper *kinyan*, witnesses, etc. This would have resulted in the reversal of all the business transactions that had been conducted over a period of several decades, and would have created chaos in the socio-economic order of the Marrano community in particular, and the Jewish community in general. The Maharashdam, and others, decided that all transactions which had been carried out by the Marranos were valid, even after their return to Judaism. His argument is instructive: "Otherwise the Marranos would be placed in an impossible situation, since those with whom they had done business would now protest that their obligations had been contracted according to the law of the land and not according to the law of the Torah and hence were invalid. This is clearly unreasonable. What is done is done; from now on, they will have to meet all the requirements of Jewish law.[60] This was the approach of the great scholars when dealing with basic problems concerning the entire public. At the root of their decision lay the consideration of the public needs in general and not only those of the individual in question.

The framework, tools, and principles which served as the basis and the content of the power and authority of the Jewish community during a period of approximately seven hundred years represent one of the most striking phenomena in the history of the Jewish political tradition. The halakhic scholars and communal leaders established a framework for Jewish autonomy under alien sovereign rule, and developed a full range of halakhic norms in the sphere of Jewish public law which granted absolute power and authority to the new form of Jewish internal rule—the *kahal* or the federations of *kehillot*. This authority was even greater than that characteristic of the earlier forms of government under the King or *Nasi*. At the same time, the rabbis shaped, consolidated and established this authority and granted it spiritual power through a system of regulations and restrictions, so that it would not become arbitrary and dictatorial, but would preserve the basic principles of justice and equity found in the *halakhah* and the *aggadah*, reflecting the spiritual character of Judaism.

Its Significance Today

With the spread of the emancipation nearly two hundred years ago, the kehillah, as an autonomous Jewish entity, came to an end. Both external and internal factors contributed to this termination, but we shall not discuss them here. Owing to this change, which took almost two centuries to come about, we were overtaken by consequences both trying and distressing: this great creation in the spiritual and practical life of the Jews was lost, and its image distorted. Hence we no longer have recourse—neither in practice nor in theory, neither for the sake of education nor for study—to the great values which were the fruit of that great era; and we make virtually no use of them for the consolidation or enrichment of our spiritual and practical life today.[61]

Decisions of the Supreme Court and the Rabbinical Courts

Some halakhic cases in the realm of government and administration, from the time of the *kehillah*, have indeed found renewed practical use today through the decisions of the Supreme Court and the Rabbinical Courts in Israel. A few examples are cited here.[62]

In one case, a city employee was dismissed for improper conduct. The employee appealed to the Supreme Court, sitting as a High Court of Justice, to invalidate the dismissal, arguing that he was not given the opportunity to explain or to answer the charges made against him. The Municipality, on the other hand, argued that, according to the existing law, it was under no obligation to grant the employee a hearing before dismissing him—and, indeed, the paragraph concerned so indicated. However, the Supreme Court accepted the employee's argument and invalidated his dismissal, quoting halakhic sources and basing its decision on the following three principles of Jewish law: a) a person can be dismissed from a public position only if he commits an offense, and not on the basis of hearsay alone; b) communal leaders are to be considered as judges, and hence they cannot make arbitrary decision but must consider each matter individually; and c) the communal leaders, who are regarded as judges, must act in accordance with the basic principles of judicial procedure: it is a fundamental halakhic rule that a person cannot be judged in his absence, and that the accused has the right to appear and to present his case.[63]

In another case, the Supreme Court ruled that a council member elected through a party list is free to express opinions which differ from those of the party he represents, as long as his action stems from serious considerations and not from irrelevant motives. A council member is regarded as a judge, and must base his decisions on his own discretion and understanding, "for he knows only that which his eyes can see."[64] On the basis of this same principle—that a person elected by the community is to be considered as a judge—the Supreme Court ruled that when the election committee appoints the chairmen of the polling committees, it must treat all citizens equally and must not discriminate against any citizen or group of citizens, relying on the power of the majority, for the chairman need not be a member of the majority in order to conduct fair elections; in fact, it is perhaps preferable that he represent the minority.[65]

Another interesting problem was brought before the Rabbinical District Court (acting as arbitrator) involving three political parties which stood for election to the municipal council under a joint list. The parties had made a written agreement that if only two out of the first three candidates on the list were elected, the second would resign in favor of the third. Indeed, as they feared, only two were elected, but the second candidate refused to resign. He argued before the Rabbinical court that the agreement had no legal validity, for several reasons: the obligation to resign had been made before the elections took place, and was therefore invalid because it concerned a presumed future event ("a matter as yet non-existent"); moreover, the agreement was invalid owing to the defect of *asmachta* because it was based on the conviction—common to all candidates before election—that more than two would be elected and there would be no need for any resignation. Furthermore, it was argued, there had been no proper *kinyan* as required by Jewish law. The court rejected all these arguments, basing its decision on the responsa cited above which indicates that any communal act is fully valid even if there is no *kinyan*, even if it involves such defects as a presumed future event, *asmachta*, etc.[66]

This decision was appealed in the Rabbinical High Court of Appeals. The appellant argued that the decision should not be based on the *halakhah* which states that communal acts do not require a *kinyan*, for this *halakhah* applies only to communal leaders—town leaders and representatives—whereas here the agreement was between political parties and their representatives and hence, like partnerships, it is subject to private law in which a *kinyan* and other provisions are required. the High Court rejected this argument and, in addition, made an important contribution to Jewish public law:

> If the *halakhah* is such that there is no need for a *kinyan* in communal affairs, and the community has such authority that the restrictions placed on individuals do not apply to it (such as the restrictions placed on presumed future events, *asmachta*, etc.), there is nothing more clearly *communal* in nature than the case under consideration—the selection of the communal leaders.[67]

The Rabbinical High Court reaffirmed the decision of the Rabbinical district Court that the second representative must resign in accordance with the prior agreement, adding, in conclusion, the following significant remarks:

> In conclusion, we must add and say to the litigants that, as public servants, and when acting in this capacity, they should not argue that the obligations which they undertook are not binding because their validity can be disputed under law. Promises and obligations, especially in communal affairs, are holy and must be fulfilled to capacity, in accordance with their original intent, wording and spirit. Public servants shall not go back on their word and bring ruin on the public by insisting on the strict letter of the law.[68]

From the examples given, it is clear that the significance of the achievements of the halakhic scholars in the sphere of public law during the period of Jewish autonomy has retained its value for today's problems. There is, of course, an essential difference between the political sovereignty of Israel today and the internal rule of the medieval *Kehillah* which lacked such sovereignty. But there is also an important similarity between the Jewish historical reality today and the historical reality in the heyday of the *Kehillah*. Both are based on a conception of autonomy and sovereignty in which the people and the community, and not the king, or the single ruler, are central. Therefore the issues and principles of Jewish public law which emerged during that era can also serve as a basis for the solution of problems arising out of the rebirth of Jewish sovereignty. The spirit and the force of these principles can help us continue to solve the many new problems which arise.

Where are these Historical Realities to be Found in the Curricula of Studies?

This is precisely the problem. We have not as yet benefited from the creative process described above in the solution of the many and varied problems related to revived Jewish sovereignty, as a process which represents a further phase in the great legal-halakhic activity of Jewish autonomy in the *kehillah*. This fact stems from many factors, but principally from a lack of knowledge and awareness, which is, indeed, painful.[69] But what is more painful is the fact that not only has the legal-halakhic material which formed the powre and authority of the *Kehillah* failed to serve as a real source of creativity and inspiration for us today, but knowledge of this historical fact is disappearing, as though it had never existed, from the hearts and minds of the educators and their students. We feel compelled to pose the following simple but penetrating question: where is this historical reality to be found in the Jewish history curricula which determine what our children will learn? Is it not time that we placed these great periods of the Middle Ages in their full and proper historical perspective?

These were, of course, also difficult times, with pogroms, plagues, both black and white, crusades, and massacres. But these were not the outstanding features of this era. The central phenomenon was the life and creativity of the community and the individual within the framework of Jewish internal rule, based entirely on Jewish law, its principles and sources. This led to tremendous creativity in all areas of law—public and private—and in the various branches of the philosophy of law. Of course, life was not a bed of roses, and there were not a few negative incidents involving both individuals and the leadership as a whole, as has been noted above. But these were only a part of an almost "normal" reality, a reality which comprised both animation and social tension, reflecting life and not an abstract, theoretical study of the good versus the bad, the just versus the unjust. An accurate, objective description of the history of this great era can reveal to us and our young people a living, breathing community coming to grips with the problems of its time and overcoming them. Through such study and knowledge, our youth will become proud of its past, will become proud of the *galut* which has been so denigrated. It will become proud of the community whose scholars and courts, in the most adverse circumstances and despite continued persecution, maintained a social structure in which, while the majority ruled and the minority had to submit, the majority could not, and moreover was not entitled to, exploit this privilege in order to rob the minority of its basic rights.

This same youth will know not only what happened, or could have happened, to Baruch of Mainz as related in the poem by Saul Tchernichovsky, but also, and more importantly, about Rabbi Baruch ben Samuel,[70] one of the judges of Mainz, who fiercely defended the right of a person not to pay taxes beyond his means, and transformed the Talmudic saying, "The majority cannot be rogues" into a cornerstone of Jewish democratic theory. The majority merely by virtue of the fact that it *is* a majority, cannot arbitrarily violate the basic rights of the minority. This was true not only in Mainz but in all the communities of the Jewish diaspora, and particularly in Spain, North Africa, Turkey, and the Balkan countries. Most of the legal-halakhic material which served as the basis of Jewish public-administrative law was found in the thousands of responsa of the rabbis of Spain and the Oriental countries, and it was they who stood at the head of its development and advancement. We should do well to bring before our children this spiritual, social and practical reality which is part and parcel of medieval Jewish history.

Yehezkel Kaufman showed great perception in noting this in his book *Golah ve-Nechar*.[71]

> The common denominator between autonomy in the diaspora and in Eretz Israel was the desire to live according to Jewish law. Throughout the generations of exile, this desire served as the basis of Jewish autonomy. This desire, as we have seen, grew out of the ideal of living according to the Torah. Judaism, which recognizes only religious law, did not recognize pagan-secular law. An integral part of the desire to live according to the Torah was the desire to live according to the legal system laid down by the Torah. Hence, throughout the generations of exile, the Jews longed for legal autonomy. Legal self-rule was, in effect, what distinguished the Jewish community from a religious community and transformed it into a national-political entity. This recognition by the alien state of the right of

the Jews to be judged according to their own legal system was of tremendous significance. First of all, as a result of this recognition, the Torah remained a kind of political constitution, even in the diaspora. The study of the torah had great social value, its scholars were viewed as leaders, and the houses of learning were respected by the people. In addition, the Jewish community was recognized as a special political entity. Legal autonomy is what actually made the Jewish people in the diaspora a "state within a state.

A Clarification of Relations between Religion and State

This reexamination of Jewish history in the diaspora and of Jewish law as it continued to be applied throughout the centuries has had a direct impact on the vast and complex network of relations between religion and state today. It is a fact that the movement of national renaissance could not have arisen, nor could it have endured and struck roots among the people, had it not been for the prayers and the longing of the Jews throughout all centuries for a future redemption, for Eretz Israel—the Land of Israel—and for Jerusalem, both the "physical" and "spiritual." The source of all these lay in the Torah and its commandments. This is true despite the fact that a number of the observant Jews and religious leaders refused to participate in the early stages of the Zionist movement. But it is also an historical fact that the Zionist movement arose within a Jewish reality which, for nearly a century, had not enjoyed any form of autonomy. Jewish autonomy had come to an end after the emancipation, when the Jewish community ceased to exist as a body ordering the lives of its members and was reduced in scope to become the Jewish community as we know it today, dealing with matters of man's relationship to God—centered around the synagogue and the rabbi—and with matters among men, centered around philanthropic, charitable and communal aid institutions. The Jewish community lacked any autonomous character, and its public life was integrated into the life of the public at large. The Zionist movement, which aspired to Jewish independence, viewed the Jewish environment from which it arose as the negation of this basic object, and assumed this state of affairs to have been typical of the Jewish community throughout its existence in the diaspora. It therefore rooted itself in the early periods of Jewish independence and sovereignty in Eretz Israel, and all the generations which followed were presented in a negative light, characterized by persecution, pogroms and massacres.

Perhaps, in order to do them justice, we should try to understand those who presented generations of Jewish history in this manner and who believed that what was required was revolution and conflict, which are inherent in, and lead to, radical change; but this rejection of entire periods of Jewish history led to dissociation from the past, to a lack of roots, to obliteration of earlier periods and creation of an interim almost totally void of belief in the Torah and *mitzvot*, and of a proper appreciation of the spiritual heritage of those generations. This reality had a strong impact on the religious Zionist movement. Religious Jewry did indeed preserve the continuity of Torah and *mitzvot* in relations between man and God. However, in the light of the post-emancipationist reality in which the observant Jews lived, a reality centered around prayer, the Sabbath, *kashrut*, etc., the entire religious struggle within the Zionist movement was confined solely to these. The vast portion of halakhic life intrinsic to autonomous communal life—problems of majority versus minority, the freedom of the individual, ethics and law, etc. (not to mention halakhic jurisdiction and judicial systems)—was almost totally discarded as being irrelevant to contemporary conditions.

This explains the startling fact that, throughout the period of religious Zionism, almost until the establishment of the State of Israel, virtually no thought was given and, in any case, no action was taken, to introduce Jewish law and jurisdiction in the pre-state Jewish community in Eretz Israel nor, in fact, after the establishment of the State. As a result, the confrontation between religion and state has been limited to the narrow sphere of family law and to the observance of the Sabbath and *kashrut*, as if *halakhah*, throughout its history, had had nothing to say on matters of law and justice, leaders and leadership, taxation and elections, basic rights and the freedom of the individual, possession and ownership, criminal responsibility and laws of torts, methods of punishment and the treatment of offenders, to mention only a few. This fact added significantly to the strained atmosphere surrounding the entire question of the proper relation between religion and state.

A practical consideration of solial and ethical values in daily life would have had a tranquilizing and unifying effect on the various camps in Israeli society and would have imbued that society with the spirit of the Torah, thus helping to create mutual understanding on the many controversial issues. The law of the Jewish state and halakhic law come into contact only in matters of family law, the Sabbath, *kashrut*, and autopsies—matters in which there is an almost unlimited range of personal standpoints and in which everyone not only vehemently defends his own position but views it as something which is both inviolable and a matter of conscience. We can state with near certainty that there is a close relationship between this regrettable and distorted restriction of the contact between spiritual and social life in Israel and the limitation and disportion of the study of history and *halakhah* in the schools. The correction of these flaws in the field of education would have a salutary effect on social and communal life in Israel.[72]

Notes

1. Y. Baer. "*Ha-Hathalot ve-ha-Yesodot shel Irgun ha-Kehillot ha-Yehudiot be-Yemei ha-Benayim*" (The Beginnings and the Foundations of the Organization of the Jewish Communities in the Middle Ages). Zion. Vol. 15 (1950), p. 1.

2. *Tosefta Bava Mezia*. 11,23: Babylonian Talmud. *Bava Batra* 8,2. See: Menachem Elon. *Ha-Mishpat ha-Ivri: Toldotav, Mekorotav, Ekronotav* (Jewish Law: History. Sources. Principles) (Jerusalem. 1973). vol. 2. p. 558ff. (Hereafter: *Jewish Law*).

3. On this see: *Jewish Law*, Vol. 1. p. 32ff.

4. B. Akzin. *Torat Ha-Mishtarim* (Jerusalem. 1968). p. 104.

5. Akzin. *ibid*., pp. 104-105.

6. *Piskei HaRosh*. *Bava Batra*. ch. 2. par. 11.

7. For details see: *Jewish Law*. vol. 2. pp. 561ff.. 581ff.

8. That is. in a contractual obligation. or when the obligation stems from the actions of another. such as the obligations of him who causes damage to recompense the injured party: see: *Jewish Law*. Vol. 2. p. 482

9. On the methods of creation in Jewish law. using these legal sources. see: *Jewish Law*. Vol. 2.

10. See. for example. Responsa of Maharam of Rothenburg. cited in Mordekhai. *Bava Mezia*. 457-458.

11. See: *Jewish Law*. Vol. 2. p. 572. note 59.

12. *Tosefta Bava Mezia*. 11. 23: Babylonian Talmud. *Bava Batra*. 8. 2.

13. Maharam of Rothenburg. cited in the Responsa of Rabbi Judah Minz. 7.

14. Resopnsa of Rosh. Klal 6. par. 5 and 7.

15. *Tashbetz*. part 1. 123.

16. Responsa of Rashba. part 3. 411.

17. Responsa of Rashba. part 3. 417: part 7. 490.

18. *Tashbetz*. part 1. 133; compare with: *Tashbetz*. part 1.123.

19. Babylonian Talmud. *Moed Katan*. 16. 1. See: Responsa of Rashba. part 3. 411. 417; part 7,490; *Tashbetz*. part 1,123.

20. Responsa of Rabbi Elijah Mizrahi. 53 (Jerusalem Darom edition. 1938. pp. 145-146).

21. Responsa of Rabbi Elijah Mizrahi. 57. *ibid*.. p. 186.

22. Compare this with the view of Rabbi Menahem ben Solomon Meiri who believed that the approval of a "distinguished person" was required only for a *takkanah* enacted by tradesmen. but "the entire population of the town can issue ordinances without this approval. for they can revoke his appointment." (*Bet ha-Behirah*. *Bava Batra*. 9. 1). See also: *Jewish Law*. vol. 2. p. 610 and note 234.

23. *Hazon Ish*. *Bava Batra*. par. 4. sub-par. 8. The author of *Hazon Ish* used similar reasoning to justify the authority of the trade unions over their members: "...The authority of craftsmen is comparable to that of townsmen. and just as townsmen have the authority of a court. so do the craftsmen have the authority of a court with respect to their fellow craftsmen. *Takkanot* enacted by them have

the validity of the takkanot of a court, for according to these *takkanot* a man can obtain a lien on his fellow's property and can sell this property in order to receive what is due to him. There is no need for a *kinyan*; rather, the *takkanah* of the court serves in place of a *kinyan*. Thus, all craftsmen, acting together, have the same authority as townsmen. This may have been a *takkanah* of the sages designed to grant the townsmen the authority of a court, and to grant all the members of a single trade the authority of a court." (*ibid.*) And, further on (*ibid.*, sub-par. 10): "...and if all the craftsmen agreed, their decision is as significant as a *takkanah* enacted by the entire community, which has the same power as a *takkanah* of the scholars of the generation over all of Israel."

24. On the extent of the parallel between the status of the communal leaders and that of the court see the subsequent discussion, and note 31. Another interesting argument, based on a *sevarah*, in favor of public, as opposed to private, agreement is to be found in the statement of Rabbi Joseph Colon (Maharik) quoted in connection with note 55.

25. Indeed, several of the sages also based the authority of the *kahal* on the similarity of this form of rule to that of the King or *Nasi*. See: *Jewish Law*, Vol. 1, p. 42ff., as well as *Hatam Sofer*, cited on p. 48, note 148 (*ibid.*). See also: *ibid.*, vol. 2, p. 558, note 1, and p. 580, note 65.

26. See: *Jewish Law*, Vol. 2, p. 564ff.; p. 570, note 53; pp. 580, 595-607.

27. Rabbi Elijah ben Hayyim, Responsa *Mayyim Amukim*, 63; *Jewish Law*, Vol. 2, p. 571ff.

28. Responsa of Rashbash, 566, 112.

29. *Jewish Law*, Vol. 2, p. 573. With regard to the concept of *asmakhta*, see: *Jewish Law*, Vol. 2, p. 257, note 51; *The Principles of Jewish Law* (ed. M. Elon, 1975), pp. 171-174. The power of the *kahal* was sometimes greater than that of the court—*Jewish Law*, vol. 2, p. 573, note 70. See also the subsequent discussion.

30. Rabbi Israel Isserlein, *Terumah ha-Deshen, Pesakim u-Ketavim*, 214.

31. *Shulhan Arukh, Hoshen Mishpat*, 37, 22, according to Rabbi Moses Isserles (Rema). Of course, the parallel between the elders of the *kahal* and the judges holds true only for those powers granted to them as leaders of the community. See: *Jewish Law*, Vol. 2, p. 571, note 57.

32. Responsa of Rashbash, 566. In this respect, the power of the *kahal* is greater than that of the court, for if a court errs in its assessment, its sale is void. For a detailed discussion, see: *Jewish Law*, Vol., 2, p. 573, note 70.

33. Responsa of Rashba, part 2,279.

34. Responsa of Maharah, *Or Zarua*, 222.

35. This principle is cited in the Babylonian Talmud, *Bava Batra*, 100, 1, with regard to an entirely different matter: If a majority choose a site for a public road, their choice stands, because, in so doing, they rob someone of his property or rights, because they have no right of way over that land. Here the expression is used to signify that the majority is limited in its decision-making power in that it cannot infringe on the basic rights of the minority. See: *Jewish Law*, Vol., 2, p. 618, note 272.

36. Responsa of Rashba, part 5,178.

37. Responsa of Rashba, part 3,398.

38. Responsa of Maharam of Rothenburg, Prague, 106, etc.

39. *Ibid.*

40. Responsa of Rabbi Elijah Mizrahi,*op. cit*, pp. 145-146.

41. See Proverbs 3:17; Responsa of Maharashdam, *Orakh Hayyim*, 37; *Hoshen Mishpat*, 421.

42. Responsa *Divrei Rivot*, 68; 224.

43. Responsa *Lehem Rav*, 2; also Responsa of Maharshah to Rabbi Solomon Ha-Kohen, part 2,95; part 3,76. It seems to have been commonly accepted that only those who paid some tax had the right to vote. See: Responsa of Maharam of Rothenburg, Berlin, 865, and the Responsum of Maharam cited in the Responsa of Rabbi Judah Minz, 7.

44. Rabbi Menachem Mendel Krochmal, Responsa *Zemah Zedek*, 2.

45. Mishnah, *Menahot*, 13, 11.

46. Babylonian Talmud, *Menahot*, 104, 2.

47. In Leviticus 2:1 it is written: "When a person [*nefesh*] presents an offering of meal to the Lord." The word *nefesh* (soul) does not appear with regard to the other sacrifices. See, for example (Leviticus 1:14): "If his offering to the Lord is a burnt offering of birds . . . ."

48. Compare this with the statement by Rabbi Joseph Trani (Responsa of Maharit, part 1,69): " . . .all those who pay taxes are equal—the rich man who gives of his wealth, and the poor man who gives of the little he possesses—for the poor man is as careful with his penny as the rich man is with his pound, because payment is according to the amount of money each possesses."

49. In the course of his argument, Rabbi Menachem Mendel Krochmal has difficulty in reconciling his conclusion with the statement of the Rosh (Responsa of Rosh, Klal 7, par. 3) that "If a community imposes an ordinance (ban) in fiscal matters, the "economic majority" rules . . .It is illogical that a simple majority composed of those who contribute only a small portion of the taxes should impose a ban on the wealthy." In order to reconcile his own conclusion with that of the Rosh, Rabbi Krochmal explained the opinion of the Rosh through a restrictive interpretation, similar to that of Rabbi Joshua Walk Katz (S'ema on the *Shulhan Arukh, Hoshen Mishpat*, 163, sub-par. 13): "It may be said that the decision of the Rosh that the 'economic majority' should rule applies only to those cases in which the majority of the people who contribute the smaller share of the money wish to enact ordinances against the will of the minority which contributes the greater part, but he did not state that the few wealthy men are to be considered a majority with the authority to impose ordinances on the majority of the community. It could also be that he believes both sides to be of equal weight in such cases and that they must come to a compromise among themselves on such matters. This requires further examination." Therefore, Rabbi Menachem Mendel concludes that the majority must be composed of both an "economic majority" and a simple majority. The opinion of "*Hazon Ish*" is instructive. He, too, was surprised at the decision of the Rosh, and believed that a simple majority alone should rule. He says (*Hazon Ish, Bava Batra*, 5, 1, p. 154): "If for the purposes of tax assessment, the community chose seven city elders and the majority of the community agreed upon these seven, and the wealthy members agreed upon seven different men, it appears that the decision of the majority of the community is to be accepted, and there can be no distinction between rich

and poor; for they are all taxpayers . . .and Rabbi Asher's argument that the poor cannot enact ordinances binding on the rich is invalid, for the poor would not base their decision on their own interests but rather on truth and justice in the public interest. If they are to be suspected of increasing the burden of the wealthy and lightening that of the poor, then, were the wealthy to have the power of majority, they, the wealthy, would be open to suspicion. From this it follows that the statement of the Rosh does not refer to tax assessment, and his intention in this matter needs to be further examined." See also the opinion of "*Hazon Ish*", op. cit., p. 154, explaining the view of Rabbi Israel Isserlein cited in *Terumat ha-Deshen*, 344.

50. Babylonian Talmud, *Hagigah*, 22, 1.

51. See: *Jewish Law*, Vol. 2, p. 805ff.

52. Responsa of the Rosh, 6,5; 6,7. See also the opinion of Rabbi Samuel De Medina (Responsa of Maharashdam, *Yoreh Deah*, 117) on the decision of the Rosh: "In my humble opinion, it seems that we can say that even the Rosh, who uses the Torah sentence 'By a majority you are to decide,' does not think that we are bound by the Torah to follow the majority in general public affairs but uses the sentence as an indication only: Since the Torah states that we should follow the majority in matters of precepts and Torah, it follows logically that in all matters in which there is a disagreement we should follow the majority."

53. *Tashbetz*, part 1, 123.

54. See *Mishnah Sanhedrin*, 5,5.

55. Responsa *Lev Sameah* of Rabbi Abraham Aliggeri, *Hoshen Mishpat*, 5.

56. Responsa of Maharik, 179 (first response, Lemberg edition; Warsaw edition, no. 181). There, Maharik cites the verse (Proverbs 3:17) as follows: "The ways of God (*darkei ha-Shem*) [instead of 'her ways' (*darkeha*)–*the ways of wisdom*] are ways of pleasantness, and all her paths are peace." This is not a printing error, for the same text appears in the original edition of the Maharik, Venice, 5279 (1519).

57. See for example, Maharashdam, *Orakh Hayyim*, 37, and *Hoshen Mishpat*, 421 (quoted above, referred to in note 41), which among other things, explains his view that the vote of a wealthy man carries more weight than that of a poor man, for otherwise "we would not be following 'the ways of pleasantness." Other sages, as we have seen above, do not agree with Maharashdam on the weight of a poor man's vote; we must assume that they disagreed in their interpretation of the expression "ways of pleasantness." Compare the opinion of Maharik with that of Rashbash, quoted above, referred to in note 32.

58. Responsa of Ribash, 399.

59. See above, referred to in note 37.

60. Responsa of Maharashdam, *Hoshen Mishpat*, 327. This was the ruling of Maharival, Maharit and others. See: M. Elon, *The Principles of Jewish Law* (Jerusalem, 1975), "Conflict of Laws," p. 717ff.

61. For a full-length discussion of this see: *Jewish Law*, Vol. 1, p. 65ff.

62. Cited here are several examples of cases in which the principle adopted was that communal leaders are to be viewed as judges. Here are also judgments which rely on Jewish legal sources to establish other principles of administrative

law. For example: On the right to plead one's case, see the judgments cited in the following note; on the administrative authority's obligation to give grounds for its decision and the citizen's right to have access to the files of the public authority, see: H.C. (High Court of Justice), 142/70. *Shapira vs. The District Committee of the Bar Association, Jerusalem*, P.D. (*Piskei Din*) 25 (1), p. 325, pp. 333-335.

63. H.C., 290/65. *Altagar vs. the Mayor and the Municipality of Ramat-Gan*, P.D. 20(1), p. 29. In the judgment, among others, is cited (pp. 39-40) the opinion of Rabbi Moses Isserles, who wrote the *Mappah* on the *Shulhan Arukh* (Responsa of Rema, 108): "Therefore it is clear that we cannot judge a matter without hearing the argument of the accused, for the Bible (Deuteronomy 1:16) states: 'Hear out your fellow men.' And although this is a simple matter, we can also derive it from the ways of God, for all His acts are just and His ways are pleasant and His paths are peaceful. First he asked Adam: 'Who told you that you are naked?' then He asked Cain: 'Where is your brother Abel?'—in order to hear their arguments. So much the more so should this apply to simple men. Therefore our sages ruled: 'I will go down and see' (Genesis 18:21) to teach the judges not to rule before they hear and understand, and from this we learn that even if it is clear to the judges that the defendant will be found guilty, they must listen to his arguments first..." See also: H.C., 3/58, 9/58. *Berman vs. The Minister of the Interior*, P.D. 12, p. 1493, p. 1507; H.C., 295/72. *Bachar vs. the District Rabbinical Court of Rehovot*, P.D. 27(1), p. 568, pp. 572-573.

64. H.C., 24/66. *Malkah vs. Sari Levi*, P.D. 20(1), p. 651, p. 657.

65. H.C., 311/65. *Marziano vs. the Polling Committee–Local Council of Ofakim*, P.D. 19(3), p. 393, pp. 396-398.

66. File 1390/5726, *The Federation of Agudat Israel and Poalei Agudat Israel, Rehovot vs. NRP, Rehovot Branch*, P.D.R. (*Piskei Din Rabbaniim*), 6, p. 166.

67. Apeal/5727/96. *The National Religious Party in Rehovot vs. the Federation of Agudat Israel in Rehovot and the Federation of Poalei Agudat Israel in Rehovot*, P.D.R. 6, p. 173, p. 176, at the bottom of the page.

68. Ibid., p. 181.

69. See: *Jewish Law*, Vol. 1, p. 74ff.

70. One of the three judges who signed the judgment in the Responsa of Maharah *Or Zarua*, 222, cited above, referred to in note 34.

71. *Golah ve-Nechar*, part 1, p. 518.

72. See: *Jewish Law*, Vol. 1, p. 65ff and p. 88ff. M. Elon, "*Mi-Baayot Ha-Halachah ve-ha-Mishpat be-Medinat Israel*" ("Problems of Halakhah and Law in the State of Israel"), Publications of the Society for the Study of the Jewish People in the Diaspora, under the auspices of the President of Israel, published by the Institute for Contemporary Jewry, The Hebrew University, Jerusalem, 1973, Series 6, No. 7, p. 9ff.; M. Elon, "*Baayot u-Megamot be-Yahasei Halakhah u-Medinah*" ("Problems and Trends in the Relationships between *Halakhah* and the State"), *Amudim* (publication of the religious kibbutzim), 1974, pp. 202-207, 256-264.

Criminal Law

[21]

SELF-INCRIMINATION IN JEWISH LAW — A REVIEW-ESSAY *

By Arnold Enker

Professor Kirschenbaum has given us a valuable addition to the rapidly growing literature in Jewish Law. This book is a thorough study of the Jewish law of self-incrimination, both in its historical perspectives and its extremely varied legal developments. Future writers on this topic will find themselves referring to this volume time and again.

The book is organized primarily into two parts. The first is "An Historical Study" in which Professor Kirschenbaum examines the Jewish law of self-incrimination at each significant stage of history from the Biblical period, through the Tannaitic and Amoraic Eras, and on into the Post-Talmudic and Medieval Rabbinic Ages. Particularly cogent and persuasive is the author's treatment of the theory that early tannaitic law accepted self-incriminating statements and that the rule against self-incrimination is a development of late tannaitic and early amoraic times. One by one, he examines the arguments in support of this thesis and convincingly demolishes them.

Also strong is Professor Kirschenbaum's exploration of the relevant Biblical sources although he is in this instance much more guarded in his conclusions. The treatment of the Achan episode in the book of Joshua is thorough and excellent. But I cannot agree that the two incidents in which King David executed persons on the basis of their confessions might lend support to the view that the Biblical requirement that guilt be established by two witnesses "was construed loosely, as an alternative or supplement to confes-

* A review essay based on a book by the same title written by Aaron Kirschenbaum and published by the Burning Bush Press, New York. 1970.

sion".[1] The evidence that David was acting in a judicial capacity seems to me particularly weak, especially in the case of Amalekite who reported Saul's death. And the fact that the incidents involved the killing of the king in one and of the sole surviving heir to the throne in the other [2] render the cases a very weak foundation for conclusions as to the nature of Biblical criminal procedure in general. Out of what seems to be an over-abundance of caution, Professor Kirschenbaum concludes that the issue must continue to "remain an open question to the critical scholar".[3]

Equally stimulating are those chapters treating of legal matters. The author's research is extensive. Starting with the basic tannaitic rule that a defendant cannot be convicted on the basis of his admission of guilt, and extending on into the amoraic discussions of the rule that a witness cannot disqualify himself from giving acceptable testimony by confessing to having violated the law, Professor Kirschenbaum guides the reader on through the wide range of circumstances that have concerned the Jewish Law at just about every stage of its development.

In this review I would like to develop some of the legal discussion a bit further.

The issue of self-incrimination in Jewish Law occurs in two contexts. The first concerns the defendant charged with committing an offense. The defendant cannot be convicted of the offense on the basis of his confession. His conviction can be obtained only on the testimony of two witnesses.

The second rule does not concern defendants in criminal cases but witnesses in any case. Ordinarily, a person who has been proved to have committed certain specified offenses is disqualified by law from serving as a witness. However, a witness does not become disqualified on the basis of his admission that he committed one of the disqualifying offenses. Disqualification of a witness,

1. Page 33. References are to the book under review unless otherwise indicated.
2. This point, originally made by the Ralbag, is reserved by the author until the chapter on Post-Talmudic Exegesis, (pp. 66—67), apparently in order to remain within the historical framework of the book's early chapters.
3. Page 33.

just as conviction of a defendant, may be had solely upon the testimony of witnesses.

The underlying assumption of this book is that there exists a close relationship in Jewish Law between these two rules. In the author's words, the rule concerning the witness' confession is "an extension" of the doctrine concerning the confessing defendant.[4] In support of this view Professor Kirschenbaum can muster an incompetent to testify to the facts in dispute in the case. The con-commentators.[5] I propose to examine this assumption more closely, for from a legal point of view these two rules seem to me to raise completely different problems and to relate to totally different situations.

The most obvious and elementary difference between the two rules concerns the immediate consequences of each. When a defendant charged with a crime wishes to confess to the accusation, Jewish Law rejects his confession thereby excluding from the court's consideration an item of evidence that, while perhaps not conclusive, is certainly of probative value. The very opposite is the result in the case of the confessing witness. Here, too, the witness is offering probative evidence concerning the matter at hand. But here, the witness' confession, if allowed, would render him a רשע incompetent to testify to the facts in dispute in the case. The consequence of the rule rejecting the witness' confession is to prevent such disqualification of the witness and render the rest of his testimony admissible.

The rule rejecting a defendant's confession, then, results in the exclusion of otherwise probative evidence while the consequence of the rule rejecting a witness' confession is the inclusion of probative evidence that would otherwise have been excluded. Such a contrasting situation strongly suggests the possibility that, their similarities notwithstanding, the two rules may not really be related

4. Page 50.

5. For a survey of the major sources, see *The Encyclopedia Talmudit*, entries
אדם קרוב אצל עצמו
and
אין אדם משים עצמו רשע.

to each other and that in fact they are concerned with totally different problems.

The thesis that the two rules are distinct also can command authority in its favor. The witness rule, as Professor Kirschenbaum teaches us, is amoraic in its documentary origin, while the tannaim discuss only the rule of the confessing defendant. Of greater significance, the statement of the witness rule in the amoraic sources is in the form אין אדם משים עצמו רשע and, as its legal basis we are given the rule אדם קרוב אצל עצמו. Neither of these expressions appears in the tannaitic sources given us by Professor Kirschenbaum.

So, too, Maimonides, the great systematizer renowned for precision in his choice of terminology and organizational scheme, very clearly and sharply separates the two rules. The confessing defendant rule is treated in הלכות סנהדרין[6] where procedure is discussed; the confessing witness rule is set forth in הלכות עדות[7] as a part of the rules on disqualified witnesses. The former is attributed by Maimonides to Biblical decree, quite clearly the Biblical requirement that two witnesses testify to the offence in question;[8] the latter rule is attributed to the principle that אין אדם משים עצמו רשע without any

6. Chapter 18, rule 6.

7. Chapter 12, rule 1.

8. At one point in the text, the author states:

> The scriptural decree mentioned by Maimonides would appear to be the dogmatic disqualification of a kinsman, including the defendant as his own nearest kinsman, from acting as a witness, coupled with the passage from Deuteronomy (19: 15—16)... which requires the testimony of a minimum of two eye witnesses in order to convict a man for a crime. (p. 63)

Maimonides' text not only offers no support for including the reference to the disqualification of a kinsman but explicitly refers to the two-witness rule solely.

> It is a scriptural decree that the court shall not put a man to death or flog him on his own admission (of guilt). This is done only on the evidence of two witnesses.

Elsewhere, the author cites the Rashbash's view that it would be "far-fetched" to define the scriptural decree referred to by Maimonides as the kinsman rule. (p. 68) Professor Kirschenbaum's inclusion of the rule disqualifying a relative from testifying appears to be based on his view that it is the combination of the two-witness rule and the rule disqualifying kinsmen from testifying that prevents us from treating the confessing defendant as one of the two required witnesses, see pp. 40—41, a view which will be discussed below.

indication whether this principle is Biblical in origin. And finally, in the case of the defendant's confession, Maimonides, albeit hesitatingly, suggests a reason for the rule, namely, fear that the confession is false; he makes no attempt to explain the policy behind the rule that rejects the witness' self-disqualifying confession.

There is still more explicit authority for the proposition that the two rules are entirely distinct; I so read the three responsa of the Rashbash cited by Professor Kirschenbaum,[9] particularly the last of the three. Professor Kirschenbaum reads the Rashbash as asserting that the rule excluding confessions applies only to witnesses but that a defendant's confession is acceptable, and is amazed that the Rashbash would assert a position so contrary to all accepted authority and to the views of Maimonides whom he quotes. The very force of Professor Kirschenbaum's argument suggests that he has attributed to the Rashbash too extreme a reading. The Rashbash, especially in Responsum 544, seems to be saying simply that the principle of אין אדם משים עצמו רשע applies only to confessing witnesses whereas the disqualification of a defendant's confession is based on a different rule. This not only seems to be the plain literal meaning of the Rashbash's responsa, but allies the Rashbash with the view I have here attributed to Maimonides as would be expected of him.

According to the thesis presented here, then, the rule excluding a defendant's confession is based on the Biblical requirement that conviction be based on the testimony of two witnesses. On the other hand, the rule preventing a witness from disqualifying himself from testifying is based on the distinct principle, applicable solely to witnesses, that a person may not testify concerning one of his relatives. The witness, being related to himself, is disqualified from testifying concerning himself; he therefore, cannot disqualify himself from testifying concerning other persons.

We will now examine each of these sets of doctrines separately.

The classical Jewish Law governing trial procedure differs from

9. Pages 68—72. Incidentally, a typographical error in note 47 refers to Responsum 521 of the Rashbash. The corrected reference should read Responsum 531.

the Common Law system in two significant respects. First, in Jewish Law the parties are incompetent to testify. This does not mean that they are not heard by the judge and have no opportunity to present their views and contentions before the court. But the law distinguishes quite sharply between the litigants and the witnesses, and their respective communications with the court differ one from the other. Litigants plead; witnesses testify.

At the initiation of the proceedings, the parties-litigants address the court themselves, stating their respective claims. The judges examine the statements, and, when appropriate, question the parties. Based on the various rules governing the evaluation of the pleadings and the weight to be accorded the various types of claims, the judges decide whether the case presents a triable issue.[10]

The witness' role is to establish those relevant issues of fact that remain in dispute after the pleadings. Here, too, Jewish Law differs from the Common Law system familiar to us, in that, generally speaking, it does not authorize the trier of the facts to evaluate the evidence freely. In the Common Law system all competent and relevant evidence is heard and, at the end of the trial, the judge and jury weigh the evidence and resolve what to reject and what to accept. In so doing, the trier of facts is relatively free of formal rules ascribing fixed weight to certain kinds of evidence.

In the Jewish Law, at least in its classical formulation which is what here concerns us, the court has much less freedom in evaluating the evidence; it is governed by formal rules to a greater degree. Thus, if two witnesses testify to a given fact and their testimony stands up under cross-examination, the fact is to be regarded as established and the court cannot reject the testimony.

And if there is a conflict in the testimony between two different groups of witnesses, each of which group's testimony withstood cross-examination successfully, the court is not free to prefer the

10. For an interesting discussion of the views of Jewish Law and of other legal systems on this matter, joined with a specific statutory proposal, see משרד המשפטים, הצעת חוק הראיות 83 (1952) (הצעת המיעוט).

testimony of one group over the other on the ground that the weight of the evidence favors one side.

The above description applies generally to both civil and criminal matters. Criminal matters differ from civil suits primarily in regard to the first of the two rules under consideration, namely, that in criminal matters the defendant's admissions of guilt will not be accorded any weight. But it is against this general background concerning pleadings and proof in Jewish Law that we can better understand the two rules concerning self-incriminating statements.

First, the rule excluding the defendant's confession. In the legal framework described above, the rule excluding a defendant's confession is neither remarkable nor extreme. Assume that two witnesses have testified against the defendant. What role is left for the defendant's confession? Under the formal rules of Jewish Law the answer is none. The testimony of the two witnesses being valid, it is adequate to assure a conviction and, indeed, leaves the court no choice but to convict. The defendant's confession adds no weight to the witness' testimony. If two other witnesses were to testify exonerating the defendant, his confession as we have seen could not be used to corroborate the first group and thereby prefer their testimony over that of the latter group. The defendant's confession then is an unnecessary extra. As stated so very concisely by the Rivash in his famous responsum:

„אבל בדיני נפשות לפי שורת הדין אין חשש בהודאת פיו שהרי אינו מתחייב מיתה על פי עצמו רק על פי עדים ואין הודאתו מעלה ומורדת..." [11]

Suppose, however, only one witness were present. Could the confessing defendant join him to provide the necessary two witneses? The answer again is no; the defendant is a party to the proceedings

11. See page 87. The existence of a relationship between the rules of pleading and procedure and the rule rejecting the defendant's confession is strongly suggested in the Rivash's responsum. The Rivash's decision to allow the confession induced him to instruct the inquiring court to alter the order of proof and the procedures relating to pleadings.

and therefore cannot be a witness. He may be heard in pleading but not in testimony.[12]

The only possible way in which the defendant's confession could be heard is, then, not as testimony, but as pleading. If the defendant's plea of guilt were to be accepted that would be the end of the case; there would be no need, indeed there would be no occasion, for hearing the witnesses. Under these circumstances, then, the question of the acceptability or nonacceptability of a defendant's confession in Jewish Law is not really a question of admissibility as that term is used in the Common Law system, but whether the defendant may be convicted on the basis of his confession alone.

Thus reformulated, the rule rejecting the defendant's confession as a basis for conviction is readily understandable, and in this legal context, Maimonides' suggestion that the policy ground underlying the rule rejecting the defendant's confession is the fear that the confession may be false is plausible. The confession, in Jewish Law, would be offered not as merely one among many items of evidence which could be weighed and considered against the rest of the evidence. The issue is rather whether to convict the defendant on his confession alone. A party in civil litigation is permitted to admit liabiity; but when punishment is at stake, the dangers of false confessions are sufficiently great to warrant especially strict procedures which forbid conviction and punishment based on the confession alone.[13] Indeed, our law today does not permit the conviction of a defendant on the basis of an out of court confession

12. In the view accepted by Professor Kirschenbaum, the defendant would have been able to join with one witness to provide the necessary two witnesses were it not for the dogma that he is related to himself (p. 41). As we will see below, Rava, who takes a leading part in the amoraic discussions under consideration, drew a sharp distinction between the defendant and the witnesses. It was a premise of Rava's system that parties were not potential witnesses.

13. Interestingly, in recommending that the court accept the confession, the Rivash was careful to state:

> in order that the matter be clarified by his own statements *in conjunction with additional item sof proof*... (Emphasis added.) See the full quotation at page 87.

alone.[14] And there is a growing tendency in the case of an incourt guilty plea to require the prosecutor to present to the court at least a summary of the evidence in order to assure the court that the plea is grounded in reality.[15]

The above analysis is irrelevant to the case of the witness who in the course of his testimony against someone else admits facts that would render him a רשע and disqualify his testimony. The rule against accepting a defendant's confession protects him from any possible punishment, and the issue before the court is not

14. Perhaps the leading Israeli case is Cr. App. 290/59, *Anonymous* v. *The Attorney General*. 14 P.D. 1489. Justice Landau cites Maimonides' suggestion of a reason for the rule. Under the analysis offered here the reference to Jewish Law by Justice Landau was appropriate. We will see later that the United States Supreme Court has referred to Jewish Law on this subject inappropriately.

The rule against conviction upon an-out-of-court confession alone is accepted in the United States as well. A leading case is *Wong Sun* v. *United States*, 371 U.S. 471, 83 Sup. Ct. 407 (1963). See also 7 Wigmore, Evidence §§ 2070—71 (3d ed. 1940): McCormick, Evidence §§ 75, 110 (1954). The English rule is less strict. See the discussions in Cr. App. 290/59, and in Wigmore and in McCormick, supra.

15. Rule 11 of the Federal Rules of Criminal Procedure provides:

> The court shall not enter a judgment upon a plea of guilty unless it is satisfied that there is a factual basis for the plea.

See *McCarthy* v. *United States*, 394 U.S. 459, 463 (1969). Standard 1.6 of the American Bar Association Minimum Standards for Criminal Justice, Standards Relating to Pleas of Guilty, recommends that a judgment of conviction should not be entered on a plea of guilty "without making such inquiry as may satisfy [the court] that there is a factual basis for the plea". See also the American Law Institute, Model Code of PreArraignment Procedure, Tent. Draft No. 5, §450.4(3) (1972). For a discussion of the problems created by undue reliance on the guilty plea without more detailed development of the facts in the case, see Samuels, *The Guilty Plea and Sentencing: Proposed Improvements*, 115 Sol. J. 120 (1971). Some, but not all, of the problems considered therein are cured by sections 75 and 136 of Israel's Code of Criminal Procedure which require the parties to plead the facts rather than legal conclusions such as "guilty".

Section 138 of Israel's Code of Criminal Procedure provides that facts admitted by the defendant at pleading are to be treated as proved unless the court decides not to accept the plea or the plea is withdrawn.

> עובדה שהנאשם הודה בה יראוה כמוכחת כלפיו זולת אם ראה בית המשפט
> שלא לקבל את ההודיה כראיה או שהנאשם חזר בו מן ההודיה לפי סעיף 137.

It has been suggested that this language forbids the court from taking evidence in order to satisfy itself as to the correctness of the defendant's admissions and that, having accepted the plea, the court must treat the admitted facts as proved and may not inquire further into the matter.

An excellent treatment of the general problem can be founded in Christie and Pye, *Presumptions and Assumptions in the General Law: Another View*, 1970 Duke L.J. 919, 926—31.

whether to punish the witness but whether to accept his testimony. There is therefore no particular reason to be exceptionally strict because of possible lingering doubts concerning the truthfulness of the confession as we were when punishment was the issue.

Moreover, there is less reason to discredit the witness' self-incriminating statement than there was in the case of the accused. First, since there is no possibility of punishment resulting, the psychological motivations mentioned by Maimonides in the case of the defendant are here absent. Second, and more significantly, the witness' admission of guilt of a disqualifying offense is often an integral part of his total overall testimony, and from the point of view of the total credibility of his statements it would be exceedingly difficult for the court to give credence to part of his testimony yet disbelieve his disqualifying admission. Indeed, as Professor Kirschenbaum so persuasively demonstrates, the halacha treats of several situations in which the witness' admission is highly credible, so much so that for certain purposes the court is prepared to believe him. Nonetheless, the admission will not be accepted to disqualify the witness.[16] Quite clearly, then, the basis for the rule in modern terms is not its lack of credibility, but its lack of competency based on external policy considerations.[17]

16. From Maimonides' treatment of the Mishna in Yebamot 25a, we may infer his view that the witness' self-incriminating statement is rejected even though it is likely true. When one witness testifies that a certain woman's husband is dead she is free to remarry but the witness may not marry her. The reason offered by Maimonides for forbidding the witness to marry the woman is that he might otherwise lie in order to marry her.

רמב"ם, יד חזקה, הלכות גירושין, פרק י', הלכה י"ד: „שאנו חוששין שמא עיניו נתן בה ולפיכך העיד לה".

If the witness testifies not merely that her husband is dead but that he himself killed him, the woman is again free to remarry though not to marry the witness. But the reason for this disqualification according to Maimonides is not that he might otherwise lie in order to be able to marry her but that he might otherwise kill her husband.

„העיקר אצלנו אין אדם משים עצמו רשע לפיכך אם אמר הרגתיו תנשא [אשתו] לאחר אבל הוא לא ישאנה גזרה שכל מי שיחשוק אשת איש יהרוג בעלה וישאנה". רמב"ם, פירוש המשניות, משנה שם.

17. Maimonides' failure to refer to doubts as to the credibility of the confession in the case of witnesses is, then, not at all because this explanation of the confessing-defendant rule "did not satisfy Maimonides himself" as Professor Kirschen-

The formal basis for the rule cannot be the two-witness requirement as the witness does not stand accused in jeapordy of punishment for the offense he admits. The issue is his qualifications to testify. Rava's legal acumen is clearly reflected in the ruling. a man is related to himself. The problem is to אדם קרוב אצל עצמו, find a rule applicable to witnesses that would disqualify that portion of the witness' testimony concerning himself without disqualifying the rest. This Rava found in the rule that a witness is disqualified to testify concerning one of his relations to which he appended the ruling that the witness is related to himself and therefore cannot testify concerning himself.

Still, it must be admitted that the principle of אדם קרוב אצל עצמו is at best a formal explanation of the rule rejecting the witness' self-disqualifying admission. Logic did not inexorably require that the witness be considered related to himself. And having so ruled, Rava's additional ruling to the effect that the witness' testimony could be rejected in part and accepted in part is even less dictated by logic's imperatives. It is plausible to suggest that the rule is a legal construction designed to prevent witnesses from disqualifying themselves, thereby depriving the court of relevant testimony and denying litigants their legal rights.

Our analysis, to summarize, yields the conclusion that we are actually talking about two different rules, each dealing with distinct problems and apparently directed at different ends. The rule rejecting a defendant's confession has nothing to do with any notion of disqualification for relatedness; such disqualification applies only to witnesses. Where punishment is not at issue, parties are always permitted to admit the charges against them despite being related to themselves. It is apparently a special ruling for cases involving punishment applying to such cases a strict reading of the two-

baum argues (p. 63), an argument that overshoots the mark for it fails to explain why then Maimonides did offer the explanation in הלכות סנהדרין, but is attributable to the fact that the explanation based on questionable credibility applies only to the confessing-defendant rule, while the confessing-witness rule is explained on grounds other than credibility.

witness requirement, and may be based on the fear that standing alone the confession is too slender a basis for conviction.[18]

Conversely, the rule rejecting the witness' confession seems to have nothing to do with the first rule. Disqualification of a witness with the consequent loss of his relevant testimony is what is at stake, not possible punishment, so that exaggerated concern over possible false confessions is no longer in order. Instead, the rule is based on the disqualification for relatedness. While the two rules may be said to use similar techniques, namely, disallowance of a speaker's adverse statements about himself, both the legal and the likely policy bases for the two rules are distinct.

I would now suggest the significance of the differences between the analysis presented here and that more commonly accepted, by examining two issues dealt with by Professor Kirschenbaum — one theoretical, the other practical — and showing how each analysis leads to different conclusions.

We have already noted the formal nature of Rava's ruling **אדם קרוב אצל עצמו**. Professor Kirschenbaum asserts the view that Rava's dictum "should not be taken literally" but was intended to be understood "metaphorically".[19] I am not sure that I understand what metaphor is intended here, but in any event I think that one must take Rava quite literally. Rava, as we will see in a moment, held a clear conception of the difference between a defendant and a witness. He knew that the rule excluding a defendant's confession could not furnish a legal basis for preventing a witness' admission of guilt from disqualifying him. Accordingly, in order to save the witness' testimony, he turned to the rules governing witnesses to find a basis for rejecting the admission. He found such a basis

18. Those who maintain the view that the rule **אדם קרוב אצל עצמו** applies to parties as well as witnesses encounter great difficulties in explaining why parties in civil cases may admit liability. See the different views assembled by Professor Kirschenbaum at pp. 78—81. The artificial constructions they are forced to erect suggest the merits of the simpler explanation offered here, namely, that disqualification for relatedness is limited to witnesses, that ordinarily a party may admit his liability, and that the rule disqualifying a defendant's confession is a special rule in criminal matters.

19. Page 58.

in the rule disqualifying a witness from testifying concerning his relatives, and declared that the witness' confession is incompetent since he is related to himself.

Professor Kirschenbaum reaches the conclusion that Rava is being metaphorical in asserting אדם קרוב אצל עצמו from an analysis of two problems. In the first he discerns a logical difficulty in Rava's reasoning. He says,

> Of greater interest and in need of a more extended analysis is Raba's formulation of the juridic reason that a man may not render himself a *rasha*. The reason given, 'A man is a *Qarob*, kinsman, unto himself; hence no man may incriminate himself' is surprising, for it runs counter to what we would expect logically. Were we presented with the fact that the law disqualifies a defendant and his *qerobim*, kinsmen, from acting as witnesses at the trial and then informed that these two disqualifications are interrelated, it would have been reasonable for us to assume that the disqualification of the defendant himself was axiomatic and the disqualification of the relatives was a logical extension of this axiom. The talmudic formulation, on the other hand, starts from the dogmatic disqualification of the kinsmen and derives the disqualification of the defendant himself by identifying him as one of those relatives![20]

The logical difficulty exists only on the assumption that "these two disqualifications are interrelated" and that the talmudic formulation "derives the disqualification of the defendant himself by identifying him as one of those relatives". The thesis suggested in this review rejects that derivation and bases the confessing-defendant rule on grounds that are distinct from the confessing-witness rule.

20. Pages 55—56.

The second issue that merits the author's attention in this context[21] is the talmudic discussion of disqualification of an entire group of witnesses based on the presence of a single disqualified relation amongst them. Replying to the suggestion that the accused himself witnessed the events at issue and is therefore to be included among the witnesses, and that being related to himself he is disqualified to testify, which in turn disqualifies the entire group, Rava replies by asserting the distinction between witnesses and those who perform the acts which are the subject of the ligitation, *i.e.*, the defendant.[22]

On this basis, Professor Kirschenbaum correctly concludes,

> Though a man is said to be a 'kinsman' to himself, there is a basic difference between him and his 'other' relatives... The defendant's own statements in court never attain the legal status of 'testimony' to begin with and thus could never bring about the rejection of any group of witnesses.[23]

But at this point the author concludes that "the qualitative distinction between the accused himself and his kinsman" indicates that "kinsman" is being used metaphorically in the dictum **אדם קרוב אצל עצמו**.

The author's analysis which bases the rejection of the defendant's confession on the "kinsman" rule runs into difficulty when it confronts Rava's assertion of the difference between witnesses and parties. To resolve that difficulty it treats Rava's use of the term "kinsman" nonlegally, metaphorically. However, it is precisely because Rava intends us to understand him quite literally when he states **אדם קרוב אצל עצמו** that the defendant if counted as a witness, would disqualify the group. If the defendant were only metaphorically related to himself he would not endanger the qualifications of the other witnesses even were he to be counted in their number. Rava avoids the disqualification of the group, not by reducing the force

21. Pages 56—58.
22. The source in B. Makkot 6a.
23. Page 58.

of his ruling that אדם קרוב אצל עצמו that might have resurrected the possibility that the witness could disqualify himself by confessing to being a *rasha* — but by asserting the distinction between the witnesses and the parties. The latter are not witnesses; the rule disqualifying the entire group of witnesses if one witness is related to the parties does not encompass them.

At this point it is appropriate to stress the fact that it is the very same Rava who asserts the principle פלגינן דיבורא in order to avoid disqualification of the confessing witness. Rava's views comport with the thesis advanced in this review. Aware of the complete separation in Jewish Law between defendants and witnesses, Rava could not treat the witness as partaking of both categories, *i.e.*, as a witness insofar as he testifies against someone else and as a defendant insofar as he implicates himself. Rava, therefore, treats him as a witness in all respects. His testimony against someone else is competent. But as he is related to himself, he is incompetent to be a witness concerning himself. The results is that he cannot disqualify himself as a witness and his testimony against someone else stands unimpaired.[24]

The second question we will consider is whether the extensive material in Jewish Law dealing with confessions and admissions is of any practical relevance to the problems faced by our contemporary legal system. The subject of the validity of confessions was a major controversial issue in the United States during the last decade, and indeed, the Supreme Court of the United States, in two leading decisions, cited Jewish Law as authority for a view that

24. The view offered in the text is contrary to that of ראב"ד who, at least in Meiri's interpretation of his views, asserts that the self-incriminating witness is to be regarded as a defendant with respect to the self-incriminating part of his testimony. ראב"ד does so in order to resolve the difficulties in the Talmudic text in B. Sanhedrin 10a. However, in order to accomplish this purpose he is required to create a legal principle עדות שבטלה מקצתה בטלה כולה for which there is no other basis to the best of my knowledge. The view offered in the text is not inconsistent with the interpretation of ראב"ד offered in יד רמה. In any event, it is clear from the sources that Maimonides rejects ראב"ד's view. So too, Rashi. The sources are to be found in B. Sanhedrin 10a and the commentaries thereon, and in Maimonides' Code of Jewish Law, Laws of Witnesses, chapter 12, rule 2. ראב"ד's dissent from Maimonides' ruling can be found there, too.

excludes confessions.[25] More recently, the subject has become very controversial in England, while in Israel the issues continue to be discussed though much more calmly. Does the *Mishpat Ivri* really have anything to contribute to these discussions?

Professor Kirschenbaum's treatment of this question is cautious and brief.[26] While he offers "the wisdom and insights" of Jewish Law "for reflection and as a relevant contribution to the discussion",[27] he is careful to suggest possibly qualifying social and historical factors, and concludes with an eloquent statement of the implications of the religious faith that forms the framework for Jewish Law.

On the basis of the analysis of Jewish Law outlined here I would suggest that the Jewish Law treating confessions is not particularly relevant to the confessions debate, primarily because the procedural and evidentiary premises of the Jewish legal system which developed these rules are so radically different from our own that the legal issues posed are equally different. As we have already seen, the issue in Jewish Law is in reality the sufficiency of a confession standing by itself as a basis for conviction. In contemporary law the question is not the sufficiency of the confession standing alone but whether it is admissible, whether the trier of the facts should hear this item of evidence along with the rest of the evidence and

25. *Miranda* v. *Arizona*, 384 U.S. 436, 458 n. 27, 86 S. Ct. 1602, 1619 n. 27 (1966); *Garrity* v. *New Jersey*, 385 U.S. 493, 497 n. 5, 87 S. Ct. 616, 619 n. 5 (1967).

There is an irony in Mr. Justice Douglas' reliance on the halacha in support of his views concerning self-incrimination Professor Kirschenbaum quite correctly points out that as regards witnesses the Jewish Law of self-incrimination and its American counterpart yield opposite results, for while the Jewish Law principle prevents disqualification and renders the testimony admissible, the American rule has become a vehicle whereby witnesses avoid testifying by invoking the possibility that their testimony will incriminate them (pp. 110—111). The device used in American law to achieve the same result as is reached in Jewish law is the immunity statute whereby the witness is granted immunity from the consequences of his testimony thereby eliminating the basis for any possible self-incrimination. Mr. Justice Douglas has been one of the leading opponents of such legislation. See his dissenting opinion in *Ullmann* v. *United States*, 350 U.S. 422, 440, 445—54, 76 S. Ct. 497, 507, 510—15 (1956). This suggests the risks involved in citing foreign legal sources on the basis of superficial similarities.

26. Pages 133—37. Compare former Associate Justice of the United States Supreme Court Arthur Goldberg's remarks in his Introduction to the book.

27. Page 134.

evaluate it freely. There is no evidence that Jewish Law, when it operates on the basis of free evaluation of evidence, would reject confessions absolutely. Indeed, the evidence is to the contrary.

My second qualification is based on the fact that the Jewish Law excluding confessions is the Sanhedrin law applying Biblical rules. Professor Kirschenbaum sets forth in his book the many grounds which would permit deviating from Biblical law. Emergency measures, with emergency defined so broadly that the state of emergency may exist for generations, is a common technique. And the king in his courts, concerned as he is with the practical problems of punishing crime, is not bound to apply Biblical law. Clearly modern courts do not function as a Sanhedrin but are more analogous to the king's courts which are free not to follow Biblical procedure so that the Jewish Law itself would not seem to call upon our courts to reject confessions totally.

Professor Kirschenbaum, too, recognizes these limitations but concludes,

> It is evident from the pages of this study that they [the Rabbis of the Talmud] and their medieval successors consistently applied the law against self-incrimination to all cases that did remain within their jurisdiction.[28]

Yet, if one examines the cases referred to in the light of the analysis offered here, namely, that we are really talking about two separate rules, one concerning defendants and the other concerning witnesses, one finds that it is only the confessing-witness rule, which as we have noted results in the inclusion rather than the exclusion of testimony, that is consistently applied. The confessing-defendant rule, which would exclude evidence from the court's consideration, was not regularly applied.

But even if our analysis would suggest that the *Mishpat Ivri* is not particularly relevant to the contemporary debates concerning confessions, we have seen that it is most relevant to another, albeit far less controversial issue, namely, whether a modern court should convict a defendant of a crime based on his confession or plea of

28. Page 135.

guilty exclusively. While there is no room in the contemporary system of proof for the absolute exclusion of confessions and guilty pleas, an increased sensitivity to their limitations as proof and the introduction of a requirement that the judge ascertain what other evidence exists to be weighed with the confession before entering the conviction would be a warranted lesson to learn from the Jewish Law.

Professor Kirschenbaum's book, then, is to be commended not only for its consistent treatment of a fascinating group of legal questions, but also because it has opened up for discussion a much more fundamental issue. Those of us who hold Jewish Law dear and who pray to see its rebirth not only in academic circles but in the law by which we order our daily affairs, have the special obligation to be certain that it is truly the *Mishpat Ivri* we are elaborating, and that our desire to be relevant to the issues of our day does not cause us to misinterpret the Jewish Law. As we have seen, two possible interpretations of the Jewish law of confessions, each having authority and reason in its support, lead respectively to differing conclusions concerning the lessons to be learned from the *Mishpat Ivri*. Yet even here, perhaps it would be appropriate to conclude אלו ואלו דברי אלקים חיים.

[22]

The Jewish Law Annual, Vol.IX

THE ROLE OF PUNISHMENT IN JEWISH CRIMINAL LAW: A CHAPTER IN RABBINIC PENOLOGICAL THOUGHT*

by

AARON KIRSCHENBAUM**

A. *The Problem*

1. The impracticality of the classical Jewish law and its helplessness in coping with social problems involving crime and punishment are proverbial. An example of this is the rule that no man can be convicted of a crime unless there were a fore-warning and its rejection on the part of the accused — both almost in the same breath.[1]

Testimony was limited to *eye*-witnesses, at least two in number; "seeing the crime together, they must testify together, and before the same tribunal."[2]

Circumstantial evidence, no matter how convincing, is insufficient for conviction — as illustrated by the Rabbi Simeon b. Shetaḥ incident.[3]

Moreover, if one or more witnesses is found to be a relative or to be otherwise disqualified, the entire group of witnesses must be disbanded.[4]

There are numerous qualifications that citizens must possess in order to be acceptable as valid witnesses. "Ten types of people are disqualified from acting as witnesses, they are: women, slaves, minors, the mentally deficient, deaf-mutes, the blind, lawbreakers, the shameless [by whose conduct it is seen that they possess no sense

* This is an English version of an article in Hebrew that appeared in *Tel Aviv University Law Review* 12 (1987), 253-266.

** Professor of Jewish Law, Faculty of Law, Tel Aviv University.

1 Maimonides, *Judges*, *Sanh*. 12:12.

2 *Ibid*., "Testimony" 4:1.

3 *Y. Sanh*. 37b.

4 Maimonides, *ibid*., 5:3.

of dignity], relatives, and interested parties; ten all told."[5]

"Two [witnesses] are as strong as one hundred, and one hundred as two"; therefore if two groups of witnesses, regardless of their respective sizes, contradict each other, the case is thrown out of court.[6]

On one hand, criminal procedure is rigged extravagantly to bring about the acquittal of the accused, for Scripture commands, *and the congregation shall save [the accused].*[7] So much so that, as is known, "A *Sanhedrin* which executes someome once in seven years is called 'bloody'; R. Eliezer b. Azariah says: Once in seventy years."[8] But on the other hand, the Torah is replete with prohibitions the violation of which carries the capital penalty; Maimonides finds their number to be thirty-six.[9]

How did the Rabbis understand their legal system which, on the one hand, makes the punishment of criminals well-nigh impossible and, on the other, contains so many capital crimes?

2. The famous declaration of Rabbis Tarfon and Akiva that, by ingenious tactics in the examination of witnesses, they would abolish capital punishment[10] raises the query as to how these pious rabbis understood the oft-repeated biblical mandate, *and he shall surely die.* Did they then arrogate to themselves a morality higher than that of Sacred Scripture?

3. And finally, Maimonides and the other great authorities of the Middle Ages who address themselves to practical problems frequently invoke royal prerogative and resort to the exigency jurisdiction of the rabbinic courts.[11] Although such measures are reassuring in that they were instrumental in the maintenance of law and order,[12] they do place in bold relief the inadequacy of the classical

5 *Ibid.*, 9:1. followed by a detailed explanation of each type.

6 *M. Makk.* 1:7; *B. Yoma* 83a; *B. Yoma* 18:3.

7 *M.B.Y. Sanh.* 4-5, Maimonides, *Judges*, "*Sanh.*" 11-12.

8 *M. Makk.* 1:10.

9 Maimonides, *ibid.*, 15:10-13.

10 *M. Makk.*, *ibid.*

11 E.g., Maimonides, *Judges*, *Sanh.*, 18:6.

12 E.g., R. Isaac b. Sheshet, *Responsa Rivash* II, 234-239. Cf. S. Assaf, *Ha'onashim aḥare Ḥatimat Hatalmud* (Jerusalem: Ṣifriyah Mishpaṭit,

criminal procedure.[13]

What are we to make of all this?

The explanation usually proffered for the "romanticism" that characterizes rabbinic (i.e., tannaitic) penology is the historical setting in which the Rabbis found themselves. The Jewish community had been deprived of its jurisdiction over criminal matters "forty years before the destruction of the Holy Temple",[14] that is approximately one hundred years before Rabbi Akiva and his colleague made their famous declaration. Hence, since "the dirty work" of criminal punishment was in the hands of the Roman authorities, so the argument goes, these rabbis could allow themselves the luxury of irresponsibility in matters of law and order.[15]

This explanation, however, ignores the great piety of the Rabbis and their extreme conservatism when it came to preserving traditional teachings.[16] It also ignores the feverish activity with which R. Akiva sought to achieve the restoration of Jewish independence.[17,18] Surely, had he succeeded he could ill-afford the luxury

---

1922).

13 It should be noted that only the king himself or only the court itself could decide, at their discretion, when circumstances justified deviation from scriptural law.

14 See below.

15 For example: P. Dykan (Dickstein), *Criminal Law* (Hebrew; Tel Aviv: Yavneh, 1966), 618; G.F. Moore, *Judaism in the First Centuries of the Christian Era: The Age of the Tannaim* (Cambridge: Harvard University Press, 1950) II.187; B. Cohen, "Evidence in Jewish Law", *Recueils de la Société Jean Bodin* 16 (1965), III; H.H. Cohn, "The Penology of the Talmud", *Jewish Law in Ancient and Modern Israel* (New York: Ktav, 1971), 61-62.

16 *M. Eduy.* 1:3; *B. Sukk.* 28a; S. Mendelsohn, "Capital Punishment", *Jewish Encyclopaedia* III, 558 (criminal traditions preserved by the Rabbis whose antiquity is confirmed by Josephus); see further: B. Rabinowitz-Teomin, "Capital Trials According to Torah Law and According to Royal Prerogative" (Hebrew), *Hatorah Vehamedinah* 2 (1952), 45-81.

17 R. Akiva ardently supported the Bar-Kokhba rebellion in its struggle for Jewish liberation from Roman rule: *Y. Ta'an.* 4:5; *B. Sanh.* 97b.

18 For an accurate description of the term, "hilkhata lemashiḥa", cf. *Talmud Encyclopaedia* (Hebrew), IX.388.

of irresponsibility in matters of law and order.

In any event, responsibility or irresponsibility, how did these Rabbis read Sacred Scripture? Thus, our study is not an historical one. We do not intend to study the state of the administration of justice at that time. Our study, rather, is an attempt to grasp the penological theory of the rabbis — of the *Tannaim*, the *Amoraim* and of the *Rishonim* (primarily, but not exclusively, of Maimonides).

B. *The Ran's Approach*

Our point of departure is a thesis proposed by rabbi Nissim of Gerondi (the *Ran*), the Spanish talmudist of the fourteenth century, in a sermon in which he attempted to reconcile the contradiction between the opposition of the Prophet Samuel to the appointment of a king and the positive commandment laid down in Deuteronomy to do so.[19] In the course of his exposition, the Ran distinguishes between the law and procedure of the classical (biblical-talmudic) criminal code (*mishpaṭ amiti tsodeḳ be'atsmo*, "the authentic law inherently just") and the king's administration of criminal justice (*haṣiddur hamedini*, "the maintenance of law and order"). He says:

> Our *Torah* is unique among the normative systems of the nations of the world. Its laws and commandments do not have as their purpose the maintenance of society but rather the descent of the Divine effulgence upon our nation and its communion with us. They seem to be of a nature similar to the sacrificial offerings and the Temple service.[20] There is no doubt that the divine Effulgence has descended and been joined unto us by those deeds though they defy human logic. This should not surprise us for just as we do not understand numerous natural phenomena though their existence is a fact, so do we not fathom the causes for the descent of the divine Effulgence and its being joined unto us. It is in this respect that our holy *Torah* is unique, differing from the normative systems of the nations of the world, for they have no relationship to it [the Effulgence] but only to the maintenance of their society.
>
> I am therefore of the opinion, and it is a correct belief, that just as the non-rational commandments have nothing to do with maintaining

19 *Derashot Haran*, ed. E.L. Feldman (Jerusalem: Makhon Shalem, 1977), 11, pp.190-191. Translation my own (A.K.). See the recent discussion in Y. Ahituv, "The *Ran* and the *Torah* State" (Hebrew), *Amudim (Tammuz*, 1986), 256-260.

20 *Cf.* Abbaye's statement, *Sanh.* 51b.

the political stability of society — they have their justification solely in bringing down the Divine Effulgence — so the civil code of the *Torah* has everything to do with combining to bring down the Divine Matter upon our nation and to maintaining our society Indeed, it is possible that the civil laws of the *Torah* are directed more to that elevated purpose than to the maintenance of our society, for this latter purpose could be achieved by the king whom we shall appoint over us. The duty of the judges and courts, however, were to govern the people in accordance with the authentic law inherently just in order to draw upon us the Divine Matter, whether they deal adequately with ordering the activities of the masses or not.

Because this is so, it is possible to find in some of the laws and ordinances of the nations measures more effective for the establishment and maintenance of law and order than in the laws of the Torah. This is not to our detriment, for whatever is lacking with regard to law and order may be filled by the king.

Thus, the king's administration of criminal justice is practical in nature, created to cope with the everyday ordering of society; it is parallel to the criminal codes of other nations. But the classical biblical code is above considerations of societal utility. "Inherently just", it is nothing less than a body of ritual whose mystical effect is to bring down the Divine Effulgence upon the Chosen People. Indeed the criminal code of Scripture is no less a ritual than the sacrificial offerings of the Holy Temple and, like them, is non-pragmatic in purpose and non-utilitarian in nature.

We make no attempt to expound upon the mystical ramifications of the *Ran*'s thesis. In line with his approach, however, we wish to advance the following argument: the rabbis of the Talmud and their medieval successors regarded the criminal law of the *Torah* as primarily a mighty instrument of character training, religious indoctrination and spiritual edification,[21] and only secondarily (and sometimes not at all) as of practical import.[22]

21 *Midrash Bereshit Rabbah* 44:1; Maimonides, *Guide of the Perplexed* 3:26. Cf. *Novellae Rashba, Bava Batra* (Jerusalem, 1963), III, 120.

22 Cf. M. Greenberg, "Some Postulates of Biblical Criminal Law", *Yehezkel Kaufman Jubilee Volume* (Jerusalem: Magnes Press, 1960), 5, part II.

C. *Jewish Law as an Educative Force*

Corroboration of the *Ran's* thesis may be found in the law of the Stubborn and Rebellious Son, in which restrictive interpretation rendered the "law" totally inoperative.

Scripture ordains:

> If a man have a stubborn and rebellious son, that will not hearken to the voice of his father or the voice of his mother, and though they chasten him, will not hearken unto them; then shall his father and mother lay hold on him and bring him out unto the elders of his city and unto the gate of his place; and they shall say unto the elders of the city: "This our son is stubborn and rebellious, he doth not hearken to our voice; he is a glutton and a drunkard." And the men of the city shall stone him with stones that he die; so shalt thou put away the evil from the midst of thee; and all Israel shall hear and fear (*Deut.* 21:18-21).

Halakhic *midrash*, selectively cited, yields the following restrictions:

If a man have a stubborn and rebellious son: "a son" — but not a daughter; "a son" — but not a full-grown man; whilst a minor is exempt, since he does not come within the scope of the commandments ... The extreme limits of a "stubborn and rebellious son" are only three months ... If he ate any food except meat or drank any drink except wine, he does not become a "stubborn and rebellious son", for it is written, *he is a glutton* [which implies meat] *and a drunkard* [which implies wine] ...

If one of them [his father or his mother] had a hand or finger cut off, or was lame, dumb, blind or deaf, he does not become a "stubborn and rebellious son". Because it is written, *Then shall his father and mother lay hold of him* — this excludes those with hands or fingers cut off; *and bring him out* excluding lame parents; *and they shall say* — excluding the dumb; *this our son* — excluding the blind; *he will not obey our voice* — excluding the deaf-mute.[23]

Rabbi Simeon declares: "The Rebellious Son neither was nor will ever be. Why, then was [the law] written? 'Interpret it and receive a reward therefore'." In other words, the criminal nature of the scriptural passage was negated; it was viewed as a subject for theoretical interpretation, moral education, spiritual edification.[24]

23 *B. Sanh.* 68b-71b.

24 Scripture's declaration: *and all Israel shall hear and fear* must,

Rabbi Jonathan demurs, "I saw him and stood upon his grave." The Talmud, however, mentions no detail of the extraordinarily bizarre series of restrictive interpretations with which R. Jonathan takes issue. May we not assume, therefore, that R. Jonathan took the Rebellious Son to be a rather rare occurrence? Whereas R. Simeon viewed it as expunged from criminal code and as taking the role of a dire warning regarding juvenile delinquency, R. Jonathan viewed it as *essentially* educational but not *exclusively* so.[25]

The same may be said regarding the "laws" of the Idolatrous City (*Deut.* 13:13-19, teaching the vital necessity of resisting all temptation to idolatry) and of the Leprous House (*Lev.* 14: 33-53, with the religious message it was meant to convey).[26]

The numerous capital crimes found in Scripture are not far behind. Idolatry, adultery, incest, murder, blasphemy, and the others, were undoubtedly paragraphs in the criminal code.[27] but the numerous details as to what constitutes the criminal act, the evidence required for conviction, and the judicial procedure to be followed must have convinced the Rabbis that teaching was uppermost in the mind of the Divine legislator, the penalties only of minor significance.[28] Thus, for example, how else would the Israelite be taught that certain types of incest are sins somewhat less severe than the desecration of the Sabbath but much more serious than eating pig?[29] Punishment was thus rarely meted out, but the serious nature of the infraction was duly impressed upon the people.[30]

---

following R. Simeon, be understood in a similar manner. Cf. *B. Sanh.* 89a.

25 R. Judah demurs on one detail, but not on the general thrust rendering the "law" of the Stubborn and Rebellious Son inoperative; cf. *B. Sanh.* 71a.

26 *Ibid.* For a modern presentation of the thesis of the *Ran*, see Rabbi J.B. Soloveitchik, *Halakhic Man*, trans. L. Kaplan (Philadelphia: Jewish Publication Society of America, 1983), ch.VI.

27 The expression "Interpret it and receive an award therefor" is found in another criminal context: *B. Sanh.* 51b.

28 Cf. Maimonides' Commentary to M. Hor. 3:8.

29 Maimonides' Commentary to *M.* Ab. 2:1. Rabbenu Jonah, *Sha'arei Teshuvah*, gate 3.

30 See Moore, *supra* note 15, at p.186. Rabbi M. Feinstein has expressed

The pedagogic role of *Torah* law was uppermost with Rabbis Tarphon and Akiva;[31] they therefore did not feel that they were arrogating to themselves a morality higher than that of Moses by abolishing a capital punishment ordained by God. Rabban Simeon B. Gamaliel is not recorded as opposing any of the myriads of details held by Rabbis Tarphon and Akiva. His argument was that an *open declaration* to the effect that — in practice — there were no capital crimes and that all was educational, hortatory and inspirational, would encourage crime. Better that the *possibility* of capital punishment remain on record (though in actuality as a mere secondary element in the criminal law).[32]

Contrast this with the way the *Torah* chose to educate the citizen in matters of assault and battery. Had the interpretation of *An Eye for an Eye* been a literal one, one who assaulted his fellow would resemble one who murdered him in that ransom could be paid and composition could not be made. Since the Oral Tradition, however, interpreted the *lex talionis* as referring to monetary compensation, one who assaults his fellow is regarded as having committed a tort: the law has no interest in punishing him but rather in obtaining compensation for the injured party. Nevertheless, the *Torah* expressed this monetary penalty (for damages, for pain inflicted, for medical treatment, for the unemployment suffered, and for the humiliation undergone) using the expression *An eye for an eye* in order to teach that one who maims the limb of his fellow "deserves to lose his limb or to have it maimed."[33]

Little wonder then that the *Torah* is replete with *leges imperfectae*, e.g. general prohibitions, prohibitions violated passively, violations amenable to correction, prohibition of acts though they be not performed in a manner rendering the actor criminally liable, rabbinical prohibitions of acts *ab initio* though they are valid *de*

---

the same idea in a different form: see *Iggerot Mosheh*, *H.M.* II, 68.

31 Compare: "R. Akiva says ... You are not responsible for *zavim*", *M. Zab.* 2:2.

32 *M. Makk.* 10:1. Compare our treatment with G.S. Blidstein, "Capital Punishment — The Classical Discussion", *Judaism* 14 (1965), 163-167.

33 Maimonides, *Tort*, "Assault and Damage", 1:3. The literature — halakhic, legal and historical — is vast and is of no immediate concern to us.

facto. All these prohibitions are bereft of criminal sanctions and non-prosecutable, but prohibitions nevertheless, enuciated to educate the Israelite, to refine his character, to elevate him and to bring him closer to his God.

This is the *Ran*'s approach. Scripture's criminal law is perceived as a religious ritual similar to the sacrifical offerings in the Holy Temple. The Temple cult is subject to a most comprehensive and detailed analysis by the Rabbis of the Talmud. For what purpose? "May our Holy Temple be speedily rebuilt": may our former glory be restored with the Kohen, Levite and Israelite taking their proper place therein. Envisaged is an ideal society in its ideal condition. Similarly was the penal code perceived by the Rabbis: study, erudition, analysis. For what purpose? "May our Holy Temple be speedily rebuilt for this purpose as well." May the former glory of the law of Scripture be restored: an ideal society in its ideal condition, where a *Sanhedrin* which executes someone once in seven (seventy) years would be considered "bloody".[34]

In sum, whereas law is ordinarily perceived as a system for the maintenance of order and the meting out of sanctions, scriptural law is perceived as essentially educative, spiritually elevating.

The secondary role of criminal sanctions in Scripture is well illustrated by the style of their formulation. The Rabbis insisted that the prohibition of a crime be expressly mentioned in the sacred text, never to be implied from the punishment which is being threatened. To their way of thinking, it was not enough to cite, for example, that a murderer shall be put to death (*Numbers* 35:18), for then one could conclude (technically) that one who murders and has been put to death has paid his debt to society, to the law, to God. The Rabbis insisted upon seeking (and finding) a second verse, "Thou shalt not kill" (*Ex.* 20:13), which prohibits murder absolutely, regardless of any sanction and independent of any punishment,[35] for education, not punishment, was uppermost in their minds.

It comes as no surprise, then, that extreme formalism is a chara-

34 It is interesting to point out that the Talmud does not pose the question, "Are we studying these laws for the Messianic era?" with regard to the sacrifical cult and the criminal code, though their operation depends upon the rebuilding of the Temple.

35 Cf. S.M. Paul, *Studies in the Book of Covenant in the Light of Cuneiform and Biblical Law* (Leiden: E.J. Brill, 1970), 122-123.

cteristic of Jewish law. The average man, the man in the street, finds it easier to follow clear-cut rules with fixed measurements and standards; criteria based upon the amorphous "reasonable man" cannot serve to guide him in his behaviour. And Jewish law is for the man in the street, not for lawyers and judges.[36] Similarly, the "laws of Heaven" play a significant role in Jewish law, again, for education and spiritual up-lifting, not penalties and sanctions, are of prime significance.[37]

D. *The Constitutional Structure of the Judiciary According to Jewish Law.*[38]

How then does Jewish Law cope with crime? In addition to (1) the classical law whose main function, as we have seen, is spiritual and educational, the Jewish code provides for three other concurrent criminal jurisdictions: (2) the rabbinical courts exercising exigency jurisdiction, (3) the law of the king, over and above the royal power to penalize sedition and treason, and (4) the heavenly court meting out divine punishment (not to be taken lightly by the reader).

The following extract from the Code of Maimonides, Tort (Neziḳin), "Murder" ch.2, serves us well in our description of the constitutional structure of the Jewish judicial system in its entirety.

1. If one person kills another himself, such as by striking him with a sword or with a deadly stone, or by strangling him, or by thrusting him into a fire, he must be put to death by the court, seeing that he himself killed another in some manner.

36 Rabbi I. Herzog, *The Main Institutions of Jewish Law, I. Property* (London: Soncino, 1980), "Appendix: Moral Rights and Duties in Jewish Law", 379. Also: M. Silberg, "Laws and Morals in Jewish Jurisprudence" (translated with introduction by B. Porath), *Harvard Law Review* 75 (1961), 323, newly translated as chapter VI of *Talmudic Law and the Modern State*, translated by B.Z. Bokser (New York: Burning Bush Press, 1973), 53-54.

37 Modern critical scholars, approaching the Bible from an entirely different point of view, have reached similar conclusions; C. Carmichael, *The Laws of Deuteronomy* (London: Cornell University Press, 1974), 258.

38 See: Y. Blidstein, *Ekronot Medini'im Bemishnat Harambam* (Bar Ilan University Press, 1973), 123-130, for a comprehensive treatment of the subject of this chapter.

2. If, however, one hires an assassin to kill another, or sends his slaves to kill him, or ties another up and leaves him in front of a lion or another animal and the animal kills him, and, similarly, if one commits suicide, the rule in each of these cases is that he is a shedder of blood, has committed the crime of murder, and is liable for death at the hand of Heaven; but there is no capital punishment at the hands of the court.
3. Regarding any of these or similar murderers who are not subject to being condemned to die by verdict of the court, if a king of Israel wishes to put them to death by royal decree for the benefit of society, he has a right to do so. Similarly, if the court deems it proper to put them to death as an emergency measure, it has the authority to do as it deems fit, provide that circumstances warrant such action.
4. If the king does not kill them, and the needs of the time do not demand their death as a preventive measure, it is nevertheless the duty of the court to flog them almost to the point of death, to imprison them in a fortress or a prison for many years, and to inflict severe punishment on them in order to frighten and terrify other wicked persons, lest such a case become a pitfall and a snare, enticing one to say, "I will arrange to kill my enemy in a roundabout way, as did so-and So; and then I will be acquitted."

A number of observations must be made.

(1) "The court", sometimes called "*Sanhedrin*", applies the formal laws of Scripture as interpreted by the Oral Tradition. It is this law which the *Ran* was referring to as *mishpaṭ amiti tsodeḳ be'atsmo*, "the authentic law inherently just"[39] — classical Jewish law. It is formulated in paragraphs 1 and 2 of the citation from Maimonides.

(2a) A king may exercise his royal prerogative to protect the life of his subjects when the times call for it.[40] It is to this prero-

39 *Supra*, at the opening of section C.

40 The royal prerogative is only regarding murder. This appears to be the doctrine of Maimonides on the basis of *Tort*, "Murder", 2:1-4, cited in the text, and of *Judges*, "Kings" 3:1. Cf. Blidstein, *supra* note 38, at 124. See further: J.D. Bleich, *Contemporary Halakhic Problems* (New York: Ktav, 1983), II. 351 n.11. Bleich cites the opinion of a number of *Rishonim* that the royal prerogative was not limited to cases of murder; it is doubtful whether Maimonides is to be numbered among them. As to proofs adduced against Blidstein's interpretation of Maimonides, which we have adopted, we may say: (1) Apparently Maimonides interpreted *Y. Sanh.* 6:3 (which would indicate that the King's prerogative included the power to prevent and punish homosexuality) as aggadic,

gative that the *Ran* refers as *haṣiddur hamedini*, and which we have translated as "the maintenance of law and order"; its avowed purpose is "for the benefit of society" *(yishuvo shel olam)*. As opposed to the classical law in paragraph 1, this may be viewed as the practical Jewish law. (It is in addition to the powers the king possesses to punish those who rebel against his authority).

(2b) The *Torah*-court, the *Sanhedrin*, was also empowered to deviate from the formal classical criminal procedure as an emergency measure. Moreover, this power was not limited to cases of murder; it could be invoked for any serious violation of the *halakhah*. Again, its justification was not limited to "the benefit of society" *(yishivo shel olam)*; it could be invoked in order to take precautions or preventative measures against violations of *Torah*-law or morality *(lemigdar milta)*. Such measures are also regarded as part of practical Jewish law.[41] The words "emergency measure" are a translation of the Hebrew expression *hora'at sha'ah*, literally, a "time measure". This phrase, a "time measure", is of two connotations:

(a) A temporary measure. A deviation from *Torah* law may never be decreed for a limitless time, for such a decree would constitute a violation of the biblical prohibition of a human institution adding to divine *Torah* law (*Deut.* 4:2).

---

or, at least, the words, "David our Master" as an aggadic allusion to the verse in Psalms; (2) Maimonides, explaining the actions of Joshua and David regarding criminal confessions, states: "As to Joshua's execution of Akhan and David's execution of the Amalekite stranger on the basis of their confessions, these were emergency measures or the exercise of the royal prerogative." This should be understood as stating that Joshua had Akhan executed as an emergency measure and David had the Amalekite stranger executed as an exercise of the royal prerogative. The proof: according to the *halakhah*, those executed by the king are beheaded; Akhan was stoned to death.

41 *B. Sanh.* 46a; Maimonides *Tort*, "Murder", 4:8-9, *Judges*, Sanh. 18:6 and 24:4, "Kings" 3,8,10; *Responsa Rashba* III, 393, cited in Bet Yoṣef, *H.M.*, 388 (at end); *Derashot Haran* 11; *Talmudic Encyclopaedia*, *supra* note 18, s.v. "*bet din*", III, 150, esp. 173, and s.v. "*hora'at sha'ah*", VIII, 512; Y.M. Ginzburg, *Mishpaṭim Leyisra'el* (Jerusalem: Harry Fischel Institute, 1957), 1-70; N.S. Hecht and E.B. Quint, "Exigency Jurisdiction Under Jewish Law", *Diné Israel* IX (1978-1980), 27-99.

(b) A measure taken because times demanded it, though it may be extended in time. (In any event, it may be decreed without limit).[42]

There are some significant differences between the royal prerogative of the king and the exigency jurisdiction of the court on the one hand, and classical *Torah* law on the other. Classical Jewish legal procedure ordains that the witnesses fulfil all the requirements detailed above, at the beginning of chapter A; the institution and conduct of proceedings are fixed — not subject to the discretion of the authorities; the witnesses must accuse and the court must try; the punishment meted by the court is mandatory.

Not so the royal prerogative of the king and the exigency jurisdiction of the court: their tribunals have discretion as to the opening of the case to begin with, as to defining the crime, the conducting of the case, and the hearing of witnesses — if at all.[43]

As to what constitutes a situation sufficiently serious as to justify invoking exigency jurisdiction, the sources are insufficiently clear. Apparently it was left to the king to decide and similarly to the court to determine when to invoke these emergency powers.

It seems that if both the king and the courts invoking their emergency powers were empowered to deal with a problem, the royal prerogative took precedence. Thus, if one hires an assassin to kill another or murders someone in the presence of witnesses whose forewarning was technically flawed, although the court could have tried the murderer if it felt that the times demanded such action, the king, if he wished, could take over the prosecution. We surmise as much, for it is Maimonides 'practice' to mention the king before the court; moreover the courts themselves were duty-bound to pay homage to the king. (The *Ran* states explicitly that if a king is regnant, the courts are limited to the administration of criminal justice in accordance with the rules of the classical law).

42 These words hold true equally for temporary measures decreed by a prophet and by a court: *Rashi*, *Yev.* 90b, *s.v.* "*veligamer*". Both connotations may be found in Maimonides: *Knowledge*, "The Fundamentals of the Law", 9:3, *Judges*, Sanh. 24:4, and *ibid*., "Rebels", 4:2. See further Rabbi Z.H. Chajes, *Collected Works* (Hebrew; Jerusalem: Divre Ḥakhamim, 1958), I: "*Torat Hanevi'im*", ch.VI.

43 Cf. Chajes, *ibid*., ch. VIII and R. Moses Ṣofer, *Responsa Ḥatam Ṣofer*, O.H., 28.

(3) God, too, presides over an independent concurrent judicial tribunal. Heavenly sanctions, such as Extirpation (*karet*)[44] and Death at the Hand of Heaven (*mittah biyde hamayyim*), play a great role in Jewish law — *halakhah*, not merely *aggadah*. Thus, the *Mishnah* which states: "He who was twice flogged [for two transgressions, and sinned again,] is placed by the court in a cell and fed with barley bread, until his stomach bursts,"[45] refers to violations which carry the *karet* penalty. According to R. Nehunniah b. HaKanneh, the *karet* penalty enters into the hierarchy of *kam lei be-derabbah minei*.[46] All those guilty of *karet* offences and receive lashes for them are relieved of the *karet* penalty.[47] All violations of *karet* offences, *mittah biyde shamayyim* offences, as well as those liable according to the laws of Heaven in civil matters (chiefly in tort liability), are disqualified from acting as witnesses.[48] A litigant has an affirmative defense against his opponent if the latter is liable according to the laws of Heaven; his seizure of the latter's assets does not fall into category of unjust enrichment.[49] Maimonides enumerates the *karet* and *mittah biyde shamayyim* offences; they are thirty-nine in number.[50]

The judgment of the Almighty resembles classical *Torah* law in its rigidity and inexorability (God's Quality of Law); it resembles the royal prerogative and exigency jurisdiction of the courts in its flexibility and adjustability (God's Quality of Mercy — a flexibi-

44 As to the nature of *karet* see *Rashi*, *Ket*. 30b, *s.v.* "*zar she'akhal terumah*"; *idem*, *Shab*. 25e, *s.v.* "*vekaret*"; Maimonides, *Knowledge*, "Repentance", 8:1; Nahmanides, *Lev*. 18:19; *idem*, "*Sha'ar Hagemul*". See further H. Albeck, *Seder Kodashin* (Jerusalem: Mossad Bialik, 1959), Introduction to Tractate Keritot, 243ff.

45 *B. Sanh*. 81b.

46 *B. Pes*. 29a; *B. Ket*. 30a. The law, however, does not follow this opinion of R. Nehunniah b. HaKaneh; *arg*. Maimonides, *Tort*, "Theft", 3:2.

47 *M. Makk*. 3:15 as determined by R. Ada B. Ahavah in the name of Rav; *B. Makk*. 23a; Maimonides, *Judges*, *Sanh*., 17:7.

48 Maimonides, *Judges*, "Testimony", 10:3; R. Meshullam of Bordeaux, *Sefer HaHashlamah* (13th century, Provence), *B.K.* 6a, in the name of his father R. Moses b. R. Judah; similarly Meiri, *Bet Habeḥirah* —*B.K.* 56a.

49 *Talmudic Encyclopedia*, *supra* note 18, *s.v.* "dinei shamayyim 6," VII, 395.

50 Maimonides, *Judges*, *Sanh*., 19:1-2.

lity which makes repentance possible).[51]

E. *Jewish Criminal Law in its Complete Form*

In the citation of the *Ran*, *supra* section B, reference was made to *tikkun hasiddur bamedini* which is analogous to the criminal justice of other legal systems. The maintenance of law and order — the apprehension of criminals, their indictment, prosecution, judgment and punishment — as understood by secular law, was accomplished — such at least was the opinion of halakhic scholars — by the invocation of the royal prerogative or of the exigency jurisdiction of the courts.

As is evident from a plain reading of Maimonides, this administration of criminal justice is an integral part of Jewish criminal law. We may and we have translated its components as: "the royal prerogative", "the judicial function of the monarch"; "emergency powers", "exigency jurisdiction". Note that these translations carry no connotation of illegality. Scholars sometimes refer to them as "extrajudicial powers", "extralegal remedies" — which give the impression that we have here deviations from the law. This perception has its origin in the statement by the *tanna*, R. Eliezer b. Jacob: "I have a tradition that the court may, [when necessary,] impose flagellation and pronounce [capital] sentences even where not [warranted] by the *Torah*; yet not with the intention of disregarding the *Torah* but [on the contrary] in order to safeguard it."[52] Indeed, this statement was made from the point of view of *Torah*-law of "the authentic law inherently just" (*mishpat amiti tsodek be'atsmo*), which, we have indicated, is sacred in nature, created to bring down the Divine Effulgence on God's people. We, however, seeking to describe the Jewish criminal law in its complete form, must not view the king's justice and the court's exercise of its emergency pow-

51 For the general framework, see A. Büchler, *Studies in Sin and Atonement in the Rabbinic Literature of the First Century* (New York: Ktav Publishing House, 1967).

52 Literally, "to make a fence round it"; *B. Sanh.* 46a. Cf. *Y. Hag.* 2:2. Further: M. Elon, *Hamishpat Ha'ivri* (Jerusalem: Magnes Press, 1973), 421.

ers as opposing *Torah* law but rather as complementary to it.[53]

How is it complementary? Basic to rabbinic thought were two fundamental concepts: (a) An élite nation which is made of God-fearing and God-loving people, clamouring to open the Gates of Heaven and passionately aspiring to communion with God — a nation where crime is an unusual occurrence, the criminal a rare individual; (b) An ideal legal system, "inherently just", with exact definitions of crimes, rigid guide-lines in the administration of justice, a highly formalized criminal procedure. Thus, a review of Maimonides *Tort*, "Murder" ch. 2:1, *supra* section D, reveals an ideal *(i.e.*, unrealistic), exact, narrow definition of the criminal act; and this is combined with rigid rules of evidence and formalistic procedure.

Paradoxically, we have, on the one hand, a society of high-minded and holy men, and, on the other, a legal system of many severely punishable crimes. This paradox finds its explanation in the rabbinic view — of The *Tannaim*, *Amoraim*, *Gaonim*, *Rishonim* and *Aḥaronim* — that the Divine Law was perceived as a spiritual entity, to educate, elevate, and sanctify the Jew.*

F. *The Heavenly Court*

It would be misleading to limit the administration of Jewish criminal justice to two institutions, the court (administering *Torah* law or taking emergency measures) and the monarchy, without mentioning a third arm of the judiciary, functioning concurrently with

53 I wish to express my gratitude to my friend, Professor Arnold Enker of the Bar-Ilan University Law School, who suggested some of these valuable insights.

* In the Hebrew original of this article (see note *supra*, at the beginning), we appended a study of the history of Jewish criminal law as presented by the classical sources — the talmudic and midrashic corpora as well as the literature of commentaries, codes and responsa. We found it noteworthy that the halakhists could agree on no single source to the effect that someone was condemned to die on the basis of the classical system of rules, regulations, requirements and restrictions. Wherever a sentence of death is mentioned as having been carried out, it was not done on the basis of *Torah*-law; and wherever *Torah*-law is invoked in a practical case it is done in order to exonerate the accused and not to condemn him.

them: the Heavenly Court presided over by the Lord of Justice Himself. This Tribunal was invoked (especially, but not only) when the other two institutions were unable or unwilling to cope with crime.

Even after the Jewish community of Palestine was deprived of juridical autonomy — specifically in capital cases — anarchy posed no serious threat.

> It was taught in the school of Hezekiah: From the day the Temple was destroyed although the *Sanhedrin* was abolished ... He who is worthy of stoning either falls from the roof or is trampled to death by a wild beast; he who merits burning either falls into fire or is bitten by a serpent; he who is worthy of decapitation is either delivered to the [gentile] Government or brigands attack him; he who is worthy of strangulation is either drowned in a river or dies of suffocation.[54]

But even before the Temple was destroyed, whilst the *Sanhedrin* was still functioning, we are told, R. Simeon b. Shetaḥ saw a man pursuing his fellow into a ruin, caught him with his sword in hand with blood dripping from it, and the murdered man writhing. Having failed to see the actual act of murder, he left the suspect to the hands of Heaven, for none may be prosecuted on a capital charge on the basis of circumstantial evidence — no matter how convincing. And "it is related that before they moved from the place a serpent came and bit [the murderer] so that he died."[55]

And even after the Temple was destroyed, "R. Tarfon and R. Akiva say: were we members of a *Sanhedrin*, no person would even be put to death."[56] Indeed, our thesis is that, as mentioned, these rabbis did not view the Law of Moses as a criminal code. Rather it was essentially a mighty instrument for the education, refinement, and spiritual elevation of man. All well and good. but what of the maintenance of law and order? What of men of violence and murderers? The Jewish mind was at rest, for the King of Kings, the Guardian of Israel who punisheth the wicked, will deal with them.

54 *B. Sanh.* 37b. Parallel: *B. Makk.* 10b. *Talmudic Encyclopedia, supra* note 18, *s.v.* "dine shamayyim", VIII, 382; "ḥayyave keritot", XIV, 548; "ḥayyave mittot bet din", XIV, 580. See H.H. Cohn, "Ira Dei Judaeorum" (Hebrew), *Tel Aviv University Law Review* 1 (1971), 13-24; *idem*, "Divine Punishment: Bibliography", *Encyclopedia Judaica, ad loc.*

55 *B. Sanh.* 37b.

56 *M. Makk.* 1:10.

The Heavenly Court was thoroughgoing, efficient and unlimited in means of enforcement. This is the thrust of a *midrash* recorded in the name of R. Simeon b. Laḳish.

> *And if a man lie not in wait, but God cause it to come to hand; then I will appoint thee a place whither he may flee* (*Ex.* 21:13). It is to this that Scripture alludes: *As saith the proverb of the ancients: Out of the wicked cometh forth wickedness ...* (*I Sam.* 24:13).
>
> Of whom does the [former] text speak? Of two persons who had slain, one in error and another with intent, there being witnesses in neither case. The Holy One, blessed be He, appoints them both [to meet] at the same inn. He who had slain with intent sits under the step-ladder, and he who had slain in error comes down the step-ladder, falls and kills him. thus, he who had slain with intent is [duly] slain, while he who had slain in error [duly] goes into banishment.[57]

The Talmud cites a *baraita* which relates that forty years before the Temple was destroyed, the *Sanhedrin* was exiled and took up residence in *Ḥanut*.[58] This is explained by R. Naḥman b. Isaac: "Because when the murderers were as prevalent that they could not be properly dealt with judicially, they said: Rather let us be exiled from place to place than pronounce them guilty[59] [of capital offences], for it is written, *And thou shalt do according to the sentence, which they of that place which the Lord shall choose shall tell thee* (*Deut.* 17:10) — which implies that it is the place" [i.e., only residence there empowers *Sanhedrin* to function].[60]

R. Naḥman b. Isaac's statement is somewhat incomprehensible. The prevalence of murderers calls for greater judicial activity, not for its cessation. Moreover exile from its official residence did not affect the exigency powers of the *Sanhedrin*.[61] On the contrary, the times undoubtedly demanded action; not surrender.

57 *B. Makk.* 10b. Cf. *Mekhilta* to *Ex.* 21:13.

58 *B. Sanh.* 41a. In *B. A. Zar.* 8b, R. Ishmael cites this *baraita* in the name of R. Jose his father. *Rashi* states that *Ḥanut* was the name of a place in Jerusalem; cf. *Y. Sanh.* 1:1 and 7:2.

59 The Aramaic expression, " ... them", in the original in all likelihood refers to the murderers *(Rashi)*. Some take it to refer to the judges of the Sanhedrin, whose puishment would have been great had they remained in session in the Hewn-Stone Chamber and not prosecuted the culprits.

60 *B. A. Zar.* 8b.

61 Compare: *Tosafot*, *s.v.* "ella", *A. Zar.* , *ibid.*, and *s.v.* "*miyyom*", *Ket.* 30a.

We leave the historical problems to the historians.[62] The statement of R. Nahman b. Isaac, who lived many years after the destruction of the Temple — and in Babylonia — reflects the despair of the Jewish spiritual leadership, a despair emanating from the feeling of helplessness in the face of the deterioration of a society ruled by violence. The exile of the *Sanhedrin* constituted a public declaration of the bankruptcy of the rule of law in Israel. This declaration spelled the end of the criminal courts.[63] This bankruptcy was not only of the authorities; it signified primarily the downfall of societal law and order. With the disappearance of an elite society of God-fearing and God-loving citizens, whom we described in chapter E, the situation changed and would have condemned the *Sanhedrin* to be bloody indeed.

Only the exigency jurisdiction of the courts — with all the problems therein — remained to cope with the proliferation of murderers, plunderers and men of violence. The House of Jacob had no alternative but to depend upon its Father who is in Heaven. It comes as no surprise then that the Rabbis assumed a posture of resignation.[64] Many years before Jews had given expression to this in an extreme form;[65, 66] and many, many generations to come would they sustain themselves with this faith.[67, 68]

62 See the literature cited in H. Mantel, *Studies in the History of the Sanhedrin* (Hebrew; Tel Aviv: Dvir, 1969), 164 n.11; S.B. Hoenig, *The Great Sanhedrin* (Philadelphia: Dropsie College, 1953), 109-113, 211-213; Cohn, *supra* note 15, at p.86.

63 *Tosafot, s.v. "melamed", A. Zar.* 8b.

64 Cf., however, *Tosafot, s.v. "miyyom", Ket.* 30a.

65 See *I Maccabees* 2:29; cf. J. Goldstein, *I Maccabees* (New York: Doubleday-Anchor, 1976), 5-6, 234-237.

66 Concerning the view of the Rabbis of reward and punishment, see E.E. Urbach, *The Sages — Their Beliefs and Concepts* (Hebrew; Jerusalem: Magnes Press, 1971), ch.11.

67 The eleventh principle of Maimomides' Thirteen Principles of the Faith.

68 In sum, then, Maimonides *Torts*, "Murder and the Preservation of Life", ch.2, para.1, reflects the classical law which makes most acts of murder non-prosecutable; para.2 refers to the heavenly court; paras. 4a and 5 describe the law of the king; and para.4b refers to the rabbinical court exercising exigency jurisdiction.

G. *A Concluding Note*

The role of punishment in the classical Jewish criminal law, *Torah*-law, is sacral, mystical, educational; its purpose is to elevate man spiritually and to bring him near to Divine Law.

The purpose of the "law" of the Stubborn and Rebellious Son is to deter youth from delinquency, from the breach of discipline and of traditionally ordained behaviour. The purpose of the "laws" of the Idolatrous City (*Deut.* 13:13-19) is to teach Israel the horror of idolatry and paganism. The ritual of the Leprous House (*Lev.* 14:33-53) sought to discourage the Israelite from uttering malicious gossip *(lashon hara)*[69] and to impress upon him God's grace in bringing His nation to the Promised Land.[70]

The halakhic provision rejecting self-incrimination in capital cases stresses how careful one must be when human life is involved[71] or alternatively, teachers that life is the Lord's and man's soul does not belong to him, so that his spoken word (the criminal confession) may not bring his life to an end.[72,73]

We have seen that, whereas the classical criminal law — *Torah*-law — is central to Jewish thought and philosophy, its place is in the House of Study *(bet hamidrash)*; the practical Jewish criminal law — of secondary theoretical significance — has its place in the court *(bet din)*, either as part of the royal government or in the *Torah* court exercising its emergency powers.

> For these [classical *Torah*] rules apply to the *Sanhedrin* alone — thus has God decreed; but in the Law of the King no attention is to be paid to them. Royal law is only interested in the truth [not in the spiritual implications of the (classical) criminal process] and meting out punishment for the infraction of the King's law. [It therefore] admits testimony by relatives, even confessions of the accused, without the [formal] forewarning.
>
> Were you to reject this and insist upon following the *Torah*-law of

69 *B. Arak.* 16b.

70 *Lev. Rabbah* 17:6.

71 Maimonides, *Judges, Sanh.* 18:6.

72 Commentary of R. David b. Zimra *(Radbaz)*, *ad loc.*

73 This exposition is a modest sample of the method employed by Maimonides in section III of his *Guide* and by the *magnum opus*, *Sefer HaHinukh*.

the *Sanhedrin*, the world would disintegrate.[74]

This view is fraught with far-reaching implications, inasmuch as the authorized interpreters of the *Halakhah* perceive the criminal law to be essentially and educational and spiritualizing, the application of *Torah*-law in capital cases is out of the question.[75]

As a result of the exposition of our thesis, the religious nature of Jewish Law takes on an added dimension. Heretofore the religious nature was evident from (1) the classification of religious-ritual violation ("sins") as "crimes", (2) the reliance on Heaven as one source of crime-prevention and law-enforcement, and (3) the "religious" *halakhah* and the legal halakhah as complementing each other.

To this we may now add a fourth aspect illustrating the religious nature of Jewish Law, namely the perception of its criminal code as a body of ritual whose religio-educational significance overrides and overshadows its societal function of creating and supervising law and order.

74 R. Solomon b. Adret, *Rashba*, as cited in *Bet Yoṣef*, *H.M.* 388. Compare: *Responsa Rashba* IV, 393.

75 Illustrative of this is the attitude, for example, of modern rabbinic authorities regarding the classical prohibition of accepting criminal confessions; see Y.M. Ginzburg, "Self Accusation according to *Torah* Law" (Hebrew), *Hatorah Ve-hamedinah* 9-10 (1958), 82.

Unjust Enrichment

[23]

The Jewish Law Annual, Vol. III

UNJUST ENRICHMENT

by

NAHUM RAKOVER*

I. "*One derives a benefit and the other sustains no loss*"

1. *Introduction*

In Jewish law "unjust enrichment"[1] embraces all those situations in which one person derives a material benefit from another without being legally entitled thereto. The central question is whether and to what extent the person from whom the benefit is derived (the donor) may require something in return from the recipient of the benefit. Since no agreement exists on the matter, no action can lie in contract. Likewise an action in tort will not be available when the donor has not been injured by the recipient's enjoyment of the benefit. Is there no other way for the donor to assert a right to a *quid pro quo*?

The nature of the benefit and the manner in which it is obtained can vary considerably. It may or may not be accompanied by a loss sustained by the other party. A person who parks his car in a lot belonging to a neighbour may or may not have to pay a charge, depending first on whether he generally pays for parking his car,—for if he does not, he has derived no material benefit,—and secondly on whether the lot is intended for parking at a charge,—for if not, he may plead that the other has not sustained any loss.

Again, a benefit may be occasioned by an act not of the recipient but of the other party. A may make improvements to B's property either through mistake or intentionally. If he does so without thought of receiving anything in return, he is certainly not entitled to be recompensed. If, however, he intended to get something in exchange, will he be entitled to be paid for the improvements? That B gave no thought to the matter may also be relevant. If B would himself have made the improvements in any event, A's act has saved him money. If not, B has

---

* LL. M., Dr. Juris.: Adviser on Jewish Law, Ministry of Justice, Israel.

[1] The Hebrew phrase for "unjust enrichment" was coined by Cheshin J. in reliance on *Jer.* 17:11—"*he that getteth riches, and not by right,* shall leave them in the midst of his days."

gained nothing and to charge him with payment involves interference with his freedom to decide whether and when he will lay out money and for what purpose.

There may also be circumstances in which the outlay of money for another's benefit is of significant social and moral importance, for instance, in saving the life of a person or his property. Is the donor entitled to be reimbursed for his outgoings? Are such worthy acts of assistance to be encouraged by ensuring that the expenditure involved is recoverable? Moreover, in personal "rescue" cases, has the rescuer any claim to be reimbursed where the rescued person protests against the rescue and states that he will not make any payment? Is a person the master of his own fate to demand of others not to help him and so avoid payment?

From the viewpoint also of the recipient questions will arise about the amount he must pay. Is the criterion to be the benefit obtained or the money spent, which may be less or more than the benefit?

According to Jewish law four main categories of cases are distinguished: (1) where the one party derives no benefit and the other party sustains no loss; (2) where the one derives a benefit and the other sustains a loss; (3) where the one derives a benefit and the other sustains no loss; (4) where the one derives no benefit and the other sustains a loss.

As to the first two, the Gemara in *Baba Kamma* 20a—where the main Talmudic discussion of the subject occurs—states that the law is very simple: in the first no payment is required but in the second it is. The third category is the subject of extended debate, whilst the last is not dealt with expressly in the Gemara but is debated by the early post-Talmudic authorities.[2]

The *Gemara* as above elaborates a number of general rules in connection with the third category, along with definitions of "recipient" and "loss". The obligation to pay and the amount to be paid under the second category are treated elsewhere in the Talmud in reference to

---

[2] Cases of actual damage were not dealt with, except such as are illustrated by that where lettable premises are occupied by persons who would not otherwise rent premises. Whilst the *Toṣafot* to *B.K.* 21a s.v. *Zeh* does not require him to pay for his occupation, *Rif* (*B.K.* 9a, Vilna ed.) would make him pay because he causes financial loss. *Rosh* explains that the obligation can be based on the fact that "he has eaten the other's loss", which is different from the case where a person closes up another's house and does not go into occupation (*Piṣke HaRosh* to *B.K.* 2:6). See also the *Hagera* and *Naḥlat David* to *B.K.*, *ibid.*

specific fact situations, such as improvements made to another's property, salvage and so on.

The first part of the present paper is concerned with an analysis of the principle embodied in the third category and its applicable rules. Other aspects, a discussion of which is necessary for an over-all view of unjust enrichment in Jewish law, have been considered in separate studies, and the conclusions are briefly summarized in the second part.[3]

The usual Common Law classification of obligations into contract and torts has led to "enjust enrichment" being treated under the rubric of quasi- or implied contract,[4] but there is a certain artificiality about this and in recent years a tendency has shown itself to regard it as an independent class. In Israeli law until 1979 the subject was not regulated by any particular statute. Several enactments—for instance the Guarantee Law, 1967 (section 9), the Land Law, 1969 (section 21), and the Agency Law, 1975 (section 10)—make provision for their respective purposes.

So long as there was no single enactment devoted to the subject, Israeli case law in the main drew upon English law in reliance on article 46 of the Palestine Order in Council.[5] No clear criteria exist in English Law for the right to claim in unjust enrichment. The view taken by Lord Mansfield, the father of quasi-contract, that the principles of natural justice and equity require restitution,[6] is very general in import. The Israeli Ministry of Justice recently published a bill on unjust enrichment,[7] the Explanatory Note to which states that in a number of respects Jewish law has been followed: a person who makes improvements to the property of another is entitled to restitution; the principle of "one derives a benefit and the other sustains no loss" serves as a consideration to exempt from payment for the benefit; and the right of the salvor to indemnity.[8] [9]

---

[3] *Infra*, 25-32.

[4] For what follows, see D. Friedmann, *The Law of Unjust Enrichment* (Heb.) (Tel Aviv: Avukah Press, 1970), and regarding our present subject, *ibid.*, 41-48. See J. P. Dawson, *Unjust Enrichment* (Boston: Little Brown & Co., 1951) and Goff and Jones, *Law of Restitution* (London: Sweet and Maxwell, 1966), ch. 1.

[5] Recently a Bill (No. 1361 of 31 July 1978, *Hatsa'ot Hok* 307) has been tabled which proposes to abolish reliance on English law and replace it by reference to the Jewish sources of justice and equity. See Sinclair's note, *infra*, 165-169.

[6] See Friedmann, *supra* n. 4, at 8.

[7] Bill No. 1353 of 5 July 1978, *Hatsa'ot Ḥok*, 266. See further *infra*, 80-83, for the texts of the Bill and the Law eventually enacted.

[8] See Silberg J. in *Zim v. Maziar* (1963) 17 P.D. 1319, 1933: "When the decisive question regarding a legal conclusion is one of philosophical outlook...we may and indeed

2. *The Talmudic discussion*

Where one person's benefit is involved in another's loss the Talmud found no difficulty in holding that the recipient must make restitution. But where benefit and no loss occur the question of paying for the benefit is more complicated.

The discussion begins with R. Yoḥanan's attribution to the Tanna R. Yehudah of the view that in three instances a person is prohibited[10] from deriving benefit from another's property and must pay for the benefit he obtains.[11] According to the *Toṣafot ad locum* the basis for this rule is a rabbinical regulation (*taḳanah*): "although it would seem right to say that a person may enjoy a benefit if another does not thereby sustain any loss, the Rabbis nevertheless instituted the rule that the first must pay since no one may enjoy the property of another without agreement." The requirement to pay, it appears, does not follow from any rule of law but from a desire generally to discourage the use of another's property without his consent. The *Gemara*, however, rejects R. Yoḥanan's attribution of the rule and says that there is no evidence that R. Yehudah stated it, since each of the three instances mentioned may rest on different grounds.[12]

The basic discussion of various aspects of the problem is, however, to be found in *Baba Kamma* 20a-21a, from which it appears that the rabbis were considerably exercised in reaching a solution. There the question is whether rent must be paid for occupying another person's premises without his agreement. The *Gemara* analyses the different possibilities and concludes that the question will only arise with regard to premises not intended for letting, where the occupier usually rents property. The argument proceeds as follows. Where the premises are not for letting

---

must draw upon our ancient sources since these alone truly reflect the basic conceptions of the Jewish people in 'its entirety'." See also the judgments of Cohn J. and Kister J. in *Yekutiel v. Bergman* (1975) 29 P.D. (II) 764, 769.

[9] For bibliography on the Jewish law of unjust enrichment, see N. Rakover, *Otsar Hamishpat* (Jerusalem: Harry Fischel Institute, 1975), 436. See also I. Herzog, *The Main Institutions of Jewish Law* (London: Soncino, 1970), II. 49-59; J. Webber, "Observations on some Cases of Unjust Enrichment", *Diné Israel* 2 (1970), 24-42; Y. Rottenberg, "Unjust Enrichment", *Encyclopaedia Judaica*, XV. 1683-1687.

[10] See *Maimonides, Responsa* (ed. Blau), 444, on the question how a prohibition arises in money matters.

[11] *B.M.* 117b.

[12] *Maimonides, loc. cit.*, also points out that R. Yehudah's alleged view is inconsistent with the rule that a person who occupies another's premises without agreement need not pay rent. See also *Hatam Sofer*, Responsa on *Ḥoshen Mishpat*, para. 79. But see *Responsa Hare Beṣamim*, II. 245.

and the person concerned would not rent another place, he has no benefit and the owner loses nothing; hence no payment is exigible. Where the premises are for letting and the person might rent elsewhere, he benefits and the owner loses; hence payment must be made. Several views are cited on the point and then an attempt to attribute these to Tannaim is dismissed and the question therefore is held to have been an open one in the Tannaitic period. Thereafter the Gemara proceeds to cite various traditions from which it emerges that most Amoraim held that a person occupying premises without agreement is to be treated in accordance with the principle (hereinafter called "the exemptive principle") that where "the one derives a benefit and the other sustains no loss", no payment for the benefit need be made.

Neither Maimonides nor Karo expressly lays down a generalised rule based on the exemptive principle; they confine themselves to the particular factual situation discussed in the *Gemara*.[13] As Maimonides puts it, "a person who occupies without agreement the premises of another, which are not for letting, does not have to pay rent although he normally rents property, since the one benefits and the other does not lose."

3. *The "manner of Sodom"*

The exemptive principle and the rule that "one may be compelled not to act in the manner of Sodom" (i.e. not to adopt a dog-in-the-manger attitude) are often treated in association. It may be noticed that the rule is mentioned in a number of places in the *Talmud*[14] where the question of acting or not acting in relation to another's property occurs before anything is actually done, whereas the exemptive principle is applied where an act has already been effected. The difference is apparent in the fact that the Talmudic references to the one never mention the other.

The earlier post-Talmudic authorities, however, stress that the circumstances in which the rule will apply are those which give rise to the exemptive principle.[15]

4. *The legal basis of the exemptive principle*

Is it to be inferred that the exemptive principle will operate by reason of the rule? According to several scholars the answer is in the affir-

[13] *Maimonides, Hilkhot Gezelah Va'avedah* 3:9; *Shulḥan Arukh, Ḥoshen Mishpat*, 363:6.

[14] E.g. *Erub.* 49a, *Ket.* 103a, *B.B.* 12b, 59a, 168a. See the instructive contribution of A. Lichtenstein on the rule in *Hagut Ivrit Ba'Amerikah* 1 (1972), 362-382.

[15] *Maimonides, Hilkhot Shekhenim* 7:8; *Rashi* to *Ket.* 103a and to *B.B.* 12b; Commentary attributed to R. Gershon, *Or Zeruʿa; Novellae Rashba* to *B.B.* 12b; *Rashbam* to *B.B.* 59a; *Yad Rama* to *B.B.* 168a.

mative.[16] It is possible to show that the early authorities[17] speak of the rule and the exemptive principle in one breath, as it were. But what they really say is that the rule applies because of the exemptive principle and not vice versa.[18] All that the early post-Talmudic authorities aver is simply that the rule will apply where one benefits and the other does not lose. It may well be that the exemptive principle operates not because of the Manner of Sodom Rule, but because a party suffering no loss has no cause of action at all against the person who benefits, and it is unnecessary to call the rule in aid. Where, however, it is desired to prevent *ab initio* an offending act, the rule may have to be invoked.[19]

The exemptive principle can also be explained in other ways without recourse to the rule. Where there is no loss, there is nothing, it may be said, to which an obligation to pay can attach.[20] Or it may be urged that although in strict law a duty to pay may exist,[21] a waiver is deemed to be imported because no loss has been suffered.[22]

---

[16] See *Pene Yehoshuʿa* to *B.K.* 20a, relying on the *Toṣafot*. See also *Novellae* of R. Ḥayyim of Telz to *B.K.* 39 and *B.B.* 109, and *Levush Mordekhai* to *B.K.*, para. 15. See also note 18 below.

[17] See note 14 above.

[18] The *Toṣafot* to *B.B.* 12b, s.v. *Kegon*, however, seems to imply that they held the exemption from payment arises under the principle that one may be compelled not to act in the manner of Sodom. *Encyclopaedia Talmudit, Zeh Neheneh,* note 8, also cites Maimonides (see note 15 above) to this effect but the matter is not clear. According to the *Toṣafot*, there are two forms of the rule, one arising under strict law and one by virtue of rabbinical regulation.

[19] In the case of the unauthorised occupation of premises, the rule is not applied *ab initio* against the owner who has suffered no loss: *Toṣafot* to *B.K.* 20b; *Rema* in *Shulḥan Arukh, Ḥoshen Mishpaṭ*, para 363, contrary to R. Eliezer b. R. Yoel Halevi, cited in *Mordekhai* to *B.K.* 2:16. *Rema*'s reason is that the owner might let the premises. See *Responsa Divre Malkhiʾel*, III, 157, rejecting this last view and distinguishing the case where the owner can put an end to the occupation or use of his property at any time without the need for any act by the occupier from the case where the owner may be suffering loss because such an act is needed. In the latter case the rule does not apply.

[20] As may be inferred from the reason given by R. Ammi in our Gemara for exempting the recipient: "What harm has he done to the other? What loss has he caused him?" See *Novellae* of R. Shimon to *B.K.*, 19:3, and *Levush Mordekhai, op. cit.*

[21] Since the recipient holds something belonging to the donor and despite the absence of any agreement as to payment. See *Birkat Shmuʾel, B. K.* 14:2-3, and *B.B.*, 7.

[22] *Maḥane Efrayim, Hilkhot Gezelah* 10. See the discussion on the question whether minor orphans can make a valid waiver where *Nimuḳe Yoṣef* to *B.K.*, chapter 2, argues that as the exemptive principle applies to minors who cannot make a valid waiver the principle is not based on waiver. On the other hand *Toṣafot* to *B.B.* 143a holds that in some cases a waiver can be made by minors. And see also *Responsa Rashba*, II 152. S. Albeck, *Dine Hamamanot Batalmud* (Tel Aviv: Dvir, 1976), chapter 4, seeks to rest the obligation to pay and the exemption from payment on the parties' resolve (*gemirat daʿat*) as to payment: see *infra*, 33-48.

5. *Protesting the benefit*

One important limitation on the exemptive principle occurs where a person declares that no one should benefit from his property.

In the *Gemara* the duty to make payment for any benefit obtained from Temple property is derived from the principle that because of the special nature of the property involved any benefit derived therefrom without knowledge is treated in the same manner as private property used with the owner's knowledge. The *Toṣafot ad locum* explain that the Divine wish is that no one should benefit in the course of committing sacrilege.[23] For that reason, the recipient must pay. There are commentators, however, who explain the ruling by arguing that the use of Temple property effected without protest from the competent authority is like the use of private property with protest.[24] Hence where the owner makes protest, the recipient of the benefit must pay although no loss has been suffered. Others again understand the phrase "use of property with knowledge" as meaning an implied agreement to pay.[25] Accordingly if no such agreement can be implied (even if protest is made) payment will not be required.

The rule in the Codes is that if the owner tells the occupier to leave and the latter refuses, he must pay rent.[26] Karo, basing the rule on *Ṭur*, says that this is obvious. This rule has been extended even to property not for letting and to an occupier who would otherwise not rent property.[27]

6. *Intention to pay for benefit*

(a) Another limitation on the exemptive principle arises when the recipient discloses an intention to pay for the benefit he obtains.

The *Toṣafot ad locum* derive this rule from the case where a person whose property encircles that of a neighbour puts up fences which run

---

[23] The *Toṣafot* to *B.K.* 21a dispute the view they attribute to *Rashi* that occupation without knowledge involves payment. See *Responsa Terumot Hadeshen*, para. 317, where the explanation given of Rashi's view are difficult to reconcile with what he actually says.

[24] This is the view of R. Yashayahu in *Shiṭah Meḳubetset* to *B.K.* ibid.

[25] *Rashba* in *Shiṭah Meḳubetset, ibid.*, and in his *Novellae*, in the name of R. Hananel.

[26] *Ṭur, Ḥoshen Mishpaṭ* 363:6; *Shulḥan Arukh, Ḥoshen Mishpaṭ*, 363:6. *Minḥat Pitin ad loc.* points to an inconsistency between *Karo* and *Rema* on this matter and resolves it by saying that where it is wholly impossible to let the property, both would agree that the occupant is exempt even if told to vacate.

[27] *Sema* to *Shulḥan Arukh, ibid.*, 14. See *Bi'ur Hagera ad loc.* 13. But *Naḥlat David* opposes this view, relying on *Rashba*, note 25 above: the obligation to pay only arises where the owner has so stipulated but not where he has merely protested the occupation.

along three sides of the neighbour's property and then the latter erects a fence on the fourth side. R. Jose said that the neighbour must pay for his share in the entire fencing. The *Gemara* tries to infer the exemptive principle from this case on the ground that had the first person erected the fourth fence, the neighbour would inferentially have been exempt from payment. The *Toṣafot* query the inference since the erection of the fourth fence by the first person does not affect the exemptive principle: Why should the neighbour pay if he erected the fence? In erecting that fence the neighbour has indicated that he is satisfied with the expenditure for the fencing. Hence the situation is different from that where a person occupies another's property and has not indicated that he is prepared to pay.[28]

The reasoning and conclusion of the *Toṣafot* were challenged in the 16th century by R. Shlomo Luria[29] on the ground that disclosure of one's readiness to pay is immaterial in the circumstances, since no loss has been occasioned to the other. Luria reasons that payment for the fencing arises because the burden on the first person is increased by the extension of the fencing, and therefore only in such circumstances will the disclosure of an intention to pay have effect.

A still later authority[30] is critical of the *Toṣafot* and holds that the reason for the obligation to pay in the fencing case is the financial gain of having a fully fenced property, whereas the exemptive principle is concerned with some indeterminate benefit.[31]

(b) Various explanations have been advanced for the obligation to pay where an intention to do so is present, as decided by the *Toṣafot*. A 19th century *responsum*[32] deals with the case of a person who bottled scent water and affixed a label which another person was using for production under government licence. After arguing that the defendant was to be charged because he had shown that the plaintiff's expenditure in obtaining the licence suited his own interests, the conclusion is reached that as long as "there are outgoings and acts beneficial to both parties,

[28] This also explains *M.B.B.* 1:4, regarding an obligation to pay on the collapse of a wall dividing the premises of joint owners and the rebuilding of the wall by one of them (see *Toṣafot* to *B.B.* 5a, and *Yam Shel Shlomo* to *B.K.*, Chapter 16.)

[29] *Yam shel Shlomo, ibid.* See *Encyclopaedia Talmudit, ibid,* note 67: *Ketsot Haḥoshen*, para. 158, 6.

[30] *Ḥelkat Yo'av, Ḥoshen Mishpat*, para. 9.

[31] See the distinction made by R. Ch. Eigash (*Markheshet*, 2:35) between the case where the benefit no longer exists, when the exemptive principle applies and where the benefit was created by the two parties and still exists and where the expenses should be shared and the exemptive principle is out of place.

[32] *Responsa Divre Malki'el*, 3. 157.

they are partners and can compel each other to contribute"—but only where the outgoings and acts were essential and for the common good. In any other situation, either may refuse to contribute to a benefit which he does not want. Hence where a recipient shows an intention to pay outgoings, he cannot plead that they were against his wishes and he therefore becomes a partner therein.

When a claim is made in respect of a unilateral benefit, no obligation to pay will arise *ab initio*, but if an intention to pay is disclosed that is equivalent to a legal undertaking to do so.

Another modern authority, R. Shimon Shkop,[33] explains the obligation to pay in the fencing case in two different ways. First, if the recipient has shown his readiness to share the outgoings, the other suffers a loss if payment is not enforceable. That is particularly so in the case of occupying premises where the owner could let the premises to the occupier at a rent and where the premises are not for letting. Another explanation is that the indication makes the recipient not merely a recipient of a benefit but enriches him. These two explanations are meant to demonstrate that the exemptive principle is not involved. Whilst the first stresses the loss of the one party, the second is based on the distinction between a mere recipient of a benefit and one who is financially enriched by the amount he had in mind to pay.

(c) The *Shulḥan Arukh* rules in accordance with the view of the *Toṣafot*: "where premises not for letting are involved, no rent need be paid provided the occupant has not disclosed that he would pay rent, were he not allowed to take up full occupation. Where he does disclose such an intention, he must pay."[34]

Manifestation of intention will only have this effect if it is made to the true owner, as may be gathered from the case mentioned in the *Gemara* of A who rents (lettable) property from B, which is found to belong to C. A must pay C the rent. If therefore the property were not for letting,

---

[33] *Novellae* to *B.K.* 19:5 and 6; 20:1-2.

[34] *Ḥoshen Mishpaṭ* 363:8. *Arukh Hashulḥan, Ḥoshen Mishpaṭ* 373:19, limits the rule: disclosure of intention will only be effective where the person would otherwise rent premises; otherwise the intention must be express. As to the date when the intention is to be disclosed, some take the view that it may occur during occupation (*Maḥane Efrayim, op. cit.*, 9) and some even after the occupation has ended (*Perishah* to *Ṭur, Ḥoshen Mishpaṭ*, 363, 7). See *Responsa Noda Biyehudah*, vol. 2, *Ḥoshen Mishpaṭ* 24, distinguishing between a disclosure of intention as to partial payment and intention as to full payment; in the first instance, the duty to pay the value of the whole benefit will only arise if the expenses have been excessive, whereas in the second, payment must in any event be made.

A would not be bound, although he had disclosed to B (not C, the owner) a readiness to pay.[35] The *Shulḥan Arukh* adds that the rent paid to B, on the mistaken impression that he is the owner, is recoverable by A,[36] but this view has been disputed.[37]

7. *Prevention of foreseeable profit*

For the exemptive principle not to apply, must the loss of the other party be actual or is it enough if he is prevented from obtaining a profit which he anticipated?

For the *Gemara* the answer is simple: "loss" includes the prevention of an anticipated profit. When R. Ḥisda posed the problem whether one who occupied premises unbeknown to the owner must pay rent, the *Gemara* asks whether the premises were for letting and the occupier generally rents premises. If so, the occupier derives a benefit and the owner sustains a loss,—and payment must be made.

The criterion of anticipated profit was not, however, determined objectively. Thus a person who does not usually derive a profit from his property, where for example he does not normally let, will not be deemed to have suffered any loss, although others generally let property of the kind in question. Moreover, even if he had in the past let the property but no longer does so, the situation is treated as at the time when the recipient derives his benefit; thus the owner suffers no loss.[38]

The concept of "loss" is also limited by prescribing that prevention of anticipated profit will only occur when the owner could actually obtain it but not where he or his agent are for instance absent and cannot in fact let the property, for then no question of anticipated profit will arise. The same applies where the owner is available and wishes to let the property but there are no people wishing to rent, in which event the property is deemed not to be for letting.[39]

The category of lettable property is, however, significantly broadened by R. Eliezer Bar Natan (*Ra'avan*) holding that a person who does not

[35] See *Shiṭah Mekubetset* to *B.K.* 21a.

[36] *Ḥoshen Mishpaṭ* 363:9. See *Novellae* of *Rashba* to *B.K.* 21a.

[37] *Ḥelkat Yo'av*, *Ḥoshen Mishpaṭ* 9. See *Or Sameaḥ*, *Hilkhot Gezelah* 3, 9; *Birkat Shmu'el*, *B.K.*, 14:2; *Novellae* R. Sh. Shkopf, *B.K.* 19:5 and *B.B.* 4:3.

[38] *Nimuke Yosef*, *B.K.* Chapter 2, cited as the law by *Rema* in *Shulḥan Arukh*, *Ḥoshen Mishpaṭ* 363:6.

[39] See *Hagahot Asheri* to *B.K.* 3:6 (in the name of *Ra'avia*) who followed *Rema* in *Shulḥan Arukh*, *Ḥoshen Mishpaṭ* 363:10. But see the criticism of *Bet Aharon (Valkin)* to *B.K.* 21a, and its refutation by Y. Flakser, "Yishuv Piṣke Marama", *No'am* 13 (1970), 55-62. See also *Responsa*, *Terumot Hadeshen* 316, which needs explanation.

personally need some property of his will normally let it out, and by the more generalised presumption that today houses are deemed to be for letting, whether or not they are in fact let at the material time.[40]

8. *Loss preceding enjoyment of benefit*

(a) A benefit may become possible initially by a preceding loss which has ceased when the benefit is enjoyed. Is the initial loss a relevant element? The *Toṣafot* to our *Gemara* cites a case from *Ketubot* 30b of a person who has stuffed food into the throat of another, the rule being that although no loss has been sustained (since if the food is "returned" it would be unpalatable and valueless) payment must be made. The *Toṣafot* to our *Gemara* explain the inconsistency on the ground that the other has benefited by reason of the first person's original loss, which brings into operation the principle of "the one benefits and the other loses" and therefore payment for what has actually been consumed must be made. The *Toṣafot* in *Ketubot*, however, offer another explanation. Since the food retains some value, payment must be made because of the partial loss sustained. Another view is that the two acts are treated as occurring simultaneously.

(b) It would seem from the *Toṣafot* in *Baba Kamma* that a preceding loss will create an obligation to pay for any subsequent benefit. That, however, is inconsistent with the decision of a later medieval authority[41] in the following case. A feudal lord after expropriating the house of A, a Jew who had fled from the lord's domain, allowed B, another Jew, to occupy it. A claimed rent from B. The exemptive principle was held to apply since the house must be treated as being not for letting since, if B were to vacate it, it might be given over to a non-Jew and no rent could then be obtained. According to the *Toṣafot* in *Baba Kamma*, B should have had to pay rent since his benefit was preceded by A's loss (the expropriation).[42] A suggestion to remove the inconsistency has been made by interpreting the *Toṣafot* to have distinguished the forced feeding case, where the two acts presumptively occurred together (as suggested above) from the expropriation case, where that was not so, A's loss occurring irrespective of B's benefit, for which reason B would not have to make payment.[43]

---

[40] See *Ra'avan B.K.* 21a, cited as the law by *Rema, op. cit.*, 363:6.

[41] *Mordekhai* to *B.K.*, chapter 2, 17, cited by *Rema, op. cit.*, 363:3.

[42] *Maḥane Efrayim, Hilkhot Gezelah* 13.

[43] *Responsa Bet Shlomoh Ḥoshen Mishpat* 122.

(c) The *Shulḥan Arukh* deals with a case where A has deposited a pledge with a non-Jewish money-lender and B who is in need of funds gets A to allow him to borrow on the security of the pledge.[44] If the pledge is destroyed, B will not, it is held, have to pay A its value. *Prima facie* B's benefit (release from his debt to the money-lender) arises because of A's loss (destruction of the pledge) and he ought to pay according to the *Toṣafot* in *Baba Kamma*. B's benefit, however, occurred after A's property no longer existed and therefore the ruling is to exempt B from payment.[45]

9. *Benefit involving lesser loss*

(a) Will the recipient of the benefit have to pay the value of the benefit or the value of the loss, where the loss is less than the benefit?

Our *Gemara* cites a *Mishnah*[46] dealing with a house of which the upper part is owned by A and the lower part by B. The house collapses and A asks B to rebuild his part so as to enable him to rebuild the upper storey. B refuses. The *Mishnah* decides that A is entitled to rebuild the lower part and occupy it until B reimburses him for the outlay. R. Judah,[47] however, observes "one who occupied another's property without his agreement must pay rent", inferring that A will have to pay B rent although B has suffered no loss in the circumstances (because of his refusal to rebuild his part). The *Gemara* seeks to treat R. Judah's view as contradicting the exemptive principle but eventually distinguishes this case because the alteration ("the blackening of the walls") of the rebuilt part entails a loss and renders A liable to pay rent.

On this basis most of the earlier authorities decide that the value of the benefit and not merely that of the loss must be paid.[48] And that is also the ruling in the *Shulḥan Arukh*.[49]

[44] *Shulḥan Arukh, Hoshen Mishpaṭ* 72:44.

[45] See *Bet Shlomoh, op. cit.* The rule has been followed where a person insures his part of a house held jointly with another but mistakenly the insurance covers the entire house. The joint owner cannot claim any part of the insurance moneys if the house is burnt down. Recourse to the rule has also been made where one has paid insurance premiums for another's property: *Responsa, Erets Tsvi (Te'omim), Hoshen Mishpat* 15, and *Responsa Avne Tsedeḳ, Ḥoshen Mishpaṭ*, 7.

[46] *M.B.M.* 10:3.

[47] The rabbis who oppose R. Yehudah admit that an obligation would occur for detriment due to "blackening" (see below) but give exemption for another reason,—the house is encumbered to the upper part.

[48] R. Meir Halvi holds that only the sum of the loss should be paid. See *Nimuḳe Yoṣef B.K.* Chapter 2. See *Responsa Noda Biyehudah* Vol. 2, Chapter *Ḥoshen Mishpaṭ* 24, that this is all the view of Maimonides. Note the distinction made in *Responsa Amude Esh*, 67.

[49] *Ḥoshen Mishpaṭ* 363:7. See *Toṣafot* to *B.K.* 21a; *Novellae ad loc.; Nimuḳe Yoṣef* to *B.K.*, chapter 2, in the name of *Ritba. Piṣḳe Harosh* to *B.K.*, chapter 2, 6. See also

(b) An 18th century authority[50] explains this last ruling on the ground that the exemptive principle rests on the rule that a person may be compelled not to act in the manner of Sodom and the rule is not applicable where there is a loss, even a minor one. Another explanation[51] is based on the view that where there is a loss a person will always be diligent in protesting against the use which another makes of his property, however small the loss he thereby sustains. Even when he does not know of the use, he is presumed to have protested, and this presumption brings the case into the rule discussed in para. 5 above.

10. *Benefit involving loss to other property*

Does the recipient of a benefit pay only where the loss is in respect of the property he has used or does his obligation extend to other property which is affected?

A 19th century scholar[52] had the following case put to him. A stole a book containing instructions how to paint and copied its contents. Apart from the question of copyright, the application of the exemptive principle is discussed in the *responsum*. If the book was new and was damaged in the course of the "theft", then the rule regarding lesser loss as above will apply. If the book is not damaged but the owner sustained loss by A now being able to compete with him in painting, it is problematic whether A must pay. A comparison is made with the case where one uses a shop of another without agreement and the shop is not for letting, but the owner does business from another shop, which may be affected. Is the damage too remote for liability to arise or is the owner's concern over the loss caused to him sufficient ground for charging the "guilty" party?[53]

The tendency is to make the recipient liable. Our *Gemara* itself asks: "What has he done to him? What loss or injury has he caused him?", the inference being that irrespective of the place of the loss the recipient is chargeable. Some of the authorities also take for granted the view that

---

Responsa Yeshu'ot Ya'akov, *Hoshen Mishpat* 4. *Gidule Shmu'el* to *B.K.* chapter 2, deals with the question, whether he should pay the value of the benefit or the sum the owner could have got.

[50] *Pene Yehoshu'a* to *B.K.* 20b. A parallel question arises on the taking of property without intention to steal: *Shulḥan Arukh, Ḥoshen Mishpat*, 363:3 and *Sema, ibid.*, 7.8. See N. Rakover, "Fundamental Problems in the Jewish law of Theft", *Sinai* 49 (1961), 27-29; *Responsa, Amude Esh*, 66b; *Responsa, Divre Malki'el*, 3:157.

[51] *Responsa, Amude Esh*, 67a.

[52] *Ibid.*, 66b.

[53] See text to note 51 above.

the loss need not arise in connection with the same property, but without going into the matter. In one 18th century case,[54] a writer sent to printers a commentary of his on two Orders of the Talmud. He complained that the printer had used the type set for his work to print a text with the commentaries of Rashi and the Toṣafot. The printer was adjudged to pay for the benefit he had obtained from using the type on the grounds that had he not acted as he did, the writer may have sold more copies of his own book without the competition presented by the printer's publication.

A somewhat similar case is that of the bottled water labels, already mentioned, where the defendant was ordered to pay on the principle that in the event of a lesser loss the entire benefit reaped must be accounted for. In the instant case, moreover, the whole question of passing-off was also a vital consideration. The damage caused concerns also increase of tax payments, and possible damage to commercial reputation.[55]

11. *Recipient providing a benefit*

Towards the end of our *Gemara* the argument takes a new line. A further reason for exemption is reported in the name of Rav. Unoccupied premises are apt to fall into decay and a person who goes into occupation even without agreement will prevent this and may even according to R. Yoṣef[56] put the premises into good condition.

This argument bases the exemptive principle on the benefit which the owner may derive from the recipient. It constitutes a revolutionary turn because, if that were so, the application of the exemptive principle would be severely limited; and some authorities do indeed draw this conclusion.[57] But neither Maimonides nor Karo mention this aspect of the matter and thus inferentially do not accept the limitation.[58]

---

[54] *Noda Biyehudah, Responsa*, Vol. 2, *Ḥoshen Mishpaṭ* 24. *Cf.* Kister J. in *Agudat Hakormim v. Yekev Hagalil* (1960) 22 P.M. 77.

[55] See *Divre Malkhi'el* 3, 157.

[56] The Gemara explains that if premises are not used for a residence, but for storing things, the reasoning of R. Yoṣef will not apply.

[57] See *Shiṭah Mekubetset* to *B.K.* 21a *per* R. Yeshayahu; *Aliyot Darkenu Yona* to *B.B.* 4b; *Or Zeru'a, B.K.*, 120-121; *Ra'avan* to *B.B.* (ed. Ehrenreich, 28): *Torat Emet*, 129. For the reasons of those who oppose this conclusion, see *Novellae Rashba* to *B.K.* 21a; *Piṣke Harosh* to *B.K.*, chapter 2:6; *Nimuke Yoṣef* to *B.K.*, chapter 2; *Yam shel Shlomoh* to *B.K.* 2:16.

[58] *Maimonides, Hilkhot Gezelah Va'avedah* 3:9; *Shulḥan Arukh, Ḥoshen Mishpaṭ* 363:6. See *Bi'ure Hagera ad loc*; *Naḥlat David* to *B.K.* 21b. But *cf. Sema, op. cit.*, 15.

12. *Causation of benefit*

The benefit derived may be the result of an act by the recipient or the donor or a third element. It is clear from the examples given in the *Gemara* that the exemptive principle applied even when the recipient's own act brings about the benefit and that the charging principle of "the one benefits and the other loses" operates even when the benefit comes from the donor's act: in the fencing case an attempt is made to show that the exemptive principle does not operate when the owner puts up the fence on the four sides so that the recipient has to pay (but the attempt fails on the ground that the other party is deemed to suffer a loss). On the other hand the classic example of the exemptive principle is the occupation of premises without agreement where the recipient benefits entirely from his own act.

The above rules, however, are not confined to the acts of the two parties immediately concerned. They extend to benefits due to an extraneous element, as in the forced feeding case,[59] except that on one view the recipient will only be chargeable if his person and not merely his property is affected.[60] This view is stated in connection with the question whether when wool is dyed the improvement due to the dyeing is independent of the wool. Rabina poses the question where the wool belongs to one person and the dyes to another whilst an ape does the dyeing.[61] Is the improvement treated as a separate item from the wool, in which case the person to whom the dyes belong may ask the person to whom the wool belongs to give him back the dyes, or is the improvement not a separate item and the owner of the wool may say that he has nothing belonging to the owner of the dyes. The *Toṣafot ad locum* ask how it is possible to press the second of these alternatives and exempt the owner of the wool from payment, unlike other cases of enrichment, whereas in the feeding case although the benefit was not occasioned by the recipient, he engaged in it in his person. An alternative answer is that the dyeing of the wool is not deemed to be a benefit since it is only decorative. The answer is that in the instant case the wool is not improved by the act of the recipient or his "agent" but by a third party. Accordingly a distinction is made as to whether the benefit accrues or does not accrue to the person of the recipient.

The distinction in most explanations is challenged by the

---

[59] *Ket.* 30b and the *Toṣafot ad loc.* See also *Piṣke Harosh* to *B.K.* 9:17.

[60] *B.K.* 101a and the *Toṣafot ad loc.*

[61] *B.K.* 19b; 55b; *Ket.* 30b.

authorities.[62] *Shakh* rejects it since it is not mentioned in the Talmud and confines the exemption to cases where a third party intervenes, but where the benefit comes about from the donor alone the recipient will have to pay because of the general rule that a person who improves the property of another is entitled to have his expenses reimbursed.

13. *Conclusions*

The question whether the principle "the one gains and the other does not lose" is exemptive or not is treated in the *Gemara* as being without Mishnaic precedent and open to varying views. In holding that the principle is exemptive, the authorities do not lay down a general rule but one confined to the specific fact situation discussed—unauthorised occupation of premises. In addition the principle is circumscribed and its application beyond the limits indicated may yield results which differ considerably from those which emerge from the Talmud and the authorities.

The legal foundations for the exemptive principle vary: that the donor has no cause of action at all; or that even though he may have a cause of action, he will be restrained from acting in the manner of Sodom.

In applying the principle the "no loss" circumstances must be carefully defined. Whilst the loss of an anticipated profit is sufficient to remove the exemption, where the property concerned is such that normally it is not a source of profit, though it might be and though other people might treat it so, no loss will occur; the same is true where the profit is not practically possible.

The kind of property from which a profit may be derived is extended by the presumption that today houses are generally for letting, without the burden of proof being on the owner.

The loss need not be co-extensive with the benefit. Even if it is less the donor is entitled to all the benefit the recipient may obtain.

Two further rules of importance are established. If the donor protests the recipient's benefit, it must be paid for. If the recipient indicates any intention to pay for the benefit should he not be allowed to enjoy it freely, an obligation to pay will arise.

Thus the exemptive principle is limited and all cases in which the recipient should rightly pay for his advantage are excluded.[63]

---

[62] *Shakh* to *Shulhan Arukh, Hoshen Mishpat* 391:2. *Cf. Mahane Efrayim, Hilkhot Nizke Mamon* 2:4; *Helkat Yo'av, Hoshen Mishpat* 9. See also *Markheshet* 2:35; *Novellae* R. Sh. Shkop to *B.K.*, 19:7; *Responsa, Bet Shlomoh, Hoshen Mishpat* 122.

[63] The view that the recipient is not exempt unless he also benefits the owner by the use he makes of the property would render the exemptive principle almost without effect, but it has not been accepted.

II. *Other aspects of unjust enrichment*

In addition to the exemptive principle of "one derives benefit and the other sustains no loss", discussed in part I, there are other aspects of Jewish law on unjust enrichment.

Some of these aspects have been dealt with by the present writer in publications of the Ministry of Justice of Israel, Research in Jewish Law series: "Transacting business with another's property" (No. 45), "Agent who receives benefit in consequence of his agency" (No. 46), "Indemnity for salvage of property" (No. 50), "Indemnity for rescue of a person" (No. 51) and "Compensation for withholding another's money" (No. 52).

1. *Transacting business with another's property*

There are various situations where, whilst the owner of property may suffer no loss from another's use of it, he is nevertheless entitled to recompense. One of these situations occurs when a person lets the property of another and receives the rent. The source of the rule is to be found in the observations of R. Jose in *Mishnah B.M.* 3:2, regarding the man who hires an ox from his neighbour and then lends it to another and the ox dies. The hirer may have made a profit from lending the ox, and R. Jose asks, "How can one do business with his neighbour's ox? The ox must be returned to its owner."

The legal basis for R. Jose's rule is sometimes explained by reference to the injustice of hiring out another's property and depriving the other of his property; and sometimes to quasi-agency, the person who obtains the benefit acting as it were as agent of the owner. The latter approach is characteristic of the rabbis who are not satisfied with merely deciding that the rights of one person pass to another but attempt to give the matter a legal complexion.

Whilst R. Jose was concerned with a specific situation, the earlier post-Talmudic authorities extended his rule by analogy to the case of a person who hires out another's property, holding that the hire price belongs to the owner, and also to the case of the unauthorised subletting of land, although some authorities sought to limit the latter to where the owner actually suffers some loss from the subletting.

Later authorities do not appear to extend the rule substantially further but more recently the possibility has been considered of applying it to the case where a stranger has effected insurance at his own cost and the question of the destination of the insurance money arises. The similarity between insurance and the lending of the ox is twofold. First, just as in the latter case the profit arises from the act of the hirer lending the ox, so with insurance the profit arises from the act of a tenant in insuring the property. Secondly, in both instances the profit derives from the monetary loss of the person involved—the hirer in having to pay the hire money to the owner without receiving anything from the borrower, and the tenant in having paid the insurance premiums.

The parallel has nevertheless been held not to apply. The owner's right to the insurance money does not rest on R. Jose's rule. The distinctive features of the ox-hiring case are not present in the insurance case. In the former, the owner's right to the hire money arises out of the hirer's obligation or the sub-hirer's use or possession of the ox; in the insurance case the person paying the premiums enters into a personal transaction with the insurance company quite distinct from the hiring of the thing hired and therefore does not transact any business directly with the owner's property. The latter therefore has no call on the insurance money. Alternatively, whilst in the ox-hiring case it may be unjust to do business with another's property, in insurance it is unjust for one to pay the premiums and for another to reap the benefit therefrom.

In applying R. Jose's rule to modern problems, a number of distinctions are made, some substantive, emphasising unjust enrichment aspects, and some formal. Where the owner claims all the profit made from his property, it is essential, for instance, to establish whether indeed the property is the source of the profit. Analysis of R. Jose's rule has taken it out of the conceptual realm of abstract justice and prevented its over-extension involving injustice to others.

2. *Agent who receives benefit in consequence of his agency*

Here the question is—how should the benefit arising from the act of a person representing another be treated? To whom does the benefit belong? Is the fact that the benefit arose out of agency activity determinative of the rights of the parties? Although possibly in agency law, the agent's act may not give any right to the principal, the latter is nevertheless entitled to receive or participate in the benefit because it is he who has been the "cause" of it. Alternatively, whilst the principal has a right to the benefit, the agent also has a right since but for his action the principal would have nothing, the benefit not being an integral part of the agency activity. If the right of the one in the benefit the other has received is recognised, there falls to be determined when he is deemed to be the "cause" to entitle him to the benefit. Juridically the problem falls within the bounds of unjust enrichment.

The rule that has emerged is that, irrespective of agency law, where a person has been the "cause" of a benefit he is entitled to enjoy it. First elaborated in the Palestinian Talmud, the rule was adopted by some of the earlier post-Talmudic authorities. Its history in the Shulḥan Arukh and the glossators is interesting. Whilst it did not receive explicit mention in the basic text, the glossators give it prominence as a point to be considered in the appropriate circumstances, in particular where the third party gives additional consideration, or where an agent has varied his agency. Reflection led to a number of distinctions depending on the connection between the benefit and the agency activity. The possibility of applying the rule to a benefit occasioned by mistake was also examined.

Some of the later rabbis held that the principal's right did not arise in strict law but resulted from rabbinical *takanah.*

The solution of sharing the benefit was not proposed under the exemptive principle—when the recipient would take all—nor under the rule relating to doing business with another's property—when the owner would get all. In the present context the agent not only enjoys a benefit from his agency but makes a profit. Accordingly, his obligation is greater than that of a person who only enjoys a benefit. On the other hand, he does not make his profit at the expense of the principal and therefore all of it cannot be said to be due to the latter. Thus the agent and principal have equally strong rights; both have contributed to creating the profit, the one by his activity and the other by his property.

The broadening of the rule would have far-reaching consequences, but beyond the situation where the third party gives additional consideration or where the agent varies his agency, no broadening of the rule was undertaken.

The law relating to the agent who obtains a benefit from his agency is examined from the viewpoint both of agency law and of unjust enrichment. In certain circumstances, an agent so benefiting may be in breach of trust or even criminally liable and be deprived of the advantage.

3. *Indemnity for salvage of property*

Is the voluntary nature of salvage significant to the salvor's right to indemnity? On the one hand, in doing what he did the salvor has acted piously in observance of a *mitsvah* (precept), unlike one who simply intervenes with regard to another's property and unasked enhances its value. Perhaps for this reason his rights are superior. Salvage should moreover be encouraged, and if the rules of law do not allow for proper compensation, they call for amendment. On the other hand, the doing of a pious act is its own reward and further monetary payment is superfluous. What connection is there between the pious act of the salvor and his monetary rights? His rights may be lesser than that of one who unasked improves another's property, since the latter presumably acted as he did in anticipation of being rewarded, whilst the former did not or waived any such right.

Regard must also be had to whether or not the owner was present when the salvage occurred and the salvor made any stipulation with him. What, further, is the position where the salvor is unsuccessful either because his efforts end in failure or because the property was salvaged without his effort? Does a person who whilst salvaging his own property salvages also his neighbour's, have any right to be paid in full or proportionately? Still another question is whether the salvor's right must be distinguished as between payment for his efforts and reimbursement of his outgoings and losses.

The source of the law is a *Mishnah* in *B.K.* 10:4: "If one was coming along with a barrel of wine and another with a jar of honey, and the jar of honey cracked, and the first emptied his wine and scooped up the honey in his barrel—he may only have the value of his services. But if he said, 'I am going to save your honey but you pay me for my wine', the other must pay him."

This Mishnaic rule that where a salvor makes no stipulation as to payment, he is only to be paid for the services he has rendered, is subject to significant reservations which make the rule exceptional, whereas the salvor's right is much wider.

The Talmud understands the Mishnah to be concerned not with the case where the property would be lost but for the salvor's action. If it is impossible to save the property, the salvor is entitled to all of it under the rule of *hefḳer* (renunciation of property), or at least to the value of what he lost in the course of the salvage.

The early post-Talmudic authorities introduced a further reservation—the Mishnaic rule does not apply where the owner is not present; in that event the salvor is entitled not only to payment for his services, but also to the value of his loss. His right is further extended to entitle him to full indemnity of his outgoings when, without his intervention, the owner would have used the salvor's property to effect his salvage.

The Mishnaic distinction between payment for services rendered and payment for losses incurred by the salvor requires clarification. The exemption as regards the latter when the owner is present and the salvor has made no stipulation is explained on the ground that the owner can argue that he could have salvaged his property with such expense. Thus, whenever this argument cannot be raised, the salvor is entitled to be paid for his losses, i.e. payment for services includes all the necessary outgoings, whereas the value of the property lost in the course of the salvage is confined to those outgoings which the owner might not have been ready to expend, for which reason stipulation must be made.

Accordingly the Mishnaic rule restrictive of the salvor's rights will apply where salvage was possible and effected in the owner's presence without his being consulted and the salvor acted freely of his own choice; he will then be entitled to payment for his services, i.e. his necessary outgoings as to which no stipulation need be made.

The owner may be exempt from payment if he voices opposition to the salvage. But where he knows that in any event the salvage will be carried out (because, for instance, it is involved in saving others) or his opposition is merely aimed at avoiding due payment for his outgoings, it will not be taken at its face value and have no effect.

The legal basis for salvage indemnity, as it emerges from a survey of the sources, lies on one view in *taḳanah* since in strict law, arguably, the salvor only acted to save the owner trouble and is not entitled to payment; and in order to encourage such acts a duty to pay was instituted by *taḳanah*. The "Rule of Court" (*tenai bet din*), referred to in the *Toṣefta B.K.* 4:26-27, which entitles a salvor to payment for his losses, may, it is suggested, be the source of the *taḳanah* as against the Mishnaic rule of law.

The connection between the rules relating to salvage and returning lost property has been one of reciprocal effect. The possibility in the case of lost property to stipulate payment in the presence of three persons is extended to salvage as an alternative to stipulation with the owner himself. Conversely, the importance of the owner's presence in salvage is extended to lost property.

The salvage rules illustrate the process whereby a deficiency in the law is remedied by *taḳanah* to obviate the possibility of one person enjoying a benefit at the expense of another. This regulation is in contrast to the law regarding improvements made to another's property without asking the owner.

4. *Indemnity for rescue of a person*

The rescue of persons is in Jewish law not merely a matter of moral sensibility. Very often the act will entail expenditure by the rescuer or damage to a third person's property. Rescue and salvage are similar in several respects. Both rest on religious precept and accordingly involve a voluntary act without any legal obligation between the parties to do the act or any agreement as to indemnifying the salvor or rescuer.

In contrast to salvage, however, an individual may not abandon his life or person. Again, salvage and rescue may be distinguished with regard to the obligation to incur expenses: whereas in salvage it is possible to set-off value against value, in rescue there is no measuring rod.

A guiding consideration is the encouragement of acts of rescue. The Talmud already prescribes under *taḳanah* that the rescuer is not bound to compensate any third person who has suffered a loss in the course of the rescue. Raba said (*Sanh.* 74a): "If one was pursuing another pursuer to save (the latter's victim) and broke some utensils, whether of the pursuer or the pursued or of any other person, he is not liable for them. This should not be so in law, but if you do not so rule, no man will save his neighbour from a pursuer."

As regards indemnity for the rescuer's expenses, the Talmud is not explicit but the early post-Talmudic authorities derived the rule in various ways. In order to encourage rescue, it was prescribed that the costs entailed must be paid immediately and without reservation. Opposition by the person rescued to payment was ignored. Similarly, where in the course of rescuing one person another is also rescued, the latter will not be heard to say that even had he himself not been rescued the rescuer would have incurred expenses, since every person could argue so and this might endanger people.

5. *Compensation for withholding another's money*

The persistent fall in money value has sharpened problems concerning the unlawful taking of money and delay in payment of money due. Two purposes are served in providing for compensation in such cases—to make up for the owner's loss resulting from his inability to use his money and to impose sanctions for delay in payment. If profit is made, a further cause of action may be found in the rules regarding the transacting of business with another's property or under unjust enrichment.

On the other hand, a number of difficulties will occur if compensation is exigible. Under the law of theft, the value at the date of the theft is alone payable and any betterment belongs to the miscreant. Again, any compensation payable may fall within the prohibition of usury; in that case the fact that the money was not "lent" willingly must be borne in mind.

The rules here are also not based on strict law but on *takanah* and binding custom, having regard to the rabbis' awareness of the profitable use to which money can be put.

The observation in the Palestinian Talmud that a person can only complain but not more of another who renders "his pocket idle" is in conflict with and therefore restricted by other tannaitic and talmudic rules.

For the post-Talmudic authorities the discussion revolves around two questions—whether tort law applies to charge the "withholder" with damages and whether the additional payment partakes of usury. As to the first, the balance of authority is that compensation is payable for the loss entailed by preventing profitable use of the money. (Some authorities would charge the "withholder" on the principle of "the one benefits and the other suffers loss".)

As for usury, money withheld at the wish of the owner is distinguished from money forcibly withheld, as is also payment made for the right to retain money from payment made by way of "fine" or compensation for the loss incurred by the owner. Reference may be made to a formula, attributed to R. Jacob of Orleans, one of the Tosafists, which is incorporated in bills to provide ab initio for payment of a fine, which is indicative of rabbinical awareness of the need to resolve halakhically problems arising in trade and commerce.

A further distinction is made between "consumer" loans and money due in connection with employment, commerce and the like. This distinction is of current importance since most advances of money are today not in the nature of consumer loans but are made for other purposes, generally through banks, and are not "loans" in the halakhic sense. Even as regards loans, the view taken by some would permit compensation for withholding repayment.

The fall in money value, characteristic of our time, is an important consideration in respect not only of the hardship which delay in payment may entail but also of the legal basis of the obligation to indemnify. The traditional authorities concentrated on the question of compensation for loss of the prospective profitable use which the owner might have made of his money. Today it is not this loss only but the actual intrinsic loss from the fall in money value which is predominant, with its repercussions as to the tort and unjust enrichment liability of the "withholder" and as to usury. Thus the necessity arises for *takanot* to augment the strict law. Three centuries ago it became customary in Poland to compensate for market losses (*peseida deshuka*). Although attempts were subsequently made to narrow the scope of this custom to the special circumstances in which it arose, modern conditions justify its wider application, since all and not only business men are affected. Thus the rabbis long ago treated the withholding of payment, which involves a loss of profit to the owner, as a form of theft.

[24]

The Jewish Law Annual, Vol. III

CONCEPTS OF *ZEH NEHENEH*... IN THE ANALYTIC SCHOOL

by

NORMAN SOLOMON*

The purpose of this article is to demonstrate the approach to halakhic discussion which characterizes what I have elsewhere[1] named the Analytic School. I shall do this by presenting the significant elements in the published *shi^curim* of Rabbis Shim^con Shkop and Ḥayyim Rabbinovitz on the subject of *zeh neheneh vezeh lo ḥaṣer.*

The Analytic School

As the work of most followers of the Analytic School is unknown to most academic students of Jewish Law, and the very existence of the School is clearly perceived by few, it will not be out of place if I use this opportunity to characterize the School briefly.

Ḥayyim Soloweicyk (1853-1918) is undoubtedly the "father figure" of the School, and his *Ḥidushe R. Ḥayyim haLevi al haRambam*[2] its classical expression. Through his influence, and that of his pupils and colleagues at Wolozyn prior to 1892, his way of study spread through the Yeshivot of Lithuania and much of White Russia, and by the outbreak of the Second World War had achieved the dominant position it holds in the Yeshiva world to this day. The special mark of Soloweicyk's method is his rejection of casuistry in favour of attention to the refinement of legal concepts. In his *Ḥidushim*[2] he presents us with questions of the traditional type on Maimonides' Code. In answering them, however, he departs from conventional casuistry (*pilpul*) by proposing a "*ḥaḳirah*", through the resolution of which the question is made to fall away. The "*ḥaḳirah*", about which I have written at length elsewhere,[3] is a pair of alternative definitions of a halakhic concept; by the choice of

---

* Rabbi. The Hampstead Synagogue, London.

[1] In an unpublished Ph. D. thesis for Manchester University, 1966. Two sections have been published in *Diné Israel* (Tel Aviv): "*Ḥilluq* and *Ḥaqira*: A Study in the Method of the Lithuanian Halakhists", in Volume IV (1973), lxix-cvi; "Definition and Classification in the Works of the Lithuanian Halakhists" in Volume VI (1975), lxxiii-ciii. This unpublished thesis will shortly be published as *The Analytic Movement:* Hayyim Soloveitchik and his Circle. South Florida Studies in the History of Judaism, Scholars Press, University of South Florida, Tampa.

[2] First edition Bresc 1936, and frequently reprinted.

[3] *Diné Israel* IV, *loc. cit.*

the correct alternative a difficulty or series of difficulties is avoided, or a problem or series of problems solved.

It is obvious that this method involves a conceptual rather than a casuistic approach. This conceptual approach, so different from that of the majority of earlier halakhists, is now the norm in most *yeshivot*, particularly those of Lithuanian provenance, though its influence on the actual decision-making process in the *Bate Din* has been much less strong. It is certainly necessary for the academic student of Jewish Law to familiarize himself with it, both in order to establish a bridge of understanding with the yeshiva world, and in order to assess better the inner logic of halakhic concepts as seen by people largely unfamiliar with Western legal systems.[4]

The two scholars whose work I shall consider in this article were both, successively, leading lights of the Yeshiva of Telshai, Lithuania. Rabbi Shimᶜon Shkop (1860-1939) was a disciple and colleague of Soloweicyk at Wolozyn. In 1884 he was invited, together with Rabbi J. L. Bloch, to join Rabbi Eliezer Gordon in the re-establishment of the Yeshiva at Telshai, where he remained until 1903, sending forth a stream of distinguished disciples, including Elchanan Wasserman, M. A. Amiel, and Joseph Kahaneman, all of whom were instrumental in disseminating his methods. His successor at Telshai was Rabbi Ḥayyim Rabbinovitz (d. 1931), sometimes known as "Reb Ḥayyim Telsher", who appears to have been the dominant intellectual personality at Telshai until his death, and whose writings display even more sharply, if less systematically, than those of Shkop, a concern with the definition of concepts. Neither of the works which I shall quote was published within its author's lifetime, though sections may have been circularized amongst the Yeshiva students in manuscript or cyclostyled form. However, there is certainly no reason to doubt the statement of Rabbi M. M. Shkop[5] that the bulk of the material included in the volume of his father's *Ḥidushim* I am making use of here was written between 1894

---

[4] This is not to suggest that the Analysts were not indirectly influenced by Western developments. It is certainly no coincidence that they are roughly contemporary with such jurists as, say, Austin or Kelsen. The relationship indeed is not unlike that between Roman and early Jewish Law; there is certainly interaction, which it is fascinating to trace in detail where possible, but each system has an inner logic of its own. Of the Rabbis mentioned in this article only Eliezer Gordon is known to have had first-hand knowledge of Western Law; but undoubtedly many of the students at Yeshivot could have mediated ideas, even if in a general and imprecise way.

[5] Introduction to *Ḥidushe Rabbi Shimᶜon Yehudah haKohen al Masekhtot Baba Kamma, Baba Metzia, Baba Bathra* (New York: Moimester, 1947).

and 1905, that is mainly at Telshai. It seems reasonable to suppose that Rabbinowitz's *Shiᶜurim* were composed, and certainly that they were perfected, during his period in Telshai, even though some of the material may have originated in his period at Slobodka prior to 1903, for it was there that he undoubtedly established his reputation for penetrating logical analysis. For my present purpose, at any rate, I shall assume that despite the reverse order of publication, Shkop's work belongs to an earlier period than that of Rabbinowitz.

R. Shimᶜon Shkop on Zeh neheneh...

Shkop's discussion—or rather, discussions[6]—of the principle of *zeh neheneh...* is to be found in the nineteenth chapter of his *Novellae on Baba Kamma.*[7]

The *Gemara*[8] discusses whether someone who occupies another's premises without the express agreement of the owner is liable to pay rent.

There are four possible cases.

i) If the trespasser has premises of his own, thus derives no material benefit from his act of trespass; and the owner does not rent out premises, and thus suffers no loss as a result of the trespass.

ii) If the trespasser derives no benefit, as above; but the owner suffers loss, as otherwise he would let his premises at a profit.

iii) If the trespasser would otherwise need to rent somewhere to live, and is therefore deriving benefit from his act; but the owner suffers no loss, as he would in any case not be letting his premises.

iv) If the trespasser derives benefit, as above; and the owner suffers loss, as otherwise he would let his premises at a profit.

The *Gemara* rules that in the first case no payment has to be made, and that in the fourth case payment must be made. The third case is a classical illustration of *zeh neheneh vezeh lo ḥaṣer*—"one benefits but the other loses nothing"—the "exemptive principle" the development of which in the rabbinic sources is expounded in Dr. Rakover's lead article in this volume. Reference should be made to his exposition, much of which will be assumed in what follows.

---

[6] The chapter is divided into eight sections. A footnote to the third, the contents of which overlap those of the first two, indicates that it was copied from another '*Ḳuntreṣ*'—presumably one of the sets of cyclostyled notes which circulated in the Yeshivot before the printed work became available.

[7] See note 5.

[8] *B.K.* 20a.

The *Gemara* does not discuss the second case, but the "*Rishonim*" do, and it is with their debate that Shkop is primarily concerned. This is characteristic of the Analytic School, for its members see themselves primarily as exponents and interpreters of the words of the *Rishonim*, rather than as definers of talmudic legal concepts *per se*.

The *Rif* and others hold that in this case—viz. where A has no benefit from living in B's house, though B suffers damage or loss thereby—A is obliged to pay rent to B. *Rashba*[9] maintains that there is no such obligation. He bases his objection on a *Mishnah* in the last chapter of *Baba Metzia*, which deals with the obligations of two men, one of whom owns and lives in the upper storey of a dwelling while the other owns and lives "in the house"—i.e. downstairs. What remedy has the tenant of the upper storey if the whole building collapses and the lower tenant refuses to rebuild his part? To the suggestion of the Tanna Kama that he should rebuild the downstairs and live in it himself until the downstairs man pays, Rabbi Judah counters that this cannot be permitted, and the *Gemara* explains that this is because his use of the downstairs would cause loss to the downstairs man, for it would at least involve "blackening of the walls". Rabbi Judah's own remedy, according to the *Mishnah*, is that the upper storey tenant should rebuild the whole, but then refuse to budge from downstairs until the downstairs tenant pays his share of the expenses. Now the only difference between Rabbi Judah's remedy and that of the Tanna Kama, seeing that in both cases loss (the "blackening of the walls") is caused to the downstairs tenant, is that if the Tanna Kama's remedy is followed the upstairs tenant benefits from living downstairs, for he has nowhere else to live; whereas if Rabbi Judah's remedy is followed, the upper tenant, though causing loss, does not himself benefit thereby, for he has somewhere else, viz. the rebuilt upper storey, in which he could live if he wishes. But surely, argues *Rashba*, nothing would be gained by Rabbi Judah's suggestion, which after all still involves loss to the downstairs man, unless we are to assume that if someone causes loss to another in these circumstances without involving a corresponding benefit to himself he is not liable to make restitution; and this directly contradicts the *Rif*'s ruling.

Shkop disposes of the *Rashba*'s problem by means of a characteristic *ḥaḳirah*. We must distinguish between the right, which Mr. Upstairs does not possess, to benefit from the property of Mr. Downstairs; and the right, which Mr. Upstairs does have, of preventing Mr. Downstairs

---

[9] *Novellae ad loc.*

from benefiting from his, Mr. Upstairs', having erected the house without Mr. Downstairs' obligatory contribution. In following the remedy of the Tanna Kama Mr. Upstairs would be deriving unjustified benefit from Mr. Downstairs' property, and as the recipient of such a benefit would be liable to make restitution for damage caused. But if he were to adopt the remedy of Rabbi Judah this liability would not arise, since he would be deriving no benefit at all from Mr. Downstairs' property, but by living in it simply be exercising his right of coercion on Mr. Downstairs in respect of Mr. Downstairs' obligation to pay for restoration of the property. It is thus perfectly consistent with the *Mishnah* to maintain that in general one must make restitution for loss caused by use of another's property even if one derives no benefit from that use.

It will be apparent from the preceding paragraph that Shkop's prime concern is not that of the casuist who avoids contradiction by pointing to some more or less arbitrary facet of one case to distinguish it from another, but that of the legal analyst who tries to discover the essential logic of the concepts with which he works.

This emerges even more clearly from his subsequent[10] attempt to clarify the legal basis of the exemptive principle itself. Jacob Joshua Falk (1680-1756), who in many ways stands out as a precursor of the Analytic School, had suggested[11] that the exemptive principle was a consequence of the rule of *kofin al midat Ṣedom*; that is, since a person may be forced by the law to yield his rights for the benefit of another where no loss is caused to himself (as Rakover so neatly puts it, one may be compelled "not to adopt a dog-in-the-manger attitude"), it follows that if the second person had helped himself to the benefit without the express consent of the donor, the donor could have no claim for payment for a benefit which the law would in any case have forced him to yield to the other. Shkop's objection to this is that the Talmud assumes that the exemptive principle is operative even with regard to *Heḳdesh*, i.e. sacred property where the "manner of Sodom" rule is irrelevant; it is also clear from a later statement in the same paragraph that a similar objection would arise from the consideration that the "manner of Sodom" rule is not relevant in cases of squatting[12]—a person cannot be forced to allow someone to live on his premises, even though he is not using them himself and would not in any case let them for profit—and the squatting

[10] "Subsequent" only in the sense that it is printed later, viz. in section 3—see note 6.

[11] *Pene Yehoshuʿah ad loc.* See also *B.B.* 12b, *Tos.* s.v. *Kegon.*

[12] See *Toṣafot B.K.* 20b s.v. *ha itanei.*

case is after all the main one in connection with which the Talmud discusses the exemptive principle of *zeh neheneh...*

Shkop therefore maintains that the exemptive principle is independent of the "manner of Sodom" rule despite their frequent association. He proposes instead that the exemptive principle is a *ṣevara*[13]—a rational, or common-sense, principle that no claim can lie where no loss has been suffered, i.e. that there can be no claim for payment for benefit where the donor has not been involved in any loss. This is similar to the rationale offered by Rabbi Mosheh Mordekhai Epstein (1866-1933)[14] for the principle in his *Levush Mordekhai*, the earliest work of the Analytic School to be published, though in all probability not the first to be committed to writing.

What is of significance here, apart from the details of the formulation of the legal basis of the principle, is that it has been put forward at all. Here are two of the first generation analysts concerning themselves—perhaps independently, though we cannot be sure—with clarifying the legal concept involved in *zeh neheneh...* With notable exceptions—Falk is one, Aryeh Loeb HaCohen[15] almost the only other—this type of activity simply was not undertaken by the traditional talmudic commentators and lawyers. Yet within the Analytic School it is normal. When one reads, for instance, the article on *zeh neheneh...* in the *Encyclopedia Talmudica*, one cannot but be faintly amused by the

---

[13] '*Ṣevara*' is several times used in the B.T. (e.g. *Ber.* 35a) where no scriptural verse or legal principle can be found to support a rule, and indicates that it is a matter of reason or common sense. Shkop surely uses the word here in this sense, though it is tempting to speculate as to whether he (or for that matter the Amoraim who used the same expression) had some sort of Natural Law concept in mind. Here, for instance, is a statement of his (*op. cit.*, p. 1) which is highly suggestive of Natural Law: "The fact that a pit becomes his (in respect of liability for damage it might cause) in virtue of his having dug or uncovered it, is because he has prepared the cause of the damage and thus become its owner; just as in matters pertaining to individual rights it is agreed both by the Laws of the Torah and the Laws of the Nations that whoever brings a new thing into the world thereby acquires all the rights in it."

[14] *Levush Mordekhai Baba Kamma* was published in Warsaw in 5661 (1901) by J. Z. Unterhaendler—more than twenty years before any other Analytic work. Epstein studied at Wolozyn, where he no doubt came under the influence of Soloweicyk and his circle. From 1893 until he moved to Palestine in 1923 he lectured at Slobodka, where he and Rabbinovitz were together until Rabbinovitz' departure for Telshai in 1903. It therefore seems impossible that Rabbinovitz was unacqainted with Epstein's printed work, though he does not cite it. Most probably, even in those cases where he puts forward similar ideas, he did not feel indebted to Epstein.

[15] Aryeh Loeb HaKohen of Styria (d. 1813). Author of *Shev Shemaʿtata, Ketsot Haḥoshen, et alia.* Another name to be added is that of Jacob of Lissa (d. 1832), whose numerous works include *Ḥavot Daʿat* and *Netivot Hamishpaṭ*. See below, note 24.

compiler's presentation of some of the preceding definitions of the basis of *zeh neheneh...* as part of talmudic law. His sources are, of course, clearly indicated—but one does constantly have to remind oneself of their lateness, and of their fundamental difference of approach from that of the earlier generations of rabbis. It is instructive to contrast articles in the *Encyclopedia Talmudica* with those in pre-Analytic encyclopaedias, such as Goitein's *Keṣef Nivḥar*[16] or Medini's *Sede Ḥemed.*[17] It is not just that the contributors to *Encyclopedia Talmudica* have a more scientific approach to their subject, or that they write with an awareness of Western concepts of law; they are in fact heavily and directly indebted to followers of the Analytic School, and see talmudic concepts through their eyes.

Shkop, having demonstrated to his satisfaction that the exemptive principle is a legal axiom that no claim can lie where no loss has been suffered, devotes the rest of his *shiᶜur* to a consideration of difficulties arising in statements of the *rishonim* on various aspects of unjust enrichment. In each case the solution—or one of the suggested solutions—depends on establishing that the benefit enjoyed by the one party has not resulted from any loss to the other party, and can therefore not constitute the basis for a claim. In contrast with Rabbinovitz, whose approach we shall examine next, Shkop does not constantly question and test his hypothesis; having once established it to his satisfaction, he merely applies it straightforwardly to a succession of cases.

R. Ḥayyim Rabbinovitz on zeh neheneh...

Rabbinovitz' *ḥakirah* superficially resembles that of Shkop and Epstein, but there is an important additional element in his presentation, which we are fortunate to have in at least two versions.[18]

There are two ways, says Rabbinovitz, in which the exemptive rule may be understood, as follows:

i) Since the owner suffers no loss on account of the benefit the user has derived from his property, it would be an act "after the manner of Sodom" if a claim for compensation were to be made against the

---

[16] First published at Prague, 1827/8, by M. I. Landau.

[17] Published from 1890 onwards in Warsaw, by J. Lev.

[18] *Op. cit.*, 39 and 172. The Hebrew texts are appended to this article. The second, in his *shiᶜur* on Baba Batra, seems to me the later version, especially as it is formulated in such a way as to lead naturally to acceptance of the idea of the dependence of the exemptive principle on the "rule of Sodom". As I point out later, the notes on Baba Kamma are still undecided on this.

beneficiary. But *kofin al midat Ṣedom*—we coerce a person not to act "after the manner of Sodom", and thus we forbid the owner to bring any action against the beneficiary.

ii) The exemption does not arise from any extraneous consideration, such as the "rule of Sodom", but is of the essence (*meᶜiḳar hadin*) of the act of benefiting. For benefiting can only result in an obligation towards the owner of an object if the owner has suffered loss. But in the squatting case, the beneficiary has derived his benefit from the object only, but in no way from the owner. The only liability for compensation which could arise would be towards the object itself, therefore, and not towards the owner; and as this is manifestly nonsense, no liability for compensation arises at all.

The first of these alternatives is very similar to the theory of J. J. Falk, rejected by Shkop, as we explained above—though in fact Rabbinovitz does not cite either of them. Unlike Shkop, moreover, he does not reject the theory categorically on the grounds of its apparent inapplicability to the squatting case.

The second alternative invites comparison with Shkop's theory, explained above, that the exemptive principle is a self-evident *ṣevara*, or rational principle. Rabbinovitz does not appear to regard the exemptive principle as self-evident[19] until he has clarified the legal essence of the act of deriving benefit involved in the case under discussion. To Rabbinovitz, therefore, it is not the mere fact that the owner loses nothing that exempts the beneficiary from liability to compensate; rather, it is that since nothing has been taken from him he is not a party to the case at all. The case is now between the beneficiary and the object, and the object not being a legal person no claim can lie.

Before we look at the way Rabbinovitz makes use of his *ḥaḳirah* the following points must be noted.

a) The expression *meᶜiḳar hadin* and its cognates are characteristic of the Analytic School, and particularly of Rabbinovitz. One is led to feel the law is something external, something objective, our task being to reveal clearly what is there already. Amongst the members of the Analytic School the belief that the Torah is the pure Word of God leads to regarding it, as a legal system, as a sort of "object" independent of all extraneous matters, and where the only way to increase our understanding is by closer attention to its detail "as it is".

---

[19] The expression "self-evident" here is my own. On *ṣevara*, see above note 13.

b) Rabbinovitz takes for granted here that there can be no such thing as an obligation towards an object *per se*. This assumption should be seen in the light of his analysis of tortious liability earlier in the volume.[20] There, taking as an example liability arising from damage caused by a person's ox, he asks whether liability arises from the defendant's negligence, or whether the liability is really that of the ox, or other property, but which in practice must be discharged by the owner. His rationale for the latter alternative—which in fact he ultimately rejects in favour of the former—is that it would be unreasonable to impose an obligation on the defendant to make any payment where he himself has not "derived a benefit" which could function as the basis for that obligation. It would seem, therefore, that when, in our case, Rabbinovitz lays down that a defendant can have no obligation towards an object, and does not even discuss whether there can be an obligation towards the plaintiff simply in his role as owner of a piece of property towards which there is a *prima facie* obligation, he is really deriving this from his earlier conclusion that tortious liability is a direct personal obligation.

c) His distinction between "claims against a person" and "claims against an object" must likewise be seen in the context of other Analytic discussions of matters *in rem* and *in personam*.[21] In modern western jurisprudence we find the *rem/personam* distinction used in connection with rights, judgments and execution as well as actions, in which connection it is found in Roman Law. There are several examples of its use in rabbinic literature, the most striking being the distinction between the effects of the two types of adjuration—*shevuʿah*, which effects a restraint on the *person* who utters it, and *neder*, which effects a taboo in the *object* itself. The Analysts use the distinction widely without discriminating between, for instance, legal and religious contexts.

Now let us see how Rabbinovitz makes use of his *ḥaḳirah*. Unlike Shkop, who, having decided which of the alternatives to adopt, proceeds to apply it straightforwardly to several cases, Rabbinovitz constantly retests his hypothesis, attempting to explain the passages under discussion according to both alternatives if this is possible.

Our first example is from his *Novellae on Baba Kamma*, and concerns the squatting case. The plaintiff does not normally let the premises, and

[20] Rabbinovitz, *op. cit.*, 14. Shkop, *op. cit.*, in his opening chapter, has practically the same *ḥaḳirah*.

[21] See my discussion of this in *Diné Israel* IV (1973), lxxvi-lxxx.

thus loses nothing as a result of the defendant's unauthorized occupation; the defendant derives benefit, as otherwise he would need to rent accommodation. The *Gemara* asks: Can (the defendant) say "What loss have I caused you (so why should I pay rent?)", or can (the plaintiff) claim "You have derived benefit (and must therefore pay me)"? *Toṣafot*[22] examines the plaintiff's claim in relation to the discussion in *Baba Bathra* 12b of the claim of a firstborn brother to receive his double share of a land inheritance in the form of two adjacent plots. One view expressed there is that he may insist on receiving adjacent plots, for *kofin al midat Ṣedom*—it would be "in the manner of Sodom" if his brothers were to refuse to allow him to have adjacent plots, for they would gain no advantage from such a dog-in-the-manger attitude, and he would suffer disadvantage by having to take plots with no common border; the other view is that the brothers can insist on a higher valuation (*kenikhṣe devar Maryon*) of the specially selected second plot, for they may argue that they are being deprived of potentially better land. *Toṣafot* maintain that the plaintiff in our case could uphold his claim despite the ruling in B.B. that *kofin al midat Ṣedom*, for it might be that the "rule of Sodom" cannot outweigh his right as an owner to exclude whom he will from living on his premises; conversely, the defendant's case is consistent with the view in B.B. that a higher valuation may be demanded, for there it is a matter of deciding *ab initio* whether the firstborn may receive adjacent plots, but here the question of rent arises only *post factum*.

Now, says Rabbinovitz, if the rationale of *zeh neheneh...* were that the one who has derived benefit can have no liability towards the owner who has suffered no loss, *Toṣafot* would not be justified in pointing to the owner's right of exclusion as grounds for his claim for rent; whatever his rights, he has not in fact suffered any loss. So, says Rabbinovitz, the underlying concept of *zeh neheneh...* is the rule of Sodom, and therefore the owner's right is relevant, rather than the absence of any loss on his part.

Rabbinovitz then—and this is characteristic of his method—attempts to interpret the same *Toṣafot* in accordance with the other "side" of his *ḥaḳirah*, viz. that *zeh neheneh...* is based on the impossibility of a liability to one who has suffered no loss, and does not arise from the "rule of Sodom". It is a necessary part of ownership (*ʿiḳar baʿaluto babayit*—compare his use of the word *ʿiḳar* above) that one has rights of

[22] *B.K.* 20b, *Toṣafot* s.v. *Itanei.*

residence, just as the owner of a field has a right to its fruits. Therefore—and unfortunately Rabbinovitz is not quite explicit here—the owner in our case may be regarded as suffering a loss, viz. the loss of his (unexercised) rights of residence, and it is this to which *Toṣafot* point in distinguishing between our case and that in B.B. on the grounds that here the owner had a right to exclude the squatter from his premises in the first place.

So far no conclusion has been reached, nor is any reached by Rabbinovitz from several other passages of *Gemara* or *Toṣafot* which lend *prima facie* support to one side or other of the *ḥaḳirah*. One of these attempts is nevertheless interesting in view of Shkop's rejection of the primacy of the "rule of Sodom" on the grounds that it is inapplicable to *heḳdesh*. Rabbinovitz quotes the relevant passage—it is a *Mishnah* from the end of Chapter 5 of *Meilah* cited in *B.K.* 20b—and argues in just the same manner as Shkop (to whom he does not refer) that since the *Gemara* uses the exemptive principle with reference to the *Mishnah*'s case of one who has derived benefit from *heḳdesh* without *heḳdesh* thereby suffering any loss, the *Gemara* must assume that the principle is not based on the "rule of Sodom"; it would be absurd to suggest that the beneficiary is exempt from making payment to *heḳdesh* simply because *heḳdesh* ought not to have taken a dog-in-the-manger attitude and deprived him of its use, for there is a strong religious prohibition against the use of *heḳdesh* by a layman. However, Rabbinovitz does not regard this as a conclusive argument. We may hold, he says, that the exemptive principle is legally based on the "rule of Sodom" despite the fact that in some particular instance the "rule of Sodom", for extraneous reasons, could not apply. I think that what Rabbinovitz is saying, though he is not explicit, is that property law has a logic of its own, which retains its integrity despite the fact that in particular instances a person's actions ought to be influenced by other, e.g. religious, considerations. Thus for our purpose it is irrelevant to say that *heḳdesh* could not be forced to allow a benefit to someone else at no cost to itself, for what prevents our insisting on this generosity is not property law as such, but religious law.

Rabbinovitz goes on to discuss the situation where the owner has some legitimate objection to the use of his property by another even where no loss is caused to himself. Surely if the reason for the exemptive principle were merely the inapplicability of a claim for compensation where no loss has been caused, it would apply here; whereas if the principle were based on the "rule of Sodom" it would not apply, since there could be no coercion against a legitimate objection of the owner to the use of his property. That there can be no coercion in such a case Rabbinovitz demonstrates from the instance of A opening (= making) a window overlooking B's courtyard in such a position that although at present it causes no *hezek reʾiyah* it may do so at a later stage when B has erected further buildings on his site. The *Rosh*[23] rules that B may not object to the new window, but that his right to demand its removal at a later stage is not prejudiced; for the time being it is *zeh neheneh vezeh lo ḥaṣer. Rashba*[23] and others, however, reject this view and support B's right to object, on the grounds that though he suffers no immediate loss to his property he is put in the disadvantageous position that if at some future date he should wish to erect a building he would have to sue A for removal of the window. Jacob of Lissa[24] makes the point that the fact that A is making use of "the air" of B's courtyard without payment would in itself confer upon B a right of objection if not that *kofin al midat Ṣedom.* At any rate, says Rabbinovitz, we see from this that a legitimate objection is sufficient to prevent the application of the "rule of Sodom"; the absence of a case for compensation, on the other hand, would not affect the situation.

I cannot understand why Rabbinovitz does not take the same line with this case as he did with the *Toṣafot* on squatting. Surely, just as he maintained that that case could be explained in terms of the owner's actual loss—viz. loss of his rights as an owner—this one could have been explained in terms of B's actual loss, viz. his disadvantage with regard to future claims. Indeed, it is only the *Rosh*, not the *Rashba* and the others who uphold B's right of objection, who considers this a case of *zeh neheneh...* at all.[25] It seems to me that what in fact has happened is that the editors of Rabbinovitz's lectures have run together material produced on different occasions, and that this last discussion was written by Rabbinovitz before he had compiled the previous one; in all likelihood his final conclusion would have been that the window case, like the squatting one, could be understood in accordance with either interpretation of *zeh neheneh...*

On the other hand, he may finally have concluded that *zeh neheneh...* is primarily a consequence of the "rule of Sodom". Certainly he tends strongly to this view in his lecture on *zeh neheneh...* in *Baba Bathra*,

---

[23] *Ḥoshen Hamishpaṭ* 154:16 indicates the sources.

[24] *Netivot Hamishpaṭ, loc. cit.*, para. 17.

[25] Jacob of Lissa, as an *Aharon*, can be discounted in this context.

where the same *hakirah* is examined in some other contexts, as well as in some of those we have already referred to. What seems to clinch the argument for him there is the consideration of a case in which the beneficiary reaps a material benefit[26]—such as an enclosure to his property which he has indicated through his own actions that he wants. Since the donor is suffering no loss at all on account of the material benefit enjoyed by the beneficiary, if the principle of *zeh neheneh...* were based on the inadmissibility of a claim for compensation when no loss had been suffered, it would apply regardless of the extent of the benefit enjoyed. If, on the other hand, it is a consequence of the "rule of Sodom", it is reasonable that though a person may be coerced into letting someone else derive some benefit from his property when it does not involve any loss for him, this would not be the case if the benefit were so great that, in effect, as Rabbinovitz puts it, "a visible part of his property would be added to someone else's".

On the whole, Rabbinovitz's lectures as they have come down to us—i.e. in the form of a work not finalised by its author—present us not so much with conclusions as with suggestions and alternative ways of interpretation. As the individual lectures—let alone their constituent parts—are undated, it is not possible to trace the development of his thought. In particular, the two groups of notes on *zeh neheneh...* present us with "work in progress" rather than with a consistent picture.

Nevertheless, there is no doubt at all as to the consistency of purpose, despite the inconclusiveness of much of the discussion. It is obvious that to Rabbinovitz the aim of his researches is the analysis of the basic concepts of Jewish Law. Conceptualism, not casuistry, is his ideal. Whereas in Shkop one finds that after a brief discussion as to the meaning of a

---

[26] The actual expression is '*mishtarashe leh*'. It is taken from *Hullin* 131a, where it denotes the benefit accruing to someone whose debt to the government has been paid by confiscation of his crop including the tithes which would otherwise have been due. Rabbinovitz argues that there is a similar "material benefit" involved—i.e. a benefit which saves expenditure he would otherwise have been prepared to make—in such a case as that where a neighbour has demonstrated by his actions that he would have been prepared to erect a high wall which his neighbour has in fact erected. His demonstration of his readiness to have paid had it been necessary removes him from the category of *zeh neheneh* and establishes a liability towards the neighbour who erected the wall to his benefit but without consulting him. (The squatting case, Rabbinovitz explains, is different, for even though the squatter is a person who would normally rent his own accommodation, he would certainly attempt to find free accommodation if possible.) What Rabbinovitz is saying is that the neighbour, through indicating what he wants and is prepared to pay for, is making a commitment—almost a contract—to pay his share. This seems to be rather like the Common Law notion of quasi or implied contract—see the references in note 4 of Rakover's article above.

particular concept a decision is reached, and then applied in a more or less conventional manner to the solution of problems, Rabbinovitz subjects his analysis to a series of tests, frequently inconclusive, and leaves one in no doubt throughout the *shiᶜur* that the subject under discussion is the concept, rather than the individual case. This is borne out by the way in which almost every paragraph starts with some such phrase as "With regard to our *ḥaḳirah*..." or "But perhaps that does not demonstrate conclusively (sc. that such-and-such an analysis of a concept is correct)..."

But both Shkop and Rabbinovitz differ profoundly from earlier and conventional Rabbis in stressing the need for analysing concepts. This may be seen very clearly in their language, for new thoughts demand a new vocabulary. I therefore append, in the original rabbinic Hebrew, the words in which Shkop and Rabbinovitz set out their basic *ḥaḳirah* with regard to *zeh neheneh*... For anyone familiar with conventional rabbinic Hebrew the novelty will be obvious. And of course the terminology is quite different from that which would be employed in a modern Hebrew legal journal.

APPENDIX

1. חדושי רבי שמעון יהודא הכהן בבא קמא סימן יט

...בפני יהושע רצה לומר שהטעם דפטור בזנוזל״ח הוא משום דכופין על מדת סדום, וזה אינו דהרי גם בהקדש מדמי הש״ס ושם לא שייך זה, אלא ודאי שהוא סברא שלא יתחייב רק אם חברו חסר היינו שאין תביעה על הממון רק אם בעל הממון מתחסר.

2. חדושי רבי חיים מטעלז בבא קמא

והנה למ״ד זה נהנה וזה לא חסר פטור, יש לחקור אם טעם הפטור הוא דכיון דהבעלים אינו חסר כלל בהנאתו הוי זה מדת סדום אם יתחייב הנהנה לשלם וכופין אותו על מדת סדום או דילמא אין טעם הפטור דהוי מדת סדום, אלא הוי פטור בעיקר דין נהנה, דעיקר החיוב מדין נהנה רק כשחסרים הבעלים מהנאתו שאז חשיב דנהנה מהם ושייך ע״ז חיוב תשלומין, אבל היכא דבהנאתו אינו מחסר לבעלים כלל לא חשיב נהנה מן הבעלים אלא רק נהנה מן החפץ ולא שייך ע״ז חיוב תשלומין כלל.

3. חדושי רבי חיים מטעלז בבא בתרא

והנה יש לחקור בדין פטור דזה נהנה וזה לא חסר, אי הוי משום דלא לקח מהבעלים מאומה, דרק היכא שלקח הנאה מהבעלים חייב לשלם, וכן להיפך כשזה כן חסר אפילו היכא שחסר רק קצת חשבינן כבר שנהנה מהבעלים כיון שהבעלים חסרים בהנאתו של זה, אבל היכא שבהנאתו אינו מחסר את הבעלים לא חשיב שלקח הנאה מהבעלים אלא ממונו בלבד, ולכן פטור; או דנימא דמטעם עדיין א״א לפוטרו, שכל התשמישים והזכותים של החפץ והממון שייכים גם לבעליו וכשנהנה מהם חשיב נהנה מן הבעלים, והא דפטור היינו משום דכופין על מדת סדום.

The Duty to Rescue

[25]

THE BYSTANDER'S DUTY TO RESCUE IN JEWISH LAW

Aaron Kirschenbaum

ABSTRACT

In Judaism, the bystander's duty to come to the rescue of his fellow-man who is in peril is religious, ethical and legal. A citizen is expected to engage in the act of rescue both personally and with his financial resources. He is required, however, neither to give his life nor to place his life in substantial jeopardy to save his fellow. Moreover, there is no ethical requirement to donate an organ in behalf of another; nevertheless, such an act is today regarded as of especial nobility and piety. Although failure to come to one's neighbor's rescue incurs no criminal sanction, the legal nature of the duty is evidenced by (1) the right of the rescuer to sue for all financial losses incurred as a result of the rescue operation, (2) the rescuer's immunity to liability, and (3) the exemption he enjoys from all positive legal, civil, and ritual duties while he is actively engaged in the rescue operation.

In the early hours of the morning of March 14, 1964, a young woman named Kitty Genovese was attacked on her way home in Queens, New York. The unknown assailant made several separate attacks on her over a period of about forty minutes, and she finally died of the stabs he had inflicted on her. As the police subsequently ascertained, at least thirty-eight neighbors had heard her screams for help, some may have also seen her struggle, yet no one intervened—not even to call the police.

This example of neighborly inaction generated widespread discussion and analysis. Newspaper reporters made special reports of the incident. The University of Chicago Law School sponsored a "Conference on the Good Samaritan and the Bad—The Law and Morality of Volunteering in Situations of Peril, or of Failing to Do So". The American Psychological Association (in 1966) held a special session devoted to the problems of the "unconcerned bystander." Numerous studies, papers and articles were written with the Kitty Genovese incident as their point of departure.

Social scientists and legal scholars, philosophers and moralists have shown widespread interest and concern in learning how people really behave in situations which thrust them into the potential role of one's brother's keeper—and why. Much time and effort have been invested in discovering how society, by the values it fosters and the code of behavior it sponsors, affects that behavior—allowing for indifference and actually cultivating a desire not to get involved, or, on the contrary, encouraging active intervention to assist a fellow human being in peril and thus transforming the unconcerned bystander into a Good Samaritan.

With these questions in mind, we turn to the Jewish legal system to learn how historic Judaism coped with these vital problems.

I. BIBLICAL EXEGESIS

The talmudic ethico-legal duties of the innocent bystander, *i.e.,* one who happens to find himself in the presence[1] of a person in peril—in danger of being victimized by a crime or in distress caused by some natural threat or catastrophe—are summarized by Maimonides (1135-1204) in his *Code* as follows:

> If one person is able to save another and does not save him, he transgresses the commandment *Neither shalt thou stand idly by the blood of thy neighbor* (Leviticus 19:16). Similarly, if one person sees another drowning in the sea, or being attacked by bandits, or being attacked by wild animals, and, although able to rescue him either alone or by hiring others, does not rescue him; or if one hears heathens or informers plotting evil against another or laying a trap for him and does not call it to the other's attention and let him know; or if one knows that a heathen or a violent person is going to attack another and although able to appease him on behalf of the other and make him change his mind, he does not do so; or if one acts in any similar way—he transgresses in each case the injunction, *Neither shalt thou stand idly by the blood of thy neighbor* (*ibid.*) . . .
>
> Although there is no flogging for these prohibitions, because breach of them involves no action, the offense is most serious, for if one destroys the life of a single Israelite, it is regarded as though he destroyed the whole world, and if one preserves the life of a single Israelite, it is regarded as though he preserved the whole world. (Maimonides, *Torts,* "Murder and Preservation of Life" 1:14, 16)

The scriptural words upon which Jewish law bases the obligation to come to the assistance of one in peril, *lō' ta'amōd 'al dam rē'ekā,* are found in the following context:

> Ye shall do no unrighteousness in judgment; thou shalt not respect the person of the poor, nor favor the person of the mighty; but in righteousness shalt thou judge thy neighbor. Thou shalt not go up and down as a talebearer among thy people; neither shalt thou stand idly by the blood of thy neighbor: I am the Lord. (Leviticus 19:15-16)

The Jewish interpretation, found in the Talmud (*B. Sanhedrin* 73a), is the unique contribution of rabbinic teaching to the exegesis of the Leviticus passage. Although its literary formulation emanates no later than from the third century C. E., thereby antedating Maimonides by at least nine hundred years, the early talmudic masters ("Tannaim") who transmitted it regarded it as hoary tradition. It is thus from time immemorial that the verse, *Lō' ta'amōd 'al dam rē'ekā* has served as the traditional Jewish version of what modern lawyers refer to as "the law of the Good Samaritan".

As if to fortify the Good Samaritan principle, the *Tannaim* went further and enlisted the law of lost articles, as follows:

> Whence do we know [that one must save his neighbor from] the loss of himself? From the verse (Deuteronomy 22:2) *And thou shalt restore it to him.* (*B. Sanhedrin,* 73a)[2]

Examining both tannaitic statements, this one and the one cited by Maimonides above, later scholars attempted to formulate the particular contribution of each one. Thus the later rabbis in the Talmud itself raise the question of the apparent superfluity of two verses teaching the same duty to rescue. They come to the conclusion that the verse, *Thou shalt not stand idly by,* broadens the duty from the person to the purse, *i.e.,* it obligates the bystander to go to extraordinary lengths to save the victim—even to the extent of actually hiring help—whereas the duty to rescue derived from the law of lost articles would have been limited to one's personal ability—no more (*B. Sanhedrin,* 73a). Early medieval scholars raise the converse question: If *Thou shalt not stand idly by* is all encompassing, what need did the *Tannaim* have to derive anything from *Thou shalt restore it to him*? Their answer: The latter verse includes the duty to come to the assistance of one who is in distress but not in any peril, *e.g.,* one who is lost in a forest but would eventually be able to find his way out.

Other medieval scholars add that the duty of rescue is not limited to circumstances creating a clear and present danger; even if the peril is somewhat obscure and doubtful, the duty to enter into a rescue operation is not thereby diminished. Whether the duty exists *vis-à-vis* a person attempting suicide or one whose negligence created the peril is a matter of dispute among the rabbinic authorities of the past four centuries (Kirschenbaum, 1976:14).

II. THE LEGAL NATURE OF THE OBLIGATION TO RESCUE

In the second paragraph of the Maimonidean passage quoted at the beginning of the previous section, it is stated that the innocent bystander who deliberately fails to come to the aid of one in peril is not subject to legal punishment.

Why is this so?

Does this indicate that the *Halakhah* (Jewish law) regards the duty of the Good Samaritan as simply a moral one?

Classical Jewish law, *i.e.,* the authoritative talmudic exposition of the formal law of Sacred Scripture, prescribes flogging for the breach of any negative commandment whose punishment is not otherwise specified. The infliction of stripes, however, is limited to those prohibitions whose violation involves an overt act; prohibitions whose violation comes about through covert inaction do not entail flagellation, certainly not the death penalty.

This limitation, however, is more of an indication of classical Jewish penological theory than it is of the nature of the prohibitions which are thereby excluded. Earthly punishment, in Jewish theory, is aimed at the active, flagrant violation of the law; it is not employed to induce general obedience to the law nor to force citizens to do their duty.

Hence in the context of Jewish legal teaching, the Maimonidean comment, already quoted,

> Although there is no flogging for these prohibitions [of standing idly by the blood of one's neighbor], because breach of them involves no action, the offense is most serious, for if one destroys the life of a single Israelite, it is regarded as though he destroyed the whole world, and if one preserves the life of a single Israelite, it is regarded as though he preserved the whole world. (Maimonides, 1949:1:14–16)[3]

is no mere pious mouthing but an ethical imperative of the first magnitude.

It is a fact of history that in Jewish society—biblical, talmudic and medieval—non-prosecutable injunctions, by their sheer religious weight, were effective in their deterrent power.

It would be misleading, therefore, to interpret the lack of judicial punishment in Jewish law for the innocent bystander who fails in his duty to come to the rescue of his fellow-man in distress as indicating that the duty is merely moral. Rather Jewish law views such failure as nonfeasance, a formal offense of inaction (*delictum mere omissivum*) where action is a duty required by law.

III. THE EXTENT OF THE OBLIGATION TO RESCUE

A. In Monetary Terms

We have already seen that, according to the Talmud, had the duty of the bystander to come to the rescue of his fellow-man in peril been derived as an extension of the law regarding the restoration of lost property, it would have been limited to the personal ability of the rescuer. *Thou shalt not stand idly by . . . ,* however, implies an all-encompassing duty—including one's financial resources as well.

But this obligation does not represent a lien on the property of the bystander; the duty remains a personal one. Thus, although one's financial resources must be utilized *without apparent limit*[4] in order to save the victim, the rescuer has the right to sue the rescued party in order to recover the money expended (R. Meir Halevi Abulafia, *Yad Ramah—Sanhedrin* 73a). This holds true even if the victim protests, wishes not to be rescued, and later refuses to compensate the rescuer.[5] On the other hand, even if the latter is destitute and may subsequently plead bankruptcy, the duty of the rescuer remains unchanged (R. Asher b. Yehiel, d. 1327, *Sanhedrin* 8:2).

The rescuer's right to compensation for expenditures and losses incurred are alluded to rather briefly and superficially in the sources. It seems to me that rabbinic authors found it unnecessary to go into detail because the talmudic references to the law of lost objects as being relevant to the duty to rescue people in peril meant to them that the rules of compensation which obtain in restoring lost objects to their owners—which are spelled out in great detail in the Talmud, commentaries and codes—could be applied, where necessary and appropriate, to cases involving the saving of life—with proper provision being made occasionally for the special significance of the latter.

An examination of the rules of compensation for the restoration of lost property yields the following conclusions:

1. The actual act of rescue, being the fulfillment of a religious duty (*mizvāh*), warrants no monetary compensation (*Tosafot, s.v. im, Bava Mezia,* 31b).

2. If the act of rescue takes place during working hours and, therefore, requires the sacrifice of the rescuer's pursuit of a livelihood, he is entitled to a minimal wage.[6] If this is unsatisfactory to him, he must receive court permission for full compensation for the loss involved in leaving work. If the court is not in session, the law of lost objects declares that his own economic interests take priority over the economic interests of his fellow (*M. Bava Mezia* 2:9). This declaration is obviously inappropriate in the case of the peril of one in distress; it seems clear that in the latter case full compensation for the labor of the rescuer would be the rule.[7]

3. Expenditures made legitimately by the rescuer would also be recoverable in full (Maimonides *Torts,* "Robbery and Lost Objects," 13:19; *Tur* and *Shulhan Arukh H.M.* 267:26).

4. The cost of damages and disabilities incurred by the rescuer in the course of the rescue operation, however, could *not* be recovered by the rescuer. The Jewish law of tort obligates the tortfeasor, and the tortfeasor only, for damages incurred; no one else—not even the one as interested as the rescued party himself—is so obligated.[8]

Although the above is but a broad outline, it suffices to give us a general view of how Jewish law copes with the problems of the losses incurred by the Good Samaritan.

The personal nature of the duty that one has to rescue has led at least one later medieval authority to limit the rescuer's right to recover the losses he incurred in the course of his rescue operation in a number of ways.

1. The rescued party must, it is true, compensate his rescuer for his losses. But if the former is bankrupt, he need not make said compensation, *even if he subsequently comes into fortune* (*M. Peah* 5:4 and *Tur Yoreh De'ah* 253(4)).

2. The rescuer's right to be compensated for his losses exists *only if the rescue operation is successful*! If he failed in his attempt, his right for compensation is, at most, that of a minimum wage for labor expended.[9]

3. The obligation to compensate the rescuer for his losses *devolves upon the rescued party himself and upon no one else, not even his close relatives* (R. Asher b. Yehiel, *Sanhedrin* 8:2).

It is relevant to note that these three limiting rulings were not regarded as discouraging bystanders to do their duty. On the contrary, the very reasoning behind them is:

> . . . for the reason [the bystander] is going to such lengths, even to the extent of incurring monetary losses, is not that he is doing so in behalf of his fellow [who is in peril] exclusively, but rather he is also doing so in his own behalf to save himself [*i.e.*] to discharge the obligation placed upon him by [the Holy One], may He be blessed. Moreover, his [heavenly] reward is a very great one indeed. (R. Samuel b. Moses di Medina of Salonica, d. 1589, *Responsa Rashdam,* Y.D. Resp. 204)

B. At the Cost of the Rescuer's Life

Much more complicated is the question, to what extent the bystander is duty-bound to come to the rescue of one in peril when such action would endanger his own life. Is self-sacrifice a legal duty? Jewish law answers in the negative, but a word of explanation is called for. The explanation concerns itself with two tannaitic passages. On the one hand, one may not commit murder to save one's own life.

> R. Johanan said in the name of R. Simon b. Jehozadak: By a majority vote it was resolved in the upper chambers of the house of Nithza in Lydda that in every [other] law of the *Torah,* if a man is commanded: "Transgress and suffer not death," he may transgress and not suffer death, excepting idolatry, incest [which includes adultery] and murder. (*B. Sanhedrin* 74a)

It is generally agreed that this conference at Lydda took place during and in the face of the Hadrianic persecutions which posed a most serious threat to Jewish religious life in Palestine *ca.* 135 C.E. (Graetz, 1908:154–156, 428–430; Halevy, 1918: 371–372).

On the other hand, one need not sacrifice one's own life to save someone else's.

> If two are travelling on a journey and one has a pitcher of water—if both drink, they will die, but if one only drinks, he can reach civilization.—
>
> The Son of Patura taught: It is better that both should drink and die, rather than that one should behold his companion's death.
>
> Until R. Akiba came and taught: *That thy brother may live with thee* (*Leviticus* 25:36)—thy life takes precedence over his life. (*B. Bava Mezia* 62a)

Not much is known about (Judah?) the son of Patura. He probably lived about the end of the first century or the beginning of the second century C. E. Rabbi Akiba himself died during the Hadrianic persecutions. Thus, the two tannaitic teachings, that of the conference at Lydda and the one emanating from the controversy between the Son of Patura and R. Akiba, are more or less contemporaneous.

In order to understand the reasoning behind these two statements, we cite the following passage regarding the refusal of the Rabbis to allow one to commit murder in order to save his own life.

> And how do we know that this principle applies in the case of murder, *i.e.*, that murder may not be committed to save one's life?
>
> It is common sense.[10] Even as one who came to Rava and said to him, "The governor of my town has ordered me, 'Go and kill so-and-so; if not I will slay thee'."
>
> Rava answered, "Let him rather slay you than that you should commit murder. What makes you think that your blood is redder than his? Perhaps his blood is redder than yours." (*B. Yoma* 82b; *B. Sanhedrin* 74a)

The apparent contradiction in the two passages produces the principle that, all things being equal, one may not decide—*by affirmative action*—whether one's life takes precedence over that of one's neighbor: In the first passage, affirmative action would have been tantamount to declaring that one's blood was redder than that of one's fellow. In the second passage, the affirmative act of giving the pitcher of water to his companion would have been tantamount to declaring that his companion's blood was redder than his own—a declaration which Jewish ethics is not prepared to endorse. There are situations in life where inaction is the lesser of two evils (Kirschenbaum, 1976:27).

Our exposition heretofore has been devoted to a situation where the Good Samaritan can save his fellow-man only at the price of his own life. Under such circumstances rabbinic law exempts the citizen from the duty of self-sacrifice and absolves him from any moral blame.[11,12]

C. *At the Risk of the Rescuer's Life*

Is one obliged to come to the rescue of his neighbor in distress if the rescue operation *may* involve a risk to one's life and to one's well being?[13] How serious must the risk be in order to qualify it under the exemption of self-sacrifice? Or, at what point does the danger to the life or the well-being of the bystander become so remote as to be inconsequential in the face of one's duty to save someone in peril?

This question as to whether the Good Samaritan need put his own life in *possible* danger to save his fellow from *certain* death is the subject of sustained controversy among rabbinic authorities. Summarized briefly, *rabbinic law today declares officially that there is no such duty,* but qualifies this declaration in a number of ways: (1) it exhorts the citizen, "One must not overly protect oneself"; (2) it urges each case to be judged on its own merits, "It seems that everything depends upon the individual circumstances"; (3) the volunteer who does endanger his life and limb is extolled as acting above and beyond the call of duty and as performing a saintly act (*middat hasidût*); (4) the degree of jeopardy which legally exempts the bystander from his duty must be a most substantial one, great enough to deter him from saving his most precious possessions had they been in similar circumstances; and (5) exceptionally, the medical practitioner is expected to treat patients even under circumstances which represent serious danger to his own life.

D. At the Cost of the Rescuer's (Non-Vital) Limb

> If a tyrant says to a Jew, "Allow me to amputate one of your limbs" (an amputation which represents no danger to life), "or else I will kill your fellow Jew," some [authorities] say that he is obligated to allow his limb to be amputated since he would not die. (R. Menahem Recanati, d. early 14th cent., *Sefer Recanati* 470)

This rather startling decision, which makes contributions of organs for transplanting obligatory under Jewish religious and ethical law, is the product of an Italian legalist and mystic of the late thirteenth and early fourteenth centuries. The startling nature of the decision is also evident from the fact that about two hundred and fifty years later it is quoted verbatim and sent to *Radbaz* (Rabbi David b. Zimra, d. 1573, one of the leading rabbinic authorities of his day) with a request for his reaction.

Refuting the proof-text offered by his Italian predecessor, Rabbi ben Zimra maintained that no precedent could be cited for such an obligation. Indeed, there was always the possibility that an operation of this sort might prove to be dangerous to the life of the individual. And he concluded:

> Moreover, it is written, *And her* [*i.e.,* the *Torah*'s] *ways are ways of pleasantness* (Proverbs 3:17); the laws of our *Torah,* therefore, must be in consonance with reason and intelligence. How can one imagine that a person would allow his eye to be blinded or his hand or foot to be cut off so that his fellow not die?

> I, therefore, see no justification for his decision. It is an act of saintliness (*middat hasidût*) [*i.e.*, above and beyond the legal requirement], and happy is the man who can live up to it.
>
> If, however, there is a possible risk of life, then [one who agrees to the amputation] is a foolish saint (*hasid shoteh*),[14] for the *possible* danger to oneself takes precedence over the *certain* danger to one's fellow.
>
> I have written what appears in my humble opinion [to be the correct understanding of the law]. (*Responsa Radbaz* III, 1053 [628])

Radbaz' responsum persisted to this century as the leading decision on the matter. Thus, even according to those who maintained that one is obligated to place oneself in jeopardy in order to save another, Judaism ordained neither a legal obligation nor a moral imperative to actually amputate or donate a limb or an organ to save someone else's life. On the other hand, although an operation of this kind invariably involved a measure of danger to the amputee or donor, the tendency of the authorities was not to denigrate the volunteer but rather to view his act—albeit with some hesitation—as a saintly one.[15] However, as these operations of transplantation became routine, with concomitant decrease in danger, rabbinic hesitation to grant approval to them has become markedly less, and the saintliness of the act has been receiving increasingly greater recognition and appreciation.

This tendency has reached its culmination in the responsum of Sephardic Chief Rabbi of Israel Ovadia Yosef, published only a few years ago (Yosef, 1976:25–43).

On the basis of talmudic texts and post-talmudic opinions, Rabbi Yosef, too, sees in *Radbaz* the decisive arbiter settling the question raised: (1) One is not obligated to put oneself in serious jeopardy to save one's fellow. (2) One may not donate a vital limb, if the transplantation represents serious danger to the donor.

However, recognizing present-day transplantation procedure as involving a degree of danger to the donor *less* than that contemplated in the strictures of *Radbaz*, Rabbi Yosef rejects the prohibition of one colleague and overcomes the hesitation of another and permits, nay, gives his blessing to the donation of a kidney to a patient in dire need thereof in the following words:

> But according to the information we have received from competent and God-fearing physicians, the danger [to the donor] involved in extracting a kidney is generally very small. Inasmuch as *Radbaz* and those of his school hold, therefore, that under such circumstances the *mizvāh, Thou shalt not stand idly by,* obtains, it follows that we must allow a healthy person to donate one of his kidneys, to save the life of his fellow Israelite whose life is seriously threatened by a disease of the kidneys. Great is the *mizvāh* of saving human life, and it [the *mizvāh*] will afford the donor the protection of a thousand shields. In any event, the donation must be performed by competent physicians; and he who fulfills a *mizvāh* shall know no evil. (Yosef, 1976)

The essential legal-ethical limitations on the obligation of the bystander to come to the rescue of one in peril, then, are based upon the real possibility that the life of the bystander may be endangered (*Cf.* Jakobovits, 1959:96–98). Hardship, suffering and great inconvenience, it is clear, cannot serve as bases of exemption,[16] neither can the fact that the would-be rescuer would undergo personal humiliation in order to accomplish the rescue serve as a basis for his exemption from the *mizvāh* of *Thou shalt not stand idly by* (R. J. I. Unterman, 20th cent., *Shevet mi-Yehudah,* pp. 20–21, *contra* the possibility raised by R. Shelomoh Kluger, d. 1869, *Hokhmat Shelomoh, H. M.* 426:1). Thus, although it would be extravagant to characterize Jewish law as *obligating* one to contribute an organ to save someone's life, it is clear that, as a result of modern medical advancement, Jewish religious authorities regard such contribution as a meritorious act of the highest order.

IV. ENCOURAGING THE WOULD-BE RESCUER

A. Exemption from Other Duties

The basic rule of Jewish law declares that all ethical, civil, religious and ritual positive duties are suspended if their implementation or fulfillment would create or sustain danger to human life.[17] "Would" is interpreted most broadly: "would certainly" (*vadai*), "would probably" (*safek*). Similarly "saving life" is interpreted as including "prolonging life substantially" (*hayyei 'ōlām*) and "prolonging life minimally" (*hayyei sha'ah*).

This was made abundantly clear by the Rabbis of Israel before the third century in their exposition of the laws of the Sabbath, one of the most sacred institutions of Judaism.

> [Although the preparation and administration of medicines involve the violation of the Sabbath restrictions in human activity], R. Matthia b. Heresh said: If one has pain in his throat, he may pour medicine into his mouth on the Sabbath, because it is a possibility of danger to human life, and every danger to human life suspends the [laws of the] Sabbath. (*M. Yoma* 8:6)

Speed is of the essence.

> Our Rabbis taught: One must remove debris [*i.e.,* an act ordinarily forbidden on the Sabbath] to save a life on the Sabbath; and the more energetic one is, the more praiseworthy is one; and one need not obtain permission from the rabbinical court. (*B. Yoma* 84b)

Hesitation is sinful.

> They have taught: The energetic one is praiseworthy, the [authority who is] consulted—insulted, and the inquirer—a murderer. (*P. Yoma* 8:5)

B. Immunity from Tort Liability

In order to appreciate the interest Jewish law evinces in encouraging the innocent bystander to be a Good Samaritan, it is necessary to present a brief exposition of some of the more salient features regarding tort liability.

The basic law of torts in Jewish law is clear:

> Man is always [in the category of one who has been] "forwarned" [and hence liable for damages] whether [he acts] inadvertently or willfully under coercion or voluntarily, whether awake or asleep. (*M. Bava Kamma* 2:6; *B. Sanhedrin* 72a; Maimonides *Torts*, "Assaults and Damages" 1:12; 6:1)

The high regard with which the *Halakhah* (Jewish law) holds private property and protects it from damage, trespass and theft is vividly illustrated by the talmudic interpretation of an episode in David's career.

> Scripture says: *And David longed and said, Oh, that one would give me water to drink of the well of Bethlehem, which is by the gate. And the three mighty men broke through the host of the Philistines and drew water, out of the well of Bethlehem that was by the gate*, etc. (II Samuel 23:15–16). [And David refused to drink the water for it was acquired through "the blood" of men]. (*B. Bava Kamma* 60b)

Now, in rabbinic psychology, "water" conjures up an association with *Torah* (divine law), and "the gate" is the courthouse, *i.e.*, where *Torah* is studied, expounded and applied to life. David's longing for water, therefore, is interpreted as a desire to understand a problem of scriptural law; and he sent his inquiry to the rabbinic scholars of his generation at "the gate," *i.e.*, at the House of Study.

What was his difficulty?

> Rabbi Huna said: [The problem was this: In his battle with the Philistines,] there were [near the battle-field] stacks of barley which belonged to Israelites but in which the Philistines had hidden themselves, and what he asked was whether it was permissible to rescue oneself through the destruction of another's property.
>
> The answer they dispatched to him was: [Generally speaking] it is forbidden to rescue oneself through the destruction of another's property; you, however, are King, and a king may break [through fields belonging to private persons] to make a way [for his army] and nobody is entitled to prevent him [from doing so]. (*Cf. B. Sanhedrin* 20b)

We may disregard, for our purposes, the royal prerogative and the concession to military exigencies. The answer—as it applies to the ordinary citizen—is somewhat startling: "Generally speaking, it is forbidden to rescue oneself through the destruction of another's property." The definitive law is thus as follows:

> Even if one is in mortal danger and must steal from his fellow in order to save his own life, he may do so only on condition that he intends to make subsequent payment. (*Shulhan Arukh Hoshen Mishpat* 359:4)

In other words, although "nothing may stand in the way [to impede] the preservation of human life" (*'ēn dāvār ha'ōmed bifnei pikūah nefesh*), the destruction of someone's property *without intention to compensate* is not necessary for the preservation of life. The same preservation of life could be accomplished by the same indispensable destruction of property if said destruction is perpetrated *with* the intention to compensate (*e.g.*, *Yad Ramah, Sanhedrin* 73b).

With this cursory presentation of tort liability in Jewish law, we have arrived conceptually at our central problem: What is the legal position of an innocent bystander, intent upon fulfilling Scripture's command not to stand idly by the blood of his neighbor, who, in the course of his act of rescue, commits a tort?

The Code of Maimonides expounds the position of Jewish law in this matter.

> If one chases after the pursuer in order to rescue the pursued, and he breaks objects belonging to the pursuer or to anyone else, he is exempt. This rule is not [a matter of] strict [*i.e.*, biblical] law [of torts], but is [an enactment, *takkanah*] made in order that one should not refrain from rescuing another or lose time through being too careful when chasing a pursuer.[18] (Maimonides *Torts*, "Wounding and Damaging," 8:4)

The fourth century talmudic source of this provision clearly recognized that the biblically ordained strict principle of near-absolute tort liability[19] was being violated here. Thus, Rabbah (or Rava) in the Talmud justifies this "violation" as being in the public interest.

> For if you were not to rule thus [but rather make the rescuer liable], no one would put himself out to rescue a fellow-man from the hands of a pursuer.

Lest one be inclined to give an inordinately narrow interpretation to this exemption from tort liability and to limit it strictly to a bystander intent upon saving a victim from a criminal act and to nothing else, we hasten to add that said exemption applied to all would-be rescuers from natural catastrophes as well as man-made harms.

Actually, the Talmud records a much earlier exemption from tort liability granted in the interests of rescuing a human being in trouble. The exemption is embodied in one of the ten stipulations made with the Israelites by Joshua when he apportioned the Land to them in accordance with their tribes. It is limited to the alleviation of the condition of a person who is lost in the woods or in the thickets of a vineyard and cannot find his way back to his settlement.

He who sees his fellow wandering in the vineyards is permitted to cut his way through when going up and to cut his way through when coming down and ruin thereby the place upon which he is treading until he brings him into the town or onto the road. And just as it is meritorious to do so in behalf of his fellow, so it is meritorious to do so in behalf of oneself. So also one who himself is lost in the vineyard may cut his way through when going up and cut his way through when coming down until he reaches the town or the road [for it was in accordance with this understanding that Joshua apportioned the Land to Israel]. (*B. Bava Kamma* 81b)

That the paramount motive underlying Joshua's stipulation was the eagerness of the law to facilitate the rescue of a person who has lost his way and to give this consideration top priority is evident from the talmudic exegesis of the above-cited passage.

What is the meaning of "so also"? [Is the latter case not obvious?]

You might have thought that this is only the case of a *fellow-man* wandering, in which case [the rescuer] knows where he [the rescuer] is going, that he [the rescuer] may cut his way through, whereas in the case of being lost himself, when he [the lost person] does not know where he is going, he [the lost person] should not be permitted to cut his way through but should have to walk round about the boundaries. We are therefore told that this is not so. (*B. Bava Kamma* 81b)

The whole point of Joshua's stipulation is the creation of immunity to tort liability (*i.e.*, for the destruction of branches and vines).

We have thus arrived at the official encouragement Jewish law gives to people who come to the assistance of their fellow-citizens in order to rescue them from peril. This encouragement takes the form of (exceptional) immunity from liability for any tort committed in the course of the rescue operation.[20]

C. Religious Incentives

Religious incentives to save someone in peril are dual in nature: coercive and hortatory.

Saving human life is a religious commandment, and Jewish traditional law ordains physical coercion for the fulfillment of one's religious duties.[21]

As our inquiry into the Jewish religious law of the bystander comes to a close, reference must be made—albeit superficially—to the socio-psychological impact of the religious concept of *mizvāh* ("commandment") and its profound hortatory effect on Jewish behavior.

R. Hanania b. Akashya said: The Holy One, blessed be He, desired to make Israel acquire merit; He, therefore, multiplied for them *Torah* and commandments; as it is written (Isaiah 42:21), *The Lord was pleased for His righteousness' sake, to make the teaching [Torah] great and glorious.* (*M. Makkot* 3:16)

This *mishnāh* epitomizes the traditional Jewish attitude toward each and every commandment of God as embodied in Scripture[22] as a mark of divine favor granting the Jew the privilege of serving his Creator by fulfilling His wish: the more commandments, the more ways in which this privilege is granted.

> The deed is the test, the trial and the risk. What we perform may seem slight, but the aftermath is immense. An individual's misdeed can be the beginning of a nation's disaster . . . Even a single deed generates an endless set of effects; initiating more than the most powerful man is able to master or to predict. A single deed may place the lives of countless men in the chains of its unpredictable effects. . . .
>
> Just as a man is not alone in what he *is,* he is not alone in what he does. A mitsvah is an act, which God and man *have in common.* We say: "Blessed art Thou, Lord, our God, King of the universe, who has sanctified us with *His* mitsvot" . . . The spirit of mitsvah is *togetherness.* We know, He is a partner to our act. (Heschel, 1962:284, 287)

And, as for the would-be rescuer who fails, it would be best to remember the words of Edmond Cahn:

> . . . and herein too there is a truthful commentary on the consequences and outcomes of morally righteous conduct. For the rescuer all too often fails of his rescue and injures or kills himself in the effort. There can be no guarantee of success. Some will be saved, others will be lost. The only guarantee we have—the only one we are entitled to—is that attempts of this kind glorify our existence which without them would be like grass and like dust. (Cahn, 1959:196)

VI. ANALYSIS AND CONCLUDING SUMMARY

> Danger invites rescue. The cry of distress is the summons to relief. The law does not ignore these reactions of the mind in tracing conduct to its consequences. It recognizes them as normal. It places their effects within the range of the natural and probable. The wrong that imperils life is a wrong to the imperilled victim; it is a wrong also to his rescuer. (Cardozo, 1921)

These memorable words were used by Judge Benjamin Cardozo for the limited purpose of extending the liability of a railway company for damages beyond those suffered by the actual victim to those suffered by a would-be rescuer (*Wagner v. International Railway Co.*, 232, N.Y. 176 [1921]). They may be used with equal effectiveness to express the spirit of Jewish law, which, regularly compelling active benevolence between man and man, makes it incumbent upon a bystander to come to the aid of someone in peril.

In this respect, Jewish law is similar to the law of most European countries but differs from Anglo-Saxon law.[23] This duty to rescue is derived from the peculiar interpretation the talmudic rabbis gave to two biblical verses,

Thou shalt not stand idly by the blood of thy neighbor (Leviticus 19:16), and *And thou shalt restore him* [a person who is losing his life] *to himself* (Deuteronomy 22:2). It obtains even if the success of the rescue operation is in serious doubt from the onset or cannot accomplish more than a brief prolongation of life.

Indeed, with the scriptural mandate clearly enunciated in the Talmud, Jewish religious authorities—ethicists in the first instance—have during the past eighteen hundred years examined every aspect of the duty: its extent, its applicability, and its enforceability, leaving us with a veritable heritage of thought and concern regarding this ethico-legal imperative.

Thus, the Maimonidean formulation of the Jewish law of the Good Samaritan does not restrict the duty to rescue to outsiders *witnessing* or *finding* a person in distress. It extends the duty to anyone informed or aware of the danger to another's life. The essential criterion is "if one person *is able* to save another." Ability is determined by a combination of factors: geographic proximity, mental awareness, know-how and physical disposition. Nor does Jewish law distinguish between a natural danger and a man-made one. An innocent bystander is required to go to great personal effort, even to suffer hardships and to incur serious financial loss, in order to save the life of his fellow. On the other hand, he is not duty-bound to give his own life or limb to save his fellow.

Moreover, the duty required by the scriptural commandment, *Lō' ta'amōd 'al dam rē'ekā*, is a general obligation. It is not based upon any special relationship based on law or contract between the bystander and the person in distress, such as parent and child, husband and wife, guardian and ward, guide and tourist, policeman, fireman, or lifeguard and public, shipmaster and crew or passenger, master and servant, host and guest, *etc.* (Rudzinski, 1966:92–93).[24] Although the duty of the physician to his patient may be somewhat different in this respect, the essence of *lō' ta'amōd* remains a general human one.

Again, although the innocent bystander who willfully fails to come to the rescue of those in peril is, according to Jewish law, liable neither to civil suit nor criminal prosecution, the duty of the Good Samaritan in Judaism may not be relegated to the realm of mere religious morality and personal conscience.

The legal nature of the duty of rescue is evidenced in a number of ways:

1. Although the duty to rescue is independent of the financial condition of the person in peril, the rescuer has the right to sue the person rescued for all financial losses the former incurred as a result of the rescue operation.

2. The bystander actively engaged in the rescue operation is exempt from all other positive legal, civil, religious and ritual duties.

3. The rescuer is immune from liability for any tort committed in the cause of his effort to save the victim in peril. Not only may the rescued party

not sue him (a possibility in the present Anglo-American law!); no one whose property has been destroyed may bring an action for tort against him.

In conclusion, three points arise for our careful consideration.

1. As a result of the breakdown of the forceful role played by traditional religion in modern life, the religious undertones accompanying legal imperatives have lost their power to encourage citizens to perform their duties without direct legal sanctions. Has this radical transformation which society has undergone affected the willingness and readiness of people to come to the rescue of those in distress? Should religious authorities work for the introduction of positive criminal and civil provisions[25] making for a statutory duty to come to the rescue of one in peril?[26] Of course, legislation of this type would be faced with such practical difficulties as (1) establishing the degree of the bystander's awareness of the victim's dangerous condition, (2) defining the degree of proximity between the bystander and the victim (*e.g.*, the only available surgeon is in one city and the dying patient in another), (3) in the case of attempts at rescue that aggravate a situation, distinguishing between an innocent, upright bystander and an officious troublesome meddler, and similar anomalies. But legislation is always faced with these kinds of difficulties. On the other hand, does the lack of such legislation really signify that citizens are in fact callous to the plight of those in peril? In other words, legislation, in order to be enforceable, would in all likelihood be aimed at acts of indifference that are blatant and reasonably easy to prove. But such instances of Bad Samaritanism are rather rare; where they do occur, the adverse publicity and public scorn would probably be potent educative as well as penal forces. Is legislation then, necessary? Would not the adoption of the provisions of Jewish law—guaranteeing the Good Samaritan compensation for his losses, exemption from all other duties that devolve upon him at the time, and immunity from tort liability—be sufficient in putting society, as expressing itself in its legal system, on record as creating a legal duty to rescue and as holding said duty in the highest regard?

2. A second question which modern religious authorities must face is the lacuna in traditional law and society regarding the dependents of an innocent bystander who dies or is disabled as a result of his rescue attempt. Traditional Jewish society had its established ways of caring for widows and orphans. Some welfare states have their ways. Would it not be proper for religious leaders to press for special provisions whereby the community would regard these dependents as entitled to specific benefits?

3. Regarding Good Samaritan behavior, a social psychologist makes the following remarks:

> We don't know whether there are differences between cultures, between emergent societies and established societies, between cultures in which the

father dominates, those in which the mother dominates, or, as in our case, the children dominate; between urban groups and rural groups, between religious, God-intoxicated Bible Belts and agnostic, cocktail-intoxicated groves of academe, even between the criminal and the conformist. (Freedman, 1966:171)

Were the law to be a mere reflection of the behavior dominant in a given society, psychiatric and sociological observations such as the one just quoted would constitute the last word in the matter. Law, however, does help shape social attitudes and personal behavior.[27] Indeed, religious law and ethical norms are built principally for such purposes. Thus, Judaism, through its code of behavior, has been striving continuously throughout its history to shape human conduct and to raise human conduct to the highest ethical level possible. Ironically, though, just at a time when Western society—as opposed to traditional Judaism—is experiencing a strong movement to limit the role of law in intervening to enforce "morality" (*e.g.*, in questions involving abortion, adult homosexuality, or the use of drugs), there is strong dissatisfaction with the (*e.g.*, Anglo-American and Israeli) legal indifference to the plight of the person in peril (*Cf.* Sheleff, 1976:190–208).

It is our hope that the study of the Jewish law of the innocent bystander—how the law places duties upon him, encourages him to fulfill them and protects him as he discharges them—may serve as a positive contribution to modern legal thinking.[28]

NOTES

1. "Presence" in all its possible meanings: physical proximity or various degrees of knowledge and awareness with the concomitant ability to rescue the victim or to ward off the danger.

2. Because they viewed the suffix *it* as superfluous, the *Tannaim* interpreted it as meaning *him,* and therefore understood the verse as commanding, *And thou shalt restore him* [a person who is losing his life] *to himself.*

3. Numerous mss. and early editions do not have the word "Israelite." On the history and significance of these variants see Urbach (1971: 268–284).

4. "*Thou shalt not stand idly by* means that thou shalt not hinder thyself. Rather *go to any extent necessary* in order to save the life of the fellow" (italics provided for the translation of *hazōr 'al kōl ha-zedadîm*) (*Rashi, Sanhedrin* 73a).

5. R. Meir b. Barukh, d. 1293 (*Responsa Maharam Rothenberg,* IV:39) referring specifically to a captive who is redeemed and then obligated to compensate his rescuers for their expenditures on the ransom. The principle is then extended to all who must be rescued under the scriptural law of *Thou shalt not stand idly by,* including a patient who refuses treatment; the physician is obligated to treat him and may subsequently receive his fee (determined by the courts or by the current rates) despite the protestations of the patient; R. J. Engel, d. 1920 (*Gilyonei Hashas, Sanhedrin* 73a).

6. *Kefoel batel,* "as an unemployed laborer," the definition of which is the sub-

ject of extended discussion; for a digest of the opinions involved in this definition, see *Talmudic Encyclopedia* (Hebrew), XI, "*Hashavat Avedah*", pp. 82–84.

7. Full compensation for losses sustained by the rescuer in the absence of court permission or in the absence of explicit warranty by the rescued party when circumstances of speed and anxiety preclude the possibility of making such warranty is also evident from *Rosh* (*Bava Mezia* 2:28).

8. The *obligatio* of the rescued party to reimburse his rescuer for his labor and expenditures, as that of an owner of a lost object to reimburse the one who found and returned it to him, is, in all probability, that of an implied contract of labor. (See further *B. Bava Mezia* 101a and Maimonides *Torts* ["Robbery and Lost Objects" 10:4] for the rabbinic analogue to *negotiorum gestio*.) Such contracts in Jewish law do not cover disabilities of the laborer incurred in the course of his employment.

9. This ruling is derived *a fortiori* from the case of an unsuccessful attempt to salvage someone's property (see *B. Bava Kamma* 116a [bot.]).

10. Heb., *sevara,* the legal-human logic of the ethico-religious authorities.

11. In other words, the whole purpose of the obligation, *Thou shalt not stand idly by,* is the preservation of life. If its fulfillment can be accomplished only at the sacrifice of life (of the would-be rescuer), then its purpose has been undermined and frustrated. Under such circumstances the obligation falls away.

12. What is the status of the citizen who, above and beyond the call of duty as defined by rabbinic law, elects to give his life to save another's? The question arose in Jewish history with regard to martyrdom for any reason other than those prescribed by religious law, namely the avoidance of idolatry, or incest and adultery, or of murder. Maimonides (*Knowledge,* "Fundamentals of the Law", 5:4) considered such self-sacrifice as sinful; the *Tosafot* (*Avodah Zarah* 27b, *s.v. yakhol,* at end) regarded it as meritorious. "The Ashkenazi talmudists were instinctual rather than rationalistic in their attitude to martyrdom—an attitude characteristic of most medieval German Jewry. The Tosafists reacted negatively to the problem as it is viewed in the *halakhah.* They recoiled—"Heaven forbid!"—from such formal halakhic reasoning that does not require martyrdom of a person forced to worship an idol in private, and they demanded obligatory *Kiddush Ha-Shem* (*Tos. Av. Zar.* 54a)" (Lamm, 1972; *cf.* Jacobs, 1957).

13. Regarding the hero of the New Testament story (Luke 10: 30–37), it has been aptly pointed out "that the original Good Samaritan extolled by St. Luke was fortunate in not arriving on the scene until after the thieves had set upon the traveler, robbed him and beaten him half to death. The Samaritan cared for him and showed him great kindness, but he did not put himself in any peril by doing so. Perhaps this is about as much as can be reasonably asked of the ordinary mortal man" (Barth, 1966:163).

14. Allusion is being made to the following talmudic passages: "[R. Joshua] used to say: A foolish saint . . . brings destruction upon the world. What is a foolish saint like? *E.g.*, a woman is drowning in the river, and he says, 'It is improper for me to look upon her and rescue her'" (*B. Sotah* 21b on *M. Sotah* 3:4).

15. *Middat hasidût* is a talmudic expression (*e.g., B. Hullin* 130b). It is usually translated "a saintly act," "saintly conduct"—the connotation being that the extraordinarily pious act is evidence that the one who performed it is of saintly character. A few years ago, a team of psychiatrists undertook to study donors in renal homotransplantations to find out how they had become involved, how they had made their de-

cisions, what surgery had meant to them, and how they had fared emotionally and psychiatrically about a year (on the average) thereafter. Among their findings was, I believe, a new dimension in *middat hasidût*. During the immediate postoperative period, usually a month or two, the donors received a good deal of attention from families, friends, even strangers who had heard of their sacrifice. Soon thereafter, after they ceased to be celebrities, they noted certain changes in their attitudes or ideas of themselves which they considered more lasting. A typical example is the statement of a forty-year-old male donor, four weeks postoperatively. "I feel better, kind of noble. I am changed, I have passed a milestone in my life, more confidence, self-esteem . . . In every way I am better. For realizing how far I could go for others, I am up a notch in life . . . I value things more, big and small things . . . I come in contact with others a bit more. My pleasures are bigger and have more meaning." Another representative quotation, this time of a fifty-nine-year-old female donor, eighteen months postoperatively: "I am a better person for having done it, more understanding, not nearly as critical. I have improved in many ways, even am more respectful of myself as a person. I feel, if I can do this, I can do anything" (Fellner and Marshall, 1970:269–281). Viewed in this dimension, *middat hasidût* should be translated (in the words of Sorokin) as "creative altruism"—"creative" in the sense that the self is realized with the help of others, for the biological need to help is fulfilled by the very act of altruism (Titmuss, 1970:212; see also, Sorokin, 1954). Making provision for expressions which characterize the modes of thinking of our secular society, we perceive *middat hasidût* as conduct which sometimes engenders and nurtures saintliness, rather than conduct which reflects and evidences it. This perception of *middat hasidût* would be in line with the doctrine popular among the medieval moralists according to which inner disposition is very often created or conditioned by one's external actions, and not *vice versa*.

16. ". . . and it goes without saying that one is obligated to undergo all sorts of suffering if thereby his fellow's life is spared or saved" (R. Abraham Gombiner, d. *ca.* 1683, *Magen Abraham, O. H.* 126). All suffering short of actual torture is probably meant (R. Z. Waldenberg, 20th cent., *Responsa Ziz Eliezer:* IX, 9a).

17. He whose perverted sense of values leads him to forget this basic rule can never be more than "a foolish saint"; see above.

18. Maimonides' formulation is a rewording of a dictum of Rabbah, or his disciple Rava (Textual readings vary; *cf. Tosafot, Ketubot* 30b, *s.v. rav ashi*), both prominent rabbis of fourth century Babylonia; the dictum is found in *Bava Kamma* (117b) and *B. Sanhedrin* (74a).

19. For if, as we have seen, one may not save himself by destroying or by appropriating another's property, it follows *a fortiori* that one may save others by such measures.

20. The solution, of course, is eminently sensible; and really much ado should not be made of it. See the similar provisions of the Czechoslovak Civil Code of 1964 and of the Civil Code of the Republic of China, in its General Principles of 1929 (both cited by Rudzinski, 1966:117–119). I should like, however, to contrast this *premedieval* dictum with the Anglo-American law of today. In an article entitled, "The Good Samaritan and the Bad," Professor Gregory (1966:28) of the University of Virginia Law School, puts it bluntly:

> Our law says [he declares] that you do not have to volunteer to relieve others from danger not due to your own fault; but if you *do* volunteer – if you engage in some activity that is followed by harm to such another – then a court may let a jury scrutinize what you did and call it actionable negligence – *no matter how hard you tried* [italics provided]. Many people aware of this think it much wiser to do nothing at all. If you are not under a duty to "fease," the non-feasance can never be held actionable. But if you do engage in feasance toward anybody, then under most circumstances you must "fease" carefully. Moral: Don't ever "fease" unless you have to!

Israeli law is not much better (*Cf.* Yadin, 1970:260–262). Professor Gregory is not very proud of his legal system. In a footnote, he writes, "Of course, I do not want to be understood as advising people never to help others who are in danger or distress." He does not; but the law implicitly does. See also Prosser (1971:340–343) who correctly attributes this serious lacuna to the general Anglo-American reluctance to countenance non-feasance as the basis of any liability. I might add that, technically speaking, the Good Samaritan is liable to tort action instituted by the very person he saved! Compare this with the talmudic statement of the fourth century just cited: Our talmudic Good Samaritan, duty-bound to come to the rescue of his fellow, is exempt from liability for the objects he broke whether they belonged to the pursued or to any other person.

21. Although the primary source (*B. Ketubot* 86a) ordains said coercion for the fulfillment of *positive* commandments, it is evident from *Tosafot* (*s.v. akhpie, Ketubot* 49b and *Bava Batra* 8b) that the commandment *Thou shalt not stand idly by,* would also be subject to coercion (1) either because it is a commandment – albeit formulated negatively – to do something positively or (2) because the supplementary commandment, *Thou shalt restore him to himself* (see above), informs *Thou shalt not stand idly by* with positive characteristics – similar to the commandments of *zedakāh* cited by *Tosafot.* Some authorities maintain that there is no distinction between positive and negative duties; all duties may be enforced by coercion (R. Pinhas Horowitz, d. 1805, *Sefer Hafla'ah,* and R. Akiva Eger, d. 1837, *Novellae,* both on *Ketubot* 49b). Other authorities, however, maintain that coercion to perform positive commandments is the exclusive prerogative of the courts and may be carried out in the extreme, whereas the physical prevention of the violation of the negative commandments is the duty of any private citizen but may not be carried out in the extreme (R. Aryeh Leib Heller, d. 1813, *Meshovev Netivot* 3:1, para 3).

22. Traditionally numbering six hundred and thirteen (*B. Makkot* 23b).

23. Except in certain states of the United States.

24. To Rudzinski's list, we might add the comrade relationship in the Israeli Defense Forces which had become well-nigh legendary. Israeli army solidarity dictated that in and after any battle, raid or skirmish, no soldier – dead or wounded, known or unknown to his rescuer – was left in the field. It is a known fact that soldiers retrieved their comrades often at great personal risk. One of the traumas of the Yom Kippur War was the weakening of this quasi-legal obligation.

25. The Portuguese provision regarding the duty to rescue, for example, is unusual in that it appears in a *civil* code, and "the failure to come to the aid of the

attacked results in liability for damages (*sera possible de dommages-intérêts*)" (Rudzinski, 1966:99).

26. *Cf.* Rudzinski, (1966:119-124): "Is the introduction of such a legal duty desirable?" The proposal refers to ethico-legal provisions of the *Halakhah*; there is no intention, of course, to foster the legislation of its moral provisions (*middat hasidût*).

27. Despite the inevitable discrepancy between the real behavior in a given society and its respective ethical ideal, "many aspects of the actual conduct seem to be colored or permeated somehow by the predominant ethical system" (Sorokin, 1962:II, 480).

28. See Kirschenbaum (1976) for full documentation. Research for this study was made possible by grants from the Memorial Foundation for Jewish Culture and the Israel Commission for Basic Research.

ABBREVIATIONS

B. = Babylonian Talmud
R. = Rabbi
b. = *ben,* son of
d. = died
M. = Mishnah
H. M. = Hoshen Mishpat
O. H. = Orah Haim
P. = Palestinian Talmud

REFERENCES

I. Primary Sources

Note: Unless otherwise noted, the citations from the classical sources of Jewish law are taken from the standard editions. The following translations (with slight modifications) were used:

The Hebrew Bible:

1917 *The Holy Scriptures.* Philadelphia: Jewish Publication Society of America.

The Talmud:

1948 Epstein, Isadore (editor). *The Babylonian Talmud.* London: The Soncino Press.

Maimonides:

1949 Obermann, Julian *et al* (editors) *The Code of Maimonides.* New Haven and London: Yale University Press.

All other translations are by the author.

II. Literature

Barth, Alan
1966 "The vanishing Samaritan." Pp. 159–169 in Ratcliffe (1966).

Cardozo, Benjamin
1921 *Wagner v. International Railway Co.*, 232, N.Y. 176.

Cahn, Edmund
1959 *The Moral Decision: Right and Wrong in the Light of American Law.* Bloomington: Indiana University Press (A Midland Paperback).

Fellner, Carl H. and Marshall, John R.
1970 "Kidney donors." Pp. 269–281 in I. Macauley and L. Berkovitz (editors). *Altruism and Helping Behavior.* New York and London: Academic Press.

Freedman, Lawrence Z.
1966 "No response to the cry for help." Pp. 171–182 in Ratcliffe (1966).

Graetz, Heinrich
1908 *Geschichte der Juden.* Vol. IV, 4th edition, edited by S. Horovitz. Leipzig: Oskar Leiner.

Gregory, Charles O.
1966 "The good Samaritan and the bad: the anglo-american law." Pp. 23–41 in Ratcliffe (1966).

Halevy, Isaac
1918 *Dorot Harischonim: Die Geschichte und Literatur Israels (Hebrew).* Frankfurt/M: Louis Golde.

Heschel, Abraham Joshua
1962 *God in Search of Man: A Philosophy of Judaism.* Philadelphia: Jewish Publication Society of America and Meridian.

Jacobs, Louis
1957 "Greater love hath no man . . . the Jewish point of view of self-sacrifice." *Judaism* 6. Reprinted, pp. 175–183 in M. M. Kellner (editor), *Contemporary Jewish Ethics.* New York: Sanhedrin Press, 1978.

Jakobovits, Immanuael
1959 *Jewish Medical Ethics.* New York: Bloch.

Kirschenbaum, Aaron
1976 "The 'good Samaritan' and Jewish law." *Diné Israel* 7:7–85.

Lamm, Norman
1972 "Kiddush ha-shem and hillul ha-shem." *Encyclopedia Judaica.* Jerusalem and New York: Keter and Macmillan.

Prosser, W.L.
1971 *The Laws of Torts.* 4th Edition. St. Paul, Minn.: West.

Ratcliffe, J.M., Editor
1966 *The Good Samaritan and the Law.* Garden City, N.Y.: Doubleday Anchor.

Rudzinski, Aleksander W.
1966 "The duty to rescue: a comparative analysis." Pp. 91–134 in Ratcliffe (1966).

Sheleff, Leon (Shaskolsky)
1976 "Morality, criminal law and politics." *Tel Aviv Studies in Law* II: 190–228.

Sorokin, Pitrim A.
1954 *The Ways and Power of Love.* Boston: Beacon Press.
1962 *Social and Cultural Dynamics.* 4 Volumes. New York: Badminster Press.

Titmuss, Richard M.
1970 *The Gift Relationship: From Human Blood to Social Policy.* London: George Allen and Unwin.

Urbach, Ephraim E.
1971 "'Kol Ha'Meqayyem Nefesh Ahat. . .'—development of the version, vicissitudes of censorship, and business manipulations of printers" (Hebrew) *Tarbiz* 40:268–284 (with English summary).

Yadin, Uri
1970 "The bad and the good Samaritan" (Hebrew). *Mishpatim* 2:252–267.

Yosef, Ovadia
1976 "A responsum permitting kidney transplants" (Hebrew). *Diné Israel* 7:25–43.

Rescue and Restitution

Ernest Weinrib

The English common law (and its American and Commonwealth progeny) is notorious for its refusal to recognize a general duty to rescue persons in peril.[1] No matter how desperate the other's circumstances (he is, say, drowning off the dock where I am standing) and no matter how easy it is to save him (the lifeline lies at my feet), I need not bestir myself on his behalf. The saving of life, even if achievable at no real cost to the rescuer, is a charitable act demanded by conscience, not by law. A well-known judgment expressed this conclusion by referring to Jesus' parable (Luke 10:30) of the Good Samaritan who tended to the wounds of the man robbed on the highway from Jerusalem to Jericho:

> The priest and Levite who passed by on the other side were not, it is supposed, liable at law for the continued suffering of the man who fell among thieves, which they might, and morally ought to have prevented or relieved.[2]

The unintended irony in these words is that the priest and the Levite seem in fact to have been obligated to assist the wounded traveller. The Talmud at *Sanhedrin* 73a quotes the following *baraita*:

> From where do we know that if a man sees his neighbor drowning, mauled by animals, or attacked by robbers, he is bound to save him? From the verse, "You shall not stand idly by the blood of your neighbor" [Lev. 19:16].

In Jesus' parable, members of the Jewish religious elite violated a norm of Jewish law that the Samaritan—outsider and enemy—practiced.

The difference between the Talmud and the common law respecting the duty to rescue reflects a difference in the normative structure of the two systems. The common law insists that breach of the duties incumbent on defendants be correlative to the violation of rights enjoyed by plaintiffs. Omissions in the face of an independently arising danger do not violate rights.[3] The bystander's failure to act is merely the withholding of a benefit. And benefits—no matter how urgently needed—are within the gift of the donor.

Talmudic law, on the other hand, is a jurisprudence of obligation rather than of rights.[4] It starts with *mitzvot*, directives aimed at the actor's conduct. The decisive consideration for the common law, that the bystander who fails to rescue does not violate the endangered person's rights, is irrelevant to talmudic law. All that matters is the commandment

[1] For a discussion of the common law position on rescue, *see* my "The Case for a Duty to Rescue," *Yale Law Journal, 90*, 247–293 (1980).

[2] *Buch v. Amory Manufacturing Co.*, 69 N. H. 257, at 260 (1897).

[3] On the philosophical underpinnings of the common law position, *see* my "Right and Advantage in Private Law," *Cardozo Law Review, 10*, 1283–1309 (1989).

[4] *See* Robert Cover, "Obligation: A Jewish Jurisprudence of the Social Order," *Journal of Law and Religion, 5*, 65–74 (1988).

Ernest Weinrib • University of Toronto, Faculty of Law, Toronto, Ontario M5S 1A1 Canada.

not to "stand idly by the blood of your neighbor," which the rabbis understood as mandating rescue.

In this article, I want to reflect on the differences between the common law and the talmudic duty. I look first to one aspect of the uniqueness of the talmudic duty to rescue, specifically, the rescuer's obligation to expend money if necessary. This gives rise to the question of whether the rescuer is entitled to reimbursement of his expenses. Lastly, I deal with the contrasting conceptualizations that underlie possible answers to this question.

To a modern lawyer, the talmudic obligation to rescue is remarkable for being inconsistent not only with the common law but also with the standard critique, namely Jeremy Bentham's attack on the common law rule.[5] "In cases where a person is in danger, why," Bentham asked, "should it not be made the duty of every man to save another from mischief, when it can be done without prejudicing himself, as well as to abstain from bringing it on him?" The common law, he observed, imposes no duty to warn the person walking with lit candle into a room strewn with gunpowder, or to use water at hand to quench the fire in a woman's headdress, or to pull the drunken man's face out of a puddle. "Who is there that in any of these cases should think punishment misapplied?"

Bentham's rhetorical questions suggest that legal duties of affirmative action should have two characteristics. First, an omission to rescue another should be punishable at law. Second, the duty should be restricted to cases where the rescue can be accomplished without prejudice to the rescuer. Thus, he would impose punishment for failure to perform an easy rescue.

Neither of these features are present in the talmudic obligation to rescue. The Talmud attaches no sanction to the violation of the duty. The reason is that the commandment not "to stand idly by the blood of your neighbor" has a peculiar structure. It is a negative commandment that is transgressed through inactivity.[6] Under talmudic law the violation of a "negative commandment in which there is no deed" is not punishable.[7] Strictly speaking, the commandment "You shall not stand idly by the blood of your neighbor" does not establish an affirmative duty to rescue but a negative duty not to not rescue. The transgression is neither that one fails to do some act that a positive command requires nor that one does some act that a negative command forbids. Although the duty has been violated, there is no specific act that the transgressor did or ought to have done for which the punishment can be exacted.

This treatment of punishment mixes elements that appear in the common law and in Bentham's criticism. The common law uses the distinction between act and omission to claim that omissions do not violate rights and therefore are not the stuff of duties correlative to rights. Bentham, on the other hand, focuses only on the consequences without regard to whether they flow from acts or omissions. Thus, he favors a duty backed by punishment as an incentive to desirable outcomes. Like Bentham, the Talmud postu-

[5] *See* Jeremy Bentham, *An Introduction to the Principles of Morals and Legislation*, in his collected works (James H. Burns & H.L.A. Hart, eds.; London: Athlone Press, 1970), pp. 292–293.

[6] Maimonides, *Mishneh Torah*, Laws of Murder and the Preservation of Life, 1:16.

[7] Maimonides, *Mishneh Torah*, Laws of Sanhedrin 18:2 (drawing on *Sanhedrin* 16a, *Temurah* 3a, *Makkot* 16a, *etc.*)

lates a duty to rescue; and like the common law, it regards the act–omission distinction as important. But unlike Bentham, the talmudic duty triggers no punishment; and unlike the common law, omission is significant not in itself but only when encased in a negative commandment. The result is a duty whose violation attracts no legal sanction.

Moreover, the Talmud does not limit the duty to what the rescuer can do (in Bentham's words) "without prejudicing himself." In the talmudic exegesis, the bare obligation to rescue is deduced from Deuteronomy 22:2, interpreted as "You shall restore him to himself." The prooftext "You shall not stand idly by the blood of your neighbor" serves the further purpose of requiring the potential rescuer to "take the trouble of hiring men" if he is unable personally to save the imperilled individual. Rescue can be an expensive proposition. In this respect, too, Jesus' Good Samaritan perfectly conforms to the legal requirements: he renders first aid to the traveller and transports him to the closest inn, wherein he finances his convalescence.

Thus, in disagreeing with the common law position the Talmud both falls short of and exceeds Bentham's prescriptions. It falls short of them by making the duty to rescue legally unenforceable. It exceeds them by requiring the rescuer to incur whatever expenses are necessary.

One might think that combining burdensomeness and unenforceability in this way brings the talmudic duty to rescue closer to the common law's distinction between moral and legal duty. In a sense, the judge's comments about Jesus' parable turn out to be correct after all: because the duty to rescue is not actionable, the priest and the Levite were not "liable at law" to the wounded traveller. To regard the talmudic duty as moral rather than legal, however, is to misconceive the talmudic position. The duty to rescue is not merely a matter of conscience. Despite the absence of a legal sanction, the directive not "to stand idly by the blood of your neighbor" is as legal as any other norm of Jewish law. Because Jewish law embodies a jurisprudence of obligation, the legal character of the duty to rescue lies in its very existence as a duty, even if its breach is not subject to sanction.

Precisely because the duty is fully legal, one can raise a quintessentially legal issue with respect to the expenditures required of the rescuer. According to the Talmud, the rescuer who cannot save the imperilled person on his own must "take the trouble to hire men." The urgency of the hour obligates the rescuer to make expenditures on behalf of the imperilled person. Can the rescuer sue the person he has saved for reimbursement of his costs? The Talmud does not expressly say whether the rescuer's expenditures accrue permanently to the benefit of the person saved, or whether they merely tide him over the emergency and must be reimbursed once normal life resumes. To put the question in the terms of Jesus' parable, is the Good Samaritan entitled to have the traveller reimburse him for the costs of lodging and the value of the first-aid supplies?

To address this question, we must turn to self-defense, also discussed in this section of the Talmud. At *Sanhedrin* 74a, the Talmud quotes the rules that apply when property is damaged in the course of an attack by one person ("the pursuer") on the life of another ("the pursued person"):

> A pursued person who breaks utensils is not liable if they are the utensils of the pursuer: he is liable if they are the utensils of anyone else. He is not liable if they are the utensils of his pursuer, so that [the pursuer's] property should not be more dear to him than [the pursuer's] person. He is liable if they are the utensils of anyone else, because he saves himself through the property of another.

Note the comment that the pursued person who breaks the utensils of a third party while escaping the pursuer is liable for the damage "because he saves himself through the property of another." A third party here and a potential rescuer seem to stand in the same relation to the endangered person: both have the resources of salvation. Were the third party present, he would be obligated to incur costs in assisting the pursued person. Accordingly, the pursued person acting in self-defense helps himself to the resources that rescuers are duty-bound to expend on his behalf. Given this parallel between the rescuer and the third party, the liability of the pursued person to the third party for his loss indicates that the rescuer can also claim reimbursement. As in both situations the imperilled person has been saved "through the property of another," the property owner's entitlement to compensation should be the same in each case.

This in fact was the conclusion of the medieval talmudist R. Asher ben Yechi'el.[8] Equating the rescuer who must "take the trouble to hire men" with the third party whose utensils are broken by the pursued person, R. Asher elegantly drew from the latter a principle applicable to both. He reasoned that in neither situation are the resources of others freely available to the imperilled person:

> The person saved is obligated to reimburse the rescuer for his expenses, for no one is obligated to save the life of another with his own money if the person saved has money... If one were not obligated to save the pursued person with one's own money, the pursued person would not be liable for breaking the utensils. The other's property would be subject to the obligation to rescue and the pursued person would have broken them legitimately in order to be saved.[9]

The liability of the pursued person for the broken utensils shows that one's property is not subject to an encumbrance for the benefit of endangered persons. Similarly, the resources the rescuer expends are completely his own; they are not impressed with a charge in favor of endangered persons. Reimbursement for the rescuer follows from liability for breaking utensils while pursued.

Is R. Asher's argument sound? The difficulty with it is that one cannot transplant the reimbursement principle to the rescuer until one has elucidated its basis in the situation of pursuit. R. Asher focuses on the Talmud's justification for reimbursing the third party, "because (the pursued person) saves himself through the property of another." These words, however, can be understood, in two different ways, only one of which expresses a rationale applicable to the rescuer.

The first possibility is that the utensil owner's entitlement to reimbursement is a consequence of what the pursued person has *done*. In breaking the utensils, the pursued person has used the property of another for his own purposes. Although the pursuit gives special urgency and motivation to the pursued person, his legal position with respect to

[8] Also known as Rosh, Germany/Spain, 1250–1327 C.E.

[9] Rabbenu Asher *ad Sanhedrin* 73a.

the third party is simply that of someone who has converted another's property to his use. The requirement of compensation is a recognition that, even under the desperate circumstances of avoiding attack, the pursued person continues to be responsible to others. According to this view, the legally salient element is the pursued person's *act* in breaking the utensils.

The second possibility is that the entitlement is a consequence of what the pursued person has *received*. He saved himself by breaking the utensils, and thus realized a benefit at someone else's expense. Unless he compensates the owner of the utensils, he will have been unjustly enriched.

These two bases of recovery are conceptually distinct. A person can be enriched without having acted on another's property. Think, for instance, of the contractor hired by my neighbor, who paves my driveway by mistake; I realize a benefit from this although I have been entirely passive.[10] Conversely, one can use another's property without thereby being enriched. Assume, for instance, that someone thinks he is under attack but in fact is not. If he breaks another's utensils while "defending" himself, the harm he causes is unaccompanied by the realization of any benefit.

Thus, the Talmud's statement that "he saves himself through the property of another" is equivocal. We do not know whether to emphasize the verb "saves" and thereby focus on the pursued person's role as actor, or to emphasize the object "himself" and focus on his role as recipient of a benefit. Because the pursued person who breaks utensils is both actor and beneficiary, the distinction between the two roles does not matter.

In the rescue situation, however, the actor and the beneficiary are no longer identical. The imperilled person is the passive recipient of the benefits generated by the rescuer's expenditures. We cannot say that the rescued person "saves himself through the property of another"; he does not save himself at all. If the rescuer is entitled to recover his losses, as R. Asher argued, it must be because benefit rather than act is decisive in the case of pursuit.

Indication that benefit is not decisive, however, comes from the Talmud's treatment of the rescuer who saves an imperilled person by damaging the goods of some third party. In this variant of the pursuit situation, different persons play the roles of actor and beneficiary. Immediately after enunciating the principle of compensation for saving oneself through the property of another, the Talmud continues:

> A pursuer who is pursuing a pursuer to save [the person the latter is attacking] and who breaks the utensils of the pursuer or of the pursued or of anyone else is not liable. That is not in accordance with strict law [*min hadin*], but unless you say so, it will turn out that nobody will rescue anyone from a pursuer.

This very concentrated passage contains two stages: the final holding and the solution that reflects the real legal contours of the situation. At the end of the day, the rescuer is relieved of any liability for property damage, because liability would be a disincentive to rescue. But the Talmud expressly terms

[10] The Talmud discusses unrequested improvements to land at *Baba Mezia* 101a.

this consequentialist disposition of the issue a deviation from the strict law.[11] From a rigorously juristic point of view, the rescuer who damages the property of a third party ought to be liable. Presumably this liability results from his having effected the rescue "through the property of another."

If so, the statement "he saves himself through the property of another" is oriented toward the act of using another's property rather than toward the benefits flowing from such use. The rescuer in this situation has not received the benefit of the rescue. He is liable in strict law because he has committed the act of breaking the utensils. Liability can rest only on what he has done, not on what he has gained.

Thus, one can argue that the rescuer who "takes the trouble to hire men" is not entitled to recoup his disbursements from the rescued person. R. Asher's reasoning to the contrary assimilates the money that the rescuer expends to the utensils that the pursued person breaks. The pursued person must reimburse the owner of the utensils because he has "saved his life through the property of another." R. Asher's reasoning gives this phrase a restitutionary interpretation. The rescuer's liability at strict law for breaking utensils, however, may indicate that the person who uses the property of another to save a life is liable for what he has done, not for what he has gained. Seen in this light, the rescuer's entitlement to compensation need not follow from the pursued person's liability for the broken utensils.

Why does it matter whether the rescuer is entitled to recover his disbursements? Of course, the answer to this seemingly mean-spirited question affects the weight of the burden incumbent on the rescuer. If the rescuer can recover his disbursements from the person he has saved, the duty to rescue is less striking. Instead of requiring altruistic sacrifice, the duty triggers what the economists call a Pareto-superior move, in which no party is worse off and one party is better off.

At stake, however, is a deeper problem. We noted at the beginning that the talmudic approach to rescue differs from the common law in being duty-based rather than rights-based. The issue of compensation for disbursements tests the limits of that distinction.

Talmudic law presents a jurisprudence of obligation because of the centrality of *mitzvot*. As the fundamental norms governing what one should do or abstain from doing, *mitzvot* are divinely ordained specifications of duty. The rabbinic jurists elaborate the *mitzvot* and apply them to the particularities of human life. The obligation to rescue is a *mitzvah* that directly originates in the biblical command not to "...stand idly by the blood of your neighbor." The allocation of rescue costs is an issue that arises in the juristic elaboration of that *mitzvah*. Even if the *mitzvah* itself embodies a jurisprudence of duty rather than of right, does the same apply to the process of elaboration?

This question directs us to what is implicit in the reasoning of the talmudists. Of course, R. Asher does not explicitly refer to rights. One can nonetheless ask whether the idea of a right is presupposed in his discussion.

[11] Maimonides, *Mishneh Torah*, Laws of Wounding and Damaging 8:14 terms this deviation a legislative reform (*takkanah*).

In this connection the distinction between liability for what one has done and liability for what one has gained is significant. Duty, "that *action* to which a person is bound,"[12] is a concept governing the person as actor. One can formulate the failure to act as the breach of one's duty. Liability for what one has gained, however, cannot be based on the antecedent breach of a duty, because the recipient of the benefit may have been completely passive. Rather, restitutionary liability rests on a right to which the claimant is entitled.

Requiring the rescuer to bear the costs of rescue would be the most extreme expression of a jurisprudence of duty. Whereas the talmudic duty to rescue makes the physical safety of others an obligatory end of one's action, the obligation to "take the trouble of hiring men" would signify that the status of safety as an obligatory end implies a duty with respect to the means as well. Moreover, the expenditures of rescue could be categorically distinguished from the utensils broken by the pursued person: because the owner of the utensils is a passive party, he does not fall under the action-based strictures of the duty to rescue. On this view, compensation for the utensils does not imply compensation for the rescuer's disbursements.

R. Asher's reasoning, however, implicitly starts with the notion of right rather than duty. The duty to reimburse is the reflex of a right originating in the rescuer's proprietary entitlements. For R. Asher, the central issue is whether the rescuer's property is subject to an encumbrance. R. Asher argues that the pursued person's liability for the broken utensils shows that someone who is in danger has no property interest in the resources of salvation. Therefore, imperilled persons would be unjustly enriched if they did not reimburse rescuers who have expended those resources on their behalf. At the heart of this reasoning are the rights that flow from ownership and the notion of unjust enrichment that is the corollary of such rights.

R. Asher's view brings the Talmud's conception of rescue closer to that of other legal systems. The question for each is how they regulate the transfer of the resources of salvation. The common law carries the logic of the rescuer's ownership of these resources to the extreme by making their disposal entirely a matter of the rescuer's discretion. Bentham's suggested duty of easy rescue compels a transfer only when the rescuer's expenditure is so minimal as to be without real value to him. As R. Asher construes it, talmudic doctrine shares with the common law and with Bentham's critique a commitment to protecting the rescuer from loss. The key difference is that they do so by restricting the obligation *ex ante*, whereas talmudic law maximizes the advantage to the imperilled party by allowing compensation *ex post*.

R. Asher's reasoning, to be sure, antedates the modern preoccupation with rights. Moreover, it operates with reference to the talmudic duty to rescue which is a conspicuous example of Judaism's jurisprudence of obligation. Nonetheless, the idea of rights exercises a gravitational pull on legal reasoning even within this jurisprudence. Instead of pushing the notion of obligation to its extreme, R. Asher formulates a restitutionary claim that implicitly depends on the idea of rights. So understood, his reasoning points to the fundamental role of rights in legal argument.

[12]Kant, I., *The Metaphysical Elements of Justice* (Indianapolis: Bobbs-Merrill, 1965 [trans. by J. Ladd, orig. ed. 1797]), p. 23 (*emphasis added*).

Economic Analysis

[27]

THE JUST PRICE DOCTRINE IN JUDAIC LAW — AN ECONOMIC ANALYSIS

Aaron Levine

Interest in the "just price" doctrine in the economics profession finds expression mainly in the work of economic historians. Investigations in this area have typically focused on the normative rules medieval schoolmen formulated for market behavior [1]. Sparsely treated, however, has been the rich contribution of the Talmudic literature and Judaic law on the various aspects of the "just price" doctrine [2].

Economicts generally feel that study of the just price question properly belongs to the sphere of religion, ethics, or normative economics, and modern economic analysis has little to contribute to this area.

The purpose of this article will be to demonstrate that modern economic tools can provide: 1) a useful framework for system-

1. For a classical exposition of the Just Price doctrine of the medieval schoolmen v. Raymond de Roover, "The Concept of Just Price: Theory and Economic Policy", *The Journal of Economic History*, Vol. XVIII, no. 4, December 1958, pp. 418—434.

2. C.F. Roman A. Ohrenstein, "Economic Self-Interest and Social Progress in Talmudic Literature", *The American Journal of Economics and Sociology*. Jan. 1970, pp. 59—70;

Ahron Shapiro, "Rabbinical Responsa and the Regulation of Competition", *The American Journal of Economics and Sociology*, Jan. 1970. pp. 71—76;

M. Tamari, "Competition, Prices and Profits in Jewish Law" (Hebrew) in H.Z. Hirschberg ed., *Memorial to H.M. Shapiro;* Bar-Ilan University. Ramat-Gan, 1972, pp. 130—146;

Aaron Levine, "The Free Enterprise Model — An Halakhic View", Proceedings, Association of Orthodox Jewish Scientists (forthcoming). For an extensive survey of economic regulation in Judaic Law v. R. Ezra Basri;

Ethics of Business Finance and Charity, According to Jewish Law, (Hebrew), Vol. I and II, Rubin Mass, Publisher, Jerusalem (1974, 1976).

atically presenting and analyzing the diverse elements subsumed under this doctrine; and 2) a vehicle for articulating and extraplorating the line of thougt Judaic law would take on the various moral issues raised by this doctrine.

Economic Framework for Analyzing the Just Price

Modern economic analysis posits that market price or value is determined by the interaction of *aggregate* supply and demand forces. The role an individual seller plays in determining market price depends entirely on the market structure he finds himself operating in. At one polar extreme, stands the market structure of monopoly. Here, the firm and the industry are one and the same. Assuming the seller is a profit maximizer, he will select the price-output combination that would best promote his goal. The monopolist is thus a price seeker and plays a role in *determining* value. At the other end of the continuum stands the market structure of perfect competition. Here, a large number of firms offer a homogeneous product for sale under conditions of perfect knowledge, freedom of entry and resource mobility. The individual firm in this market structure produces an insignificant portion of the total market supply and perceives market price as a datum. Price is determined by the *aggregate* forces of supply and demand, outside the influence of the individual firm. The firm faces here a horizontal demand curve, meaning that it can sell all it can produce at the prevailing norm and would lose all its patronage to competitors if it chose to sell above market price. Standing in an intermediate position in this range of market structures is the type of marketplace that typically prevailed in the medieval period. Economists would call it a modified form of monopolistic competition. Here, many sellers offer a similar but not identical product for sale under conditions of imperfect knowledge and other bottleneck factors. The product differentiation characteristic of each marekt signifies that each seller faces a downward sloping demand curve. Competitive price here would not gravitate toward a single value, as it does under perfect competition, but would rather be described as a range of values. Elasticity of demand would determine, in the final analysis, the extent of this competitive price range.

What follows from the above discussion of value theory is a convenient classification of ethical prescription for the marketplace into two separate categories: (1) normative rules designed to influence the *determination* of value itself and: (2) normative rules governing market conduct once value has already been established by the impersonal forces of supply and demand.

Subsumed under category I is the formulation of guidelines for: 1) price and wage controls; 2) interferences with the aggregate forces of supply and demand; 3) the ethics of profiteering as a result of a *change* in market price; and 4) the latitude the individual seller enjoys in setting a price for his own product in the absence of a competitive norm.

Belevant moral questions subsumed under category II include: 1) the formulation of a taxonomy of grounds for invalidating or otherwise modifying transactions concluded at prices that diverge from the market norm; 2) the ethics of selling *below* market price: 3) and the ethics of engaging in price discrimination on the basis of the terms of payment.

Use of our framework will limit our discussions to moral issues relating directly or very closely to pricing at either of the two relevant stages. Ethical problems in market conduct not relating to price will not be dealt with here.

Normative Rules in Judaic Law Relating to the Determination of Value

The criterion adopted by Judaic law in determining the legitimacy of interfering with the natural process of market determination of value is evidently promotion of social welfare and the preservation of religious practice.

Promotion of social welfare, as discussed below, requires the community to safeguard the economic interests of both producers and consumers. Should the vagaries of supply and demand forces relegate either of these groups into a position of economic deprivation, remedial intervention should be undertaken.

Judaism's concern for the subsistence needs of the masses finds expression in the Rabbinical ordinance requiring each Jewish community to enforce a profit rate limitation of 16.2/3 for vendors dealing in commodities essential to human life (Chayei Nefesh) [3].

Similarly rooted is the Talmudic ordinance against hoarding. Prescriptions against hoarding take the form of disallowing market purchases of essential commodities in excess of normal consumption needs. Producers, though, may normally withold any part of their crop from market sale. Nonetheless, during a period of famine, producers are subject to a quota in regard to the amount of produce they may store. The quota allows the producer to store no more than one year's supply of foodstuff for himself and his family [4].

Though the Jewish community is not mandated to enforce profit rate limitations on its industry other than the chayei nefesh sector, price and wage control fall within its legitimate legislative authority [5]. Such legislation becomes effective law, according to R. Moses ben Joseph de Trani (1500-1580) of Safed, by means of a simple

3. V. Baba Batra 90a; Asher ben Jechiel (1250-1328); *Rosh Baba Batra* V:28; Jacob ben Asher (1270-1340);

Tur Choshen Hamishpat 231:27;

Maimonides (1135-1204), *Yad, Hilkhat Mekhira* XIV:1; Joseph Caro (1488-1575), *Shulchan Arukh, Choshen Hamishpat* 231:20. Which commodities are to be regarded as essential and hence subject to regulation was disputed among the Talmudic codifiers. R. Vidal Yom Tov of Tolosa, 14th century Spanish expounder of Maimonides' teachings, posited that only foodstuff itself is to be regarded as essential to life and hence subject to regulation. Products essential for the preparation of food (machsherei okhel nefesh) are not subject to price regulation (v. *Maggid Mishnah Yad,* op. cit.). A diametrically opposite view was advanced by R. Joseph Carro (op. cit.). Only products not essential even in the preparation of foodstuff are not subject to regulation. Commodities used in the preparation of foodstuff are considered as foodstuff itself and subject to price control. Finally, a third taxonomy was advanced by R. Joshua ben Alexander Ha-Kohen Falk (1555-1614) of Lemberg. While vendors of foodstuff are subject to a 16 2/3% profit rate limitation, the allowable profit margin is widened up to 100% for sellers of products used in preparation of foodstuff. Products not even used in the preparation of foodstuff need not be regulated at all. (V. *Smah, Sh. Ar.; Choshen Hamishpat* 231, note 36).

4. V. *Sh. Ar.*, op. cit. 231:24.

5. Moses ben Joseph de Trani, *Responsa MaBit* Vol. 1, no. 237.

majority of those eligible to vote. R. Moses posits that the simple majority rules applies even according to the authorities that require more than a simple majority when the legislative matter would benefit some segments of the community at the expense of others. Price and wage legislation involves the determination of *relative* gains and not the generation of absolute losses and gains [6]. Judaic law thus allows the community's notion of equity in the distribution of income to determine the disposition of gains from productive activity.

The welfare of the business sector was also a vital concern of the Talmudic Sages. Appreciation of the fact that the viability of the community's economic life hinges heavily upon the prosperity of the business sector finds expression in the Talmudic dictum that public prayers are offered, even on the Sabbath, when commodity prices drop dangerously low [7].

In a similar vein, it is reported in Taanith 20b that it was the custom of R Huna to send his representative to the marketplace every Friday toward evening to buy up the unsold portion of the perishable vegetables purveyed by the local gardeners. He subsequently would "dump" the excess supply into the river. R. Huna's motivation in subsidizing the gardeners, the Talmud relates, was to insure that they would continue to supply the town with vegetables in the future. Unless they could earn reasonable profits for their efforts, they could not be expected to continue their enterprise.

Invoking the economic incentive argument as a justification for subsidizing the producer leads, in our view, to the proposition that a subsidy of this sort is in order only when its objective is to prevent the producer's earnings from falling below his opportunity cost. Here, in the absence of the subsidy, the producer would turn his efforts elsewhere. Should his current earnings, however, contain elements of economic rent, denying him the subsidy would

6. Moses ben Joseph de Trani, *Responsa MaBit* Vol. 1, no. 237.
7. V. Baba Bathra 91a.

not generate the above distorting effect, as his present enterprise would still represent his best market alternative.

Another basis for interference with the market process of value determination in Judaic law is the preservation of religious practice. The classical. historical example of intervention of this sort is recorded in the Mishnah Kirithuth 1:7. Noting the exorbitant price of birds of the type needed for the fulfillment of the sacrifical requirements of women who gave birth, R. Simeon b. Gamliel the Elder (d. 70) set out to remedy the situation. Motivated by a grave concern that the exorbitant price of birds would lead to a wholesale neglect of the sacrificial obligation, this Sage boldly changed [8] the law governing the sacrificial requirements of women who gave birth. To this end he proclaimed that a woman who had five definite births need bring one sacrifice only and would thereby become ritually pure. Formerly, each birth required a separate sacrifice. The effect of the proclamation was quite dramatic. With the demand for sacrificial birds dropping off markedly, their price gravitated to a resonable level.

To insure a plentiful supply of essential products in Eretz Israel the Sages required producers to sell their products directly to consumers [9]. Middlemen were not entitled to a markup unless they worked to process the product they purchased [10].

With the same objective in mind, the Talmudic Sages prohibited the exporting or transferring of essential produce from Eretz Israel [11]. Included in the interdict was the prohibition against exporting from one province to another province within the geographic boundaries of Eretz Israel [12].

Insofar as the above laws apply only to Eretz Israel and not to Jewish settlements elsewhere [13], the basis of this intervention was

8. R. Simeon B. Gamliel here relied on the principle "eth La'asoth Lashem, heferu Thorathecha" (V. Tefereth Yesrael, ad locum).

9. V. Baba Bathra 91a; Maimonides, *Yad*, op. cit. XIV:4 *Sh. Ar.* op cit. 231:23.

10. Samuel b. Meir (1085-1158), *Rashbam*, Baba Bathra 91a.

11. V. Baba Bathra 90a.

12. *Sh. Ar.*, op. cit., 231:26.

13. Joshua ben Alexander Ha-Kohan Falk, *Smah, Choshen Hamishpat* 231, notes 42, 44.

apparently to promote the settlement of Eretz Israel. Tamari, in his analysis of the laws restricting the markup practices of middlemen takes the above position too[14].

The Ethics of Selling at the Market Norm

In the absence of a legal price established by communal legislation, selling at the prevailing norm presents no moral issue in Judaic law. This is evidenced from the ruling that even in the regulated Chayei Nefesh sector, the 16 2/3% profit constraint is relaxed when the market price rises above its current level. For example, suppose an individual buys wheat at harvest time at $2 a bushel. Now, a month later, the market price of wheat rises to $4 a bushel. Given the rise in the market price, the buyer may sell his wheat at $4 a bushel, nothwithstanding the 66 2/3% markup he realizes thereby[15].

The Ethics of Monopoly Pricing

What latitude does the monopolist enjoy in pricing his product in accordance with the demand conditions his product faces? The ethics of monopoly pricing analytically dichotomizes into two cases, one involving elastic demand and the other involving perfectly inelastic demand.

Selling at whatever price the market will bear in the former instance apparently presents no moral issue in Judaic law. This is evidenced from the long standing sanction given to the communal practice of auctioning the privilege of performing a public ceremonial function of a religious character to the highest bidder[16]. With the ceremonial honor put up for sale unavailable elsewhere, the competitive bidding among the auction participants *determines*

14. M. Tamari, "Competition, Prices and Profits in Jewish Law" (Hebrew) in H.Z. Hirschberg, ed. *Memorial to H.M. Shapiro* (Bar Ilan University, Ramat-Gan, 1972), p. 133.

15. Jacob ben Asher, *Tur*, op. cit. 231:26; Joseph Caro, *Sh. Ar.*, op. cit. 231:20.

16. Meir Ben Isaac Eisenstadt (1670-1744), *Panim Me'irot* Vol. II No. 25; V.R. Ezra Basri, *Ethics of Business Finance and Charity*, According to *Jewish Law*, part two, (Sucath David Publisher, Jerusalem 1976), p. 172.

value. Hence, no moral issue is raised here. Capitalizing on "site" value[17], auctioning a rare painting and selling the patent rights of a new invention for whatever price the market would bear provide other examples of monopoly pricing under conditions of elastic demand.

Exercising monopoly power when faced with a perfectly inelastic demand curve does raise a moral issue in Judaic law. Analysis of the following Talmudic passage in Baba Metzia 58b bears this out:

> It has been taught, R. Judah b. Bathyria (midd first cen.) said: The sale of a horse, sword and buckler on (the field of) battle are not subject to ona'ah, because one's very life is dependent upon them.

Given the life threatening environment of the battlefield zone, the vendor of implements of war enjoys a captive market. The buyer, for all intensive purposes, will not hazard to investigate market alternatives amidst a raging battle. The vendor therefore enjoys a monopolist position here.

With the vendee's demand for a horse or weapon in the battlefield zone described as perfectly inelastic, he certainly receives subjective equivalence for whatever price he agreed to pay for these articles. This is the reasoning of R. Judah b. Bathyria. Whether his ruling represents mainstream Talmudic thought is a

17. Real estate transactions are not subject to the full scope of ona'ah regulations. This exclusion proceeds from exegetical interpretation of the biblical source of ona'ah: "And if thou sell a sale unto thy neighbor or acquirest aught of thy neighbor's hand" (Leviticus XXV:14) — something that is acquired (by being passed) from hand to hand (is subject to ona'ah regulation), thus excluding land, which is not moveable (v. Baba Metzia 56b). Nachmanides (commentary at Leviticus XXV:14) points out that insofar as a biblical interdict against ona'ah is mentioned explicitly in connection with real estate transactions, the exemption cited above must be taken to refer exclusively to the restitution procedure normally provided for in ona'ah cases. Hence, real estate transactions are subject to the prohibition against ona'ah, though not to its prescribed restitution procedure.

What follows as a corollary from our analysis of the ethics of monopoly pricing is that the interdict is violated only when the real estate transaction involved an authentic opportunity cost, i.e., property of the same general characteristics was available in the market place at a price above or below the transaction price at hand. No moral issue, however, is involved regarding the price differential attributed to "site" value.

matter of dispute among the early decisors. R. Hai ben Sherira [18] of Pumbedita (939-1038) and R. Isaac ben Jacob Alfasi [19] of Algeria (1013-1103) ruled that R. Judah b. Bathyria's opinion represented a minority view and should therefore be rejected. R. Hananel b. Hushul, 11th century North African decisor, however, ruled in accordance with R. Judah ben Bathyria [20].

The acceptability of R. Judah ben Bathyria's opinion, according to Moses Ha-Kohen of Lunel, 13th century decisor, hinges heavily upon the validity of assimilating his battlefield case with the fugitive-ferryman case discussed in Baba Kama 115a. Here, the Talmud relates that in the event an absconding criminal agreed to pay a ferryman an above market price to provide him with conveyance across a river, the former is entitled to recoup from the ferryman the differential involved [21].

The point of similarity between the two cases is obviously that in both instances the buyer's interest in the product involved is price inelastic, i.e., he would agree, for all intense purposes, to pay any price the seller insists on. In the ferryman-fugitive case, given that the conveyance averts the fugitive's imminent capture, the latter certainly receives subjective equivalence in his transaction with the ferryman. Nonetheless, remove his fugitive status, this same individual's demand for the conveyance would properly be described as price elastic and he would presumably not valuate the service above market price. With his price inelastic demand reflecting transitory subjective value, the fugitive is entitled to recoup from the ferryman any amount he paid him above the competitive norm. Similarly, remove the condition of war, the vendee would presumably not agree to pay the price he paid for the implements of war.

Though Moses Ha-Kohen advances no specifics as to why the assimilation should be rejected, two points of dissimilarity, in our

18. Hai ben Sherira, *Ketab-al Shira wa-al Baye*, translated into Hebrew by Isac al Bargeloni, *Sefer ha Mekkah ve ha Mimkar*, Venice (1602).

19. *Rif*, Baba Metzia, IV.

20. *R. Hananel*, Baba Metzia 58b.

21. V. Bezalel Ashkenazi (1520-1591), *Shetah M'kubetzet*, Baba Metzia 58b.

view, stand out. Firstly, whereas the demand inducing factor in the battlefield case affects all market demanders equally, causing the *aggregate* demand schedule for implements of war to shift upward, no such similar upward *shift* of the demand schedule occurs in the fugitive-ferryman case. In the latter case, the demand inducing factor uniquely affects the fugitive's subjective evaluation of the ferryman's services, leaving the aggregate market demand for the service unaffected. Secondly, whereas a competitive norm exists for the services of the ferryman at the time the fugitive contracted for his services, no competitive norm exists when an individual transacts for weapons on the battlefield.

What proceeds clearly from the school of thought that accepts the analogy between the fugitive-ferryman case and the battlefield case is the general principle that exercise of monopoly power when the relevant aggregate demand schedule is price inelastic is ethically immoral.

Normative Rules Governing Market Conduct Once Value Has Already Been Determined

The ethics of the price terms of transactions concluded within the framework of a competitive norm are governed in Judaic law by the laws of ona'ah [22]. These laws provide a taxonomy of grounds for invalidating or otherwise modifying transactions concluded at a price that diverges from the prevailing norm. Though constituting a separate interdict, an ona'ah offense is regarded in Judaic law as a violation of property rights and is classified as a form of theft [23]. Three degrees of ona'ah have been identified by the Sages:

(1) First degree ona'ah occurs when the discrepancy between the sale price and the market price is more than 16 2/3% [24]. Here,

22. V. *Sh. Ar.*, op. cit. 227; for an extensive bibliography of Rabbinical Responsa dealing with various aspects of ona'ah law v. Basri, op. cit., pp. 159—181.

23. V. Baba Metzia 61a: Jacob ben Asher, *Tur Choshen Hamishpat* 227:1; Joshua ben Alexander HaKohen, *Smah*, *Sh. Ar.*, op. cit. 227 note 1.

24. V. Baba Metzia 50b.

grounds exist for invalidating the original sale. Nullification rights in the above case, according to Maimonides (1135-1204) and R. Joseph Caro (1488-1575), rests exclusively with the plaintiff. Should the latter express a desire to uphold the transaction, despite the price discrimination involved, the offender must accept this and may not, in turn, invalidate the sale [25]. Selecting this option does not, however, avail the plaintiff of any claim for the restoration of the ona'ah involved. Plaintiff may either void the transaction or accept it as it was originally concluded [26].

Another opinion in the above matter is expressed by the Spanish Talmudic decisor, R. Jonah ben Abraham Gerondi (c. 1200-1263). In his view, as long as the plaintiff does not uphold the transaction, the offender too is given the prerogative of voiding it. The offender's rights in this matter proceed from the magnitude of the price discrimination involved. Since the concluded price diverged more than 16 2/3% from the market norm, the offender may insist that the original transaction be treated as an agreement consumated in error (mekach ta-ut). Once the transaction is, however, upheld by the plaintiff, the offender loses his right to void the sale. Denying the offender *full* nullification rights here follows from the fact that he, the offender, enjoys no such rights when his offense consists of the less severe crime of contracting for a sale price involving less than first degree ona'ah. Conferring him with full nullification rights when his offense is graver runs counter to all cannons of equity [27].

(2) Second degree ona'ah occurs when the sale price differs from the market price by exactly 16 2/3%. Here, the transaction remains binding. Neither of the parties involved may subsequently void the transaction on account of the price discrimination. Plaintiff, however, is entitled to full restitution of the ona'ah involved [28].

25. Maimonides, *Yad*, op. cit. XII:4; Caro, *Sh. Ar.* op. cit. 227:4.

26. Asher ben Jechiel, *Rosh*, Baba Bathra V:14 understands this to be the view of Isac ben Jacob Alfasi of Algeria (1013-1103).

27. Quoted in *Rosh*, op. cit.; also quoted in Nissim ben Reuben Gerondi (1340-1380) of Barcelona, *Ran*, Baba Bathra 84a.

28. Baba Metzia 50b.

(3) Finally, third degree ona'ah occurs when the sale price differs from the market price by less than 16 2/3%. Here, the transaction not only remains binding, but in addition, the plaintiff has no legal claim to the price differential [29].

The Basis of the Ona'ah Claim

The basis of the ona'ah claim requires explanation. Given both the assumption of rationality and the voluntary nature of the agreement, would plaintiff have freely entered into the original transaction unless he felt certain he was receiving in exchange equivalent *subjective value?* What then is the basis of his subsequent ona'ah claim? Strategic to the resolution of the above dilemma is the legal presumption of what the buyer and seller intend to accomplish with their transaction. Under the supposition that the the basic intent of parties to a transaction is to exchange value of *equal objective* or market worth, the legitimacy of the ona'ah claim is readily apparent. Given the above presumption of intent, any discrepancy between the transaction price and the market norm signifies that the original objective was not realized. Had plaintiff been aware of the full range of market alternatives available to him at the time he consumated his ona'ah transaction, he would have either withdrawn from the ona'ah transaction altogether, or would have insisted upon a modification of the price terms of the agreement. Plaintiff clearly incurred an opportunity cost as a result of his ona'ah transaction.

That plaintiff's claim is rooted in the certainty that he incurred an opportunity cost as a result of his ona'ah transaction is seen clearly from R. Asher ben Jechiel's (1250-1327) analysis of third degree ona'ah.

Noting the absence of any provision for legal redress in third degree ona'ah cases, R. Asher speculates whether it might be permissible, in the first instance, to contract into third degree ona'ah. Pivotal to the resolution of this question, in R. Asher's view, is the

29. Ibid.

definition of market price. Is market price to be understood as a single value, or is it to be defined as the range of deviations of less than 16 2/3% from the price of this moot transaction. Adopting the former view leads to the conclusion that knowledge of the market norm prohibits either party from contracting into a price agreement that diverges even slightly from it. The absence of legal redress for third degree ona'ah would then be explained by the presumption that when the degree of ona'ah involved is of such a relatively small amount, plaintiff waives his claim to restitution. The presumption follows from our inability to fix the value of the article sold. While some experts would insist that ona'ah took place, others would just as vehemently deny it. With experts divided as to whether ona'ah occurred, and if it did by how much, we may safely presume that the victim of this possible price discrimination waives his right to restitution.

Adopting the latter view, however, leads to the conclusion that third degree ona'ah is not price fraud at all. Denying legal restitution here follows from the fact that the concluded price, though at variance with the prevailing norm, falls, nevertheless, within the legal price range. Why price should be defined as a range of values rather than by a single value is defended by R. Asher on the grounds that even when the buyer and seller are fully aware of the prevailing norm, each would, on occasion, to their own disadvantage contract into a price agreement at variance with this norm. The vender, for instance, would offer to sell his wares below the prevailing market price when his merchandise represented to him unwanted inventory, or when he has an urgent need to raise cash. Similarly, the buyer, finding a product to his keen liking would, on occasion, offer to pay for it a price above the market norm. Given these facts, market price should not be defined as a single value, but rather as a range of deviations around this value.

Though offering no definitive resolution of the above dilemma, R. Asher urged the following guideline for third degree ona'ah cases: Cognizant of the prevailing norm, an individual should not contract into a price agreement that even departs slightly from this value. Should an individual fall victim to third degree ona'ah, on the other hand, he should accept his loss graciously and express no complaint [30].

Implicit in R. Asher's analysis of third degree ona'ah is the realization that the competitive norm in a heterogeneous product market does not gravitate toward a single value. With each seller facing a downward sloping demand curve, the competitive norm can only be described as a *range* of prices. This insight provide R. Asher with his first approach in explaining the absence of legal redress in third degree ona'ah cases. With a similar but by no means identical product available in the marketplace for a price less than 16 2/3% of the moot transaction, we may safely presume that plaintiff waives his legal claims against the offender. Quality differences and other features that differentiate the products being compared make it debatable whether the moot transaction represented in reality an inferior value. What follows as a corollary is that the basis of the ona'ah claim when the price differential involved is 16 2/3% or more is the certainty that plaintiff incurred an opportunity cost as a result of his transaction. Here, division among experts as to whether the moot transaction represented an inferior value would not occur. Consequently, the ona'ah claim is honored.

Judaic law apparently adopts R. Asher's first approach to third degree ona'ah as evidenced by the prohibition against contracting in the first instance, into third degree ona'ah [31]. What follows by logical extension is the opportunity cost basis of the ona'ah claim.

Viewing the ona'ah claim as an opportunity cost claim leads directly to the proposition that when the product market involved is homogeneous in nature, plaintiff is entitled to restitution of the price differential even when the degree of ona'ah was only third degree. Extrapolating from R. Asher's discussion of third degree

30. Asher ben Jechiel, *Rosh. Baba Metzia* IV:20.

31. V. Maimonides, *Yad*, op. cit.; Jacob ben Asher, *Tur*, op. cit.; Joseph Caro, op. cit.; Nachmanides, *Commentary on Leviticus* XV:14; Ezra Basri, *Ethics of Business Finance and Charity* (Hebrew), part two (Jersalem, Sucath David Publisher, 1976), p. 160. For a variant view v. Aaron Ha-Levi of Barcelona, *Sefer Hachinuch*, mitzvah 337.

ona'ah, R. Jechiel Michael Epstein reached this same conclusion [32].

Another proposition proceeding from the opportunity cost hypothesis is that the ona'ah claim should be honored even when the per unit price of the product involved is not well defined. An example of such a situation is provided by R. Moses Isserles' (1525-1572) analysis of ona'ah claims in the wool and milk markets. Here, it was apparently the custom of vendors to charge their customers different prices in accordance with the size of their purchases. Nonetheless, the per unit price *range* could be determined in each of these markets. With the per unit price range determinable, the legitimacy of the ona'ah claim, according to R. Moses Isserles, could be evaluated [33].

Proceeding as a corollary from the opportunity cost hypothesis is the notion that plaintiff's plea is honored only when we may reasonably presume he was ignorant of the alternative market opportunities open to him at the time he entered in the ona'ah transaction.

That the presumption of imperfect knowledge is what lends credibility to the ona'ah claim is evidenced by the following considerations:

(1) The laws of ona'ah apply only when the price divergence involved falls within the margin of error.

Individuals freely entering into market transactions are presumed, by Judaic law, to have an *approximate* notion of the value of the article involved. Hence, price agreements which diverge enormously from the prevaling norm are not regarded as having occurred as a result of ignorance of market conditions on the part of the participants involved. Divergent price agreements are, quite to the contrary, interpreted as representing a tacit understanding between buyer and seller to treat the price differential as a voluntary gift transfer. Credence is given to plaintiff's ona'ah claim only when the discrepancy between the sale price and the prevailing

32. R. Jechiel Michael Epstein, *Arukh Hashulchan, Choshen Hamishpat* 227:21.

33. R. Moses Isserles, *Darkei Moshe, Tur, Choshen Hamishpat* 209. This view is advanced to dispute R. Joseph Caro's position on this matter.

norm falls within the margin of error. Here the three categories of ona'ah become applicable [34].

(2) Plaintiff is given a limited amount of time to register his ona'ah complaint.

When the buyer is defrauded, a lapse of sufficient time to allow him the opportunity to show his purchase to an expert assessor forfeits for him any legal recourse against ona'ah [35]. This time span, as the foremost medieval Talmudic commentator R. Solomon ben Isaac (1040-1105) pointed out, provide plaintiff with sufficient time to ascertain whether or not his purchase involved ona'ah. Silence beyond this interval is therefore taken as an implicit waiver of his legal claims against ona'ah [36].

In contrast, when the seller is defrauded, he may exercise his legal claim against the buyer until time elapses sufficient for him to ascertain the market price of the good he sold. Should the article involved not be generally available in the marketplace, the seller's ona'ah claims extend until we are certain he witnessed a market sale of an article of the same type involved in the moot transaction [37].

The role the presumption of imperfect knowledge plays in legitimizing the ona'ah claim is further illustrated by the householder and selling on trust exemptions.

(3) When a householder sells his articles of personal use, he is not liable to ona'ah claims. The privileged status of the householder is rationalized by R. Hisda of Babylonia (217-309) on the basis of the presumption that any one dealing with him realizes that the latter would not dispose of his personal articles unless he could sell them above market price [38].

34. Joseph Caro, *Sh. Ar.*, op. cit. 220.

35. V. Baba Metzia 49b; Asher ben Jechiel, *Rosh*, Baba Metzia IV:15; Maimonides, *Yad*, op. cit. XII:5; Jacob ben Asher, *Tur*, op. cit. 227:15; Joseph Caro, *Sh. Ar.*; op. cit. 227:7.

36. Solomon ben Isac, *Rashi*, Baba Metzia 49b.

37. V. Baba Metzia 50b; Maimonides, *Yad*, op. cit. XII:6; Jacob ben Asher, *Tur*, op. cit. 227:10; Joseph Caro, *Sh. Ar.*, op. cit. 227:8.

38. V. Baba Metzia 51a.

Given the above rationalization of the househodler's favored treatment, R. Asher limited the exemption to instances where the buyer was aware that he was transacting with a householder. When the buyer can establish that he was unaware that the seller was a householder, the presumption that the former waives his claims against ona'ah is patently invalid [39].

(4) When a vendor sells his wares on trust he is not subsequently liable to ona'ah claims [40]. Selling on trust, according to Maimonides, requires the vendor to divulge to his prospective buyer his cost price and his proposed profit margin. Should the vendee agree to these terms and consummate the transaction with a symbolic act (kinyan), a subsequent finding that the cost price involved ona'ah does not allow plaintiff to modify the original transaction in any manner. Agreeing to allow the vendor a specified profit margin demonstrates on the part of the buyer a disconcern with what the objective market value of the commodity is. Given that eralization of the agreed upon profit rate required the sale to be concluded at the stipulated price, subsequent ona'ah claims are denied [41].

It should be noted that when the presumption of imperfect knowledge is made, all victims of ona'ah are placed on an equal footing. No distinction in Judaic law is made between the casual market participant and the shrewd dealer. When victims of ona'ah are entitled to restitution or nullification rights, these rights apply even when the plaintiff turns out to be a shrewd businessman. Business acumen does not generate a legal presumption of awareness of the market norm at the moment the sale was consummated. Conversely, no special considerations or additional rights are con-

39. Asher ben Jechiel, *Responsa Rosh*, K'lal 102, quoted by Jacob ben Asher, *Tur*, op. cit. 227:27 and by Joseph Caro, *Sh. Ar.*, op. cit.

40. V. Baba Metzia 51b; Jacob ben Asher, *Tur*, op. cit. 227:37; Joseph Caro, *Sh. Ar.*, op. cit. 227:27.

41. Maimonides, *Yad*, op. cit. XIII:5. For a variant view of what constitutes selling on trust. V. R. Israel of Krems (Fl. mid 14th century), *HaGaot Ashri*, Baba Metzia IV.

ferred to the novice or infrequent market participant when he is victimized by ona'ah [42].

Though the ona'ah claim is rooted in the presumption of imperfect knowledge on the part of the plaintiff, certainty that he was aware of the market norm at the time he entered into the ona'ah transaction does not *automatically* invalidate his subsequent ona'ah claim. This is evidenced from the ruling of the Germanic Talmudic codifier, Mordechai ben Hillel Ha-Kohen (1240-1298) that a victim of second degree ona'ah retains restitution rights against the offender even when it can be established that he was aware of the market norm at the time the sale was finalized. Here, far from constituting an implicit waiver of his rights, plaintiff's failure to register any complaint when he negotiated the sale could very well manifest on his part an artful design against the offender. Viewing his options, plaintiff could have indeed concluded that his optimal strategem required him to *delay* his protest until after the sale was finalized. Demanding that the transaction be concluded at the market norm might provoke the offender to break off negotiations altogether. Bargaining with him, on the other hand, to reduce the price differential, might prove sucessful, but would at the same time reduce the degree of ona'ah involved from second to third degree. With no restitution rights provided for plaintiff in third degree ona'ah cases, pursuit of this course of action would effectively disallow him to recover the differential. Most attractive to him would therefore be to allow the sale to be concluded with second degree ona'ah. Once finalized, he would then assert his restitution rights.

A variation of the above case occurs when the concluded sale involves first degree ona'ah. In this instance, certainty that plaintiff was aware of the prevailing norm at the time he entered into the sale invalidates his subsequent claims against the offender. Insofar as first degree ona'ah cases do not generate for the plaintiff

42. V. Baba Metzia 51a; Asher ben Jechiel, *Rosh*, Baba Metzia IV:17; Maimonides, *Yad*, op. cit., XII:8; Jacob ben Asher, *Tur*, op. cit. 227:14; Joseph Caro, *Sh. Ar.*, op. cit. 227:14.

restitution rights, his silence at the time he entered into the sale cannot be construed as a ploy to recover the price differential involved. Plaintiff's failure to protest is therefore taken as an implicit waiver of his claims against ona'ah[43].

Subjective Value and the Ona'ah Claim

Nascent in R. Asher's analysis of his second approach to third degree ona'ah is an anticipation of the modern economic concept of consumer surplus. This notion is concerned with the relationship between market price and subjective value. Given that market price is determined by the interplay of *aggregate* supply and demand forces, the *subjective* esteem an individual demander attaches to the said product may or may not coincide with this norm. When the consumer's subjective evaluation of the product falls below this norm, he obviously rejects the product. When his subjective evaluation of the product either coincides with or exceeds the market price, the consumer will buy the product. In the latter instance, he will enjoy a windfall as well. The difference between the maximum price the consumer would willingly pay to obtain the product, rather than do without it, and the actual transaction price provides a measure of this windfall or consumer surplus. Does a given market price generate at least some amount of consumer surplus to the great majority of those patronizing the product at that price? Economic theory answers in the affirmative. The prevailing norm represents the market's evaluation of the *marginal* unit of the product. Given the assumption of diminishing marginal utility, this evaluation will afford consumer surplus to the great majority of the actual patrons of the product.

With the market price of the commodity affording some consumer surplus to a vast number of its patrons, the legitimacy of presuming

43. R. Moses Isserles, *Rema*, op. cit. 227:27 quoting Mordechai ben Hillel Ha-Kohen (Baba Metzia IV:307); David ben Samuel Ha-Levi (1586-1667), *Turei Zahav, Sh. Ar.* ad locum; Jacob ben Moses Lorberbaum (1760-1832), *Nitivot Hamishpat, Sh. Ar.* ad locum note 4; Jechiel Michael Epstein, *Arukh Hashulchan*, op. cit. 227:9. For a variant interpretation of Mordechai v. Joshua Ha-Kohen Falk, *Smah, Sh. Ar.*, ad locum and Aryeh Loeb ben Joseph Ha-Kohen (1745-1813, *Ktzot, Sh. Ar.* ad locum.

that the vendee realized subjective equivalence in his transaction when the degree of ona'ah involved was less than 16 2/3% becomes evident.

Symmetrically, the prevailing norm may or may not allow the individual producer to recover his costs. Given that market price under competitive conditions gravitates towards the marginal cost of producing the last unit demanded, the prevailing norm will allow the more efficient producers in the industry to more than recover their costs. This latter fact gives credence to the presumption that the producer would, at times, sell unwanted inventory below market price in order to recover his outlays *faster* than his normal selling activities would permit him to. Hence, the vendor's ona'ah claim is denied when the price differential involved is less than 16 2/3%.

Though subjective value enters explicitly into R. Asher's rationalization of the lack of the restitution procedure in third degree ona'ah, subjective value plays no role in assessing first and second degree ona'ah claims. This is evidenced from the following considerations:

(1) An explicit declaration on the part of the plaintiff that the article he is acquiring is subjectively worth to him the entire sum demanded by the seller does not, according to Talmudic decisors, invalidate his subsequent ona'ah claims[44].

(2) Barter transactions are not subject to ona'ah regulation. The Talmud in Baba Metzia 47a exegetically derives this exemption from the Biblical source of the ona'ah prohibition. "And if thou *sell* aught unto they neighbor, ...ye should not wrong one another" (Leviticus XXV:14). By use of the term *sell,* the verse is taken to refer solely to money transactions. Barter transactions are hence excluded from ona'ah regulations.

44. V. Aryeh Loeb ben Joseph ha-Kohen, *Ktzot, Sh. Ar.,* op. cit. 227 note 1; Ephraim Nabon (d. 1735), *Machanah Ephraim, Hilkhat Ona'ah,* chap. 20. These opinions were advanced to dispute R. Yom-Tob ben Abram Ishbili's view on the matter (v. Novalae *Ritvah,* Kiddushin 8a).

Basing his analysis on Maimonides' treatment of the barter exemption, R. Jechiel Michael Epstein of Belorussia (1829-1908) in his authoritative work Arukh Hashulchan, Choshen Hamishpat (pub. 1884-93), rationalizes the exclusion by pointing out that money transactions differ in essence from barter exchanges. When money is the medium of exchange, the clear intent of the parties involved is to exchange equal objective values. Given this intent, the prevailing norm serves admirably to determine whether or not the objective was realized. Barter transactions, on the other hand, are predicated on the existence of a double coincidence of wants. With neither of the articles involved in the exchange constituting a commonly accepted medium of exchange, the intent of each party is clearly to acquire something of greater subjective value to himself that what he has to offer in exchange. The laws of ona'ah therefore do not apply to barter exchanges[45].

Price Cutting

Another moral issue relating to pricing policy that arises within the context of a competitive market is the ethics of the business tactic of price cutting. In this regard the Mishnah in Baba Metzia 60a relates:

> R. Judah said: A shopkeeper must not distribute corn or nuts to children, because he thereby accustomes them to come to him; the Sages permit it. Nor may he reduce the price; but the Sages say, he is to be remembered for good...

Insofar as Talmudic decisors follow the majority view of the Sages[46], competitive price cutting apparently presents no moral issue in Judaic law. This indeed is the position taken by both Tamari[47] and Basri[48].

45. R. Jechiel Michael Epstein, *Arukh Hashulchan*, op. cit. 227:21.

46. V. Maimonides, *Yad*, op. cit. XVIII:4; Jacob ben Asher, *Tur*, op. cit. 227:18; Joseph Caro, *Sh. Ar.*, op. cit. 227:18; E. Basri, op. cit. p. 177.

47. Tamari, op. cit. p. 137.

48. Basri, op. cit. p. 177.

The ethics of competitive price cutting, as it appears to us, is a more complicated issue. Is price cutting an ethical business practice even when its effect is to financially ruin a rival firm, securing for the firm employing this tactic a monopoly position? In what follows, we will not take a particular position on this issue, but merely indicate some of the complexities involved.

The ethics of predatory price cutting should apparently be viewed within the context of the view Judaic law takes regarding ruinous competition in general. In this regard, an Amoric dispute concerning the right of an established firm to restrict free entry is recorded in Baba Batra 21b. R. Huna would confer an established firm monopoly status in the closed alley of its location, while R. Huna ben R. Joshua would allow a rival to locate even in close proximity to an established firm. R. Moses Schreiber (1762-1839) posited that the above disputants are in basic agreement as each refers to different circumstances. R. Huna's protectionist philosophy is restricted to instances where the effect of the new entry would ruin, not merely reduce, the livelihood of the established firm. The free entry advocacy of R. Huna ben R. Joshua, on the other hand, is confined to instances where the effect of the new entry would be merely to reduce the profit margin of the entrenched competitor and not to deprive him of his livelihood entirely [49]. Though one of the foremost contemporary Talmudic decisors concurs with the protectionist philosophy espoused by R. Moses Schreiber [50], a large number of other authorities do not regard *deprivation of livelihood alone* as valid grounds for conferring a territorial monopoly [51]. The divergence of opinion surrounding the issue of freedom of entry would apparently apply to the ethics of predatory price cutting as well.

49. R. Moses Sofer, *Responsa Chatam Sofer, Choshen Hamishpat* no. 78.
50. R. Moses Feinstein, *Responsa Igrot Moshe, Choshen Hamishpat,* no. 38.
51. V. R. Ephraim Zalman Margoliath (1762-1828), *Responsa Beit Ephraim, Choshen Hamishpat* no. 26; R. Mordechai Jacob Breisch, *Responsa Chelkat Yaakov* no. 65; R. Isac Arieli, *Einayim Lamishpat, Baba Bathra* 21b.

Another consideration in assessing the ethics of predatory price cutting is the circumstances under which it occurs. Price cutting is clearly both predatory in *motive* and *effect* when the firms involved are operating under very similar cost conditions and one firm decides to sell *below* cost for the purpose of driving its rivals out of business. A much less reprehensible form of this tactic occurs when a firm sells *above* cost, but is able to undersell its rivals by virtue of its superior efficiency. Disallowing the price cutting tactic here effectively *subsidizes* inefficiency and retards the rate at which new technology can be introduced and integrated into the economic system. Insofar as conferring a firm with a territorial monopoly, within the context of the discussion in Baba Bathra 21b, does not *of necessity* involve the subsidization of inefficiency, the controversy surrounding that issue is irrelevant in assessing the ethics of efficiency-based predatory price cutting. With protecting inefficiency decidedly injurious to consumer welfare, efficiency based predatory price cutting is perhaps a legitimate practice. Should the efficient firm decide at some later time to take advantage of its monopoly position by raising its price, communal legislative authority could at that time impose upon it appropriate restraints.

Credit Buying and Cash Discounts

We will now turn to the remaining element in category II, price discrimination based on the terms of payment.

Charging above market price for a credit purchase represents another form of price discrimination explicitly prohibited by Talmudic law. Insofar as the price differential involved reflects a compensation the seller realizes for accepting a delay in payment due him, the transaction violates the prohibition against usury [52]. The above prohibition was relaxed somewhat by the early Talmudic codifiers when the competitive norm for the subject article was not clearly defined. Here, the seller may engage in a modest price dis-

52. V. Mishnah, Baba Metzia V:3.

crimination as long as he does not explicitly tell the buyer of his policy of charging more for credit purchases than when payment is immediately made. With the degree of price discrimination small, the premium the seller realizes for credit purchases could be easily attributed to factors other than a desire on his part to be compensated for the delay in payment. The nature of the sellor's pricing policy becomes, however, obvious, when he charges a significant premium for credit purchases. The latter practice is therefore prohibited, notwithstanding the absence of a clearly defined norm for the article involved [53].

Charging a premium for credit purchases is prohibited, according to the Germanic Talmudic codifier Mordechai ben Hillel Ha-Kohen, under certain conditions even when the credit transaction was concluded at the current market norm. This occurs when the vendor initiates an offer to sell his product *below* the current market norm for an immediate payment. Once such an offer is made, the parties may not proceed to conclude the transaction on credit terms at the current market norm. Nevertheless, in the event the buyer accepted the seller's original offer and the transaction became legally binding on both parties, the parties may alter the terms of the sale from cash to credit at the current market norm [54].

The renter of real estate may engage in explicit price discrimination in the form of charging a higher rental when payment is made at the termination of the lease than when it is made at the beginning of the leasing period. Price discrimination of this nature is rationalized in the Talmud in Baba Metzia 65a on the grounds that rent is legally due at the termination of the lease. Hence, the premium rental charged when payment is at the termination of the lease does not amount to an additional payment the renter realizes for tolerating a delay in payment due him [55].

53. V. Jacob ben Asher, *Tur, Yoreh De'ah* 173:1—2; Joseph Caro, *Sh. Ar., Yore De'ah* 173:1—3.

54. R. Mordechai ben Hillel Ha-Kohen, Baba Metzia, V:317, quoted by R. Moses Isserles, *Rema, Sh. Ar.*, op. cit. 173:3.

55. V. Mishnah, Baba Metzia V:3; Jacob ben Asher, *Tur*, op. cit. 176:10; Joseph Caro, *Sh. Ar.*, op. cit. 176:6.

Wage agreement, according to R. Vidal, may call for the worker to receive a higher compensation when payment for the stipulated work is made at the completion of the work than when it is made before the work starts. Insofar as wages are legally due only at the completion of the stipulated work, the premium the wage earner realizes when he is paid at the completion of the stipulated work does not amount to a differential reward for tolerating a delay in receiving his wages [56].

56. R. Vidal Yom Tov of Tolosa, *Maggid Mishnah, Yad, Hilkhat Malveh VeLoveh* VII:8.

Name Index

www.ingramcontent.com/pod-product-compliance
Lightning Source LLC
LaVergne TN
LVHW102107300926
849161LV00014B/3068
* 9 7 8 0 8 1 4 7 3 0 4 9 2 *